Bali & Lombok

1st Edition

by Mary Justice Thomasson-Croll

WILEY

Wiley Publishing, Inc.

Published by:

WILEY PUBLISHING, INC.

111 River St.
Hoboken, NJ 07030-5774

ISBN 978-0-470-49776-0

Editor: Melinda Quintero
Production Editor: Jonathan Scott
Cartographer: Andrew Murphy
Photo Editor: Richard Fox
Production by Wiley Indianapolis Composition Services
Front cover photo: Rice terraces near Ubud © Russell Kord / Alamy Images.
Back cover photo: Surfing in Lombok © Fadil Aziz / Alamy Images.

For information on our other products and services or to obtain technical support, please contact our Customer Care Department within the U.S. at 877/762-2974, outside the U.S. at 317/572-3993 or fax 317/572-4002.

Wiley also publishes its books in a variety of electronic formats. Some content that appears in print may not be available in electronic formats.

Manufactured in the United States of America

5 4 3 2 1

CONTENTS

LIST OF MAPS — vii

1 THE BEST OF BALI — 1

1 The Best Unique Balinese Experiences...1

2 The Best Temples ...2

3 The Best Diving & Snorkeling...3

4 The Best Beaches ...4

5 The Best Activities for Kids ...4

6 The Best Resorts ...5

7 The Best Villas...6

8 The Best Dining...6

9 The Best Spas ...7

John Hardy's Bali...8

2 BALI IN DEPTH — 10

1 Bali Today ...10

Bali's Royal Regency Past ...11

2 Looking Back at Bali...11

3 Bali: Center for the Arts...16

Bali's Craft Villages at a Glance...19

4 Balinese Architecture...20

Buying Textiles ...20

5 Religion & Spirituality ...22

What's in a Name?...23

6 Lay of the Land ...25

7 Eating & Drinking in Bali...26

Eating at the Kaki Lima...28

3 PLANNING YOUR TRIP TO BALI & LOMBOK — 30

1 When to Go...30

Nonreligious Festivals ...31

Odalan Ceremonies & Festivals ...33

2 Entry Requirements...35

Online Traveler's Toolbox ...35

3 Getting There & Getting Around ...37

A Note on Addresses ...40

4 Money & Costs...40

The Value of Indonesian Rupiah vs. Other Popular Currencies...40

Getting Your Money's Worth When Changing Currency...41

5 Health ...42

Purchasing & Using Travel Insurance in Bali & Lombok...44

6 Safety...45

7 Specialized Travel Resources ...45

8 Sustainable Tourism...47

9 Staying Connected...49

10 Tips on Accommodations...50

BALI & LOMBOK

CONTENTS

4 SUGGESTED BALI & LOMBOK ITINERARIES 52

1 The Regions in Brief..............52
2 The Best of Bali in 1 Week........55
3 The Best of Bali in 2 Weeks.......56

Suggested Lombok Itineraries......57
4 Bali for Families 57

5 ACTIVE VACATION PLANNER 59

1 Organized Trips & Tours 59
2 Activities A to Z 61

*Alternative Health & Wellness
A to Z* 62

6 KUTA 72

1 Getting There & Getting
Around 72
Fast Facts: Kuta 73
2 Where to Stay.....................73

3 Where to Dine 79
4 Exploring Kuta 84
5 Shopping 87
6 Kuta After Dark....................90

7 SEMINYAK & CANGGU 93

1 Getting There & Getting
Around 93
2 Where to Stay.....................96
3 Where to Dine 101
The Best of Eat Street 106

4 Exploring Seminyak 108
5 Shopping 109
6 Seminyak After Dark 114
7 Canggu.......................... 115
A Day in Denpasar............... 116

8 SANUR & THE NEARBY ISLANDS 120

1 Getting There & Getting
Around 120
Fast Facts: Sanur................. 120
2 Where to Stay................... 121
*A Brief History of Tourism in
Sanur* 122
3 Where to Dine 130
4 Exploring Sanur................. 134

5 Shopping 138
6 Sanur After Dark 139
7 Nusa Lembongan, Nusa
Ceningan & Nusa Penida......... 140
*Walking from Tamarind to
Mushroom Beach*................ 144
Nusa Ceningan 149

9 THE BUKIT PENINSULA 154

1 Jimbaran Bay.................... 154
2 Uluwatu 165

*Pecatu Indah Development &
the New Kuta* 170

3 Nusa Dua 174

*The Nusa Dua Seaweed
Farmers* 182

*Balinese Dance Performances
on the Bukit Peninsula* 183

*Ashes to Ashes, Dust to Dust:
Cremation*. 184

4 Tanjung Benoa. 185

10 UBUD   189

1 Orientation 190

Fast Facts: Ubud 190

2 Where to Stay. 191

3 Where to Dine 201

Cafes, Coffee & Tea 204

4 Exploring Ubud 207

Learning to Love the Earth. 215

5 Around Ubud 217

6 Shopping: Island of the
Goods 218

*Dance & Cultural
Performances*. 222

7 Ubud After Dark 224

11 CENTRAL MOUNTAINS   225

1 Exploring the Central
Mountains 225

2 Danau Batur 226

*A View of Danau Batur &
Penelokan* 228

3 Bedugul & Danau Bratan,
Buyan & Tamblingan 234

4 Munduk 237

5 Gunung Batukaru 240

12 EAST BALI   243

1 Exploring East Bali. 243

Fast Facts: East Bali. 246

2 Klungkung (Semarapura). 247

*Dining & Breaking Records in
Karangsem Regency* 248

3 The Sidemen Valley 249

4 Bangli & Gunung Agung 251

5 Padangbai 254

6 Manggis 257

Festivals in & Around Tenganan 258

7 Candidasa 260

8 Amlapura 263

9 Amed. 265

10 Tulamben. 268

13 NORTH BALI   271

1 Getting There & Getting
Around 271

2 Tembok, Sembirenteng
& Tejakula. 271

3 Air Sanih & Surrounding
Villages 275

4 Singaraja 276

5 Lovina 278

6 Pemuteran. 284

Pemuteran's Biorock Project. 285

14 WEST BALI — 288

1 Getting There & Getting Around 288

Fast Facts: West Bali 288

2 Tabanan 288

3 Tabanan to Negara 293

4 Negara & Around 296

5 Taman Nasional Bali Barat 298

15 LOMBOK — 303

1 Lombok in Depth 303

Frommer's Favorite Lombok Experiences 304

2 Getting There & Getting Around 307

Specialized Lombok Tours 311

Fast Facts: Lombok 312

3 West Lombok 313

4 Senggigi 316

5 The Southwest Coast & Islands ... 322

Lombok's (& the World's?) Greatest Wave 324

6 North Lombok 324

Tips for Trekking Mount Rinjani 329

7 Central Lombok 330

Lombok's New International Airport 331

8 Kuta & the South Coast 332

Up in the Air: A New Megaresort for Lombok? 332

Surfing on Lombok's Southern Peninsula: Ekas Bay 333

Bau Nyale Festival 335

9 East Lombok 336

Cultural Riches & Ancient Traditions in East Lombok 338

16 THE GILI ISLANDS — 339

1 Getting to, Between & Around the Gilis 338

Fast Facts: The Gili Islands 343

2 Gili Air 344

3 Gili Meno 347

4 Gili Trawangan 349

The Five Best Dive Spots on the Gilis 355

17 FAST FACTS — 358

1 Fast Facts: Bali & Lombok 358

2 Airline Websites 360

18 BASIC INDONESIAN — 361

1 Basic Grammar 361

2 Essential Words & Phrases 361

INDEX — 365

General Index 365

Accommodations Index 372

LIST OF MAPS

Suggested Bali & Lombok
  Itineraries 53

Kuta 74

Seminyak 94

Sanur............................124

Nusa Lembongan, Nusa
  Ceningan & Nusa Penida 141

The Bukit Peninsula 156

Nusa Dua & Tanjung Benoa 175

Ubud & Surrounding Villages 192

Central Mountains...............227

Danau Batur 229

East Bali 244

North Bali.......................272

West Bali........................289

Taman Nasional Bali Barat &
  Gilimanuk 299

Lombok..........................308

The Gili Islands..................339

ACKNOWLEDGMENTS

Without Elizabeth "Bossy Boots" Brown's organizational skills, this book would have been rough sledding. A lifetime of travel has given this alumna of well-established publishers the unwavering spirit and natural curiosity needed to assist on a book about complex and fascinating Bali and Lombok. My endearing and faithful assistant Uchee Ramang is also to be thanked, as are a talented and diverse group of island experts too numerous to mention. Special thanks also go to the Balinese and Indonesians who put up with all of our silly questions with typical grace and charm, and to Melinda Quintero for patiently editing the answers.

—Mary Justice Thomasson-Croll

HOW TO CONTACT US

In researching this book, we discovered many wonderful places—hotels, restaurants, shops, and more. We're sure you'll find others. Please tell us about them, so we can share the information with your fellow travelers in upcoming editions. If you were disappointed with a recommendation, we'd love to know that, too. Please write to:

Frommer's Bali & Lombok, 1st Edition
Wiley Publishing, Inc. • 111 River St. • Hoboken, NJ 07030-5774

AN ADDITIONAL NOTE

Please be advised that travel information is subject to change at any time—and this is especially true of prices. We therefore suggest that you write or call ahead for confirmation when making your travel plans. The authors, editors, and publisher cannot be held responsible for the experiences of readers while traveling. Your safety is important to us, however, so we encourage you to stay alert and be aware of your surroundings. Keep a close eye on cameras, purses, and wallets, all favorite targets of thieves and pickpockets.

ABOUT THE AUTHOR

An intrepid traveler by nature, **Mary Justice Thomasson-Croll** left the States after 2 years with an NBC news affiliate to take up a post with the Hong Kong bureau. She spent 18 glorious years covering the incredible evolution of Hong Kong and Southeast Asia. Six years ago MJ (as she is known to friends) moved to Bali and has since fallen in love with the island and its gentle people and ways that are a far cry from her former city life. Writing from her bijoux house on the beach, MJ posts to many publications that include *Travel + Leisure, Tatler,* the *South China Morning Post,* and *Luxe Guides.* MJ holds a degree from Christie's Fine Arts in London, as well as a BA from George Washington University in Washington, D.C. She is currently working on a screenplay loosely based on the events surrounding the handover and hangover of Hong Kong in 1997.

FROMMER'S STAR RATINGS, ICONS & ABBREVIATIONS

Every hotel, restaurant, and attraction listing in this guide has been ranked for quality, value, service, amenities, and special features using a **star-rating system.** In country, state, and regional guides, we also rate towns and regions to help you narrow down your choices and budget your time accordingly. Hotels and restaurants are rated on a scale of zero (recommended) to three stars (exceptional). Attractions, shopping, nightlife, towns, and regions are rated according to the following scale: zero stars (recommended), one star (highly recommended), two stars (very highly recommended), and three stars (must-see).

In addition to the star-rating system, we also use **eight feature icons** that point you to the great deals, in-the-know advice, and unique experiences that separate travelers from tourists. Throughout the book, look for:

(Finds)	Special finds—those places only insiders know about
(Fun Facts)	Fun facts—details that make travelers more informed and their trips more fun
(Kids)	Best bets for kids, and advice for the whole family
(Moments)	Special moments—those experiences that memories are made of
(Overrated)	Places or experiences not worth your time or money
(Tips)	Insider tips—great ways to save time and money
(Value)	Great values—where to get the best deals
(Warning!)	Warning—traveler's advisories are usually in effect

The following **abbreviations** are used for credit cards:

AE	American Express	**DISC**	Discover	**V**	Visa
DC	Diners Club	**MC**	MasterCard		

TRAVEL RESOURCES AT FROMMERS.COM

Frommer's travel resources don't end with this guide. Frommer's website, **www.frommers. com**, has travel information on more than 4,000 destinations. We update features regularly, giving you access to the most current trip-planning information and the best airfare, lodging, and car-rental bargains. You can also listen to podcasts, connect with other Frommers.com members through our active-reader forums, share your travel photos, read blogs from guidebook editors and fellow travelers, and much more.

The Best of Bali

Bali is an island so rich in its diversity and spirituality that it simply can't be described in words alone. Many have tried and wound up with little more than clichés— "Morning of the World," "Dawn of Civilization," "Island of the Gods." This is a land full of mysticism, spirituality, and pleasure and the lucky Balinese live their lives confident in the knowledge that they do so in a form of paradise.

Bali consistently wins travel accolades and its high-profile resorts consistently fill the Top 10 of the "Best of . . . ," "Hot List . . . ," "Readers' Choice . . . ," and all manner of other lists. The island itself, outside of the resort awards, ranks yearly as either the best island destination or one of them, in the same strata as Maui, St. Barts, and Capri. This guidebook can take you as far as the pristine beaches and mountaintop sunrises but only open eyes can catch the magic of Bali, through chance encounters and serendipity. You'll leave speechless.

1 THE BEST UNIQUE BALINESE EXPERIENCES

- **Participating in a Ceremony** No matter where you are staying in Bali, you can, if you wish, get yourself invited to a ceremony either through a friendly villa staff member or your hotel concierge. Don't forget your sash and sarong. Pick up the spiritual vibe, keeping in mind that "ceremony" is often just a word that replaces "celebration."
- **Watching a Balinese Dance Performance** Bali's highly stylized traditional dances have evolved from ancient Hindu rites and often take the performer into a trancelike state. The best way to see it is in a temple but performances at public theaters and even on hotel grounds can be equally entrancing. Don't pass up an opportunity to see the rarely performed *Oleg Tambulilingan* if you get the chance. It is a sexy virtuoso duet depicting a randy male bumblebee courting a coy lady bee.
- **Calling on a Balian** What is a Balian you say? The simplest explanation is a

medicine man or a spiritual healer. Balinese see them for illness, emotional distress, and all manner of problems. At the moment you will hear the name **Ketut Lyer** bandied about as the healer made famous by Elizabeth Gilbert's book, *Eat, Pray, Love.* Eager seekers form lines running round the block of his Ubud home-cum-practice, so don't bother going there. Instead ask a Balinese friend or someone at your hotel where they recommend you go, as every good Balinese has a Balian. Appointments aren't necessary and there are normally no phone calls you can make to even find your special healer. It's all about just showing up on a first-come, first-served basis, trying your luck, and leaving a donation. Any good Balian worth his salt doesn't discuss money with a client. What you leave is what you decide to leave and many Balinese without much spare cash leave rice and simple offerings. See box, "Alternative Health & Wellness A to Z," p. 62.

- **Eating with Locals at a Warung** Warungs, or roadside cafes, serve up some of the best local food on the island. Pull up a well-worn wooden stool to a group table and pick your food from the buffet. One of the best warungs is in Seminyak, the **Warung Sulawesi** (p. 107), where flavors of Bali are mixed with the piquant offerings of far-flung Indonesian islands. In Ubud, even though it is well discovered, go for the suckling pig at **Ibu Oka** (p. 206).

Ask anyone where it is and they will point you in the right direction.

- **Strolling in a Village in the Morning** Local color is at its brightest in the mornings in a village in Bali. Take a leisurely stroll and you will see children in uniform walking hand in hand to school, moms bringing back the day's provisions from the market, and men and women placing offerings throughout the village and in the temples. It's a stunning start to your day in paradise.

2 THE BEST TEMPLES

Take a guide and you will understand far more about each temple. As the layout and style of most temples is the same, it is the history that brings out the life in them. Always be appropriately dressed and observe temple rules.

- **Pura Luhur Uluwatu** This is a dramatically perched sea temple on the cliffs above the legendary surf break Uluwatu. It is possibly Bali's most spectacular shrine. The best time to visit is at sunset. Be sure to take in the nightly Kecak show and mind the gap—the railings are few and far between. See p. 166.

- **Pura Goa Giri Putri** This is quite an extraordinary experience. You enter the cave, on one side of the mountain, on your hands and knees through a small gap in the rocks, and then pass 450m (1,500 ft.) inside the mountain only to come out the other side on to a beautiful valley. A visit here justifies a day trip to Nusa Penida on its merits alone. See p. 151.

- **Pura Gunung Kawi** Bali's "Valley of the Kings" is hewn in the cliffs, and on both sides of the river are massive commemorative monuments to 11th-century kings and queens. Strictly speaking, Gunung Kawi is not a temple, but it is nevertheless considered a holy place. A visit here is an unforgettable experience. See p. 208.

- **Tirta Empul** This temple is built around a sacred spring, Tampak Siring, and its two bathing spots have been used by the Balinese for a millennium. It is believed that the springs have magical powers and bring good health and prosperity. Pack your bathing suit, go at sunrise, and experience the springs as the Balinese do. See p. 209.

- **Pura Ulan Danu Bratan** This temple sits on the edge of Lake Bratan and is worth a visit if only for its beautiful surroundings. The part of the temple that gets all the attention is the 11-roof *meru*, situated on a point of land, jutting out into the lake. Sadly, the lake and the surrounding area can get overrun with litter from visiting tourists. See p. 235.

- **Pura Luhur Batukaru** This is one of the six axial temples sacred to all Hindu Balinese and one of the most ancient sacred sites on the island. Majestically nestled in the jungle, at the head of the valley on the slopes of Batukaru, this is a wonderful place to wander round in wonder. See p. 241.

- **Pura Lempuyang** Only for the fit and willing, it takes some 1,700 winding steps up through the forested slopes of Mount Lempuyang to reach Pura Lempuyang, and the views on to Mount Agung are divine. See p. 263.

- **Pura Besakih** This makes the "Best of" solely because of its importance and spectacular ceremonies. It is the largest and the holiest, known as the "Mother Temple" and translates literally as the "Temple of Spiritual Happiness." Go early, avoid the crowds, and take your own guide. See p. 252.
- **Pura Tanah Lot** Otherwise known as Pura Pakendungan, this temple sits dramatically on a rock, surrounded by black sand and pounding surf, and is possibly the most picturesque and most photographed temple on the island—especially so at sunset. It is reachable only during low tide. It can get very busy with coach-loads of tourists so it is best seen in the early morning. See p. 290.

3 THE BEST DIVING & SNORKELING

- **Nusa Penida** This island is the nearest dive site for those staying in the south of the island. It is a 40-minute boat ride from Sanur and benefits from the main deep water channel current running down the Lombok Strait. The main draw is from July to November when there is a high chance of swimming with the large Mola-Mola, or oceanic sunfish, or around the same time, you may find manta rays. See p. 150.
- **Bloo Lagoon** This small, white-sand bay just outside Padangbai is not normally a recipe for finding interesting fish, but the treasure-trove of marine life here includes sharks, stonefish, scorpionfish, and nudibranches. One of the highlights of this dive spot is its night dives. See p. 255.
- **Gili Biaha** This island is a 25-minute boat ride north of Candidasa and has some of Bali's most stunning diving. Here you will find a vast diversity of fish, sharks, and frequent pelagic visitors set against a backdrop of chiseled black walls with beautiful, healthy corals and often superb visibility. Go to the Shark Cove and you are almost guaranteed to see a white tip shark or two. See p. 255.
- **USAT Liberty** Certainly the most famous and most popular dive site in Bali, this wreck lies between 3m and 37m (10 ft.–120 ft.) from the surface and can be enjoyed by serious divers and snorkelers alike. It is easy to reach from the shore and hosts over 300 species of fish. Go for a night dive. See p. 269.
- **Menjangan Island** Situated in the West Bali National Park, 10km (6 miles) offshore, this deer-inhabited island offers deep coral reef walls only 45m to 90m (150–300 ft.) from shore, with a diversity of gorgonian fans and plenty of small and medium-size fish on view. The protected island is reached by boats staffed by ex-fishermen from the area. The high visibility coupled with the gentle currents make this an exceptional place for the whole family. See p. 299.
- **Belongas Bay** This bay in south Lombok has many excellent dive sites and pristine and as yet unpolluted reefs. There is plentiful macro life and an abundance of mackerel, tuna, barracuda, napoleon wrasse, and white and black tip reef sharks. You may even get to see hammerhead sharks. See p. 68.
- **The Gili Islands** Located off the west coast of Lombok, and with over 20 accepted sites, this is an ideal location to base yourself if you want to spend the day sub aqua. The Gilis are famous for their turtles and if you are quick and fortunate, you may even get to swim with them. See chapter 16.

4 THE BEST BEACHES

The image of Bali as a beach destination has likely taken hold from its surf-dominated origins back in the 1970s. And while there are many beautiful stretches, they are less typical and planning your beach trip requires thought—not least because the rip and swell that lure surfers pose a less hospitable attraction for swimmers.

- **Kuta Beach at 66**   While this is not necessarily the prettiest place to lie nor indeed the safest place to swim, Kuta Beach at 66 attracts people from all of the world to soak up the atmosphere and rays and watch the bods on the beds. Settle down on a sun lounger and the world will pass by. See p. 86.
- **Ku de Ta**   While more a bar than a beach, treat it as the latter and book one of the four-person sun loungers and kick back for the day with top-drawer service on tap. See p. 101.
- **Sanur Beach**   Similar in style to Nusa Dua, Sanur retains its old-world charm and connection to a more authentic Bali than Nusa Dua, with mile after mile of traditional warungs competing with top-class resorts set on the boardwalk. This is a great spot for sailing, kite surfing, and kid-friendly swimming. See p. 120.
- **Bingin Beach**   Of all the amazing golden beaches on the Bukit, this remains as charming and original a spot as you can get. Untroubled to date by overzealous developers, and with surfers doing a daily show out front, this is a perfect beachside experience. See p. 166.
- **Nusa Dua Beach**   As perfect, friendly, and enticing a beach setting as anywhere. The offshore reef provides the protection, and the never-ending five-star hotels fronting the boardwalk provide the setting for lazing on or by the beach with immaculate service immediately at hand. Dinghies and kayaks abound. See p. 174.
- **Pantai Pasir Putih (White Sand Beach)**   This idyllic spot, off the tourist trail, is a closely guarded secret. Just beyond Candidasa, it is a perfect crescent beach protected by two high promontories with a dozen picturesque warungs serving cold beer and prawns. It is the closest Bali comes to the Caribbean with azure waters and gentle breezes. See p. 260.
- **The Gili Islands**   Near perfect, soft white sand beaches surround the Gili islands. Quite how they managed to retain their innocence for so long is a mystery. Take a 3-day break here. See p. 339.

5 THE BEST ACTIVITIES FOR KIDS

- **Surfing**   Teenagers can take part in many of the surfing and kite schools on the island, depending on the time of year and the prevailing winds. Sanur is the best area for learning to kite surf and Kuta Beach for wave surfing. See p. 69.
- **Waterbom**   Your kids will love you for taking them to this water park, but be forewarned, once you take them you will never hear the end of it. The management have rigged this: They offer you a discount card on exit for a repeat visit within 7 days. This place is great fun, exhilarating, and well managed with surprisingly good food. Your saving grace after this generous day out with the kids is that they will be so knackered they will hit the sack early. See p. 87.

- **Bali Safari & Marine Park** Kids of all ages will love the zebras, rhinos, and wildebeest roaming as free as they are going to get this side of the savanna. Add in the animal rides and daily shows and this makes a terrific break from the sea and surf for the kids. See p. 134.

- **Green Camp** Let your children have their own natural discovery of the wonders of Balinese culture and the great outdoors from planting rice, picking cocoa, and making chocolate, or just climbing one of the hundreds of coconut trees that dot the landscape of this cool camp. If they like getting dirty (and what kid doesn't) this is their place. For parents, you can exhaust and educate at the same time. The camp is seasonal and courses are weekly or daily, drop-ins are welcome. See p. 215.

- **Bali Bird Park** Certainly one of the best managed bird parks and rehabilitation centers in the world, this is an experience that all ages will relish. The Bali starlings, birds of paradise, and Komodo dragons are each worth the trip in their own right, never mind all together. See p. 134.

- **Bali Tree Top Adventure Park** Tree Top will test the bravery and agility of all from 6 to 60. Budding Tarzans of all ages are catered to in the wondrous setting of the Bedugul Botanical Garden. The six levels range from brave kids to super-hero. A must for the outward bound. See p. 235.

- **Menjangan Resort** Take the safari jeeps with rooftop seating around the estate to view the deer, monkeys, and wild boar in the hedgerow. There is world-class snorkeling at Menjangan Island, horse riding, trekking, and bird-watching to keep any child amused. You can even stay in charming cabins in the mangroves—great for inspiring botanists. See p. 301.

6 THE BEST RESORTS

- **The Legian Hotel** Nothing tops being in the swankest part of town at one of Bali's most glamorous hotels. From the beautiful Seminyak beach front, soak up the sun, take in the view, and plan your activities for the next day. Chances are they will remain a beautiful pipe dream. See p. 96.

- **Desa Seni** While certainly not one of the more costly nor extravagant choices, at this bijoux resort your soul is nourished in a way that sometimes money just can't buy. From the incredibly tasteful layout, to the complimentary yoga classes and organic dining sourced right from the resort's own gardens, you will leave relaxed and restored. See p. 115.

- **Bulgari** With a world full of exotic locations, Bulgari chose Bali and a stunning cliff top near Pura Luhur Uluwatu for its first sortie outside Italy. Extravagant, possibly brash, but definitely daring, this high-roller's resort literally cut itself into a cliff side. The prices are as steep as the inclinator that leads you down to their private beach, but they deliver as only Bulgari can. See p. 169.

- **Amandari** Or is that Aman darling? It's hard to beat the perfectly positioned Amandari with its spectacular deep valley views over terraces down to the rushing water of the Ayung river. The hotel retains a reverence for its local community and while they are very PC, they aren't above making sure that your wish is their command. See p. 191.

- **The Chedi Club** At the Chedi Club, a complimentary minibar and sunset cocktails are just a few of the lovely freebies. Add in your own designated 24-hour butler and you can see how spoiling the Chedi Club can be to its lucky members—or is that guests? See p. 191.

- **Puri Ganesha** Puri Ganesha is in a class of its own. Evenings spent at the main house or restaurant chatting about life, loves, and the pursuit of happiness always end on an upbeat note. The most decadent trait of this hideaway haven is the tranquility by day, but don't expect it by night. See p. 285.

7 THE BEST VILLAS

- **Atas Ombak** The unique beachfront position, surrounding sweeping lawns, and immaculate gardens make this villa a stellar choice. The deal is made even sweeter by its proximity to Seminyak and all of the great shopping and dining. See p. 100.
- **Villa Mana** This is a villa on a different scale, from its .8-hectare (2-acre) lawn and sweeping rice paddy views to all manner of tricks and toys. It is a super-spot for throwing a megaparty or just entertaining family and friends with plenty of room for the children to frolic. See p. 115.
- **Villa Des Indes** This place outclasses any other villa on the island by the sheer magnitude of its remarkable collection of Indonesian artifacts, antiques, and museum-quality paintings. Everything about it is reminiscent of luxury travel of a bygone era, even down to the sterling silver and crystal cocktail glasses. See p. 100.
- **The Istana** Sitting on the cliff top, the Istana, or "palace," has jaw-dropping views of the Indian Ocean, and rock-star status. You pay the price for the privilege. See p. 171.
- **Villa Bulan Putih** On Bingin Beach, a favorite for surfers and sun seekers alike, this villa has all the ingredients including beachfront position, a sprawling lawn, and tasteful decor. It's the kind of place that you check into but you don't want to check out of. See p. 172.

8 THE BEST DINING

- **La Lucciola** This is the most elegant beachside dining experience in Bali. Accessed over a charming footbridge and sitting on one of the prettiest stretches of Seminyak Beach, this is a wonderful place for a leisurely meal at any time of the day. Mellow, magical, and memorable. See p. 103.
- **Nutmegs** Picturesque Nutmegs overlooks a spacious garden filled with frangipani trees and hundreds of candles that twinkle under the stars. The open kitchen remains wondrously calm given the level and variety of cooking on offer. See p. 102.
- **Sardine** Quite possibly Bali's most charming restaurant. Built entirely of bamboo with a stunning rice paddy view in the posh Petitenget area of Seminyak, the design is as innovative as the daily changing menu. Fresh sardines feature high on the menu. See p. 103.
- **Sarong** Running the gamut of Asian cuisine, this buzzing Seminyak eatery draws crowds like bees to honey. What makes it great? Superbly decadent decor of chandeliers, soft lighting, plenty of mirrors, and an expansive bar—people-watching nirvana. See p. 103.
- **Sip** A better French bistro outside of France would be hard to find and with

over 100 wines and champagnes on offer, it is a crowd-puller for the GM's and restaurateurs that run the competition. See p. 104.

- **Private Dining at Tugu Hotel** One of Bali's grandest treasures is the Tugu, and if you book ahead you can enjoy two magnificent dining experiences. For the flamboyant, you can dine like an imperial king and have a dinner in the 300-year-old Kang XI period temple that is set up in the red Chinese dining room. For the more traditional, and dare we say humble, have authentic Balinese and Javanese cuisine in their warung with its open kitchen and wood-burning stoves. Both are charming. See p. 119.
- **Echo Beach, Canggu** Sunday nights on the beach here are famous for their seafood barbecue with picnic tables and stools by the waterfront, lots of gregarious groups of friends and families and live rock and roll. The scene would suit the '60s but it is family friendly. See p. 115.
- **Jimbaran Bay** A visit to Bali will not be complete without a trip to Jimbaran

for seafood. Come at sunset, dip your toes in the sea, watch the local families splashing in the waves, have a beer, and settle down to seriously delicious seafood barbecue by candlelight. See p. 162.

- **Kayuputi at St. Regis** Grab a private cabana overlooking the white sand beach, settle into the white overstuffed cushions, and choose from the seasonal selection of Sturia and Prunier caviar and oysters. Enjoy the ocean breeze and ask the award-winning sommelier for his recommendation while you peruse the menu. Make lunch hour a day out and in the end hope the breeze blows your bill away. See p. 179.
- **Mozaic** Chris Salan's restaurant in the heart of Ubud has become the most coveted fine-dining experience on the island. His six-course tasting menus, with optional wine pairing, should be on everyone's Ubud itinerary. Crayfish sourced from Java cooked with curry butter and passion fruit cream is the kind of consistent innovation that makes it a shining star and gets three from us. See p. 201.

9 THE BEST SPAS

- **Beach Massage** Sometimes the best things in life are almost free and a 5-buck massage on the comfort of your own beach lounger is pretty close to both. At just about any tourist beach in Bali you will find wizened women with strong hands and hearts who will approach you for massages. Chances are you won't be disappointed.
- **Theta Spa** The best treatment rooms in this hip destination spa in Kuta have floor to ceiling windows overlooking the beach that let you look out while nobody else can see in. All the treatments use natural ingredients with honey being a favorite, and after a bit of

pampering you can hang at the spa bar—a magnet for the tanned and trendy. See p. 85.

- **Jari Menari** The award-winning Jari Menari's name, "Dancing Fingers," immediately gives the wrong impression that a massage here is going to be on the delicate side. With all male masseuses it couldn't be further from the truth. The "Four Handed" massage has two gifted practitioners working in rhythmic harmony. See p. 109.
- **Thallaso at Ayana** Seawater is considered holy by the Balinese who use it not only to receive the ashes of their loved ones but also to cleanse temples and

Tips ## John Hardy's Bali

John Hardy, founder of the Green School (p. 215), is a bon vivant, visionary, and Canadian gone Balinese. Here are his principles for living and exploring Bali.

Walk   You can walk safely everywhere; you could walk across Bali and never walk on the road. So, get off the road and walk. There is always a path down to the river; there is always a path across the river up the other side.

Bike   Get on a bicycle. If you are too hot or tired to ride uphill, take a bus up the hill and ride downhill—any hill. You really can't get lost if you ride downhill; eventually you will end up at the ocean. I recommend any road down from Kintamani. If you can say the word Ubud, you can get there.

Get a Guide   If you can afford a ticket to get here, you can afford a guide. Nothing fancy, just someone you've convinced to show you Bali—the sister, cousin, uncle of the person that is running your hotel. Go to temple; go to the mountains; go anywhere, such is the magic of the guide.

Get Dressed   When the Balinese called the gods down, they called them to bless all souls on the planet. This is magic, so get dressed for it. Ask a Balinese person to help you get the proper temple attire. Every Balinese person, rich or poor, has it and goes to temple. And so should you.

Eat Temple Food   The food in the temple is amazing and made as an offering—you will not taste this anywhere else. If there is any way you can talk your guide into getting you temple food, it's worth the effort.

even themselves. You needn't go that far to have a holy experience. In the world's largest aqua-tonic seawater therapy pool at the Ayana, you have a priceless view of the Indian Ocean and experienced hands to lead you. See p. 155.

- **Uluwatu Spa at the InterContinental**   A day in the sun is good for the mind and fabulous for the spirit, though less wonderful for the bod. If you have overindulged on vitamin E, don't despair and go for the treatment named in your honor, the "Sun Goddess," good for lads and ladies alike: a hydrating facial, aloe and lavender body wrap, and all-over moisturizing rub down. Keeps your body primed for its next bout of abuse. See p. 155.

- **COMO Shambhala**   "The Source" therapy rooms have full frontal views of the Ayung river gorge. Treat yourself to the Hot River Stone Massage where stones collected on-site are warmed and used to gently massage those aching knots in your body. After mine I embarrassingly answered, "Rock on . . ." See p. 194.

- **The Jiwa Spa at the Conrad**   After a day at the beach, book in for the signature treatment "Ocean Flow" that combines elements of flowing strokes with acupressure similar to the movement of ocean waves. See p. 185.

- **The Remede Spa at St. Regis**   The Remede Spa is deliciously indulgent and open to nonresident guests. Maximize your time by using the Aqua Vitale pool set in the elegant spa courtyard. Be sure to take advantage of the complimentary Jacuzzi, steam, and sauna. Carpe diem. See p. 183.

- **Four Seasons Sayan** The new Watsu Pool at the Four Seasons was built specifically for their water therapy guru Elisa Senese who practices Watsu Waterflow therapy and craniosacral balancing. Elisa's mild movements bring you into a weightless state intended to make you feel as cosseted as being back in the womb. See p. 214.

- **Maya Ubud Spa** Go for the oversize circular baths and outdoor bales that hang serenely over the edge of the river. Listen to the sound of chirping cicadas and birds and relax after your treatment of choice in a jasmine- and frangipani-infused bathtub. See p. 214.

Bali in Depth

Bali is 153km (95 miles) east to west and 111km (69 miles) from tip to toe. Though small, a rich millennia of history has fostered an artistically diverse population, with virtually all of the Balinese being skilled craftsmen, dancers, or artists, and a spiritually blessed life, with more temples than houses, and ceremonies that last for days or even weeks. The island has beaches, volcanoes, terrace after terrace of rice paddies, mountain treks, arts and crafts, rivers and rafting, ceremonies and blessings, mountaintop sunrises, and beachside sunsets. Whichever Bali you are looking for, it is waiting to be found. Ask a typical visitor or expat what Bali means to them and you'll get many answers. Small does not mean limited.

1 BALI TODAY

Against a tumultuous historic backdrop, and in an otherwise Muslim-dominated archipelago, Bali has somehow managed to not only retain its Hindu independence but has flourished as a tourist paradise. The Balinese amalgam of Hindu traditions, Buddhism, and ancient Javanese practices and their acceptance of different lifestyles, has led many outsiders to call this place home or at the very least to return time and time again. Recent efforts by politicians to impose Sharia law and far-reaching antipornography measures in Indonesia indicate that support for an Islamic state is still strong in some areas of this vast nation. Thankfully, the Governor of Bali has gone on record as declaring that the law will not be enforced in Bali, although for cultural and historic reasons rather than for the economic benefits that tourism brings. Bali has seen a huge inflow of foreign investment in recent years. Luxury resorts and multimillion-dollar villas are commonplace, even despite the fact that only Indonesian citizens can own land in freehold title. Foreigners investing in Bali adhere to different ownership forms, which all have time limits on the control of the land in question—though it is possible to own a patch of paradise.

The country as a whole has seen improvements in infrastructure, telecoms, education, and health, and Bali, while still lacking many modern facilities, is beginning to develop as well. That being said, the roads remain potholed, the litter piles up by the side, and many locals still use the rivers for all aspects of their daily ablutions. Though this peaceful island has been dealt various blows in recent years, not least the bomb attacks of 2002 and 2005, the resolve and determination to carry on has been rewarded with a resurgence in popularity. Bali is now increasingly global and, noticeably, travelers are emerging from Russia and China, competing with the traditional Australian, Japanese, and European markets.

While many Balinese have deserted the rice fields to work in the tourist industry and the double-edged sword of tourism has wrought many changes, the island's culture has survived intact, and is perhaps stronger than ever. As with any undiscovered paradise that isn't so undiscovered anymore, many people criticize this little

Bali's Royal Regency Past

Bali is divided into one municipality, Denpasar, and eight regencies. Each regency has a capital, which further consists of a number of districts, divided into villages and then comprised of a *banjar,* or a series of *banjar,* which are the local, traditional neighborhood organizations.

Today's regencies have historic roots. The south coast at Gelgel was settled by the son of the last Rajah of Majapahit who declared himself the King of Bali or the Dewa Agung. The Dewa, in an attempt at some form of orderly rule, subdivided the island into principalities, which he then gave to his relatives and generals to govern. Over time, these principalities became increasingly independent and their descendants became princelings and then rajahs of smaller kingdoms. Many of the princelings set out to extend their influence and lands beyond their limited principalities and conquered, among others, the neighboring lands of Lombok and Sumbawa.

The arrival of the Dutch in the 17th century with their superior arms, organized forces, and willingness to trade were fundamental in Bali's development by not allowing any one dynasty to dominate. The local regencies took the somewhat pragmatic approach of recognizing Dutch supremacy and engaging in trade treaties while retaining, or more accurately being allowed to retain, their local autonomy. The Dutch themselves had their eyes on greater prizes, notably the Spice Islands, and they largely left Bali to its own devices. However, with the increasing interest of the British in the region, Bali became strategically important, given the proximity to the Dutch lands and plantations in nearby Java. The regencies of Buleleng, Jembrana, and then Karangesem, Gianyar, and Bangli all submitted themselves to Dutch control leaving the remaining three of Badung and Tabanan in 1906 and Klungkung in 1908 to fall in the dreadful *puputan.*

Ancestors of the royal families still live and work in what is left of their palaces although they now use their old homes as hotels or guesthouses or antiques shops. But the Balinese, with the caste system still relevant if not completely intact, retain their regents as the center of their community.

island for not being what it was. And while certainly it is not the island of Walter Spies and Charlie Chaplin, it is an enchanted isle, where the Bali you want to find is there—so long as you wish to discover it.

2 LOOKING BACK AT BALI

EARLY HISTORY

While Bali's recorded history is scant, even in the last 100 years, there is evidence of a Stone Age people dating to around 2,500 B.C. and the arrival of the first migrations of the Austronesian people. These rice-eating travelers of Chinese and Malayan descent arrived via the maritime trade routes of Southeast Asia via Taiwan and the Philippines, cultivating rice as they went. They first introduced and developed the complex irrigation system, *subak*, which survives to this day.

A Bronze Age people of Chinese and Vietnamese descent from the Dong Son area of Vietnam arrived in the 3rd century B.C., who brought bronze, copper, and iron. Their first sites were in the northwest at Cekik near what is now Gilimanuk and also inland at Sembiran. Evidence from these sites indicates a population of fishermen, hunters, and farmers. Their graves show evidence of metallurgy and that they had by this stage acquired the skills to cast or smelt copper, bronze, and iron themselves.

The lasting influence for much of Bali came from the Indian traders who arrived around the 1st century A.D. These mainly peaceful merchants also brought Hinduism. By the 5th century, a Hindu kingdom had been founded in Bali.

Bali's history, as a whole, is populated with many different groups of people; much of these diverse communities lived self sufficiently and independently from each other. Indonesia claims to be a mix of some 250 ethnic groups, and the Balinese have their own special genetic blend of Chinese and Malay, with traces of Polynesian and Melanesian mixed in with Indian and Javanese.

Among the diverse groups that arrived in Bali after the original Chinese settlers, were a group of only some 400 who arrived from the village of Aga, in East Java, around the 8th century. They settled in the remote mountainous area around Gunung Agung and their communities prospered. Bali Aga societies survive intact and to this day decry and resist most forms of outside influence—with little or no contact with the outside world, their arcane ways are still evident in their original colonies of Campuhan, Taro, Tegalalang, and Batur. Their societal structures exist on rigid and ancient rules and visits by outsiders and tourists can still be a daunting and occasionally harrowing experience. They remain a tough and

hardened society, far removed from much of Bali that most visitors know.

The topography of the island therefore gave way to two forms of living, the people of the mountains and the people of the sea. It is the gentrified southern and coastal people, with their civilizing Javanese customs and easy natural resources, that has given Bali its overarching identity.

By the 11th century, the influence of the Javanese, with their then predominately Hindu beliefs, was being felt more and more. Initially they came peacefully and shared reciprocal political and artistic ideals. This union of the two islands, Bali and Java, was cemented under the rule of Javanese King Airlangga, whose mother moved to Bali shortly after his birth. This informal connection allowed Bali to remain semi-autonomous for the next 200 years until King Kertanegara conquered Bali in 1284.

Though his reign was short lived (he was murdered about 8 years later), his son, the great Vijaya, founded the Majapahit dynasty, which lasted from 1293 to 1520. The influence of this dynasty reached as far afield as the Malaysian peninsula and the very eastern extent of what is now the Republic of Indonesia. The Majapahit bequeathed to Bali many of the features of its present-day society, from the style of royal rule, to its architecture, and the structures of its temples. It also brought the principles of the caste system, which are adhered to today.

The ascendancy of Islam and its spread into Java in the late 15th century caused the Hindu Majapahit dynasty to falter and ultimately disintegrate into feuding sultanates. The last Javanese Majapahit king high-tailed it to Bali, taking with him many of the court's intellectuals, artists, and priests. This wave of culture and spirituality formed the basis of Balinese society that we see today as a rich and cultured heritage.

Included in this exodus was the great priest Nirartha who, it is believed, introduced many of the complexities of Balinese religion and was a founder of many of the major temples on the island. Bali's Hindu influences and the unique way of life have managed to withstand the dominance of Islam for centuries since. Bali remains the only non-Islamic island in the whole of Indonesia.

THE ADVENT OF COLONIALISM

Marco Polo in 1292 and Vasco de Gama around 1512 were known to have reached Indonesia, but the first European to set foot on Bali is credited as the Dutchman Cornelis de Houtman in 1597. He, like many others since, was captivated with the island and when it came time to leave, it is said that it took him almost a year to round up his crew. The Dutch were more driven by financial gain than cultural pleasures and the control of the Spice Islands, the Moluccas, was a higher priority than the beauty and charms of Bali. The Dutch, while not taking any forceful control, established trading posts in Bali instead.

Dutch colonial control expanded across the Indonesian archipelago in the early part of the 19th century, including an increasing presence in Bali. By then, Bali's independent kingdoms we know today, Klungkung, Karangasem, Buleleng, Jembrana, Tabanan, Mengwi, Badung, Gianyar, and Bangli, had taken shape. The Dutch were intent on adding the whole of Bali to their colonial ambitions and set about its capture. It took separate and simultaneous wars from 1846 to 1849, and the actions of various Balinese kings using the colonizers to advance their own local ends, for the Dutch to take control of even just the north of the island. And it was not until the wars of the rajahs, from 1884 to 1894, that the Dutch finally extended their rule to the east. Karangasem and Lombok fell in 1894 and finally the Rajah of Gianyar, in a ploy where self interest took precedence over island sovereignty, was convinced by the new Lords of Ubud, to make peace with the Dutch.

The south refused to yield to Dutch rule and while some of the older guard preached peace, they were overruled by a group of headstrong young princes who defeated the Dutch in a surprise attack. Needless to say, the Dutch did not take this lightly and a larger force was dispatched to Bali to make a stand against the stubbornly resistant and proud southern kingdoms of Tabanan, Klungkung, and Badung. And yet, the Dutch were still seeking justification for an all-out assault.

In 1904, a Chinese schooner struck the reef near Sanur. The Dutch government made what were essentially unreasonable demands for compensation, which was refused by the Rajah of Badung, with the support of Tabanan and Klungkung. A dispute over the rights to plunder the cargo ships (traditionally held by the Balinese) presented the Dutch with the reasoning needed to launch a new attack. In 1906 the full force of the Dutch navy rocked up at Sanur, initiating the Badung War. After blockading the southern ports and having had various ultimatums ignored, the Dutch mounted large naval and ground assaults and in September they marched on the palace of Badung.

At the palace, the Dutch were not met by expected resistance, but instead by a silent procession with the rajah at the lead dressed in white cremation garb, armed only with a kris, followed by his supporters. His march stopped some 100 paces from the Dutch and then a priest plunged the kris into his chest. The rest of the procession followed suit and proceeded to either kill themselves or others in the procession, all of whom had voluntarily entered into a rite known as *puputan*. Sensing certain defeat at the guns of the heavily armed Dutch, the noble Balinese decided not to suffer the ignominy of defeat or surrender but rather had their death rites applied and took part in a ritual mass suicide. Despite the Dutch pleas for them to surrender, this *puputan* ended in the deaths of an estimated 4,000 Balinese men, women, and children. That same afternoon a similar event took place at the palace of Pemecutan. The Rajah of Tabanan and his son surrendered, but both committed suicide 2 days later in a Dutch prison. The last remaining regency, Klungkung, brokered a peace deal.

Not surprisingly, the atrocity of the *puputan* garnered worldwide condemnation and even a member of the Dutch Upper House of Parliament labeled the scandal the "extermination of a heroic race." Holland's image as a responsible and evenhanded colonial power was seriously compromised.

The deal that had been brokered with Klungkung fell apart when the Dutch attempted to take monopoly control of the opium trade. Riots erupted in Gianyar and the Dutch sent the troops back in, forcing the rajah to flee to Klungkung. He attempted an all-out attack, initially by himself, armed only with a ceremonial kris believed to wreak havoc on the enemy. He was brought down by a single bullet. His six wives, seeing the death of their beloved, turned their kris on themselves and committed suicide. They were then followed by the others in the procession coming out of the palace. With this last *puputan,* the Dutch could finally claim victory over the island.

The victory proved to be spiritually and morally empty and the Dutch governors were able to exercise little influence. Local control over religion and culture generally remained intact. For most commoners, life went on whether they were being ruled by their new colonial masters or their previous rajahs.

The advent of tourism and travel after the Great War brought new influences and greater worldwide attention to Bali. The island became home to anthropologists Margaret Mead and Gregory Bateson, and artists Miguel Covarrubias and Walter Spies. Musicologist Colin McPhee, in his book *A House in Bali,* fostered the Western image of Bali as "an enchanted land of aesthetes at peace with themselves and nature." Celebrity visitors such as Noel Coward and Charlie Chaplin, Barbara Hutton and Doris Duke, helped make Bali synonymous with a latter-day Garden of Eden. It was at about the same time that Pandit Nehru, the reflective and scholarly first Prime Minister of India, described Bali as the "Dawn of the World." Western tourism landed on the island.

THE ROAD TO INDEPENDENCE

Dutch rule over Bali came later than in other parts of the East Indies, such as Java and Maluku, and it was never as well established. Despite the long road to colonization, the Dutch period lasted only until Imperial Japan occupied Bali in 1942, for the duration of World War II. After Japan's Pacific surrender in August 1945, the Dutch attempted to return to Indonesia, including Bali, and to reinstate their prewar colonial administration. But Indonesia and Bali resisted, this time armed with Japanese weapons. One of the many heroes of the time was the wartime resistance leader Colonel I Gusti Ngurah Rai who spent the war years tormenting the Japanese. His death in an almost suicidal attack, considered the final *puputan,* is another footnote in the heroic history of Bali and its warriors.

The Dutch tried to maintain their colonial rule for another 4 years before finally conceding that they no longer had a role as masters in the East Indies. The Republic of Indonesia that had been originally constituted by Sukarno and Mohammed Hatta, in the immediate aftermath of WWII, now included Bali and the other

12 island states the Dutch had attempted to retain. On December 29, 1949, with the inclusion of these last states in the Republic of the United States of Indonesia, the curtain came down on the Dutch East Indies.

POST-COLONIAL INDONESIA: FROM 1949 ONWARD

The tentative federation, led by Sukarno and Mohammed Hatta, attempted to consolidate this 17,000-island nation. The road to peace and prosperity was not without its troubles. Sukarno, who had been a revolutionary, moved from democracy to autocracy and on to authoritarianism. Regional and factional problems led him eventually, in July 1959, to dissolve the assembly and assume full dictatorial powers. Increasingly, Sukarno was becoming pro-Communist and received aid from Communist sources. He made little secret of his desire to make amends for centuries of Western colonialism in Southeast Asia and he was perhaps driven more by this than any actual Communist sympathies. In 1963, he went as far as to make a stand against the formation of the federation of Malaysia, seeing it as a puppet for continued British rule. He was ultimately unsuccessful and failed to bring the disputed, now Malay lands, of northern Borneo into the Indonesian Republic.

The economic cost of this failure on the fledgling economy coupled with his alienation from the West and resulting lack of financial support when it was most needed, created hyperinflation, which lasted throughout the early part of the decade. The resulting social unrest and his failing health weakened his iron grip on the country.

Matters came to a head on the night of September 30, 1965, when eight senior generals were taken from their houses, supposedly by a group of Communist renegade army divisions, and either summarily executed or taken to Halim airport where they met the same fate. The later justification that these actions were taken to prevent an army-led coup did not convince many. A certain General Suharto convinced the other surviving generals to plan their own countermove and in a surprisingly easy manner, regained control of the military faction. Sukarno stayed in power but Suharto had emerged as a major political figure.

The backlash against the Communists in 1965 after the attempted coup is one of the bloodiest in Indonesian history. Bali was the scene of some of the worst atrocities, where mobs rounded up suspected Communists and sometimes just clubbed them to death. As many as 500,000 suspected Communists or ethnic Chinese were massacred in Indonesia with about 100,000 in Bali alone—at the time, 5% of Bali's population. Sukarno, who had enjoyed unprecedented levels of popularity, was on his way out. Finally in 1966, Sukarno fled the presidential palace and only nominally remained president for another year.

Under Suharto, the military gained far-reaching influence over national affairs. For the next 3 decades, until his undoing by the economic crisis of 1997, Indonesia enjoyed a period of sustained prosperity, even despite Suharto's embezzling autocracy and his cronies' horrific graft. Fortunately the economic meltdown had an upside: the resulting riots and protests brought an end to Suharto's military-led rule and in June 1999, Indonesians enjoyed their first free parliamentary election since 1955. They overwhelmingly ousted the incumbent.

Indonesia achieved a tentative peace under a provisional democratic government headed by President Megawati, daughter of Sukarno. She inherited political instability and an economy in crisis, but she addressed corruption and the military's human rights record. However, her rule only lasted until 2004 when she was defeated by the former military general Susilo Bambang Yudhoyono, otherwise known as SBY. His coalition government,

based on his moral code of honesty and anticorruption, has also come out on top in the elections of 2009.

3 BALI: CENTER FOR THE ARTS

Everybody in Bali seems to be an artist.
–Island of Bali, 1937, Miguel Covarrubias

Having been mainly left alone up to the 20th century, "Bali's Golden Age" under the patronage of the then dominant Gelgel kings, this small island developed its own distinctive arts, which remain touchstones of the culture and Balinese psyche and life. Tellingly, the Balinese language has no word for art or artist.

Under a regency decree, whole villages became dedicated to one craft or artistic discipline. From this we have **Ubud** and **Batuan** for paintings, **Mas** for woodcarvings, **Celuk** for silver and gold markets, and **Batubulan** for stone carvings. Outside of royalty, the temples were the main patron of the arts. Art has always played an important role for the temples and their ceremonies, which can be entirely given over to one form of artistic expression.

The tradition of art in Bali has largely been one of anonymity. Each individual had his craft that he performed, and class or caste was irrelevant. Artists carried out their craft to serve their community and temple not for their own personal aggrandizement. Princes, goldsmiths, and drivers would perform different parts in the same orchestra or even dance. The creation or the performance was for the glory of the village and the community rather than for personal fame. This lack of posterity permeates many aspects of Balinese life, and while they revere and remember the spirits of the dead, the Balinese do not themselves seek immortality—just as their wood carvings will eventually rot, their soft sandstone sculptures will crumble, and termites will eat their canvases.

Much of the way art was expressed, certainly in paintings, has changed with the circumstances. The temples and rajahs are no longer the island's biggest art patrons. A new class of customer has arrived with new demands: the tourist. In the mid-1920s, with the arrival of international artists such as Walter Spies and Rudolf Bonnet, a very traditional style of painting (*wayang* style), where images are depicted as two dimensional figures, emerged as a new distinctive art movement. What remains today is a combination of traditional artisans using conventional methods and time-honored customs and new and expressive art forms that are increasingly experimental.

PERFORMING ARTS

Dance, theater, and music all blend together in Balinese culture, and no Balinese would think of a show that separated each of the component parts. The generic term for this traditional theater, as with the style of painting, is *wayang,* which literally means shadow. Dance, drama, and music also play a central part in ritual ceremonies and temple blessings. Their history is told and passed down through the generations in the many dramatic tales performed on a regular basis. Until the advent of television, this was how history was told.

Theater

Of the many forms of theater, *Wayang Kulit* is the most well known and most often performed. This is a dance with shadow puppets, featuring intricately cut figures, originally made from buffalo parchment, called *kulit,* meaning leather or skin. The puppeteers project the images against a screen and depict tales from the Hindu epics, accompanied by a gamelan ensemble.

Other similar types of theater are **Wayang Arja,** a puppet opera set to music telling romantic stories. In **Wayang Golek,** wooden doll puppets are operated from below by rods. **Wayang Karucil** is somewhere in between Golek and Kucil, and the puppets are made from thin bits of wood. **Wayang Beber** uses illustrations and scrolls along with a narrator who sings and tells the story.

Dance

As with theater, Balinese dance mainly portrays stories from Hindu epics, the **Ramayana** being the most common. There are over a dozen differing styles of dance and all can be incredibly powerful with many of the performers entering true trancelike states. Balinese dancing originated with religious dance, although has become increasingly theatrical, with characters that were once demons or devils now more for the amusement of the crowd.

Each movement in a dance is made up entirely of prescribed gestures. This leaves little room for improvisation, though there is much that can be enhanced by the individual dancer or troupes' interpretation, emotional intensity, and expressiveness of their features. During any dance, watch the dancers' faces, and particularly the eyes. Like many displays of art, there are certain aspects that cannot be taught.

Among the many different varieties of Balinese dance, the following are the most important: **Kecak,** or the Ramayana Monkey Dance, is the most famous and most powerful. A circle of up to 150 men, wearing only a checked cloth, chant rhythmically "cak cak cak cak cak" while throwing their arms up in the air, dancing round the circle or rocking on the ground, over and over, to and fro. It tells the tale of a monkey king and his warriors. Walter Spies worked with the local dancer Wayan Limbak to turn the dance into a more dramatic performance though it comes as no surprise that *kecak* was originally a trance ritual and had groundings in exorcisms. One of the most famous places to see this is at sunset at **Pura Luhur Uluwatu** (p. 166) surrounded by real monkeys who are as naughty as some of the characters being portrayed.

Barong and *Rangda* or the Barong and Kris dance has been mainly adapted for tourists and is a fight between good and evil with the King of the Spirits *(barong)* overcoming the demon queen *(rangda)* after the wicked queen has cast a spell on the Barong and his supporters making them stab themselves with their daggers (kris). The Barong however is able to make the daggers cause no harm and they stab themselves with no effect, but spectators, especially those in the front row, are usually left feeling as though they have witnessed some form of exorcism—the dance's original purpose.

Legong is a graceful dance performed by young girls. *Baris* is a traditional war dance in which a solo dancer depicts the feelings of a young warrior prior to battle. *Topeng* is a masked drama with tales of mythical kings and gods. A narrator, who wears a half mask, tells the story accompanied by the gamelan with dance, fight, and a bit of humor. *Wayang Wong* is a shadow dance in which the players wear masks and tells an aristocratic love story between Rama and Rawana with soft delicate music. It was originally only ever performed in four royal palaces and has always been considered the most aristocratic of plays.

Music

Bali is renowned for its profusion of musical performances and the variety of its instrumental ensemble, the **gamelan:** a group of players with xylophone-like instruments, drums, and gongs that can range up to 50 in number. Each gamelan orchestra has its own specific tuning and is considered a single entity. All Balinese music is based around the gamelan, an integral part of all ceremonies and performing arts. The sound is easily identifiable and identified with Bali. Musical styles vary regionally: The music of western Bali, for example, uses gamelan made from bamboo, called *jegog,* which grows to enormous sizes and can take up to four men to carry one instrument. There are some 25 types of varying sizes of gamelan in metal, bronze, or bamboo. Of the various different styles, the **Gong Keybar,** introduced in the early 1900s is nowadays the most popular form. If you're curious to see the manufacture and production of gamelan instruments, visit **Tihingan** (p. 248) in east Bali.

PAINTING
Wayang Style

The classic Balinese style is **wayang,** which takes its origins from the shadow puppets of the same name. Clear rules determine the shapes, colors, and even the positioning of the characters—noble on the left, evil on the right, just as they are in a performance. Paintings were traditionally on *langse,* which were broad rectangular cloths used as wall hangings in temples or curtains in palaces, or on *ider-ider,* which were similar to scrolls. This style of painting continues to flourish thanks to the drive of **Nyoman Mandara** in the 1960s and his government-sponsored painting school.

Other traditional styles are *Batuan,* which is strongly *Wayang*-based and involves hundreds of painted images of Balinese life; *Keliki* is similar to an old *Batuan* style showing mythical characters engaged in the struggle of good against evil, though the *Keliki* paintings are rarely larger than 20cm × 15cm (8 in. × 6 in.). The *Pengosekan* style deals with nature, plants, and insects and emerged as recently as the 1960s with influences that could certainly be ascribed to "flower power."

Walter Spies and Rudolf Bonnet helped evolve more abstract terms of expression during the 1920s. Their arrival coincided with a seismic cultural shift as the increasing Dutch colonial influence removed the power and money from the rajahs and the temples. This meant that the rajahs were no longer the main patrons and financial supporters of artists and as such could no longer dictate the traditional styles. This two-pronged influence led to a huge change and an explosion in the whole artistic movement. No more were artists retained purely for the benefit of the temple or the palace with their constrained and preordained styles. Now they had to cut their cloth for a new style of buyer, the tourist. This new freedom of expression brought individual displays of talent leading to fame for the likes of **I Gusti Nyoman Lempod** and **Sudjojono** whose work now commands hundreds of thousands of dollars. I Gusti Nyoman Lempod's paintings are full of energy and characterize everyday life as well as religious themes. Two other Balinese artists of note are **Nyoman Gunarsa** and **Made Wianta** who are considered to be the pioneers of Balinese contemporary art.

Pita Maha & the Modern Style

Spies had originally been enticed to Bali from Java at the behest of the royal family. With Bonnet and one of the local princes, Cokorda Gede Agung Surapati, he established the **Pita Maha,** an artists' cooperative that allowed artists to develop their own expressive style and to even sign the canvas. Pita Maha means literally "great vitality," but it also means "ancestor," which resonates particularly well with the Balinese. Here they sponsored and controlled the quality of work of selected artists and sold pieces through their gallery. In later years many of the paintings they sponsored were donated to the **Puri Lukisan** (p. 210), the oldest museum in Ubud. The war and Spies's incarceration, for his fondness for certain young Balinese boys, disrupted the movement. Bonnet's

Bali's Craft Villages at a Glance

As with art, so are crafts specific to individual villages. Be careful where and from whom you buy as many artifacts are now imported and may be machine- rather than handmade. And again, as with art, some of these are very hard to tell from original works.

Basketware & Painting: Batuan
Carving: Penarukan
Coconut & Bone Carving: Bangli; Tampaksiring
Gamelan Instruments & Gongs: Blahbatu; Sawan; Tihingan
Jewelry: Tampaksiring; Ubud
Masks: Mas; Puaya
Pottery: Pataen; Pejaten; Ubung
Puppets: Puaya
Silver & Gold: Budakeling; Celuk
Stone Carving: Batubulan
Temple Decorations (umbrellas, wind chimes, and so on): Sukawati
Weaving: Belayu; Beratan; Gianyar; Mengwi; Sidemen; Tenganan
Woodcarving: Jati; Mas; Pujung; Tegallalang; Ubud

return in the 1950s never quite reclaimed the past glories, nor did the Ubud Painters group, which replaced Pita Maha. The 1950s saw the further input of **Arie Smit** who developed a Matisse-style of painting with lots of bright colors, fish or frogs on bicycles, and ducks with hats. Many of his paintings now hang in the **Neka Museum** (p. 210).

CRAFTS
Textiles & Weaving

Prized for their stunning beauty, variety, and role in traditional costume and ceremony, the traditional textiles of Bali and Indonesia are woven, twined, batiked, tie-dyed, embroidered, and embellished works of art and are among the best treasures to acquire while visiting Bali and Lombok—and anywhere else in Indonesia. Fine, authentic, handmade textiles originating from all of the far-flung islands of the Indonesian archipelago are available in antiques shops, boutiques, galleries, and markets. Religious paraphernalia, shrines, dancers, priests, masks, and offerings are all wrapped, bound, draped, or ornamented with specifically prescribed textiles, redolent with symbolic meaning. Bali is by no means unique in this regard. Throughout Indonesia, traditional textiles are ritual objects, stored wealth, trade goods, bride wealth, and tokens of prestige.

Bali itself is extraordinarily rich in textile traditions. *Ikat* cloths have patterns dyed into the individual threads before they are woven, with the design only appearing on the loom. The effect creates jagged borders between one color and the next and bold patterns in a wide range of color palettes. Most *ikat* now is made in Gianyar Regency and around **Klungkung** (p. 247). Traditional markets in large towns are a good place to shop, or go directly to *ikat* workshops to buy ready stock, and to watch the weaving process first hand.

Tips **Buying Textiles**

When you look at textiles, in general, it's best to start at the high end (and perhaps come back to it). Develop an eye for the kind of cloth you like, then shop around. First, try the galleries at five-star hotels and reputable antiques shops in Ubud and Seminyak for antique textiles, and then visit markets and boutiques for contemporary pieces. You may well return to the high-end shops, and obtain good value there, because their owners know the world market, and are adept at sourcing the very finest examples. They are also more likely to identify textiles correctly as to origin, age, and quality. Expect reputable galleries to offer literature and anecdotal information about collectible textiles. They are your best source of accurate information.

Use your eyes. Judge for yourself. You are choosing a work of art. Ultimately, your feeling is the best guide. Whatever type of Indonesian textile you choose to acquire, choose well, and then rest assured that you have acquired an object of lasting value, for both its visible and invisible attributes.

Songket is fashioned with threads of cotton, silk, gold, or silver that float on the base cloth in a variety of patterns. Again, east Bali, especially **Klungkung** (p. 247) and **Sidemen** (p. 249), are among the best places to find good contemporary *songket.*

Geringsing textiles are woven only in **Tenganan** (p. 257), using a painstaking double-*ikat* technique, in which both the warp and weft threads are patterned prior to weaving. The quality of antique pieces has never been matched by contemporary weavers, although a revival is underway. Antique and high-quality new pieces fetch thousands of dollars.

Wood

Wood carvings and craft is a particular specialization of the Balinese. Historically, wood carvings were for ornamentation in palaces, temples, and houses of high caste. With increasing tourist demand, attention has lately been turned to the more portable, less ghoulish, and less antidemonic items. There are plenty of carved Buddha heads, and Garudas as well as traditional styles of furniture, all mainly in local woods such as belalu, suar, or even teak. Be on the lookout for sandalwood, for its delightful and lasting fragrance. Such pieces tend to be small and detailed, with a propensity for elephants, and are slightly more pricey than other carvings. A lot of the intricate doorways that you see in many villas these days are imported from Java, the local ones having been snatched up a long time ago.

4 BALINESE ARCHITECTURE

Balinese architecture has developed characteristic gorgeous gates, airy pavilions, mystical statues, and romantic gardens. This holds true even in the 21st century, where we find Bali at an architectural crossroads between Mannerist splendor and minimalism, and ever at the cutting edge of international tropical design.

The buildings, tropical gardens, and temple umbrellas that leaped off the travel posters in the last days of the 20th century are still to be found, albeit beneath a thick veneer of other new and differing styles. The "New Look," for which Bali is now equally famous, is a result of decades of experimentation with modernism and the notion of "New Asia."

All Bali's many looks somehow derive from the island's architectural traditions of outdoor living, pavilions in all shapes and sizes, and walled compounds. "Bali style" is essentially a courtyard architectural style, inherited, no doubt, from the Chinese, with indigenous and the Hindu-Javanese influence. The original architectural style of Bali, which can still be found in the mountain villages near **Lake Batur,** was simple and almost severe: low-eaved, high-pitched-roof single unit dwellings made of bamboo and timber sitting on packed mud or stone plinths. The dwellings are arranged on terraces, according to clans and castes, and set in rows, aligned with the mountain-to-sea axis. Villages such as **Belantih, Songan,** and **Terunyan** still exhibit this style. Similarly the temples of this mountain Bali culture (called Bali Aga) were almost Zen-like in their austerity (the old **Pura Puseh** at Bayung Gede, is one example).

As classical Javanese Hinduism was introduced into Bali in waves, starting as early as the 10th century, and as people started to populate the flatter coastal regions the rows of simple, single hut dwellings grew into courtyards of multi-purpose pavilions—following the South Indian model—which eventually grew walls and gates in the Chinese or Javanese style. Chinese influence had been strong along Bali's north coast through trade since the beginning of the first millennium, and that region's architecture retains a strong Chinese character. The terraced sanctuaries and worshiping grounds of the animistic ancients slowly became Hindu temples, but retained much of their original nature; shrines remained oriented toward the mountains, the abode of the pre-Hindu gods, even as they grew towers, gates, and shrines, modeled on Hindu-Javanese prototypes.

At the beginning of the 20th century, when many Balinese palaces were razed after the series of horrific *puputan* of 1906 and 1908, Dutch colonial architectural styles started to take hold. Influence in the north, with neoclassical bungalows, is still visible in **Singaraja** and the mountain village of **Munduk;** other examples are in **Denpasar** in the south. The building of the Art Deco **Hotel Denpasar** in 1935 could be seen as the start of the modern era of Balinese architecture. From then on, all the island's princes—always keen to adopt, absorb, and adapt—wanted colonial-style pavilions and little *pensiones,* modeled on the Hotel Denpasar, sprung up across the island.

Other "princes" had started arriving in Bali by the 1930s: a colony of foreign artists and scholars who wanted to live like the Balinese, but in a palatial manner. Many settled near Ubud, where local prince Tjokorda Agung Sukawati proved a great patron and mentor (he was a cofounder of the Pita Maha Art Foundation). Walter Spies invented the modified *wantilan,* the traditional cock-fighting pavilion found in every town square, during this time, in an attempt to get his baby grand piano between the columns of his home. The Balinese Dream Home movement started during this Happy Valley–esque prewar era. The **Le Mayeur** home (p. 135) is now a museum, and Spies's home in Ubud is now the **Hotel Tjampuhan** (p. 198). Musicologist Colin McPhee's home is now the **Taman Bebek Villas** (p. 196) in Sayan. And the **Hotel Denpasar** still stands, largely untouch. Within a brief period of time Bali began exporting ideas for tropical resorts to the entire world. Even the Brutalist Bali Hyatt in Sanur, completed in 1973, provided a platform for the next generation of tropical hotel design stars who went on to create culturally referenced resorts highlighting local architecture and materials around the globe. The main lobby of the **Bali Hyatt** (p. 121) remains today as the largest single pavilion on the island, a masterpiece in coconut and bamboo.

Since the 1930s, a trend to do better than the Balinese at creating glamorous architecture and interiors was embraced by dream-home owners, hotel developers, and architects—both foreign and Indonesian.

Hotels became the new temples of Bali, just as the Balinese were deserting their traditional architecture in favor of more Western home designs. Balinese villages and south Bali suburbs today are littered with examples of Hindu wedding cake, Ghost Train Gothique, and Imelda Marcos Modern interspersed with pure Hindu-Balinese temples, and the occasional Majapahit palace and traditional courtyard home.

5 RELIGION & SPIRITUALITY

Though Balinese faith is not guided by any particular creed, dogma, or scripture, it literally and figuratively colors every aspect of Balinese life. Religion encapsulates both faith and nationality; life is religion and religion is life. The religion, practiced by all but 5% of the island's population, is a variant of India's Hinduism called Hindu-Dharmaism, that teaches that every living organism has both good and evil spirits. But what the Balinese seek most of all is to be Balinese, and to develop harmony with their family, community, ancestors, gods, and demons in the belief that this conduct will ensure their reincarnation as a happier, nobler being.

TEMPLES

The temple is the single most important institution on the island. Bali is commonly called the island of a thousand temples, although this is an understatement as every house, village, many crossroads, and irrigation points have a temple. Most *pura* ("temple" in Sanskrit) share a common architecture, being larger or smaller versions of the previous one you saw. The temples' structure, layout, and days of celebration (and how to celebrate), have been ordained for centuries. All temples are laid out on the *kaja-kelod* line: They are oriented from the mountain (holy), or *kaja*, seaward (profane), or *kelod*. There are temples for the

harvest, for the rain, for life, for death, and for just about every aspect of daily life you can think of. To see the temples in their true light, you must see them during their ceremony time when they are adorned in bright colors and ceremonial garb, offerings are made, and the gamelan sings.

Major Temples

Bali has nine major temples, known as the directional temples or *kahyangan jagat,* that protect the island from evil spirits. The directional temples occupy auspicious locations, whether the side of a mountain, a cave, or cliff top. The nine temples are **Pura Besakih** on the western slopes of Gunung Agung, **Pura Sambu** on the southern slopes of Gunung Agung, **Pura Goa Lawah,** and **Pura Lempuyang** on the slopes of Gunung Lempuyang; in the central mountains, **Pura Luhur Batu Karu** on the southern slopes of Gunung Batukaru, **Pura Ulun Danu Bratan** at Bedugul, and **Pura Ulun Danu Batur** at Kintamani; on the Bukit, **Pura Luhur Uluwatu;** and in the south, **Pura Masceti** near Sanur.

The next group of important temples are the sea temples, built in the 16th century by the legendary Hindu monk from Java, Nirartha. These sea temples are on the western coast of Bali and run counterclockwise from Nirartha's supposed point of arrival. They start at **Pura Gede Perancak** just to the south of Negara, and lead down to **Pura Rambut Siwi** to the east of Negara. The sea temples continue to **Pura Tanah Lot,** on south to **Pura Luhur Uluwatu** at the southwestern extremity of the Bukit Peninsula, round to **Pura Mas Suka** at the southern tip, then to **Pura Sakenan** at Pulau Serengan, an island between Benoa and Sanur, and finally to **Pura Pulaki,** just northeast of Gilimanuk.

Village & Family Temples

Every village has at least three temples. The three distinct types of village temple are the **Pura Puseh,** the temple of the village founders, the **Pura Desa,** the village temple, and the **Pura Dalem,** the temple of the dead, which will normally be just outside the village.

Family temples are small shrines in each home where daily prayers and handmade offerings are given. Many Balinese believe that the spirits of their ancestors remain in their family temple.

CEREMONIES

Prescribed ceremonies last anywhere from 3 to 42 days, depending on the importance of the occasion. Shrines are dressed with cloth and painted brocade or *salang* (carved wood painted with gold), and sometimes Chinese coins, are hung in the four corners of the shrines.

The ritual ceremonies and festivals in Hindu Balinese can be classified into five types: **Dewa Yadnya,** rites related to the worship of gods such as a temple anniversary or *odalan;* **Rsi Yadnya,** in reverence to prophets or priesthood, including the ancestors before they have been deified; **Pitra Yadnya,** rites related to death; **Manusa Yadnya,** rites of passage (from conception to just before death); and **Buta Yadnya,** sacrifices to placate the negative or demonic forces that bring misfortune to man.

Temple Celebrations

The timing of celebrations are based on one of two calendars in use in Bali, although predominately it is the *wuku* or the *pawukon,* which is a year of 210 days, rather than the *saka* calendar brought by the Majapahit, which follows the series of 12 lunar months. Annual temple festivals occur with both. Auspicious dates for such things as launching a new fishing boat or getting

What's in a Name?

The Balinese have no common last names. Everyone is given a last name about 3 months after they are born that symbolizes what their parents would like them to be or a trait that they see in their newborn. For example, babies perceived to be smart are often called **Samarta** or **Pradnyana.** If the parents are hoping for a peaceful baby they might give the last name **Santi.**

First names tend to follow castes. First names are all the same for the **Sudra** caste, about 90% of the population, the average worker. The full name of a Balinese person indicates caste, birth order, and gender. All male names begin with an "I," pronounced "eee" and all the female names begin with a "Ni" pronounced "nee." I or Ni is followed by one of four given names depending on birth order. The first born within a Sudra caste family is Wayan (pronounced Why-on), then Nyoman (pronounced Nyo-m'on) or Nengah (pronounced Neng-aah), then Made (Ma-day), and last would be Ketut (pronounced Ketoot). If you hit number five you go back to Wayan again.

(Tips) **Some Local Customs to Live By**

When on Bali, don't point with your finger, point with your thumb, which is considered polite. Take off your shoes before entering someone's home. Don't even contemplate going into a temple without the proper dress of a sarong and sash. Being gentle and polite, like the Balinese themselves, will get you a lot farther with whomever or whatever situation you are dealing with.

married are determined by these calendars. As neither follow the Western calendar, festival dates change from month to month and year to year.

Bizarrely, and slightly out of character, **cockfights** are an integral part of religious ceremony. Villagers are obliged to keep fighting cocks and to donate them to the cockfights that follow the ceremonies. The men take great care of their fighting cocks, fawning over them and massaging them and occasionally even letting them fight each other. Cockfighting has its origins in blood sacrifices, although the more skeptical might suggest that the gambling surrounding the cockfights nowadays is more the reason for keeping this tradition alive. In 1981 the government made all forms of gambling illegal. Cockfighting now takes place in more remote locations than in the past and can be easily dismantled in a moment's notice. Betting can go up to 1 to 2 months wages in a single fight.

The dedication or inauguration day of a temple is considered its birthday *(odalan)* and the celebration takes place every 210 days; this is the most important regular ceremony for a temple. The ceremonies continue into the evening with either *pendet* or *rejang* dances, led by the priests and by elderly women who act as assistants to the priests. Many spend the whole night in the temple. The two most important ceremonies are the purification ceremony, **Panca Wali Krama,** which takes place once every 10 years, and the **Eka Dasa Rudra,** the greatest ceremony of all taking place only every 100 years.

Common to all temples are *galungan* (10 days) and *kuningan* (the final day of *galungan*), which take place every 210 days and celebrate the triumph of light over evil and the creation of the universe. As these are common to all temples, this is also a public holiday—although not for quite the full 10 days.

For more on the major Balinese holidays, see p. 31.

Life Cycle Rites

The other ceremonies at the temples are ritual life cycle rites, starting at birth and ending at death and cremation. Until the 42nd day of a child's life, the mother and child are both still considered impure and cannot enter temples. One curious custom is that the Balinese do not let a baby touch the ground until the 105th day ceremony.

Another ceremony partly unique to the Balinese is tooth filing for adolescents: It is believed that it is tooth shape that distinguishes gods and humans from birds and animals. The purpose of this *matatah* is to remove impurity by eliminating or reducing the Sad Ripu, or the six weaknesses or deadly sins: lust, greed, anger, drunkenness, confusion, and jealousy. The Sad Ripu are symbolically eliminated by flattening the two upper canines, teeth that most resemble an animal's, and the four incisors. The lower teeth are left alone, as they represent desire and passion, which should not be killed completely. Every Balinese will have his teeth filed and it can even happen after death.

6 LAY OF THE LAND

GEOGRAPHY

Only 37km (23 miles) separates Bali from Lombok, but there is some 1,300m (4,265 ft.) of vertical drop in the Lombok Strait. This almost trivial distance belies an evolutionary lifetime in the development of plants and animals. The deep ridge forms part of the fabled **Wallace Line,** the imaginary boundary drawn in 1859 by Alfred Russel Wallace, which runs between the far west coast of Australasia through to Southeast Asia and separates our natural world in two parts. On one side you will find only those animals and fauna similar to Australia, such as marsupials or cockatoos, and on the other, Bali side, are monkeys and woodpeckers. Wallace's observations provided Darwin with information that accelerated his thesis on the *Origin of the Species.* Quite bizarrely, even birds observe this line.

Bali's place at the edge of the Indo-Australian and northern Eurasian tectonic plates is indeed explosive, and little wonder that the island is dominated by volcanoes. A volcanic mountain range stretches all the way across the island; a northern and southern plain surround this mountain range, with the northern being narrower and hillier, making rice growing more difficult, while the southern plain is rich and intensively cultivated, with terraced rice fields dominating the landscape.

Gunung Batur remains a very active volcano and erupted three times in the 20th century, in 1905, 1926, and 1963 and continued spouting until 1974. The highest mountain, **Gunung Agung,** was quiet for almost 150 years, but erupted quite spectacularly with little warning in 1963, killing some 2,000 and destroying much of the local vegetation and surrounding villages. It also lowered itself by some 200m (656 ft.).

While Bali was made famous by its surf, the images of a golden sand playground are often wide of the mark, as the majority of the popular **coastline** of the west is dominated by rocks or black volcanic sand. Golden beaches and coral reefs are rarer than the pervading tourism image of Bali suggests, and are the exception rather than the rule. The north coast has much coarser sand and the east has mainly stones and pebbles, although there are some hidden gems.

FLORA & FAUNA

Huge banyan trees grow majestically in the grounds of temples or other holy places. Tamarind trees are typically found on the north coast, and in the highlands acres of clove trees planted by Suharto to make cigarettes, still smoked today, grow in abundance.

Some 15 varieties of bamboo grow on Bali alone, which are used in anything from baskets, satay sticks, and furniture to great 3,000-sq.-m (32,291-sq.-ft.) buildings. Mangrove trees hug the shores near Sanur and further south towards Tanjung Benoa. While on the Bukit, where the land is arid, flame and acacia trees create a shrubland.

The most important of all crops on Bali is rice. Rice has shaped the culture and the landscape, and it is no coincidence that the word for rice, *nasi,* also means meal. It is the main crop of the island and is grown in such abundance that even as the cornerstone of the staple diet for all, there is sufficient left over for export. In the last part of the 20th century, attempts were made to increase the number of crops per year from two to three using artificial nutrients and fertilizers. What was overlooked however was the complex system of irrigation, *subak,* developed over hundreds of years, and the interdependence of each *sawah,* or rice field. The disturbance of this shared irrigation between farmers, who themselves may not have been fully aware of just how developed and interdependent they were, has had in some cases, crippling results.

The west has coconut plantations. Most of the original taller coconut varieties are now being replaced with the dwarf hybrids that have higher yields. Coconut trees are extremely valuable to the community, not only for the coconuts, but also for their many byproducts. Other crops include fruit and vegetables around Bedugul. With heights of around 1,200m (3,937 ft.), the cool temperatures together with the nutrient-rich soil are ideal conditions for most vegetable growing. These cool temperatures are also ideal for coffee and Indonesia is the fourth largest producer of coffee globally. Although most of the coffee grown is in Java and Sumatra, Bali does also play a small part in the export. Coffee plantations are in the central mountains around Munduk, theBatukaru, and even Kintamani.

On the western side of the Wallace Line, Bali is the natural home to mammals associated with the Indo-Asian continent although the last tiger seen here was apparently shot dead in 1937. However, Bali is still rich with the likes of deer, civets, wild buffalo, and more monkeys than you would care to shake a stick at—not least because they would likely take it from you and shake it right back. Furthermore, Bali has over 300 species of birds such as swallows, starlings, and sea eagles. The underwater world, especially around Nusa Lembongan and Penida, contains some of the greatest varieties of fish and shellfish in the world such as the Mola-Mola, sea horses, manta rays, dolphins, and sharks.

7 EATING & DRINKING IN BALI

The rich array of food found in the rest of Asia is, to many, sadly lacking in Bali. But then again, many who come to Bali don't experience authentic Balinese cuisine. However, though food plays a central role in Balinese ceremonies and offerings, food is seen more as a staple of life rather than a luxury. This is reflected in the manner in which the daily ration is served, usually portable and often without too much experimentation and choice. Balinese meals tend to be eaten quickly and without fanfare. People simply eat when they are hungry and dining out or in groups is not a normal social convention. Festivals are the major exception, when food is prepared in an elaborate and decorative manner and eaten communally, marking the occasion as something out of the ordinary.

Most of the daily staples center around rice, accompanied by vegetables and a small amount of either fish or meat, with a range of spices and chilies, usually cooked in the early morning, and consumed whenever the need arises. Coconut remains central to Balinese cooking and can be either grated or squeezed to produce cream, or the oil is used for frying. The husks can be used for cooking in an open fire which, when barbecuing fish, can sometimes be an overpowering flavor. Other spices and herbs common to Balinese cooking are ginger, *galangel* and turmeric, lemongrass, chili, and lime with palm sugar and tamarind to sweeten it all up.

Given their Hindu origins, the Balinese rarely eat beef although this is also partly due to the inability to keep meat fresh, given limited refrigeration.

LOCAL DISHES

Warungs in Bali and Indonesia are best described as the equivalent of a French cafe. Almost all locals will buy at least one meal a day at their local warung. You should at some stage consider eating at one. The obvious dish to choose is **nasi campur,** rice with a mix of whatever else

> **Warning!** **A Dish You Might Want to Avoid**
>
> Beware of **sate anjing,** made from dog.

has been cooked that day. You go to the counter, where the dishes are on display behind a glass screen, armed with a pointing finger (about the only time pointing is acceptable in Bali), and point out what dishes you want. The options will usually include roasted and/or curried chicken, tempeh, sweet and sour pork, fried fish, various steamed greens, and *urap,* a pungent, warm salad of steamed vegetables with coconut and spices.

A similar way of serving an array of food is **padang** style, which originated in Sumatra, where all the dishes for the day are laid out on a table and you help yourself. Hygiene can be an issue here as many customers take from the communal dishes using only their hands and dishes will then be served to subsequent customers. You'll see the same array of food with side dishes of *sambal,* but in general the dishes tend to be very spicy. A favorite *padang* dish is *rendang,* a spicy stew, usually beef or mutton, slow cooked in coconut and spices until the sauce is almost fully absorbed by the meat.

For more freshly cooked foods, **bakso** is a soup of noodles and meatballs, served as an anytime snack. **Bakwan** has spicy wontons. **Soto ayam** is chicken soup with noodles, topped off with egg, tomatoes, and spices typically for lunch.

The perennial favorite, for when you cannot think of what to eat or just want something simple, is *nasi goreng,* fried rice with vegetables and chicken and/or prawns. Alternatively, *mie goreng* has noodles rather than rice as the base. **Gado gado** is a vegetable salad served with a spicy peanut sauce dressing and usually crispy prawn crackers.

For a snack, there is plenty of choice. **Tempeh** is crunchy shelled soy beans mixed with a special strain of yeast to form a small flat cake, then fried. Spring rolls, **lumpia,** are large crispy pastry skins filled with meats and/or vegetables with mild spices then deep fried. **Sate** (satay) is ubiquitous on the island and makes a great snack. It is made of either chicken, beef, goat *(kambing),* or fish, which is threaded on bamboo skewers and grilled over coconut husk coals, then usually served with a spicy peanut sauce *(saus kacang).* Sate lilit is minced meat or fish with spices on lemongrass skewers—possibly the most delicious way of serving *sate.*

Palm sugar and coconut are the anchors on the sweet side. You will find black sticky rice, *bubuh injun,* served in hot sticky sauce of palm sugar and coconut cream. Rice flour cakes are popular and at breakfast you may also see Balinese pancakes, which are coconut pancakes dipped in palm sugar. Other dishes use bananas such as *godoh* or *pisang rai,* which are fried or steamed bananas, respectively, coated in coconut.

The menu and preparation changes for ceremonies. Much care and attention is given to not only the preparation of food but also the choice of dishes appropriate to serve as offerings to show commitment to communal social obligations. Among those traditionally served are *babi guling, bebek betutu,* and *lawar* as they require much preparation; they are usually undertaken by the whole community. At large festivals, you can see whole teams working through the day making the ceremonial dishes.

Babi guling is spit-roasted whole stuffed baby pig presented intact on the table for feasts or banquets. The spicy filling is made of, among other things, chili, turmeric, ginger, *galangal,* onions, and garlic all basted in coconut oil and a bit more turmeric. Duck, or *bebek,* is best served as ***bebek betutu,*** covered in a spicy paste, wrapped in banana leaf, and slow cooked in pit of embers. ***Lawar*** remains one of Bali's most famous local dishes and, as it must be consumed immediately, is not found in restaurants. Made from pig's blood and spices, together with an assortment of other goodies, *lawar* can be found in every village in Bali. The meat distinguishes the type of *lawar*—chicken, duck, beef, pork, turtle, or even dragonfly but thankfully turtles are now rarely used.

DRINKS

Fresh young **coconut milk** is refreshing and healthy. Drill a hole, drink the juice, then scrape the juicy coconut flesh from the inside of the shell. A variety of drinks are based on young coconut *(kelapa muda)*. ***Es campur*** is somewhere between a drink and a dessert—shaved ice topped with sweet condensed milk and a variety of *agar-agar* based jellies. Similar is *es buah,* which has chopped fresh fruit. *Es rumput laut* adds locally harvested seaweed.

Fresh **juices** *(jus aneka buah)* are available everywhere. Fresh lime juice *(jus jeruk nipis)* is a good thirst quencher, as is fresh watermelon *(semangka)* or orange juice *(jus jeruk),* sometimes confusingly made from tangerines, which tastes even better. When ordering, make sure you ask for any sugar to be served on the side. Many times you will ask for a fresh fruit juice only for it to be loaded with extra sugar.

You will find many places selling Bali ***kopi*** (coffee) and it is normally wonderful. Generally, Balinese coffee is processed using the wet method, which results in a sweet, soft coffee with good consistency. However, while the coffee is good here, the way it is served and presented can leave a little to be desired. For some reason they seem to overpowder and then underfilter the coffee, leaving large dollops of ground coffee in your mug.

Beer, Wine & Moonshine

Bali sits outside the normal ways of the rest of the Muslim-dominated country and therefore alcohol, though expensive, is accessible. Imported wines and spirits tend to be expensive, as import duties are on a value basis which was raised to 300% in 2008.

The locally produced wines are Hatten and Wine of the Gods, with white, red, and rose varieties, from grapes grown in Bali. There is also Two Islands, red and white

Eating at the Kaki Lima

Kaki lima are small carts along the roadside and in busy areas around towns and markets that turn out a variety of quick, inexpensive meals.

Martabak is a deep-fried chicken or duck egg omelet with spices and ground meat. Carts selling *martabak* usually also sell *putu,* a small green colored roll like a pancake, filled with palm sugar, and *terang bulan,* larger pancakes with sweet chocolate-flavored condensed milk, nuts, and other toppings.

Kaki lima also sell fried rice or noodles (*nasi* or *mie goreng*). *Bakso* is a spicy and delicious soup with noodles, meatballs, and other local snacks such as *gorengan,* a selection of deep-fried tofu, tempeh, and savory pastries.

Use caution when eating at the *kaki lima,* as quality and hygiene can vary, as they have little access to running water to properly wash their plates.

The Rijsttafal

Rijsttafel is an Indonesian feast, described as the "Crown Jewel of Indonesian Cuisine" and is translated from the Dutch as "rice table." Up to 40 dishes are served in small proportions and accompanied by rice. It originated in colonial times when the Dutch felt they needed a banquet that represented the multiethnic nature of the East Indies archipelago. Popular dishes include egg rolls, *gado gado, sambal,* and pickles, satay of all types, fish, fruit, vegetables, and nuts enhanced by coriander, basil, bay leaves, cardamom, *galangal,* and lemongrass.

wines, made from Australian grapes imported as grape juice and then fermented and bottled here. The roses with plenty of ice are perfectly drinkable, the rest are more an acquired taste.

One shining bright light, literally, as its name means "star," is the local beer, **Bintang,** served ice cold everywhere. The other locally produced beer, by a Western-owned firm, is **Storm Beer,** both dark and light.

Home brews *arak, brem,* and *tuak* are popular among the locals but are basically moonshine. *Arak* is an extremely alcoholic brew made from rice, and distilled and fermented until it becomes a clear white spirit. Alcohol content varies greatly but it is usually just strong and not particularly tasty. It can be served either with ice or mixed with local honey and fresh limes or added to cocktails to disguise the taste. However the whole *arak* production was completely closed down in June 2009 as one rogue manufacturer added methanol to his batch which resulted in at least

27 deaths, among them four foreigners, and the blindness of many others.

Brem is a rice wine and has not been affected by methanol; white rice produces the white *brem* and black rice is used for red *brem*. Usually sold while still "young," the white tends to be slightly sour and the red, quite sweet, similar to a light port wine.

Tuak is made from juice extracted from the aren palm. When fresh, it is a light pink color and not alcoholic; the sweet drink with a strange odor is popular with locals, especially at feasts and parties. The alcoholic variety is made from *tuak* that has been mixed with palm sugar, poured into earthenware containers, and buried. Once fermented, the *tuak* turns a lighter color and has varying degrees of alcoholic content, depending on the strength of the original brew and the length of time underground. The smell and flavor are quite pungent and vaguely rotten. Along with *arak*, it is definitely an acquired taste.

Planning Your Trip to Bali & Lombok

A little planning can make the difference between a bum trip and a great journey. When should you go? What festivals or special events will occur during your visit? What's the best way to get there? How much should you plan to spend? What safety or health precautions should you take? This chapter answers these and other questions.

1 WHEN TO GO

WEATHER

Bali lies between latitude 08 45S and longitude 115 10E, which places it firmly in the topics. Accordingly, average year-round temperatures are a balmy 26°C to 29°C (80°F–85°F) varying only with altitude. The average temperatures in the central mountains are 18°C to 24°C (64°F–75°F). Days are generally 12 hours long year-round.

In general, Bali and Lombok have similar weather, though Lombok is dry and receives less rain than Bali. The hot and sticky **rainy season** lasts October to March with downpours that can obscure all visibility. The wet season brings daily rain with the worst falling between December and February. From June to August, the temperature drops slightly and

there is usually a refreshing cool breeze in the air. Humidity is high during the rainy season and better in the dry season.

The popular **dry season,** referred to as "summer" by the locals even though it is the southern hemisphere, is cooler and much more pleasant. The best time to visit is during the dry season from April to October. This is also **high season** together with Christmas and New Year, when most hotels and villas will charge higher rates. December and January are characterized by sudden and short thunderstorms in the afternoon, though sometimes it can rain for days, flooding all the rivers and roads. For up-to-date information on weather in Bali go to www. accuweather.com.

Average Bali Temperatures, Rainfall & Humidity

Month	Low C/F	High C/F	Rainfall mm/in	Humidity	Season
January	26/79	32/90	300/12	85%	Wet
February	26/79	32/90	280/11	75%	Wet
March	25/77	32/90	215/8½	70%	Wet
April	25/77	33/91	100/4	65%	Dry
May	25/77	32/90	85/4	60%	Dry
June	23/73	31/88	75/3	60%	Dry
July	21/70	31/88	55/2	60%	Dry
August	23/73	31/88	40/1½	60%	Dry
September	24/75	32/90	90/3½	65%	Dry
October	25/77	33/91	100/4	75%	Wet
November	26/79	32/90	150/6	80%	Wet
December	26/79	32/90	295/12	85%	Wet

Nonreligious Festivals

For an exhaustive list of events beyond those listed here check http://events.frommers.com, where you'll find a searchable, up-to-the-minute roster of what's happening in cities all over the world.

Bali Spirit Festival (www.balispiritfestival.com): A yoga festival based in Ubud over a week in March or April.

Bali Arts Festival (www.baliartsfestival.com; **Taman Werdhi Budaya Arts Center**, Jl. Nusa Indah, Denpasar; ✆ **0361/227176**; www.artifoundation.org): A month-long (typically June–July) festival in Denpasar. Dancers from all over Bali gather for the opening grand parade. Events include traditional dances, music, and night markets. Special foreign groups are also invited to perform.

Senggigi Festival: A week-long cultural festival in July in Lombok's tourism central.

Sanur Kite Festival: Typically held over 3 days during July or August depending on the wind in Kesiman, near Sanur. Daily competitions are attended by thousands of locals and teams from overseas keen to win a prize.

Negara Bull Races (**Bali Tourism Board** in Denpasar ✆ **0361/223602**): Traditional bull races occur every other Sunday from July through October in Parancak.

Nusa Dua Festival: A week-long festival in August offering an insight into Balinese culture and customs with art, cultural, and sporting events.

Sanur Village Festival (www.gotosanur.com): A weekend festival in August that celebrates Sanur with music and dance.

Kuta Karnival (www.kutakarnival.com): A week in September of surfing competitions, games, music, and food in Kuta.

Ubud Writers Festival (www.ubudwritersfestival.com): A festival to exchange ideas and celebrate writing in Bali and the world; 1 week in October.

LOW, HIGH & PEAK SEASON

Low: January 9 to June 30; September 16 to December 20. Low season is a great time to negotiate deals on accommodations and find cheap hotel packages.

High: July; September 1 to September 15; Chinese New Year and Easter week. Accommodation is hard to find and almost as expensive as peak season. Roads aren't as congested as at peak, but it is still difficult to get around with ease.

Peak: August; December 20 to January 9. Although the weather in August is cooler than the rest of the year and there is very little rain, December's weather is hot and humidity is high. During peak season, Bali is bursting at the seams with tourists. The roads become heavily congested and dinner reservations are hard to get. Expect to pay almost double for accommodations; shopkeepers will drive a hard bargain.

PUBLIC HOLIDAYS

Most of the major Christian, Muslim, Hindu, and Buddhist holidays are celebrated in Bali. The government also sets a few additional days every year during the year, though Islamic holiday dates change year to

Med Medan: the Kissing Ritual

This protective ritual takes place a day after the "Day of Silence" (Nyepi) that occurs according to the full moon every year. Young boys and girls from the area of Sesetan (south Denpasar), gather in the streets and are divided into two facing lines. When a whistle is blown the two sexes advance to one another until they exchange kisses. For those who get too amorous, parents, friends and relatives are on hand to thrown cold buckets of water over them.

year. **January:** 1 New Year; **February:** 14 Chinese New Year (2561), 26 Maulid (Birth of the Prophet); **March:** 16 Nyepi Balinese New Year (1932); **April:** 2 Good Friday, 28 Waisak Day (Buddha's birthday); **May:** 13 Ascension Day; **August:** 17 Indonesia Independence Day; **September:** 11 and 12 Eid-ul-Fitr Muslim festival to end Ramadan, 13 shared holiday by government decree; **November:** 17 Idul Adha, cattle sacrifice and hajj pilgrimage; **December:** 7 Islamic New Year (1432), 25 Christmas.

MAJOR RELIGIOUS EVENTS & FESTIVALS
On Bali

Festivals and religious events are important features in the social landscape of Bali, and are also permanent fixtures in Balinese daily life. Celebrations in Bali follow a lunar calendar rather than the Western calendar. Thus many major festivals fall on different dates over the years. Read more about the Balinese calendars on p. 23.

While the temple festivals (see below) are pretty to witness, a village festival is a rare treat. Most villages have their own annual festivals generally exclusive to their village. They can be enormous spectacles and worth a visit. Take a guide to explain the traditions and help with translations as most people who attend don't speak English. Look out for the **Med-medan** in Denpasar (see below), **Ngerebeg Ceremony** in Tegalalang, **Usaba Sambah festival,** which includes the *makare kare* and *maayunan* in Tenganan (p. 258).

Galungan (May 12, 2010; Dec 8, 2010; July 6, 2011), the most prestigious festival (similar to Christmas on the Western calendar), occurs every 210 days and lasts for 10 days. The festival celebrates the coming of the gods and ancestral spirits to earth to dwell again in the homes of their descendents. Festivities are characterized by offerings, dances, new clothes, plenty of feasting, and visits to family and friends. The celebrations end with **Kuningan** (May 22, 2010; Dec 18, 2010; July 16, 2011) where the families bid their farewells to the gods and spirits.

Every village in Bali celebrates Galungan and Kuningan by adorning the outside of their houses with a *penjor,* a decorative tall bamboo pole, about 8m (26 ft.) high, with palm leaves, rice stems, coconuts, and corn. At the end of each of the poles hangs a *sampian,* a beautiful plaited palm leaf creation. Some poles are decorated with lights similar to a Christmas tree. The poles are usually installed on the Tuesday before Galungan, they should be removed and the ornaments burned after 42 days.

Tawur Kesanga or **Ogoh-Ogoh day,** occurs the day before Nyepi (see below). Villagers hold a large exorcism-celebration at the main village crossroad. Throughout the month of March, you will see villages making large *ogoh-ogoh,* fantastic 4½m to 6m (15 ft.–20 ft.) papier-mâché effigies. Neighboring villages compete to build the scariest and largest *ogoh-ogoh* imaginable. After sunset, the villages carry their *ogoh-ogoh* on a bamboo platform through the streets to the sound of gamelan. When they arrive at the crossroad, the *ogoh-ogoh* are held aloft to a crescendo of noise from drums, gongs, cymbals, and voices. In order to start the new year with a clean slate, tradition demands that evil spirits are woken up and driven away from the island by loud clashing noise. The carnival ends with the *ogoh-ogoh* being lead to the beach where they are burned, but more recently, given the cost of manufacture, they have been sold on to collectors.

Nyepi (March 16, 2010; April 4, 2011), the day following the dark moon of the spring equinox, opens a new year of the Saka calendar. It is the Balinese equivalent to New Year's Eve in the Western calendar. It is celebrated by "a day of silence," fasting, and meditation, which begins at 6am and ends the following day at 6am. During the day, people respect strict rules set centuries ago: no working, no entertainment (even love making), no traveling, no talking, no TV and radio, no eating, and no lights— most *banjar* cut off power to the area, though they will give electricity to families who have babies or young children. People are not allowed to leave their houses and security guards, called *pecaleng,* patrol the streets to ensure no one disobeys the rules. The airport is closed and no flights are allowed to land or take off during the day. Hotels are allowed electricity to feed their guests but are not allowed to let their guests leave the property. The traditional "fear" is that evil spirits may still have not left the island and any sound will draw them to your house. By being silent, the evil spirits will leave in search of noise.

Saraswati, the fifth day of the Indian month Magh (Jan–Feb), is a day devoted to the goddess of knowledge, arts, and literature, Dewi Saraswati. To mark the occasion, offerings are placed on books and shrines. Students and teachers attend special ceremonies in schools and universities.

On Lombok

The main religious event on Lombok is the **Bau Nyale Festival** (Feb or Mar; p. 335). The Lingsar Temple is the site of a mock war in October for **Perang Topat** (p. 315).

ODALAN CEREMONIES & FESTIVALS

An **odalan** is the anniversary of a temple's founding and is the best time to visit. These festivals can last a day or more. Temples are beautifully decorated with flowers, palm leaves, flags, and *penjor.* Offerings of food, flowers, and prayer are made and music is performed. Some of the smaller temple anniversaries aren't as spectacular but will be less crowded. Below is a list of *odalan* celebrations throughout Bali by temple. Dates are fixed year to year. *Pura* means "temple."

JANUARY
2: Pura Puseh and Pura Desa, **Gianyar;** Pura Luhur Dalem Segening, **Tabanan.**
6: Pura Dalem Tarukan Linggih Pajenengan Ida Dalem Tarukan, **Gianyar;** Pura Penataran Dalem Ketut, **Gianyar;** Pura Puseh Manikaji Desa Peninjoan, **Bangli.**
13: Pura Srijong, **Tabanan;** Pura Rambutsiwi, **Jembrana.**
27: Pura Dalem Puri, **Besakih.**

FEBRUARY
6: Pura Maspait, **Jembrana.**
10: Pura Penataran Agung, **Karangasem;** Pura Penataran Peet, **Klungkung.**

MARCH
1: Pura Jati, **Jembrana.**
3: Pura Kehen, **Bangli;** Pura Yogan Agung, **Badung.**
23: Pura Masceti, **Gianyar.**

APRIL
27: Pura Beratan, **Klungkung.**

(**Tips**) **Etiquette for Visiting Temples & Ceremonies**

You may be allowed to enter certain temples, even at ceremony time, but be sure to respect temple etiquette: Wear a sarong and sash and observe all signs regarding temple rules. Ladies are not allowed to enter if they are menstruating, are pregnant, or have given birth within the past 6 weeks.

You are able to enter some ceremonies but don't just go charging in—ask one of the *pecalang* (those dressed in checked black and white sarongs) if you can go in first. Do not stand higher than a priest during a ceremony as this is disrespectful.

MAY

13: Pura Lempuyang Luhur, **Karangasem;** Pura Batukaru, **Tabanan;** Pura Kentel Gumi, **Klungkung.**

14: Pura Ulunsari, **Badung.**

15: Pura Segara, **Badung.**

17: Pura Dasar, **Klungkung.**

22: Pura Pekendungan, **Tabanan;** Pura Bukit Jati, **Bangli;** Pura Sadha, **Badung;** Pura Sakenan, **Badung;** Pura Taman Pule, **Gianyar;** Pura Samuan Tiga, **Gianyar.**

26: Pura Tanah Lot, **Tabanan.**

JUNE

1: Pura Andakasa, **Karangasem;** Pura Goa Lawah, **Klungkung;** Pura Uluwatu, **Badung.**

2: Pura Gede Perancak, **Jembrana.**

16: Pura Silayukti, **Karangasem;** Pura Air Jeruk, **Gianyar.**

26: Pura Pasek Gelgel, **Buleleng;** Pura Dalem Pemuteran, **Klungkung;** Pura Pedharman Bhujangga, **Besakih;** Pura Taman Sari, **Tabanan;** Pura Dalem Tarukan, **Bangli;** Pura Benua Kangin, **Besakih;** Pura Merajan Kanginan (Ida Betara Empu Berabah), **Besakih.**

27: Pura Parangan Tengah, **Nusa Penida.**

30: Pura Petitenget, **Badung;** Pura Kereb Langit, **Badung.**

30: Pura Bendesa Mas Kepisah, **South Denpasar;** Pura Natih, **Batubulan;** Pura Puseh, **Kerobokan;** Pura Desa Silakarang, **Singapadu;** Pura Dalem Petitenget, **Kerobokan;** Pura Dalem Pulasari, **Gianyar;** Pura Kubayan, **Pedungan;** Pura Pasek Gelgel, **Tabanan;** Pura Pibon, **Denpasar;**

Pura Pasek Lumintang, **Denpasar;** Pura Panti Penyarikan Medahan, **Tampak Siring;** Pura Pasah Agung, **Kediri.**

JULY

6: Pura Dalem Puri, **Gianyar;** Pura Dalem Kediri, **Singapadu;** Pura Dalem Desa, **Sukawati;** Pura Dalem Desa Singakerta, **Ubud;** Pura Dalem, **Sukawati;** Pura Paibon Pasek Tangkas, **Ubud;** Pura Puseh Ngukuhin, **Gianyar;** Pura Pemerajan Agung Ki Telabah, **Tabanan;** Pura Karang Buncing, **Gianyar;** Pura Dalem Desa Bubunan, **Buleleng;** Pura Luhur Pedengenan, **Tabanan;** Pura Pucak Payongan, **Ubud;** Pura Tanah Kilap Griya Anyar Suwung Kauh, **Denpasar;** Pura Selukat, **Gianyar.**

7: Pura Sari, **Kapal.**

21: Pura Puseh, **Desa Sukawati;** Pura Pasek Gelgel, **Buleleng;** Pura Maospahit, **Denpasar;** Pura Bendesa Manik Mas, **Tegalalang;** Pura Panti Pasek Gaduh, **Denpasar.**

31: Pura Puseh and Pura Desa, **Gianyar;** Pura Luhur Dalem Segening, **Tabanan.**

AUGUST

4: Pura Dalem Tarukan Linggih Pajenengan Ida Dalem Tarukan, **Gianyar,** Pura Penataran Dalem Ketut, **Gianyar;** Pura Puseh Manikaji, **Bangli.**

11: Pura Srijong, **Tabanan;** Pura Rambutsiwi, **Jembrana.**

SEPTEMBER

4: Pura Maspait, **Jembrana.**

8: Pura Penataran Agung, **Karangasem;** Pura Penataran Peet, **Klungkung.**

27: Pura Jati, **Jembrana.**
29: Pura Kehen, **Bangli;** Pura Yogan Agung, **Gianyar.**

OCTOBER
19: Pura Masceti, **Gianyar.**

NOVEMBER
23: Pura Beratan, **Klungkung.**

DECEMBER
9: Pura Lempuyang Luhur, **Karangasem;** Pura Batukaru, **Tabanan;** Pura Kentel Gumi, **Klungkung.**

10: Pura Ulunsari, **Badung.**
11: Pura Segara, **Badung.**
13: Pura Dasar, **Klungkung.**
18: Pura Pekendungan, **Tabanan;** Pura Bukit Jati, **Bangli;** Pura Sadha, **Badung;** Pura Sakenan, **Badung;** Pura Taman Pule, **Gianyar;** Pura Samuan Tiga, **Gianyar.**
22: Pura Tanah Lot, **Tabanan.**
28: Pura Andakasa, **Karangasem;** Pura Goa Lawah, **Klungkung;** Pura Uluwatu, **Badung;** Pura Taman Ayun, **Badung.**
29: Pura Gede Perancak, **Jembrana.**

2 ENTRY REQUIREMENTS

VISAS

Procedures in Bali, Lombok, and Indonesia can change without given notice. For up-to-date information, contact the nearest Indonesian embassy or consulate in your country. For a list, go to www.indonesia.go.id.

Visitors from the Australia, Canada, New Zealand, United Kingdom, United States, and most of Europe can get **Visas**

Online Traveler's Toolbox

www.asiawebdirect.com: A guide to booking a hotel room in Bali
www.balidiscovery.com: Award-winning website with up-to-date information on everything you need to know about Bali for your holiday
www.baliguide.com: An insider's guide to Bali
www.bali-paradise.com: Complete online travel guide to Bali
www.baliplus.com: Bali's biggest little guide book online, with up-to-date information on exhibitions, festivals, and just about everything
www.balistarisland.com: A one-stop travel agency to Bali
www.balitourismboard.org: The official tourist board website
www.baliwww.com: The best online guide to Bali with an excellent blog
www.gili-paradise.com: The best online resource for the Gili Islands
www.i-escape.com: All the details on the best hip hideaways
wwwistylemagazine.net: I Style Magazine's website for great fashion and home decor shops
www.indo.com: Comprehensive travel guide to Indonesia
www.kecak.com: Booking portal for Bali and Lombok hotels
www.thelombokguide.com: The definitive guide to Lombok
www.theyakmag.com: Bali's most fashionable rag with the latest in fashion, food, and accommodation
www.whygo.com: Best deals on flights to and accommodation in Indonesia

on Arrival (VOA) through Ngurah Rai International Airport or the seaports of Padangbai and Benoa in Bali and Selaparang Airport in Lombok. For stays of 7 days or less, the charge is US$10; for stays of up to 30 days, the charge is US$25 payable by credit card and most major currencies. For stays of longer than 30 days, a tourist or business visa must be arranged before arrival.

Your passport must be valid for at least 6 months from the date of your arrival; your passport must also have at least two blank pages.

Overstays are charged US$20 per day for up to 60 days. Overstay violations are liable to 5 years imprisonment or a fine of Rp25 million.

Any person holding a passport from the following countries is eligible for a **free visa.** Those holding valid passports will be granted a 30-day visa short-visit permit on arrival at any Indonesian international gateway without charge: Brunei Darussalam, Chile, Hong Kong SAR, Macau SAR, Malaysia, Morocco, Peru, Philippines, Thailand, Vietnam, and Singapore. Your passport must be valid for at least 6 months from the date of arrival and you need to be in possession of an onward or return ticket.

REGISTRATION IN BALI & LOMBOK

On arrival at your hotel or villa on either island, you must register yourself and your family with the police. This will be automatically done if you stay in a hotel but those staying in private houses or villas should hand over their passports to the villa staff who will do this for you. You will also be asked to pay Rp50,000 per person (you do not have to pay this in a hotel). Failure to register can lead to a hefty fine.

If you decide to move locations during your stay, you must bring your passport with you to register in each accommodation.

The hotel may not be willing to allow you to stay otherwise.

CUSTOMS REGULATIONS

Customs allows you to bring in, duty free, 200 cigarettes, 50 cigars, or 100 grams of tobacco; cameras and film; 1 liter of alcohol; and perfume clearly intended for personal use. Forbidden are guns, weapons, narcotics, pornography (leave it at home if you're unsure how it's defined), televisions, fresh fruit, Chinese medicine, and printed matter with Chinese characters. Plants might also be confiscated.

On arrival at the airport all bags are screened for alcohol. Anyone caught carrying alcohol over their duty free allowance will find it either confiscated or will have to pay a high duty penalty. Rates are not fixed and can be negotiated!

What You Can Take Home

The export of tortoise shell, crocodile skin, and ivory is prohibited. For information on what you're allowed to bring home, contact one of the following agencies:

Australian Citizens: Australian Customs Service at © **1300/363-263,** or log on to **www.customs.gov.au.**

Canadian Citizens: Canada Border Services Agency (© **800/461-9999** in Canada, or 204/983-3500; www.cbsa-asfc.gc.ca).

New Zealand Citizens: New Zealand Customs, The Customhouse, 17–21 Whitmore St., Box 2218, Wellington (© **04/473-6099** or 0800/428-786; **www.customs.govt.nz**).

U.K. Citizens: HM Customs & Excise at © **0845/010-9000** (from outside the U.K., 020/8929-0152), or consult their website at **www.hmce.gov.uk**.

U.S. Citizens: U.S. Customs & Border Protection (CBP), 1300 Pennsylvania Ave., NW, Washington, DC 20229 (© **877/287-8667;** www.cbp.gov).

MEDICAL REQUIREMENTS

There are no inoculation or vaccination requirements for visitors to Bali and Lombok. Visitors arriving from parts of Africa, however, may be screened for yellow fever.

It is wise to get vaccinated for typhoid and hepatitis A and B. All travelers should also be up to date on their tetanus immunizations.

---

3 GETTING THERE & GETTING AROUND

For specific details on getting to and around **Lombok,** see p. 307. Practical advice below for navigating Bali is also applicable to Lombok.

GETTING THERE BY PLANE

Denpasar Airport, aka **Ngurah Rai International Airport** (**DPS;** ✆ **0361/ 751011**) is 13km (8 miles) southwest of Denpasar. For airport information and connection to airline reservations counters, call ✆ **0361/751011,** ext. 1454. When you leave Bali, you pay an airport departure tax of Rp150,000 paid at immigration.

Most visitors from the U.S. and Canada fly here via Taipei on **China Airlines,** Bangkok on **Thai Airways,** Jakarta on **Garuda Indonesia,** Singapore on **Singapore Airlines,** Tokyo on **Japan Airlines,** Hong Kong on **Cathay Pacific,** or Seoul on **Korean Air.** Bali is served from Europe by **Cathay Pacific** via Hong Kong; tickets can be purchased from **British Airways, Singapore Airlines,** or **Air France.** Flights from Australia and New Zealand can be booked through **Qantas.** For a full listing of airlines serving Bali and Lombok and their websites, turn to p. 361.

GETTING AROUND

Bali is made up of three main roads that circumnavigate the island and hundreds of smaller roads that traverse the countryside. It takes approximately 3 hours to travel the length and breadth of Bali. Road conditions on the main roads are generally good but can be heavily populated with slow traveling trucks. The conditions of the minor roads are generally determined by the weather. During the rainy season, road conditions fall foul of torrential rain and heavy traffic leaves the roads covered in potholes and debris.

Although there is a good public transport system here, journeys tend to be very long and don't take in smaller destinations.

By Private Car & Driver

The best way of seeing the sights of Bali is by hiring a car and a driver. It gives you the freedom to explore the backwater of this picturesque country. Plenty of car-hire agencies on Bali offer day services or weekly rentals; your hotel or villa may have its own cars and drivers available for you as well. Having a driver takes away the stress of having to navigate the small roads around the island; they can also help with any translations as once you leave the main areas very few people speak any English.

Tips **The Best Way to Avoid a Traffic Accident**

Any foreigners involved in even minor traffic violations or accidents may be vulnerable to exploitation. You should therefore think seriously about employing a private driver or hiring a car with a driver.

> **⚠ Warning!   Driving Infringements**
>
> Always ensure that you have the car documentation with you as well as your international driver's license. The police carry out regular spot checks and you'll be fined for any infringements. Not wearing a seatbelt while driving or as a passenger or not wearing a helmet on a motorcycle is also an infringement. Stay calm during all dealings with the police, do not argue with them, and do not offer them a bribe. They are less interested in whether you have committed a traffic violation and more in what you have in your wallet. A standard fine should be Rp50,000 but police will try to get as much money as they can from you. Do not flash a full wallet of cash, as you might not see it again.

Drivers on overnight stays will find their own suitable accommodation at very little cost to you. You will be expected to pay the driver's food and accommodation but the cost of the vehicle, insurance, and petrol should be included in the price. Expect to pay about Rp350,000 to Rp450,000 a day, open to negotiation.

Before hiring a car and driver make sure that they have all the relevant paperwork and insurance in place and agree on all costs ahead of the rental period. Also make sure that they have a good command of English and are knowledgeable about the island.

By Rental Car

To rent a car you are supposed to have an International Driving License or a locally issued tourist driving license together with a copy of your passport. However, most rental businesses will rent you a car with a copy of your home national driver's license.

One-month licenses are issued on the spot for Rp150,000 at the **Foreign License Service,** Jl. Gunung Sanghiang, Denpasar (𝄞 **0361/422323**). You will also need to show a copy of your passport and your home national driver's license.

Before you drive away in your car, ensure that the car has all its registration documentation (Surat Tanda Nomor Kendaraan Bermotor or **STNK,** vehicle registration certificate) and copies of any insurance policies.

You must be vigilant at all times when driving in Bali. The Balinese rarely stop to check for on-coming traffic, which can often cause the driver to slam on their breaks or swerve to avoid a collision. At night, many motorcycles and cyclists rarely have lights on and street lighting is limited. Traffic lights are not always observed. Accidents are common. Vehicles are left-hand drive. The national speed limit is 70kph but you won't find many areas to do this.

Expect to pay between US$18 to US$45 a day for vehicle hire, though the bigger agencies will charge a lot more. Prices will either be in rupiah or U.S. dollars. The cheapest form of transport is a Suzuki jeep which should cost about US$18 a day; a Toyota Kijang should cost about US$22 a day; a top of the range limousine-style Suzuki costs US$45. These prices should include some insurance but always check what insurance you are getting before agreeing to a price.

International chains on the island include: **Avis,** Jl. Danau Tamblingan, Sanur (𝄞 **1800/656545** or 0361/282635; www.avis.com), and **Hertz,** Ngurah Rai airport (𝄞 **0361/768375;** www.hertz. com). Local companies include: **Baliwww**

Car Rental (🕾 **0361/731520;** www.bali www.com/car_rental) in Denpasar; **Bali Car Hire** (🕾 **08/11380699** or 0361/418381; www.balicarhire.com), also in Denpasar, a reliable company with a good variety of cars available; and **CV Amertha Dana,** Legian (🕾 **0361/753518;** www.amerthadana.com), which does not have new cars but their rates are good and service very attentive, and they rent motorcycles.

By Motorcycle

The easiest, cheapest, and fastest way to get around Bali is by motorcycle. However it is also the most dangerous with daily accidents and weekly motorcycle deaths.

Plenty of companies on the streets will hire you a motorcycle if you have a driving license. It should cost you about Rp50,000 a day for a basic 110-125CC scooter, less if you are hiring long term. Surfer racks should be available at no extra cost.

Always check the motorcycle first to make sure that everything is working: brakes, indicators, and wheels; also ensure that you have the right insurance and vehicle registration documents, which you need to carry with you at all times. All motorcyclists must wear helmets and these should be supplied at the time of rental for no extra charge. Ensure the helmet fits properly. If you cannot find one that fits, buy one.

By Taxi

Metered taxis are the best and most convenient way of getting round **southern Bali** if you haven't got your own car and driver. Costs start from the initial fee of Rp5,000 for the first 2km (1¼ miles) and then the meter ticks up Rp5,000 per kilometer thereafter. If you want to make any stops allow for about Rp20,000 per hour waiting. To rent a taxi for the day, agree on a price ahead of time and let the driver know what you expect from him. Most of them will want to show you their friends' shops and businesses, if you don't want to do this be very clear at the outset and be firm. If you haven't hired a car for your holiday but would like to head off somewhere for the day, some taxis are happy to take you on half-day or full-day excursions. Allow Rp450,000 for a full day. **Made Sueta,** owner of his own Ngurah Rai Taxi (🕾 **08/123947919**), is a fount of knowledge and would be happy to guide you around Bali.

Taxi numbers are: **Bali Taxi/Blue Bird Taxi** 🕾 0361/701111; **Komotra Taxi** 🕾 0361/499449; **Ngurah Rai Taxi** 🕾 0361/724724; **Wahana Taxi** 🕾 0361/244555; and **Golden Bird Bali** 🕾 0361/702000.

By Bemo

Blue and brown vans called *bemo* operate as buses in Bali. They have regular routes, but these aren't really written down and they make numerous stops. A long-distance journey will likely include at least one transfer. Most tourists save the headache and go for private transport. *Bemo* are better for short hops (around town, for example) than long distances. Destinations and stops are posted in the front window. Denpasar is the main transportation hub for the entire island. A typical trip costs Rp5,000 to Rp10,000. Negotiate before riding. You pay before you alight.

By Bus

Perama Tours (🕾 **0361/751551;** www.peramatour.com) runs a shuttle bus that serves all the main towns and cities in Bali and also covers Mataram and Senggigi in Lombok (🕾 **0370/635928**). These are easy to catch, cheap, safe, and a comfortable way to explore. Unfortunately, they are very slow. If you need to travel between main towns they are a good mode of transport but they do not stop at small villages or well-known sights en route.

> (Tips) **A Note on Addresses**
>
> The spelling and naming of most Indonesian geographical features, villages, towns, and even streets varies considerably as there is no standardized form that meets both popular and official approval. Names can be spelled many different ways, even on signboards in front of various government offices. There are three overlapping and concurrent address systems for any given location: old street name and number, new street name with new numbers, and *kampung* (neighborhood) name with block numbers. For instance Jalan Diponegoro (an Indonesian hero) is often referred to by its other names Jalan Gusti Ngurah Rai (from local history) or Jalan Raya Sesetan Gang II (the *kampung* name and alley number). To top it off, numbers do not always follow and you are just as likely to find 22 next to 133.

4 MONEY & COSTS

The unit of currency in Indonesia is the **rupiah,** from the Sanskrit word for wrought silver, *rupya.* Coins come in denominations of Rp25, 50, 100, and 500. Notes are Rp1,000, 2,000, 5,000, 10,000, 20,000, 50,000, and 100,000; the largest denomination is worth about US$10 (£5.90). The rate of exchange is relatively stable. At press time, the average was about **Rp10,000 to US$1.** Look to www.xe.com for the most up-to-date currency rates.

We've listed prices according to how each individual establishment lists them, typically either in rupiah or U.S. dollars.

Though you can order rupiah before leaving home, it is not necessary. Denpasar airport on Bali and Selaparang airport on Lombok have plenty of money changers in the arrival terminal and ATMs once through Customs.

Cash is king in Bali and Lombok. Wherever you go you will need it, whether to pay for parking, entrance to museums, tips, or taxi rides, or to buy knickknacks, you will need to have low denominations of cash. Although Rp100,000 bills are useful for high-priced items, smaller shops and taxis do not carry large amounts of change. There seems to be an expectation that the customer should provide appropriate change, rather than the other way round.

The maximum amount of currency that you can bring into Bali is US$10,000 in cash.

ATMS

ATMs are everywhere in south Bali. Withdrawals can be made with credit cards and some debit cards on the Maestro and Cirrus networks. Most ATMs dispense money

The Value of Indonesian Rupiah vs. Other Popular Currencies

Rp	US$	Can$	UK£	Euro (€)	Aus$	NZ$
10,000	$1	C$1.12	£.65	€.72	A$1.16	NZ$1.46

Getting Your Money's Worth When Changing Currency

Although there are good, honest money changers there are also many unscrupulous vendors. Here are a few tips when using money changers:

- Make sure you do your own calculations. Do not rely on the staff. Some calculators can be tampered with.
- Check to see if there is a commission fee. Be cautious that you may have a good rate of exchange but have to pay a hefty commission rate. If the commission is low, ensure that you are getting a good exchange rate.
- Count the money yourself. Better still, count it twice. Do not pass it back to the staff to recount as you may find a few notes missing after leaving the shop.
- The money changers should give you a receipt. If they don't, insist.
- Be warned of counterfeit bills. If a note doesn't feel right, ask for another one. Do not accept any damaged currency.
- Be sure to count zeros on a note. Rp10,000 is roughly equivalent to US$1 and Rp100,000 is US$10.

in multiples of Rp50,000 which is extremely annoying when withdrawing large amounts of cash. A few machines will dispense Rp100,000 notes. All ATMs are clearly marked which denominations they pay out.

Some banks will only allow maximum withdrawals of Rp1,250,000 at one time but will allow up to three withdrawals in a day. Others will allow Rp3,000,000 at one time with a maximum of Rp6,000,000 withdrawal in a day. The best ATM we have found is Permata Bank, where you can withdraw Rp3,000,000 in Rp100,000 notes up to a maximum of two withdrawals. These ATMs are in the Circle K on Jalan Laksmana in Seminyak, on Jalan Legian near the turning to Jalan Double Six in Kuta, Jalan Tamblingan in Sanur, and Jalan Raya Ubud in Ubud.

Withdrawal charges depend on your bank in your country. Cash advances on credit cards are treated as loans and accrue interest daily. You will be charged a transaction fee, too. Withdrawals made with

debit cards should only be charged a transaction fee. Inquire at your bank for rates. Sometimes it is better to pay for things on a credit card directly rather than paying in hard cash.

The best banks to withdraw money from are Bank Central Asia (BCA), Bank Lippo, Bank Mandiri, Bank Negara Indonesia (BNI), and Permata Bank. Outside the main tourist areas you will not find many ATMs. It is always best to take cash with you.

On Lombok you will find ATMs in Mataram, Senggigi, and Praya. Be sure to have enough cash before arrival.

CREDIT CARDS

All high-end hotels, shops, restaurants, and nightclubs accept credit cards. Visa and MasterCard are the most commonly accepted cards but some do take American Express and Diners Club. Merchants may charge a 3% to 5% surcharge for credit transactions. Payments are usually in rupiah but some companies have been known to charge in U.S. dollars, particularly large hotel chains. If this is the case, ask them to clarify what exchange rate they are using as you may be better off paying in cash.

FOREIGN EXCHANGE

Most major currency can be exchanged in banks, hotels, and authorized money changers in the main tourist areas. Rates depend on the currency and the denominations you are holding. U.S. dollars are the preferred currency but euros and sterling are also popular. U.S. bills issued before 2006 will receive a lower rate than newer ones. Sometimes any old, folded, or

damaged notes will not be accepted due to the high risk of the note being forged.

Money changers generally offer the best rates and are the most convenient. Daily opening times vary from 9am until 10pm. Double-check your money before leaving as there are money changing scams, especially in the Kuta (on Bali) area. State-sponsored **Wartel Telecommunications Service** offices are the best. Banks generally offer the next favored rate but going into a bank is time-consuming and often exhausting. Hotels offer the lowest rate of exchange. Cashing traveler's checks requires a passport.

5 HEALTH

Taking simple precautions such as getting vaccinated, using mosquito nets and insect repellents, and watching what you eat and drink can greatly reduce the risk of exposure to a number of diseases that thrive in the tropical climate.

Consult your doctor before leaving. Besides the routine vaccinations recommended in your own country, you may need to get the following vaccinations at least 4 to 6 weeks before your trip to allow time for your vaccines to take effect: hepatitis A and B, typhoid, and tetanus-diphtheria.

SWINE FLU

Several cases of **swine flu** have been reported in Bali. The Balinese Health Department, proficient in dealing with matters of epidemics, is currently working with the Denpasar Airport Health Office. Any planes that now arrive in Bali from countries confirmed to be infected with the H1N1 virus will be sequestered briefly at a remote aircraft parking area where the plane and its passengers will be sprayed with disinfectant. Passengers will then disembark and be subjected to thermal

scanners to determine if any have an elevated body temperature which, if discovered, would earn a more thorough medical examination by the airport's H1N1 containment team. Although this sounds like a lengthy procedure, it is all undertaken very quickly and without much delay.

BUG BITES & OTHER WILDLIFE CONCERNS

Dengue fever is a viral infection that typically causes flulike symptoms, including fever, muscle aches, joint pains, headaches, nausea, and vomiting, often followed by a rash, is transmitted by Aedes mosquitoes, which bite during the daytime, especially in the morning and late afternoon.

Malaria is another common disease transmitted by Anopheles mosquitoes, which are most active after sundown. Malaria is common in Lombok and eastern part of Indonesia, but not in Bali. You are recommended to take malaria prophylaxis. Purchase your antimalarial drugs before travel as some of the recommended antimalarial drugs are not always available over the counter. Discuss with your doctor at least 3 to 4 weeks before traveling as some of the malaria prophylaxis need to be taken 2 weeks before entering the malaria area.

A few cases of **rabies** have recently occurred in Bali and the local government has been actively vaccinating dogs to help control the disease. Although there is no official recommendation by the government for humans to get the rabies vaccine, it may be worthwhile for those spending a lot of time in rural areas, working in veterinarian positions, or anyone who may come into contact with bats and monkeys. If you do get bitten or scratched by a monkey or bat during your travel, you must go directly to the hospital and take vaccination procedures against rabies.

DIETARY RED FLAGS

You can't drink the water from the taps on Bali and Lombok, but bottled water is cheap and readily available. Just about every hotel will supply you with a couple bottles or a jug of boiled water—to be extra cautious, use it to brush your teeth as well. The ice in Bali is generally okay to use as the production is government controlled. Stay clear of ice in nontourist areas where it could be locally produced.

One of the most common illnesses that affects travelers is **diarrhea,** which usually occurs with a sudden change in diet. Infectious agents are the primary cause and people traveling from developed countries to developing countries experience rapid and dramatic change in the type of organisms in their gastrointestinal tract. To prevent traveler's diarrhea, avoid foods or beverages from street vendors and small warungs that look questionable (the presence of other tourists and locals eating is always a good sign), avoid raw or undercooked meats and seafood. Keep yourself hydrated. Any electrolytes solution or tablets will help hydrate you and assist with maintaining the right balance of minerals in your body. For more serious cases, antibiotics can be prescribed at any pharmacy.

Some travelers will also be diagnosed with a stomach bug that we like to call **Bali Belly,** more akin to an acute case of gastroenteritis, which can be caused by a bacterial or parasitic infection. It is usually passed on by the fecal-oral route. Symptoms include abdominal pain, nausea, vomiting, and diarrhea. The illness can last a few days or a few weeks and can leave the victim bedridden and too ill to move. Consult a doctor immediately.

SUN EXPOSURE

The equatorial sun can burn your skin faster than you think even on cloudy days. In July, the climate feels cooler due to the cool breezes but this is the time when most are unaware of the dangers of the sun. Limit exposure or liberally apply a high factor sunscreen. The sun is at its strongest between 11am and 2pm. Always keep hydrated. **Popcari Sweat** and other similar rehydrating drinks are sold everywhere but water remains the number-one priority.

WHAT TO DO IF YOU GET SICK AWAY FROM HOME

We list hospital and emergency numbers in the "Fast Facts" sections throughout this book. Plenty of English-speaking doctors are available on Bali; the better qualified doctors can be found in the more touristy areas of Bali and Lombok. If you do need a doctor, ask your hotel or villa concierge first, as they likely have one on call.

Apotek, Indonesian pharmacies, can be found on most busy streets in Bali and Lombok. They stock some Western brands but mostly local medicine. **Kimia Farma** is a Japanese pharmacy chain that stocks well-known medicinal brands and toiletries. They also have a doctor on-site who can prescribe antibiotics for less serious illnesses.

If you suffer from a chronic illness, consult your doctor before departure. Pack prescription medications in the original

Purchasing & Using Travel Insurance in Bali & Lombok

A visitor should be aware that along with the "normal" range of issues that need consideration with regards to health and precautions in the tropics, attention should be paid to ensuring a viable exit strategy in the event of serious illness or accident. As Indonesia is still developing, the standards of medical care are not as sophisticated as those in neighboring developed countries such as Singapore and Thailand. Frequently the issues that one faces require swift decisions and immediate action. In order to ensure one's personal safety in all situations it is essential to hold a good travel Insurance policy.

When purchasing a policy, gather clear information on how to initiate an evacuation, should it prove necessary. Insurance companies are obliged to meet requirements in order to authorize an evacuation and this can be a time-consuming process when medical reports are required to verify the nature of the problem. Discuss this with the potential provider and be sure you understand their requirements. Take a worst-case-scenario approach. "What if" you are incapable of contacting the company yourself? How would someone else do this on your behalf?

Over time we have developed an approach that we suggest you follow.

1. Have several copies of any membership card or policy you hold in different parts of your luggage.

2. Always carry a copy in your wallet or bag. If you are unconscious or incapable of response, hospital staff will seek something to confirm you have medical coverage. Make it easy for them or anyone else who finds it to contact your insurer.

3. Carry a copy of the claim form with you, all companies require these to be filled out and you don't want to be caught without one.

4. It is important to have a copy of contact phone numbers of family and friends who will help you if need be; keep this in the same place as the insurance information.

5. Make a photocopy of your passport and other essential documents and keep them in a separate place from your originals, or even better keep a password-protected thumb drive with scanned copies of your essential documents with you.

–Richard Flax
Head Bali Emergency Response Team

containers with pharmacy labels in carry-on luggage, otherwise they may not make it through airport security. Carry a copy of your prescription form and any other paperwork detailing what the drugs are for and who they have been prescribed to.

INSURANCE

We highly recommend that you have an insurance policy in place before arriving in Bali and Lombok. Make sure that it covers medical expenses. While the hospitals in Bali (less so in Lombok) are good, there are some services that they cannot supply and in these cases you may be evacuated to Singapore for further medical attention. Some policies do not cover "dangerous activities," which can include surfing, scuba diving, bungy jumping, horseback riding, and some watersports. For further information visit www.frommers.com/planning.

6 SAFETY

While Bali is one of the safest places to travel in Asia, there is no denying that **traffic** plays the most serious threat to a visitor's life. Pavements are constantly abused by cars and motorbikes who see them as quick routes when traffic is at a standstill; at night beware the many gaps in the pavements that have been known to catch the compos and non compos mentis alike. Drivers think nothing of driving at high speeds through villages and towns, overtaking on bends, braking hard or swerving to avoid chickens, dogs, and potholes. If you feel uncomfortable, ask your driver to slow down, and then ask again. Many drivers think that all visitors to the island like them to drive fast and will therefore show their appreciation for this at the end of the day. Your safety is more important.

With regards to riding a motorcycle, always wear a helmet and be vigilant at all times especially at night when dogs prowl the streets, kids cycle their bikes without headlights, and locals walk and gather in nonlit areas. Most riders on the island learn to ride a motorbike at an early age—you'll see some as young as 9 or 10 ferrying their younger brethren—and they do not have to sit for any road test examinations.

The basic rule you need to keep in mind is that as a foreigner the accident is always your fault. The thinking being that if you had not been here, the accident would not have happened. Take our advice and book a driver.

If you are staying rurally, the local **banjar** will take pride in the low crime rate and very often will take matters into their own hands should they find any impropriety among their own. Only after they have had their time with the perpetrator, will they call the police.

While much of Indonesia still relies on graft or back handers for the smooth conduct of business, crime itself remains low and especially so in the tourist world. However do take the usual safety precautions you would anywhere. Violent crime is rare, pickpockets are not. Exercise considerable caution by using a money belt, particularly in crowded tourist areas, and being careful not to flash large wads of cash. Most hotels or villas will provide you with a safety box; use it. If nothing else, make sure your suitcase has a good lock on it.

Given the world we live in, and not withstanding the lack of crime, there is still much emphasis on security and you will encounter standard—if sometimes only rudimentary—security checks at most hotels and restaurants. Don't be alarmed, they search everyone and will usually also wish to have a peak in the boot or under the bonnet of your car. Take the slight intrusion in your stride. It is for everyone's benefit.

If you have an issue, contact your consulate (p. 359).

7 SPECIALIZED TRAVEL RESOURCES

In addition to the destination-specific resources listed below, please visit Frommers.com for additional specialized travel resources.

GAY & LESBIAN TRAVELERS
The Balinese are Hindu, unlike the rest of Indonesia, which is predominately Muslim. In Bali you will find a relatively rich

gay scene although not one that is openly flaunted. While homosexuality is accepted, any public display of romance, whether straight or gay, is frowned upon. The Indonesian legal age of consent for straight and gay sex is 16.

Bali is now a gay-friendly place, and it is unlikely that gays will encounter any problems while on holiday, especially in the touristy areas of the south. The best place to base yourself is in Seminyak, with its open gay scene and plenty of gay-owned and gay-friendly accommodations, bars, and nightclubs. There is also a fabulous gay cruising area north of Petitenget beach.

For up-to-date information on the best places to stay and Bali's gay scene check the following websites: www.bali-rainbows.com; www.utopia-asia.com; www.rainbowtourism.com; www.balifriendlyhotels.com; and www.baligayguide.com.

Lombok, a Muslim island, frowns upon homosexuality and you will find it difficult to find suitable accommodations and accepting people. The only exception is the Gili Islands, where there is a slightly more laid-back attitude.

TRAVELERS WITH DISABILITIES

Bali and Lombok's hilly terrain, strong sea currents, and narrow streets with little parking may not make ideal conditions for travelers with disabilities but that shouldn't stop anyone from traveling here. What the islands lack in infrastructure they make up for with caring people and a willingness to help.

Two well-established companies can arrange all your travel needs, suitable accommodations, and any equipment hire. They also have a full-service bus with a lift facility. Special caretakers can be arranged through these websites at a cost of approximately US$20 a day. Contact **Bali Access Travel,** Jl. Danau Tamblingan 31, Sanur (© **0361/851990;** www.baliaccesstravel.com), or **Bali Mobility and**

Tours, Jl. Danau Tamblingan 54, Sanur (© **0361/2817-8054;** www.balimobility.com).

Bali International Diving Professionals (© **0361/270759;** www.bidp-balidiving.com), based in Sanur, are an experienced International Association for Handicapped Divers (IAHD; www.iahd.org) qualified dive team and have specially modified boats to assist with divers with disabilities.

FAMILY TRAVEL

Bali is an ideal family destination—the whole family, whether you have very young children or older children, will find something to suit their tastes in Bali. Lombok less so, as it is does not offer the same variety of activities and is much less developed than Bali.

Hotels and restaurants are well equipped for kids and babies. Nearly all hotels have cots and high chairs and if a restaurant doesn't have a kid's menu they are generally happy to make something simple for them to eat. Babysitting is easy to organize both night and day and reasonably priced. Some of the larger hotels have specialist kids' clubs with designated children check-in. Generally, kids up to the age of 12 are allowed to share a hotel room for free, though some hotels will charge a nominal fee.

With regards to children's admission, most places offer family packages at great discounts. Children under 4 are usual free but not always, especially at water parks or animal parks.

Most supermarkets stock baby food and toiletries, albeit very expensive as most is imported from the West. There is no need to bring prams as there are very few places to use one. If you are thinking of trekking with your very young child, bring a baby carry-pack.

To locate accommodations, restaurants, and attractions that are particularly kid friendly, refer to the "Kids" icon throughout this guide.

> (Tips) **Do It on a Beach or in a Jungle: Your Bali Event**
>
> Few places can compete with Bali as a destination for a major celebration—weddings, birthdays, anniversaries. Local planners will assist with everything from paperwork, to flowers, catering, entertainment, like cultural performances and music, so you can kick back and enjoy the ride. The island has hundreds of wedding and event planners, but the best are **Karen** at Cherange (info@cherange.com; www.cherange.com), and, if I do say so, myself, **MJ** (mj.mjpr@gmail.com; www.mjprevents.com).

WOMEN & SINGLE TRAVELERS

For the female traveler, Bali is a safe island to discover on your own or in a group. On the whole, Balinese men are fairly benign to the appearance of Western women however we are seeing an increase in visitors from neighboring countries who have come to work on the building sites and in the fields that think nothing of wolf whistling, cat-calling, and making lewd propositions. Most of them are harmless but you should be vigilant when walking around at night in areas where these men hang out. The only people to be wary of are the **Kuta cowboys,** men who prey on woman looking to establish a relationship. For them, this is an opportunity to obtain some much-needed funds and have some fun at someone else's expense.

While traveling around the island, dress appropriately so as not to offend. While tight shorts and bare shoulders are acceptable on the beaches, they are frowned upon in the more rural areas.

For those traveling to Lombok, as long as you are respectful of their Muslim culture and dress appropriately you should not be bothered.

Bali and Lombok are generally safe and single travelers face no real threat or dangers. That said, don't throw common sense out of the window. Women on their own, in particular, should still be careful especially when out alone in the evening. Both men and women should beware of nightclubs where there have been a few cases of people having their drinks spiked. Never leave your drink unguarded or with a stranger.

STUDENT TRAVEL

Check out **STA Travel** (✆ 800/781-40404 in the U.S; www.statravel.com; and ✆ 0871/2300040 in the U.K.; www.statravel.co.uk) for the best advice, cheap flights, and accommodations for Bali and Lombok.

8 SUSTAINABLE TOURISM

With its exceptional natural sites and indigenous cultures, Indonesia could become one of the world leaders in ecotourism with Bali playing a key role. However ecotourism development in Bali is still far from its potential, although increasing awareness and a more educated traveler has made this sector the most

interesting growth segment of tourism in Bali today.

Historically, Bali attracted the rich, the cultured, and the bohemian, seeking the idyllic island life. Yet, this paradise situation eventually gave way to the advent of cheaper travel brought on by a new wave of tourists, many initially seeking the surf of Kuta. Low-end hotels and guesthouses quickly sprang up to cater to this new market.

To counter this tourist insurgency, the government of the day had a plan: containment. The maxim being that tourist revenues were good, but tourism on the whole was bad. The government attempted to keep this growing wave within the confines of a government-sponsored tourist enclave, Nusa Dua, but this proved to be short lived. Not only did tourism persist beyond the artificial boundaries, but it soon became clear that focusing tourism in one area at the expense of all others not only created an imbalance in tourist revenues but also led to an uneven and unsustainable demand for water, waste-disposal, and road use, not to mention negative ecological impact and coastal erosion.

Rolling forward to today when one would hope some lessons had been learned, the demand for basic utilities and the need to dispose of the waste and effluence of the millions of tourists leads many of the grand hotels of Seminyak and Kuta to still directly pollute the immediate seas and beaches on which their revenues rely.

The effects on the social strata and structure of Bali has been, to date, much contained, due in many parts to the self-policing and self-appointed village council, the *banjar.* They rule over social laws and are a necessary ally for any hotel, villa, or other business. Woe betide any who challenges their authority without just cause.

Tourists too have reacted against their irresponsible past. The noisy few that pollute the streets and bars of Kuta are slowly being outnumbered by a responsible and growing majority seeking the peace and natural charms of the original Bali. This is evidenced by the increasing number of eco- and socially responsible semi educational resorts. The **Aman hotel group** is possibly the most high profile

tourist-dependant business that prides itself on bringing more to a community than it can take away.

Bali is now seeing a huge development in ecotourism resorts. While some of them are extremely good others make promises they do not follow through on. While in no way an exclusive list, we recommend the following accommodations, which are all trying to do something positive for the local environment: **Menjangan Resort** (p. 301), **Munduk Moding Plantation** (p. 238), **Puri Lumbung Cottages** (p. 239), **Sarinbuana Eco Lodge** (p. 242), and **Udayana Eco Lodge** (p. 171). Some newer resorts are fully off the grid, powered by solar or wind and even charge separately for air-conditioning such as **Gili Eco Villas** (p. 352).

Among more dedicated offerings is **C Bali** (p. 232) and the village ecotourism network **JED** (p. 59) with their four initiatives in Sibetan, Kiadan Pelaga, Tenganan, and Nusa Ceningan.

The waters around Bali and Lombok offer some of the best diving in the world, however the coral reefs and the marine ecosystems face increased pressures from sedimentation, pollution, over fishing, reef bombing, cyanide fishing, and exploitative recreational activities. Various initiatives and teams of dive schools are working together to help promote the rejuvenation of damaged reefs, educate fishermen about safe fishing practices, and protect the reefs from any further erosion. The **Gili Eco Trust** (www.giliecotrust.com; p. 356) works with all seven of the dive schools in the Gili Islands to outstanding success. In Permuteran, **Reef Seen Aquatics** (p. 284) have built the largest "Biorock" installation in the world while working with the local community to create other successful restoration projects. The World Wildlife Federation in Indonesia is working with Friends of the Reef to help protect the reef in the **West Bali National Park** (p. 298).

9 STAYING CONNECTED

Bali generally has good network coverage. In the mountains you may find patches where there is limited network coverage but you are never far from a phone line that works. The cheapest way to make any international calls is through **Skype** (www.skype.com) or any voice-over Internet protocol services.

In Lombok, phones are available in the cities and all tourist areas and all mobile phones work in these areas, too. In some of the more remote areas, particularly close to mountains, signals can fail.

TELEPHONE DIALING AT A GLANCE

To place a call from your home country to Bali: Dial the international access code (011 in the U.S. and Canada, 0011 in Australia, 0170 in New Zealand, 00 in the U.K.), plus Indonesia's country code **(62),** the city or local area code (**361** for Kuta/Seminyak, Jimbaran, Nusa Dua, Sanur, and Ubud; **362** for Lovina; **363** for Candidasa; **370** for Lombok and the Gilis), and the six-digit phone number (for example, 011 62 362 000000). **Mobile phone numbers** do not have a city or local area code, and begin with an 8 followed by a long string of numbers. Dial Indonesia's country code (62) followed by the number.

To place a call within Indonesia: You must use the area code if calling between states. For calls within the country, area codes are all preceded by a **0** (for instance, 0361 for Kuta/Seminyak, Jimbaran, Nusa Dua, Sanur, and Ubud, 0363 for Candidasa, 0370 for Lombok, and so on). Dial the city or area code preceded by a **0,** and then the local number (for example, 0362/000000). For mobile phones, add a 0 to the number.

To make a landline call to a local landline phone, do not include the local code (that is, dial 1234567 not 0361/1234567).

To place a direct international call from Indonesia: Dial the international access code **(00),** plus the country code, the area or city code, and the number (for example, to call the U.S., you'd dial 00 1 000/000-0000). International country codes are: Australia, 61; Canada, 1; New Zealand, 64; U.K., 44; U.S., 1.

To reach the international operator: Dial 102.

CELLPHONES

Nowadays, most mobile phones have the technology to work overseas. While this is a benefit, the cost of using your home mobile phone is prohibitively expensive. Instead, buy a local SIM card from one of the thousand **wartels** (phone shops) that surround the islands and use it in your phone. Bali and Lombok offer a variety of networks, each of which has different benefits. Try to establish from the seller which is the best for your needs and what promotions are available for each network. Expect to pay around Rp50,000 for your SIM card alone. You will then need to buy some credit—start off with Rp1,000,000.

INTERNET ACCESS

Wi-Fi access is increasingly common in Bali. More and more hotels, restaurants, and cafes offer Wi-Fi—especially in the south. Not all offer it for free, some still charge and you are also encouraged to buy a drink or something to eat.

Inland, in the central mountains, network coverage is limited and what Internet service is available is so painfully slow that it's not worth the effort. Wartels, supermarkets, and restaurants up and down the coast offer Internet access. You can pay anything between Rp10,000 and Rp30,000 an hour for the service.

For Lombok, Internet access and Internet cafes are available in cities and all tourist areas. In the villages and remote locations, there is usually no Internet and often no computers.

10 TIPS ON ACCOMMODATIONS

Bali accommodations range from bungalows that cost Rp40,000 (yes, US$4) to luxury villas at US$1,000 a night. An increasingly popular trend for families and groups is to rent a villa, which can go from US$100 up to US$5,000 per night and are usually served by a retinue of staff. On the lower end, and for a more local experience, are *losmen* (traditional homestay, a bastardization of the Dutch word *logement*) or rustic bungalows. In the better homestays, expect a clean and simple room with a double or two single beds. They usually don't have air-conditioning, but they will have a fan. Better places will have an attached bathroom with a cold-water shower, Western toilet, and hand basin. The lower budget places will sometimes have a squat toilet and *mandi* (a bucket of water to splash over your body).

Many villas and bungalows have open-air bathrooms, often set in a lush garden. They are definitely a very Balinese experience, but may also shelter little uninvited guests and are best avoided if you have low tolerance for critters.

Bali's resorts and fine Western hotels cost a fraction of what luxury accommodations would elsewhere. Promotional and Internet rates are available at all hotels in Bali and Lombok. Paying the rack rates, or published rates (which are listed in this guide), even in high season, is almost unheard of. Especially in the off season, it pays to shop around; you can show up at the front desk of even the largest hotels and ask for the best rate.

Almost all hotels charge a 21% tax (10% government tax and 11% service)

on top of the quoted rates. Some hotels tack on a charge in high season—the 2 or 3 weeks around Christmas and New Year's, plus the months of July and August. Some establishments might charge only 17% tax and some only the 10% government tax with no service added. Check when you are booking.

VILLAS

Bali is becoming increasingly famous for its **private villas** complete with staff. Indonesia's low labor costs, at one-third the already low levels of Thailand, result in single villas employing teams from five to over 30 people.

We're proponents of the villa option, as opposed to a hotel or resort, because you receive more space, privacy, and exclusivity for your money. Plus, if you are traveling for longer than a week with kids or in a group larger than two, a villa can end up as a bargain in cost and convenience.

Some villas and hotels are decadently over the top. We are talking private spas and helipads—you know, the necessities. Almost all stand-alone villas come with pools, gardens, and a full-time fleet of staff that usually includes a round-the-clock cook, housekeeper, gardener, and babysitter. Other standard features include air-conditioning, kitchens, stereo systems, satellite televisions, and IDD telephones. Most include an airport pickup and transfer; some have same-day laundry service, grocery shopping and restaurant delivery services, car and motorbike rentals, and catering. All villa compounds offer 24-hour reception and security. None of the villa complexes are beachfront but all are close to the action.

Not every place sold as a "villa" actually fits the bill. Prices vary widely: Some operators claim to go as low as US$30 a night (which usually just means a stand-alone hut on hotel grounds), but realistically you'll be looking at upwards of US$200 a night for a decent location and a private pool. At the top of the range nightly rents can easily go north of US$1,000 a night. The general rule "you get what you pay for" applies.

Most villas will have breakfast or a light snack ready for you on arrival. You then order your meals from a menu and they buy the groceries for you. Private villas normally have a higher quality of food, presentation, and service, but are much more expensive. Most stand-alone villas will buy your groceries, prepare your meals, and will charge between 10% and 30% in addition to the grocery bills. As a rule of thumb, the more expensive the villa the higher the additional expense on meals, but there are exceptions. Do the math first.

Look carefully at who is running the villa (run by the owner? local company? Western company? local staff who answer to an overseas owner?) and who you are renting through (directly from the owner? a management company? an established villa agent? one who just opened a month ago after his friend Nyoman told him how easy it was?). Each has its pros and cons. If it's an agency, see if it's been reviewed in the foreign press.

Ask how long the villa has been taking commercial guests. Villas normally take a year or so to get to best service levels. Also, in the first 6 to 12 months of operation great villas may offer introductory rates that are priced below market to gain awareness of their new offerings.

Estate Agents

Elite Havens, Jl. Raya Semer, Banjar Semer, Kerobokan (© **0361/731074;** fax 0361/736391; www.elitehavens.com), is the leading luxury villa agency in Bali.

Bali Villa Worldwide (BVW), Jl. Laksmana 3B, Oberoi-Seminyak (© **0361/732013;** fax 0361/736705; www.balivillaworldwide.com), manages a selection of top-notch properties available for rent all round Bali.

BaliOn, Pantai Seseh, Canggu (© **0361/742-4015;** www.balion.com), a family-run agency with a broad selection of budget to luxury choices on the island.

Bali Tropical Villas, Jl. Raya Seminyak, Gang Lalu 7, Seminyak (© **0361/732083;** fax 0361/732083; www.bali-tropical-villas.com), is run by Anita Lococo for over 15 years. There is nothing she doesn't know about most properties on the island, she has even written books on the subject.

Bali Experience, Jl. Banjar Anyar Kaja 89, Kerobokan (© **0361/844-5934;** fax 0361/847-5160; www.bali-experience.com), has an easy-to-navigate website that makes choosing even harder as there are so many wonderful properties.

Suggested Bali & Lombok Itineraries

Though Bali is about half the size of Jamaica and smaller than Delaware, you'll never tire of temples to visit, beaches to discover, and trails to hike. In truth, there's so much here for the visitor to do that a week or even two will not seem enough time to enjoy island life—just ask any of the expats who now call Bali home. Still, you can cram a lot of activity in 2 weeks or less, thanks to Bali's extensive tourism infrastructure and an endless array of outfitters ready to take you wherever you want to go. Since the island is so small, you don't need to constantly move hotels throughout your trip. You can cover a lot of ground by taking day trips from the major tourism hubs of Kuta, Seminyak, and Ubud.

1 THE REGIONS IN BRIEF

BALI

Physically, Bali is divided in half, east to west, by a volcanic mountain chain, and north to south by deep river gorges. Black volcanic sand is the norm, but white sand beaches periodically dot the coast, with some of the most spectacular either on the **Bukit** or hidden in the **east.** The island is dominated by two active volcanoes, **Gunung Agung,** the apex of Balinese religious and cultural belief, and **Gunung Batur,** with its twin calderas and shimmering lake. The **northwest** is given over mainly to national park, the **central mountains** to coffee and crops, and the remote **east** with its pebble beaches and crystal clear seas, to diving and snorkeling.

SOUTH BALI The triangular wedge of tropical lowlands south of Ubud to the Bukit Peninsula is the most developed area of Bali. The tourist hub of Seminyak-Legian-Kuta is next door to the international airport and provides a convenient first stop and a good base for day trips. **Kuta** is perhaps the most developed, with the cheapest digs on the island. The tourist influx means this is the place to come for nightlife, which attracts a younger, backpacking crowd, but you'll find much better fine-dining options in Seminyak. Unfortunately, Kuta Beach has a very strong current, which makes swimming difficult and dangerous, but it's a surfer's paradise with rip curls and challenging waves. **Seminyak** is certainly Bali's chicest "village," home to the majority of the island's expats and upscale accommodation. See chapters 6 and 7.

Denpasar is Bali's capital, with a population of over a half-million. Though most visitors completely bypass the city for more idyllic surrounds, it is home to the Bali Museum (p. 116), one of the island's best for a general overview of Balinese history and culture.

Though **Sanur** has a history of hosting international visitors that dates to the beginning of the 20th century, it maintains a level of tranquility near impossible to find in the

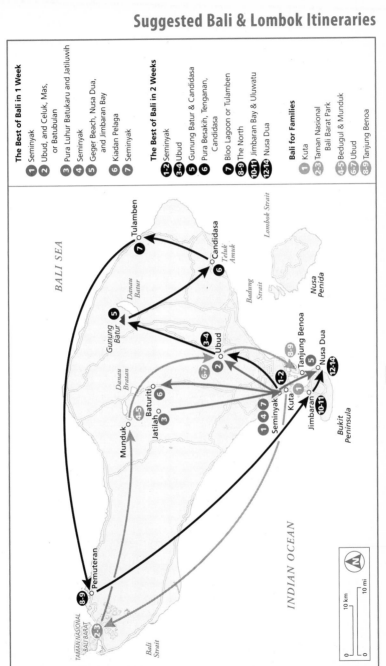

The Best of Bali in 1 Week

1. Seminyak
2. Ubud, and Celuk, Mas, or Batubulan
3. Pura Luhur Batukaru and Jatiluwih
4. Seminyak
5. Geger Beach, Nusa Dua, and Jimbaran Bay
6. Kiadan Pelaga
7. Seminyak

The Best of Bali in 2 Weeks

1-2. Seminyak
3-4. Ubud
5. Gunung Batur & Candidasa
6. Pura Besakih, Tenganan, Candidasa
7. Bloo Lagoon or Tulamben
8-9. The North
10-11. Jimbaran Bay & Uluwatu
12-14. Nusa Dua

Bali for Families

1. Kuta
2-3. Taman Nasional Bali Barat Park
4-5. Bedugul & Munduk
6-7. Ubud
8-9. Tanjung Benoa

tourist mania of Seminyak-Legian-Kuta. Surfing, windsurfing, scuba diving, and snor-keling are the main attractions here. Just off shore are the islands of **Nusa Penida, Nusa Lembongan,** and **Nusa Ceningan,** which provide some of Bali's finest scuba diving and are an easy boat ride from the mainland. See chapter 8.

BUKIT PENINSULA   This dollop of land just to the south of the airport is not only a favorite among globetrotting surfers, but also hot on the list of hotel and resort develop-ers. **Jimbaran Bay,** just past the airport, is famous for its beach lined with seafood res-taurants. **Nusa Dua** is a government-sponsored and -built walled high-end resort that sits above the eastern cliffs and is soon to be joined by a similar new development, Pecatu Indah, on the west. In the meantime, the surf still rages at **Uluwatu,** one of Bali's, and indeed the world's, most famous waves. See chapter 9.

UBUD   Simply put, Ubud's raison d'être is to be Balinese. The island's rich culture—with traditions, artistry, and spirituality that encompass seemingly every aspect of daily life—thrives here in a multitude of temples, museums, art galleries, and artisan villages. Money and development in Ubud is funneled toward preserving traditions and encour-aging cultural innovations; international chain companies are kept at bay. You cannot visit Bali without seeing Ubud. See chapter 10.

CENTRAL MOUNTAINS   Volcanic **Gunung Batur,** with its double caldera, is the big-gest draw for visitors to the central mountains. But as a visitor, your experience of the mountain may be sullied by overly aggressive touts and busloads of tourists. Certainly the view from the top at sunrise will be worth it. Don't overlook the other highland charms hidden in villages on the volcano's slopes. Bring your hiking shoes and warm clothes—it's a different world up here. See chapter 11.

EAST   The volcanic chain of mountains that dominate Bali's landscape are home to the center of the Balinese world: **Gunung Agung.** On the drive up to the mountain and **Pura Besakih,** Bali's largest and holiest temple, you'll pass through one of Bali's most scenic areas, the **Sidemen Valley.** East Bali also has its fair share of gorgeous coastline and some of Bali's greatest scuba diving and snorkeling is right off the shore of **Tulamben** and **Amed.** See chapter 12.

NORTH   North Bali's string of seaside villages and resorts are cut off from the south by the mountains. See chapter 13.

WEST   The western half of Bali is dominated by the **West Bali National Park,** with its hiking and bird-watching, and supreme diving off **Menjangan Island.** See chapter 14.

LOMBOK

WEST   The west coast is Lombok's most developed area and the home of the majority of islanders. The cities of **Ampenan, Mataram,** and **Cakranegara** serve as the main jumping off point to the rest of the island. Both the port and airport are here. See p. 313. **Senggigi,** just north of the cities, is Lombok's main tourist hub with the most hotels and resorts on the island, as well as the home base for many of the island's outfitters. See p. 316.

SOUTHWEST   This peninsula remains Lombok's least developed area in terms of tour-ism and thus provides the unique opportunity to explore hidden bays and deserted beaches. See p. 322.

NORTH   This is the seat of **Gunung Rinjani,** Lombok's sacred volcano and destination for many of the island's tourists. See p. 324.

CENTRAL   The cooler central region of Lombok presents your best opportunity for shopping. Small artisan villages that produce *ikat* cloth, baskets, and pottery are scattered among the hills here. See p. 330.

SOUTH   A new megaresort has been proposed for south Lombok, which has possibly some of the finest beaches in all Indonesia. The surf here is also internationally renowned. See p. 332.

EAST   To see the least developed and least visited area of Lombok, come to the east. The villages here are home to a very traditional society of Sasak people. You can also catch a ferry to the islands of Komodo and Flores from here. See p. 336.

THE GILI ISLANDS   These three tiny islands (**Gili Air, Gili Meno,** and **Gili Trawangan**) have no cars, scant electricity and running water, and little connection to the outside world. Therefore, they're very popular among backpackers, surfers, and anyone looking to go off the grid for a while. Aside from scuba diving, the main draw here is the potential to spend all your time with your feet in the sand. See chapter 16.

2 THE BEST OF BALI IN 1 WEEK

Most people stay in **Seminyak** (chapter 7), especially when short on time. Seminyak has the biggest variety of hotel options per square meter than anywhere else in Bali and can't be beaten for its arterial access to surfing, beaches, shopping, and nightlife. Plus, its proximity to the airport makes getting back less of a hassle.

Day ❶: Beach & Shopping
After breakfast, head to **Ku de Ta** (p. 101) and grab one of their sun loungers. Spend the morning soaking up the sun and scanning the surfers. For some retail therapy, head down Jalan Laksmana and Jalan Raya Seminyak where there are plenty of places to pick up gifts to take home and threads for the beach. Catch the sunset at **Breeze** (p. 102), the beachfront bar of the **Samaya** (p. 97). For dinner, stroll down Eat Street (Jl. Laksmana) and take your pick of any of the dozens of restaurants.

Day ❷: Arts & Culture
Start with an early rise and head to **Tirta Empul** (p. 209), and bathe in the magical waters. Next stop is **Pura Gunung Kawi** (p. 208), one of Bali's oldest temples. Head to the center of Ubud for lunch and visit the **Neka Museum** (p. 210) and the **ARMA Museum** (p. 210). On the way back to Seminyak, cruise through **Mas, Batubulan,** or **Celuk** (p. 217) to browse for jewelry, woodcarving, and stone carving. After a full day, enjoy room service or an early dinner at your hotel.

Day ❸: Explore the Countryside
Start with an early visit to **Pura Luhur Batukaru** (p. 241) and soak in the spirits and the cool jungle air. Then head for a trek around the mystical rice paddy fields of **Jatiluwih** (p. 240). The cool western uplands, overlooking half the island, offer magnificent views. As you wind your way back to Seminyak, notice the coffee, coconut, cacao, clove, jack fruit, banana, and papaya (to name a few) growing here. Head to the beach for a quiet dinner at **Gado Gado** (p. 101) or **Ma Joly** (p. 84) in Tuban.

Day ❹: Pamper Yourself
Book a spa outing a day in advance. Head to **Desa Seni** (p. 115) and start your day with a Pilates or yoga class. Enjoy a healthy light lunch of ingredients from their organic garden. For dinner, head to **Bumbu Bali** (p. 187) in Tangung Benoa

where you will awaken out of your coma with spicy Balinese cuisine and a local *barong* dance with banging gamelans.

Day ❺: Beach Bliss

Head to **Geger Beach** (p. 180) for the day to swim in the safe shallow waters, take a stroll down the beach to watch the seaweed farmers at work, and have a massage while you top off your tan. For sunset supper, head to **Jimbaran** (p. 154) beach for the festive holiday-like atmosphere—complete with mariachis.

Day ❻: Give Back to Bali

Spend the day with JED (a local ecotourism mininetwork) at the traditional village **Kiadan Pelaga** (p. 236) in the central

mountains. You will learn about the process of growing and making coffee, see dry rice paddy fields, and meet the members of a small community. The villagers will prepare a traditional Balinese feast for you. All proceeds go right back to the village.

Day ❼: Last Minute Sun, Shopping & Spa

Don't get stuck at Ngurah Rai Airport buying your batik and baskets at 10 times the cost. Enjoy your last day as a shopping spree in Seminyak instead. And, be sure to soak up that last bit of sun or splurge on a final spa treatment to prepare you for your flight home.

3 THE BEST OF BALI IN 2 WEEKS

If you have 2 weeks to spare, you can take a more leisurely and complete tour of the island.

Days ❶ & ❷: Seminyak

Lounge at the oceanfront pool at the luxurious **Legian** (p. 96), followed by a sunset visit to the temple **Tanah Lot** (p. 290). The next day, take a surf lesson at the **Rip Curl School of Surf** (p. 85), followed by a sunset cocktail and dinner at **Ku de Ta** (p. 101).

Days ❸ & ❹: Ubud

After the 1-hour drive to **Ubud** (chapter 10), base yourself at either the **COMO Shambhala** (p. 194) or the **Chedi Club** (p. 191)—worth every rupiah. Take a morning trek through the rice paddies and then check into one of many local spas. Tuck into a gourmet French meal at **Mozaic** (p. 201) for dinner. The next day, peruse the numerous shops on Monkey Forest Road and take a break at the **Monkey Forest** (p. 217), where you can feed the monkeys a few bananas. Late in the afternoon, take the 1-hour drive to Penelokan, a town that sits on the outer crater's edge of

Gunung Batur (p. 54). The best of the local accommodations is the **Lakeview Hotel** (p. 228).

Day ❺: Gunung Batur

Make the 2-hour ascent of Gunung Batur, an active volcano. At the top, you can boil eggs in pockets of erupting steam and walk along one of the volcano's ridges. In the afternoon, hire a car for the 2-hour trip to check-in to **Candidasa** (p. 260), on Bali's east shore. The boutique **Alila Manggis** (p. 258) has good value accommodations, beachside massage pavilions, and one of the area's best restaurants, Sea Salt.

Days ❻ & ❼: The East

Take a day trip to **Pura Besakih** (p. 252), Bali's most important temple, and spend the afternoon wandering **Tenganan** village, followed by dinner at **Vincent's** (p. 262) in Candidasa. The next day, go diving or snorkeling at the **Bloo Lagoon.** If you're an advanced diver, sign up for the famed wreck dive at **Tulamben** (p. 268).

Suggested Lombok Itineraries

It's a 25-minute flight or a 2-hour boat ride to Lombok, meaning this neighboring island demands more than a few days of your time.

Spend at least 2 days on Lombok. Base yourself in **Senggigi** (p. 316), the tourism hub, and take scuba-diving trips along the coast. Hire a driver to take you on a shopping tour through the island interior. If you're really ambitious, you can make it the **Gili Islands** (chapter 16) to spend the night, but these dots of sand are best savored over a few days and without a rush.

With a little more time you can scale sacred **Gunung Rinjani** (p. 328)—the shortest treks are 2 days and can go as long as 4. Or, head the opposite direction and go to the south coast, perhaps the most beautiful strip of sand and rock in all of Indonesia. Use **Kuta** (p. 332) as a base for exploring the beaches, surf, and back roads, and witness the sunset.

Lombok is also a key transportation point for travel to islands east, such Komodo and Flores. Lombok-based **Sunda Trails** (p. 311) can take you there.

Days ❽ & ❾: The North or Lombok

To truly get away from it all, head to either Bali's **northern** (chapter 13) beaches by car or the neighboring island of **Lombok** (chapter 15) via plane or boat. In the north, stay at the **Matahari Beach Resort** (p. 285), which provides bungalows with traditional Balinese facades and a Michelin star–worthy restaurant. On Lombok, the most luxurious choice (and a good value) is the **Oberoi** (p. 326), with a gorgeous swimming pool and a secluded beach.

Days ❿ & ⓫: Jimbaran Bay

Hire a car to the romantic yet local area of **Jimbaran Bay** (p. 154), home to a number

of the world's top resorts. The cream of the crop are the **Karma Kandara** (p. 172) and the **Four Seasons Resort at Jimbaran Bay** (p. 160). Visit the cliff-side temple **Uluwatu** (p. 166) at sunset, followed by a grilled lobster and shrimp dinner at **Menega Café** (p. 165), the best seafood hut on Jimbaran beach.

Days ⓬–⓮: Nusa Dua

End your holiday by winding down beachside or poolside at any number of the resorts in this five-star enclave (p. 174). Visit **Bumbu Bali** (p. 187), one of the island's top restaurants, which offers authentic Balinese cuisine and cooking classes.

4 BALI FOR FAMILIES

Bali is an excellent choice for family holidays. With so much on offer, you are quite literally spoiled for choice. To top this, the Balinese love kids and slather them in attention. Your children will be enchanted by the local color that surrounds them from the picturesque underwater world to the noisy ceremonies. Most resorts cater to kids with clubs, programs, and classes like kite making and Balinese mask painting and you can often get discounted interconnecting rooms and children's meals.

Day ❶: Kuta

Start your children's trip off with a rip and sign them up for a half-day surfing lesson at **Rip Curl School of Surf** (p. 85) or with **Marcy** (p. 86). Either way, you can lounge on a beach chair while they have their lessons.

For the afternoon, head to the water park **Waterbom** (p. 87). Have dinner at **Papa's** (p. 80) and order an explosive volcano pizza—lit at your table, it burns for 2 minutes before the kids get to blow it out.

Days ❷ & ❸: Taman Nasional Bali Barrat Park in Menjangan

It's a 3-hour drive from Seminyak, but be a good troop leader and lead your scouts on a 2-day adventure to the 1,000-hectare (2,471-acre) **Taman Nasional Bali Barat Park** (p. 298). It's worth it. Stay at the family-friendly **Menjangan Jungle and Beach Resort** (p. 301) in a hut in the mangroves. Snorkel off the coral reef walls of Menjangan Island. After lunch, take a jeep tour of the park where wildlife, including deer, monkeys, wild chickens, and wild boar, gather at the watering holes.

Fill your second day with an early morning bird-watching tour, kayaking at high tide, horseback riding, and trekking. Your hotel will help you organize all your activities.

Days ❹ & ❺: Bedugul & Munduk

Your drive to Bedugul and the beautiful **Botanical Garden** (p. 235) will take you through bamboo forests. After the gardens, head to the **Bali Tree Top Adventure Park** (p. 235), where the whole family can try their hands at a variety of adventure circuits with and all sorts of active play. In the afternoon check into the **Puri Lumbung Cottages** (p. 239), which has stunning panoramas of the rice fields and coast.

Days ❻ & ❼: Ubud & Surrounding Area

There are three choices for the day here and even if you're running a democracy, it's going to be hard to choose given the names alone: the **Elephant Park** (p. 216), the **Bali Bird Park** (p. 134), or the **Safari Park** (p. 216). Check in to the luxurious **Chedi Club** (p. 191) in time for their scrumptious afternoon tea (included in the price) or the **Alam Sari** (p. 197), with activities for the kids like painting, kite making, mountain biking, and swimming. In the morning, either go to the **Monkey Forest** (p. 217) and spend some time with those pesky relatives or go **rafting** (p. 215). In the afternoon stroll the streets for some shopping or just enjoy the hotel pool and relax.

Days ❽ & ❾: Tanjung Benoa

Spend your final family time in the relaxed setting of the **Conrad** (p. 186). Heaps of activities here for the kids include water-skiing, windsurfing, snorkeling, banana boating, and jet-skiing. Check your young ones into the all-day kids' club while you grab a bale and catch up on some reading. The resort even has spa treatments specifically for children so that the entire family can pamper themselves at once. On one of your nights here, hire an in-house babysitter and dine at either **Rin** (p. 187) or **Spice** (p. 187) and take a romantic moonlit walk along the promenade.

Active Vacation Planner

Bali and Lombok offer travelers a fantastic opportunity to combine lazy luxury with heart-pounding adventure and even a bit of personal enrichment. The azure seas of the Indian Ocean that frame the island provide the coral reefs and world-famous waves sought by professional divers and hardened surfers alike, and the climate provides lush green jungles that climb up a picturesque volcanic mountain range ideal for hikers and trekkers. If you seek artistic adventure or personal and spiritual enrichment, the many varied communities centered around Ubud will help you learn about the island's artistic heritage and, should you wish, let you seek introspection. You may also find your peace on a yoga mat.

While the essence and charm of Bali and its culture remains, you are never far from a developed tourist infrastructure to assist you with your adventure. The island offers almost too many options to list in a summary.

1 ORGANIZED TRIPS & TOURS

INDONESIA- & BALI-BASED TOUR OPERATORS

Independent travelers tend to view organized tours as antithetical to the joy of discovery, however there are not many undiscovered places in Bali. Besides, leaving the details to someone else frees up substantial time to concentrate on something else—like your actual vacation. Most tours include local guides, all land transportation, accommodation, meals, and any gear that may be required. Lombok, though, can be problematic for an independent traveler simply due to the language barrier. However, it remains largely "undiscovered" (by Bali standards) by foreign tourists.

Organizing a specialized tour in Bali from your hotel or villa is as easy as calling your concierge or villa manager. Nearly any tourism business, from restaurants and car rental outfits to hotels, can arrange virtually any trip you can dream of. These are small islands with a very tight-knit tourism infrastructure and community. Chances are if your point of contact cannot arrange the trip him- or herself, they'll know exactly who to call. Such is the Balinese sense of hospitality.

BALI **Bali Discovery Tours** ★★ (✆ 0361/286283; www.balidiscovery.com) is one of the island's largest and most established tour operators and offers customized and off-the-shelf tours. These guys really know their stuff and have been doing it for about 20 years. Their website has up-to-date news on what's happening on the island and a comprehensive list of practical tips and advice to make your holiday a success.

JED ★ (**Jaringan Ekowisata Desa;** ✆ 0361/737447; www.jed.or.id) is an ecotourism nongovernmental organization that works with four traditional Balinese villages (Pelaga Kiadan, Sibetan, Tenganan, and Cenigan). They organize day visits to experience village life as well as overnight stays with a village family. This is a very local affair with local guides, local food, and all profits going to the local communities.

Sobek ★★ (℃ 0361/287059; www.balisobek.com) is a well established and ethical adventure tour company that arranges and runs white-water rafting, cycling, and trekking all over Bali. Sobek invests heavily in providing the highest safety standards of all companies on the island. All the staff receive on-going safety training and language courses to ensure the highest of standards are met.

ABL Tours and Travel (℃ 0361/731520; www.baliwww.com) is one of the busiest leading tour operators. They can assist with organizing custom-made tours, villa and hotel accommodation, and even weddings.

Bali Adventure Tours (℃ 0361/721480; www.baliadventuretours.com) can arrange fun day and overnight itineraries to volcanoes, the jungle, and rural villages.

LOMBOK & THE GILI ISLANDS   Sunda Trails (℃ 0370/647390; www.sundatrails.com) offers off-the-beaten-track tours to remote villages on Lombok and the nearby islands. They specialize in creating tailor-made programs for those looking for something a little bit different from the usual packages available.

Island Promotions (℃ 08/1805305632; www.gili-paradise.com) provides accurate and up-to-date information on transport, accommodation, and activities for the Gili islands. They have a reliable booking service to plan activities before you arrive.

INTERNATIONAL TOUR OPERATORS

Asia Transpacific Journeys (2995 Center Green Court, Boulder, CO 80301; ℃ 800/642-2742 or 303/443-6789; fax 303/443-7078; www.asiatranspacific.com) deals with small groups and custom programs that include luxury accommodations. Tours to Bali can take in the island of Komodo on a traditional Indonesian schooner or trekking in the central mountains.

Backroads (801 Cedar St., Berkeley, CA 94710; ℃ 800/462-2848 or 510/527-1555; fax 510/527-1444; www.backroads.com), the cycling and hiking specialist, organizes trips round the island taking in the village communities, the fantastically rich underwater world, and the beaches and scenery of Bali.

Carrier (No. 1 Lakeside, Cheadle, Cheshire SK8 3GW; ℃ 01244/897551; www.carrier.co.uk) was voted by Condé Nast Traveler readers as the number-one favorite tour operator. Their service is second to none. Based in the U.K., Carrier can organize luxury stays in villas and hotels throughout Bali.

Elegant Resort (The Old Palace, Chester CH1 1RB; ℃ 01244/897551; www.elegant resorts.co.uk) is a renowned luxury resort tour operator that arranges accommodation and packages staying in all the best resorts in Bali.

G.A.P. Adventures (19 Charlotte St., Toronto, Ontario M5V 2H5; ℃ 888/800-4100 in the U.S. and Canada, 0844/410-1030 in the U.K.; www.gapadventures.com) is a sustainable adventure travel organization based in Canada with affiliated travel agents all over the world (check the website for a detailed list). They specialize in holidays for independent travelers looking for something unique.

Intrepid Travel (11 Spring St., Fitzroy, Victoria 3065; ℃ 613/9473-2626 or 877/488-1616 in the U.S.; fax 613/9419-4426; www.intrepidtravel.com), a popular Australian operator, is probably the best choice for an off-the-beaten-track tour of Asia. Intrepid caters their trips to the culturally discerning, those with humanitarian goals, those in search of comfort and adventure, those on a budget, or those looking for a looser structure and lots of options. Its name is its motto, and with some of the best guides in Asia, these folks will take you to the back of beyond safely and in style.

i-to-i (© 800/0111156 in the U.K. or 800/985-4852 in the U.S.; www.i-to-i.com) is a globally recognized travel organization that places volunteers in overseas projects that assist local communities. Packages include surfing and teaching English or working with orphans and the disabled in Bali.

Kuoni (Kuoni house, Dorking, Surrey RH5 4AZ; © 01306/747002; www.kuoni. co.uk), a well established U.K.-based firm, specializes in long haul trips.

Responsible Travel (www.responsibletravel.com) is the leading ethical travel agent, a joint initiative with Conservation International. They work with local communities to create authentic experiences throughout Bali and Lombok.

Thomas Cook (© 0871/895-0055; www.thomascook.com), organizes package holidays to suit all budgets and tastes. Great for those on a budget and with kids. They are the number-one travel agent for Bali.

Trailfinders (48 Earls Court Rd., London W8 6FT; © 0845/954-6060; www.trail finders.com) is undoubtedly the leading travel agent in the U.K. and Ireland for holidays to Bali and Lombok. Their specialty is honeymoons and weddings.

2 ACTIVITIES A TO Z

PERFORMING ARTS & CRAFTS SCHOOLS

Ever since the days of Walter Spies in Ubud, Western artists have discovered profound inspiration in Bali's landscape. Of course, the Balinese were doing it long before the Westerners caught on.

The **Suly Resort & Spa,** Jl. Cok. Rai Pudak, Br. Yangloni, Peliatan (© 0361/976185; www.sulyresort.com; Rp100,000 per person per hour), has joined with Bali Global Ashram Foundation to create an education platform where visitors can take classes in pottery, painting, dance, wood carving, kite making, and cooking to name a few. Classes are run by professional and well-known Balinese instructors.

PERFORMING ARTS The multicultural center **Pondok Pekak,** Jl. Monkey Forest, Ubud (© 0361/976194), essentially a library, is a resource center that brings locals and Westerners together. They offer a wide range of community activities for children and adults largely focused on the *Sanggar* (traditional music and dance organization). Programs include gamelan and dance (*legong* and Frog dance) lessons. There are also a selection of traditional Balinese workshops, which allow visitors to learn about fruit carving, Indonesian language, and mask carving.

The **Mekar Bhuana Conservatory,** Jl. Penyaringan 24, Sanur (© 0361/842-7030 or 08/1999191104; www.balimusic.org), runs a selection of courses on gamelan and Balinese dance.

Tjokorda Raka Swastika, Puri Saren, Ubud (© 0361/975753), an accomplished musician who has played with and taught many of the best orchestras in Bali, is now running courses on gamelan and any other musical instruments that form part of the *gong kebyar.* Pak Tjokorda Raka is an excellent teacher for all levels. Classes are held in his house on the grounds of Puri Saren, Ubud's Palace.

POTTERY Italian Marcello and Michela Massoni head **Gaya Ceramic and Design** ★★, Jl. Raya Sayan, Ubud (© 0361/7451413; www.gayafusion.com), which produces pottery for famous brands like Armani and Bulgari. They offer a selection of courses and a residency program with instructors from all over the globe.

Alternative Health & Wellness A to Z

Bali was recently voted the "Asian Spa Capital of the Year" by *Asia Spa*. Bali hosts numerous alternative therapies for wellness and spiritual enlightenment. Here are some of the best people and most unique offerings on the island.

Astrology   **Salena Bulan** (📞 **08/1338106349;** salenabulan@gmail.com), in Ubud, has been passionately studying astrology for over 17 years. With an emphasis on Jungian psychological and reincarnation evolutionary astrology, her approach is more psycho-spiritual than predictive.

Ayurveda   **Uma Inder** (📞 **08/1236206136;** uma_inder@hotmail.com), in Ubud, is an Ayurvedic Practitioner and Panchakarma Specialist in women's health. Uma offers consultation, treatments, and self-care educational programs. She is also an ayurvedic doula with experience in fertility awareness, conscious conception, lactation support, and pre/post natal wellness programs.

Balian   A Balian (p. 1) is a traditional Balinese healer. Two favorites are: **Cokorda Rai** (📞 **08/1805477388**), in Ubud, who reads auras and energy; **Pak Sirkas** (📞 **361/742-1169**), in Canggu. **Pak Ketut Arsana** is the founder of Ashram Munivara, dedicated to the teachings of Shiva. Contact him through Ubud Bodyworks Healing Centre, Jl. Hanoman 25, Ubud (📞 **0361/975720;** www.ubudbodyworkscentre.com). The most famous Balians at the moment are **Wayan** and **Ketut Liyer** from the book *Eat, Pray, Love*. You can visit them but with so many Western tourists calling on them, they have somehow lost their charm. Wayan is based in her shop Traditional Balinese Healing in Ubud on Jalan Jembawan; Ketut still practices from his house in Pengosekan. Ask any hotel or villa for directions as the street does not have a name.

Herbs & Medicinal Plants   **Lilir** and **Westi** (📞 **08/123816020**), in Ubud, are a Balinese couple whose families go back nine generations as medicinal plant healers. Both do early morning herb walks through the rice fields, drinking tea and teaching about the medicinal plants found along the way.

The **Sari Api Ceramic Studio,** Jl. Suweta, Ubud (📞 **0361/977917** or 08/124660919), allows guests to explore their creativity using clay. Beginner's classes for both kids and adults give an introduction to throwing clay on a wheel as well as hand building. Studio space can be rented out to skilled potters.

SILVERSMITHING & JEWELRY   **Studio Perak,** Jl. Hanoman, Ubud (📞 **08/123651809;** www.studioperak.com), employs traditional Balinese silversmithing. Husband and wife Ketut and Joanna have developed their own courses for visitors to try their hands at making Balinese styled jewelry. Try their 3-hour course and make a ring or pendant. Children from 8 years are also welcome.

TEXTILES   **Threads of Life**'s ★, Jl. Kajeng 24, Ubud (📞 **0361/972187**), courses explore the history, weaving, dyeing techniques as well as the traditions of *ikat* and batik using handspun threads and natural dyes. The money goes to support local communities. Classes run between Rp50,000 and Rp150,000.

Holistic & Intuitive Healing **Frederique Nault** ((08/123920615; healing@indosat.net.id), in Kuta, is a qualified naturopath whose innovative treatments are drawn from a comprehensive range of powerful healing methods, such as craniosacral therapy and energy psychology, personally tailored to suit the individual's needs. **Dr. Susan Spillman** ((08/1337812502; www.baliartsandtours.com), in Ubud, starts sessions with an in-depth discussion of your concerns and then employs energy work and/or Quantum-Touch—primarily used for pain relief or reduction.

Meditation **Frank Wilson** (Brahma Kumaris World Spiritual University, the Meditation Shop; (**08/1805398000;** www.themeditationshop.org) offers rajah yoga meditation for relaxing, refreshing, and clearing the mind and heart. **Pak Kadek Suambara** ((08/5237131444) in Ubud offers meditation and laughter yoga. The **Bali Usada Meditation Foundation** can be reached at (**0361/289209** (Ngurah Rai 328, Bypass Sanur, Denpasar).

Natural & Raw Food Counseling **Mark Ament** ((08/1916743272; mark@healingvibes.com), in Ubud, is a specialist in healing through living foods and internal cleansing and offers powerful techniques to lose weight and overcome severe allergies and chronic depression.

Oils **Gabrielle Souczek** ((08/180564426), in Ubud, performs Raindrop Technique essential oil massages designed to push toxins out of your tissue, oxygenate your cells, repair DNA, eliminate viruses, bacteria, and inflammation, release emotional issues, and leave you feeling vibrant.

Sound Healing **Swami Bodhi Arun** ((08/5935174112), in Ubud, accompanies meditation with the vibration and sound of crystal quartz bells.

Tarot Readings **Jan Merril** ((08/17356013; janmerrills@gmail.com), in Ubud, is a gifted tarot reader, who will bring insights into your current and future life. Or learn to read the cards yourself in an intimate full-day course.

The best place to learn about the rich history of Batik and the techniques of the trade is with Bali's own batik artist **Ketut Sujana** ((0361/979097 or 08/123762280). Ketut offers hands-on courses for individuals or groups. His workshop is behind his studio in Lungsiakan, on the main road opposite Fly Café outside Ubud. Ketut charges Rp50,000 an hour. Allow about 3 hours for your first course.

BIKING ★★

Bali seen from a bike is far more engaging than one seen from a speeding car. There will not be one village where the children don't stop what they are doing to wave and cheer you on. With 1 week in Bali and a good guide you may be able to circumnavigate the island's full distance of 410km (255 miles). Stick to the back roads as much as you can. Avoid the main road north up the west coast, the main artery for tired lorry drivers going in and out of Java.

> ## (Tips) Bali Sports Online
>
> To find out what is happening in the sports world of Bali at any time check out
> the Sanur-based Bali sports online magazine at **www.stiffchilli.com**.

A full-day tour with a reputable company will cost anything from about Rp350,000 and will generally include bike, lunch, and a local English-speaking guide. Multiday tours either circumvent the island completely or pass through the mainly uncluttered roads less traveled of the mountainous center and flats of the east.

Look into the fully guided tours presented by Thailand-based **Spice Roads** (www. spiceroads.com), specialists in off-road adventures and touring remote villages. Not for the fainthearted, these 10-day trips will teach you as much about the island as they will about yourself. And at just over US$1,500, including your bike, guide, and accommodation, they are an exhilarating and inexpensive way to see the island.

U.S.-based **Pedaler's Pub & Grille** (www.pedalerspubandgrille.com) does a 7-day tour called the "Bali Paradise Ride" which takes you from Ubud, down to Candidasa, and up round the east coast on fairly empty roads and back via Kintamani for US$1,595 including your guide, accommodation, meals, and van support en route.

Wayan, the energetic and enthusiastic owner of **Balibike.com ★** (© 0361/978052) does a great day trip from Kintamani back down to Ubud on "only his known secret roads." He will collect you from as far afield as Kuta and take you to Kintamani for breakfast with a view over Lake Batur. You then head mainly downhill back to Ubud for the most delicious lunch, home cooked by his wife, before he returns you to your hotel. Groups reach up to 20 but with a couple of guides, with one at the back to encourage stragglers. The cost is Rp400,000 from Kuta and Rp350,000 from Ubud which includes your bike, helmet, breakfast, lunch, and transfers.

Bali-based **Archipelago Adventures** (© 0361/844-4624; www.archipelago-adventure. com) will do 1-day trips on the back roads. They charge US$65 per person if there are only two of you, but less if there are larger groups.

Lombok has a similar terrain to Bali but there are far fewer accommodation options and once you leave the established tourist west coast, you may well have to rely on your own canvas, or homestays. However, while there are extra hardships and a whole heap of extra planning required, the rewards can be greater. The roads are a lot less clustered and you will encounter little traffic once north of Senggigi. If you are planning on cycling on Lombok, a guide will be a good idea. One word of warning: The coastal areas are not as flat as they are in Bali.

With a little bit of initiative, some research, and armed with a detailed map, you can head out on your own and explore. You will find basic accommodations along your route without having to book in advance and there are plenty of places to buy water. You will however miss out on some of the history and local knowledge that a local guide usually provides. Look to do no more than 80km (50 miles) in a day.

A reliable company in Lombok is **Lombok Biking Tours** (© 0370/692164), on the main street in Senggigi next to Bumbu Café. Tours are designed for the fit and unfit alike. They will do a 2-hour guided tour for Rp100,000 per person.

ACTIVE VACATION PLANNER

5

ACTIVITIES A TO Z

BIRD-WATCHING

Bali and the surrounding islands are a haven for twitchers. With the successful reintro-duction of what was once the world's most endangered species, the eponymous Bali starling, now back and flying free, the island can hold its head up high.

The most well known and idiosyncratic tours are with Victor Mason who runs **Bali Bird Walks** ★ (✆ 0361/975009; www.balibirdwalk.com), along with his partner Su and her brother Pink. They have been the best birding guides for the past 15 years. Depending on conditions and demand they will take you on a tour of the rice fields around Ubud (for US$33 per person including lunch). They also do walks around Batu-karu or if you want they will head for the sea and wetlands.

Friends of the National Park Foundation (**FNPF**; ✆ 0361/977978; www.fnpf.org), is a nonprofit organization that works with local communities to assist with the preserva-tion of wildlife in Indonesia. They own over 20,000 hectares (49,421 acres) on Nusa Penida where they have set up a bird sanctuary. They are currently working on two recovery programs for the Bali starling and the lesser sulphur-crested cockatoo with some success. Either come for a day of bird-watching with a dedicated guide or stay the night on the island.

BOATING & SAILING ★★★

Several smaller islands are easily accessible from Bali and Lombok, making these two a wonderful base for exploration. The sailing season for many traditional Indonesian boats is May to September. While a lot of the more established boats are booked up almost a year in advance, an increasing number of charter and sail companies are sprouting up. A lot of the shorter trips, typically 5 days, give or take, will focus on the Komodo islands while the longer ones venture out in to the Banda Sea.

The **Royal Bali Yacht Club** (www.royalbaliyachtclub.com) is all dinghies and lasers on Serangan Island, a reclaimed bit of scrubland on the road to Sanur. They also have a small facility in Sanur in front of the Mecure hotel on the beach. Visitor membership is only Rp250,000; they have various boats for hire and will provide lessons at pretty low rates (Rp50,000 per hour per person). If you want to sail, or take the kids for the day, it's fun, safe, and low key.

Some of the larger hotels in **Sanur** and **Nusa Dua** have their own accompaniment of lasers, dinghies, and catamarans for you to use. If your hotel does not, you will easily find various places along the beach that will hire them. However, you will find no sailing, nor boats for hire anywhere on the west coast of Bukit peninsula as there are few places to safely land them.

In a different league from many other boats, with prices to match, are the offerings of **Silolona** (✆ 0361/287326; www.silolona.com), **Ombak Putih** (✆ 0361/766269; www.ombakputih.com), **Raja Laut** (www.rajalaut.com), and newcomer **El Aleph** (✆ 08/1337700668; www.elalephcruising.com). These are luxury cruises in traditional Phinisi-styled boats, offering educational adventures that take you to some of the most beautiful, and, other than by boat, inaccessible spots in the archipelago. If you have managed to tuck any money away, pretend this is your rainy day and take a trip on one of these before your number is called.

Pitched somewhere in between the high-end charter boats and the mass-market day trips is a journey on what is affectionately known as the Pirate Ship or the **Bulan Pur-nama** ★★★ (www.bulan-purnama.com). They do both charters and individual cabins and will hire it out for in the region of €1,000 a day, with diving and on-board staff included. This traditional Phinisi wooden boat runs dive and surf charters through the eastern islands, including Komodo to Moyo then Lombok or even Labuan Bajo to Komodo. Home anchorage is Gili Trawangan, and they also organize Gili Island cruises, starting in Bali. For the less ambitious, try a day trip on a large charter yacht: **Sail Sensations** (✆ 0361/725864; www.sailsensations.com) will take you to Lembongan for the day; the **Waka** (✆ 0361/723629; www.the-waka.com) will do the same on a catamaran.

Websites **www.baliintaran.com/bali-cruises** and **www.balicruises.com** are useful, though are ultimately booking agents. They will have new and updated information on available boats and may be able to better fit your individual dates and requirements.

COOKING ★

Several half-day and full-day cooking courses are on offer in Bali. The day typically starts with a visit to a local fresh food market to learn about all the ingredients that go into creating a Balinese dish. The chef will then explain the techniques that are used to put together your dish and once cooking is over, you are rewarded with eating your creation. Look into the following schools: **Alila Manggis** resort in Manggis (✆ 0363/41044; www.alilahotels.com); **Bambu Bali** in Nusa Dua (✆ 0361/771256; www.balifoods. com); and in Ubud, **Casa Luna** (✆ 0361/973282; www.casalunabali.com) and **Mozaic** (✆ 0361/975768; www.mozaic-bali.com). Hotels may also arrange classes on request. **Hanging Gardens** (p. 194) is one of note.

FISHING

While much fun can be had by going out at 5am on a *jukung* with a local fisherman, the fishing consists of throwing a simple baited line out the back of a boat and trolling the current or alternatively using a hand line. It is not exactly adrenalin-filled and your time will be spent either puttering out and back at about 4 knots or sitting watching your local friend doing all the fishing, but you will be fascinated by just how many fish they catch using this method.

Given the amount of marine life and the virtually guaranteed chance of success, it is somewhat surprising that there are so few game fishing boats. If you do find someone to take you out, make sure the boat you go with has a covered area, looks shipshape, and you have plenty of sunscreen and liquids. Most boats will leave from either Benoa or Padangbai harbors; costs will range from US$80 to US$200 per person for 4 hours and will usually take no more than four people, although some can take as many as eight. Species you are likely to find include Spanish mackerel, wahoo, mahimahi, all sizes of tuna, sail fish, and barracuda.

Established operators are **Bali Fishing** (www.bali-fishing.com) or **Ena Fishing**, Jl. Tirta Ening 1, Sanur (✆ 0361/288829; www.enafishing.com). Ena also does a night trip leaving at sundown and returning 4 hours later. They have also recently added a freshwater fishing trip to Lake Buyan although the fish here are smaller than those in Lake Batur.

Another option and labeled as "fishing at its finest" is **Yos Dive** (✆ 0361/773774, 0361/775440, or 0361/775438; www.yosdive.com), based out of Tanjung Benoa. Trolling for 4 hours from a power boat for between two and four fishermen at a time will cost US$200 per person. They also will charter a covered power boat for the day, with driver for US$625, including fuel and lunch.

Possibly the best boat is operated by **Blue Water Safari** (✆ 0361/723479; www. bwsbali.com). You can charter the whole boat for Rp5,500,000 for 4 hours or Rp8,000,000 for 8 hours. They provide you with the latest kit and they use GPS and a

ACTIVE VACATION PLANNER

ACTIVITIES A TO Z

fish-finding technology to locate the shoals. A half-decent picnic lunch is included. The boat carries up to 10 passengers, but only four lines can be used at a time.

While Lombok has many fishermen, fishing is simply a necessary fact of life. Most fishermen or boat owners however will be only too delighted to take you out. Prices for a few hours should be about Rp400,000 depending on fuel usage. **Lombok Marine** (© 0370/692225; www.lombokmarine.com), in Mataram, will take you to Desert Point or possibly to deep water spots beyond the Gilis. This is on a traditional *jukung* and not a speedboat with any facilities other than an awning.

GOLFING ★★★

You could make golf the sole reason for a trip to Bali. The island has world-class 18-hole courses and a charming 9-hole course. They are all different in style; one in the cool of the mountains, three others fringed by the sea, and the **Bali Beach** 9-hole course (© 0361/287-7333; www.balibeachgolfcourse.com) in the flat lands of Sanur.

The Indonesian Open, the first PGA tour event to visit Bali, was played, to much success, in 2009 at the newest of the courses, **New Kuta Golf** (© 0361/848-1333; www.newkutagolf.com) at Pecatu.

The longest admired of Bali's courses is the Greg Norman–designed **Nirwana** (© 0361/815960; www.nirwanabaligolf.com) at Le Meridien, facing Pura Tanah Lot. This course has won many accolades over the years, among them Best Golf Course in Asia 2005 by *Asian Golf Monthly*. Another course is the **Bali Golf and Country Club** (© 0361/771791; www.baligolfandcountryclub.com) in Nusa Dua.

Prices reflect the high quality of the courses, but check with your hotel, as many have discounted arrangements. Book ahead. Pro shops mainly sell only golf accessories and clothing although they do provide very good golf club and sometimes shoe hire at differing levels and price points.

Somewhat surprisingly given the level of tourism on the island, Lombok has two decent courses. The **Lombok Golf Kosaido Country Club** (© 0370/640137) close to the Oberoi Hotel, was designed and is owned by the same people who have brought you the Bali Handara Kosaido course. The other, the **Rinjani Country Club Golf & Resort** (© 0370/627396) is actually on the side of Mount Rinjani, only 20 minutes from Mataram. Both thankfully are far more competitively priced than their Bali counterparts, with prices ranging from US$65 to US$85 including greens fee and caddy, although a buggy is extra and costs US$25 at Kosaido. You have to walk at Rinjani. Both will rent you clubs and even shoes.

HIKING & TREKKING ★★

The year-round temperate climate, the challenging but not daunting terrain, the fascinating culture, and the layers of history at every turn make both Bali and Lombok wonderful places to explore on foot. The islands are also small enough that you'll never feel like you're in the middle of nowhere and the prospects of getting totally lost are pretty limited. Hiking is best (and safest) during the dry season (Apr–Oct).

Most peaks, if they are your goal, are scale-able in less then 8 hours, and many can be done in less than 4. The one great trek that takes you furthest from regular habitation and requires careful preparation is **Mount Rinjani** (p. 328) on Lombok. This challenging excursion will take 3 or 4 days, leaving from Senaru, and most definitely requires a guide.

The majority of other mountain treks necessitate a guide as you will want to be at the summit by sunrise. You therefore will need to head out in darkness at any time from 2am onward. You should be provided with both a head and hand torch. Sunrise, when you get there, is quite a magical and a sublime experience—weather permitting. It is not a wonder that the Balinese consider the peak of **Mount Agung** (p. 253) the island's most sacred spot. Indeed so much so, you are not allowed to climb at certain times of the Balinese year. Climbing Mount Agung is a pilgrimage for all Balinese and at some stage in their life, they will undertake it at least once.

Trekking agents for Bali include **Bali Adventure Tours** (© 0361/721480; www.baliadventuretours.com); **Clipper** (© 08/123802675; www.clipperdiscovery.com); **Sobek** (© 0361/287059; www.balisobek.com); and Gede from **Bali Sunrise Tours** (www.balisunrisetours.com), an old original.

For Lombok, many tour agents and trekking offices are based in Senggigi, Senaru, Sembalun Lawang, and Sembalun Bumbung. **Lombok Rinjani Trekking** (© 0370/6686625; www.lombokrinjanitrekking.com) offers fully equipped treks. Ensure you check in with the official **Rinjani Trek Management Board** (© 0370/641124 or 08/11390047; www.lombokrinjanitrek.org) for all aspects of trekking and guides on Mount Rinjani.

SCUBA DIVING & SNORKELING ★★★

BALI Bali is situated in the heart of the Indo-Pacific, the world's richest marine biogeographic zone. Due to the Indonesian throughflow, Bali receives plankton-rich waters which foster a diverse underwater ecosystem.

Pelagics (open-ocean marine life) include manta rays, whalesharks, and, July to mid-November, Mola-Molas (the weird-but-wonderful ocean sunfish). The reefs are ideal for snorkeling with profuse hard and soft corals, gorgonian and other seafans, coral bushes, and sponges including some massive barrel sponges. Altogether more than 2,000 species of reef fish thrive in Bali's waters, and then you'll find eels, crabs, lobsters, turtles, starfish, shrimp, and nudibranches, mimic octopus and wonderpus, ambon scorpionfish, rhinopias, and ghost pipefish. Truly, the list goes on.

LOMBOK While diving at Gili Trawangan, Gili Meno, and Gili Air is quick, fun, and easy, it's nowhere near on par with the diving in the south of Lombok itself.

At Belongas Bay you'll find pristine reefs, plentiful macro life, and an abundance of fish not to be found elsewhere around Lombok. You'll spy mackerels, tunas, barracudas, napoleon wrasse, white and black tip reef sharks, and eagle rays. Plus, there's the possibility of sighting hammerhead sharks. Sekotong can have strong currents and so some of the pinnacles are for experienced divers only. During the dry season, there are often reports of more than 100 hammerhead sharks in Magnet area.

OUTFITTERS Most scuba outfitters on the islands can arrange trips to any of the dive sites. The most popular, one-stop local outfitters are:

At **Aqua Marine Diving,** Jl. Raya Petitenget, Seminyak (© 0361/738020; www.aquamarinediving.com), combined British ownership with the expertise of local dive staff make for an unbeatable combination. Aqua Marine runs day trips to fully inclusive intensive underwater safaris to the island's best sites. **Skubaskool,** Jl. Dyanapura/Abimanyu 9, Seminyak (© 0361/733845; www.skubaskool.com) is a well-run French operation (although they all speak great English) with packages (13 days/12 nights and 22 dives) that enable you to circumnavigate the island.

Other PADI dive centers include: **Abyss Adventures,** Jl. Danau Poso 36b, Sanur (© 0361/271317; www.abyssadventures.com); **Bali Crystal Divers,** Jl. Tamblingan 168, Sanur (© 0361/286737; www.crystal-divers.com); **Eurodive,** Lipah Bunutan,

Amed ((C) 0363/23605); **Menjangan Resort,** West Bali National Park, ((C) 0362/94708; www.menjanganresort.com); **Mimpi Resort Menjangan,** Banyuwedang ((C) 0362/94497; www.mimpi.com); **Paradise Palm Beach Bungalows** in Tulamben ((C) 0362/22918; www.paradise-tulamben.com); **Scuba Seraya Resort,** Desa Tukad Dabu, Tulamben ((C) 0361/283922; www.scubaseraya.com); and **World Diving Lembongan,** Pondok Baruna, Jungutbatu ((C) 08/123900686; www.world-diving.com).

The only dive company in south Lombok is **Dive Zone,** Senggigi ((C) 0370/6603205; www.divezone-lombok.com).

INSURANCE   Most holiday insurance policies don't cover scuba diving; some don't cover snorkeling either. The best idea is to have **DAN** (Divers' Alert Network; www.diversalertnetwork.org) membership and coverage which provides evacuation for diving and nondiving related incidents, and dive-related medical treatment. You get peace of mind and an expert in diving-related injuries/problems at the end of the phone, no matter where in the world you find yourself.

WHEN TO DIVE   In Bali, the rainy season runs from October to March. The monsoon patterns, lunar calendar, and seasonal upwelling of rich, cold water in the Lombok Strait (between Bali and Lombok) generally means that April to June and September to November offer the best seasons for diving. July to August and December to January are very good, while February to March usually have the least to offer. While we do see manta rays year-round, the best season is April to May and for Mola-Mola is August to October.

SURFING ★★★

Bali shot to surfing prominence on the back of Albert Falzons 1972 epic *Morning of the Earth.* The opening shots of this now infamous surf movie featured the trademark cave of Uluwatu (but the wave itself was actually Australia's Winki-Pop, contrary to popular belief). Now after years of adventure, exploration, and intrepid traveling against nature and all odds, Indonesia is one of the most sought after and cherished surfing destinations on earth, with Bali its base station and beating heart.

Sitting roughly in the middle of the Indonesian archipelago's 17,000-plus islands, Bali lies 8 degrees south of the equator and enjoys two distinct seasons. The shorter, hotter wet season runs from December through to the end of March while the more popular and longer season runs from April through to the end of November. Bali has breaks on both the east and west coasts, meaning hungry wave seekers can find offshore conditions on this world-famous surfing island every day of the year. Now that the east coast waves of the wet season are becoming more popular and well known, surfing tourists are starting to visit in larger numbers at this time of year, too. With the quality and consistency of waves in Bali it is possible to escape the masses by venturing further away from the more famous spots.

THE BREAKS   As far as surfing real estate goes, pound for pound, mile for mile, Bali's **Bukit Peninsula** (p. 155) is only perhaps equaled by the meccalike North Shore of Oahu, in Hawaii. **Uluwatu** (p. 167) lies on the southwest corner of Bali and is the home to one of the most sacred Hindu temples on Bali. **Padang Padang** (p. 168) is one of the country's heaviest and most dangerous waves. Just north is **Bingin** (p. 168), a short and hollow ride, suited to tube-riding and the flamboyant trickery displayed by the cunning local surfers who govern the place. On the east coast, **Sanur** (p. 138) is a high-quality surfing area in the most picturesque of settings. **Sri Lanka** (p. 183) is another highlight to this surfing wonderland. The beach is immaculate, a rarity in these parts, and carries the polished persona of a private resort-style beach. **Nusa Dua** (p. 183) can get big—really big. With a take-off zone the size of a football field, the heaving chunks of ocean swell provide aquatic thrills to the willing and can deliver the uninitiated into a world of unforeseen pain. Join the throngs of tourists and locals at **Kuta Reef** (p. 86), easily spotted from your plane window to the north of the ocean-intruding runway.

Lombok is home to the infamous **Desert Point** (p. 324), voted by Australian surf bible, *Tracks* magazine, as the best wave on earth. Notoriously fickle and affected by the strong currents ripping through the Lombok trench (the world's second-deepest stretch of ocean) many surfers camp out here for months on end waiting for magic to happen. Now within easy striking distance from Bali, particularly if you own a helicopter, when the waves get good here the word gets out pretty quickly. In stark contrast to Desert Point, **Ekas** (p. 333) has a variety of waves for beginners all the way through to advanced surfers.

OUTFITTERS & INFORMATION   Most of the surfing outfitters on the islands will be able to set you up with a full surfing itinerary. Some of the best equipped are: **Tropicsurf** (© **07/54554129** in Australia or 08/1916766607 in Bali; www.tropicsurf.net), headed by Jack Chisholm (ask for Jack), offering private guided and personalized coaching services. The only surf school worldwide to be inducted into Australia's surfing hall of fame, Tropicsurf is the global leader in surf coaching, for beginners to world champions, and is the best upmarket service in Bali. Marcy, a handsome suntanned New Zealander, has 20 years coaching experience in Bali alone. **Marcy's Surf Coaching** (© **08/123859454;** marcymeachin@hotmail.com) is the true original and he will get you on your feet in no time. Best one on one, but he'll also do groups. **Girls Surf Retreats** (© **08/1916766607;** www.girlssurfretreat.com) offers surf, fitness, yoga, and spa pampering retreats with a maximum of six guests. Women only. **Surf Goddess Retreats** (www.surfgoddessretreats. com) is run by girls for girls. The company organizes all inclusive, "surfari" packages, including yoga and spa treatments. Special care is also placed on the accommodation and food, which are second to none. The **Rip Curl School of Surf** (© **0361/735858;** www. schoolofsurf.com) is an internationally respected surf company that organizes surf and paddle boarding—the latest craze to hit the shores—courses for beginners and experienced surfers.

Surf Travel On-line (© **0361/750550;** www.surftravelonline.com) features up-to-date information on surf packages, boat charters, and surf camps in Bali, Lombok, and throughout Indonesia.

YOGA & SPIRITUAL JOURNEYS ★

Muslims are barred from practicing yoga due to its connection to Hinduism, though yoga is not a religion. As Bali is not of the Muslim majority, yoga is openly practiced and advertised. With such a large expat community, you will see advertisements for private yoga classes posted up on community boards in coffee shops and local hangouts. A majority of the resorts, hotels, and villas on Bali will offer some form of yoga, either from an in-house teacher or as host to yoga retreats. Do not expect to find much by way of yoga offerings on Lombok, an island of Muslim majority.

The **Yoga Barn** (© **0361/970992;** www.theyogabarn.com) is a rustic, spiritual space, set amidst terraced rice paddies, in the middle of Ubud. It is an inspiring and beautiful environment for the nourishment of body, mind, and soul.

Throughout the island you will find small and large retreats, some dedicated to holistic practices and others offering a broad spectrum of related activities. One of the most prominent services is **Bali Spirit** (© 0361/970992; www.balispirit.com). Contact them directly to discuss extended holistic practice; yoga and meditation retreats; and detox centers. Their extensive list of practitioners and retreats makes them the one-stop shop for the best services on the island.

One World Retreats (© 0361/289752; www.oneworldretreats.com) is a travel service that specializes in tracking down retreats and workshops led by world-renowned yoga and Pilates teachers.

In the north, **Zen Bali** (© 0361/289752; www.zenbali.com), combines ayurveda, pranayama (breathing practices), yoga, and mediation with beauty treatments. Leading practitioners are on hand to provide assistance; this retreat offers unique and specialist programs for beginners and the advanced.

Bali is home to several spiritual communities that welcome visitors. The **Gandhi Ashram**, in Candidasa (© 0363/41108; www.ashramgandhi.com), is a community of followers of Mahatma Gandhi. They practice their founder's beliefs through prayer, meditation, and yoga. Visitors and volunteers are welcome to join the community.

The **Nirarta Centre** (© 0366/24122; www.awareness-bali.com) is tucked up in the hills of the Sidemen Valley. This center focuses on one-to-one self-guided or guided seminars to assist with personal development.

WHITE-WATER RAFTING

Bali has two main rivers for rafting that are both category III: the Ayung, just outside Ubud and the Telaga Waja in the foothills of Mount Agung, which is only a category III due to its distance from help. And while these are not going to challenge the most intrepid of rafters, the scenery, backdrop, and occasional adrenalin rush, especially in the rainy season, justifies their position as the number-one organized adventure tour on the island. Remarkably, something like 10% of all visitors to the island go white-water rafting—that makes some 250,000 of you.

There are only some five or so fully licensed, properly registered and insured rafting companies. Three of them are **Bali Adventure Tours** (© 0361/721480; www.bali adventuretours.com), **Bali View Rafting** (© 0361/795-5879; www.baliviewrafting. com), and the original and still the most popular **Sobek** (© 0361/287059; www.bali sobek.com). Increasingly more companies are getting licensed as the authorities start to enforce and police slightly better, so there will be others that become legitimate.

Each raft journey takes about 2 hours and is suitable for ages 6 and up. Some outfitters have their own lunch place at the end with warm showers and fresh towels. Be prepared for a long walk down many, many steps (I stopped counting at 450) and up thankfully not quite as many (though I was no longer counting by then).

Prices do range between the rafting companies; generally you will pay between US$50 and US$72 for adults and US$30 and US$52 for children. Family packages will range from US$150 to US$200 depending on what promotions they are running at the time. Sometimes, it is better to book through an agent. **Bali Discovery Tours** ★★★ (© 0361/ 286283; www.balidiscovery.com) often runs Internet promotions where you can make large savings off the published price.

Kuta

Just a 10-minute drive from the airport, Kuta is a popular destination for budget travelers and Aussies who hop over for long weekends or holidays. Some might say that Kuta is a den of iniquity, with all the bars, drag queen shows, and Kuta cowboys waiting to find a foreign woman who will give them a taste of the good life. Kuta is not by any stretch of the imagination, the "real" Bali. Over the years, Kuta has fallen victim to rampant commercialization, which has drastically changed the environment from a small fishing village lining a pristine beach to a hopping city with blaring disco music. Kuta is really more for a younger crowd looking for action. If that describes you, then by all means stay awhile.

After World War II, Westerners and Balinese became intoxicated by the idea that Kuta could become a popular tourist destination yielding great profits for both local and foreign investors. In 1936, Bob Koke, a young Hollywood photographer and the first professional surfer in Bali, arrived with his future wife, Louise Garret.

Their original plan was to paint and photograph Bali's wild natural scenery, but they became so enchanted that they decided to stay and open a small bamboo and thatch roof hotel.

By the late 1960s, Kuta became a favorite for hippies and other intrepid travelers from Australia and Europe. By the 1970s, surfers began arriving in earnest. Development continued at a slow pace until the 1980s, when numerous restaurants and hotels started going up. And by the 1990s, the environmental impact of the proliferation of businesses generated bad traffic jams, illegal immigrants from other Indonesian islands, hawkers, and serious waste management problems. The biggest burden fell on the farmers who were forced to sell their fields due to the construction of buildings that ultimately resulted in the cut-off of their water supply. Those who insisted that they wouldn't sell could no longer cultivate their crops. It was the end of an agrarian era for Kuta, which is now one of the most developed areas in Bali.

1 GETTING THERE & GETTING AROUND

Kuta is near the airport, and most hotels offer free airport pickup. If hiring a cab, go to the airport's official taxi counter, where you'll pay a set fare, typically Rp60,000.

Kuta is a big rectangle. The two main north-south streets are **Jalan Pantai Kuta** and **Jalan Legian.** They're connected east-west by **Jalan Benesari, Poppies Gang I,** and many quaint *gang* (alleys). You can easily meander in and out of these small alleys and do some window-shopping or take the reasonably priced blue-and-yellow metered taxis. The horse and buggies *(cidomo)* are ridiculously overpriced: From Pantai Kuta near Hard Rock Hotel to Jalan Double Six (about 6km/3¾ miles), the cost is Rp150,000—equivalent to an average local weekly salary!

Taxis are available everywhere in Kuta, but be sure to ask them to put on the meter. Most taxi companies are reputable, such as **Blue Bird** and **Komotra** taxis, but beware of the white taxis who often try to scam naive tourists.

Recent street name changes in Kuta include: Jaalan Pura Bagus Taruna is now Jalan Werkudara; Jalan Segara is now Jalan Jenggala; Jalan Kartika Plaza is now Jalan Dewi Sartika; Poppies Gang II is now Jalan Batu Bolong; Jalan Stria is now Jalan Kediri; Jalan Pantai Kuta is now Jalan Pantai Banjar Pande Mas; Jalan Padma is now Jalan Yudistra. Locals, business owners, and maps will use a combination of these names.

(Fast Facts Kuta

ATMs **ATMs** are on practically every corner in Kuta.

Currency Exchange Storefront exchange services line most streets and offer the best rates. **Central Kuta Money Changer** on Jalan Pantai Kuta, Suci Arc Street 19 (© **0361/762866**), generally offers good rates. Several authorized money changers are in Kuta Square and Kartika Plaza.

Hospitals In Kuta, try the **Bali International Medical Centre (BIMC)**, Jl. Bypass Ngurah Rai 100X (© **0361/761263**), open daily from 8am to midnight; sometimes they will send someone to your hotel. Another option in Kuta is the **International SOS Bali**, Jl. Bypass Ngurah Rai (© **0361/710505**).

Internet Access Some restaurants and cafes have free Wi-Fi for customers. Internet cafes generally charge between Rp10,000 and Rp37,000 per hour.

Pharmacies Of the many choices available in Kuta, **Kimia**, Jl. Raya Tuban 15 (© **0361/757483**; 24 hr.), is the biggest and usually offers more foreign brand medications than smaller pharmacies.

Police The **Tourist Police** (© **0361/763753**) main station is on Jalan Pantai Kuta and is open 24 hours a day.

Post Office The main post office is on Jalan Raya Tuban, far from the town center. Some postal agents are around town (at Jl. Selamet; Mon–Thurs 7am–2pm, Fri 7–11am, Sat 7am–1pm) or at your hotel can send mail for you.

Safety Pedestrians must watch for **reckless motorbike drivers** who use the sidewalks to avoid traffic on Jalan Legian. You'll also be harangued by some of the most **aggressive touts** on the island, and the beaches are crowded with so-called masseurs. Kuta is known for some unsavory folks who are adept at **picking pockets** or **snatching purses** off shoulders. The **Kuta Cowboys** are the young men who hang out on the beach all day surfing and at night look for girls to hang out with. For the most part they want to practice their English, flirt, and have fun. However if drugs become apparent or if you feel threatened in any way whatsoever, leave the scene immediately and head back to your hotel. It can't be emphasized enough that drugs are illegal in Bali and the consequences are dire.

Tourism Information The Bali Department of Tourism operates a **visitor information** center at Jalan Benasari 36B (© **0361/754090** or 08/123928098).

---

2 WHERE TO STAY

Compact Kuta and Tuban (or South Kuta Beach as it was renamed in 2009) offer hotels anywhere from five-star fabulous to the fringes of ferocity from one door to the next. On

ATTRACTIONS ●

AJ Hackett **3**
Bali Bomb Memorial **21**
Bali Slingshot **31**
Marcy's Surf Coaching **6**
Paradiso Bowling & Billiard Center **30**
Pro Surf School **18**
Rip Curl School of Surf **7**
Waterbom **32**

ACCOMMODATIONS ■

Alam Kul Kul **16**
Bali Niksoma **8**
Discovery Kartika Plaza Hotel **34**
Hard Rock Hotel **29**
Holiday Inn Resort **40**
Hotel Santika **36**
Kupu Kupu Barong **38**
Padma Hotel **9**
The Patra Bali Resort & Villas **41**
Poppies Cottages **25**
Ramada Bintang Bali Resort & Spa **37**
Villa Coco **2**
Villa de daun **20**

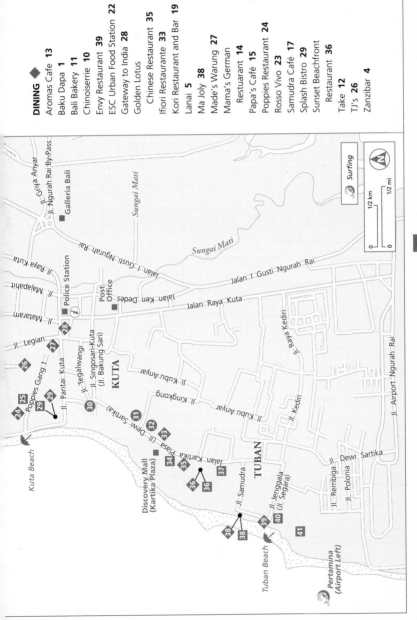

DINING

Aromas Cafe **13**
Baku Dapa **1**
Bali Bakery **11**
Chinoiserrie **10**
Envy Restaurant **39**
ESC Urban Food Station **22**
Gateway to India **28**
Golden Lotus
  Chinese Restaurant **35**
Ifiori Restaurante **33**
Kori Restaurant and Bar **19**
Lanai **5**
Ma Joly **38**
Made's Warung **27**
Mama's German
  Restaurant **14**
Papa's Café **15**
Poppies Restaurant **24**
Rosso Vivo **23**
Samudra Café **17**
Splash Bistro **29**
Sunset Beachfront
  Restaurant **36**
Take **12**
TJ's **26**
Zanzibar **4**

KUTA

6

WHERE TO STAY

Jalan Raya Kuta, along the stretch of beach north from Tuban through to Legian, you'll predominantly hit large beach resorts for families, several stylish and secluded boutique digs, and loads of simple garden hotels that present great value. Snake around the nearby alleyways and you'll discover some hidden treasures, as well as the most basic of bed-and-breakfasts and party-style pads reserved for insomniacs.

KUTA
Expensive

Bali Niksoma ★   Perfectly positioned between Legian and Seminyak, this boutique resort has a superb two-tiered pool and minimalist cottage-style rooms. Super-size bathrooms have separate his and her vanities. Resort facilities are limited to a restaurant and small spa. Comparatively, this resort is a little pricey for what you get, but the beachfront location (with amazing pool) and proximity to shops, nightlife, and restaurants is what this place is really all about.

Jl. Padma Utara Legian Kaja, Legian. ✆ **0361/751946.** Fax 0361/766476. www.baliniksoma.com. 57 units. Peak season US$265–US$1,090; high season US$245–US$1,070; low season US$225–US$1,050. AE, MC, V. **Amenities:** Restaurant; bar; gym; Jacuzzi; 2 outdoor pools; room service; sauna; spa; Wi-Fi (for a fee). *In room:* A/C, TV/DVD, stereo or CD, hair dryer, minibar.

Discovery Kartika Plaza Hotel   This is one of Kuta's long-time hotels right on the main strip. Their classic oceanfront rooms feature dark varnished furnishings and spectacular views of Kuta Beach, just steps away. The style is a complementary blend of modern-minimalist with ethnic accents—adorned with beautiful Balinese carvings. A private outdoor veranda has daybeds for enjoying the intoxicating environment. The newly upgraded "Ocean suites" have beautiful rattan furnishings, state-of-the-art equipment, and great views of the massive pool. The spacious marble bathrooms with large bathtubs invite you to totally unwind in absolute luxury.

Jl. Kartika Plaza, Kuta. ✆ **0361/751067.** Fax 0361/753988. www.discoverykartikaplaza.com. 318 units. High season US$245–US$995; low season US$220–US$975. AE, DC, MC, V. **Amenities:** 3 restaurants; pool bar; lounge; babysitting; kids' club; concierge; gym; Jacuzzi; 2 outdoor pools; room service; sauna; tennis and squash court; watersports; Wi-Fi. *In room:* A/C, TV, stereo or CD, hair dryer, minibar.

Hard Rock Hotel (Kids)   No doubt an American icon and the only one of its kind in Indonesia. Take a walk down memory lane with Mick Jagger, Janis Joplin, and other rockers whose photographs decorate the walls of this beachfront hotel. The rooms have an Art Deco style in soft pastels and include great rock memorabilia. Check out the loft rooms which have a deluxe master bedroom and an additional bedroom on the second floor. The facilities include Bali's largest freeform pool with a real sand island at the center, water slides for kids, a recording studio, and a climbing wall.

Jl. Pantai, Banjar Pande Mas, Kuta. ✆ **0361/761869.** Fax 0361/761868. www.hardrockhotels.net. 418 units. Year-round US$240–US$460 standard; US$620 suite. AE, DC, MC, V. **Amenities:** 4 restaurants, Splash Bistro (p. 82); 3 bars; kids' club; concierge; health club; outdoor pool (w/swim-up bar); room service; spa; Wi-Fi. *In room:* A/C, satellite TV w/on-demand movies, fridge, minibar.

Villa de daun ★★ (Finds)   Among the chaos of high-octane Kuta sits this new exclusive retreat of 12 luxuriously appointed villas. Owners Michelle and Jimmy have captured the vibe of the island with stylish live-in pads with indulgent bathrooms, and private swimming pools and gazebos. Add 40-inch plasma TVs with knockout Bose sound systems, gourmet kitchens complete with fridges that stock the iciest drinks on the planet, and lavish king-size beds perfect after a day out bargaining with the locals. You're breaths away from the bevy of shops, restaurants, and local nightlife but a good 500m (1,640 ft.) walk to the beach. Get in if you can.

Jl. Raya Legian, Kuta. 🕐 **0361/756276.** Fax 0361/750643. www.villadedaun.com. 12 villas. High season $350–$450 1-bedroom, $550 2-bedroom, $650 3-bedroom; low season $300–$400 1-bedroom, $500 2-bedroom, $600 3-bedroom. AE, MC, V. **Amenities:** Restaurant; babysitting; room service; spa; Wi-Fi (restaurant and lobby only). *In room:* A/C, TV/DVD, stereo or CD, hair dryer, minibar.

Moderate

Alam Kul Kul   First opened in 1989, this popular beachfront resort is best known for its excellent Italian restaurant Papas, which was probably one of the first pizzerias in the area. The resort has undergone a massive renovation; the modern and comfortable rooms are great for families and while pristinely clean and modern, still offer a relaxed and casual ambience. The resort fronts Legian beach, though you have to cross a very busy road in front before you hit the sand.

Jl. Pantai Kuta, Legian. 🕐 **0361/752520.** Fax 0361/766861. www.alamkulkul.com. 80 units. High season US$185–US$285; low season US$150–US$250. AE, DC, MC, V. **Amenities:** 2 restaurants, Papa's Café (p. 80); bar; babysitting; concierge; outdoor pool; room service; spa; Wi-Fi (for a fee). *In room:* A/C, TV, hair dryer, minibar.

Padma Hotel ★ (Kids)   You've got all you need at the Padma, a self-contained compound just the right distance from the fray for peace and quiet, but close enough to go play and shop. There's something for the whole family here, including a good kids' club, daily activities, a roster of day trips, the fine Mandara Spa, and cultural classes such as egg painting and musical demonstrations. Garden rooms have parquet floors and Balinese furnishings. Standard rooms all have balconies and great views. Family rooms open onto a patio and central garden. There is a quiet, tout-free grassy spot between the pool and the beach where the kids can frolic.

Jl. Padma 1, Legian. 🕐 **0361/752111.** Fax 0361/752140. www.padmahotels.com. 406 units. High season US$165–US$390 standard, US$1,225 villa; low season US$140–US$365 standard, US$1,200 villa. AE, DC, MC, V. **Amenities:** 7 restaurants; 2 bars; babysitting; kids' club; concierge; gym; outdoor pool; room service; spa; tennis; watersports; Wi-Fi. *In room:* A/C, TV/DVD, movie library, hair dryer, minibar.

Ramada Bintang Bali Resort & Spa★ (Kids)   This resort is set on more than 6 hectares (15 acres) of tropical gardens extending down to the beachfront of South Kuta. The "Romantic" rooms are ideal for honeymooners or any couple seeking something out of the ordinary. The cozy rooms have elegant netting over the bed, parquet floors, and ethnic accents throughout. Bathrooms feature marble floors and a nice bathtub. The excellent activity program includes yoga, aqua aerobics, beach volleyball, and water pillow fights. Kids have their own special program to keep them busy so moms and dads can have a relaxing holiday in paradise.

Jl. Kartika Plaza, Kuta. 🕐 **0361/753292.** Fax 0361/752015. www.bintang-bali-hotel.com. 402 units. High season US$155–US$685 standard, US$1,435 suite; low season US$120–US$650 standard, US$1,400 suite; extra bed US$35. AE, DC, MC, V. **Amenities:** 2 restaurants; coffee shop; lounge; 2 bars; babysitting; kids' club and children's play group; concierge; gym; health club; Jacuzzi; outdoor pool; room service; sauna; spa; tennis court; Wi-Fi (for a fee). *In room:* A/C, TV, hair dryer, minibar.

Villa Coco ★ (Kids)   This place is great for families, couples, or groups who want to be beachfront near a safe patrolled surfing beach, restaurants, and nightlife. The property has direct access to Legian beach and also backs onto the famous Jalan Double Six shopping street. The affordable one- and two-bedroom garden and pool villas have their own entrances and small gardens and lawns. Though there is no restaurant, you do have

24-hour room service and breakfast, lunch, or dinner can be served poolside. Individual barbecues, cooked at your villa, are a good value and reflect the no-nonsense style of the Australian owners.

Jl. Double Six, Gang Villa Coco, Seminyak. ✆ **0361/730736.** Fax 0361/734828. www.villacoco.com. 15 units. Peak season US$160–US$640; high season US$130–US$540; low season US$110–US$475; extra bed US$35. AE, MC, V. **Amenities:** Restaurant; pool bar; babysitting; outdoor pool; room service; Wi-Fi. *In villa:* A/C, TV/DVD, movie library; stereo or CD, kitchenette, minibar.

Inexpensive

Poppies Cottages (Finds) These newly renovated cottages were originally built in 1980. The beautiful wooden interior and marble open-air bathrooms with sunken tubs make this a wonderful find. The rooms are a bit small for the price, but everything is very clean and comfortable. The small central pool resembles a natural pond, surrounded by verdant garden nooks perfect for lounging. The cozy poolside bar is a great place for lunch or a refreshing cocktail. Guests can also conveniently dine at **Poppies Restaurant** (p. 82), just across the alley.

Jl. Legian, Gang Poppies I-19, Kuta. ✆ **0361/751059.** Fax 0361/752364. www.poppiesbali.com. 20 units. High season US$86; low season US$73; extra bed US$15. AE, DC, MC, V. **Amenities:** 3 restaurants; pool bar; babysitting; outdoor pool; room service; Wi-Fi. *In room:* A/C, fan, TV/DVD, movie library; stereo or CD, hair dryer, minibar, MP3 docking station.

TUBAN (SOUTH KUTA BEACH)

Holiday Inn Resort ★ (Kids) Don't let the motel name of this newly refurbished resort deter you. Ultra-contemporary in style and set on sun-kissed Segara beach, this hip hotel delivers the latest in all things "concept" in its category. This resort is as fabulous for families as it is for fashionistas with its range of facilities. The five Family and six Kids Suites have beds shaped like sail boats with captain's wheels, circus tent wardrobes, bean bags, and giant plasma TVs with Wii and Xbox, plus super stylish interconnecting rooms for the grown-ups. The resort's Baruna Suites and split-level villa-esque Arjuna suites (most of which face the ocean) are sleek, modern, and super-spacious in design. While the kids are reveling in the Teen-Zone or Rascals underwater club, adults can enjoy the spa or lounge at one of the restaurants.

Jl. Wana Segara 33, Tuban. ✆ **0361/755577.** Fax 0361/754549. www.bali.holidayinn.com. 195 units. High season US$145–US$215; low season US$125–US$195. AE, MC, V. **Amenities:** 2 restaurants, Envy (p. 83); coffee shop; lounge; pool bar; babysitting; kids' club; concierge; gym; outdoor pool; room service; spa; Wi-Fi (for a fee). *In room:* A/C, TV/DVD, hair dryer, minibar, MP3 docking station.

Hotel Santika (Value) All the rooms at this charming boutique-style hotel were renovated in 2004 with natural stone and wood, including attractive granite bathroom counters with marble floors. The overall effect is a warm and homey environment—a refreshing change from other area hotels. The Garden bungalow features four-poster beds, an outdoor shower, terrazzo floors, and serene garden views. All bungalows have Kamasan paintings hanging above the beds or on the walls. The Ocean Front Suites are secluded from the rest of the property and have private swimming pools and lovely ocean views. It is certainly very good value for money.

Jl. Kartika Plaza, Tuban. ✆ **0361/751267.** Fax 0361/751260. www.santikabali.com. 171 units. Year-round US$175–US$350; extra bed US$50. AE, DC, MC, V. **Amenities:** 3 restaurants, Sunset Beachfront Restaurant (p. 82); 2 bars; lounge; babysitting; kids' club; 3 outdoor pools; room service; spa; tennis court; Wi-Fi (for a fee). *In room:* A/C, TV, hair dryer, minibar.

Kupu Kupu Barong ★★ (Finds)   The Ma Joly disguises the secret garden gem of Kupu Kupu Barong. Tucked behind voluptuous gardens, these high-end suites blend modern conveniences with local artistry and romantic panache. The Master Suites are decked with private pantry, living room, and an indulgent king-size bedroom with bathrooms larger than some spas. Special mention is due to the luxurious L'Occitane amenities, a bath the size of a plunge pool, complimentary Evian water, and the beachfront location. Perch yourself at the bar or lounge on plush double daybeds set on private island decks and drink in the Campari-colored sunsets—cocktail in hand, of course. *Note:* Although this resort welcomes families, it is better suited to adults.

Jl. Wana Segara, Tuban. ✆ **0361/753780.** Fax 0361/753781. www.kupubarongbeach.com. 11 units. High season US$285 and up; low season US$235 and up. AE, DC, MC, V. **Amenities:** Restaurant, Ma Joly (p. 84); bar; babysitting; concierge; outdoor pool; room service; spa. *In room:* A/C, TV/DVD, movie library, stereo or CD, hair dryer, minibar, MP3 docking station.

The Patra Bali Resort & Villas ★   This hidden treasure has become a prime luxury get-away for the elite. A long list of kings, queens, and heads of state have stayed here. Situated right next to the airport, you might wrongly assume that the noise would be unbearable, but in truth, it's quite peaceful here. The rooms are attractively decorated in traditional Balinese style with exquisite wood furnishings, marble bathrooms with huge bathtubs, and private balconies overlooking a tropical landscape. The luxurious private villas are ideal for families or couples seeking solitude. Many of the villas have private plunge pools and 24-hour butler service. There is also a large seaside swimming pool and a private club exclusive to guests.

Jl. Ir.H.Juanda, South Kuta Beach. ✆ **0361/751161.** Fax 0361/752030. www.patrabali.com. 228 units. Peak season US$250–US$460 standard, US$360–US$1,810 villa; high season US$225–US$435 standard, US$335–US$1,785 villa; low season US$190–US$400 standard, US$300–US$1,750 villa; extra bed US$40. AE, DC, MC, V. **Amenities:** 2 restaurants; coffee shop; 2 lounges; pub; babysitting; kids' club; concierge; gym; outdoor pool; room service; spa; tennis court; Wi-Fi (for a fee). *In room:* A/C, TV, hair dryer, minibar.

KUTA

6

WHERE TO DINE

3 WHERE TO DINE

KUTA

Expensive

Golden Lotus Chinese Restaurant ★ (Finds) CHINESE   Kuta's best kept secret. Inside the Bali Dynasty Hotel, this elegant restaurant serves some of the finest Cantonese and Szechuan cuisine in Bali. Many guests also frequently stop in for all-you-can-eat dim sum, which include 60 varieties for only Rp85,000 (Sun 10am–2:30pm). The stir-fried beef and the fried prawns with yellow bean curd sauce are absolutely scrumptious.

In the Bali Dynasty Hotel, Jl. Kartika Plaza. ✆ **0361/752403.** Reservations recommended. Main courses Rp85,000–Rp105,000; set menu Rp105,000 and up for 6 dishes. AE, MC, V. Daily 11:30am–2:30pm; 6–10pm.

Ifiori Restaurante INTERNATIONAL   Directly opposite Discovery Mall and adjacent to Waterbom Park, this modern Italian diner is a great spot for lunch or dinner. Dare I say it serves the best garlic bread on the planet? Try the chili-and-garlic-crusted squid, *calamari fritti piccanti*, or the *melanzane alla Ifiori*, a combination of baked eggplant, minced lamb, and grated cheese. They do a great *osso buco* and grilled swordfish. Take the coffee cheesecake with an *affogato* for dessert. You get a choice of inside air-conditioned dining or outdoors among the bustle, plus computer access, Wi-Fi, satellite TV, tourist information, and they'll even send your postcards for you. A DJ spins nightly.

Jl. Kartika Plaza 20. © **0361/750175.** www.ifioribali.com. Reservations recommended. Pasta Rp67,000–Rp153,000; meat Rp74,000–Rp149,000; fish Rp75,000–Rp115,000. AE, MC, V. Daily 11am–2am.

Mama's German Restuarant ★ (Value) GERMAN   Mama's opened in 1985. By offering substantial German home cooking at low prices, it has proved to be a popular hangout with travelers and has become a Kuta institution. In addition to hot dogs, burgers, French fries, and ice cold beer, the menu bursts with authentic German dishes including roast pork *(Schweinebraten)*, Vienna schnitzel, rolled beef *(roulade)* with cabbage and dumplings, German sausages, German meat balls *(frikadellen)*, spit-roasted chicken, pork roast, and huge pork knuckles. Mama's also has a beer garden and a separate Dining Club with a cocktail bar, a large billiards table, and live music in the evenings. Mama's serves imported draft beer and German schnapps, along with a limited but well-priced wine list.

Jl. Legian. © **0361/761151.** www.bali-mamas.com. Reservations recommended. Main courses Rp54,000–Rp120,000. AE, MC, V. Daily 24 hr.

Papa's Café ★ (Kids) ITALIAN   The sound of crashing waves mixes easily with the grinding espresso machine at Papa's beachfront restaurant. The standards here are above-average with the vegetables sourced from Bedugul and the meats all imported from Australia. A favorite dish is the Kintamani Volcano Pizza, stuffed with beef, ham, spicy sausage, pepperoni, and salami, and pumped with air until it resembles a mountain and arrives flaming at the table. Top it off with the award-winning chocolate cake with peanut brittle. Each night features live in-house music.

In the Alam Kul Kul (p. 77), Jl. Pantai Kuta. © **0361/755055.** www.papascafe.com. Reservations recommended. Volcano pizza Rp115,000; pasta Rp79,000–Rp199,000; steak Rp145,000–Rp170,000; seafood platter for 2 Rp499,000. AE, MC, V. Daily 8am–midnight.

Rosso Vivo ★ ITALIAN   Wandering sophisticates will home in on the brilliant red umbrellas lining this small oasis beachfront eatery. Fresh salads, seafood, homemade pasta, Milanese-inspired meat dishes, and delectable desserts are a brilliant entree to poolside cocktails and a ringside view as the sun says *"ciao."* Ideal for romantic dinners, afternoon tea, and tapas accompanied by nightly jazz with local musicians from sunset onwards.

In the Kuta Seaview Hotel, Jl. Pantai Legian. © **0361/751961.** www.kutaseaviewhotel.com. Reservations recommended. Main courses Rp65,000–Rp240,000; set menus US$35–US$75. MC, V. Sun–Thurs 7am–1am; Fri–Sat 7am–2am.

Samudra Seaside Café (Value) INTERNATIONAL/INDONESIAN   Though this place offers a good variety of Western food, their specialty is Indonesian cuisine so if you want to try *nasi goreng* (fried rice with veggies and egg), *satay campur* (chicken, beef, seafood, and fish with peanut sauce on skewers), or any other local delicacy, this is the place. The Western food is just okay. Every Tuesday they offer a set menu and Thursdays they have a big Italian buffet. There are great views of Kuta Beach across the road, so you can watch a fabulous sunset while you dine.

Grand Istana Rama hotel, Jl. Pantai Kuta. © **0361/752208.** Reservations recommended. Main courses Rp60,000–Rp130,000; Tues set menu Rp140,000; Thurs buffet Rp150,000. AE, MC, V. Daily 11am–11pm.

Take ★★ (Finds) JAPANESE   This authentic Japanese restaurant serves up just about
the finest Japanese food on the island. Every evening, from 6pm onward, the place is
packed with Koreans and Japanese who come to dine on the freshest fish and daily
imported seasonal food. The owner is often on hand to give advice on what is good.
There is so much to choose from, and the picture menu will steer anyone who is not
familiar with Japanese food in the right direction.

Jl. Patih Jelantik. ✆ **0361/759745.** www.ramarestaurants.com. Reservations recommended. Main
courses Rp9,000–Rp498,000. AE, MC, V. Daily 11am–midnight. Also on Jl. Padma, ✆ **0361/750760.**

Moderate

Bali Bakery ★ CAFE   Locally owned Bali Bakery has a huge selection of bakery items
and a full menu. The air-conditioned comfort makes it a prime destination for escaping
the heat on Jalan Raya Kuta; locals will head here for everything from a simple milkshake
to a three-course dinner.

Jl. Imam Bonjol. ✆ **0361/755149.** Main courses Rp35,000–Rp100,000. MC, V. Daily 7:30am–10:30pm.

Chinoiserie ★ (Finds) CHINESE   For out-of-the-ordinary Chinese food with a modern twist you can't beat this newcomer—nor its striking red frontage. Young Singaporean
owner, hotelier, and restaurateur Bernard Foo has put panache and loads of chi-chi into
Chinoisserie with a stunning decor (he also has an interior decorating business which is
perfectly evident). The cuisine is really more authentic Singaporean fare, better known as
Peranakan, which is a combination of cooking styles—think Chinese, Malay, Indian, and
Thai with a smattering of Indonesian and Western influences. Thankfully, MSG is MIA
here with sauces that are light and fragrant and dishes that range from dim sum to duck
pancakes to feast on.

Jl. Sunset 7. ✆ **0361/808-8777.** Main dishes Rp40,000–Rp118,000. MC, V. Daily 11am–11pm.

ESC Urban Food Station BISTRO   There's not much you won't find at this eatery
with some 200-plus items on its nearly 24/7 urban fare menu. You can Wi-Fi over breakfast waffles and New York City bagels with a steaming Driscoll coffee, nosh on salads and
pastas, or tuck into the Longhorns Texas BBQ to revive you after a bout of shopping or
a night on the town. Portions are massive.

Jl. Legian 61. ✆ **0361/756362.** www.escbali.com. Main courses Rp50,000–Rp100,000. MC, V. Daily 7am–
5am. Grill available after 6pm only.

Gateway to India INDIAN   This superb, family-run, Indian restaurant is always
busy. Customers can sit at the front and watch the activity on the street while relishing
their Madras fish or *tikka masala.* The restaurant has an a la carte menu of over 200
dishes. Favorites include mixed vegetable *pakora,* tandoori chicken Madras, vegetable
biryani, and other meat, fish, and vegetable specialties. This successful little restaurant
has outlets in Seminyak, Nusa Dua, and on Jalan Sunset.

Jl. Pantai Kuta 11, 3rd floor. ✆ **0361/754463.** Reservations recommended. Main courses Rp50,000–
Rp75,000. MC, V. Daily 11:30am–11pm.

Kori Restaurant and Bar ★ INTERNATIONAL/STEAKHOUSE   Valet parking
in the narrow and chaotic Poppies Gang II? Finery uncharacteristic of Bali abounds at
this chic venue. Sit in the dining room, replete with linen and silver, or on one of the
more romantic cushioned bamboo platforms that bridge the narrow garden oasis. The
light lunch menu features *malai köfte,* spicy vegetarian fritters in a curry sauce, or the

mouth-burning Bali chili burger (if you dare). The dinner menu successfully mimics a Western steakhouse. Try the mixed grill of U.S. beef loin, spare ribs, pork cutlet, and Nuernberger sausages; or order the Singapore chili crab, savory and spicy fresh black Bali crabs served with a bib. At the high end of the menu is the giant seafood grill, cooked and served on a hot lava stone.

Poppies Gang II. ℂ **0361/758605.** www.korirestaurant.co.id. Reservations recommended. Main courses Rp30,000–Rp140,000. AE, DC, MC, V. Daily noon–11pm.

Lanai INTERNATIONAL This beachside hangout, formerly known as Benny's, has undergone a metamorphosis and now has a sushi bar and panini menu. This is where the crowds converge at sunset for a beer, or take a break from the beach for a fresh fruit juice over a game of backgammon. The menu has a good choice of snacks, Indonesian food, sandwiches, pizzas, and pasta. Particularly recommended is the sesame-crusted ahi tuna with wasabi mayo, lamb *shawarma* pita wrap, Lanai burger, and blueberry cheesecake.

Jl. Double Six. ℂ **0361/731305.** Reservations recommended. Main courses Rp46,000–Rp68,000. MC, V. Daily 8am–11pm.

Poppies Restaurant ASIAN/INTERNATIONAL Poppies Restaurant is so famous it even had two lanes named after it. Established around 1973, it serves Asian and Western dishes of fresh fish and seafood, soups, curries, lobster, steaks, and vegetarian dishes like a delicious veggie curry with brown rice. Poppies gets its veggies from Organic Nature, one of Bali's pioneers in organic farming.

Poppies Gang I. ℂ **0361/751059.** www.poppiesbali.com. Reservations recommended. Men must wear shirts. Main courses Rp46,000–Rp148,000. AE, MC, V. Daily 8am–11pm.

Splash Bistro (Kids) INTERNATIONAL/INDONESIAN You can have it all here, served poolside, from nachos to grilled sirloin to burgers. There are also some excellent Indonesian dishes on the menu like traditional oxtail soup. The huge wood-fired pizzas come with an assortment of toppings. Kids can play in the massive swimming pool while you rock out to old and new songs, sip cool cocktails, and enjoy the great food. It's an all-American dream.

In the Hard Rock Hotel (p. 76), Jl. Pantai Kuta. ℂ **0361/761869.** Main courses Rp50,000–Rp150,000. AE, MC, V. Daily 10am–10pm.

Sunset Beachfront Restaurant INDONESIAN/INTERNATIONAL This restaurant has excellent food, which you can enjoy while watching one of Kuta's fabulous sunsets. Try one of their special stone dishes with your choice of fish, lamb chops, or steak served on a piping hot stone. You cook your meal yourself. Other choices include wood-fired oven pizzas, delicious salads, and exceptional Indonesian dishes like *nasi goreng.*

In the Hotel Santika (p. 78), Jl. Kartika Plaza. ℂ **0361/751267.** Main courses Rp65,000–Rp145,000. AE, MC, V. Daily 7am–11pm.

Inexpensive

Aromas Cafe VEGETARIAN Aromas is a long-established, vegetarian restaurant, with an extensive menu from India, Thailand, the Middle East, Mexico, and Europe. Check out the generous sandwiches made with quality whole grain and rye breads, and the innovative juices, shakes, and salads. Not to be missed is the Provençal mushrooms, cheese, and herbs topped with flaky pastry, and the sticky date pudding with butterscotch sauce. Aromas does not use eggs and all ingredients are carefully sourced. All food preparation takes place on the premises, using purified water and minimum quantities of dairy products. On-site internet and Wi-Fi is free.

Jl. Legian. ✆ **0361/751003.** Main dishes Rp45,000. MC, V. Daily 8am–10:30pm.

Baku Dapa INDONESIAN   If you are wondering where to go late at night when you need a good food fix among the bars of Dhyana Pura, check out Baku Dapa. This authentic little warung has been serving consistently good Indonesian food at low, low prices for many years. Baku Dapa is renowned for its *sop buntut* (oxtail soup), probably the best in town. Typical Indonesian dishes on offer include *nasi goreng,* chicken satay, *gado gado* with peanut sauce, *tempe goreng* (fried soybean), and piping hot *tahu goreng* (fried tofu), accompanied by a selection of fresh and fiery homemade chili *sambal,* and followed by *pisang goreng* (fried banana with honey).

Jl. Dhyana Pura. ✆ **0361/731148.** Main dishes Rp15,000. No credit cards. Daily 24 hr.

Made's Warung ★★ (Finds) INDONESIAN   This is a longtime Bali favorite, and for good reason. If it's busy, and it often is, don't be surprised if you end up sharing a table. *Gado gado,* satay, and curries are all recommended, and the price is right. Fun surprises on the menu include a bagel with smoked marlin, tofu burgers, and Caesar salad. Don't pass up the daily specials, particularly the fresh fish. Beverage choices range from iced coffee and juice to very potent booze concoctions (be warned).

Br. Pando Mas. ✆ **0361/732130.** www.madeswarung.com. Main courses Rp12,000–Rp30,000. AE, MC, V. Daily 10am–midnight. Also in Seminyak (p. 105).

TJ's ★★ MEXICAN   TJ's is one of Kuta's legends, open since 1984. TJ's famous margaritas were the first in Bali and many say they are still the best. Some of the loyal staff has been at TJ's from the very beginning, and the customers are a mix of tourists, regulars, and old friends; people come back year after year. If you want a taste of Kuta history, you might just find it wrapped in an enchilada, served with a spicy salsa, and toasted with a margarita. The food is excellent, with a wide range of delicious starters and main courses including dips, nachos, buffalo wings, quesadillas, tacos, enchiladas, tostadas, fajitas, salads, and baked potatoes followed by some truly wicked deserts such as the delectable mango cheesecake with raspberry sauce.

Poppies Gang 1/24. ✆ **0361/751093.** www.tjbali.com. Main courses Rp35,000–Rp55,000. MC, V. Daily 11am–11pm.

Zanzibar ★ (Finds) (Kids) INTERNATIONAL   Zanzibar is a funky and fun restaurant with tables on a raised terrace and second-floor balcony overlooking the beach. This is a good place to do lunch, or to enjoy a snack, a cappuccino, or an ice-cold beer, and is also the perfect choice for a meeting place, a game of pool, or to check your e-mail. From 5pm on, Zanzibar fills up with punters to pay homage to the setting sun. You won't go hungry either, with a wide choice of the best real Italian pizzas in town, a fine selection of pasta, sandwiches, Indonesian food, vegetarian food, meat and fish, and a superb mezze platter. A bit more upmarket than the other beachside restaurants on the strip, Zanzibar serves chilled sounds from the DJ box and free snacks from the bar on Sundays from 5pm until 8pm.

Jl. Double Six. ✆ **0361/733528.** Main courses Rp45,000–Rp80,000. MC, V. Daily 8am–11pm.

TUBAN

Envy Restaurant ★ ITALIAN   Envy is a fabulous destination for sunset cocktails and late night lounging. The brilliant, Italian-inspired menu covers the spectrum of delicious beachside flavors, such as poached jumbo prawns with a tropical citrus dressing, squid ink spaghetti, Australian Wagyu beef, and the most sensational pizzas from the stone hearth oven. Special mention goes to the lethal tiramisu. The lava-lamp-like bar top morphs in color as the sun sets and you'll insist on trying as many fashionable cocktails as you can muster. Watch the envious parade of locals and tourists on the esplanade that fronts the restaurant as you listen to chilled and sensual grooves by the resident DJ.

In the Holiday Inn Resort (p. 78), Jl. Wana Segara 33. (℃) **0361/752527.** www.envy-bali.com. Reservations recommended. Pizza Rp58,000–Rp78,000; pasta Rp78,000–Rp98,000; small plates Rp78,000–Rp98,000; grill Rp30,000–Rp445,000. AE, DC, MC, V. Daily 10am–midnight.

Ma Joly ★★★ (Finds) (Moments) FRENCH/INTERNATIONAL   Ma Joly is five-star dining—you'd pay double the price for food not nearly as good elsewhere. This superb beachfront restaurant is hidden away at the end of a quiet road in Tuban and is well worth navigating to no matter where you are staying in Bali. The refined and uncompli-cated menu appeals with rabbit and langoustine with fennel and walnuts; the must-try grilled entrecote of Angus beef served with salty caramel, star anis, and mint; a selection of fine wines; and sensational desserts. *Tip:* This is a perfect place to be seduced by the Segara beach sunset.

In the Kupu Kupu Barong (p. 79), Jl. Segara. (℃) **0361/753708.** www.ma-joly.com. Reservations recom-mended. Lunch Rp95,000–185,000; set menu Rp200,000 and up, includes 4 courses and coffee; dinner Rp150,000–Rp195,000; set menu Rp300,000 and up for 4 courses and coffee. AE, MC, V. Daily 7am–10:30pm.

KUTA

6

EXPLORING KUTA

4 EXPLORING KUTA

Apart from surfing and sunbathing on **Kuta Beach** ★, and shopping there isn't a great deal to do in Kuta, so book a tour to destinations across the island with Kuta as a hub.

The **Bali Bomb Memorial,** on the site of the original Paddys on Jalan Legian, com-memorates the 202 lives taken during the tragic bombing that occurred on Bali on October 12, 2002. At the center of the memorial are the names of all the people who were killed. The attack was the deadliest act of terrorism in the history of Indonesia.

BOWLING & SNOOKER   **Paradiso Bowling & Billiard Center** (℃ **0361/758882**), on Jalan Kartika Plaza, has an 18-lane bowling alley and a spacious billiard center with 38 snooker tables.

BUNGY JUMPING & SLINGSHOT   **AJ Hackett,** Jl. Arjuna, beside Club 66 (℃ **0361/731144;** www.ajhackett.com/bali; daily noon–8pm, Fri–Sat 2pm–4am; US$79 for one jump, certificate, and T-shirt), jumped into the Guinness Book of World Records in 1987 by being the first and only person to bungy jump 110m (361 ft.) from the Eiffel Tower. Since then he has built a global business for all those thrill seekers out there. Try your hand at bungy jumping off the Kuta tower, on your own or with a bicycle or even a motorbike. The sky's the limit.

"Get in, sit down, shut up, and hang on" is the catchphrase of the **Bali Slingshot.** Situ-ated beside Kuta Centre in Tuban (℃ **0361/736151;** admission including T-shirt US$25; package for two persons including T-shirts and video US$59), the slingshot is a bit like a reverse bungy. A capsule that accommodates up to two people is lifted to two huge vertical towers by gigantic bungy cords. The cords are stretched to capacity before the capsule is released and catapulted 50m (164 ft.) skyward in less than 2 seconds, spinning on its own

axis at its maximum height before decelerating into a series of bounces and being lowered
back down to its launch pad.

SPAS   Kuta has plenty of spas and massage outlets, most in the resorts. Spas are open daily. **Cozy ★**, Jl. Sunset, Block A3 (© **0361/766762;** foot reflexology Rp76,000, body massage Rp86,000; MC, V; 11am–10pm), is popular for cheap massages and has a ground-floor bar for freshly made juice and tea. The few massage tables are partitioned by curtains only—but with these prices who's complaining.

In Villa de daun (p. 76), the **DaLa Spa** (single treatment US$32–US$65, package for single US$86–US$210, package for couple US$159–US$389; AE, MC, V; 9am–10pm) is a seductive boudoir-cum-spa parlor. Delicious treatments include a chai bath and Balinese coffee and chocolate scrub.

In Kupu Kupu Barong (p. 79), the beachfront **Gaya Spa** (single treatment US$40–US$60, package US$105–US$158; AE, DC, MC, V; 9am–10pm) is unpretentious but seriously good. Expert therapists know exactly how to unhinge those niggling knots and knead your body with great precision. They do fantastic massages like the deeply therapeutic stone massage with Reiki.

The **Jamu Traditional Spa ★★** (body treatments US$65–US$80, massage US$25–US$65, package US$80–US$160; AE, MC, V; 9am–9pm) in Alam Kul Kul (p. 77) draws inspiration from age-old healing practices found across the Indonesian archipelago. *"Jamu"* refers to the herbal elixirs that local women consume in their pursuit of natural health and beauty and which is still widely used to this day. Using only natural ingredients such as fresh fruit, flower blossoms, and indigenous herbs and spices, Jamu offers such exclusive treatments as the Papaya Kemiri Mint Body Wrap and the Fruit and Nut Facial. They also run Jamu Spa School with 1-week certificate courses so you can take home the artful massage and indulge your family and friends.

Treatments at **Patra Bali Resort** (p. 79; single treatment US$15–US$45, package US$85–US$150; AE, DC, MC, V; 8am–10pm) include complimentary use of the spa's Jacuzzi. If you really want to unwind, be sure to try one of their treatment packages like the Refreshing Mind Package—2 hours and 15 minutes of pure bliss—or the Sunset Package—4 hours of total pampering from head to toe.

The new beachfront **Tea Tree Spa** (single treatment Rp460,000–Rp730,000, signature Rp1,060,000; AE, MC, V; 9am–9pm) in the Holiday Inn Resort (p. 78) has a range of aptly titled therapies such as "Because You Deserve It," "Hold My Calls," and "Out for Lunch."

The **Theta Spa ★★★**, on the beach of Ramada Bintang Bali Resort, Jl. Kartika Plaza (© **0361/755-726;** www.thetaspa.com; single treatment US$15–US$89, package US$101–US$138; AE, MC, V; 10am–10pm) is a tucked-away destination spa worth making a special effort to experience. All massages and treatments use natural products. If you're a couple, try Theta Honey Love, a chocolate and almond scrub. Afterwards you are wrapped in Borneo honey and left to soak in a bath of milk and flower petals.

SURFING ★   Surfers from all over the world are drawn to Kuta's breakers, which are at their best between May and September. Kuta beach can be an ideal place to learn with its soft sandy beaches, consistent rip, and its normally friendly breaks.

Rentals & Schools   Plenty of surf shops line the main drag that will help with board rental or tide information. Your hotel can arrange a private or group lesson, but we suggest the following schools and teachers:

The **Rip Curl School of Surf,** Jl. Arjuna (© **0361/735858;** www.schoolofsurf.com; from US$49 for an hour lesson, board hire US$5 for 4 hr. or US$10 for 8 hr.) was

> ## (Warning!) Swimming Kuta Beach at 66
>
> Unfortunately, the Kuta surf makes recreational swimming virtually impossible.
> Even past the breakers, the current can be too strong. Pay close attention to
> swimming warnings and restrictions, and be very careful if you do swim. Only
> swim in between the flags on Kuta beach. Sometimes lifeguards will be on duty
> but do not rely on them. Several people die every year in the water.

established in 1998 and has an international reputation for offering great service. The professional, predominately Indonesian team provides courses for kids, novices, and day trips for the more advanced. They will even teach you paddle boarding if you can balance long enough and can stand the abuse from the surfing contingent.

Learn to surf with one of the top surf schools in Bali, voted "Best Surf School in Bali" for 3 consecutive years by *Magic Wave Surf Community Magazine.* **Pro Surf School,** Jl. Pantai Kuta (© **0361/7441466;** www.prosurfschool.com; lessons start from €32), offers comprehensive surfing lessons for beginning, intermediate, and advanced surfers, as well as surf trips around Bali.

For those looking for their own surf guru, you can experience the thrill of surfing taught by professional surfers who know all the ins and outs of each break—and they may even share some secret locations if you promise not to tell. **Marcy's Surf Coaching ★★★**, Jl. Arjuna (© **08/123859454;** marcymeachin@hotmail.com; lessons start at Rp400,000 per hr.), is the name of the outfit run by a New Zealander who has been living and surfing in Bali for the last 20 years. Marcy (arguably also a life coach) will get you up on a surfboard on day one. For advanced surfers, he will work out a program, and for the proficient, he will take you to some of the best, uncrowded surfing areas in Bali. Marcy specializes in one-to-one coaching. You may recognize him in the water—he's the one shouting "Paddle, paddle, paddle!"

Jack Chisholm ★★★ (© **08/1916766607;** jack@tropicsurf.net; prices upon inquiry) spends his time between the Maldives and Bali and manages Tropicsurf (p. 70) in Bali, specializing in a variety of surfing holidays. Jack is also an enthusiastic photographer and filmmaker who captures his idea of the very essence of beauty when a wave and a surfer are in natural unison. Jack runs all-girls surf retreats and attempts, very badly (sadly), to play the guitar.

The Waves   Kuta Reef (best swell: west or southwest; **best size:** 3 to 5 ft.; **best winds:** southeast) is an easy short boat ride out from the beach at Tuban. This is a fantastic wave, best a couple of hours after low tide on the incoming. Many local and international surfers cut their teeth on this wave early in their trips before heading to more advanced reef break options. Still, Kuta Reef is a really fun wave when it's on; patience and good manners are the key to surfing happiness out here. This wave can be spotted from the beach and the short boat ride (easily negotiated with boatmen from shore) adds an element of Indo adventure to your daily surf.

If the swell is up, then head around to the north of the runway and you will find **Airport Rights (best swell:** west or southwest; **best size:** 3 to 6 ft.; **best winds:** southeast), a long right breaking for over 100m (328 ft.). It's really good at 3 to 5 feet and is a lonely right on a coast of infamous lefts. Take the same boat as you would for Airports surfed on higher tides with a strong swell running.

Airport Left (**best swell:** south; **best size:** 4 to 5 ft.; **best winds:** southeast) is a short wave running out in front of the airport runway at Tuban. It is often packed with Japanese surfers seeking a mellow, less threatening and competitive surfing experience for their annual holidays. Despite the short length of ride and the crowd factor, it can still be a fun place to surf.

A WATER PARK (**Kids**)   If the kids aren't getting enough of a kick out of the busy beach at Kuta, take them to **Waterbom** ★★★, Jl. Kartika Plaza (✆ **0361/755676;** www. waterbom.com; adults US$23, children 2–12 years old US$13, family US$66; daily 9am–6pm). Right in the heart of Kuta is a tropical adventure park that caters to children and adults. The 3.8-hectare (9½-acre) site is designed around a tropical garden and includes exhilarating water rides, slides, and trails. For those who would prefer to keep themselves dry there are plenty of other options: a spa, a climbing wall, shops, and a poolside bar. The food court has good Italian, French, Indonesian, and American outlets. *Tip:* Once you have purchased your tickets, if you go into the souvenir shop you can purchase another ticket for around US$10. The ticket is valid for 7 days after purchase to get entry back into the park.

---

5 SHOPPING

Shopping in Kuta isn't nearly as swank as in Seminyak. What you will find is surfer gear, cheap sarongs and printed batik shirts and shorts, beaded belts, designer knock-offs, and tourist knickknacks. Don't be fooled by the first price offered, because prices are generally three times what they should be, so be prepared to bargain hard. On **Poppies Gang II** you'll find everything from tie-dyed sarongs, shorts, swimsuits, knock-off cologne, hats, and wristwatches. Traffic-jammed **Jalan Legian** also has a large selection of shops and restaurants. **Jalan Pantai Kuta** has a few good fashion and accessories shops. **Kuta Square** has international brand knock-off stores including Nike, Polo, and Armani—don't get suckered into paying high prices.

The **Discovery Mall** (www.discoveryshoppingmall.com) has a multitude of high-end shops, along with a good selection of international restaurants, cafes, and banks. The **Galleria Bali** (✆ **0361/761945;** www.dfsgalleria.com) is the oldest luxury shopping mall in Bali but is currently undergoing renovations. You can find duty-free goods like Chanel, Coach, and other big brands (designer labels here are the real deal). Galleria Bali has a variety of affordable restaurants that serve both international and Indonesian food. Free shuttle service is offered from many Kuta hotels. **Istana Kuta Galleria,** in a strategic area between Kuta and Legian, consists of 250 shops and many good Indonesian and Western restaurants.

Most stores are open daily, 9am to 9pm.

BOOKS

For books, stop by **Periplus,** with locations in Discovery Shopping Mall (✆ **0361/ 769757**), Kuta Square (✆ **0361/763988**), Carrefour (✆ **0361/8477336**) in Seminyak, and even at the airport.

KUTA

6

SHOPPING

CLOTHING

On Jalan Legian, you'll find a mix of classier shops like **Uluwatu** (© **0361/751933**) which produces handmade lace clothing called *krawang*. Their product line includes women's clothing, nightwear, and bed and table linens. **Body & Soul** (© **0361/767169**) is another great shop with trendy Hong Kong–inspired clothing for women. The styles are youthful and fresh with smaller sizes but there are a few items for fuller-figured women. Their Bambini line offers a good selection of really cute fashions for children 3 to 8 years old with an emphasis on girlie clothes and a few styles for boys, too. Another shop worth visiting is **Decollage** (© **0361/758510**), a boutique with handbags, funky shoes, accessories, and hip clothing.

On Jalan Pantai Kuta, **Emily the Strange** (no phone) offers a variety of great tees, tanks, hoodies, sweatshirts, dresses, bizarre collectible toys, and fun accessories; **Skin** (© **0361/765020**) is for those seeking unisex clothing in cotton, silk, and linen.

In Kuta Square, **Milo's** ★★ (© **0361/754081**) is the one exception that's worth checking out for beautiful designer clothing for men and women. Milo, an Italian born designer, finds great inspiration for his exclusive designs from orchids and other flowers indigenous to Bali. Dresses, blouses, and skirts come in a mix of elegant floral motifs in satin and silk. This is high-end couture, so be prepared to pay up to US$400 for designs. A great shoe store for big-size men and women's shoes is **Maju Jaya** (© **0361/751184**). Women's sizes go up to European 45 and men's to 46. Most of their shoes are leather with a good selection of sandals, closed shoes, dress shoes, and children's shoes. Prices go from Rp75,000 on up.

Mambo   Mambo has a great selection of bright, happy street wear. An Australian franchise, the shop stocks a wide range of quality garments for men and ladies in chic, casual, colorful, and fun styles. Mambo is probably best known for its board shorts, but also offers a good variety of men's shirts, pants, and T-shirts, and ladies tops, reversible short pants, sundresses, and skirts of a high standard of workmanship at reasonable prices. Jl. Pantai Kuta and Jl. Legian. © **0361/752275.**

Paul Ropp ★★   Paul Ropp is a name that you will see on every fashion street in Bali. Instantly recognizable in Bali, Paul Ropp designs for someone who wishes to stand out in a crowd. Accordingly, bright yellows, burnt oranges, fiery reds, and shocking pinks are categorized within a Fire theme; turquoises, sapphires, aquamarines, violets, and sea-grass represent Water; and so on. The garments, for men and women, include long flowing appliqué skirts, baggy embroidered cotton pants, camisoles in sheer silk, loosely woven country-cotton shirts, graceful beaded evening dresses, silk crepe sarongs, and slippers garnished with jewels. Istana Kuta Galleria. © **0361/757835.** www.paulropp.com.

GROCERIES & WINE

J Cuvee, Jl. Kartika Plaza 20 (© **0361/761888**), offers a wide selection of international wines, but with recent government crack-downs on illegal wine imports, prices have escalated so be prepared to pay a lot more than what you'd pay at home.

An outlet of the French supermarket **Carrefour** is on Jalan Sunset (© **0361/847-7222**), and stocks everything from fridges, art material, and cheap clothing to Western and local food and produce. They have an excellent fish counter and their bread is the best on the island.

Dijon ★★ (Finds)   This delightful deli offers a fantastic selection of hams, cured meat, cheeses, and antipasti; imported meats from Australia and New Zealand; and a daily selection of fish and shellfish. If you are pining for familiar foods from back home, this is the place that is likely to stock it. Their small cafe, the Corner (9am–7pm), next door, is the perfect place to grab a coffee, a quick lunch, or an early supper. A bulletin board here is filled with local news and information on all sorts of services like private yoga lessons, swimming classes for kids, and so forth. Jl. Setiabudi. (℃ **0361/759636** or 759638. www.dijon-bali.com.

HOUSEWARES & FURNITURE

Farah's Oriental Rugs & Carpets, Jl. Bypass Ngurah Rai 5 (℃ **0361/766901/2**), offers an exclusive collection of more than 2,500 handmade rugs, carpets, and *kilim*—Turkish non-pile rugs. **Vinoti Living,** in Galleria Bali (℃ **0361/752723** or 752720), has an excellent selection of high-end contemporary furniture skillfully crafted from ash and nyatoh woods. Their furniture designs are sleek with clean lines. You can also find an impressive collection of artwork, including antique look-alike objects from more remote regions of Indonesia. **Lightcom,** Jl. Patih Jelantk, inside Komplek Pertokoan Kuta Gallery (℃ **0361/769246**), offers a wide array of stunning indoor and outdoor lighting imported from the U.S., Europe, Australia, and China. Their designs are simple and very contemporary. The name says it all: the **Why Not Shop,** Jl. Nakula, corner of Imam Bonjol (℃ **0361/499001**), offers a surplus of Asian home decor items such as paintings, furniture, and lighting as well as some nice jewelry and clothing. There are some unusual finds here and everything is handmade and reasonably priced. The **Zire,** Jl. Dewi Sri 21 (℃ **0361/755431**), specializes in synthetic rattan furniture, which is both attractive and highly durable. You can choose from a variety of color schemes and contemporary designs for indoor and outdoor furnishings. They also have some attractive wooden furniture, kitchen accessories, and housewares. Another great one-stop place is **Serba Antik,** Istana Kuta Galleria (℃ **0361/769400**). They have everything under the sun from curtains, wallpaper, carpets, rugs, furniture, bed covers, upholstery, and more. The furnishings are simple yet elegant, and are beautifully crafted from fine woods and other natural materials.

Cempaka ★ Located along Bali's main thoroughfare in the heart of Kuta, adjacent to Galeria Bali, Cempaka is a stunning, high quality modern and classic furniture and housewares shop. The staff can help with designing your interior and delivering the goods wherever you live. For those just looking for a gift there is plenty to choose from. The specially designed housewares are second to none and you are bound to find something worth hauling back home. Open Monday to Saturday, 9am to 8pm. Jl. Bypass Ngurah Rai 8, Simpang Siur. (℃ **0361/766555.**

SURF SHOPS

Internationally recognized surf clothing and lifestyle brands have their anchor stores in Kuta. The massive **Curl,** Jl. Legian (℃ **0361/754455**), is one of three Rip Curl outlets in Kuta. **Quicksilver** is in the Discovery Mall (℃ **0361/757838**).

Bali Barrel This surf cult store stocks garments, accessories, and sports gear by numerous manufacturers, including Island Style, O'Neill, Quiksilver, Ocean Earth and Honey Ocean Earth, Spyderbilt, Rizt, and Volcom. The music is upbeat and loud and the central focus is a V-shaped mezzanine, displaying a selection of surfboards. The girly wear upstairs includes sandals with high heels (not exactly beach wear) and a colorful collection of kids' stuff. This is also a good outlet for purchasing high-quality eyewear. Jl. Raya Legian. (℃ **0361/767237.**

Jungle Surf   The first Jungle Surf shop opened on Jalan Legian (near Peanuts Club) in 1993 and was Bali's first big modern surf shop. Its roots go back to the late '70s when its founder, Ketut Kasih, a surfing legend and one of the very first Balinese surfers, started making and selling Bali's original board shorts. Kuta now has three of these stores to satisfy all of your surfing needs. Discounted items are upstairs in the Jalan Legian and Kuta Suci Arcade stores. Jl. Pantai Kuta. ℂ 0361/750097.

Surfer Girl   Surfer Girl is much more than just an all-girls surf store. This is a one-stop shopping destination where young women can purchase the clothing, board shorts, sandals, accessories, jewelry, and perfume that makes it easier for them to convey the personality and spirit behind their active lifestyles. Most of the popular lines of colorful beach wear and casual wear are imported from Australia. There is a collection of sandals and footwear by Reef, and a range of genuine surf wear from well-known brands designed for, and purchased by, serious surfers and surfer wannabes. Kuta Square, Discovery Mall. ℂ 0361/752693. www.surfer-girl.com.

6 KUTA AFTER DARK

Kuta is the place to be if you want to party hearty. The action begins roughly at 10pm but really gets going around 11pm and lasts until dawn every night. Don't forget your sunglasses, you'll probably need them. Plenty of clubs and bars have their own unique style, although many are more alike than not.

BALINESE THEATER

One of the highlights of being in Kuta is the multitude of cultural performances on offer at many of the four-star hotels and restaurants. The **Kuta Paradiso Hotel,** Jl. Kartika Plaza, Tuban-Kuta. (ℂ 0361/761414; www.kutaparadisohotel.com) features a nice variety of traditional dance performances with their theme night buffets, on Monday, Wednesday, and Saturday. The **Legian Beach Hotel,** Jl. Melasti (ℂ 0361/751711; www.legianbeachbali.com), presents a gamelan orchestra with elegant Balinese dancers. Performances are also held at **Banjar Tegal,** Jl. Raya Legian (no phone; Rp50,000), every Saturday and Tuesday night at 8pm. Puppet performances (*wayang kulit*) can be seen in **Banjar Buni,** Jl. Raya Kuta (no phone; Rp50,000), Monday and Thursday night at 8pm.

BARS & PUBS

Peanuts' Pub Crawl, Jl. Legian and Jl. Melasti (ℂ 0361/754226), is a great way to visit a few of Kuta's infamous watering holes. The crawl begins at Peanuts II, every Tuesday and Saturday. You get to ride in the historic Peanuts' car while barhopping. Peanuts also has a "Welcome to Bali" party every Thursday.

The sports bar at the **Stadium Café,** Jl. Kartika Plaza (ℂ 0361/763100) ensures you always know the score of your favorite team while you're on holiday.

Down in **Poppies Gang I,** you'll find a myriad of small cheap bars, always full with crowds looking for less expensive food and drinks. The **Nusa Indah** (no phone) has been around since the heady days of the '70s, and nothing much has changed. You can still get super-cheap drinks, and you never quite know who you'll meet at the long bamboo bar.

Vibrant **Q Bar,** Jl. Dhyana Pura (ℂ 0361/730927), throbs with DJ music, live drag shows, and an enthusiastic patronage of trendy gay men. It has video screens, a dance floor, and a stage. The extensive drinks menu has over 60 different exotic cocktails and shooters. Regular late-night live entertainment includes themed parties, drag shows, fashion shows, talent contests, look-alike contests, male model competitions, and masquerade balls. Shows usually begin around 11pm, but it is best to arrive early.

JALAN MELASTI The aging **Aussie Pub** (© 0361/751910) is famous for its icy cold beer and is subsequently full of all beer-loving Australians, and then some. The walls are covered in graffiti, so while you're here you can leave your mark. **Bali Rock** (© 0361/754466), opposite the Aussie pub, keeps the live music rocking to appreciative crowds. Easy to find, it's the loudest bar on the street. If *Sweet Child of Mine* gets your blood pumping, then do drop in.

JALAN DOUBLE SIX **Bacio** ★ (© 0361/7566666; www.bacioclub.com) is a great venue offering music, cocktails, wine, and tapas. Take in views of Blue Ocean Beach from the outdoor bistro, or groove to the thumping beats inside with two DJ booths and an upstairs VIP member's only lounge. The stylish bar of **De Ja Vu** (© 0361/732777; www.myspace.com/dejavubeach) is best for a sunset cocktail. Later in the night things start getting funky and spunky. The small **La Vida Loca** (no phone) club packs them in for vodka drinks, with a great live band nightly, playing mostly Latino grooves. The crowds don't really get here till after 2am. Bring your sunglasses as well as your salsa moves as most La Vida Loca's party till sunrise.

POPPIES GANG II The **Bagus Pub** (no phone) is busy day and night serving up ice-cold beers to the holiday brigade. Close to the night spots on Jalan Legian, it's great for meeting other holiday makers. **Tubes** (no phone) was established in 1986, at a time when surfers had very few places to hang out. No one anticipated just how fast the word would spread about this place by the constantly traveling surfers as they rode the waves to all the corners of the globe. Tubes is popular for playing pool and watching the feature and surf movies shown daily on a big screen. While here, enjoy some good food with a choice from two kitchens: Buffet style *nasi campur* from the traditional Indonesian kitchen, or "No Noodles . . . Western food for when you're all noodled out," offering pasta, pizzas, burgers, and baked potatoes. For an older-style Bali bamboo bar that gets raucous later at night, head to **Crusoes** (no phone). Pub-style food, drinks, and pool tables make this popular with the guys and their miniskirted cue-toting compatriots. The **Double D Sports Bar** (no phone) is an older sports bar that screens every imaginable game on the globe. The bar on the street seems to be just as busy during the heat of the day as it is in the heat of the night. Good pub food and drinks, and a friendly crowd. Opposite Sky Garden (see below), the **Engine Room** (no phone) keeps the young tourist crowd revved up and accelerated. Think fuel-injected cocktails and live bands. It's always busy and a great pit stop for well oiled revelers.

JALAN LEGIAN **Paddys Bar** (© 0361/758555) packs the crowds to the rafters nightly as DJs play the latest sounds to fired up backpackers. Buy-two-get-one-free specials keep the party moving in the right direction—or not. Opposite Paddys and Bounty (see below) is the **Espresso Bar & Pizzeria** (© 0361/752576), a tiny older bar so crowded that the band stands out on the street to play. Cold beers flow and ensure any would-be rock stars are well oiled enough to brave belting out a number—like *Mustang Sally* in c-flat. The first club along the strip to go five floors high, **Sky Garden** (© 0361/756362) is still one of the most popular any night of the week. The ground-floor base camp serves food all night long, while upstairs DJs crank out different styles of music depending on what floor you want your party plans elevated to. This is a great place to meet old friends and find some new ones if you are anywhere under your 30s. **Vi Ai Pi**

(📞 **0361/750425;** www.viaipiclub.com) is the more upmarket choice for an evening cocktail while watching the street scene unfold below. Towards 9pm it heats up even the most discerning of guests. The top floor has an air-conditioned billiard room.

JALAN PADMA The **Legian Pub** (no phone) is another raucous night spot that starts early in the evening (some folks in there appear to have started a lot earlier). There is live music or karaoke most nights, and a super-friendly bar staff that also like to jump up and sing. Be sure to try the green starfish cocktails, but only with caution. It's hard to know if it's the clientele or the passing parade who are doing the posing at **Posers** (no phone), an English-style corner pub that makes a fine meeting place over a nice cold ale. On Jalan Sahadewa, the small road linking Jalan Padma and Jalan Melasti, **Legends** (📞 **0361/ 755376**) is busy every night with the holiday crowd looking for good value drinks and food. There's a live band most nights, so if you can find your way to Jalan Sahadewa keep an ear out for the party noise—you'll be sure to find it.

CLUBS

Kama Sutra (📞 **0361/761999**) has become a local teenager hangout, at the north end of Kuta. Nightly shows feature local bands that love to do those tried-and-true cover songs; you won't find much or any original music in Kuta's clubs. The one exception is Hard Rock Hotel's **Centerstage,** Jl. Pantai Kuta (📞 **0361/761869**), which occasionally features some good live acts, but it can get pretty crowded. **Deejay Café,** Jl. Pantai Kuta (📞 **0361/755661**), is the only after club in Bali, located just behind Stars Surf Café. Their professional DJs and state-of-the-art sound system will get you in the mood to pump and grind on their huge dance floor.

Bounty It looks like an old boat, but inside the crowd is definitely young and intent on showing off their drinking and dancing skills. After midnight it is standing room only and every dance podium is packed with revelers usually doused from the regular foam parties. Although the Bounty has a Captain's wheel no one seems to be at the helm when it sails off into the long dizzy night. Jl. Legian. 📞 **0361/754040.**

Club Double Six ★ Next door to Bacio (see above) is the daddy of nightclubs—this one is legendary. On the beach at the far end of Jalan Double Six, this huge club includes a swimming pool and bungy jump. After 3am, it is the hot spot to go after everyone's been everywhere else. Local and international DJs play the best house and techno around, with a truly impressive sound system that'll have you out on the floor or hanging off the end of a bungy string. Jl. Double Six. 📞 **0361/756666** during office hours. www.double sixclub.com.

M-Bar-Go M-Bar-Go started out as one of Kuta's first stylish nightclubs. This is the hangout for kids on gap year and returning expat students—it's a young crowd. Resident and guest DJs play booming house music. Efficient staff serve a wide variety of drinks and cocktails, and the massive floor space is punctuated by long bars, comfortable sofas, and snug corners. Jl. Legian. 📞 **0361/756280.**

Rendevous Rendevous provides three floors of live entertainment, pumping house beats, and some of the friendliest bar staff around. Not a big club, but big on fun and all manner of madness and mischief. Jl. Padma Utara. No phone.

Seminyak & Canggu

It's hard to know the boundaries of where Kuta, Legian, and Seminyak begin and end because the three villages have been slowly melding into one another for the past several decades. Today one thing is clear: Seminyak is certainly in a class all its own—and the sunsets are splendid.

Seminyak is Bali's Notting Hill, Soho, or Miami Beach and has even been compared to Ibiza. If you come here in August and early September, you will see why. Chock-a-block with high-octane parties and "ump humph" music, Seminyak's social beat reverberates from Jalan Laksmana all the way to the beach, pulsing along with the rhythm of the waves. The vibe is mixed with royalty, trendy Europeans, financiers that haven't failed, and Jakarta glitterati.

As Seminyak reaches maximum capacity, Petitenget, one village over, has become the next even more upmarket locale. After that is Batu Belig and then **Canggu,** which is becoming a bit of an expat ghetto. Lack of planning throughout all of this explosive growth is a story in itself.

In the 1960s and 1970s, when foreign tourists first began arriving in Bali in large numbers, the chosen path was always via Kuta. In the 1970s, Sanur became the darling of daring travelers on the South Sea's circuit. But it wasn't long before wealthy American Charles Osborn bought 15 hectares (37 acres) of land on the beach in a sleepy little area 5km (3 miles) north of Kuta. At the time, Seminyak was all a dozy dream of sea, surf, sand, and green. Osborn hired Australian architect Peter Muller to design a private residence, but the project spun out of control and morphed into a 75-room hotel. In 1974 it was christened the Kayu Aya Hotel. A bad partnership agreement saw the hotel taken possession of by the Balinese partner and fall into disrepair. Overseas investors eventually repossessed the property from the Balinese owner in 1977 and it was bought again by local Balinese supported by the Oberoi Group. Their hope was that their new property was far enough away that they would thrive in solitary splendor forever. They were mistaken.

1 GETTING THERE & GETTING AROUND

Seminyak is about 25 minutes maximum from the airport and almost all of the villas and hotels here offer complimentary pick-up from the airport. If you're taking a cab from the airport, pay for your trip at the official taxi counter located outside the arrival hall before you travel. The approximate cost is about Rp100,000. Prices are fixed.

Seminyak has no public transport but no matter what main street you may be walking on, it is always easy to hail a cab **(Blue Bird).** Hotel cars run at a premium of Rp300,000 per hour, which is nearly as much as the cost for a local car and driver for the day.

FINDING AN ADDRESS

Every major thoroughfare has both an official and unofficial name. Also, *gang* (small alleyways) often don't even bother with names at all, though they are used as roads and

ACCOMMODATIONS ■

Alu Bali **13**
Anantara Seminyak
 Resort & Spa Bali **33**
The Dusun **19**
The Elysian Boutique
 Villa Hotel **30**
The Kayana **11**
The Kunja **8**
Laksmana Villas **25**
The Legian **26**
The Oberoi Bali **29**
The Samaya **23**
Sentosa Private
 Villas and Spa **14**
Silq **5**
The Villas Bali Hotel
 and Spa **40**
Villa Aqua **20**
Villa Bali Asri **31**
Villa Crusoe **17**
Villa Des Indes **24**
Villa Kubu **38**

DINING ◆

Biku **12**
Blossom **14**
Breeze **23**
Callego Massage
 & Warung **22**
Dewi Warung **18**
Gado Gado **34**
Ku de Ta **28**
Kura Kura Restaurant **29**
La Lucciola **21**
La Sal **35**
The Living Room **16**
Made's Warung **39**
Metis **3**
Nutmegs **15**
The Restaurant **26**
Ryoshi **36**
Sardine **4**
Sarong **9**
Sip **37**
Wah Wah **27**
Warisan **2**
Warung Bonita **10**
Warung Gossip **1**
Warung Kolega **6**
Warung Sulawesi **7**
Wild Orchid **32**

ⓦ Warning! Safety

Note that Seminyak's **sidewalks** are a hazard to your health, with so many gaps and holes that the odd partygoer and shopper have gone missing a time or two.

Every year new tales of tourists being taken down permanently by the **undertow** spread throughout the community. Be extra cautious if you are going to swim at all. Warning flags with skull and crossbones or cautionary red flags mark some of the worst areas and are in front of well-known places like the Legian Hotel. The further north you go the stronger the current and the fewer warning flags. This undertow stretches from Kuta beach, through Seminyak, all the way to Gilimanuk.

have shops and restaurants you'll want to visit. As a rule of thumb, go with the old unofficial names that everyone can understand with the exception of **Jalan Oberoi** and **Jalan Laksmana,** which seem to be understood no matter which name you use. Here are the unofficial names and their corresponding new official names: Jalan Oberoi is now called Jalan Laksmana; Jalan Raya Seminyak is now called Jalan Raya Basangkasa; Jalan Dhyana Pura or Jalan Gado Gado is now called Jalan Abimanyu; Jalan Double Six is now called Jalan Arjuna.

2 WHERE TO STAY

VERY EXPENSIVE

The Legian ★★★ If budget isn't a problem then go for broke. The beautiful people from Asia, Europe, and North America flock to the Legian and everyone seems just that much more gorgeous in the stunning surrounds. As an all-suite hotel built like a private beachfront estate, every guest room features a comfortable living room, dining area, spacious bedrooms, and a balcony. The decor is on the masculine side with rich woods and cool marbles, but the whole place is nicely appointed with Indonesian artifacts. Gardens envelope a split-level swimming pool, while refined dining is available at the oceanview, simply named Restaurant, or in the privacy of your suite. The on-site villa complex (the **Club,** p. 97) is also worth your attention.

Jl. Kayu Aya, Seminyak Beach. ⓒ **0361/730622.** Fax 0361/730623. www.ghmhotels.com. 66 units. High season US$650 and up; low season US$550 and up. AE, MC, V. **Amenities:** Restaurant (p. 102); 2 bars; babysitting; bicycles; concierge; gym; outdoor pool; room service; spa; watersports; Wi-Fi. *In room:* A/C, TV/DVD, movie library, stereo or CD, hair dryer, minibar.

The Oberoi Bali ★★ ⓕ Finds The Oberoi hotel was one of the first luxury hotels on Bali, and has long attracted celebrities, from Henry Kissinger to Julia Roberts. The native bungalows of coral stone with wood beams and thatched roofs have become the benchmark for tropical Bali style. Cozy rooms strike a great balance between high-end comforts and local style. Amenities are first class: marble bathrooms with sunken tubs facing private gardens, and goodies such as slippers, robes, and flip-flops for the beach. Private pool villas are luxurious beyond belief. The beach here has a nice expanse of sand with few

touts to harass you. Service is genuinely warm and helpful without fawning, and you can **97**
feel at ease here without forgetting that you're in Bali.

Jl. Kayu Aya, Seminyak Beach. ℭ **0361/730361.** Fax 0361/730791. www.oberoihotels.com. 74 units.
High season US$352–US$616; low season US$320–US$560. AE, DC, MC, V. **Amenities:** 2 restaurants; bar;
babysitting; concierge; gym; outdoor pool; room service; spa; tennis; Wi-Fi (for a fee). *In room:* A/C, TV/
DVD, movie library, stereo or CD, hair dryer, minibar, MP3 docking station.

EXPENSIVE

Anantara Seminyak Resort & Spa Bali ★   These oversize suites overlooking Semi-
nyak's beach are pretty much the closest you can sleep to the ocean without having to camp.
This luxurious four-story hotel (one of the tallest buildings around) resembles something
from Miami's South Beach with a hip, urban vibe rather than a traditional Balinese resort.
Decadent touches such as an outdoor balcony bathtub in each of the rooms (in addition to
an extravagantly roomy tub in the bathroom), an espresso machine, and an iPod with Bose
speakers make this a hit among a young, wealthy, globe-trotting crowd.

Jl. Abimanyu (Dhyana Pura), Seminyak. ℭ **0361/737773.** Fax 0361/737772. www.bali.anantara.com. 60
units. High season US$550 suite; low season US$450 suite. AE, DC, MC, V. **Amenities:** 2 restaurants; bar;
babysitting; bicycles; concierge; gym; outdoor pool; room service; spa; Wi-Fi. *In room:* A/C, TV/DVD, movie
library, stereo or CD, hair dryer, minibar, MP3 docking station.

The Samaya ★★   Close to half of all Samaya's guests are repeat clientele—which
comes as no surprise. Smack dab in the middle of prime beachfront Seminyak, here you
pay practically half of what you pay at other hotels in this über-trendy area. Choose from
one-, two-, or three-bedroom villas, which, although a bit tired, are within spitting distance of the beach. The Samaya also offers a new 24-villa Royal Courtyard Complex, a
90-second buggy ride from the main hotel and across the street. The new villas offer all
the modern conveniences of the moment, like flatscreen TVs in the marble tubs. Sublime
sunsets show nightly and an evening at Breeze restaurant overlooking the beach is perfect.
Recently named "Best for Romance" by Trip Advisor, each villa comes with wooden
gazebos housing daybeds that make an ideal perch for private dining or a double daybed
for a massage for two.

Jl. Laksmana, Seminyak Beach. ℭ **0361/731149.** Fax 0361/731203. www.thesamayabali.com. 46 units.
High season US$575 and up; low season US$475 and up. AE, DC, MC, V. **Amenities:** 2 restaurants, Breeze
(p. 102); 2 bars; babysitting; bicycles; concierge; gym; outdoor pool; room service; spa; Wi-Fi. *In room:* A/C,
TV/DVD, movie library, stereo or CD, hair dryer, minibar, MP3 docking station.

VILLA COMPLEXES

The Club at The Legian ★★ (11 villas; high season US$1,300 1-bedroom, US$2,400
3-bedrom; low season US$950 1-bedroom, US$2,000 3-bedroom; additional person
US$60–US$100; AE, MC, V), is the Legian hotel's (p. 96) villa complex across the
street. You have access to the Legian hotel facilities—though privacy is assured. Villas
have private pools, butler service, and a private bar.

 Tips   The Best ATMs in Seminyak

The best ATMs to withdraw money from are Permata Bank ATMs. They will allow
you to withdraw at least two lots of Rp3 million in Rp100,000 notes. Circle K on
Jalan Laksmana has one as well as several other ATMs.

The Dusun ★   This spacious complex was the second to hit Seminyak's shores and still offers great value for its location and service. The grounds have a mature garden and roomy villas with deep pools. Service is top-notch and the whole place is blissfully quiet. They also have a brand new sister property, the boutique all-villa **Kunja** (✆ 0361/ 733130; www.thekunja.com) with similar rates in Kerobokan.

Jl. Kayu Jati 8, Seminyak. ✆ **0361/734000.** Fax 0361/734-100. www.the-dusun.com. 14 villas. High season US$454 1-bedroom, US$823 3-bedroom; low season US$381 1-bedroom, US$738 3-bedroom; extra person US$20. Rates include breakfast. AE, MC, V. **Amenities:** Babysitting; bicycles; concierge; outdoor pool; room service; spa; Wi-Fi. *In villa:* A/C, TV/DVD, movie library, stereo or CD, hair dryer, kitchen, minibar, MP3 docking station.

Sentosa Private Villas and Spa ★★   Fashionistas flock to this trendy complex, with its exclusive ensemble of 38 luxury villas. The main pool is surrounded by a top-of-the-line gym, spa, and excellent restaurant and bar, Blossom. Every room has the standard amenities like the flatscreen televisions, integrated music system, and stylish marble bathrooms with sunken bathtubs, and most feature a Jacuzzi and outdoor bamboo showers. The larger villas have kitchens with full-size refrigerators. The boat available for hire would be at home in St. Tropez. Spoil yourself and make a point of booking in advance for a day trip to one of the islands.

Jl. Pura Telaga Waja, Petitenget. ✆ **0361/730333.** www.balisentosa.com. 38 villas. High season US$650 and up; low season US$550 and up. AE, MC, V. **Amenities:** Restaurant, Blossom (p. 102); bar; babysitting; kids' club; concierge; gym; outdoor pool; room service; spa; Wi-Fi. *In villa:* A/C, TV/DVD, hair dryer, minibar.

Taman Wana ★ (Kids)   The three villas here can be booked together or individually and are in one of the best nearby beach neighborhoods, Batu Belig. This is a good option for families as there is a large shallow play pool and an outdoor playground as well. The English and Italian owners are long-term Bali expats and grow organic vegetables. Thus, food is a priority here and you can expect excellent dining.

Jl. Batu Belig, Kerobokan. ✆ **0361/732527.** www.tamanwana.com. 3 villas. High season US$495 2-bedroom, US$595–US$750 3-bedroom, US$2,040 whole complex; low season US$396 2-bedroom, US$476–US$600 3-bedroom, US$1,632 whole complex. AE, DC, MC, V. **Amenities:** Restaurant; bar; babysitting; outdoor pool; room service; spa; Wi-Fi. *In villa:* A/C, TV, stereo or CD, hair dryer, kitchenette.

Villa Bali Asri ★★   Slightly off the beaten track, these villas sit in a wooded, tree-filled landscape. French owner Jean Paul doesn't let a stone go unturned in his quest for perfection. His elegantly appointed villas use local materials, Indonesian artifacts, pricey European soft furnishings, and just the right amount of color. The pools in slate gray and cool celadon green have an addictive quality that makes moving a tiresome endeavor— for those so inclined, there is a fully equipped gym on the premises.

Jl. Saridewi 39, Oberoi-Seminyak. ✆ **0361/735444.** Fax 0361/737508. www.villabaliasri.com. 11 villas. Peak season US$275–US$1,200; high season US$240–US$1,100; low season US$210–US$1,000. Meals market price; additional US$15 for dinner for maximum 4 persons. AE, MC, V. **Amenities:** Free airport transfers; babysitting; gym; room service; sauna; spa; tennis court; Wi-Fi. *In villa:* A/C, fan, TV/DVD, stereo or CD, hair dryer, kitchen, minibar.

Expensive

Alu Bali ★   This small compound of self-contained Balinese villas has dramatic lighting, great design, and excellent food. All villas come with their own kitchens and meals are cooked at your request right in your villa. The gracious hospitality comes from the fact that, while a perfectionist, the owner is also very personable. This place is definitely gay friendly—sometimes it seems like all of gay Sydney is here!

Jl. Raya Petitenget, Gang Alu, Seminyak. ℂ **0361/736445.** Fax 0361/736660. www.alubali.com. 7 villas. High season US$230–US$494; low season US$209–US$449. AE, MC, V. **Amenities:** Babysitting; bicycles; concierge; room service; spa; Wi-Fi. *In villa:* A/C, fan, TV/DVD, movie library, stereo or CD, hair dryer, kitchenette, minibar, MP3 docking station.

The Elysian Boutique Villa Hotel ★★ The Elysian Villas are the only villas recommended by both Hip Hotels (www.hiphotels.com) and Design Hotels (www.design hotels.com). An open-air restaurant overlooks a swimming pool flanked by intimate cabanas in traditional black and white check. Sliding glass doors in the guest rooms open onto the little garden and pool. Base yourself here to party with a groovy wet bar, iPod dock with iPods you can check out for the beach, and a coffee table with a built-in champagne bucket.

Jl. Saridewi 18, Seminyak. ℂ **0361/730999.** Fax 0361/737509. www.theelysian.com. 26 villas. High season US$350; low season US$300. AE, DC, MC, V. **Amenities:** Restaurant; bar; babysitting; bicycles; concierge; outdoor pool; room service; spa; watersports; Wi-Fi. *In villa:* A/C, fan, TV/DVD, movie library, hair dryer, minibar.

The Kayana These villas are part of the Royal Collection that owns the **Samaya** (p. 97). They are about as cookie-cutter as they come, but brand new and with everything you could want with modern furnishings, plunge pools, and oversize bathrooms with both an indoor and outdoor shower.

Jl. Petitenget, Kerobokan Kelod. ℂ **0361/847-6628.** Fax 0361/847-6633. www.thekayana.com. 24 villas. High season US$380 and up; low season US$350 and up. AE, DC, MC, V. **Amenities:** Restaurant; lounge; babysitting; tandem bikes; concierge; outdoor pool; room service; spa; Wi-Fi. *In villa:* A/C, TV/DVD, movie library, stereo or CD, hair dryer, minibar, MP3 docking station.

Laksmana Villas ★ Laksmana Villas are each individually owned and styled. Villa Semiblan, designed by award-winning Grounds Kent, is replete with Jim Thompson (of Thai silk fame) soft furnishings. All villas are unique and individual so check out the website and see what tickles your fancy.

Jl. Laksmana 22, Seminyak. ℂ **0361/733320.** Fax 0361/737508. www.laksmanavillas.com. 9 villas. High season US$325–US$900; low season US$225–US$775. AE, MC, V. **Amenities:** Babysitting; concierge; room service; Wi-Fi. *In villa:* A/C, TV/DVD, movie library, stereo or CD, hair dryer, kitchenette, minibar.

Silq One of the investors here is a shareholder at Indonesian *Tatler* magazine, and as such many of the guests here tend to be wealthy Jakarta families. Situated in the more upmarket area of Petitenget, the villas have floor to ceiling glass paneling for the natural light. Royal-worthy king-size four-poster beds are laid out on tasteful hardwood teak floors. The bathrooms are all Villeroy and Boch and everything is just a tad more upscale than some of its neighbors.

Jl. Petitenget 27C, Kerobokan. ℂ **0361/847-5461.** Fax 0361/847-5459. www.silqkerobokanbali.com. 17 villas. High season US$350–US$550; low season US$250–US$450. AE, DC, MC, V. **Amenities:** Restaurant; bar; babysitting; concierge; outdoor pool; room service; spa; Wi-Fi. *In villa:* A/C, TV/DVD, movie library, stereo or CD, hair dryer, minibar.

Villa Kubu ★ A favorite with the expat set around Asia, Villa Kubu has an old-world charm. Cobblestone pathways connect the complex of individual villas and no two are alike. Off the busy main roads of Seminyak the scene here manages to be serene. Staff have been here for years and often welcome back guests like long lost family members.

SEMINYAK & CANGGU

7

WHERE TO STAY

The new, spiffy spa will be a surprise to the numerous repeat guests that make their way here every year.

Jl. Raya Seminyak, Gang Plawa 33F, Seminyak. ℂ **0361/731129.** Fax 0361/735500. www.villakubu.com. 14 villas. Peak season US$345–US$525; high season US$300–US$475; low season US$265–US$435. Meals market price. AE, MC, V. **Amenities:** Free airport transfers; babysitting; room service; spa; Wi-Fi. *In villa:* A/C, fan, TV/DVD, movie library, stereo or CD, fridge, hair dryer, kitchenette, MP3 docking station.

Moderate

The Villas Bali Hotel and Spa
One of the first villa complexes in the Seminyak area, the well-known Villas Bali Hotel and Spa is a better choice than some of the new complexes in the neighborhood. One-, two-, and three-bedroom villas each have their own entrance, pool, and kitchen and are ideal for those who want to enjoy their own surroundings rather than eating out every day. The **Prana Spa** (p. 108) offers yoga retreats and fabulous treatments; **Chill** (p. 108) offers natural healing and reflexology for all of your aches and pains. If you're on a spa vacation, this is the place to stay.

Jl. Kunti 118X, Seminyak. ℂ **0361/730840.** Fax 0361/733751. www.thevillas.net. 50 villas. High season US$290 and up; low season US$260 and up. AE, DC, MC, V. **Amenities:** Restaurant; babysitting; outdoor pool; room service; 2 spas; Wi-Fi. *In villa:* A/C, TV, stereo or CD, hair dryer, kitchenette.

STAND-ALONE VILLAS

Right on the beach at Batu Belig, **Atas Ombak** ★★★, Jl. Batu Belig (ℂ **0361/730668;** fax 0361/736391; www.atasombak.com; five bedrooms; peak season US$2,550, high season US$2,250, low season US$1,500, extra bed US$20 a night; meals market price; AE, DC, MC, V), is one of Bali's most popular event villas—with good reason—for its large garden area that can accommodate up to 300 people at a seated dinner. This is a seasoned home where gracious staff, who have been with the property for generations, run the property like the gentile estate that it is.

Villa Aqua ★, Jl. Kayu Jati 20, Seminyak (ℂ **0361/730668;** fax 0361/736391; www. villa-aqua-bali.com; four bedrooms; peak season US$1,250, high season US$1,000, low season US$775, extra bed US$25 a night; meals market price; AE, MC, V), is a perfect choice for a group of friends or family without children. The villa is set on two levels and within a large walled courtyard with a 25m (82-ft.) swimming pool taking up a large part of the outdoor space. Other amenities include a Jacuzzi, steam room, and sound-proof party room with a pool table and bar. Each of the four bedrooms is spacious and intended to offer maximum privacy and discretion for couples.

There is one hidden villa on Seminyak Beach that is boho chic at its best, with a million-dollar view for less. **Villa Crusoe** ★★, Jl. Petitenget 40X (ℂ **0361/7424015;** www.balion.com; 2 bedrooms; high season US$600; low season US$450; AE, MC, V) is an old fisherman-style beach house is filled with Asian and Western antiques and objects of all origins like Tibetan carpets on teak floors and a Chinese apothecary chest that serves as a good place to store pool towels. A poolside antique *joglo* serves as a spare room.

Villa Des Indes ★★★, Jl. Astina Pura 3, Seminyak (ℂ **0361/737799;** fax 0361/736183; www.villadesindes.com; two units with two or three bedrooms; peak season US$618–US$1,450, high season US$523–US$1,250, low season US$428–US$850; rates include breakfast, other meals market price; AE, MC, V), never intended as a rental, was built to house one couple's stunning collection of museum-quality antiques and art. The villa is bordered on one side by a koi pond and on the other three sides by a 21m (69-ft.) meandering swimming pool. The splendid living and dining pavilion is in an antique *joglo,* once the property of a Javanese nobleman. A Covarrubias painting of a Balinese village at night as well as a Bateson and Meade (as in Margaret Meade) painting of a *barong* dance are just a few of the treasures you will find during your visit. Pretend to be nobility and enjoy the ride.

---

3 WHERE TO DINE

Seminyak is teeming with restaurants of every variety and price range. The majority are individual enterprises, although some of the best, like Blossom and Kura Kura, are part of villa complexes and hotels. The truly international community lends the international restaurants their authentic base.

VERY EXPENSIVE

Gado Gado ★ (**Finds**) INTERNATIONAL   A new chef and management team at Gado Gado has whipped the food and service into shape to match the stunning location. Relax at one of the tables on the timber deck above the beach and enjoy a leisurely lunch or romantic dinner. A favorite risotto was cooked to perfection and served with grapefruit, fresh mahimahi, and just the right amount of seasoning.

Jl. Abimanyu (Jl. Dhyana Pura). ℂ **0361/736966.** Reservations recommended. Main courses Rp200,000. MC, V. Daily 9am–midnight.

Ku de Ta ★★★ (**Moments**) INTERNATIONAL/MEDITERRANEAN   Everyone who is anyone makes their way to Ku de Ta when they are in Bali. It's fabulous fun and you can't beat the awe-inspiring sunsets and beachfront. The indoor and alfresco dining surrounds a plunge pool and grassy courtyard, three bars, and a rooftop lounge. Mediterranean menus are available for lunch and dinner and grazing food is served from noon until 10pm, including Asian tapas, sashimi and sushi, and oysters. August, or "high season" here is high voltage and you can't be too overdressed or underdressed for the annual "Bikini" and "White Party." A DJ spins day and night.

Jl. Laksmana 9. ℂ **0361/736969.** www.kudeta.net. Reservations recommended. Lunch Rp60,000–Rp120,000; dinner Rp230,000–Rp440,000. AE, DC, MC, V. Sun–Thurs 8am–11:45pm; Fri–Sat 8am–12:45am.

Kura Kura Restaurant ★★ (**Finds**) (**Moments**) EUROPEAN/INDONESIAN   This gem is a favorite for romantic celebrations. The breezy Balinese thatched pavilion encased in folding glass panels and surrounded by lotus ponds with the sounds of the *angklung* music and crashing waves make for a true island experience. Modern European cuisine is served on fine bone china with white linen silver service. Order their home-cured smoked salmon with anything, especially their signature blinis. Royal Indonesian cuisine and some excellent Indian dishes give a nod of appreciation to the owners of Oberoi. The not-so-gentle reminder on your bill in capital letters that says "No Tipping, Please" means the service you just enjoyed was genuine.

In the Oberoi (p. 96), Jl. Kayu Aya. ℂ **0361/730361.** www.oberoihotels.com. Reservations recommended. Indonesian Rp275,000–Rp410,000; continental Rp350,000–Rp430,000; seafood Rp300,000–Rp1,000,000; set menu Rp300,000–Rp360,000. AE, DC, MC, V. Daily 7–11:30pm.

The Living Room ★ FRENCH/ASIAN   Owned by Daniel Vannequé, the brother of the owner of Sip, this restaurant has been staked out by a regular crowd of European expats. The food isn't as beautiful as the people with an eclectic menu of French and

Asian dishes that can be hit or miss. Frogs' legs in white-wine sauce with green papaya salad are a favorite choice. The bar area and glassed-in wine cellar is where the Euros hold court until the wee hours. A superb place for occasional celebrity spotting and late-night dancing (DJ until 3am Thurs–Sun).

Jl. Petitenget 2000X. ℰ **0361/735735.** www.thelivingroom-bali.com. Reservations recommended. Main courses Rp190,000–Rp240,000; set menu Rp350,000–Rp550,000. AE, MC, V. Daily 6pm–midnight.

Nutmegs ★★ Ⓕ**Finds** PAN-ASIAN   This new restaurant at the famous dance bar Hu'u is sleek and stylish. The tables are decked out in crisp white linen, white flowers, and candles. Service is ninja-perfect. Exuberant and enthusiastic Chef Philip Mimbimi is a graduate of the Culinary Institute of America with a five-star resume and he will do back flips to make sure your experience is charmed. Go with his recommendations of the night and you won't go amiss. The key to his cooking is the freshest ingredients that can be found that day. The club **Hu'u** (p. 114) turns into party central on the weekends so time your meal carefully if you want a quiet night. Otherwise get up and party. Nutmegs is a great alternative to Ku de Ta, with Lychee Martinis that kick. Live music plays every Thursday night.

Jl. Petitenget. ℰ **0361/736574.** www.nutmegs-restaurant.com. Reservations recommended. Main courses Rp128,000–Rp528,000. AE, MC, V. Daily 11am–1am.

The Restaurant at the Legian ★★ INTERNATIONAL   Award-winning German chef Dorin Schuster serves up modern European fare with an Asian bent. He is extreme in his dedication to perfection and sources his seafood from his own fishermen in Java. The Ahi Tuna with soy and sesame marinade and cassava root chips is melt-in-your-mouth fabulous.

In the Legian (p. 96), Jl. Kayu Aya. ℰ **0361/730622.** www.ghmhotels.com. Reservations recommended. Main courses Rp260,000–Rp490,000. AE, MC, V. Daily 7am–11pm.

EXPENSIVE

Blossom ★ THAI   Already well known and respected in Bali following his earlier stint as the original chef at Ku de Ta, Chef Chris Patzold has taken over the reins here. Blossom is off the pool and rock garden of the Sentosa and the bar is Bali's classiest. Patzold's inventive take on Thai cuisine includes the sensational seared scallops with crisp duck, lime leaf, coconut, and Thai basil and the Crisp Skin Salmon Salad with watermelon and mint chili shallot dressing. Do not deny yourself the stunning bar where the well-trained staff know the value of a nimble wrist and a heavy hand. Friday evenings feature live jazz at the edge of the swimming pool.

In Sentosa Private Villas and Spa (p. 98), Jl. Pura Telaga Waja. ℰ **0361/730333.** www.balisentosa.com. Reservations recommended. Main courses Rp85,000–Rp220,000; set menu Rp490,000. AE, MC, V. Daily 7am–midnight.

Breeze ★★ EUROPEAN/AMERICAN   Hold onto your tipple with all your strength as this chic open bar sits virtually on the beach and is prone to windy weather. Chef Michael Shaheen showcases Euro-American cuisine that blends the best of the environment with his own vision. Using many indigenous ingredients, the menus are dictated by the local harvest in a "Simple, Seasonal, and Uncomplicated approach." Our favorites have been black pepper, sesame tataki, and marinated hamachi (rare) with wakame and seaweed salad, tempura nori rice cake, ponzu, and pan-seared diver scallops. The Peking duck—pan-seared confit—was delectable.

In the Samaya (p. 97), Jl. Laksmana. ℂ **0361/731149.** www.thesamayabali.com. Reservations recommended. Sandwiches Rp95,000–Rp110,000; pasta Rp85,000–Rp195,000; main courses Rp83,000–290,000. AE, DC, MC, V. Daily 7am–11pm.

La Lucciola ★★★ MEDITERRANEAN This happening beachside restaurant—a Seminyak pioneer—is lovingly referred to as "La Looch" and looks out onto one of the prettiest stretches of Seminyak beach. The new Italian chef offers classic Mediterranean fare with a touch of Asian spice. The pan seared fillet of coral trout with pancetta, marinated artichokes, wild rocket, and preserved lemon dressing is a firm favorite. Finish with a lemon and vanilla bean soufflé and a bracing expresso. The only way to get to the restaurant is through the parking lot of the famous Petitenget Temple next door—the laughter will lead the way.

Jl. Petitenget. ℂ **0361/730838.** Reservations recommended. Main courses US$15–US$25. AE, MC, V. Daily 9am–11pm.

La Sal SPANISH It's hard to find La Sal—it is on a small back lane that connects Jalan Laksmana and Jalan Abimanyu. But on the menu you will easily find a good choice of tapas such as delicious—imported and expensive—Iberico Bellota ham from acorn-fed black free-range pigs, calamari with squid cooked in its own ink, grilled chorizo sausages, crunchy mushrooms, and a delicious veal carpaccio with foie gras and Manchego cheese. The list also includes a clam casserole, garlic prawns in truffle oil, grilled king prawns, crispy pork belly with lentils and mango, twice cooked lamb shoulder, and paella. You could select from a small but good choice of wines, but why not sangria instead? Sunday evenings is Argentinian Churrasco night.

Jl. Drupadi II 100. ℂ **0361/738321.** www.lasalbali.com. Reservations recommended. Main courses US$15; set menu US$30. AE, MC, V. Daily 11:30am–11pm.

Metis ★★ FRENCH/MEDITERRANEAN This open-air 350-seat emporium houses a patisserie, bars, event space, an arts and interior shop, a jewelry boutique, and a women's fashion boutique. The French cuisine focuses on fois gras and seasonal truffles, white asparagus, and mushrooms. Vegetarians also have plenty of options.

Jl. Petitenget 6. ℂ **0361/737888.** www.metisbali.com. Reservations recommended. Lunch Rp90,000–Rp155,000; pasta Rp175,000–Rp205,000; seafood Rp185,000–Rp305,000; meat Rp170,000–Rp250,000. AE, MC, V. Daily noon–11pm.

Sardine ★★ SEAFOOD Strikingly housed in a sprawling bamboo structure overlooking rice paddies, Sardines is equally inviting for a drink or a meal. A comfortable lounge area sits next to a pond, home to a school of very rare white koi carp—the chef assures us they will not end up on your table. The menu is made of predominately fish and organic greens. The owners have taken a tip from the locals and serve surprisingly delicious *arak* cocktails—no mean feat. Sardines of course are the house specialty on the daily changing menu.

Jl. Petitenget. ℂ **0361/738202.** Main courses Rp90,000–Rp180,000. MC, V. Tues–Sun noon–1am.

Sarong ★★ PAN-ASIAN Chef Will Meyrick takes minimalism out of the equation for both his food and decor at Sarong. The appealing airy *joglo*-style pavilion is draped with gold with gilded mirrors and enormous chandeliers completing the romantic sheen. In contrast, the menu draws on the traditions of hawker or street food from India, Indonesia, China, and Thailand. Merrick elevates pedestrian favorites to sophistication. A must is the betel nut leaf starters with either salmon shrimp galangal coriander or raw tuna betel leaf with lemongrass shallots and lemon basil. Betel nut (the leaf from the arcadia palm) is a known stimulant that causes a sense of heightened alertness, similar to a cup of coffee. If you fancy tandoori, try the Zafferrani Paneer, cheese stuffed with succulent and tangy North Indian chutney. Sarong also has an excellent bar worthy of a visit on its own accord. Keep an eye on the cool crowd via the huge overhanging gilt mirror.

Jl. Petitenget 19X. ✆ **0361/737809.** www.sarongbali.com. Reservations recommended. Main courses US$15; set menu US$30. AE, MC, V. Daily 7pm–1am.

Sip ★ FRENCH   Sip is a winner despite its unlikely location across from the Bintang supermarket. Owner Christian Vannequé was France's youngest Head Sommelier at La Tour d'Argent in Paris in the 1970s and has created a wine list for wine novices and wine aficionados alike—no easy task on an Indonesian island. His Wine Climax features outstanding and rare bottles from the Old and the New World. The kitchen is run by Chef Patrick Chauchereau who worked in several two-Michelin-star restaurants in Paris before coming to Bali. Sip offers French home cooking at reasonable prices: escargot in garlic butter, homemade pâtés, traditional cassoulet (our favorite), and *tete de veau ravigotte* (boiled calf's head and tongue in *ravigotte* sauce). Meals finish with a variety of French cheeses and mouthwatering sweets.

Jl. Raya Seminyak 16A. ✆ **0361/730810.** www.sip-bali.com. Reservations highly recommended. Main courses Rp75,000–Rp295,000; specials Rp89,000–Rp155,000. AE, MC, V. Tues–Sun noon–11:30pm; closed for lunch on Sun.

Wah Wah ★★★ BURGERS   Just across the street from the Legian Hotel, Wah Wah, like its Shanghainese owner of the same name, is frankly bizarre. Its proprietor is an artist and a self-taught culinary genius who has dabbled in just about everything. His idea for his pre-club/lounge/restaurant/bar/gallery/souvenir shop is to make the best hamburgers in the world in bite-size portions and keep the drink prices reasonable. His finger food is made with Wagyu beef, fois gras, blue cheese, and other rich ingredients. He also has veggie burgers, if you must. Wah's art adorns the walls. His paintings in deep reds and greens with simple brush strokes on primarily black backgrounds exude a certain degree of sexuality. It's brazen and brash and decidedly unique.

Jl. Laksmana 11A. ✆ **08/18349809.** www.wahwahburger.com. Reservations recommended. Main courses US$13–US$35; 6-course tasting menu US$30. AE, MC, V. Daily 8am–1am.

Wild Orchid THAI   The Thai cuisine here is a modern twist of classic regional dishes like green curries and pad Thai. Pomelo is grown locally so don't miss out on the salad

---

ⓜ Moments   Balinese High Tea

Biku ★★★, Jl. Petitenget (✆ **0361/857-0888;** www.bikubali.com; main courses Rp50,000–Rp100,000; MC, V; daily 8am–11pm), is an enchanting 150-year-old Javanese *joglo* as regal as its owner, Princess Asri Kerthyasi, and her son, Tjok Gde Kerthyasa, a tea master. High tea is the main draw but don't miss out on breakfast and lunch. Start with a cup of limited edition Javanese tea. A must is the three-tiered presentation of sweets and tea sandwiches and scones with homemade jam and cream. Everything here is baked fresh daily, including the rose petal cupcakes. Don't miss Friday to Sunday, from 1 to 5pm, when you can have a mystical afternoon tea leaf reading by some of the island's leading psychics. Questions are answered and futures revealed.

> ## Warisan ★★★
>
> After 20 years of being Bali's favorite restaurant, this grande dame is having a face-lift and will be back to serve its loving public in early 2010. The Mediterranean French fare needs no improving and won't change. Keep your ear to the ground on the reopening date. Jl. Raya Kerobokan 38 (✆ **0361/731175**).

that is sweet, sour, and spicy. Presentation here is inspired: jasmine rice is served from bamboo tubes and rice paper rolls are served in cane bird cages.

Jl. Abimanyu (Dhyana Pura). ✆ **0361/737773**. www.bali.anantara.com. Reservation recommended. Main courses Rp110,000–Rp340,000; set menu Rp250,000–Rp350,000. AE, DC, MC, V. Daily 7–11pm.

MODERATE

Café Bali ★ INTERNATIONAL   You might accidentally drive right past this tremendously stylish white clapboard building on Jalan Laksmana. Don't. Dutch and French design maximize giant chandeliers, pretty table tops, comfy sofas, and classic bistro chairs to make you almost forget you were on a tropical island. The cuisine is French-meets-East, with steak frites, dim sum, sashimi, and spring rolls.

Jl. Laksmana. ✆ **0361/736484**. Main courses Rp28,000–Rp70,000. MC, V. Daily 7am–2am.

Ryoshi ★ JAPANESE   The prices are reasonable for sushi at Ryoshi, and all kinds of other Japanese fare is done just right, too (just ask the many Japanese guests). Try the butterfish sashimi, a deepwater whitefish with a rich texture and savory flavor. There are locations all over the island, but the Seminyak outlet is by far the best.

Jl. Raya Seminyak. ✆ **0361/731152**. www.ryoshibali.com. Reservations recommended. Wagyu steak Rp15,000–Rp300,000; sushi and sashimi set Rp22,000–Rp73,000; a la carte Rp12,000–27,000. AE, MC, V. Daily noon–midnight.

WARUNGS
Expensive

Warung Bonita ★★ INDONESIAN   This warung is an institution of a different sort. On the odd night you can catch Bonita in top form, dolled up, hat on, and scarf billowing under the fans. Bonita often leads an impromptu cabaret giving diners a fabulous floor show—maybe not Tony-award-worthy, but certainly enjoyable. Warung Bonita offers authentic home cooking from the islands and some Western fair as well. Try the Indonesian buffet lunch, which has attracted a loyal following among local and expat residents alike. Every Friday night features a live Balinese performance.

Jl. Petitenget. ✆ **0361/731918**. www.bonitabali.com. Reservations recommended. Main courses Rp23,000–Rp150,000. MC, V. Daily 8am–midnight.

Moderate

Made's Warung ★★ (Finds) INTERNATIONAL   This is the cream of the crop, having started from humble origins in Kuta beach, Made and Peter's place has since become a landmark at both locations. If it's busy, and it often is, don't be surprised if you end up sharing a table. Made's is a must for first-time tourists and families, who will love their popular Indonesian offerings. *Gado gado,* satay, and curries are all recommended, and the price is right. Go for the infamous Japanese dish of *shabu shabu,* available for a minimum

The Best of Eat Street

Dozens of restaurants line **Jalan Laskmana,** aka Eat Street. Establishments pop up and close like shutters during a storm. Prices are competitive at all of these establishments; part of the fun is strolling down the street before deciding where to dine. Below are a few stand-out selections; reservations are recommended at all of these busy places, all open daily.

Chandi ★★★ (© **0361/731-060;** www.chandibali.com; burgers Rp36,000–Rp48,000, vegetarian Rp26,000–Rp42,000, fish Rp42,000–Rp120,000; AE, DC, MC, V; Mon–Thurs noon–midnight, Fri noon–2am, Sat 10am–2am, Sun 10am–midnight) serves a "gastronomic twist on Pan-Asian cuisine" with organically grown greens and spices from local farmers.

Centuries of tension between Korea and Japan seem to dissipate at **Kaizan** (© **0361/747-2324;** main courses Rp35,000–Rp250,000, set menu Rp70,000–Rp250,000; AE, DC, MC, V; 9am–1am)—upstairs is Korean barbecue; downstairs is Japanese. Next door is the little brother restaurant **K2,** a traditional inn-style Japanese restaurant serving Japanese tapas.

Owned by Moroccan locals, **Khaima** (© **0361/742-3925;** www.khaimabali. com; main courses Rp49,000–Rp95,000; MC, V; 11am–11:30pm) has excellent appetizers include phyllo pastry filled with vegetables, minced lamb, tuna, chicken, or goat cheese; salads of tomatoes and bell peppers, cinnamon and carrots, or eggplant; and tagines with lamb and eggplant with couscous and kebabs. Friday and Saturday nights feature belly dancing performances that see even the most staid customers shaking their booties.

Rumours (© **0361/738720;** www.balinesia.co.id; pasta Rp23,000–Rp85,000, steak Rp42,000–Rp99,000, pizza Rp25,500–Rp46,500; AE, MC, V; 6pm–midnight) is a bit of a dive, but having a quality Australian T-bone or sirloin for about US$8 is hard to beat. Rumours only accepts reservations until 7:30pm, which should give you an idea just how popular this buzzing bistro is.

Trattoria ★ (© **0361/737082;** www.trattoriabali.com; pasta Rp43,000–Rp49,000, fish Rp46,000–Rp64,000; AE, DC, MC, V; 11am–midnight) has a simple recipe: mix delicious Italian food with reasonable prices and keep the emphasis on steady clientele rather than on haute cuisine. The plentiful, modest food stays true to the roots of the ever-present owner and his brother from southern Italy.

Last but not least, classy Italian dishes at very affordable prices makes **Ultimo** (© **0361/738-720;** www.balinesia.co.id; pizza Rp29,000–Rp45,000, main courses Rp43,000–Rp79,000, set menu Rp85,000–Rp125,000; AE, MC, V; 5pm–midnight) one of the most crowded Eat Street restaurants. Go before 7pm to avoid the crowd or you may wait for up to 30 minutes to be served.

of four people (*shabu shabu* means "swish swish"). The dish is prepared by submerging meat, seafood, or vegetables into a pot of boiling broth. Fun surprises on the menu include a bagel with smoked marlin, tofu burgers, and Caesar salad. Don't pass up the daily specials, particularly the fresh fish. Beverage choices range from iced coffee and juices to some very potent booze concoctions. Paintings, memorabilia, and nostalgic posters lend a warm and cozy feel and the tables spill out in the courtyard where tango aficionados occasionally tap their toes. Friday and Saturday nights include a live Balinese dance performance.

Jl. Raya Seminyak. ✆ **0361/732130.** www.madeswarung.com. Reservations recommended. Balinese Rp40,000–Rp45,000; Indonesian Rp25,000–Rp55,000; *shabu shabu* Rp90,000–Rp100,000. AE, MC, V. Daily 10am–midnight.

Inexpensive

Callego Massage & Warung (Moments) INDONESIAN
This warung is the daytime hangout for the gay community in Bali on Petitenget beach. The vibe is ultra casual with scattered plastic chairs and tables with sun loungers available for rent in front of the warung. Expect to see many minute Speedos as well as the odd tourist who may wonder where they landed. The food is Indonesian fare with a few uninspired sandwiches but the Bintang is cold and the atmosphere extremely chilled.

Jl. Taman Ganesha 9. ✆ **0361/730370.** Main courses Rp25,000–Rp45,000; pasta Rp15,000–Rp30,000; Indonesian Rp20,000–Rp30,000. No credit cards. Daily 10am–9pm.

Dewi Warung (Finds) JAVANESE
Across from the Petitenget Temple is a row of warungs. Facing this row, head for the one the farthest on the left. Here the cook, Ibu Dewi, serves fresh chicken soup or *soto ayam*—as delicious as it is good for you. The *sambal* that accompanies the other perfect Javanese specialties has just the right amount of spice and, like all Javanese cuisine, is not spiced hot like Balinese cuisine. It took this assignment and my close friend's advice for me to discover this jewel—now you can catch me here several days a week on my favorite pink plastic stool.

Jl. Petitenget. No phone. Main courses Rp10,000–Rp20,000. No credit cards. Daily 6:30am–9pm.

Warung Gossip INDONESIAN
Just a few minutes away from the trendy end of town, Warung Gossip serves typical fare that is just a bit more Westernized for tourist palates. A great mix of nationalities meets here on any given night and tables are jam-packed to ensure lots of eavesdropping.

Jl. Pengubengan Kauh. ✆ **0361/738765.** Rice and vegetables Rp3,000–Rp5,000; fish Rp7,500; meat Rp8,000. No credit cards. Daily 9am–10pm.

Warung Kolega INDONESIAN
This place in Kerobokan is so popular for lunch that sometimes you have to wait for a table. *Nasi campur* is the order of the day here. Kolega is well-known for its Javanese cooking and delicious treats like tempeh with soy sauce.

Jl. Petitenget 98A. ✆ **0361/732480.** Rice and vegetables Rp2,000–Rp3,000; fish Rp8,000; meat Rp6,000–Rp11,000. No credit cards. Mon–Sat 9am–8pm.

Warung Sulawesi ★★ INDONESIAN
This little gem is run by an American and his Indonesian partner who serve up some very good Indonesian food. The warung has good food at good prices and provides housing for the staff.

Jl. Petitenget. ✆ **0361/746-3052.** Rice and vegetables Rp3,000–Rp4,000; fish Rp9,000; meat Rp7,000–Rp12,000. No credit cards. Daily 9am–8pm.

4 EXPLORING SEMINYAK

Not much activity takes place in Seminyak other than lolling on the beach or shopping till you literally drop (into a hole on the street), or just enjoying your well-earned rest. Remember, the rip currents here make swimming a risky prospect. Most visitors use Seminyak as a base for day trips to explore the rest of the island.

PETITENGET TEMPLE ★★ As one of the directional temples on the island, Petitenget (along Jl. Petitenget) is a beautiful and busy site on the beach and a beehive of activity. *Tip:* Several *banjar* are attached to the temple and the best time to see it is during Melasti (once a year 3 days before Nyepi; Mar 16, 2010, Apr 4, 2011, and Mar 23, 2012) when thousands of villagers arrive marching in unison towards the temple and through to the beach to cleanse their souls.

HORSEBACK RIDING ★★★ (Moments) Sabina, the owner of **Umalas Equestrian,** Jl. Lestari 9X, Banjar Umalas Kauh–Kerobokan (℡ **0361/731402;** www.balionhorse.com; ½-hour rice field tour US$25, 2-hour beach tour US$72, 3-hour beach tour US$102; daily, by reservation, from 7am–9pm), fell in love with Bali 14 years ago. Sabina explains, "I came to Bali and everything was here, beautiful countryside, beaches, and people but I missed my horses so I came up with a plan." Umalas includes 35 stables, indoor and outdoor arenas, paddocks, a swimming pool, a restaurant, and even accommodation for those looking to book a riding holiday.

SPAS Spas are open daily. **Body Works,** Jl. Kayu Jati 2 (℡ **0361/733317;** www.body worksbali.com; massage Rp79,000–Rp289,000, infrared sauna Rp150,000–Rp320,000, facial Rp135,000–Rp319,000; MC, V; 9am–10pm), was the first spa in Seminyak in 1994 and now looks rather dated with its Moroccan-inspired design and girls dressed in sarongs and *kebaya* in blue. Cattycorner to the Petitenget Temple, Body Works enjoys much popularity simply because of its location. Blow dries, crème baths, and manicures and pedicures are the mainstays here as are Balinese massage, *lulur* scrubs, and the ever-popular aloe vera facials. The infrared sauna has the most jaded housewives of Seminyak booking in for a miracle cure.

One of the spas in the Villas Bali Hotel and Spa (p. 100), **Chill** (Classic US$13, Ultimate Chill US$18, Chill Out US$15, Holistic Chill US$23; AE, MC, V; 10am–10pm), has built a fine reputation for reflexology. The Ultimate Chill is a 90-minute indulgence concentrating on the feet, ankles, neck, and shoulders in a combination of reflexology and acupressure. Advance booking is recommended. The **Prana Spa** (ayurveda US$84–US$263, massage US$82–US$165; AE, DC, MC, V; 9am–10pm), also in the Villas Bali Hotel and Spa, sets itself apart simply by its totally incongruous Mogul-inspired architecture with turrets, towers, look-out posts to nowhere, and ornate hand-painted frescoes. Some of the treatments get their inspiration from the Majapahit royal courts and others hail from ayurvedic medicine. The hotel affiliation offers excellent spa packages and spa cuisine at the attached cafe.

When **Glo ★★★,** Jl. Kunti 119 (℡ **0361/738689;** www.glogarage.com; mani/pedi Rp110,000–Rp307,000, brows and lashes Rp110,000–Rp185,000, wax Rp46,000–Rp198,000, facial Rp380,000–Rp430,000; MC, V; 10am–8pm), opened in Seminyak women from around the island breathed a sigh of relief as finally there was a place to get European-quality manicures and pedicures and not just a foot rub and a splash of paint. The facials are some of the best on the island.

Treatments at **Jari Menari** ★★★, Jl. Raya Seminyak (✆ **0361/736740;** www.jari menari.com; four hand massage Rp440,000; MC, V; 9am–9pm), are some of the best worldwide not to mention in Bali. All male masseuses give the infamous "Four Handed Massage," which gives you the pleasure of four palms applying perfect pressure rather than just two. Tuesday massage classes teach a nine-step 25-minute massage sequence. The session starts with a 40-minute yoga class. Students watch demonstrations and then give and receive treatments. You'll be the best souvenir to give to a loved one back home.

The spa (massage US$45–US$90, ayurveda US$99, hot stone US$55–US$75, Balinese Eternal Bliss package US$120–US$210; AE, DC, MC, V; 9am–10pm) at the **Samaya** (p. 97) has a standout location on the beach—it doesn't get any more calming than this. If you're travelling as two, book into a beachfront treatment room and enjoy the Balinese Eternal Bliss couples' treatment that lasts 2½ hours. Book this package at sunset and enjoy the view—of the sunset and each other.

Overlooking the rolling surf of the Indian Ocean, the spa (massage US$65–US$120, beauty treatment US$20–US$120; AE, MC, V; 10am–9pm) at the **Legian** (p. 96) is famous for its totally self-contained single and double treatment suites, each with a private bathroom and steam room. The treatments are diverse: Chose from ayurvedic *shiro dhara,* warm stone massage, and reflexology. Excellent couples' massages are available as well as the exotic royal Javanese *lulur* and Balinese *borah* body wrap.

Spa Venus ★ (Balinese massage Rp160,000–Rp290,000, reflexology Rp160,000, detox, up to 11 days, US$550–US$950; AE, MC, V; 10am–10pm), in the Villa Kubu (p. 99), offers treatments for longer-lasting results. Massage is by blind therapists who miraculously find those spots that need the most attention. Therapies also include acupuncture, naturopathy, craino-sacral therapy, and energy healing.

5 SHOPPING

Shopping in Seminyak is rife with possibilities, if you can just forgive the bumps and grinds of making your way to your destination by car, motorbike, or on foot—a slightly more hazardous prospect. While Kuta remains the focal point for mid-range labels and surfing duds, the goods in Seminyak display local creativity and originality. The junky jewelry that was once commonplace has given way to high-end gems of immense creativity and originality at a fraction of the cost at home. Homewares are another great deal and Balinese home accessories are found in shops literally around the world from Harrods to Home Depot. Shops are typically open daily 9am to 9pm.

Seminyak has a new shopping mall at **Seminyak Square,** on Jalan Laksmana, that stocks a selection of the bigger brand names like Body & Soul (p. 88 in Kuta), Periplus, Quiksilver, and the food shop Casa Gourmet.

Periplus

The best place for maps, books, and magazines is Periplus. The number-one publisher of books on Asia has a chain of 15 bookshops around Bali. Handy stores are outside Bali Deli on Jalan Kunti; in Seminyak Square; next door to Made's Warung on Jalan Raya Seminyak; and in Kuta's Discovery Mall.

SEMINYAK & CANGGU

7

SHOPPING

Getting the Goods Home

From a small lamp to a large 6m (20 ft.) Buddha, the following shippers will arrange pick up, packing, and delivery of your goods: **Limajari,** Jl. Raya Kerobokan 100x (☎ **0361/730024;** www.limajaricargo.com), and **Rim Cargo,** Jl. Laksmana 32 (☎ **0361/737670;** www.rimcargo.com). **Sourcing Bali,** Jl. Gunung Salak 31A, Kerobokan (☎ **0361/744-8025;** www.sourcing-bali.com; Mon–Fri 9am–5pm, Sat till 3pm), will take care of all of your shipping needs and they have "personal shopping helpers" who will assist with negotiations, product selections, order placement, and payment.

JALAN RAYA SEMINYAK

Jalan Raya Seminyak starts at the junction of Jalan Raya Kerobokan and stretches the all the way down to Kuta where it turns into Jalan Legian. The street is littered with small boutiques, clothing and craft shops, and homeware shops. Here are some of our favorites, starting at the top of the road nearest to Jalan Raya Kerobokan:

G and V ★★   G and V is the vision of Giuseppe Verdacchi, an Italian architect known on the island as Beppe. It's almost impossible to describe Beppe's style since his acute eye for beauty ranges from textiles, ceramics, woven fabrics, retro-style '40s furniture and decorations, to Art Nouveau wall tiles from the Dutch colonial period. His tabletop accessories combine stone, silver, wood, and semiprecious gems like turquoise, coral, and black lapis. ☎ 0361/731916. www.gvbali.com.

Dandelion   Adorable is the word for this bambini boutique that dresses little girls in poppy red trench coats and boys in suitably striped sailor tops and shorts appropriate for boating in the Mediterranean. ☎ 0361/730375.

Haveli   Situated opposite each other on Jalan Seminyak are two Haveli homewares showrooms. The collection takes inspiration from the many travels of the owners in Southeast Asia and Europe. The rich fabrics include taffeta, silks, satins, Indian saris, and fine French linens. ☎ 0361/737160. www.havelishop.com

Bali Antique Shop ★   A stellar shop for serious collectors, Bali Antique Shop has two shops now in Bali and a sister shop in Belgium. Artifacts from Cambodia, Buddhas and monks from Thailand, and Singha heads from Sumatra are all waiting to be found. ☎ 0361/737826. www.baliantiqueshop.com.

By the Sea   Recalling visions of family seaside holidays at their best, this delightful collection of family clothing is produced in 100% cotton in fruity hues with stripes, polka dots, floral motifs, and paisley silk screen prints. ☎ 0361/732198.

Disini   The owner here is clearly French as everything is appropriately chic. Quilted bedcovers, cushions, and table linens all come with mix and match accessories. All of the natural fabrics are from Southeast Asia. Clever designs like canvas striped beach bags with matching towels are a hit. ☎ 0361/731037.

Innuendo ★   The silk, chiffon, and cotton separates sold here would sell worldwide at triple the price. Count on finding superb eclectic outfits pretty and perfect for weddings and special occasions, often with matching wraps and accessories to complete the ensemble. The cuts are irresistible and some of the silks are bias cut. Many are delicately garnished with sequins, Japanese glass beads, and Swarovski crystals. © 0361/730790. www. **111** innuendofashion.com.

Dinda Rella ★★★ It feels like Cinderella's walk-in closet here with embellished evening gowns and cocktail frocks that go from understated beige to over the top fuchsia. Evening wear is a fraction of the cost of what it would go for back home but sizes are decidedly small. Have a dress made to order in 5 working days. © 0361/734228.

Papillon Find good-quality shoes and sandals with lots of embellishment at gratifying prices here. Although they export around the world take note that the largest size for woman is US 8½. © 0361/734967.

Biasa ★★ Everybody shops at Biasa, so you know its good value and good quality. The easy, at-home entertaining wear is comfortable, cool, and suitable for Bali's tropical climate. Colorful, classy, and romantic fabrics include soft cottons, muslins, silks, and linens. The lovely scarves and accessories like sequined handbags make great gifts. Upstairs is a floor devoted entirely to menswear. © 0361/730308. www.biasabali.com.

ET Club Glam yourself up with the large selection of brightly colored bags, belts, and shoes bejeweled in beads and stones that are so popular with the Euro jet set. Order one in every color. © 0361/734795.

JALAN LAKSMANA

This is the best shopping street in Bali. Shop after shop of designer goods, to suit all tastes and budgets, are crammed into one street that stretches from outside the Legian Hotel all the way up to Jalan Raya Kerobokan. Designers from round the world, who now call Bali home, have retail spaces and showrooms selling their wares for less than you will find in your own country.

Appropriately located on the corner of a busy thoroughfare, the **Cornershop/tuckshop ★** is the expat hangout for breakfast, lunch, and coffee and also a clothing shop with men's, women's, and kid's clothing by trendy Bali-based designers. Opposite the Cornershop is a tiny shoe box of a shop called **I Love Bali**—filled with brightly colored casual beachwear. Next door is **Buddha Wear** for knitted jersey outfits in an assortment of colors. Up the steps from Buddha Wear, **Sabia** (© 0361/733995) has just the sort of things you need in Bali, St. Tropez, or St. Barts: nifty espadrilles, oversize woven straw beach bags, stylish floppy sun hats, and cool cotton kaftans. A few doors down is **Joy Jewellery ★★** (© 0361/791-4893), by Dutch owner Jenny, a longtime Bali resident. She told me that Beyoncé had just placed a large order and she was rushing to get the delivery on time. Lots of celebrities find her silver and gold jewelry addictive, but mere mortals can purchase them too at about a quarter of what they would cost stateside.

Tips Jalan Mertanadi

If you are looking to furnish your home with treasure from Indonesia, head to Jalan Mertanadi, better known as Jail House Road. The road has large warehouse-size buildings interspersed with smaller specialist shops selling an assortment of items for the home. There is a billiard specialist, large teak furniture manufacturers, model ship makers, French repro furnishing companies, as well as Indonesian antique furnishings and artifacts.

> **Finds**   **Icon Asian Arts**
>
> This innovative gallery of iconic Asian arts, thus the name (Jl. Oberoi 17; ✆ **0361/ 733875;** www.iconasianarts.com; daily 11am–7pm), is run by Bruno Piazza and his partner Susi Johnston, two seasoned figures in art, art history, Asian tribal art, textiles, design, and photography. They bring decades of experience, conscientious collection, and insight into the world of collecting Indonesian tribal art, ethnographica, excavated jewelry, animist art, tribal sculpture, and fine textiles. Their client list reads like the Forbes top 500 but they would never name drop—it's not their style. The gallery, with rotating exhibits throughout the year, adheres to the creed: Discussion, Debate, Discovery, and Authenticity.

For the latest in funky designs and an eclectic mix of accessories, nearby **Prisoner of St. Petersburg** and **Rock n Royalty** are hard to beat. While **Hakari,** over the road, is for those with a more subdued taste in clothes.

Further down the road, for fashionistas, are **Lulu, Lily Jean,** and **Magali Pascal.** Choose from elegant silk dresses, cut-off shorts, and funky accessories.

Religion   This hot underground label presents retro punk designer clothing for men and women—mainly T-shirts, jeans, stretch cotton dresses, and skirts. The sexy, carefree appliqué patchwork and cutwork, distressed textures, and overcooked screen prints and washes are bold and to some beautiful. Styles are off the shoulder, backless, painted, tied, rushed, and customized. ✆ 0361/731916.

Bamboo Blonde   Women flock to this large and airy boutique for sundresses, separates, and accessories. The clothes are as cheery as the designer Louise who can usually be found laughing up a storm as the punters raid her boutique for good quality bargains. This is Bali's answer to Top Shop. ✆ 0361/742-5290.

Simple Konzept Store ★★   The owners of this Italian boutique have worked with Prada, Armani, and other prestigious labels. This two-level shop would be right at home in Milan with an outstanding assortment of his and hers clothing and Vivienne Westwood accessories. ✆ 0361/730393.

Quarzia ★★★   This is a stylish den of fabulous men's and women's hand-painted silk separates made by an Italian husband and wife team. Simonetta is an expert in textiles who studied in Venice before moving to Bali where she uses what she calls the "charming technique of batik" on silk. Men's wrap pants and shirts and ladies dresses, robes, and silk separates are all excellent quality. ✆ 0361/736759.

Maru Gallery ★★   Situated opposite the Legian Hotel, the concept here is "Body–Art–Space," according to American owner Marina Urbas. Currently, Maru has eight international jewelry designers under its wings from Bali, Canada, France, and Italy. Materials range from the usual suspects of precious metals, diamonds, brass, stainless steel, and sterling silver, to the more exotic such as Lombok pearls, shark's teeth, and feathers. Maru has always carried the designs of Nohan, an Indonesian designer who has found success in the international and local market with his own distinctive style and fantastic craftsmanship. Aside from the owner's stunning work, one of the signature labels is Mal, designed by a Canadian woman who makes those "must have and will find

For Men

Jl. Oberoi 1 (ℰ **0361/738776**) is a hideaway gem by the former head designer from Biasa, an old Bali institution, and a favorite of wealthy Italians in town. Classic linens and cottons fill the racks in subtle tones of taupe and gray. The pashmina scarves complete the Euro look in colors to die for and prices to match.

Much further down the road is Deefusion (see below). In the corner of this furniture emporium is **Nico Perez,** another designer who dresses men effortlessly in linen. Choose from a selection of classic pastel and muted colored casual ware.

For Children

Start at the **Cornershop** (see above) for funky T-shirts and separates then head to **Clara Mia's** for sweet, flowery dresses and shirts too cute for words. **Kiki's Closet,** with kitsch kids wear in bright colors with plenty of fun patterns including polka dots, animal prints, and stripes, is popular with Versace-dressed mothers. For those with more subdued taste, plenty of beautiful embroidered and batik clothing is at **Kids A Go Go** suitable for babies and young children.

Interiors

The furniture emporium of **Deefusion** sells a selection of modern furnishings from well-known Filipino designers. The showroom will ship directly to your home from their factory in the Philippines.

JALAN PETITENGET

Studio 13 ★★★ New Sumatran designer Johnny Rimali got caught on the way from Indonesia to Paris and decided to try his luck in Bali. Success has come quickly and Johnny now sells his jewelry and bags to places like Barneys in New York and other high-end boutiques. One of his specialties is canvas and nylon totes that have become coveted items of the in-crowd. ℰ **0361/307-4113.**

Jemme Jewellery This jewelry shop is glittering with gemstones and just the right mix of extravagance and understated elegance. Luke, the English designer, mixes gemstones, cubic zirconia, silver, semiprecious stones, precious gems such as emeralds and rubies, and 18-carat and white gold. ℰ **0361/733508.**

JALAN KEROBOKAN

Ni Luh Djelantik ★★ This large and imposing shop on the intersection of Jalan Raya Seminyak and Jalan Raya Kerobokan sells ready to wear and custom-made shoes and bags in quality leather. Platforms and heels are a specialty and the Indonesian designer is gaining international recognition with Giselle, Kate Moss, and Elle McPherson all having a pair or two. Shouldn't you, too? ℰ **0361/744-6068.**

The Orchard Fine Furniture

The **Orchard,** Jl. Oberoi 33X (ℰ **0361/410397;** www.ibaldesigns.com) is home to iBal Designs. This is a one stop shop for made to order or readymade colonial furnishings and home accessories of understated elegance.

Raya Antiques ★★★   One of the most eclectic collections of antiques on the island, Raya Antiques sells everything from apothecary jars and Dutch colonial pottery to Chinese blue and white porcelain. Everything is stylish, including the owner who runs around town in one of the few vintage cars on the island. ☎ 0361/732312.

Andy's Gallery   A fun Aladdin's den of Indonesian artifacts, antique instruments, and pottery. Take your time and really explore as there are some treasures to be found for sure. ☎ 0361/742-9361.

GROCERIES

Local products are about a tenth of the cost of the same for imported products. The **produce market** near Seminyak, on the corner of Jalan Raya Kerobokan and Jalan Gunung Tangkuban Perahu, has a wide range of seasonal fruits and vegetables as well as snacks—especially peanuts—available in a dozen different ways.

Bintang, Jl. Raya Seminyak 17 (☎ 0361/730552; 7:30am–11pm, Fri from 8am), has all the basics: noodles and rice, fresh fruit and vegetables, toiletries, a limited selection of wines, and imported cheese and dairy. There is also a film-processing counter, a small pharmacy, and a magazine and book stand. Upstairs is a stationery and household section that sells kitchen goods like light bulbs and plastic glasses.

Bali Deli, Jl. Kunti 117X (☎ 0361/738686; www.balideli.net; 8am–10pm), is astronomically expensive. A box of Cheerios goes for US$10. Still, it has a huge range of deli products including meat, fish, and a wonderful choice of cheeses and other dairy, plus fresh fruit, veggies, and baked goods. A courtyard restaurant has an international menu with surprisingly good sushi, salads, pastas, "design your own" sandwiches, desserts, fresh juices, and gourmet coffee.

With good fresh produce, a decent deli counter, and some imported items that won't totally break the bank, the new **Casa Gourmet,** Seminyak Square (☎ 0361/738026; www.casa-gourmet.blogspot.com; 8am–10pm), is giving Bali Deli a run for its money. The excellent ice cream stand will keep the kiddies entertained while you do the shopping.

Grocer & Grind, Jl. Kayu Jati 3X (☎ 0361/737321; www.grocerandgrind.com; 8am–10pm), is equally good for a gourmet fix. You'll find homemade cakes, quiches, take-away sandwiches, paninis, as well as house-smoked salamis and a deli section with meat and cheese.

6 SEMINYAK AFTER DARK

Late night clubbing in Bali happens in Kuta—which is not to say that Seminyak doesn't have its fair share of revelry. The party in Kuta is very different from the one in Seminyak, which draws a much more high-end crowd. **Hypnotique,** Seminyak Square (☎ 0361/732202; www.hypnotiquebali.com), pulls in a respectable and fun crowd. **Hu'u,** Jl. Petitenget (☎ 0361/736443; www.huubali.com), rocks on the weekends with the high life from Jakarta as well as some older clubbers who enjoy music that isn't all thump and pump. **Ku de Ta,** Jl. Laksmana 9 (☎ 0361/736969; www.kudeta.net), is a perennial favorite and mandatory stop of the Bali nightlife circuit and the **Living Room,** Jl. Petitenget 2000X (☎ 0361/735735; www.thelivingroom-bali.com), is a happening spot on the weekends for European expats and wealthy tourists who come to Bali in high season like bees to honey. The latest addition is the **Red Carpet Champagne Bar,** Jl. Laksmana 42 (☎ 0361/737889; www.redcarpetbali.com)—the gals in red hot pants directly on Jalan Laskmana and watch the roving circus outside.

7 CANGGU

Canggu is Seminyak's suburbia. First discovered by surfers looking for new waves outside of Kuta, Canggu's appearance has changed from rolling rice paddies and cattle farms to rows of luxury villas. However it still retains much of its village community feel—a refreshing change from the car-laden streets of Seminyak. It's a 10-minute hop in a taxi from Seminyak. There is no public transportation here. Plenty of surfers head to the waves with their boards on bikes.

All activities in Canggu are based around surfing. This beach is not for the idle as there are a lot of rocky outcrops. Of the several surf breaks, **Canggu** (better known as Tugu; **best swell:** south/southwest; **best size:** 3–5 ft.; **best winds:** east and no wind days) is a popular spot, best during the dry season, April to October. This wave offers punchy, rippable, and super-fun right and left beach break peaks for the masses, all punctuated by a few submarine rocks and marine visitors. This is an early morning wave as lunch time winds are too strong. On lighter wind days you can surf it until dusk. Canggu is often crowded at dawn during the dry season. Look for windless days in the wet season for some off-season respite.

Echo Beach ★ is just north of the surf break and makes for an easy laid-back day in the sand or on a sun lounger. Sunday nights light up with families and live music.

WHERE TO STAY

Most people in Canngu stay in a luxury villa. The older properties tend to have large rolling gardens while the numerous newer ones can be on small plots of land, suitable for those on a budget. There are a few hotels but only one is worth mentioning.

The big Canggu splurge is the mega **Villa Mana** ★★★, Jl. Pipitan Sari, Br. Babakan, Canngu (📞 **0361/730668;** fax 0361/736566; 7 bedrooms; peak season US$1,300; high season US$1,200; low season US$1,000; meals market price; AE, MC, V). Soaring 5m (16-ft.) ceilings shelter the clean and modern design of shimmering dark woods and polished stone with contemporary Balinese art. Wooden decking surrounds the infinity pool and lounge area replete with a tricked-out bar. A whirlpool is perched above the rice paddy with a view to Mount Batukaru; just below is a playing field perfect for soccer and frolicking kids. The seven oversize en-suite bedrooms and industrial strength kitchen make this place party central.

Desa Seni ★★★ The Desa Seni (Artist's Village) is comprised of antique *joglo* and embellished with royal antiques and charming folk art. Vegetable gardens and rice fields surround the pool. Our villa, Rumah Wunga, had bedside lamps made of ox bells; the brightly painted headboard was originally a wall panel from Madura; the armoire was formerly a food storage chest from the 1920s. A twice weekly class in African rhythm and movement meets here.

Jl. Kayu Putih 13, Canggu. 📞 **0361/844-6392.** www.desaseni.com. 10 units. Year-round US$150 standard; US$290 suite; US$360 villa. AE, MC, V. **Amenities:** Restaurant (p. 119); bar; babysitting; bicycles; concierge; outdoor pool; room service; spa. *In room:* A/C, TV/DVD, stereo or CD.

Oazia Spa Villas ★★ At Oazia you get your own villa with a spa that would be more at home in a five-star resort. A dedicated personal assistant picks you up from the airport

A Day in Denpasar

Denpasar, the capital of Bali since 1960, was once an important trading center and the home of the rajahs of Badung before the colonial era. You'll likely pass through from the south on your way to the mountains. The core of the city is a crisscross of streets extending from Jalan Gajah Mada where the **Catur Muka** sculpture commemorates the Badung War. This space of land has since been turned into a peaceful park called **Puputan Badung Square.**

You can easily see Denpasar's center and many sights on a self-guided walking tour. The best time for this walk is a weekend morning when you'll face much less traffic. It will take you from 9am until about 3:30pm, including museum, temple, and dining stops. Start from Puputan Badung Square where your taxi driver can wait for you. Take in the **Jagatnata Temple,** Jl. Mayor Wisnu, dedicated to Sanghyang Widi, the supreme god, built in 1953. The white coral shrine *(Padmasana)* symbolizes the foundation of the world. Next door is the **Bali Museum** ★★ (✆ **0361/222680;** Rp2,000; daily 8am–3pm), constructed in 1910 in *puri-pura* style. The fascinating exhibits have explanations in clear English on textiles, sacred objects, the Balinese calendar, rituals, masks, costumes, puppets, and prehistoric stone sarcophagi, bronze, and other artifacts.

After the museum, go towards the Arab area to hunt for textiles and gold around Jalan Sulawesi. Head towards Jalan Thamrin to visit the **Puri Pemecutan** palace, then the **Pura Maospahit** temple, on Jalan Sutomo, north of the roundabout. A small side lane leads to this peaceful 14th-century temple. The oldest section of this temple was likely brought to Bali from the Majapahit Kingdom—though it has been rebuilt since being badly damaged in 1917 by an earthquake. After the temple, go down on to Jalan Gajah Mada to see the **Badung** and **Kumbasari** markets (corner of Jl. Gajah Mada and Jl. Sulawesi), selling fresh produce, meat, fruit, flowers, and vegetables. The second floor of Badung has textiles, temple elements, and dance costumes. Eating stalls are on the fourth floor. Kumbasari is the handicraft, textile, and souvenir market. The **bird and animal markets** and **Satria temple** are on Jalan Veteran. After the markets, you can easily head back down again towards Puputan Square.

You can watch the *kecak* dance at **Catur Eka Budi,** Jl. Waribang, Kesiman (✆ **0361/238935**), every day at 6:30pm. The **Werdhi Budaya Arts Center,** Jl. Nusa Indah (✆ **0361/227176**), also runs a daily show at 6:30pm.

Getting There Denpasar is reached from the Bypass from Sanur or from Legian and Seminyak through Jalan Imam Bonjol within a half-hour, although roads are very congested between 8 and 9am and 4 and 6pm. From the airport to Denpasar in a **taxi** should cost approximately Rp50,000.

Visitor Information The main tourist office for Denpasar is **Denpasar Government Tourism Office,** Jl. Surapati 7 (Puputan Badung Sq.; ✆ **0361/223602;** Mon–Thurs 7am–2pm, Fri 7–11am, Sat 7am–12:30pm). You can get a free city map here.

Where to Stay Though most visitors do a 1-day visit to the city, if you do decide to stay check out: the **Adinda Hotel,** Jl. Karna 8 (✆ **0361/240435;** fax

0361/235997; high season Rp250,000, low season Rp200,000; AE, DC, MC, V), with air-conditioned rooms; **Hotel Puri Ayu,** Jl. Jendral Sudirman 14A (© **0361/ 245312;** fax 0361/228851; www.puriayu.com; high season Rp600,000, low season Rp500,000; MC, V), near the main business area, commercial district, and government offices; or the **Inna Bali,** Jl. Veteran 3 (© **0361/225681;** fax 0361/235347; www.innabali.com; high season Rp450,000, low season Rp325,000; AE, DC, MC, V), the island's oldest hotel, known for serving cruise passengers in the 1930s. The **Nakula Familiar Inn,** Jl. Nakula 4 (© **0361/ 226446;** Rp90,000; no credit cards), is a family *losmen.*

Where to Dine   Visiting Denpasar provides the perfect opportunity to try authentic Balinese cuisine. Due to few tourists in the city, tastes are geared toward locals. Most restaurants and warungs can be found on **Jalan Sumartra, Jalan Veteran,** and **Jalan Teuku Umar.** The restaurants below are open daily.

For the best *babi guling* in Denpasar, keep your eyes peeled for low tables and the tell-tale pork with crispy skin—there is no sign on this gem. It's on Jalan Sutomo, beside the Maospahit Temple (no phone; about Rp15,000 a plate; no credit cards; mid-morning to about 10pm).

The **Amsterdam Café & Bakery,** Jl. Diponegoro 140 (© **0361/235035;** main courses Rp27,000–Rp100,000; MC, V [Rp100,000 minimum]; bakery 7am–11pm, restaurant from 8am) has veal cordon bleu, steaks, and great orange cheesecake. **Hong Kong,** Jl. Gajah Mada 99 (© **0361/434845** or 420320; main courses Rp18,000–Rp100,000; MC, V; 9am–10pm), has a huge menu with specialties of sliced beef with black pepper, *sapo tahu* (bean curd) seafood in clay pot, fried chicken, and, for the bold, braised sea cucumber. The **Tiara Dewata Food Center,** Jl. Mayjen Sutoyo 55 (© **0361/235733**), is a cheap and clean food court offering dishes from many regions.

The following are on Jala Teuku Umar: **Baker's Corner** (© **0361/243861** or 243863; main courses from Rp20,000; AE, MC, V; 9am–11pm), a reliable bakery-restaurant-lounge with a vast menu of international dishes; **Kak Man** (© **0361/ 227188;** main courses Rp20,000–Rp80,000; no credit cards; 11am–11pm), with *bebek tutu* (steamed duck with Balinese spices); **Raya Sayang** (© **0361/262006;** main courses Rp25,000–Rp65,000; MC, V; 11am–11pm), the best Chinese restaurant in Denpasar.

Of the warungs, try **Warung Sari Boga,** Jl. Sutomo 29C (© **081/353260759;** *nasi campur* Rp8,000; no credit cards; 6am–9pm), for its unbelievably varied textures of tofu and tempeh that look and taste like meat. **Warung Satria,** Jl. Kedondong 11A (© **0361/235993;** around Rp15,000; no credit cards; 8 or 9am–10pm), is famous for *ayam betutu* (chicken), *betutu bebek* (duck), *satay lilit* (fish), and *sambal goreng pedas* (hot sambal). **Warung Wardani,** Jl. Yudistra 2 (© **0361/224398;** main courses Rp25,000; no credit cards; 8:30am–4pm), specializes in *nasi campur.* You might also try the beef satay, *dendeng sapi* (beef cooked crisp and spicy), *hati sapi* (Beef heart), and *chendol* (made of thick coconut milk, palm sugar, red beans).

Bali Buddha & Cafe Moka

The sister restaurant to the Ubud cafe and grocer, **Bali Buddha,** Jl. Raya Banjar Anyar 25 (✆ **0361/844-5935;** main courses Rp40,000–Rp70,000; no credit cards; daily 6am–10pm), in Canggu serves up healthy, primarily organic fare, with a large selection of vegetarian dishes. The small grocer has fresh hummus and yogurt, fresh breads and muffins, and dried and fresh fruits.

A branch of **Cafe Moka,** Jl. Raya Banjar Semer (✆ **0361/844-5933;** main courses Rp35,000–Rp70,000; no credit cards; daily 8am–10pm), has freshly baked baguettes, quiche, and a very good croissant. A small deli counter serves a limited choice of sliced meats and cheeses, milk, and yogurt.

and hands you your own mobile phone with their number plugged in—for the rest of your stay your personal assistant is on call for you. A popular program is the "Women's Goddess Workshop" which includes moon cycle awareness, ritual goddess mythology, and tantra beliefs. A gourmet spa menu offers dishes like poached lobster in a dill lemon sauce and other tempting items that won't put on the pounds.

Jl. Sahadewa, Banjar Anyar, Kerobokan. ✆ **0361/844-6105.** www.oaziaspavillas.com. 3 villas. Peak season US$520–US$1,200; high season US$450–US$980; low season US$370–US$880. AE, MC, V. **Amenities:** Restaurant; outdoor pool; room service; spa. *In villa:* A/C, hair dryer, Wi-Fi.

Pantai Lima ★★ The villas here all face Pererenan black beach. Their modern design mixes Balinese style with the quirky yet sophisticated tastes of the young French owner—*tres chic.* The kitchens are overseen by no less than Sebastian Robuchon, nephew of Joel, who needs no introduction.

Jl. Srikandi, Subak Munggu, Tegallantang, Desa Pererenan, Mengwi. ✆ **0361/844-4555.** Fax 0361/844-9555. www.pantailima.com. 5 villas. Peak season US$2,200; high season US$1,750; low season US$1,500. AE, DC, MC, V. **Amenities:** Babysitting; gym; room service; tennis court; Wi-Fi. *In villa:* A/C, fan, TV/DVD, movie library, stereo or CD, kitchenette.

Tugu Hotel ★★★ (Finds) Owned by a successful philanthropic Indonesian family, this hotel could easily reopen as a living museum. Astounding antiques and art, most notably by Walter Spies and Rudolf Bonnet, from all over Bali and Java are lovingly placed throughout and in the guest rooms. As a member of the Relais & Châteaux hotel collection, this hotel is a magnet for those in the know. Book the Walter Spies suite and get into the melancholy mood of the artist who passionately loved Indonesia—much like the owners of Tugu.

Jl. Pantai Batu Bolong, Canggu. ✆ **0361/731701.** www.tuguhotels.com. 21 units. High season US$330 standard, US$475 suite, US$600 villa; low season US$285 standard, US$435 suite, US$535 villa. AE, MC, V. **Amenities:** 2 restaurants, Waroeng Tugu and Bale Sutra (see below); bar; babysitting; bicycles; gym; outdoor pool; room service; spa; watersports; Wi-Fi (for a fee). *In room:* A/C, TV/DVD, movie library, hair dryer, minibar.

WHERE TO DINE

The Beach House ★★ INTERNATIONAL   The Beach House will bring the '60s back for you. Sunday barbecues draw large groups of friends and family while a live band belts out old classics. An excellent seafood buffet is served nightly on picnic tables and benches set up on the deck and at the waters edge. The blackboard above the bar notes "Honest & Tasty Staff, No Happy Hour Just Happy Endings."

Echo Beach. ℂ **0361/747-4604.** Main courses Rp25,000–Rp50,000. MC, V. Daily 7am–11pm.

Desa Seni Restaurant ★★ INTERNATIONAL   My meal here was so memorable, I had to ask for the recipe. While they happily provided it the chances of me re-creating it are slim at best as some 80% of their produce comes from their own organic gardens on the grounds. Salads use exotic fruits and veggies and main courses stick true to simple tropical classics, with pastas, grilled fish, chicken, and vegetables all accented with local herbs and spices.

In Desa Seni village resort (p. 115), Jl. Kayu Putih 13. ℂ **0361/844-6392.** www.desaseni.com. Lunch Rp40,000–Rp65,000; dinner Rp45,000–Rp75,000. AE, MC, V. Daily 6am–11pm.

Sukerti's ★ (**Finds**) EUROPEAN   This little gem is tucked behind the hideous Legong Keraton Hotel. Despite its unimposing decor and surroundings, it serves up fantastic European fare like a Duck Liver Parfait with Mango Salsa and Consommé Jelly. Jazz music is live every Wednesday to Friday night.

Jl. Pantai Berawa. ℂ **0361/855-0056.** Main courses Rp21,000–Rp42,000. No credit cards. Daily 6–11pm.

Waroeng Tugu and **Bale Sutra** ★★★ (**Moments**) CHINESE/INDONESIAN   Hotel Tugu's two restaurants are the ultimate in intimate dining. **Waroeng Tugu,** an open-air, traditional Balinese kitchen, has authentic pots on display and antique rustic tables and chairs. Meals are cooked in front of you on a wood-burning stove. An excellent choice is the rijstaffel, with chicken curry, chicken satay, beef in coconut sauce, a prawn croquet, egg in a spicy sauce, shredded beef, bean cake, fried grated coconut, yellow pickles, a shrimp cracker—and a banana. The **Bale Sutra** dates back to 1706 when it was used by the Indonesian and Chinese Peranakan family. The stunning red dining room houses a 300-year-old Kang XI Chinese temple. Here you can dine on Chinese cuisine fit for an emperor.

In Tugu Hotel (p. 118), Jl. Pantai Batu Bolong. ℂ **0361/731701.** www.tuguhotels.com. Set menus Rp400,000–Rp500,000. AE, MC, V. Daily 11am–11pm.

Sanur & the Nearby Islands

The tranquil shores of Sanur are fringed by a series of coral reefs that have given safe haven to sailing boats and protected the golden-sand shores from storms for centuries. One of the oldest archaeological remains on the island can be found here, in Pura Belanjong, a temple built by the Buddhist king Adhipatih Sri Kesari Varmma—the first in the sequence of kings and queens of the Varmadeva Dynasty—in A.D. 914. Within this temple is a stone column crowned by a lotus cushion that bears ancient inscriptions in both old Balinese script and Kawi (similar to Sanskrit). Only partly deciphered, it is thought to refer to a military expedition against enemies in neighboring islands, perhaps Nusa Penida, or even some more distant part of the Indonesian archipelago, commemorating victory in battle. Two other similar pillar edicts have been discovered further inland near Tampaksiring and Bangli, documenting further conquests.

Nusa Lembongan, Nusa Ceningan, and **Nusa Penida** make up a group of three islands 20km (12 miles) off the southeast coast near Sanur and offer a sedate and peaceful alternative to the "mainland."

---

1 GETTING THERE & GETTING AROUND

Sanur is just 18km (11 miles) from the airport. Taxis from the airport to town will charge around Rp100,000, and **Blue Bird taxis** can be called (© **0361/701111**) for the return trip for about Rp75,000. The journey takes around 20 to 30 minutes. Plenty of Blue Bird taxis patrol the main Sanur strip, until about 10pm. It's easy to hail a cab. If you are going a long distance, it is best to fix a return journey cost. Don't be afraid to ask them to wait for a few hours, as most drivers are happy to. *Bemo* prowl the streets, operating on a hop on/hop off basis and are an economic way to tour the strip.

Your hotel or villa can arrange a car or car and driver rental. However, if you don't want to pay their commission, you can easily arrange your own from any of the rental car businesses on Jalan Danau Tamblingan, the main drag. Expect to pay from Rp220,00 to Rp550,000 a day for a rental. Some companies also offer insurance packages. Be sure to take one, as it is worth the extra money.

Locals take good advantage of the **seaside path** for morning constitutionals, and it is fun to join them and their dogs, shortly after sunrise or just before sunset, and stroll from one end to the other in the vibrant tropical glow.

Fast Facts   **Sanur**

ATMs The McDonald's, Circle K, Makro, and Hardy all have ATMs, as do the Gazebo Beach Hotel, Grand Bali Beach Hotel, Bali Sanur Besakih Hotel, and Penjor Restaurant.

Banks The following hotels have bank branches on-site: Sanur Paradise Hotel, Grand Bali Beach Hotel, and Sanur Beach Hotel. Individual bank branches are: **Bank Danamon,** Jl. Danau Tamblingan 67; **Lippo Bank,** Kompleks Ruko Sanur Raya 29-30 (℃ 0361/285250); **Bank Mandiri,** Jl. Danau Tamblingan 27 (℃ 0361/282663); **BNI,** Jl. Danau Tamblingan 19 (℃ 0361/282590); **Permata Bank,** Jl. Danau Tamblingan 77 (℃ 0361/270050).

Currency Exchange Money changers are located along Jalan Danau Tamblingan, the main drag, and in the hotels.

Hospitals & Clinics **Sanur Hospital,** Jl. Bypass Ngurah Rai (℃ 0361/289076); **Surya Husada,** Jl. Danau Buyan 47 (℃ 0361/285236); **Dharma Yadnya Private Hospital,** Jl. W.R. Supratman, Tohpati (℃ 0361/224729); **Clinic Laboratorium Sanur,** Jl. Bypass Ngurah Rai (℃ 0361/289078); **Clinic Blanjong,** Jl. Sri Kesari 15 (℃ 0361/287250).

Internet Access Many hotels and villas in the area offer free Wi-Fi. You can buy a Wi-Fi voucher at **Batu Jimbar** (p. 132) and enjoy a coffee and food while surfing in an outdoor setting. Other Internet cafes are on Jalan Danau Tamblingan or Jalan Hang Tuah.

Pharmacies **Guardian Pharmacy,** Jl. Danau Tamblingan 134 (℃ **0361/284343**); **Kimia Farma,** Jl. Bypass Ngurah Rai 232 (℃ **0361/283397**); **Apotik Sanur,** Jl. Danau Buyan 10 (℃ **0361/289312**).

Police Station The police office is on Jalan Bypass Ngurah Rai (℃ **0361/288597**).

Post Office The post office is on Jalan Danau Buyan, open Monday to Saturday 8am to 7pm.

Supermarkets **Hardy,** Jl. Danau Tamblingan 136; along the Ngurah Rai Bypass are **Makro, Sarinah Supermarket & Giftshop,** and **Yudistira Supermarket.**

2 WHERE TO STAY

EXPENSIVE

Bali Hyatt ⟨Finds⟩ With its distinctive architecture of traditional materials such as bamboo, thatch, and natural stone, Bali Hyatt captures the best of Balinese outdoor living. This oasis of vast tropical gardens, secluded lily ponds, and picturesque walkways has been seamlessly melded into the serene village life of Sanur. A vast pool connects the resort and garden to the beach. Upgrade to the Regency Club, Hyatt's "hotel within a hotel," for preferential treatment and daily continental breakfast. Many expats in Asia look at this as their preferred vacation home away from home.

Jl. Danau Tamblingan 89, Sanur. ℃ **0361/281234.** Fax 0361/287693. www.bali.resort.hyatt.com. 386 units. Peak season US$180–US$500; high season based on available rate per the day. AE, DC, MC, V. **Amenities:** 5 restaurants; cafe; 5 bars; babysitting; bicycles; kids' club; concierge; gym; Jacuzzi; outdoor pool; room service; spa; tennis court; watersports; Wi-Fi (for a fee). *In room:* A/C, TV/DVD, hair dryer, minibar, MP3 docking station (suites only).

Tandjung Sari ★★ ⟨Finds⟩ The name of this hotel comes from a small temple on the beach whose name translates as "Cape of Flowers," referring to this frangipani-clad headland.

A Brief History of Tourism in Sanur

In many ways, Sanur's history is a microcosm of Bali's modern history, particularly in regards to tourism. After initial European visitors began arriving in the 1920s, Sanur attracted a number of European artists who established homes here—among them Belgian Le Mayeur, Swiss Theo Meier, and Mexican Miguel Covarrubias. Sanur also attracted Walter Spies and Beryl De Zootes who collaborated and recorded their discoveries in *Dance & Drama in Bali*. Much of the research for the anthropological tome *Balinese Character* compiled by Margaret Mead and her third husband Gregory Bateson, was completed in Sanur during the mid-1930s.

The **Sindhu Beach Hotel** and the **Narmada Hotel,** built in the 1950s, were Sanur's first flirtation with large-scale tourism. Early travelers were delighted with the secluded seaside village, and Sanur began to attract a steady flow of international elite. The **Hotel Bali Beach** was built towards the end of the Soekarno era, with war compensation funds from the Japanese. The construction of this luxurious building, Bali's first ever high-rise, attracted both positive and negative attention: Local sightseers came to Sanur on holiday to view the symbol of Bali's entrance into the world of modernity, while travelers expressed their regret at this blot on the traditional village landscape. In response to the negative reactions a law was passed preventing further construction of any buildings in Bali to a height taller than the coconut palms. This law remains in effect today.

Balinese traditional architecture and decor derived from local arts and crafts became more popular. The **Tandjung Sari Hotel** and **La Taverna** set this trend to some extent. Favored by the early jetsetters of the 1960s, these became the haunt of celebrities, artists, and musicians. By the end of the decade, tourism was booming.

The Bali that met Australian artist Donald Friend in 1967 was dealing with the aftermath of immense social unrest, natural disasters, and rampant inflation, conditions that worked in favor for him and his friend Wija Wawo-Runtu in their acquisition of property and antiquities. These were times when the land by the sea still had little value in the eyes of the Balinese and was only used for grazing cattle or growing coconuts. The beach was also considered a dangerous place to spend time, as not only do demons inhabit the sea but the Sanur beach looks out to Nusa Penida, where the most evil spirit in Balinese cosmology, Jero Gede Mecaling, is believed to dwell.

By the end of the 1960s, Sanur became a focus for a new international set of expatriates and artists seeking their own piece of paradise and Donald's house was an integral part of the expatriate social scene. The fame and notoriety of his **Villa Batu Jimbar,** built in 1975, soon spread to a new generation of Australian artists. As the Tandjung Sari Hotel grew and new developments were built, Donald had considerable influence in evolving what became the "Sanur Style" of low-rise dwellings inter-relating with meticulously designed gardens.

The original hotel opened in 1962 as a four-bungalow extension to the family home of Wija Wawo-Runtu and has today expanded to a 26-bungalow retreat. Set amidst lush gardens on the beachfront, the individual bungalows have evolved from traditional Balinese architecture and have every comfort the guest may desire. Guests are given the kind of service only personal friends could expect, including invitations to cultural events. This is one of the best-kept secrets in Sanur.

Jl. Danau Tamblingan 41, Sanur. ☎ **0361/288441.** Fax 0361/287930. www.tandjungsarihotel.com. 26 units. Year-round US$200–US$340; extra bed US$30. Rates include breakfast. AE, DC, MC, V. **Amenities:** Restaurant (p. 131); bar; concierge; outdoor pool; room service; spa therapy; Wi-Fi. *In room:* A/C, TV/DVD, movie library, stereo or CD, hair dryer, minibar, MP3 docking station.

Waka Maya   Hidden in southern Sanur where coconut groves shade the walkways to the white sand beach, this compound of Balinese-style dwellings has been thoughtfully crafted for both comfort and inspiration. Elements of traditional and rustic art add to the feeling of seclusion, making it the ideal place to unwind, rediscover the serenity of life, and soak up Bali's special atmosphere. A massage center and spa pampers you with a combination of Balinese and Indonesian herbal spices. Relax by a pool designed along the proportions of an ancient Balinese bathing palace. Garden lovers will delight in the mysterious carved statues that peep through lush tropical plantings, ponds, and water features teeming with lilies, lotus, and fish. *Tip:* The Waka Resort is now the location for Kokolulu cancer retreats, which are based out of Hawaii. For more information go to **www.cancer-retreats.org**.

Jl. Tandjung Pingging Pantai, Sanur. ☎ **0361/289912.** Fax 0361/270761. www.wakamayasanur.com. 12 villas. High season US$171–US$335; low season US$147–US$310. AE, DC, MC, V. **Amenities:** Restaurant; outdoor pool; room service; spa; Wi-Fi (for a fee). *In villa:* A/C, hair dryer, minibar.

MODERATE

Flashbacks ★ (Finds)   This welcoming, Australian-owned place right in the middle of Sanur has nine rooms that vary from very modest to spacious and fully equipped. The design is reminiscent of traditional Balinese style in the early days of tourism. Bathrooms are worked in natural stone. This is the kind of place where you immediately feel comfortable and there is always great conversation around the main dining table. Australian barbies and long chats infused with laughter long into the night are a common occurrence.

Jl. Danau Tamblingan 110, Sanur. ☎ **0361/281682.** Fax 0361/281966. www.flashbacks-chb.com. 9 units. Year-round Rp160,000–Rp515,000. Rates include breakfast. No credit cards. **Amenities:** Cafe, the Porch Café (p. 132); saltwater pool; room service; Wi-Fi. *In room:* A/C, TV.

Griya Santrian   Owned and operated by the same family as the Puri Santrian, this resort is an easy walk to restaurants and shops along the main Sanur street. The rooms and the furnishings are a mish-mash of styles, with some simply decorated and others with floral bedcovers and rattan furnishings. The proximity to the beach where the *jukung* boats are enables guests to enjoy the tempo of village life and the local fishermen's daily routine. A gallery has regular exhibitions of art by local artists, photographers, and sculptors.

Jl. Danau Tamblingan 47, Sanur. ☎ **0361/288181.** Fax 0361/288185. www.santrian.com. 98 units. Peak season US$110–US$260; high season US$100–US$250; low season US$80–US$230; extra bed US$30. AE, DC, MC, V. **Amenities:** Restaurant; bar; lounge; Jacuzzi; 2 outdoor pools; room service; spa; watersports; Wi-Fi (for a fee). *In room:* A/C, TV, hair dryer, minibar.

La Taverna ★★   La Taverna was one of the first beachside hotels in Sanur. The rooms are a harmonious blend of Italian and Balinese styles, featuring thatched roofs, hand-crafted antiques, and terrazzo bathrooms. A wide variety of rooms are available, from

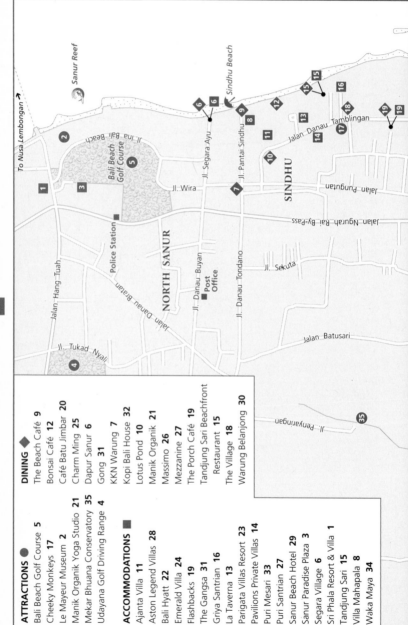

ATTRACTIONS ●
Bali Beach Golf Course **5**
Cheeky Monkeys **17**
Le Mayeur Museum **2**
Manik Organik Yoga Studio **21**
Mekar Bhuana Conservatory **35**
Udayana Golf Driving Range **4**

ACCOMMODATIONS ■
Ajanta Villa **11**
Aston Legend Villas **28**
Bali Hyatt **22**
Emerald Villa **24**
Flashbacks **19**
The Gangsa **31**
Griya Santrian **16**
La Taverna **13**
Parigata Villas Resort **23**
Pavilions Private Villas **14**
Puri Mesari **33**
Puri Santrian **27**
Sanur Beach Hotel **29**
Sanur Paradise Plaza **3**
Segara Village **6**
Sri Phala Resort & Villa **1**
Tandjung Sari **15**
Villa Mahapala **8**
Waka Maya **34**

DINING ◆
The Beach Café **9**
Bonsai Café **12**
Café Batu Jimbar **20**
Charm Ming **25**
Dapur Sanur **6**
Gong **31**
KKN Warung **7**
Kopi Bali House **32**
Lotus Pond **10**
Manik Organik **21**
Massimo **26**
Mezzanine **27**
The Porch Café **19**
Tandjung Sari Beachfront
   Restaurant **15**
The Village **18**
Warung Belanjong **30**

Surfing

Badung Strait

BATUJIMBAR

Bali Crystal

Jalan Danau Tamblingan

Sanur Windsurfing Centre

Jl. Duyung

SEMAWANG

Jl. Kesari

Jl. Karangsari
Ngurah Rai

Jl. Kusuma Sari

Jalan Ngurah Rai By-Pass

Jl. Cemara

Bali Kitesurf School

Jl. Kanda

Jl. Tirta Nusa

BELANJONG

Jl. Tirta Ening

Ena Dive Centre &
Marine Adventures

Jl. Sudamala

Jl. Tirta Nadi 2

Jl. Tirta Ening

Tambaksari

Jalan Danau Poso

Jl. Sekar Waru

Abyss
Adventures

Jl. Mertasari - Sanur Kauh

Jl. Kutat Lestari

Pura Belanjong

Jl. Pengembak

WEST SANUR

Jalan Ngurah Rai By-Pass

To Kuta

Singaraja
BALI
Ubud
Denpasar
Negara
Sanur
Gilimanuk
INDIAN
OCEAN

1/4 km
1/4 mi
0
0

economy rooms to the private bungalow-style duplex or a two-story suite with large daybeds overlooking its own private garden courtyard. La Taverna is famous for its stone-fire pizza oven, the first on the island, and all pasta and breads are made on-site. Tourists from throughout Southeast Asia hold many fond memories of this place and what it lacks in modern facilities it makes up for in its shabby-chic charm.

Jl. Danau Tamblingan 29, Sanur. © **0361/288497.** Fax 0361/287126. www.latavernahotel.com. 45 units. High season US$100–US$1,400 standard, US$200–US$600 suite; low season US$80–US$120 standard, US$150–US$600 suite. Rates include breakfast. AE, MC, V. **Amenities:** Restaurant; babysitting; bicycles; outdoor pool; room service; spa; Wi-Fi (for a fee). *In room:* A/C, hair dryer, minibar.

Mara River Safari Lodge ★ Directly "Out of Africa," this themed resort is a delightful surprise, located within the **Bali Safari & Marine Park** (p. 134). Rustic wooden boardwalks bleached by the tropical sun lead to a cluster of thatched adobe cottages; behind is a re-created tiny African oasis. Each well-appointed room looks out over this picture-perfect view of zebras and onyx grazing savanna-like pastures. A 15-minute drive from Sanur, the lodge features 39 suites from deluxe to family rooms, and directly adjoins the Tsavo Lion restaurant and Simba Bar & Lounge, where plate-glass windows separate guests from the lions outside.

In Bali Safari & Marine Park, Jl. Bypass Prof. Ida Bagus Mantra Km. 19, Gianyar. © **0361/747-5000.** Fax 0361/950555. www.mararivcrsafarilodge.com. 38 units. High season US$145–US$290; low season US$135–US$280. MC, V. **Amenities:** Restaurant; cafe; bar; bicycles; concierge; outdoor pool; room service; spa; Wi-Fi. *In room:* A/C, TV, hair dryer, minibar.

Puri Santrian ★ The Puri Santrian is owned and operated by a local family. Balinese traditions of warmth and generosity of spirit shine through the service of the courteous and attentive staff. The spacious Garden Wing rooms overlook lush gardens, with large balconies or terraces. The Beach Wing rooms, with either garden or pool views, are favored by those who want to be close to the water. The bungalows have two rooms in a traditional Balinese-style building, ideal for those who want the privacy of their own home away from home. Eastern and Western influences converge at the spa offering a wide range of treatments—from Balinese body massage, detoxifying seaweed, and volcanic mud body masks to Phytomer's exclusive European marine-elements based products.

The **Santrian Club** is a vast hotel within a hotel of 60 terraced suites overlooking manicured tropical gardens and an expansive swimming pool featuring a cascading waterfall, a pulsating whirlpool, and spacious lounging pavilions. Using quality local woods and rattan, these spacious suites have all the modern amenities including marble bathrooms. Specially assigned staff pay attention to the guests' every need and services include a complimentary American breakfast, daily fruit platter, and afternoon tea. Children and babies are not allowed in the club rooms.

Jl. Cemara 35, Sanur. © **0361/288009.** Fax 0361/287101. www.santrian.com. 183 units. Peak season US$115–US$175; high season US$105–US$165; low season US$85–US$145; extra bed US$30. AE, DC, MC, V. **Amenities:** 2 restaurants, Mezzanine (p. 130); pool bar; lounge bar; bicycles; 2 outdoor pools; room service; spa; watersports; Wi-Fi (for a fee). *In room:* A/C, TV, hair dryer, minibar.

Sanur Beach Hotel Set on one of the most pristine stretches of the beach in Sanur, this five-star resort has been hosting guests for over 20 years. The endless facilities are tailored to families with children as much as to businesses wanting to use their conference facilities. There are two tennis courts, what seems like an acre of swimming pool (with a yummy bar), a gym, spa, and just about every watersport you can think of. Rooms are well appointed but dated. You check-in here for the facilities and the view not for a luxurious room. Food and drinks cater to large groups with portions to match, but you do get a choice of buffet or a la carte. Many people who come to this resort don't wander—it's that kind of place.

Jl. Danau Tamblingan, Sanur. ✆ **0361/288011.** Fax 0361/287566. www.sanurbeachhotelbali.com. 426 units. High season US$130–US$260; low season US$100–US$230; extra bed US$30. AE, MC, V. **Amenities:** 4 restaurants; 2 bars; bicycles; kids' club; gym; outdoor pool; room service; spa; tennis court; watersports; Wi-Fi (for a fee). *In room:* A/C, TV, minibar.

Sanur Paradise Plaza   The Sanur Paradise Plaza caters to the needs of both the business and leisure traveler, with a vast adjoining convention center. The hotel is on the crossroads at the north end of the village, and the suites are in a separate area 10 minutes away. All rooms surround the tropical poolside gardens and have easy access to restaurants and bars, a fully equipped fitness center, and a traditional spa. Camp Splash! features a 30m (98-ft.) water slide and all-day activities for kids. The resort is an easy walk to the nearest beach, but most prefer to take the shuttle to a more secluded spot.

Jl. Hang Tuah 46, Sanur. ✆ **0361/281781.** Fax 0361/281782. www.sanurparadise.com. 329 units. High season US$110–US$200; low season US$90–US$180; extra bed US$20. AE, MC, V. **Amenities:** 2 restaurants; cafe; bar; kids' club; gym; Jacuzzi; outdoor pool; room service; spa; Wi-Fi (for a fee). *In room:* A/C, TV, hair dryer, minibar.

Segara Village   Parklike garden scenery and stunning ocean outlooks gracefully endow this resort, which follows a unique Balinese village concept. There are five distinct village areas, each seamlessly wrapped in tropical gardens. The newly renovated guest rooms offer warm patches of color, clean lines, and luxurious simplicity. The deluxe rooms feature a state-of-the-art entertainment facility. Three swimming pools and the pristine beach form the foundation for the resort's "fun in the sun" philosophy. The Beach restaurant and bar provides a menu of both Indonesian and international selections. An innovative Jacuzzi bar encourages guests to sip tropical cocktails while enjoying the jets of refreshingly cool water.

Jl. Segara Ayu, Sanur. ✆ **0361/288407.** Fax 0361/287242. www.segaravillage.com. 120 units. Peak season US$135–US$215; high season US$130–US$210; low season US$110–US$190; extra bed US$30. AE, DC, MC, V. **Amenities:** Restaurant, Dapur Sanur (p. 132); bar; lounge; babysitting; concierge; 3 outdoor pools; room service; tennis court; watersports; Wi-Fi (for a fee). *In room:* A/C, TV, DVD and movie library (bungalows only), hair dryer, minibar.

INEXPENSIVE

Puri Mesari   This small private hotel at the secluded southern end of Sanur is perfect for guests seeking a peaceful environment and is only a short stroll from Mertasari beach. There is an open-air sitting area and a library and a restaurant with a large selection of both Indonesian and international cuisine. At the heart of the property is the swimming pool, with a sunken bar, the ideal place to cool off with refreshments, plus a children's pool and play area. The simply elegant rooms are decorated with polished natural stone and bathrooms are made of terrazzo. The warm and friendly service is of a level that could only be provided by a family-run hotel.

Jl. Mertasari 66, Sanur. ✆ **0361/281578.** Fax 0361/285738. www.purimesari.com. 21 units. High season US$50–US$60; low season US$48–US$55; extra bed US$25. MC, V. **Amenities:** Restaurant; babysitting; bicycles; outdoor pool; room service; Wi-Fi (for a fee). *In room:* A/C, minibar.

Sri Phala Resort & Villa A great little hidden gem in a quiet part of Sanur, this recently built property comprises 12 spacious deluxe bungalows each with its own private balcony and swimming pool, with lounge and cocktail bar. Guest rooms with natural wood paneling and carved four-poster beds look out over the swimming pool and lounge area tucked into tropical gardens near the welcoming shade of a pavilion. The large bathrooms are complete with sunken tub and marble basin.

Jl. Hang Tuah III-5, Sanur. ✆ **0361/286479.** Fax 0361/289868. www.sriphala.com. 27 units. Peak season US$70–US$160; high season US$65–US$155; low season US$55–US$145; extra bed US$18, MC, V. **Amenities:** Restaurant; bar; Jacuzzi (in Garden villa only); outdoor pool; room service; spa; Wi-Fi (for a fee). *In room:* A/C, TV, minibar.

VILLAS
Expensive
Aston Legend Villas The Aston Legend Sanur is small but surprisingly sumptuous. Six private villas with one, two, and three bedrooms each have their own pool and a semi-outdoor lounge area with a kitchen, dining area, and air-conditioned bedrooms with en-suite bathrooms. The villas are furnished and decorated to be modern and minimalist, with clever combinations of local tiles, fabrics, and artifacts. The Caramel Restaurant provides delicious meals and refreshments. The Lomi Lomi Spa is replete with an exotic menu of treatments.

Jl. Cemara 33, Sanur. ✆ **0361/270567.** Fax 0361/270562. www.astonlegendsanur.com. 6 villas. Year-round US$350 1-bedroom; US$450 2-bedroom; US$600 3-bedroom. MC, V. Rates include breakfast. **Amenities:** Restaurant; bar; babysitting; concierge; outdoor pool; room service; spa; Wi-Fi. *In villa:* A/C, TV/DVD, movie library, stereo or CD, hair dryer, minibar, MP3 docking station.

The Gangsa ★★ The term *gangsa* refers to the instrument that provides the resonant melody in a traditional gamelan orchestra. Set at the heart of the village, each villa here is nestled within a private garden compound offering open-air living and a gourmet kitchen. A private swimming pool is surrounded by ample deck space for outdoor sun bathing and dining. Guests are offered cooking lessons and taken on picnics, cycle tours, and walks in the rice fields—achieving a rare insider's view of Sanur. A variety of fun and educational children's activities are available in the playroom. Children learn Balinese traditional games and pastimes such as kite-making under the supervision of a trained child minder.

Jl. Tirta Akasa 28, Sanur. ✆ **0361/270260.** Fax 0361/270262. www.thegangsa.com. 11 villas. Year-round US$330. AE, DC, MC, V. **Amenities:** Restaurant, Gong (p. 130); free airport transfer; babysitting; bicycles; kids' club; outdoor pool; room service; spa; Wi-Fi (for a fee). *In villa:* A/C, TV/DVD, movie library, hair dryer, kitchenette, minibar.

Parigata Villas Resort Set in the village of Semawang, at the south end of Sanur, each of the 18 villas here has a plunge pool and Jacuzzi. The on-site coffee shop is open 24 hours. Free shuttle service connects the enclave with a sister resort on the beach, where villa guests can use the beach club and spa.

Jl. Duyung 99, Sanur. ✆ **0361/270133.** Fax 0361/270132. www.parigatahotelsbali.com. 18 villas. High season US$475–US$875; low season US$450–US$850. AE, DC, MC, V. **Amenities:** Restaurant; bar; pool bar; babysitting; outdoor pool; room service; spa therapy; Wi-Fi. *In villa:* A/C, TV, hair dryer, minibar, Wi-Fi.

Villa Mahapala Villa Mahapala has a unique feature: The villa aligns your entire holiday experience with your zodiac sign. The villas, complete with their own private pools, offer a choice of zodiac themes, each villa being individually designed according

> **(Finds)** **Predeparture Spa & Dinner Package at the Gangsa**
>
> The Gangsa has a special afternoon in store for those who have to check out of their hotels early, with flights that don't depart till evening or late at night. Call for a pickup from your hotel. The staff at the Gangsa will store your bags so you can spend the afternoon at the spa. Afternoon tea is provided, and guests are free to lounge away by the pool, before joining in a Balinese rijstaffel dinner and being escorted to the airport.

to a particular zodiac sign. There are two categories of villas, decorated either in subtle pastel or bold colors that define femininity and masculinity.

Jl. Pantai Sindhu, Sanur. ⓒ **0361/286222.** Fax 0361/281222. www.villamahapala-bali.com. 20 villas. Peak season US$500–US$625; high season US$480–US$605; low season US$450–US$575; extra bed US$50. Rates include breakfast. MC, V. **Amenities:** Restaurant; bar; bicycles; concierge; gym; Jacuzzi; room service; spa therapy; Wi-Fi. *In villa:* A/C, TV/DVD, stereo or CD, hair dryer, outdoor pool, minibar.

Moderate

Ajanta Villa   Located just off the beach, these one- and two-bedroom villas all have private gardens and pools, and spacious interiors with luxury bathrooms with a Jacuzzi and a shower. The unobtrusive service caters to guests' every requirement. Private balconies overlook the gardens and pool. Guests seeking privacy can have meals cooked in their villa by an expert cook and dine in the secluded villa garden.

Jl. Danau Tamblingan 21, Sanur. ⓒ **0361/285953.** Fax 0361/283170. www.ajantavillas.com. 10 villas. Year-round US$210–US$250; extra bed US$25. Rates include breakfast. AE, MC, V. **Amenities:** 2 restaurants; bar; bicycles; gym; room service; spa; Wi-Fi. *In villa:* A/C, TV/DVD, movie library, stereo or CD, hair dryer, minibar, MP3 docking station.

Emerald Villa   This property offers one- to four-bedroom villas for sale and rents them out on a profit-sharing basis when the owners are away. Each villa has its own 9m (30-ft.) pool, bathrooms with indoor and outdoor showers, and kitchen. Other facilities that encourage a long-term stay include a washing machine and dryer, Internet, and a dedicated phone line for free local calls. The Emerald Villa is tucked in the back of the village, where native birds abound and there is little noise other than that of the small waterfalls that flow into the pool. Cool terrazzo floors, high ceilings, and elegantly sculpted bamboo finish add a distinctive Balinese style. Guests are appointed a personal concierge and a private housekeeper/butler.

Jl. Karang Sari 5, Sanur. ⓒ **0361/284069.** Fax 0361/270143. www.baliluxuryvillarentals.com. 30 villas. High season US$198 1-bedroom, US$225 2-bedroom, US$296 3-bedroom, US$419 4-bedroom; low season US$175 1-bedroom, US$195 2-bedroom, US$250 3-bedroom, US$310 4-bedroom; extra bed US$30. AE, MC, V. **Amenities:** Restaurant; bar; free airport transfer; babysitting; concierge; room service; spa therapy; Wi-Fi (for a fee). *In villa:* A/C, TV/DVD, stereo or CD, hair dryer, kitchen, minibar, outdoor pool.

Pavilions Private Villas ★★ **(Finds)**   Designed for people who treasure open spaces and nature, the Pavilions, tucked away discreetly at the end of a shady bamboo-lined driveway, is a well-kept secret. On the west side of the main Sanur road, this maze of gardens is an enclave of spacious villas with extra large bathrooms with double vanities, showers, and sunken baths. Personal butler service enables attention to individual preference, dietary needs, and escorted outings. The picturesque central swimming pool has an adjoining bar that serves refreshingly pure juices, properly brewed coffee, and alcoholic beverages. There is a shady massage bale or you can arrange a private spa treatment in your own villa.

Jl. Danau Tamblingan 76, Sanur. ☎ **0361/288381.** Fax 0361/288382. www.pavilions-resorts.com. 23 villas. High season US$260–US$490; low season US$220–US$450. AE, MC, V. **Amenities:** Restaurant; babysitting; concierge; gym; outdoor pool; room service; spa; Wi-Fi. *In villa:* A/C, TV/DVD, hair dryer, kitchenette (in some), minibar, MP3 docking station.

3 WHERE TO DINE

Expect all restaurants in Sanur to be open daily.

EXPENSIVE

Charm Ming ★★ ASIAN FUSION/FRENCH   Brought to you by the owners of Resto Ming, down the road, this charming restaurant is newer and in my opinion better than its counterpart—and I'm just nuts about the name. The creative menu has splendid traditional French and Asian fusion dishes. Snails with garlic butter are always a popular choice, as is the onion soup. Plenty of meat and seafood dishes are on offer for your main course. The beef bourguignon is so tender, it melts in your mouth; the prawns with Balinese spices are another good choice.

Jl. Danau Tamblingan 97. ☎ **0361/288029.** Reservations recommended. Main courses Rp45,000–Rp200,000. AE, MC, V. From 5pm.

Gong ★ BALINESE/INTERNATIONAL   Access this hideaway through the traditional Balinese door that leads into the Gangsa private villas in the depths of Sanur village. The chef of the day takes the time to explain his cooking traditions, why offerings are made before the rice is served, how the spices are crushed, the multiple uses of cinnamon, and all the fascinating little points and tips that will become the memorabilia of a holiday in Bali. He may even invite you back for a cooking lesson. Two menus are offered—one Balinese and the other international. Even for those already familiar with Balinese cuisine this is a menu full of rare treasures. *Sup labu don bayem,* a pumpkin and mixed seafood soup with wild spinach and coconut milk, warming, light, and tasty, makes a terrific starter. Their rijstaffel offers a perfect introduction to Balinese food. A daunting dessert menu of traditional sweets will tempt the glutton in you. Call for directions or ask to be picked up.

In the Gangsa (p. 128), Jl. Tirta Akasa 28. ☎ **0361/270260.** www.thegangsa.com. Reservations recommended. Main courses Rp60,000–Rp150,000; rijstaffel Rp225,000 per person (10 dishes). AE, MC, V. 7am–11pm.

Lotus Pond ASIAN/ITALIAN   The Asian menu here highlights noodle specialties and the Italian menu serves up a seafood spaghetti to die for. For regional delicacies try the green mango Thai salad and Indian samosa. For the best of Bali you can't go wrong with the rijstaffel. Bring the family—there's plenty of room and when the kids get bored they can relax or lie down in the comfy chairs of the adjoining lounge. *Tip:* The owner is an avid ceramics collector and he has set up a minimuseum here.

Jl. Danau Tamblingan 30. ☎ **0361/289398.** Reservations recommended. Main courses Rp50,000–Rp105,000; *bebek betutu* order 24 hr. in advance Rp95,000; 3-course menu Rp110,000. MC, V. 8am–11pm.

Mezzanine ★ PAN-ASIAN   A special chef is assigned to each cuisine at Mezzanine—Thai, Japanese, Chinese, and Western—and you could come back every night for a

> **Moments Balinese Dance Lessons**
>
> On Friday and Sunday afternoons, the local children come to the Tandjung Sari beach *wantilan* (adjoining the pool and restaurant) for lessons in traditional Balinese dance by some of the most famous classical *legong* dancers on the island. This regular gathering is organized by the **Tandjung Sari Foundation** (www.tandjungsarihotel.com/news.html), to foster the preservation of the arts for the future generations. Take a moment and watch the future artisans of Bali perfect their form. They will be delighted you are taking an interest.

month without getting bored. Choose from the small sushi bar, or watch the action at the teppanyaki grill. If you like traditional hot food, ask them to make it in original spicy style, as the standard here is rather subtle to please the sensitive Western pallet. The Thai chef suggested we try the Thai beef salad—*yam neua yang*—and the tofu curry and pad Thai. Salmon in black-bean sauce—*salmon yang tar-si*—is a delicious fusion, and the duck curry—*gaeng phat ed yang*—is very flavorful. The Japanese and Chinese menus offer an equal array of choice, with the standard fresh sushi, California rolls, and tofu salad. Ask for the Japanese chef's special creation. The Chinese king prawn in garlic aioli sauce and the chicken teppanyaki are divine, as is the beef tenderloin. Talk about being spoiled for choice—this is the place.

In the Puri Santrian (p. 126), Jl. Mertasari. ✆ **0361/288009.** www.santrian.com. Reservations recommended. Main courses Rp60,000–Rp200,000. MC, V. 6–11pm.

Tandjung Sari Beachfront Restaurant ★★ INDONESIAN The legendary Tandjung Sari Beachfront Restaurant does not change. The favorite spot in its heyday for hosting the who's who visiting the island, it still has retained its exquisite simplicity. There were nights when Mick Jagger and friends gathered around the bar, and nobody took any notice. The signature rijstaffel is painstakingly prepared with all the hand-ground roots and spices, and the *pepes ikan* snapper with Indonesian spices in banana leaf is a testament to the subtle flavors that once made Indonesia a favored destination of the spice-trading ships. Try a dessert reminiscent of colonial days: the *klappertart* coconut pie or Balinese crepes, *dadar unti.*

In the Tandjung Sari (p. 121), Jl. Danau Tamblingan. ✆ **0361/288441.** www.tandjungsarihotel.com. Reservations recommended. Main courses Rp70,000–Rp95,000. AE, MC, V. 6:30am–10:30pm.

MODERATE

The Beach Café INTERNATIONAL This is one of the best places to grab a bite to eat on the beach. The frittatas are an excellent alternative breakfast dish and seafood pasta is especially good, but order half the portion.

Sidhu Beach. ✆ **0361/282875.** Main courses Rp45,000–Rp89,000. MC, V. 7am–11pm.

Bonsai Café ★ INDONESIAN/SEAFOOD Plenty of similar restaurants line this strip, but this one is slightly different because of its unique bonsai garden. The oldest bonsai tree here is apparently 500 years old but most of the others range from 15 to 50 years old. The cafe serves excellent seafood and always has a selection of freshly caught fish and seafood on display.

Jl. Danau Tamblingan 27. ✆ **0361/282908.** Main courses Rp30,000–Rp68,000. MC, V. 7am–11pm.

Café Batu Jimbar ★★ CAFE   Known as the best place for wholesome organic salads, and a popular haunt for the rich and famous, this upmarket cafe is generally bustling for breakfast, lunch, and dinner. The sign of a good restaurant is its return clientele, and by the sight of all the familiar happy faces sitting out on the teak deck watching the world go by, Café Batu Jimbar has accomplished this with flying colors. Choose from the wonderful array of fresh juices or opt for some good wine from the chiller. The to-die-for mushroom soup and mascarpone cheese are served with Kayu Api crusted bread. The Batu Jimbar salad is legendary: a huge plate of green salad, asparagus, eggplant, beetroot, sweet corn, and beans served with raspberry vinaigrette. And for those needing a protein fix there is the Australian tenderloin, Angus strip loin, and lamb. The Indonesian dishes are spicily authentic, and fresh cakes are baked daily. Sunday is market day, when the local organic farmers and artisans bring their fresh wares to sell, and benches are set up with all kinds of Indonesian traditional cakes and snacks—there are even some quality hand-crafted clothes, bags, and jewelry.

Jl. Danau Tamblingan 75a. ⓒ **0361/287374.** Reservations recommended. Main courses Rp45,000–Rp145,000. AE, MC, V. 7:30am–10:30pm.

Dapur Sanur INTERNATIONAL/SEAFOOD   The beachside restaurant at Segara Village, long known as Le Pirate, has recently been renamed as the Dapur Sanur, or Sanur's kitchen. Your meal here will be of wholesome, fresh food in large servings accompanied by a delicious homemade spicy *sambal,* Balinese style. There is a daily fresh "fish market" on the beach where you can select from an array of fresh snapper, king prawns, lobster, and squid, and have it barbecued to your liking. An array of pasta and salads are available and the menu offers fresh juices and mocktails, or wine.

In the Segara Village (p. 127), Jl. Segara Ayu. ⓒ **0361/288407.** www.segaravillage.com. Main courses Rp40,000–Rp85,000. MC, V. Noon–3pm and 5–10pm.

Massimo ★★ ITALIAN   If you're seeking to spend an evening in a warm family atmosphere and to enjoy some fine Italian dining at an affordable price, then Massimo's is the place. You can't miss it as you are welcomed by a huge array of tempting gelatos on the street in front and Massimo himself is usually around to greet you. Massimo makes his own gelato, pasta and ravioli, mozzarella, and bread. The pasta with ricotta, pachino tomatoes, olives, chili, and mint, and the white and green fettuccine with four cheeses and prosciutto ham are amazing. The wood-fired pizzas have a crispy crust. Try the house's specialty, Pizza Roll, or order some *calzoni.* Kids will love the dramatic Pizza Volcano. Very quaffable Spanish and Australian wines are also available.

Jl. Danau Tamblingan 228. ⓒ **0361/288942.** www.massimobali.com. Reservations recommended. Main courses Rp25,000–Rp89,000. MC, V. 11am–10:30pm.

The Porch Café INTERNATIONAL   This is a groovy place for breakfast and lunch. Lots of delicious Aussie fare here includes homemade pies, burgers, dory fish filets, and bangers and mash. You can also choose from a selection of excellent tapas and gourmet sandwiches.

In Flashbacks (p. 123), Jl. Danau Tamblingan 110. ⓒ **0361/281682.** Main courses Rp20,000–Rp50,000. No credit cards. 7am–11pm.

The Village ITALIAN   This stylish restaurant with pristine white tablecloths and comfortable expansive lounges seems to simply beckon one in off the street. It is a rare privilege even in these times in Bali to be able to enter a walk-in, climate-controlled wine cellar and choose a wine to accompany your meal. The Venetian scallops in white wine sauce and the portobello mushrooms topped with baked cheese were hard to resist, and the memory lingered on with the crisp white wine.

Jl. Danau Tamblingan 47. (C) 0361/285025. Main courses Rp48,000–Rp85,000. AE, MC, V. 11am–11pm.

INEXPENSIVE

KKN Warung WARUNG   This warung used to be across the road from where it now stands and during the day it was a garage. At night they moved the cars out and the tables in and it became a restaurant. If you go in the evening it's best to arrive around 6pm. They do a very good *enak bebek baker, cah kangkung,* and grilled fish. They don't speak a lot of English but don't let this put you off. The *sambal* will get your motor running, so to speak.

Jl. Tandakan 5 Sindhu. (C) 0361/282424. Main courses Rp12,000–Rp30,000; grilled fish Rp7,000 per kilo. No credit cards. 11am–11pm.

Kopi Bali House INTERNATIONAL   With its striking signage stretching up over three floors of shops, it is pretty difficult to miss Kopi Bali House. The range of coffee, imported and local, absolutely dazzles. The menu is eclectic and well executed. First prize goes to the *sop buntut* (spicy oxtail soup) and smoky *ayam panggang* (chicken grilled with Balinese spices). Expats missing home can settle for classic fish and chips. The desserts are too good to be missed, with almond dacquoise and blueberry cheesecake. End with the full-bodied aftertaste of a perfectly prepared Bali coffee and the palate will be replete.

Jl. Bypass Ngurah Rai 405E. (C) 0361/270990. www.kopibalihouse.com. Main courses Rp30,000–Rp99,000. AE, MC, V. 8am–11:30pm.

Manik Organik ★ VEGETARIAN   This great little vegetarian health food restaurant serves up predominantly organic, light meals, salads, sandwiches, soups, snacks, fresh juices, as well as great coffee and teas. The home-cooked food here has no use for preservatives or additives, and they are serious about the quality of food they produce. Try their delicious pumpkin soup and their Tiny Tofu salad: roasted tofu with tamarind sauce served on a bed of mixed salad.

Jl. Danau Tamblingan 85. (C) 0361/855-3380. Website for produce only: www.manikorganik.mione group.com. Main courses Rp30,000–Rp41,000. AE, MC, V. 9am–9pm.

 Kopi Lubak

Famous for having the best Bali coffee on the island (the Arabica grown in the mountainous region of Kintamani), the Kopi Bali House is also the only place on the island where the infamous *kopi lubak* civet coffee from Sumatra is served. The coffee cherries eaten by and passed through the digestive tract of the Asian palm civet (Paradoxurus hermaphroditus) are collected and processed hygienically then given a medium roast, so as not to destroy the complex flavors that develop through the process. Jack Nicholson favored *kopi lubak* in the recent film *The Bucket List,* which has given the coffee a new-found popularity in the West— bringing smiles to many farmers in Kintamani.

Warung Belanjong ★ BALINESE   For a delicious selection of Balinese food in a clean and ordered environment, this is the place to go for lunch. The *siap betutu* is a must try—tender and succulent with a deliciously spiced stuffing, it has a subtle smoky flavor of wood fire. Try the *tum siap,* minced chicken cooked in banana leaves, or *pepes be pasih,* fresh fish grilled with spices in banana leaves. *Nasi campur* is the most popular. The menu has no pork. The Indonesian and European food is excellent and there is plenty of choice for vegetarians. The secret ingredient in the hamburgers, served Australian style, is beetroot.

Jl. Danau Poso 78. ✆ **0361/285613.** Main courses Rp16,500–Rp39,000. No credit cards. 9am–10pm.

---

4 EXPLORING SANUR

A recent addition to Sanur's cultural preservation efforts is the **Mekar Bhuana Conservatory** ★★, Jl. Penyaringan 24 (✆ **0361/842-7030** or 08/1999191104; www.bali music.org). After more than 11 years of intensive research in villages across the island, New Zealand ethnomusicologist Vaughan Hatch and his wife, *legong* dancer Putu Evie Suyadnyani, began to realize their mission of cultural preservation by opening a center where people can appreciate and learn about the endangered performing art-forms in Bali. The center has five sets of antique gamelan, a performance space, as well as an archive, and has recently released its first audio recording. Private and group courses are available. Special tours visit workshops where traditional instruments are made, and presentations of the rich array of traditional dance and ceremonial costumes can be arranged.

Bali Bird Park ★★★ (Moments)   Just 15 minutes north and slightly east of Sanur is the Bali Bird Park. The main priority of the park, other than breeding, is that all birds taken in are given the opportunity to return to the wild. All the birds have their own, well-tended environment, sympathetic to their natural habitat with different species mixed together. There are some 2,000 varieties of plants alone, and 250 different species of birds with over 1,000 birds in total. Among the rarer species are six varieties of the famed bird of paradise, which until recently, were only found in a few remote islands in Papua. Other birds include some of the world's most endangered species, the Bali starling, along with the Javan hawk, the cassowary, various types of eagle, and even a few komodo dragons. Don't forget to catch at least one of the free spectacular bird shows that run through the day. The cafe has Western and Indonesian food. They sell some of the tastiest ice cream, all made on the island, and the juices are worth every penny.

Jl. Serma Cok Ngurah Gambir, Singapadu, Batubulan, Gianyar. ✆ **0361/299352.** www.bali-bird-park. com. Adult US$24, children ages 2–12 US$12. Daily 9am–5:30pm.

Bali Safari & Marine Park ★★   Set on 40 hectares (99 acres) of splendid natural habitat, the Bali Safari & Marine Park has 400 animals from regions including Indonesia, India, and Africa. The many sensational highlights include a traditional Balinese purifying sacred bath, the story of man-eating lions in Tsavo of Kenya, and the majestic white tigers of India. This park is the latest establishment of the world-renowned Taman Safari Indonesia, a name made famous for more than 20 years of efforts in nature conversation and recreational business. Bali Safari & Marine Park is tremendously active in protecting endemic and endangered species, as well as orchestrating educational campaigns to save the animals. Shows run throughout the day and, compared to Western prices, this place is a bargain. A Jungle Hopper Package for about US$25 includes the entrance fee, Safari

(Kids) Cheeky Monkeys

Situated down a little alley, off the main drag, **Cheeky Monkeys** ★, Jl. Danau Tamblingan 82 (℗ **0361/282420;** www.cheekymonkeysbali.com; registration Rp100,000; daily care Rp150,000 for 8:30am–noon, Rp35,000 per hour after; daily 8am–4pm), is a children's drop-in center that is also a kindergarten and pre-school. They have plenty of toys, a sweet little garden with playhouses, a trampoline, a restaurant serving organic food, and indoor rooms. The lovely staff will ensure your children have lots of fun and meet other children their own age. Activities throughout the day keep your little ones entertained: art classes, cooking, storytelling, and games. The nursery can provide short-term care for visiting families with children under 6 years old; drop-ins are available from 8:15am until 4pm daily. This is the favored nursery in Sanur among the local expats.

Tram Tour, free entry to the Water Park, and unlimited access to the Theme Park Rides as well as one photo with an animal. While having lunch you can watch white tigers at play in their natural habitat. You can also stay overnight in the park (p. 126), for more animal viewing time.

Jl. Bypass Prof. Dr. Ida Bagus Mantra, Km 19.8. ℗ **0361/950000.** www.balisafarimarinepark.com. Admission Rp85,000. Mon–Fri 9am–5pm; Sat–Sun 8:30am–5pm. Pickup can be arranged.

Le Mayeur Museum ★★   The artist Le Mayeur came to Bali in 1932. His original plan was to stay for 8 months. However, he was deeply impressed by the temple rituals and dances, and further entranced by a young *legong* dancer called Ni Pollok. Bali had worked its magic, and in 1933 he returned, settled in Sanur, and ultimately married Ni Pollok, who became the main subject of his paintings. Le Mayeur's studio is now a museum and gallery. Although time and the damp seaside salt sprays have taken their toll on the art works, the museum is well worth a visit. Due to his Belgian nationality, Le Mayeur was not sent to prison camp during World War II, but placed under house arrest by the Japanese, so he was able to continue his work. His place was ransacked, but fortunately he managed to keep his paintings. Wartime shortages meant he had to use rice sack-cloth called *bagor* instead of canvas. Unfortunately, these works have not aged well.

Jl. Hang Tuah. ℗ **0361/286201.** Admission Rp5,000. Sun–Thurs 8am–4pm; Fri 8am–1pm.

CYCLING   All big hotels have rental bikes, and Sanur is the ideal place to cycle around, especially by keeping to the back roads. It is best to set out early morning or late evening, when the weather is cooler and the roads not too busy.

The best place to cycle is down the promenade. The 5km (3-mile) stretch takes you from one end of Sanur all the way to the other, passing cafes, restaurants, and fishing boats along the way. The early evening is the best time to ride the beach as you get to mix with the friendly locals enjoying the sea and sedate atmosphere. The ride itself is easy and suitable for the whole family.

There are a few places to rent bikes on Jalan Danau Tamblingan and also along the promenade itself. Prices can vary according to season. Off season the prices will be less but with the arrival of high season the prices shoot up. Don't pay more than Rp50,000.

If you would like to join a tour, the **Segara Village** hotel (p. 127) runs regular bicycle tours of Sanur.

DIVING & SNORKELING   At least 50% of Bali's dive companies are in Sanur even though the diving here is not very good. Instead, Sanur makes a great base for diving expeditions further afield. The coral reef that follows the coastline is less than 1km (less than 1 mile) off the beach of Sanur. While the waters here are okay for snorkeling, those learning to dive, and those looking for refresher courses, it is not recommended for experienced divers. There's very little coral, few fish, and often very low visibility. Another consideration is the strong current and the shallow waters at low tide.

For **snorkeling,** many boats are available for hire to go out to the reef at high tide, including glass-bottom boats if you don't want to get wet. There's usually a surface current but the boat will follow you. Don't allow the boatman to drop anchor, which is highly damaging to the reef. He should use the moorings available.

The following dive operators are reliable and always maintain their dive equipment. They also offer valid insurance cover. Be wary of people approaching you offering cheap courses. Costs generally run US$90 to US$125 for a day trip; US$525 for 3 days, 2 nights; and US$935 for 7 days, 6 nights.

Abyss Adventures, 36B Jl. Danau Poso (✆ **0361/271317;** www.abyssadventures. com), offers technical diving (and tech dive training) and recreational diving if requested. **Bali Crystal,** Jl. Tamblingan 168 (✆ **0361/286737;** www.crystal-divers.com), specializes in Instructor Development Courses (IDC) and will provide recreational diving if requested. **Ena Dive Centre & Marine Adventures,** Jl. Tirta Ening 1 (✆ **0361/288829;** www.enadive.co.id), a five-star Gold Palm PADI dive school, can arrange introduction lessons, PADI courses, and diving throughout Bali.

GOLF   The **Bali Beach Golf Course,** Jl. Hang Tuah 58 (✆ **0361/287733;** www.bali beachgolfcourse.com; 9 holes US$54; 18 holes US$67, prices include green and caddy fees and government tax; driving range Rp35,000 for 50 balls; caddies available at no extra charge but a discretionary tip of approximately Rp30,000 is welcome; club hire Rp22,000 per club or Rp175,000 for the set; call ✆ **08/1210040612** for lessons with a pro; 1-hour lesson Rp500,000, including 100 balls), is a 9-hole course in front of the Grand Bali Beach Hotel among mature, tall trees, sculptured gently rolling fairways, and water features. Subtle breaks keep the golfer guessing and are well-bunkered, leaving little room for errant shots. They also have a floodlit night driving range, the only one in Bali, open daily from 7 until 11pm.

Udayana Golf Driving Range (✆ **0361/289603;** Rp14,000 morning; Rp15,000 afternoon for 50 Balls; club rental Rp30,000 per club, Rp150,000 for set; trainer Rp100,000 for 1 hour, excludes balls and clubs; daily 7am–8pm) is another option for practice, just a few kilometers down the road west of the Grand Bali Beach Golf Course on Jalan Hang Tuah.

KITE- & WINDSURFING   Sanur has ideal conditions for windsurfing with its sheltered 5km-long (3-mile) lagoon. Sanur's protective reef creates flat-water cruising conditions inside the lagoon with waves on the reef varying from small to mast height, and the Serangan Island channel is good for speed—the wind there is always a few knots stronger than elsewhere. Rental boards are available along the beach in Sanur and generally hotels will be able to provide information on the most convenient supplier. For wind and wave information around Sanur call ✆ **0361/288011,** ext. Blue Oasis.

Bali Kitesurf School, Jl. Cemara 72 (② **0361/284260;** www.bali-kitesurfing.org; 75-min. introduction Rp350,000; 2-hr. level one Rp900,000; 75-min. level two Rp650,000; 75-min. level three Rp650,000), was the pioneering International Kite-boarding Organization center in Indonesia in 2004. Just in front of the club is a good kite-surfing spot in both seasons, during medium-low to high tide.

The **Blue Oasis Beach Club** (www.blueoasisbeachclub.com) at Sanur Beach Hotel, Jl. Danau Tamblingan (② **0361/288-011;** kitesurfing $95–$145, board rental $20–$50, kite rental $35–$70; windsurfing $65–$85, rental $25–$80) rents Hobie Cats, lasers, and windsurfing boards. Courses are also available.

SAILING　The **Royal Bali Yacht Club** aims to encourage and promote the sport of sailing in Bali by providing a forum where both experienced and beginner sailors can meet to learn or practice their skills. Boat ownership is not necessary to join the club—it's possible to join a boat-owning member for sailing. Laser races are held on several Sundays each month at times suitable to the tide and wind. Tall boats are moored at a clubhouse at Serangan. Regardless of whether you are a novice or an old salt, the club makes a special dispensation to tourists to try out the club. For the latest event calendar check **www.royalbaliyachtclub.com**. This is such a small club that if you want to speak to someone, it's best to call the Commodore directly (② **08/1353026067**).

SPAS　Spas are open daily. The stunning spa (Anom Rejuvenating Massage US$60, avocado scrub US$40; AE, DC, MC, V; 9am–10pm) in the **Bali Hyatt** (p. 121) has an Anom Rejuvenating Massage that starts with a therapeutic scrub of copra, dried coconut flesh, pine, and lavender flowers to gently remove dead skin before a combined Swedish and acupressure massage. The avocado body scrub is great for rehydrating the body, and is ideal for anybody suffering jet lag.

The **Jamu Traditional Spa** (traditional treatment US$65–US$80, contemporary treatment US$65, massage US$25–US$65, packages US$80–US$100; AE, MC, V; 9am–9pm), in the Tandjung Sari (p. 121), honors traditional local therapies. Scrubs are a favorite choice here and employ natural ingredients like candlenuts, coconut, tea leaves, as well as the blended spice mixtures of *boreh* and *lulur*—time-honored ingredients that have superb results. Two very local treatments are the Kerokan Massage, which uses a small coin-size seed to massage your back and neck, and the Selendang, a body wrap used by Indonesian women post-childbirth to help regain elasticity.

Rebab (single treatment US$35–US$75, package US$80–US$100; MC, V; 9am–6pm) in the Gangsa (p. 128) is not to be confused with a rehab spa. Instead, you will find a holistic spa with a menu of traditional Balinese healing and beauty rituals using indigenous herbs, spices, and plants. The spa's mantra of wellness is based on the Hindu belief that balance is the essence to overall physical and spiritual wellness.

The spa (the Touch US$25–US$75, the Rituals US$60–US$90, *lanang bagus* rituals US$55–US$80; AE, DC, MC, V; 8am–9pm) in the **Waka Maya** (p. 123) has aroma-therapy. Try the Sutra massage: a full-body massage combining pressure points, deep-tissue massage, and long strokes to relieve tension. You can chose your own scent like Crystal Breeze, a blend of bergamot, lemon, and musk meant to clear the mind and stimulate and uplift while restoring a sense of balance.

SURFING   The best time to surf this coast is the rainy season, September to March.

Sanur Reef   Best swell: south; **best size:** 4 to 6 feet; **best winds:** west-southwest. Turn right at the lights at Sanur and you will find yourself staring at a magically long surfing set-up once you manage to park the car. The wave itself is very long and very fun and is a favorite with the crowds on wet season big days.

Serengan   Best swell: south; **best size:** 4 to 6 feet; **best winds:** west-southwest. This wave is in an area protected from turtle poachers, you can only get access with identification. Please remember to bring it. Turn right, heading toward Sanur from Kuta opposite the Makro and weave your way along a confusing split road. Look out for oncoming traffic, too. Pass through the village of Serangan and head out onto the reclaimed Turtle Island through the boom gates and drive through the weird, desertlike ambience toward a series of shoreline warungs. A left and right break here are an easy paddle from the beach. Leave your keys and gear with a warung and be sure to buy a thank you Bintang on the way out. Check out the karaoke-style beach discos in the village of Serengan on the way home. Wear booties if you can or surf the higher tide. A secret spot just a few years ago, Serengan now attracts the masses.

SWIMMING & BEACHES   The Sanur reef makes the ocean here ideal for surfers and also people with young kids along the shore side. Sanur does not get a strong beach break like Kuta or Seminyak. Swimming is only possible at high tide as low tide exposes the reef. Swimming outside the reef is not recommended.

YOGA   Balispirit runs yoga classes at **Manik Organik Yoga Studio ★★**, Jl. Danau Tamblingan 85 (Jeni ℂ **08/1338680835** or Fira 08/176655732) daily. Classes are drop in and open level and cost Rp90,000 (buy 10, get two free). Yoga mats and blocks are provided. Private classes can be arranged, see Balispirit's Private Tuition/Personal Training page. Schedules are at **www.balispirit.com**.

5 SHOPPING

Shops are typically open daily, 9am to 9pm.

CLOTHING

Ibisa   Owned by a former fashion retailer from Sydney's trendy suburb of Paddington, this boutique is a study in cool. Lovely linen and cotton pieces in both plain and prints are perfectly lined on rails and shelves, creating a story for a more classic dresser. Jl. Danau Tamblingan, opposite Griya Santrian Sanur. No phone.

Nogo ★   This is one of Bali's best fabric and textile retailers and is a destination in itself for lovers of local textiles. There is a lot to see and learn here. A good selection of *ikat* and *endek* are available. Prepare to bargain. Jl. Danau Tamblingan 100. ℂ **0361/288765.**

GROCERIES

The Pantry   This delightful deli next door to Café Batu Jimbar (p. 132) stocks a selection of imported foods, including cheese, cold meats, chutneys, pastas, and a small and decent selection of wines. There is a good confectionery section and freshly baked breads that come from the cafe. Jl. Danau Tamblingan. ℂ **0361/281048.**

Sanur Deli & Annie Salon Pop by here in the morning for fresh Australian-style deli foods, snacks, and salads, and whopping great loaves of freshly baked German rye bread. Stock up on the deli's latest range of delicious tropical jams, pickles, and chutney, and order a cake. If you have extra time on your hands, get your hair colored and cut and have a manicure and pedicure at Annie's Salon next door. Jl. Danau Poso 67. ℭ 0361/270544.

HOMEWARES

A-Krea ★★ This is a lovely place to browse and pick up gifts. A beautiful selection of homewares and some stylish clothes and accessories can be found here. The store also stocks a selection of traditional batiks, some bamboo baskets, and seashell items. Jl. Danau Tamblingan 51. ℭ 0361/286101.

Griya Santrian Art Shop Across the road from Nogo, in what is fast becoming the pocket of luxury shopping in Sanur, is the newly opened Griya Santrian Art Shop, beside the Village Italian restaurant (p. 132). The large shop features a boutique section, upmarket handicrafts, designer jewelry, a selection of textiles, and homewares. Jl. Danau Tamblingan. ℭ 0361/288181. www.santrian.com.

Gudang Keramic ★ Samples and seconds from the Jenggala range are piled high here, making this a popular haunt for bargain hunters. A ceramics facility is attached for those who would like to try their hand at creating their own designs. Also part of the complex is an interesting selection of glass sculpture, some of which is available for sale. Jl. Danau Tamblingan. ℭ 0361/289363.

Hug A Bug On the main street, this is one of the few places catering to young children. Hug a Bug stocks books in a variety of languages as well as toys and handmade furniture, some clothing, and fancy dress. Jl. Danau Tamblingan 71. ℭ 0361/288445.

Uluwatu This two-story shop features beautiful handmade Balinese lace and a wonderful assortment of bedding, tablecloths, and a line of classic clothing. White predominates. Jl. Danau Tamblingan. ℭ 0361/288037. www.uluwatu.co.id.

MARKETS

Pasar Sindhu (Jl. Danau Tamblingan) is a bustling traditional morning market for fruit and vegetables that turns into a food market in the evenings. On the west side of the Bypass, the original **Pasar Delod Peken,** at Intaran, is even more extensive and stretches along the entire length of the road, starting at dawn every day of the week. At **Café Batu Jimbar** (p. 132) on Sunday mornings is a market that offers organic vegetables, plants, local foods, and fun stalls with a range of local produce and trendy designer articles. The nearby **Manik Organic Restaurant,** at Jl. Danau Tamblingan 85, also offers a regular organic farmers' market on Thursday evenings, from 2 to 8pm.

6 SANUR AFTER DARK

Sanur is truly magical after sunset. The last light of the day burns with a soft brilliance, and in the afterglow the clouds and the sea often reflect the rosy glow that promises good weather on the following day. Gamelan music echoes on the sea breeze from groups honing their skills. Traditional dance performances are to be seen in a number of restaurants and hotels. The Hyatt's **Piano Bar** is a cozy enclave. Elegant nightspots like the **Bali Hai Supper Club** on the rooftop of the Bali Beach Hotel and the sumptuous **Matahari** discotheque at the Bali Hyatt offer dancing and entertainment till the wee hours.

> **Tips   The Traditional Dances of Sanur:
> Ask for Them by Name**
>
> Among the more famous dances found in Sanur are the *barong* of Taman with its *telek* or *sandaran* imps; the kris dance of the Black Barong of Singgi; the *baris gede* trance dance of spear-bearing warriors of Banjar Belong; the *topeng* mask dance of Banjar Puseh; and the classical *legong* dance, which is practiced by several different groups. Ask at any hotel for details and they will be happy to investigate what is on in the region and arrange the whole trip for you.

The Beatles Bar ★★   The owner, Percy Burlace, is obviously a Beatles fan, the story being that he was the promoter of the Beatles Australian tour in the '60s. The whole place is packed with Beatles memorabilia, posters, books, and trivia. There's even a life-size model of the group. Percy owns the only gold record ("Strawberry Fields Forever") of the Beatles that Michael Jackson didn't own, a replica of which is hanging up in the bar—at least we think it's a copy. When you first go there, you have to pay Rp20,000 to join the "club." For that money, you become a life member and get a free drink. Jl. Sekuta, off Jl. Bypass Ngurah Rai 284. © 0361/289032.

Tandjung Sari   Come here for cocktails on the beach as the day draws to a close. Though the martinis are not cheap and this old lady of Sanur might be beginning to show her age, the old-world charm and class is still worth the trip. The service itself is worth it—some of the staff seem like they have been there since it opened. Sit back and watch the world go by. Jl. Danau Tamblingan 41. © 0361/288-441.

7 NUSA LEMBONGAN, NUSA CENINGAN & NUSA PENIDA

Of the three islands near Sanur, **Nusa Lembongan** is geographically closest and remains to date the only real tourist destination. Both **Nusa Ceningan** and **Nusa Penida** are largely unspoiled and for the most part unaware of the majority of developments of the 21st century. Nusa Lembongan is famed for its surf breaks and laid-back style while Nusa Ceningan and Nusa Penida are known for their nature, pristine landscapes, and traditional local life and culture. All three are famous for their world-class diving and snorkeling.

DAY TRIPS

Day trips are a popular option for the hurried, and a 1-day cruise will bring you to Nusa Lembongan with possibly 100 other similar-minded folk where you will be offered snorkeling, banana boat rides, glass-bottom boat trips, sea kayaking, and maybe even a trip to the mangrove forest or a cultural village tour. A buffet lunch and later some form of water slide will also be thrown in. The approximate price is US$90. The following are the main cruise operators serving Nusa Lembongan:

Bali Hai ★, Benoa Harbour (© **0361/720331;** fax 0361/720-334; www.balihaicruises. com; cruises 9:15am–4:15pm US$95, sunset dinner cruise 5:45–8:45pm US$45, overnight US$125–US$145 per night), the most popular of the day cruises, offers as many options as you could think of, with sailboats, diving, and sunset dinners. This is a one-stop shop.

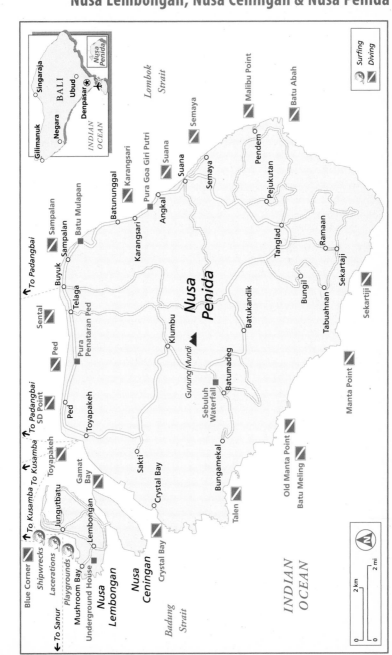

Bounty, Benoa Harbour (© **0361/726666;** fax 0361/726688; www.balibounty cruises.com; one-way US$35, round-trip US$70, day cruise 10am–4pm US$95, dinner cruise 6–8:30pm US$49; MC, V) runs similar day trips to Nusa Lembongan.

Waka Louka Cruise ★, Jl. Pulau Moyo 25x (© **0361/723629;** fax 0361/722077; www.wakaexperience.com; catamaran 9am–5:30pm US$104, dinner cruise and sailing, charter only; MC, V), a delightful catamaran, is more stylish than anything else on the market, and organizes day trips and dinner cruises on board.

Sail Sensations ★, Benoa Harbour (© **0361/725864;** fax 0361/725866; www.sail sensations.com; day cruise 9am–5pm US$85, twilight cruise 6:30–9pm US$55, over-night US$285–US$325; MC, V), part of Nusa Lembongan Resort, organizes day trips for US$95, which includes high-speed ferry, village tour, buffet lunch, snorkeling, a 5-minute banana boat ride, and, for those wishing to part with another US$17, a bicycle and car mangrove tour.

Island Explorer Cruises, Jl. Bypass Ngurah Rai 622, Suwung (© **0361/728088;** fax 0361/728089; www.bali-cruise.com; day cruises 9am–5pm US$69–US$79; MC, V), part of Coconuts Beach Resort on Nusa Lembongan, does cruise and stay packages or even just transfer only from Benoa Harbour at US$35 round-trip. The day cruise includes lunch and activities, such as a village and seaweed tour, banana boats, kayaking, fish feeding, or just leisurely sailing a yacht to the island if you prefer a slower pace. Both the Fun Ship and the Sail Boat depart Benoa at 9am but the yacht takes 2 hours while the fast boat only takes 1 hour. And, yes, the Fun Ship comes complete with its own water slide.

NUSA LEMBONGAN

Nusa Lembongan is surrounded by a beautiful marine park; the magnificent scenery includes white sandy beaches or limestone cliffs dropping vertically into azure seas with the most incredible view back to Bali and Mount Agung. At only 4km (2½ miles) long and 2km (just over 1 mile) wide, you can walk round the island in less than 4 hours. *Note:* Of the three islands detailed in this chapter, Nusa Lembongan has the most exten-sive facilities for scuba diving.

Getting There

FROM BENOA HARBOUR, BALI INTERNATIONAL MARINA **BlueWater Express** (© **0361/723479** or 081/338418988; www.bwsbali.com; one-way Rp325,000, round-trip Rp550,000; 10% discount when booking online) has speed boats that whisk you across the water in 30 minutes. The boat departs Benoa at 10am for Gili Trawangan making a quick stop at Nusa Lembongan. Return journeys leave at 1:30pm from Gili T to Benoa, stopping at Nusa Lembongan at 3:30pm. Most people who catch boats from Benoa Har-bour to Nusa Lembongan have arranged a day cruise with one of the many luxury cruising companies. You can still buy a travel ticket only without having to take part in all their leisurely activites. See also Island Explorer Cruises, under "Day Trips," above.

FROM SANUR BEACH The fast boats of **Scoot** (Lembongan Island Cruise, Jl. Hang-tuah 27; © **0361/285522;** fax 0361/286913; www.lembonganislandfastcruises.com or www.scootcruise.com; three trips daily) will take you to either Mushroom Bay or Jung-utbatu for US$45 round-trip (US$27 one-way). Local hotel transfers on Bali are included in the fee. Scoot's office is next to Dunkin' Donuts opposite the Sanur Paradise Hotel or on the beach near the departure point beside Grand Bali Beach hotel.

So-called **public boats,** very basic affairs aimed at the local trade, from Sanur beach, leave daily at 8am and 10am (90 min. one-way; Rp35,000). Coming back, the boats leave at 7:30am from Jungutbatu.

A **faster public boat** (© 0361/743-2344; Rp200,000), costs more but should get you there in about 45 minutes; daily departure from Sanur beach is at 8am in front of Ananda Hotel. Departures from Nusa Lembongan are at 10:30am, 1, and 3pm.

The **Tanis Lembongan Express** (© 08/1338737344; one-way US$27, round-trip US$45; price includes hotel pickup) takes 25 to 35 minutes from Sanur beach near Grand Bali Beach hotel; it departs at noon and 4:30pm, returning to Bali at 10:30am and 3pm. They also arrange fishing trips, surf safaris, and a day cruise which includes lunch, hotel transfers, and activities.

FROM KUTA If you're in Kuta, **Perama Tours,** Jl. Legian 39 (© 0361/751551; one-way Rp120,000, round-trip Rp230,000; www.peramatour.com), has a shuttle and boat service. A shuttle bus leaves from Kuta at 10am; the boat leaves from Sanur Beach at 10:30am taking about 40 minutes. Boats return at 8:30am the following day. Catch boats opposite Jalan Huang Tua. The office of Perama Sanur can be found at friendly Warung Pojok in Jalan Hang Tua.

Orientation

The two main beach areas are **Jungutbatu** to the northeast and **Mushroom Bay** in the southwest. The former was the original surf destination and it still has backpacker accommodations with lots of chilled bars and *nasi goreng* or pizza restaurants. Mushroom Bay has a more upmarket feel and caters to vaguely well-heeled families wanting to veer from the beaten track or couples wanting a romantic break. However, times change and the hotels of Mushroom Bay now seem slightly dated in comparison to the more recent additions on the hillside above Jungutbatu or the upscale villas just completed on the sunset side of the island. Mushroom Bay also has the added pollution of day-trippers but, notwithstanding this, it is still a very pleasant spot with a great white sandy beach and various beachside restaurants.

FAST FACTS A local **doctor** in Jungutbatu will charge you Rp300,000 for a consultation. A small nurse's clinic in Jungutbatu is slightly cheaper. Bring plenty of cash as the island has **no ATMs.** Perama Tours and **Bank Pembangunan Daerah Bali** can change currency and travelers checks. You will also be charged between 3% and 5% for use of your credit card. For Internet in Jungutbatu, expect to pay about Rp1,000 per minute. Typical speeds are much slower than advertised. **GTNET** near the western end of Jungutbatu is a good bet with seven PCs and an on-site technician, open from 10am to 10pm. A wartel phone office at Mainski Inn has Internet.

Exploring Nusa Lembongan

You can easily rent a bicycle (typically from your hotel) and spend the day pottering round the island. End the day watching a game of competitive inter-village beach volleyball or head to the Mangrove bar at the northern end of the island with a floating

---

Snorkel, Bicycle & Motorbike Rental

There is no shortage of places offering snorkeling equipment, mountain bikes, and motorbikes for rent. Typical prices are, per day, Rp20,000 to Rp30,000 for snorkeling gear, Rp40,000 for a bicycle, and up to Rp100,000 for a motorbike. No need to lock up your bike or moped—they can't go anywhere!

Walking from Tamarind to Mushroom Beach

Make a day of a stroll from Tamarind to Mushroom Beach, stopping for lunch, sunbathing, and a dip en route. Start from Lembongan Island Beach Resort and head toward Coconut Beach. Once there you will find a small shop behind which is a path that will take you over the headland for views of the sea and coastline. Stop to watch the seaweeders at work. At the end of the headland is an ideal place to swim in the clear waters. Stop off for a beer or coffee at the legendary **Blackie's Warung** ★★ and have a chat with the owner himself who is happy to share his stories of island living on Nusa Lembongan. If you want to spend the day at the beach, this is a perfect place to base yourself, on a sun lounger under the trees. Continue past Ketut's Bungalows and over the hill towards Mushroom Bay. This is one of the safest places to swim on the island as the waters are calm. Choose from any of the restaurants here if you didn't stop at Blackie's and enjoy a long leisurely lunch—beer obligatory! Bali Beach Café has a good reputation for food and if you are feeling too lazy to walk back, will happily give you a lift home on the back of a motorbike at no extra cost.

pontoon in the middle of the mangroves (though this can be slightly disappointing at low tide). Discover natural springs or learn about seaweed farming or take an organized trip in to the mangroves by canoe.

Many of the day trip boats do special trips to either the mangrove forests or the seaweed farms. These are both educational and beneficial to the locals as they receive money directly. You can make your own way to the mangrove forests and seaweed farms but as most of the locals don't speak any English and there is little to see unless you are in the know, it can be a rather unentertaining visit.

Alternatively, on the road out of Mushroom Bay towards Jungutbatu is the **Gala Gala Underground House** built by what can only be described as an eccentric. It took Made Byasa some 15 years to fashion this labyrinth by hand. It is well worth stopping at and donating a small amount of money to the upkeep. You can actually climb down inside the house and take your own personal tour through this cold and dank home and wonder how anyone could spend a night in here—never mind 15 years!

Walk, or moped, the yellow suspension bridge between Nusa Lembongan and Nusa Ceningan (p. 149) and continue on with a tour of untouched Nusa Ceningan.

The **Lulur Spa** at Batu Karang Lembongan Resort (p. 147) is Nusa Lembongan's first complete spa with facials, massages, pedicures, manicures, and hair treatments. Call ℂ **0366/24880** and ask for Lulur Spa for more information. **Alam Nusa Spa** (ℂ **08/1338377482** or 08/1337912008 for advance reservation) offers Balinese massage on Mushroom Bay near the Bali Hai.

DIVING   The many dive academies based on Nusa Lembongan serve the dive sites all round the three islands. The ones below are particularly noteworthy, although most offer a similar package at about the same price. A single dive, including all equipment, snacks, and drinks, is US$40 to US$45 and dives US$70 to US$75 for two dives. Discounts are available if you book online or are a walk-in. Due to the cool water, you may wish to hire a wetsuit. Stick to accredited dive schools and if you are in the least concerned after having chatted with them, simply move on to the next place. Though Nusa Lembongan has several dive sites around it, the majority of the better-known ones are at Nusa Penida (p. 152). Nusa Lembongan's **Blue Corner,** although deep, is a very popular drift dive, the highlight being a wall that is usually full of fish, sharks, big Napoleon wrasse, sometimes eagle rays, and Mola-Mola.

World Diving (© 08/12390-0686; www.world-diving.com) is renowned by many as one of the best dive schools in Indonesia. It is located at Pondok Baruna guesthouse in Jungutbatu. They offer introductory courses all the way through to Assistant Instructor level. This is the only dive school in Nusa Lembongan with a purpose-built training pool. **Bali Lembongan Scuba** (© 0366/24491; www.balilembonganscuba.com) is in Jungutbatu. **Bali Diving Academy Lembongan** (www.scubali.com) is on Jungutbatu beach, within the grounds of Bungalow No 7. In Mushroom Bay, **Pro Dive** (© 0361/766753 or 726823; www.prodivebali.com) has been operating on Nusa Lembongan for just over 2 years, although they have been in Bali since 1992.

FISHING   Most hotels or villas can arrange a fishing trip. The price should be around Rp500,000 for 3 hours, leaving at about 6am and returning at 9am. Most trips are in traditional *jukung,* with a hand line out the back to trawl the current. You will be amazed at just how many fish they catch on a good day. One of the local characters is **Captain Nemo** on the beach near Playgrounds. Alternatively ask any of the boats on the beach, negotiate and most will offer an authentic line fishing experience.

SNORKELING   Many operators on Jungutbatu Beach will take you out in their *jukung* with some form of sun shade. Alternatively, you can join an organized snorkeling trip with one of the diving schools; they will also rent you decent gear. Most boat operators will charge in the region of Rp400,000 for up to four people for a 2- or 3-hour trip and may take you to places such as Crystal Bay off Nusa Penida or one of the other less busy options. Most *jukung* will avoid Manta Point as the sea and currents can become too strong for these boats and novice divers. Plenty of good snorkeling is to be had all round the island and even just off Jungutbatu beach, itself. Sometimes you actually don't have to go that far.

SURFING   The best time to surf around these islands is the dry season (Apr–Oct).

Shipwrecks   **Best swell:** south-southwest; **best size:** 3 to 6 feet; **best winds:** east-southeast. This superb right-hander is at the far northern end on the Nusa Lembongan beach. It offers a relatively easy take-off, a nice barrel section, and a fun "wally" section as the wave wraps around the headland towards the beach and much shallower end section. Best (and safer) on higher tides. This wave can get crowded depending on how many surf charter boats are passing by. You can also find it with smaller numbers if you are willing to hang around for a while. Beware of a protective element courtesy of a few local surfers and expatriate residents who like to keep the waves to themselves.

Lacerations   **Best swell:** southwest; **best size:** 5 to 8 feet; **best winds:** east-southeast. This is the heaviest wave of the three main waves on Nusa Lembongan and is for the most accomplished tube-riders only. If this is not you, please don't paddle out. Only surfable on the higher tides, Lacerations serves up fast and relentless barrels, over sharp and shallow reef. Further hazards include the wire fish-traps and strong currents. It's not called Lacerations for nothing! Lacerations can get crowded with a hungry bunch of capable and skilled wave-riders. Show respect and charge when your number is called. No second chances out here.

Playgrounds **Best swell:** southwest; **best size:** 3 to 5 feet; **best winds:** east-southeast. This wave gets its name from the floating playground located just beside the break, but it could also have earned this name through the playful nature it possesses. This wave breaks both left and right and both can be good from mid- to higher-tides and is the best bet for the less proficient surfer or the one chasing a mellower experience, sans crowd. The crowds out here are generally smaller than at Lacerations and Shipwrecks.

Where to Stay

Nusa Lembongan has not quite turned its back on its surfing roots, though there are now options for surfers who want to return with their families. The island is not so unrecognizable from its early surfer days.

Mushroom Bay

Hai Tide Huts (Kids) This is a favorite place for families. The 15 traditional two-story *lumbung* huts, with simple but orderly bedrooms reached by a ladder on the upper floor, are charmingly done and in great condition belying their 1993 construction. Bathrooms are not attached but are not too far away and are kept very clean. The large swimming pool has areas for the whole family. A nice relaxed lawn fronts the sea with two-person hammocks and plenty of deck chairs to take in the view. Food is buffet style with freshly barbecued seafood, prawns, chicken, and sweet corn and a la carte pizza (starting at Rp40,000) and steak (starting at Rp65,000). Snorkeling, kayaking, and banana boat trips are available for residents, as well as a unique Semi Submersible Submarine, where you sit in a glass cabin below the waves.

✆ **0361/720331.** www.balihaicruises.com. 15 units. Year-round 1-night package US$125 per room; 2-bedroom villas US$125 per person, including cruise transfer, activities, and breakfast; additional nights US$90 per room. **Amenities:** Restaurant; bar; outdoor pool; watersports. *In room:* A/C, fan.

Nusa Lembongan Resort On a manicured peninsula facing north, west, and east in Mushroom Bay, this was until, recently, the most expensive resort on the island. Twelve well-appointed air-conditioned villas (two with an extra bedroom) have either a direct view of the sea or a garden view from a private terrace. A terrific swimming pool anchors the lounging area and the staff are attentive although possibly more enthusiastic than proficient. A bar and restaurant sit on a lovely terrace overlooking the beach, although the menu is a bit confused and heavy for such a tropical setting. Included in your price is snorkeling and use of canoes and a glass-bottom boat trip. Being at the western point, they also have a private sunset viewing deck that drops down from the garden 20m (60ft.) to the sea.

✆ **0361/725864.** Fax 0361/725866. www.nusalembonganresort.com. 12 villas. High season US$320–US$790; low season US$295–US$765. Rates include breakfast and activities. AE, MC, V. **Amenities:** Restaurant; lounge bar; babysitting; bicycles; outdoor pool; room service; spa; watersports. *In villa:* A/C, stereo, minibar.

Waka Nusa Resort On a hectare (2½ acres) of beach front, these thatched bungalows have plenty of space and rustic charm. The overall feeling is one of barefoot chic. Plenty of beachfront bales are available for lounging; the cloverleaf swimming pool is surrounded by natural stone. Rooms have air-conditioning and hot water. As part of the Waka group, the standard of service is good although they also cater to day-trippers which might annoy overnighters. Eating is semi-communal on long bench tables. The usual fare has starters averaging Rp40,000 and main courses up to Rp80,000. With your booking, you also get kayaking, bicycles, snorkeling, table tennis, badminton, and a trip in a glass-bottom boat. (The size of the glass in the bottom of the boat is about the size of an ice cooler—bring your magnifying glass.)

☎ **0361/484085.** Fax 0361/484695. www.wakaexperience.com. 10 units. High season US$194; low season US$174. Rates include breakfast and activities. AE, MC, V. **Amenities:** Restaurant; bar; babysitting; bicycles; outdoor pool; room service; spa; watersports. *In room:* A/C, minibar.

Jungutbatu

Batu Karang Resort & Day Spa ★★ This boutique offering, with its own dedicated spa, is setting new standards on the island. Australian father and son Troy and Alan Sinclair spent 4 years building this classical yet modern stone offering set on the hillside facing the surf breaks. Golf buggies take you up the hill to your suite or villa at the end of the day. All rooms have air-conditioning, Internet, satellite TV, 220-thread cotton sheets, and king-size beds. The outdoor stone baths and showers have views over the spectacular surf breaks. The resort has its own water and sewage treatment plants making it by far the most ecofriendly place to stay. A very decent open plan restaurant and bar are on the lower levels, while further up is a bar, a beautiful day spa, a 25m (82-ft.) two-lane lap pool, and a smaller swimming pool with a swim-up bar, and an infinity edge pool down below.

☎ **0366/24880.** Fax 0366/24881. www.batukaranglembongan.com. 23 units. High season US$257–US$750, minimum stay 3 nights; low season US$232–US$825, minimum stay 2 nights. Rates include breakfast. AE, DC, MC, V. **Amenities:** Restaurant, Muntigs Bar and Restaurant (p. 150); bar; lounge; babysitting; bicycles; gym; Jacuzzi; 2 outdoor pools; room service; spa; watersports; Wi-Fi (for a fee). *In room:* A/C, TV, hair dryer, minibar.

Coconuts Beach Resort This is a very charming option as each of the traditional stone bungalows rise up the hillside with wondrous views to Playgrounds, Lacerations, and Mount Agung. The style is simple but handsome: the air-conditioned bungalows have stone floors and bathrooms beautifully tiled in greens and aquamarines; up the hill are a further eight bungalows open to the elements with floor-to-ceiling blinds and curtains rather than windows that let in the sea breeze. Plus, they all get hot water. The pool is pleasant enough and the Sea Breeze restaurant has snapper filets at Rp55,000 and hamburgers at Rp35,000. The better views are higher up the hillside, which makes for a longer walk—so you have to earn it.

☎ **0361/728088.** Fax 0361/728089. www.bali-activities.com. 18 units. Year-round US$39–US$49 standard. Rates include breakfast. MC, V. **Amenities:** Restaurant; bicycles; outdoor pool; room service; watersports. *In room:* A/C, ceiling fan.

Lembongan Island Beach Villas With 11 two-bedroom villas, four with their own plunge pool and all with kitchens, this place is popular with families and groups who are happy to look after themselves. It is understandably booked all year-round as it is well priced for the standard of accommodation and level of facilities. There is no formal restaurant. As with seemingly all the better accommodations in Jungutbatu, it is on the side of the hill facing the surf breaks.

☎ **0366/24119.** Fax 0366/24490. www.lembonganbeachvillas.com. 11 villas. High season US$225 with private pool, US$205 without private pool; low season US$185 with private pool, US$165 without private pool. Rates include breakfast. MC, V. **Amenities:** Bar; babysitting; room service; watersports; Wi-Fi (for a fee). *In villa:* A/C, TV/DVD, kitchen, outdoor pool (in some).

Playgrounds At the southern end of Jungutbatu beach overlooking the surf break, these five rooms in a large house have a choice of fans or air-conditioning. Though these clean and basic rooms with satellite TV have only cold water in the showers, you still get wonderful views from the balconies on the top floor.

© /fax **0366/24524** or 08174748427. www.playgroundslembongan.com. 10 units. High season US$60–US$260; low season US$50–US$240. No credit cards. **Amenities:** Restaurant; bar; babysitting; bicycles; gym; outdoor pool; room service; watersports. *In room:* A/C (in some), fan.

Shipwrecks Beach Villa A minute walk from the beach opposite Shipwreck's surf break, this timber constructed villa offers three bedrooms overlooking a tropical garden. Each bedroom has a beautiful four-posted bed with an outside bathroom. The property does not allow children under 5 years old but it is an ideal property for older families or a collection of surfers. The villa can be rented whole or by the room.

© **08/1338032900.** www.nusalembongan.com.au. 3 bedrooms. High season Rp500,000 standard, Rp620,000 master suite; low season Rp460,000 standard, Rp570,000 master suite; extra person Rp130,000. Rates include breakfast. 2 night minimum stay. MC, V. *In room:* A/C, fan.

Sunset & the Rest of the Island

Dream Beach Bungalows This is a quiet spot with a beautiful white-sand beach on the southwestern part of the island. Of the 11 rooms, seven are single story *lumbung* style with fans and cold water showers. It's basic, erring on budget, but it has great atmosphere. The lovely restaurant serves Thai curries for Rp45,000 and usually fresh tuna every day. Music is mainly reggae on the great upstairs deck where you can have a drink or a bite, and "Don't worry about a thing."

© **08/1338737344.** www.dreambeachlembongan.com. 11 units. High season US$75–US$135; low season US$65–US$125. Rates include breakfast. MC, V. **Amenities:** Restaurant; cafe; bar; bicycles; outdoor pool; watersports. *In room:* Fan.

Lembongan Sunset Beach ★★ (Finds) A new addition to the island, and raising the bar in terms of standards and facilities, is this group of luxury villas perched on 2 hectares (5 acres) of manicured peninsula. The villas, set in their own landscaped grounds facing either west to the sunset or east to Mount Agung, are environmentally low impact: solar panels heat fresh water collected by the resort; waste water is treated; and wind power is planned for the future. The beautifully styled houses are a mix of three- and four-bedrooms all with floor to ceiling sliding windows, kitchens, and a modern feel with their use of limed coconut wood. Café Waru, the stylish bar and restaurant, serves island dishes such as fresh grilled fish and their own home-grown salads. Five shaded bales with hanging chairs overlook the ocean near the 18m (36-ft.) lap pool. Truly Nusa Lembongan has arrived.

© **08/1337122166** or 08/123670989. www.lembongansunsetbeach.com. 8 villas. High season US$300–US$700; low season US$250–US$600. MC, V. **Amenities:** Cafe; bar; outdoor pool; tennis court; watersports. *In villa:* Fan, kitchen.

Where to Dine

Restaurants are typically open daily, from 7 or 8am to 9 or 10pm.

Mushroom Bay, Sunset Beach & Dream Beach

Cafe Bali (no phone; main courses Rp35000–Rp60000; no credit cards), in the middle of Mushroom Bay, is the beach's focal point, outside of the hotels, and a great place to hang out. The simple specialties are fresh whole snapper, prawn tempura, and an assortment of decent pizzas. If you can't make it for lunch at **Warung Sunset** (© **08/123621633;** main courses Rp20,000–Rp30,000; no credit cards), on Sunset Beach, then just go for sunset drinks. Fresh, local fish is usually the daily special; choose from plenty of cold drinks, cocktails, and mocktails. They will also arrange transport home if you

149

Nusa Ceningan

This tiny island is untouched by any form of tourism and access other than by sea is via a 100m (328 ft.) bright yellow bridge from the southeastern side of Nusa Lembongan, wide enough only for either a bicycle or moped. This beautiful little place has no official accommodation other than home-stays, nor indeed any litter. What it does have is neat and well-tended stone walls, trees, and shades of old coconut plantations. It makes a very pleasant trip and you will likely not meet any other tourists. The locals are friendly and it is virtually impossible to get lost.

In the channel between Nusa Lembongan and Nusa Ceningan, no more than 500m (1,640 ft.) apart, are the **seaweed farms** that support the livelihoods of many of the islanders. Guided tours teach you about seaweed farming, ultimately drawing the conclusion that it is a lot of hard work for not a huge amount of financial gain. Seaweed farmers earn between Rp3,000 and Rp8,000 per kilo of seaweed harvested. Still, it is a living, with a fresh harvest every 4 to 6 weeks.

The **Jaringan Ekowisata Desa (JED)** ★★ (📞 0361/737447; www.jed.or.id), translated as the Village Ecotourism Network, offers educational trips with a farmer who shows you how the locals harvest seaweed. You also learn how to make food from seaweed, including cakes. A trip for two to four people is US$130 per person; five or more people US$105 per person. Price includes all transfers, overnight accommodation in a home-stay, meals, and an all-day guide. JED can also arrange trips if you are not interested in staying the night.

A great **surf break** here is called simply Ceningan, off the coast between Nusa Lembongan and Nusa Ceningan. It works when the breaks on the other side of Nusa Lembongan don't. This is also known as the Secret Spot.

can't quite make it on your own. On Dream Beach is **Café Pandan** (📞 08/1338737344; main courses Rp50,000–Rp100,000; no credit cards), another local favorite. Fresh tuna is the order of the day and Thai curries go for Rp45,000.

Jungutbatu

Most places on this strip cater to the surf crowd. The restaurant at Coconuts Beach Resort (see above), **Sea Breeze** (📞 0361/7443936 or 0361/728088; www.bali-activities.com; main courses Rp22,000–Rp150,000; no credit cards) serves Indonesian and Western food at reasonable prices with friendly service and an oceanfront bar.

The fun, if predictable, sports bar **Scooby Doo Bar & Restaurant** overlooks the bay. Enjoy a cold beer while watching the sun go down over Bali. The **Mainski Lembongan Resort** (📞 0361/9237322; www.mainski-lembongan-resort.com; main courses Rp18000–Rp82,000; MC, V) has a poolside bar that shows music DVDs on the giant screen every night and serves ice cold beers, local and international wines, and a range of fun tropical cocktails. Happy Hour is daily from 5 to 7pm. They also have a pool table, table tennis, and Wi-Fi.

Bunga Bungalows Restaurant (no phone; main courses Rp35,000–Rp50,000; no credit cards) has various tables and loungers looking out to the surf. The high point are the wood-fired pizzas from Rp35,000 to Rp50,000. Food stops at about 9pm. **Ware Ware** (𝒸 **08/123970572;** main courses Rp22,000–Rp50,000; no credit cards) offers grilled catch of the day, *nasi goreng,* and Italian and Indonesian dishes. This place is rightly popular not just for its location on a terrace overlooking the surf. **Lembongan Reef** (𝒸 **08/1338757683;** www.lembonganreef.com; main courses Rp25,000–Rp50,000; no credit cards), perched on a platform on the hillside overlooking the surf breaks, does a great catch of the day such as grilled mahimahi for Rp55,000.

Ketut Warung (Finds) THAI   Without a doubt a local treasure, not just for Madam Ketut's deliciously delicious Thai curries and soups, but also for Ketut himself—a proclaimed healer and generous host. Try the Tom Yum soup, in the simple venue with plain wooden tables and rickety chairs, followed by reflexology and a genuine healing massage by the local master. Back pains, knee joints, whatever is ailing you. The warung is just behind Mainski resort, but ask when you get close and persevere in finding this gem. If lost, ask for Ketut Malom. Definitely recommended, but don't play the grandson at Connect 4.

No phone. Main courses Rp15,000–Rp25,000. No credit cards. Daily 8am–9pm.

Muntigs Bar and Restaurant INTERNATIONAL   As with the hotel (Batu Karang Resort, p. 147), this is a notch up from the other island restaurants, although not as romantically set at night as most others that actually front the sea. Come here for great food and drink without busting your budget. The menu makes a refreshing change from the typical options of the rest. Don't forget to try their chocolate mousse. They stock a wide variety of imported wines—almost as rare as hen's teeth on Nusa Lembongan—and imported beers, and they make great cocktails.

𝒸 **0366/24880.** www.batukaranglembongan.com. Main courses Rp60,000–Rp90,000. AE, MC, V. Daily 7am–10pm.

NUSA PENIDA

Nusa Penida is the Bali, or even the Nusa Lembongan, that time left behind. It is a mainly dry and somewhat desolate landscape where nature and wildlife have been left to their own devices. Known to the outside world for being either a formal penal colony or, to the believers of Bali, as the home of Jero Gede Mecaling, the evil spirit with his horde of devils that is warded off by the Barong Landung dance around Galungang.

Nusa Penida's main attraction is the incredible flora and fauna found scuba diving the crystal clear waters or exploring cliffs that drop deep into the sea. The island straddles the Wallace Line and its northeastern shores have the most incredible view up the Lombok Strait. Birdlife has remained left alone and many endangered species have prospered.

Rich in many of the simple things, this is a charming island of natural beauty and not even the increasing number of day-trippers, neither those who come for the diving nor the Quicksilver clients in their floating pavilion, can detract from its charms.

A daily market in Sampalan is open in the early morning from about 5 to 10am selling local and imported (from Bali) fruit and vegetables.

Getting There

Most people arrive on Nusa Penida at Toyapakeh beach from Nusa Lembongan or, if arriving on the public boat from Padangbai, at the main port in the administrative capital

In the summer of 2009, one local boat going to Nusa Penida capsized and all of
the passengers died. Surprisingly, most Balinese cannot swim.

of Sampalan. Boats should leave Padangbai for Nusa Penida at 7am and 2pm (Rp30,000
one-way) from the ferry terminal but are not always reliable. They return from Nusa
Penida at 9am and 4pm. Small boat owners will also take you to the island for the right
price. Prepare to bargain. If you are only staying a night, you can even negotiate a return
fare as the boatman can usually find some cheap accommodation for the night.

Public boats depart daily from Yellow Bridge (Nusa Lembongan) at 6am in front of
Nusa Ceningan. They can be a bit sketchy at times and are usually very crowded. There
is no same-day return. The ride across is approximately 90 minutes; they only leave when
full. The current fare is Rp300,000 for charter boat transfers (**Scoot Boat** ℂ 08/
7861323761). You can always hire your own boat, ask any fisherman or inquire at any
of the big hotels on Nusa Lembongan.

FAST FACTS The police station, hospital (ℂ **0366/23582**), any banks, and the main
harbor are in Sampalan. The two main Banks, **Bank Bri** and **Bank LPD,** are on the main
street near the hospital. Neither have an ATM although they will change money for you.
Both are open Monday to Friday from 8am to 3pm. A **Western Union** (ℂ **0366/31880**)
in Sampalan should give credit card advances. The island has little or no Internet service.

Exploring Nusa Penida

Arrange a guide in advance through your hotel or villa or alternatively hire a bike and guide
when you arrive on the beach at Toyapakeh. You will easily encounter people offering to
take you on an escorted motorbike ride round the island or snorkeling. Typically, they will
charge in the region of Rp150,000 to Rp200,0000 for a full day, which should include your
bike and petrol. A trip on the back of a bike to the Bat Cave alone will cost up to
Rp100,000 per person per bike and guide/driver. If you want to rent your own bike for
your own tour of the island, a bike will cost around Rp80,000 for the day. A local chap who
takes regular tours and is knowledgeable and friendly is **Rod** (ℂ 08/1805333747).

Other trips on the island are to **Telaga,** which is the center for weaving, or to the
temples at either Semaya or at the top of Mount Mundi. Alternatively, you can swim in
a beautiful waterfall fed by a natural spring just a 2km (1¼-mile) walk from Batumadeg,
although you will have to get a guide to lead you.

TEMPLES Though known as the Bat Cave, to be honest, **Pura Goa Giri Putri** ★★
only has so many bats. Regardless, this is quite extraordinary and justifies a day trip to
Nusa Penida. About 45 minutes by bike from Toyabungkah, you arrive at a fairly feature-
less point and start climbing the 100 or so steep carved stone steps. At the top is a temple
where you make a small donation and then you will be taken into the cave. You wriggle
through the entrance, no bigger than a man hole. The cave then starts opening up and
continues on for about 250m (820 ft.) rising to some 100m (328 ft.) in height in the
middle. A series of temples in the cave are partially lit. At the far end, you arrive at the
other side of the mountain and peer out to a verdant green tree-lined valley that is almost
Provençal. You have literally just walked through the mountain.

Back at the start, you have a view up the Lombok Strait, with Bali to the west and Lombok to the east. You are effectively straddling the Wallace Line. On a clear morning, as the sun is still climbing, the view from here is breathtaking.

The main temple on the island is **Pura Penaturan Ped,** an extensive and charming temple on the road out of Sampalan with lots of carvings. Various other temples line the road, such as **Batu Mulapan,** many of them similarly carved in limestone.

BIRD-WATCHING   The interior of Nusa Penida has been mainly left alone and nature has been allowed to keep hold. This is a place for professional twitchers. The **Nusa Penida Bird Sanctuary** ★ (© 0361/977978; www.fnpf.org), part of the Friends of the National Parks Foundation (FNPF) and also now sponsored by the Begawan Giri Foundation, is on the road east of Sampalan and has possibly the most Bali starlings found in any one place. The Bali starling was at one stage the most endangered bird in the world, with only seven in the wild. The biggest challenge to rearing birds in the wild, other than poaching, is the proper water and trees to provide the right habitat. Since its inception in 2002, the Nusa Penida Bird Sanctuary has planted some 115,000 trees. The foundation has also managed to get all the villages of Nusa Penida to sign an agreement stating they will help preserve the wildlife on the island—indeed the whole island is now a bird sanctuary. Contact the Bird Sanctuary at the Bali Bird Park (p. 134) just north of Sanur for more information on organizing a birding tour.

DIVING   Though Nusa Penida is best known as a diving destination, most of the best-known dive schools are based on Nusa Lembongan (p. 144). The whole Nusa Penida and Nusa Lembongan area offers drift-diving in mild to strong currents. The water can be chilly but is often startlingly clear (with visibility between 15–40m/49–131 ft.), with gorgeous corals and prolific fish, some turtles, sharks, and, July to mid-November, Mola-Mola (the weird and wonderful-looking ocean sunfish). If you are staying on mainland Bali, you may find it easier and less hassle with boat-transport to also book diving at Nusa Penida/Nusa Lembongan with a mainland operator (p. 68).

The three main north coast sites—**SD, Ped,** and **Sental**—have many soft corals and fish, such as sweetlips, lionfish, moray eels, scorpionfish and reef sharks, plus turtles, nudis, and crabs.

Toyapakeh, Nusa Penida's most popular dive site, has good visibility and rich, impressive coral formations with big bommies and a profusion of colorful soft corals that provide excellent hiding places for Ribbon eels, banded sea snakes, and nudibranches. If you are here late afternoon, you may see Mandarin fish.

Although a small area, **Gamat Bay** has soft corals, gorgonians, and hard corals (including table corals) and is thus full of reef fish—some quite rare—commensals, and nudibranches. On the outside slope are big bommies, overhangs, and small caves that provide resting places for larger fish. This is also a cleaning station for the ever-popular Mola-Mola.

Crystal Bay ★★ is best known for sightings of Mola-Mola in the July to mid-November season, when water temp can reach 19°C (66°F). While the bay itself is quite beautiful, with good numbers and variety of fish plus gorgeous corals, it also has a **Bat Cave.** You enter from underwater then surface inside the cave, which is open to the sky, and watch the bats overhead. On the deep wall after the Bat Cave you can often see eagle rays and (if you are lucky) the wobbegong shark, only found in Bali.

Manta Point on Nusa Penida's southwest coast has dramatic limestone cliffs that descend straight into the ocean. The swell and surge however can be strong. The mantas seen here are 2 to 4m (6½–13 ft.) in size at an average depth of 5 to 10m (16–33 ft.);

> **Warning!** Dive Schools on Nusa Penida
>
> The dive school outside of Sampalan branded **Quicksilver** shows no evidence of
> PADI certification. The Quicksilver website states quite proudly that they have
> insurance coverage up to US$100 per person. An introductory dive is advertised
> at US$115 against US$45 for an accredited school such as World Diving on Nusa
> Lembongan (a short boat ride from Nusa Penida), where many accredited dive
> schools are based. See, "Diving," p. 144.

you may see other big fish such as Mola-Mola, bamboo sharks, shark rays, tuna, tiger
mackerel, and dolphins, while the smaller fish include other rays and unicornfish.

Malibu Point, on southeast Nusa Penida, lies on a very steep slope, with table corals
and big bommies. There are huge schools of rainbow runners, big trevallys, and rays.
Malibu Point is Nusa Penida's best location to see a variety of sharks.

Batu Abah, on the far side of Nusa Penida, is known for mantas and Mola-Mola. You
need a fast and sturdy boat to reach Batu Abah within a reasonable time.

MANTA POINT You have two ways to see the resident manta rays: one is obviously
from the sea but the other is from directly on the cliffs at Manta Point. The best chance
of seeing them is to get there about 8:30am or an hour thereafter. It will take you up to
2 hours to get there by bike from Toyabunkah.

SNORKELING For snorkeling, a lot of people head straight for **Crystal Bay,** making
it feel a little crowded, particularly given the island's remote location and the number of
other bays close at hand. While you should be observant of currents and not simply head
off on your own, you may find it more rewarding to pull in to some of the other bays
and snorkel there.

Where to Stay & Dine

You have few, if any, real choices for staying on Nusa Penida. For those comfortable with
braving the elements, here are your choices: **Made Homestay** (𝒞 08/5238814998;
Rp100,000 standard, Rp120,000 twin; rates include coffee for breakfast; no credit cards)
is four basic but clean bungalows of Balinese carved stone in a delightful garden. Cold
water and fans are the order of the day. The beachside **Mutiara Mas Bungalows** (𝒞 08/
1337077590; Rp120,000 no A/C, Rp150,000 with A/C; no credit cards) are just 10
twin rooms, with either air-conditioning or a fan. Facilities include a couple of bales and
even a volleyball court. It is a beautiful spot, though the dodgy (and not in the least bit
artistic) Art Market is just next door as is the charmless Quicksilver Dive Operation.

For dining, there are various local warungs but none of real note, so just pick a busy
one and hope for the best.

The Bukit Peninsula

The Bukit Peninsula dangles from the southern tip of Bali like a locket on a chain. *Bukit* means "hill" and encapsulates the whole of the tear-drop shaped area south of the airport starting at **Jimbaran Bay** on the west side, down through the beaches of **Pecatu** and the cliffs of **Uluwatu**, to the southern tip and all the way round to the east side and the government sponsored five-star tourist enclave of **Nusa Dua**, continuing up to the forgotten strip of **Tanjung Benoa.**

The Bukit with its dramatic craggy coastline and vegetation, or lack thereof, is in stark contrast to the rest of Bali with its verdant rice paddies and lush tropical jungle. And whereas rice farming is the staple crop on the rest of Bali, here there are only seaweed farms and limestone quarries, the scars of which are visible from as far afield as Ubud. Thus, the government has aggressively encouraged the development of tourism, giving incentives such as special tax breaks and government funds to established international hotel chains to sweeten the deal.

Historically, this was a fairly scary place where great herds of *banteng* (wild Indonesian cattle) and water buffalo roamed free, and where the occasional sighting of Kebo Iwa, the legendary Balinese giant and master builder, sent shivers through the collective Balinese imagination. The Dutch colonials followed the lead of the rajahs and continued the hunting tradition. The Dutch also banished criminals and undesirables to the Bukit. All this trivia leads you to laugh: Bukit is nowadays referred to by eager developers as "The Beverly Hills of Bali." Instead of sighting wild boar along these dusty roads, you are more likely to be stuck behind water-truck tanks plodding up the hills in low gear as they carry this scant resource to the villas and resorts.

1 JIMBARAN BAY

The bustling beach town and idyllic getaway of Jimbaran is just south of the Ngurah Rai International Airport, on the neck of the Bukit Peninsula, 20 minutes from Kuta and Seminyak. As this is still predominately a working fishing village, a charming diversion here is simply watching the traditional *jukung* (fishing) boats bring in their catch. Jimbaran has one of the best sandy beaches in south Bali, with clear, calm water great for swimming. Developers were quick to realize this, and thus Jimbaran now has some of the finest high-end resorts on the island. Despite development, the town still looks like a fishing village, with small mom-and-pop seafood shacks serving up some of the best fish dishes on the island—a worthy day trip for good eats alone. The best time to visit is just before sunset, although don't be overly hungry when you arrive as the food can sometimes take a while.

GETTING THERE & GETTING AROUND

Jimbaran is on the road to Nusa Dua, 1.5km (less than 1 mile) south of Kuta. **Cabs** are plentiful and cost Rp110,000. *Bemo* are not available here. **Walking** is the best way to get a feel for life in Jimbaran village. The morning provides the opportunity to see

> **(Tips)** **Taxis & Getting around the Bukit**
>
> Taxis are not easy to find on the Bukit peninsula, and though you can walk between a few of the villages, you'll need some form of motorized transport to get around most of the time. Hotels, villas, and restaurants can order a taxi for you when required. If you find yourself without a taxi, call one. Ask how long it will take for them to get you, as they are notoriously slow. Once you've got a taxi and reached your destination, have your driver wait for you for about Rp12,000 an hour. Check with your driver before you depart. See p. 39 for taxi numbers.

offerings placed in every nook and cranny, children in their uniforms heading to school, and mothers going to and from the market.

FAST FACTS At the **Kimia Farmacy,** Jl. Gunung Batur A-3 (© **0361/847-9785**), a doctor is on-site daily from 4 to 10pm to consult for any minor ailments.

EXPLORING JIMBARAN BAY

The **Puru Ulun Siwi** temple, at the village's main crossroads, dates from the 18th century and is one of the few that faces east, rather than north to Mount Gunung Agung, as is the usual practice. This is because the temple, once a primitive shrine, became a Hindu-Balinese temple fairly early in the 11th century. At this time, the holy man Mpu Kuturan still followed the custom of his native Java in orienting his temple toward holy Mount Semura in East Java. You might just catch a farmer, from the market across the street, at the temple collecting water to bless his fields for good harvests—and to keep rodents at bay. The **produce market** across the street isn't one of Bali's largest but it is one of the best. Because of its proximity to the seafood market, many of the island's chefs and their staff shop here. As a result, farmers know to bring their best and brightest produce.

SPAS Spas are open daily. Whatever treatment you chose at the **Four Seasons spa** ★★ (p. 160; single treatment US$55–US$380; AE, MC, V; 9am–9pm), you won't be disappointed. After your treatment your gracious therapists leave you to bathe in a frangipani-and-rose-petal-filled tub—something best shared between two people.

The Ayana resort (p. 160) has two knock-out spas to splurge on (single treatment US$40–US$190, package US$125–US$700; AE, MC, V; 9am–11pm): **Ayana Thallaso** ★★★ and **Spa on the Rocks** ★★★. At the Thallaso spa, you bathe in a warmed seawater-fed pool and are pummeled within an inch of your life. This treatment is meant to be invigorating, making it perfect before a night on the tiles. The next day, book into the Spa on the Rocks, which hangs on a cliff top. Pass 2 hours of your time with the "Amazing Jade" massage with warm and cold stones, a 24-point foot reflexology massage, facial, and Swedish deep-tissue massage.

Being one of the preferred hotels for conferences in Nusa Dua, the InterContinental (p. 161) has **Uluwatu spa** ★★★ (single treatment Rp250,000–Rp1,000,000, package Rp900,000–Rp2,100,000; AE, MC, V; 8am–11pm) that caters to gentlemen with "jet-setter stress relief," sport manicures and pedicures, and "Out to Lunch: Conference Delegates Delight," a 2-hour vigorous massage using steaming hot towels and specialized oils. Their package deals present a very good value in this expensive neck of the woods.

Ornate rooms, with chandeliers and dark moody colors, at **Henna Spa** ★ (single treatment Rp115,000–Rp300,000, package Rp300,000–Rp520,000; AE, MC, V; 8am–9pm)

ATTRACTIONS ●
Exo-Fly **4**
Garuda Vishnu Kencara
  Cultural Park **34**
Jimbaran fish market **2**
Paintball Bali **36**
Produce market **1**
Pura Luhur Uluwatu **28**
Puru Ulun Siwi **5**

ACCOMMODATIONS ■
Alila Villas Uluwatu **31**
Ayana Resort & Spa **17**

Bulgari Hotel &
  Resort 186 **30**
Four Seasons Resort
  at Jimbaran Bay **16**
Gending Kedis Luxury
  Villas and Spa **15**
Gong **27**
Hotel InterContinental **9**
The Istana **26**
Jimbaran Puri Bali **7**
Karang Kambar Estate **38**
Karang Putih Villa **37**
Karma Kandara Villas **33**

Kayumanis
  Jimbaran **6**
Khayangan Estate **29**
The Long House **35**
Mick's Place **19**
Mu Uluwatu **20**
Padang Padang Inn **22**
Puri Bambu **3**
Udayana Eco Lodge **14**
Uluwatu Resort **25**
Villa Balquisse **12**
Villa Bulan Putih **18**
Villa Shaba **13**

INDIAN OCEAN

THE BUKIT PENINSULA

9

JIMBARAN BAY

To Kuta, Sanur & Seminyak

Ngurah Rai Int'l Airport

Jimbaran Beach

Jimbaran

Mangroves

Jl. I Gusti Ngurah Rai

Jl. I Gusti Ngurah Rai

Jl. Uluwatu

Benoa Bay
(Teluk Benoa)

See "Nusa Dua & Tangjung Benoa" map

Mangroves

Badung Strait

Buala

Nusa Dua

Tekud Gagar

Tekud Belongmemedi

Jalan Darmawangsa–Benoa

Ungusan   Kutuh

Pura Geger

Tirta Beach

Green Bali Beach

Surfing

Gilimanuk   Singaraja

Negara   BALI

Ubud

Denpasar

Bukit Peninsula   Nusa Penida

DINING ◆
Assam Garam **12**
Bella Singaraja **10**
Cafe Moka **32**
Dava **17**
Di Mare **33**
Honzen 97 **17**
Il Ristorante **30**

Jiwa Juice **21**
Kisik **17**
KO Restaurant **9**
Menega Cafe **11**
Nelayan **7**
On the Rocks **17**
PJ's **16**
Sangkar **30**
Seafood
  restaurants **8**
Sunset Grill **23**
Tapis **6**
Yeye's Warung &
  Gift Shop **24**

in Villa Balquisse (p. 160) make for an opulent spa experience. The "Javanese Lulur Royal Ritual" is inspired by the prenuptial treatments of the Royal court of Yogyakarta. The 2-hour treatment includes a massage with handmade frangipani massage oil, followed by 45 minutes of the invigorating Lulur skin scrub with turmeric, rice, and jasmine, followed by the yogurt splash treatment. The smells are so overpowering you'll get hungry. Fortunately the spa also has delicious tapas and a wonderful fresh ginger tea.

SURFING   **Airport Rights** and **Airport Left** (p. 86), two waves near Kuta, are also easily accessible from Jimbaran Bay. Hire a boat from shore.

SHOPPING

An increasing number of higher-end retail outlets are spread out on the main access stretch, Jalan Raya Uluwatu. Shops here are spread out, so map out where you're going beforehand. Shops are open daily, typically from 9am to 6 or 7pm.

Cocoon Home   Cocoon is for your home and yourself. Attractive jewelry on sale is from Italy, Mali, and a selection of well-known Bali designers and a Canadian designer working mainly with pearls. Shop for silk scarves with batik designs, cotton sarongs, hats, and bags. For the home, you'll find salad servers and spoons made from horn and silver, and a super selection of picture frames. Jl. Uluwatu 91. (©) **0361/705054.**

Ganesha Gallery ★★   This small gallery has a big heart and attracts a flow of dealers, buyers, and admirers. The Ganesha Gallery exhibits a different local or international artist four times a year. Works by both international and local artists always emphasize a connection between the East and West, with a definite eye towards the beauty of Bali. A recent exhibition by New Zealand artist Devina Stephens left standing room only—outside the gallery entrance! In Four Seasons Resort (p. 160). (©) **0361/701010.**

Jenggala Ceramics ★★★   From humble beginnings in a small crowded workshop on Sanur Beach, Jenggala Ceramics has grown into a multimillion-dollar business that exports around the world. The studio was founded by two, now deceased, Balinese legends: Brent Hesselyn, a New Zealand designer and potter, and Wija Waroruntu, an Indonesian hotelier. Wija's daughter, Ade, has since taken over the business. You'll encounter ceramics all over Bali—from the markets to your breakfast table—but the best ones are Jenggala. Their inspiration comes from natural forms such as frangipani, bamboo, and banana and lotus leaves. The tableware collections in a variety of colors and custom-made sets can be ordered and shipped around the world. Their impressive client list includes Chef Jean-Georges Vongerichten who orders sets for his high-profile restaurants in New York, London, and Paris. Monthly exhibits include private collections as well as work of artist-in-residence, Anne van Borselen, a sculptor and a painter from

---

(Moments)   **Paint-a-Pot & Make-a-Pot at Jenggala Ceramics**

At Jenggala Ceramics, children of all ages can explore their inner Picasso by painting raw, glazed ceramic. Prices range from US$7 to US$26. If you want to handle your own clay, 2- and 4-hour sessions are priced according to the kilos of clay used. Make a reservation for a group visit of more than two people. Hours for Paint-a-Pot are 9am to 5pm; Paint-a-Pot is US$6 to US$20, Make-a-Pot is US$12 (plus cost of clay).

> ## (Tips) Fresh Fish at Home
>
> Most villas and even hotels will be happy to have you bring back a fish and cook it for you any way you would like. Hotels might charge a small fee but the chef at your villa will not. Follow these four steps to buying fish:
>
> 1: Be prepared. Bring some ice in a cooler or in a waterproof container so you can transport your fish home. This is crucial no matter how long or short the drive.
>
> 2: Use your nose. If fish smells fishy, it is. Fresh fish should not smell bad.
>
> 3: Use your hands and eyes. When picking your fish, be sure your fish has clear eyes and a firm feel. When fish start to go off, their eyes get misty and their flesh gets limp.
>
> 4: Get it gutted. Tell the seller to gut your fish for you; if you want it scaled, ask.

Holland. Visiting and local artists also present ceramics shows here. Jl. Uluwatu II. ℂ 0361/703311. www.jenggala.com.

Paul Ropp ★★ Paul Ropp started his career selling marijuana rolling papers with the U.S. flag on them in New York. He made so much money from this venture that he funded his world travels and wound up in Bali in the 1970s. He and his wife started buying and selling clothes between India and Bali. Now Ropp has dozens of shops on Bali and franchises around the world. All of his fabrics originate from over 5,000 Indian workers who operate in home industries to produce intricate, colorful silks, cottons, and wool. Each piece is a bit of bohemian Versace; embrace the company slogan: "Clothes for people who prefer to be naked." Jl. Uluwatu 80. ℂ 0361/701202. www.paulropp.com.

Tiempo This wonderful shop sells decorative art, antiques, and furniture from Java and China and some simply marvelous pieces from Sulawesi, Timor, and Nusa Tenggara. This is a place where you can find something really special to bring home from your Indonesia travels. Jl. Raya Uluwatu I 102. ℂ 0361/745-0919.

Warisan Casa The eclectic and fusion designs here utilize durable timber such as plantation teak, mahogany, and recycled teak with other materials, such as leather, fabrics, glass, and metals. Warisan strives for every product to "last for generations" while reflecting the meaning of *warisan*—Indonesian for "heritage." Standard furniture on display costs between US$100 to US$1,500. Open Monday to Friday 10am to 6:30pm; Saturday 10am to 5:30pm. Jl. Raya Bypass Ngurah Rai Kedonganan. ℂ 0361/701081. www.warisan.com.

Market

Go early to the **Jimbaran fish market** ★★★ (Kedonganan Fish Market), on the northeast corner of the main crossroads in the village, just across the street from Pura Ulun Siwi temple. The market opens at 4am and sells the highest quality and freshest seafood in all of south Bali. The market and adjacent beach at Jimbaran Bay are hives of morning activity. Colorful wooden boats with their high prows, decorated masts, and ropes covered in bright flags provide a bright burst of color. These elaborately dressed boats come from Java, Sulawesi, and Flores, and stop on every island to sell their catch. The waters nearest to Bali are often overfished, so most of the seafood comes from other nearby waters. Young boys rush to the boats to help pull them onto shore for the market stall owners to inspect the catch.

THE BUKIT PENINSULA

9

JIMBARAN BAY

Very Expensive

Four Seasons Resort at Jimbaran Bay ★★★

The very picture of luxury, the Four Seasons is on a stunning hillside overlooking the bay. Each thatched villa has a large bedroom and marble bathroom with oversize tub. The little things stand out: thick towels and fancy bathroom amenities, two sinks, garden showers, a library with Internet access, and snap-to service. Other facilities include a top-notch spa and a cooking school. The horizon pool blends seamlessly with the ocean blue and other small pools invite you to relax and escape from it all. Walk or be driven in a golf cart down to the beach. The beach club has surfing, kayaking, and catamarans.

Jimbaran. ✆ **0361/701010.** Fax 0361/701020. www.fourseasons.com. 147 units. Peak season US$880 and up 1-bedroom, US$2,100 2-bedroom; high season US$780–US$970 1-bedroom, US$1,800 2-bedroom; low season US$680–US$870 1-bedroom, US$1,600 2-bedroom. AE, DC, MC, V. **Amenities:** 3 restaurants, PJ's (p. 162); 2 bars; babysitting; concierge; health club; Jacuzzi; 2 outdoor pools; room service; sauna; spa; tennis courts; watersports. *In vila:* A/C, satellite TV, DVD, stereo w/CD player, fridge, minibar, Wi-Fi.

Expensive

Ayana Resort & Spa ★★

When I first walked into the brand-new Ayana, Made, the doorman, had a lovely frangipani lei and a greeting of "Welcome to the Ritz-Carlton" for me. Poor Made, you can understand his confusion since it was only 2 weeks prior that this property changed hands. The Ayana, as it is now known, hasn't strayed from its former management credo, since the new company is run by the former Ritz-Carlton CEO. You can still expect the same anticipatory service chasing you around the 77 hectares (190 acres) overlooking Jimbaran Bay. Each room is decorated in muted colors with a touch of sea blue to match. The resort has its own private beach. Facilities include five swimming pools, six wedding venues, renowned restaurants, private villas, and more. Do not miss treating yourself to a rejuvenating water treatment session at the **Thallaso Spa** (p. 155). The new **Rock Bar** (p. 162) has to be one of the best beach bars on the island.

Jl. Karang Mas Sejahtera Jimbaran. ✆ **0361/702222.** Fax 0361/701555. www.ayanaresort.com. 368 units. Peak season US$760 and up; high season US$674 and up; low season US$198 and up; extra charge for kids 4–11 years old US$15. AE, MC, V. **Amenities:** 3 restaurants, Kisik, Dava, and Honzen 97 (see p. 162, p. 163, and p. 163); bar; babysitting; kids' club; gym; Jacuzzi; outdoor pool; room service; spa; tennis court. *In room:* A/C, TV/DVD, iPod, hair dryer, minibar, Wi-Fi.

Gending Kedis Luxury Villas and Spa

The name of this brand-new, ridge-top villa complex translates to "bird song," in deference to the continually chirping birds nestled in the wooded ravine below. While not directly on the beach, a shuttle service is on standby to Bali's golden mile within minutes. Each villa has a spacious pool and kitchen. You can stock your own wine refrigerator in the bar at your pool, which is a nice touch. The restaurant provides good food for good value.

Jl. Karang Mas Sejahtera 100V, Jimbaran Bay. ✆ **0361/708906.** Fax 0361/848-2188. www.gendingkedis. com. 85 villas. High season US$800 and up; low season US$725 and up. AE, MC, V. **Amenities:** Restaurant; lounge; bar; babysitting; kids' club; gym; outdoor pool; room service; spa. *In villa:* A/C, TV/DVD, hair dryer, minibar, Wi-Fi.

Villa Balquisse ★★ (Finds) (Value)

"If paradise existed, it can't be far from this" is what one guest wrote in the guest book here, and how right he is. It is hard to find fault with the lavishly decorated bedrooms in warm, earthy tones filled with artifacts, furniture, and pictures lovingly collected by the owner from her world travels. The adjoining spa is an ideal place to shake off the stresses of life in the most luxurious way possible. With additional personal touches like free drop-offs to the beach in an old Volkswagen convertible, daily afternoon tea, and fruit sticks at 11am wherever you are, this little gem is hard to leave.

Jl. Uluwatu 18X, Jimbaran. *(*C)* **0361/701695.** Fax 0361/703087. www.balquisse.com. 9 units. High season US$156–US$200; peak season US$144–US$180; low season US$132–US$168. AE, MC, V. **Amenities:** Restaurant, Assam Garam (p. 164); babysitting; bicycles; outdoor pool; spa. *In room:* A/C, hair dryer, minibar, Wi-Fi.

Moderate

Hotel InterContinental ★ (Kids) The InterContinental hotel chain knows what savvy travelers want: great service and value. The InterContinental Club (Priority Club Member: free; Ambassador Club Member: $150 in addition to room rate) here fulfills both requirements. Club members are given priority immigration clearance and delivered to check-in on the Club Floor, where the first matter of business is what you want to drink. Guests who pay for Club-class rooms enjoy evening complimentary cocktails and canapés, all day tea, coffee, and snacks and an especially lavish spread for breakfast. The Club rooms are oversize and contemporary with elegant bathrooms, spacious living rooms overlooking the Club pool, and gardens. All of this is a 2-minute walk to the private beach and the other top-notch facilities. The excellent kids' club (Star Trekkers) has superb programs that leave everyone in peace. The hotel even has its own turtle release program.

Jl. Uluwatu 45, Jimbaran. *(*C)* **0361/701888.** Fax 0361/701777. www.bali-intercontinental.com. 418 units. Peak season US$355 and up; high season US$335 and up; low season US$305 and up. AE, MC, V. **Amenities:** 2 restaurants, KO Restaurant and Bella Singaraja (p. 163 and p. 163); bar; lounge; babysitting; bicycles; kids' club; gym; Jacuzzi; outdoor pool; room service; spa; tennis court; watersports. *In room:* A/C, TV/DVD, hair dryer, minibar, Wi-Fi.

Jimbaran Puri Bali ★★ (Finds) The pioneer resort on Jimbaran beach, the Puri Bali, originally the Pansea, has stylish, self-contained garden cottages scattered among lily ponds, coconut trees, and statuary, set back from the beautiful beach. Despite its top location, this is not a big resort and you won't have to fight for sun loungers or crawl your way through the crowd to get to the breakfast area. All cottages have terraces, shaded by umbrellas, with privacy-providing screens and outdoor deck showers. Rooms are done in carved teak under thatched roofing, with mosquito netting and natural linen touches. Bathrooms have sunken tubs and all the goodies. The resort is a haven of privacy and calm, a good choice for getting away from it all.

Jl. Uluwatu, Jimbaran. *(*C)* **0361/701605.** Fax 0361/701320. www.jimbaranpuribali.com. 41 units. Peak season US$270–US$580 cottage, US$680–US$950 pool villa; high season US$220–US$520 cottage, US$610–US$860 pool villa; low season US$200–US$500 cottage, US$530–US$700 pool villa. AE, MC, V. **Amenities:** 2 restaurants, Nelayan (p. 164); bar; babysitting; outdoor pool; room service. *In room:* A/C, satellite TV, DVD player, fridge, hair dryer, minibar.

Kayumanis Jimbaran Set back from a fisherman's beach beneath a canopy of coconut palms, Kayumanis Jimbaran's spacious, yet rustic, thatch-roofed villas are excellent examples of indoor-outdoor tropical living. Your villa opens onto your private pool where a waft of sea air is mixed with the sweet smell of the frangipani trees. Your personal butler is on-call 24 hours a day to appease your every whim.

Jl. Yoga Perkanthi, Jimbaran. *(*C)* **0361/705777.** Fax 0361/705101. www.kayumanis.com. 20 villas. Year-round US$550. AE, MC, V. No children 15 years old and under. **Amenities:** Restaurant, Tapis (p. 164); Jacuzzi; outdoor pool; room service; spa; tennis court. *In villa:* A/C, TV/DVD, hair dryer, kitchen, minibar, MP3 docking station, Wi-Fi.

Puri Bambu (Finds) Although Puri Bambu has no beachfront, it is in Kedonganan, a peaceful traditional village near Jimbaran, and the beach is only 5 minutes walk away. The large rooms frame lovely garden courtyards, one of which holds a decent-size pool. Be sure to take an early morning or early evening walk around the village to get a feel for the age-old traditions that make Bali so beautiful.

Jl. Pengeracikan, Kedonganan. ℂ **0361/701468.** www.puribambu.com. 48 units. High season US$65–US$95; low season US$50–US$80; extra bed US$12. MC, V. **Amenities:** Cafe; bar; babysitting; concierge; Internet; outdoor pool; room service. *In room:* A/C, TV, hair dryer, minibar.

Villas

Villa Shaba ★★ (Value (Finds) This Moroccan-inspired villa is reminiscent of a more genteel age. The five bedrooms surround a central *riad* (courtyard) with flowing fountain. The smart, open-plan kitchen and an elegant drawing room face a generous span of French doors that open to the pool sheltered by mangroves. The suites and bedrooms can be booked individually or you can take over the entire villa. A vintage convertible Volkswagen Safari is on-call to take you to the beach. Beach picnics can be prepared at a moment's notice—complete with chilled champagne and wine.

Jl. Uluwatu, Gang Gigit Sari, Jimbaran. ℂ **0361/701695.** Fax 0361/703087. www.shaba-bali.com. 3 bedrooms. High season US$330–US$390; peak season US$300–US$366; low season US$276–US$330. Rates include breakfast. AE, MC, V. **Amenities:** Restaurant; bar; free airport transfer; babysitting; bicycles; outdoor pool; room service; spa. *In room:* A/C, fan, TV/DVD, hair dryer, minibar, MP3 docking station, Wi-Fi.

WHERE TO DINE
Very Expensive

Kisik ★ SEAFOOD *Kisik* is Balinese for "cliff rising out of the ocean," and I couldn't think of a more apt (and succinct) name for this location. The restaurant awaits on the shore at the foot of the cliff, a superb sunset spot. At night hundreds of twinkling lights from local fishing boats bob out at sea. The idea here is a copy of the typical Balinese warung with superb service and five-star prices. The menu is determined by the catch of the day. Your catch is grilled in the open kitchen as you like. When the swell is large you can actually feel the mist from the surf. Ask for the corner table with killer views.

In Ayana Resort & Spa (p. 160), Jl. Karang Mas Sejahtera. ℂ **0361/702222.** www.ayanaresort.com. Reservations recommended. Fresh seafood US$20–US$40; lobster US$200. AE, DC, MC, V. Daily 6–10pm.

PJ's ★★★ MEDITERRANEAN PJ's (Pantai Jimbaran), is one of my favorite places to dine in Bali. Mediterranean-inspired dishes, seafood specialties, and crisp thin-crust pizza from a wood-burning oven are all served in a breezy seaside pavilion where the

---

(Moments) **A Night Out on the Rocks**

The **Rock Bar** ★★★ (5pm–1am) at the Ayana resort (p. 160) sits at the base of the cliffs and is so close to the water's edge that the lovely salty sea mist of the crashing waves will make you thirsty. Choose from a long list of specialty cocktails (starting at Rp95,000). Tables are also set in a special section you access via a cave entrance. DJs perform regularly. This is the sort of spot where expats bring visitors to experience the decadence of living large on the edge.

with cucumber mint salad, lime, and spicy tomato chutney. The snapper is cooked any way you like it, and, perhaps due to it's proximity to the ocean, is the best I have ever had on the island. The service is attentive but unobtrusive and the general vibe is one of relaxed indulgence. Finish off with the molten chocolate fondant with sour cherries and homemade vanilla ice cream or the chilled passionfruit cheesecake. Or have both.

In the Four Seasons Resort Bali (p. 160), Jimbaran Bay. ℂ **0361/701010.** www.fourseasons.com/jimbaranbay. Reservations recommended. Main courses US$15–US$65; set menu upon request. AE, MC, V. Daily 11am–10pm.

Expensive

Bella Singaraja ITALIAN   You wouldn't expect good Italian food at a resort in Jimbaran Bay, but Bella Singaraja surprises even the most jaded expats, like myself. The decor is, unfortunately, a bad attempt at creating a grand dining room, but the food and service more than make up for the copper chiffon curtains. It is always a good start to have a superb antipasto of Italian prosciutto, ham, and mortadella. The veal parmigiana is a fine choice, and the grilled prawns and salad are hard to resist.

In the Hotel InterContinental (p. 161), Jl. Uluwatu 45. ℂ **0361/701888.** www.bali-intercontinental.com. Reservations recommended. Main courses US$12–US$33; set menu US$45–US$75. AE, DC, MC, V. Daily 6:30–11:30pm.

Dava ★★★ INTERNATIONAL   One of this restaurant's best attributes—other than the martini bar—is its design. The entrance features an open-air reception island, seemingly floating above a free-form pool, which in turn hovers above the Indian Ocean. The setting doesn't detract from the excellent food. The chef says, like most places in Jimbaran, that he serves international cuisine with, "fresh flavors predominately from the sea." A good example of this would be the Five Flavors of the Sea starter: "Lobster, bacon, vinaigrette, orange, sprouts, salmon, lime, black bean, mint, wasabi sorbet, pearl meat, vine ripened tomato, sesame, wakame, yellowfin tuna, Chinese olive praline, caper vinaigrette, chives, Morton Bay bug tail tempura, squid ink, and lemon peel." What a mouthful! There is a great "Martini Club Assiette" where you chose three minimartinis, out of the selection of 50 on offer, for the price of one.

In Ayana Resort & Spa (p. 160), Jl. Karang Mas Sejahtera. ℂ **0361/702222.** www.ayanaresort.com. Reservations recommended. Main courses US$25–US$250 a couple; set menu US$55. AE, DC, MC, V. Daily 7–10:30am and 6:30–10:30pm.

Honzen 97 ★★ JAPANESE/KOREAN   Honzen ("wonderful food") is a traditional Japanese/Korean restaurant for top-quality dining. Choose between *tatami* or traditional seating; downstairs is sushi and sashimi and upstairs is Korean. Honzen's sashimi is off the charts compared to the rest of the island.

In Ayana Resort & Spa (p. 160), Jl. Karang Mas Sejahtera. ℂ **0361/702222.** www.ayanaresort.com. Reservations recommended. Main courses US$10–US$12; set menu teppanyaki US$70–US$120; *yakiniku* US$45–US$80. AE, DC, MC, V. Daily noon–2:30pm and 5:30–11pm.

KO Restaurant ★★ JAPANESE   Before dinner at one of the island's best Japanese restaurants, enjoy live entertainment, drinks in the sushi lounge, and light snacks of sushi or delicious *robotayaki* skewers, and tempura. Dine in a separate sushi lounge and bar, in a private dining room, or a teppanyaki area where guests watch the culinary flair of Chef Wayan Badra, trained in Kyoto with a Japanese master. Smiling, delicate girls in brightly colored kimonos show you to your table. It's only when you notice their slightly uncomfortable walk in their *tabi* (white socks) with flip flops that you recognize their Balinese origins.

In the Hotel InterContinental (p. 161), Jl. Uluwatu 45. ✆ **0361/701888.** www.bali-intercontinental.com. Reservations recommended. Main courses US$20; set menus US$40. AE, MC, V. Daily 6:30–10:30pm.

Moderate

Assam Garam ★ (Finds INDONESIAN/MIDDLE EASTERN   This charming restaurant opens onto the fertile gardens of the Villa Balquisse. This is not haute cuisine, it's honest from the heart cooking. For appetizers, it can be hard to choose from a selection of dishes like light and fresh scallop carpaccio with lime and olive oil marinade; New Zealand lamb and mint rolls; and Moroccan salad, a blend of vegetables, olives, feta, and herbs. Two pages of main courses offer Balinese delights like roasted duck with spinach, star anise chicken on ginger risotto, and the popular lamb kebab with couscous and vegetables. For dessert, it was hard to resist the almond pear tart and the delicious selection of homemade ice cream.

In Villa Balquisse (p. 160), Jl. Uluwatu. ✆ **0361/701695.** www.balquisse.com. Reservations recommended. Main courses Rp65,000–Rp105,000; kids' menu R35,000. AE, MC, V. Daily noon–10pm.

Nelayan ★★ FRENCH/MEDITERRANEAN   The Nelayan is all about the chef, and its stunning setting is icing on the cake. French Executive Chef Lionel Auvray has an impressive track record of five-star cooking around the globe. Children get their own menu and plenty of beachfront to run wild on while you enjoy the *fruits de mer.* The Lobster Extravaganza is an indulgent and delicious five courses, starting with a cocktail, followed by the *amuse-bouche* of thinly sliced lobster and avocado in a raspberry sauce. This is followed by lobster ravioli and lobster medallions in vanilla sauce. Your little banquet ends with a fresh strawberry soup with lemon sorbet.

In the Jimbaran Puri Bali (p. 161), Jl. Uluwatu. ✆ **0361/701605.** www.jimbaranpuribali.com. Reservations recommended. Main courses US$16–US$35; set menus US$25–US$50. AE, MC, V. Daily 6:30–11pm.

Tapis ★ INDONESIAN/WESTREN   This simple and chic restaurant serves inventive Indonesian cuisine and a rijsttafel. The open-air kitchen is on view in a thatched pavilion. Western dishes include all the usual pastas and seafood.

In the Kayumanis Jimbaran (p. 161), Jl. Yoga Perkanthi. ✆ **0361/705777.** www.kayumanis.com. Reservations recommended. Main courses US$18; set menus US$50. AE, MC, V. Daily 8am–10pm.

Inexpensive ★★

Jimbaran is a mecca for seafood, with over two dozen **seafood restaurants ★★** located right on the beach. The restaurants are quiet at lunchtime but as the sun goes down, crowds arrive to admire the beautiful sunsets and paddle in the sea. Once dark, torches and candles create a wonderfully romantic atmosphere. Diners grab their tables in the

---

(Tips   **Weighing in at the Jimbaran Seafood Restaurants**

You pay only for the seafood you select and your drinks. The peanuts, entree, vegetables, and platter of fruit at the end should be included. Seafood is sold by the "kilo"—many of the scales are questionable. The restaurateurs expect you to bargain and its part of the fun. But if you want to be precise, check the scales with a liter of water, which equals 1 kilo. Then you know that they aren't inflating the price.

sand. The restaurants essentially serve the same fresh catches with a few offering some choice of style of cooking.

There are now three distinct sections of seafood shacks. Those at the far end of the bay are the originals. These are locally owned and therefore have a stake in the future and reputation of the area. The newer places are near the Four Seasons and have better toilets and furniture. Some also have a full bar service. Check all prices as they tend to get better the further you go toward the end of the bay. This strip is better than between the Four Seasons and InterContinental. The third strip, closest to the airport, is best avoided, not only because they are the greatest rip-offs but also as they are possibly unlicensed by the local authorities.

Choices are crab, clams, fish, lobster, prawns, and squid laid out at the restaurant entrance on beds of ice and, given the turnover, all guaranteed fresh that day. You can either leave the staff to choose the items or you can go directly to the barbecue area and choose it yourself. It is better to pick your own, although actually identifying it when it has been cooked, is trickier. Agreeing on a price up front ensures no surprises later on and don't be afraid to try to haggle—it is expected. The restaurants are rarely expensive and are not known for ripping anyone off, so be kind. Some places suggest that they do not haggle, but the majority price it in. Keep your ears open to what the locals expats are paying per kilo. You will be amazed by the difference.

Prices are reasonable with dinner for two with beer or soft drinks approximately R150,000 to Rp250,000. Wine is available but usually only local Balinese Hatten wine, which is best drunk either very cold or very quickly. Feel free to bring your own wine and ask if they have corkage.

Look for **Menega Cafe** ★★ (© 0361/705-888; www.menega.com/cafe.html), which stands out from a row of restaurants that basically offer the same thing for its more unique grilling approach: Most places grill on coconut shells, but here they add some secret ingredient. Though you can certainly enjoy some pleasant conversation and a few Bintangs with the manager, you'll never get him to tell you the secret.

2 ULUWATU

On the southwestern tip of the Bukit, Uluwatu is perched high on a cliff overlooking the Indian Ocean. Down below are stretches of secluded beaches, few accessible by road—the only way down is by foot. Not for the fainthearted. This also happens to be one of the most famous surf breaks in the world. The views from the cliffs overlooking the break are stupendous and satisfying enough for most.

GETTING THERE & GETTING AROUND

A **taxi** from Kuta to Uluwatu takes about 30 to 40 minutes up and down winding and dusty unpaved limestone roads; cost is about Rp150,000 one-way. Make sure you have the contact number of your destination as many taxi drivers will get lost.

EXPLORING ULUWATU

Garuda Vishnu Kencara Cultural Park   We would be remiss for not mentioning this monstrosity that is unlikely to ever be completed. The park sits above Jimbaran Bay, and was intended to be the greatest cultural park in Indonesia with a 146m (180-ft.) statue of the Hindu god Vishnu. If it is ever completed it will be taller than the Statue of

> **(Moments)** **Visiting Pura Luhur Uluwatu at Sunset**
>
> Every evening at sunset (6pm) at Pura Luhur Uluwatu dancers present a thrilling performance of kecak, arguably Bali's most famous and dramatic dance. It will cost about Rp5,000 to enter the temple and an additional Rp50,000 to view the dance. Both men and women will need to rent sarongs and sashes at the entrance if you're not already traditionally dressed.

Liberty in New York City. The very park's essence is widely debated in Bali among the local population, with some saying it was intended to serve as a "Welcome to Bali" landmark for passengers arriving by plane, while others state simply that it makes a mockery of the Hindu religion. Whatever it is, it isn't working and so far only the head and torso of Vishnu have been completed. Initially commissioned in the Soeharto era, there have been too many problems to list, though current President Susilo Bambang Yudhoyono has promised to finish the project.

Jl. Raya Uluwatu, Ungasan Kuta Selatan. (✆) **0361/703603.** www.gwk-culturalpark.com. Admission Rp30,000. Daily 8am–10pm.

Pura Luhur Uluwatu ★★   Dramatically perched on a high promontory overlooking the surf at Uluwatu, this is possibly Bali's most visually spectacular shrine. Its name literally translates as "the one on the top." Like most other temples in Bali, the origin is obscure, however inscriptions signed during the reign of King Marakata date the temple to at least 1025. The temple is well known for its walet birds, who can be seen floating and darting in the breeze and perching on the sacred temple. Their nests are an important ingredient in Chinese birds' nest soup.

Dedicated to the spirits of the sea, the temple is an architectural wonder in black coral rock, and despite its age and exposure to the elements, features well-preserved stone carvings. This is one of the six directional temples on the island and is the southwest guardian against evil spirits. This is also purportedly the dwelling place of almighty deity Bhatana Ruda, god of the elements and cosmic forces. Although the temple complex is open to all, only Hindus are allowed to enter the inner temple.

Jl. Labuan Sait, Pantai Suluban, Uluwatu. Admission Rp25,000. Daily 8am–6pm.

BEACHES **(Finds)**   Though strong rip currents and shallow waters make the beaches less than ideal for swimming, they are still great for getting wet and enjoying the stunning scenery. Uluwatu is all about the **views. Balangan,** an idyllic white sand beach fringed by cliffs, is relatively quiet and is spared the annoying trinket hawkers and too many tourists. A few cafes sit near the tree line, and the water here is safe for swimming, as the waves break over the reef 200m (656 ft.) from the shore. **Bingin** ★★★ beach is pockmarked with rock and reef, forming intriguing tide pools at low tide. **Impossibles** beach is another great setting for a seaside walk at low tide, but is more well-known as a prime surf break. **Padang Padang** ★★ is archetypically enchanting, being nestled into a pocket of lava rocks; the beach entrance is through a cave crevice. This area is great at low tide for children.

PAINT BALLING **(Kids)**   **Paintball Bali,** Jl. Karang Putih 1 (✆) **0361/770300;** www. paintballbali.com; US$60 includes pickup and drop-off, 150 bullets, three waters, one soft drink, and a hot dog, value package US$40 includes 100 bullets, three waters, one soft drink, and fries; daily 9am–9pm), occupies about 3 hectares (7½ acres) of playing fields. Facilities include individual changing rooms and lockers. Have lunch off-site as the offerings here are of the hot-dogs-and-fries variety, even though some food is included in the price. Better yet, bring your own picnic.

PARAGLIDING   Take the opportunity to fly over the glittering Indian Ocean, shimmering green rice terraces, and those crazy surfers. Seeing Bali from the sky is a vibrant reminder why this island was earmarked "Island of the Gods." You don't want to go with a paragliding service that isn't up to scratch, so make sure your chosen outfitter has certification from the Bali branch of the Indonesian Aerosport Federation. I recommend tandem flights with **Exo-Fly ★**, Jl. Toyaning 24, Kedonganan (**℃ 0361/705-517;** www. exofly.com; US$69 family package, includes two adults and two children; daily fly time 2–5pm).

SPA   If you can't afford a night at the **Bulgari** (p. 169), you're not alone. The spa **★★** (daily 9am–9pm), however, could be worth a day's indulgence. This is probably one of the finest spas on Bali, housed in an antique hand-carved teak *joglo* (Javanese house) that was dismantled in Kudos on Java, and authentically re-created on-site. Go for broke with the aptly named "Unforgettable Double Bulgari Royal Lulur" for two people, which lasts 3 hours and includes two therapists per person. Prices are steep (US$93–US$975; AE, DC, MC, V) so plan on making a full day out of your pampering and use the pool and the relaxation area.

SURFING   Some of the best surfing spots in Bali and indeed the world, can be found in the sea surrounding the west coast of the Bukit. These breaks are for experienced surfers only—they are definitely not to be tackled by novices. If the size of the waves don't get you, the razor sharp shallow reef will. The best time to surf here is during the dry season (Apr–Oct).

Uluwatu   Best swell: south; **best size:** 3 to 10 feet; **best winds:** southeast. Home to the famous Uluwatu temple and its colony of crazy monkeys, a casual visitor could be forgiven for overlooking the other zoo down the cliff and in the water at **Salubuan Beach,** break point for Bali's most famous waves. This beach has four distinct sections. The furthest out is **Temples,** which likes a mid to high tide and offers long, hollow rides towards the **Peak,** a second take-off spot directly out from Wayan Gondry's famous Green Iguana warung. The next section breaks furiously over a shallow reef and is aptly named **Race Track.** Speed is the key to survival here. Beyond that, towards Padang Padang, is **Outside Corner,** which comes into its own on only the biggest days but provides some of the most incredible heart-in-mouth surfing available on the planet. If you get it wrong here you will be washed towards the dangerously jagged rocks of the cliff-line and face a tediously long and treacherous swim back to safety. Sound like fun?

THE BUKIT PENINSULA

9

ULUWATU

(Warning!) Resident Monkeys

Watch out for local monkeys at Pura Luhur Uluwatu that like to help themselves to hats, handbags, cameras, and anything else they can get their mucky hands on. They are usually happy to exchange your valuables for some fruit, but try to avoid this tedious and potentially dangerous negotiation.

Padang Padang **Best swell:** south; **best size:** 5 to 8 feet; **best winds:** southeast. Just north of Uluwatu is not only one of Bali's premier surf locations, it's also one of Bali's nicest beaches. At Padang Padang, an easy paddle out from the lagoonlike shoreline delivers you into the gaping jaws of one of the world's most celebrated left-handers. Best on bigger swells, Padang Padang is a true proving ground for local and international surfers alike. Be sure to pop into the **Sunset Grill** (p. 173) on the road linking Padang Padang with Bingin.

Impossibles **Best swell:** south; **best size:** 4 to 8 feet; **best winds:** southeast. This long stretch of reef runs north from Padang Padang down to Bingin and owes its name to the incredibly fast and long waves that explode along the "picture perfect" reef. Though widely heralded as an oasis of sorts, given the right swell period and direction, Impossibles can still deliver unbelievable waves that will be etched forever in salt across a surfer's memory. It's rare that surfers actually make it, so expect an absolute beating if you are outrun by the watery freight train and left to battle with the coming wider, wilder sets. Surf it on the mid-tides and on larger swells.

Bingin **Best swell:** south; **best size:** 3 to 5 feet; **best winds:** southeast trade winds. This is one of the best, albeit shortest, left-hand barrels available in Bali. A short, hollow, and punchy ride, Bingin is fondly followed by hordes of local and international surfers looking for an easy bit of tube time.

Dreamland **Best swell:** south-southwest; **best size:** 3 to 5 feet; **best winds:** southeast trade winds. This was once one of the most beautiful and picturesque beaches on all of Bali—fully deserving of the apt name. Now the charming, old warungs are gone and the once pristine landscape has been butchered for a monstrosity of a hotel structure to be implanted on the once amazing cliff-face (p. 170). The golf course hosted the 2008 Indonesian Cup Tournament, for those surfers who fancy a bit of golf trivia.

Wave wise, Dreamland is a mellow option surrounded by more serious waves, and thus attracts hordes of less skilled surfers. This is still a good option for a cruise session and is best on lower tides. Keep your eyes on everyone and don't forget your mouth guard as collisions are common here.

Balangan **Best swell:** south; **best size:** 4 to 8 feet; **best winds:** southeast. Balangan is a left-hand wave breaking off the headland to the north of Dreamland. It can be found easily these days owing to the signs and newly sealed roads delivering you straight to this once semi-secret location. As a fast and hollow wave, Balangan has the habit of catching surfers unaware as the bigger sets loom much further out than where the pack normally assembles. Sitting further out than the pack can pay dividends: As the big sets come your new friends will watch with jealousy as you take off free from trouble as they contemplate their own imminent smashing. Surf here on the mid- to higher tides.

(Tips) Surf Board Repairs

If you ding your board, "Cookie the Legend" will fix it for you. From the bottom of the stairs to Uluwatu Surfing Beach, go left. He's the last one in a string of warungs before you reach the cave. You can't miss it.

Tips **Sand Fleas**

Depending on the time of year and the flow of certain currents you may encounter sand fleas on Uluwatu beach. They seem to be particular to Uluwatu and nobody knows why. It could be because the water here is a bit cooler due to its depth and sand fleas migrate with the flow of currents and in cooler climes. They are invisible at first but once you start feeling the bite, and take a closer look, you'll see they look like sand. They are perfectly harmless, yet can be very annoying. Repel them with heavy-duty mosquito repellent or very strong citronella.

If you are walking around the cliff tops here, look out for the craggy rocks and be sure not to stub your toes while watching the waves. Also look out for the green snakes. They look friendly but are among Bali's most dangerous.

Green Balls **Best swell:** south; **best size:** 4 to 6 feet; **best winds:** west-northwest. Located just near the Bali Cliff Resort (on the peninsula's southern face), the main wave at Green Balls is the right-hander at the bottom of the stairs. On the other side of the channel the left-hander can get good too, with lighter winds or days when there is some north in the breeze. You can check the wave from the cliff top, which is a blessing given the 500 or so steps down to the sand. Hire a local to help you with your gear and take plenty of water. It's a long way down and in this case, what goes down must come back up.

WHERE TO STAY

The main choice of accommodation here is either a five-star-über-luxury hotel or a multimillion-dollar villa. However in recent years, many of the rustic surfer accommodations have come of age and make a good alternative for those on a budget.

Very Expensive

Bulgari Hotel & Resort 186 ★★ Only two Bulgari hotels grace the world, and one of them is here. Propped up by the brand name, Bulgari's villas come with a hefty price tag. The edge of a cliff is no natural setting for a series of villas and a monumental amount of limestone has been excavated to create sheer, gleaming walls and terraces to ensure all 59 villas on this steep incline have a sea view. This has in no way been a sympathetic development project. The result however is one of elegance and luxury.

Notwithstanding the environmental impact, this place oozes Italian chic; the distinctive, masculine Bulgari style is complemented by natural lava and palimanan stone and dark exotic woods like bangkeray hardwood and mahogany. Everything is subtle, classy, and handmade in Bali. The villas have oversize sexy black marble bathrooms and smallish bedrooms with colorful Sumbanese hand-woven bedcovers and a thrilling bed sheet thread count. Every villa has its own private plunge pool with views over the cliff tops and the sea beyond.

Jl. Goa Lempeh, Br. Dinas Kangin, Uluwatu. ✆ **0361/847-1000.** Fax 0361/847-1111. www.bulgarihotels. com. 60 units. High season US$870–US$1,580; low season US$750–US$1,460. AE, DC, MC, V. **Amenities:** 2 restaurants, Il Ristorante and Sangkar (p. 172); bar; fitness center; Jacuzzi; outdoor pool; room service; spa. *In room:* A/C, TV/DVD, hair dryer, minibar, MP3 docking station, Wi-Fi.

Pecatu Indah Development & the New Kuta

Once called Dreamland in Pecatu Indah, this development is now called New Kuta—a strange name and an even stranger place. The original name came from a white sand beach on the western coast of the Bukit peninsula, a favorite haunt for local and international tourists due to its gorgeous beach, laid-back warungs, and a slice of old Bali beach life, that many including myself considered paradise. Sadly "Dreamland" has become a nightmare. Several years ago Tommy Suharto, disgraced son of the former Indonesian president, and his rich cronies tried to develop Dreamland into something grander, but the group initially went bankrupt. Today, they are back in the chips, and the New Kuta development is going full steam ahead. The 400-hectare (1,000-acre) project is well underway and will include private residences, luxury hotels, a convention center, theme park, hospital retirement community, and an international school. The area already has a completed golf course overlooking the old Dreamland beach and recently hosted the 2009 Indonesian Open—the first PGA Golf event to be held in Bali. A huge desalination pipe to water the golf course now runs out into the surf, thus changing the breaks, and will eventually change the coastline of the area. New Kuta bills itself as "the most beautiful investment in the world." Some beg to differ.

Alila Villas Uluwatu ★★ This brand-new, top-of-the-line ecoresort has Green Globe's stamp of approval, meaning all of the materials are sustainable or recycled and the use of water and energy meets their stringent requirements. Perched upon a plateau of wild savanna landscape, every villa has a spectacular ocean view and its own pool. Each guest is assigned a personal butler who coordinates with a leisure concierge to customize experiences that meet your interests, schedule, and preferences. They also offer "Alila Journeys," half-day wellness programs that include yoga and meditation classes and self-care recommendations, Bali arts and crafts, culinary experiences, and excursions. While staying here, slip into the cliff-top Sunset Cabana for dinner at dusk and simply get inebriated on the sea air and stars.

Jl. Belimbing Sari, Banjar Tambiyak, Desa Pecatu. ✆ 0361/848-2166. Fax 0361/848-2188. www.alila hotels.com. 85 units. High season US$800 and up; low season US$725 and up. AE, MC, V. **Amenities:** 3 restaurants; babysitting; gym; outdoor pool; spa. In room: A/C, TV/DVD, iPod, hair dryer, minibar, Wi-Fi.

Moderate

Mick's Place Mick's Place in Bingin, near Uluwatu, is a surfer's dream come true. Over the past 8 years Mick has built six seriously simple Polynesian-influenced round huts on this patch of cliff above Bingin Beach. It is a great place for those who want to explore the famous surf breaks nearby, heal their senses at Mick's Yoga Sanctuary, or rejuvenate body and soul at the on-site restaurant. He also offers shopping expeditions and will even provide you with his own driver.

Jl. Pantai Bingin II, Bingin Beach. ✆ 0361/847-0858. www.micksplacebali.com. 6 units. High season US$90–US$250; low season US$70–US$200. No credit cards. **Amenities:** Restaurant; outdoor pool; room service. In room: Fan.

Inexpensive

Mu Uluwatu   These nine thatched bungalows with wooden floors and stone walls overlook both Bingin and Impossibles, yet are within walking distance of Uluwatu and Padang Padang. Comfortable digs come with king-size beds, mosquito nets, and individual bales. A saltwater pool and Jacuzzi sit on a nice wooden deck with a smashing view. The friendly French management will arrange yoga on-site; they also have mountain bikes for rent and can arrange sailing nearby.

Jl. Pantai Bingin, Pecatu. ⓒ **0361/847-0976.** www.mu-bali.com. 9 units. Peak season US$70–US$180; high season US$60–US$160; low season US$55–US$150. No credit cards. **Amenities:** Restaurant; bar; bicycles; saltwater pool and Jacuzzi; Wi-Fi. *In room:* Fan, TV/DVD (in Bintang bungalow only).

Udayana Eco Lodge ★   This is a superb choice for a very alternative holiday. The 30 hectares (74 acres) of bush land, overlooking Jimbaran and Benoa bays with views of Mount Agung, are protected by the University of Udayana as a flora and fauna refuge. All of the ecofriendly buildings rely on solar power, while an extensive rainwater storage system keeps the gardens lush and prolific. The rooms are simple bordering on spartan with rattan and tropical materials used for the few bits and pieces of furniture. The 22 types of bougainvillea on-site are home to hundreds of butterflies, and make nice playgrounds for the over 60 species of birds—the bulbul and the kingfisher being the most common sightings. The staff will give you a simple guidebook and loan you a set of binoculars. On Sundays, guests are welcome to join impromptu matches on the lodge's cricket lawn where several of Indonesia's test matches have been held. You're likely to meet some interesting and likeminded people on your stay, as we did, when we befriended a Norwegian ornithologist who aided us in our quest for the kingfisher.

Jl. Kampus Universitas Udayana, Bukit. ⓒ **0361/747-4204.** Fax 0361/701098. www.ecolodgesindonesia. com. 14 units. Year-round US$45–US$70. AE, MC, V. **Amenities:** Restaurant; bar; lounge; outdoor pool; room service; Wi-Fi. *In room:* A/C, fan.

Villas
Very Expensive

Groups are spoiled for choice in this area for entire estates that rent by the night. **The Istana** ★★, Jl. Labuan Sait, Pantai Suluban, Uluwatu (ⓒ **0361/762868;** fax 0361/ 769866; www.theistana.com; 5 bedrooms; peak season US$2,900; high season US$2,450; low season US$1,650; rates include breakfast, other meals market price; AE, MC, V) was recently renovated with little expense spared. The villa has a children's wing, games room, and private master suite with its own pool.

The stunning **Karang Putih Villa** ★★, Jl. Karang Putih 1, Banjar Kutuh Ungasan, Uluwatu (ⓒ **0361/731074;** www.elitehavensbali.com; 6 bedrooms; peak season US$2,800; high season US$2,200; low season US$1,500; rates include breakfast, other meals market price; AE, MC, V), has a colonial feel with a modern twist, elegantly furnished with Asian antiquities. The villa has its own private beach club, a floodlit grass tennis court, boules court, putting green, and helipad.

From the Sanskrit word for "Seventh Heaven," we get the **Khayangan** ★★★, Jl. Goa Lempeh, Pecatu, Uluwatu (ⓒ **0361/732013;** fax 0361/736705; www.balivillaworldwide. com; 6 villas; peak season US$4,000; high season US$3,500; low season US$2,750; meals market price; AE, MC, V), a private villa above Selonding Beach, with an unobstructed view of the Indian Ocean. This villa's unique design features 11 antique *joglo*, once the traditional homes of Javanese aristocracy. The villa has two infinity edge pools, a spa, a tennis court, and even lawn croquet.

Sunsets can be seen from the two master bedrooms fronting the ocean in the **Karang Kambar Estate** ★, Jl. Karang Kembar, Banjar Jabapura, Desa Kutuh, Kuta Selatan, Badung (✆ **65/9018-1742** in Singapore; www.bali-karangkembarestate.com; 5 bedrooms; peak season US$1,150 and up; high season US$950 and up; low season US$775 and up; rates include breakfast, other meals market price plus 10%; AE, MC, V). The villa has a private beach house on the reef, making it an ideal place to go with children when the tide is out as there are some very exotic fish in the tide pools.

The **Long House** ★★, Jl. Goa Gong, Kompleks Tiara Nusa, Jimbaran (✆ **0361/ 780-3046;** www.thelonghousebali.com; 6 bedrooms; peak season US$1,500; high season US$1,000; low season US$800; extra bed US$25; rates include breakfast, other meals market price; AE, MC, V), perched just above the village of Goa Gong above Jimbaran, was built to take advantage of a 180-degree view of endless glassy blue Indian Ocean and the volcanoes in the horizon. The villa has a spa, gym, Jacuzzi, and movie theater; there's even an elevator to get to the three stories without lifting a finger . . . well maybe just to push a button.

Villa Bulan Putih ★★★, Jl. Pantai Bingin Labuan Sait, Pecatu (no phone; www. villabulanputih.com or info@villabulanputih.com; 7 bedrooms; peak season US$1,200; low season US$900; meals market price plus 10%; AE, MC, V), is all subdued tones and minimalist modern sculpture that create a sense of calm. Nothing distracts from the stunning views beyond the French windows. A big plus is the immaculate lawn for the wee ones to wander and for impromptu ball games.

Expensive

Karma Kandara Villas ★   Karma Kandara is one of the more impressive new resorts in Bali. The villas are all privately owned, so while you are in residence you feel comfortably at home, albeit not your own. The one- to four-bedroom whitewashed poolside villas sitting above the surf are covered in bougainvillea. Most bedrooms face the sea and have semi-outdoor bathrooms with grandiose stand-alone tubs for two. The plunge pools have dark wooden decks that make a more private alternative to the resort's main pool, but the *pièce de résistance* is **Nammos Beach Club,** accessed by a private "inclinator" down the near sheer cliff face. Sitting on an impossibly picturesque beach with a fertile coral reef just offshore, this club is great for snorkeling and is exclusive to guests, albeit only thanks to its privileged inaccessibility. DJ music spins nightly. Non–resort guests can pay US$25 to use the beach club facilities for the day. A sister resort is the **Karma Jimbaran** (www.karma jimbaran.com), in Jimbaran Bay, though it's not as fabulous as this location.

Jl. Villa Kandara, Br. Wijaya Kusuma, Ungasan-Bali. ✆ **0361/848-2200.** Fax 0361/848-2201. www.karma kandara.com. 22 villas. Peak season US$760 and up; high season US$674 and up; low season US$605 and up. AE, MC, V. **Amenities:** Restaurant, Di Mare (p. 173); bar; babysitting; bicycles; kids' club; gym; Jacuzzi; outdoor pool; room service; spa; watersports. *In villa:* A/C, TV/DVD, hair dryer, minibar, MP3 docking station, Wi-Fi.

WHERE TO DINE

The most noteworthy restaurants are in the large hotels and come with large hotel price tags. A few cafes on Jalan Uluwatu are worth stopping for. Along the many beach breaks are plenty of local warungs good for a cold beer or a simple snack. Choose one that looks busy that day. Unless otherwise noted, restaurants are open daily.

Very Expensive

Il Ristorante & Sangkar ITALIAN/BALINESE   An Italian inspired and locally influenced cuisine distinguishes these two poolside restaurants in the Bulgari. Overlooking a reflection pool, the resort's signature **Il Ristorante** ★★ has masterful Italian cuisine mixing the finest Italian ingredients with the islands' organic produce. For more casual, all-day dining, the **Sangkar** combines authentic Balinese dishes—enriched with various regional influences from the Indonesian archipelago—with a selection of international specialties. The homemade cookies are delicious. You can buy the condiments to bring home, making them possibly the most competitively priced goods with a Bulgari label.

In the Bulgari Hotel & Resort 186 (p. 169), Jl. Goa Lempeh. ✆ **0361/847-1000.** www.bulgarihotels.com. Reservations recommended. Il Ristorante: main courses US$30–US$70; set menu US$170 and up. Sangkar: main courses US$20–US$20. AE, DC, MC, V. 6:30am–11pm (Il Ristorante dinner only).

Expensive

Di Mare ★ MEDITERRANEAN   Acclaimed as one of Bali's most spectacular dining venues and one of the must-see spots, the Di Mare frames the ocean and sky from atop a craggy overhang 85m (280 ft.) above a crystal lagoon. Executive Chef Raymond Saja turns out zestful Mediterranean-meets-Pacific-Rim cuisine accompanied by an exhaustive list of classic and new world wines. The kitchen uses the freshest season-driven local ingredients; fresh oysters are presented with aplomb.

In the Karma Kandara Resort (p. 172), Jl. Pura Masuka. ✆ **0361/848-2200.** www.karmakandara.com. Reservations recommended. Main courses US$16–US$50; set menu US$45–US$200. AE, MC, V. 6am–11pm.

Inexpensive

Jiwa Juice JUICE BAR   Fresh juices, salad fare, and a good snack menu are available to keep you pumped up for surfing of a different sort (free Internet). Internet access is intermittent in this neck of the woods and for that reason alone Jiwa Juice has a loyal following. The bulletin board here is chock-full of information on where to get your board fixed, available villas and *losmen* for rent, and local parties.

Jl. Labuan Sait 108, Pecatu. ✆ **0361/847-0736.** Main courses RP30,000–Rp50,000. No credit cards. Dry season 8am–10pm; wet season 8am–8pm.

Sunset Grill ★ (Finds) MEXICAN   If the thought of going Latino appeals while in Bali, this is your place. Ten-year-old Sunset Grill, the first-ever restaurant in Uluwatu, is run by Cacho, from Puerto Rico. He and his Balinese wife make killer *chimichangas* with fiery Indonesian chilies complemented by pitchers of marvelous margaritas. In the words of Cacho, "We have several rules here and people don't like that. The first is you can't be in a rush, we don't like beautiful, useless garnishes, and we never ever advertise, in fact we try to discourage business, because it gets too crowded. We only have three staff and me and 30 seats." Full meals without alcohol rarely go above US$7 and meals are rarely without alcohol. Cacho also runs a pizza delivery service called Papi's (same phone number). A word of advice, don't sit in Cacho's chair.

On the beach in Padang Padang. Cacho's mobile ✆ **08/1337406173.** Main courses Rp30,000–Rp65,000. No credit cards. From lunch until Cacho says it's closing.

Yeye's Warung & Gift Shop (Finds) INDONESIAN/INTERNATIONAL   Yeye's is not your typical warung. You've got lots of choices here, but the seafood salad of fresh local octopus and prawns is a favorite. The grilled mahimahi or snapper is served with a daily selection of fresh vegetables. If you want your fish served the local way, ask for it steamed in banana leaf with *sambal*. A few good Indian curries and Thai dishes are thrown in for good measure as are pizzas, *jaffles,* burgers, sandwiches, pancakes, and desserts, which change daily. Thursday is a much-loved night for the barbecue of chicken, seafood, sausages, steaks, and kabobs. At night there is often a surf movie playing and it can all feel a bit Beach Blanket Bingo gone Tropo.

Jl. Labuan Sait, Pecatu. ✆ **0361/742-4761.** Main courses Rp27,000–Rp32,000. No credit cards. Noon–midnight. Past the bridge at Padang Padang beach on Jl. Uluwatu; go straight a few meters.

3 NUSA DUA

Nusa Dua is a 300-hectare (740-acre) government-sponsored, self-contained, high-end tourist destination replete with manicured lawns, swaying palms, white sand beaches with pristine waters, and security gates at all entry and exit points. Virtually all accommodation here is five-star, and unlike the rest of the Bukit Peninsula with its barren shrub land and limestone cliffs, sandy soil reaches down to a long stretch of immaculate beach, protected by a reef. Coconut trees abound and remind us that before the local government fashioned this resort complex to "minimize the impact of tourism on the Balinese culture," Nusa Dua was once a coconut plantation. Also in contrast to the rest of the island, the roads are bereft of potholes, the streets are empty and litter free, and not surprisingly it can all seem a bit sterile.

The immediate vicinity lacks activities. Many tourists seem content with simple R&R and, being only a 20-minute drive from the airport, it is a convenient place to base yourself on a short break.

GETTING THERE & GETTING AROUND

Most if not all hotels in Nusa Dua offer an airport pickup service, but you can also find shuttles and cheap taxis at the airport. (Be sure to take only the official blue-and-yellow metered taxis; see p. 39.) *Bemo* from Denpasar go to Nusa Dua by way of Kuta and Jimbaran.

These big resorts make it so comfortable, you won't have to leave the grounds—but even the most starry-eyed honeymooners might want a break from expensive hotel meals. Most hotel taxis are rentable at a pricey US$11 per hour; but if you are going out for the day, it can work out to be more convenient and more cost effective to hire a car and driver from a private company such as **Amertha Dana** (✆ **0361/735406**).

Driving around Nusa Dua is confusing, making **walking** and **cycling** (most hotels rent bikes) the best, and really only, way to get a feel for the lay of the land. The hotels are all set side by side and a beachside boardwalk takes you all the way down the strip. It's about a 5km (3-mile) walk.

FAST FACTS **Prima Medika Clinic,** in Grand Hyatt Hotel (p. 178; ✆ **0361/771234**), has general clinic hours from 9am to 9pm and a 24-hour on-call service. The staff at **Kimia Farmacy,** Jl. Bypass Ngurah Rai 890 (✆ **0361/774118**), are generally helpful and can prescribe minor medication for most ailments. A doctor is on-site daily 4 to 10pm to consult for any minor ailments. The **police** office of Bualu/Nusa Dua is located at Jl. Bypass Ngurah Rai (✆ **0361/772110**). Most hotels can send letters and post cards. For parcels and any recorded items the only **post office** in the area is Udayana, Bukit Ungasan, Nusa Dua (✆ **0361/771202**).

WHERE TO STAY

With many of the hotels, there is little difference between them so it comes down to personal choice and price. It's worth considering the hotel club floors as they serve sunset

ATTRACTIONS ●
Bali Game Safari **23**
Bali Golf & Country Club **17**
Bali Star Island **15**
Pasifika Museum **13**

ACCOMMODATIONS ■
Amanusa **22**
Balé **21**
Club Med **8**
The Conrad **6**
Grand Hyatt Bali **14**
Kayumanis Nusa Dua **9**
Laguna Resort & Spa
  Nusa Dua **12**
The Nikko Hotel **23**
Novotel Coralia Benoa Bali **3**
Nusa Dua Beach Hotel
  and Spa **10**
The Royal Santrian **7**
Rumah Bali **4**
St. Regis Bali **18**
Wantilan Villas at the Bali Golf
  and Country Club **17**
Westin Resort Nusa Dua **11**

DINING ◆
Bali Collection **13**
Bumbu Bali **5**
Eight Degrees South **6**
Faces **21**
Geger Beach **20**
Italian Restaurant **22**
Kayuputi **18**
Mayang Sari Restaurant **12**
Nampu **14**
Nusa Dua Bar and Grill **19**
Nyoman's Beer Garden **16**
Ocean Terrace **12**
Piasan **9**
Raja's Bali Cuisine **10**
Rin **6**
Spice **6**
Surya Café **1**
Tao **2**
The Shore Restaurant
  and Bar **23**

BENOA
Tanjung
Benoa

Jl. Segara

Jalan Pratama

Jl. Setra
Gandamayu

Sri
Lanka

Jl. Telaga Waja

Gang Welaka

Jalan Pratama

Mangroves

Badung
Strait

To Jimbaran

CELUK

Jalan I Gusti Ngurah Rai

Jl. Pratama

Post Office ■

BUALA

Bali Golf
& CC

NUSA
DUA

Jalan Kuruksetra

Jl. Amphi

Jl. Siligata

Jl. Pantai Mengiat

Geger Beach

Amanusa
Golf Course

Nusa Dua

Pura Geger

Nusa Dua Selatan

0   1/2 km
0   1/2 mi

Gilimanuk   Singaraja

Negara   BALI

Ubud

Denpasar

INDIAN
OCEAN

Nusa Dua &
Tanjung Benoa

🏄 Surfing

THE BUKIT PENINSULA

9

NUSA DUA

cocktails, canapés, all-day refreshments, and breakfasts separate from the hotel's main buffet. With alcohol at a premium on the island, this can work out to be a good deal. Many of the hotels have beach frontage and if they don't they will usually have their own beach club accessed by golf carts with liveried staff supplying cold water and fresh towels throughout the day.

Very Expensive

Amanusa ★★★ The Amanusa has a magnificent hilltop setting overlooking a golf course and the beaches. It comes with quite a price tag, but a visit to Amanusa is an invitation to service that is gracious and intuitive, and to accommodations that are over-the-top luxurious while remaining in harmony with the surroundings. Rooms are crafted in rich redwood with four-poster beds, sunken tubs, and outdoor and indoor showers. The central 24m (79-ft.) pool is stunning; and in-house dining at the Terrace is an experience in itself, with great views and delicious local cuisine. The beach club, a short drive down the hill, offers a collection of private bales that front the Bali Golf and Country Club. Staff can arrange diversions that range from cycling excursions to island cruises to cooking classes, shopping, and adventure tours.

Bali Golf & Country Club, Nusa Dua. ✆ **0361/772333**. Fax 0361/772335. www.amanresorts.com. 35 units. Year-round US$750–US$1,150. AE, MC, V. **Amenities:** Restaurant, Italian Restaurant (p. 179); babysitting; bicycles; gym; outdoor pool; room service; spa; tennis court. *In room:* A/C, TV/DVD, hair dryer, minibar, MP3 docking station, Wi-Fi.

Balé ★ Balé means "bungalow" in Balinese, but the moniker is rather modest—this is an absolutely beautiful collection of villas set on a hill overlooking the ocean. Each villa has its own plunge pool and a daybed in the courtyard. The interiors are elegantly simple, with large bathrooms and outdoor showers. While not set right on the beach, the Balé has a shuttle that whisks you to its own private beach club in 2 minutes. The resort is popular with yuppies and gay couples. For adults seeking peace, an added bonus is that no children under 15 are allowed.

Jl. Raya Nusa Dua Selatan 76, Nusa Dua. ✆ **0361/775111**. Fax 0361/775222. www.thebale.com. 29 units. High season US$600–US$900; low season US$450–US$750. AE, MC, V. No children 14 years old and younger. **Amenities:** Restaurant, Faces (p. 179); bar; bicycles; gym; outdoor pool; spa. *In room:* A/C, TV/DVD, iPod, hair dryer, minibar, Wi-Fi.

Kayumanis Nusa Dua If the private-villa-no-children-allowed concept appeals to you but the Balé is too pricey, try the Kayumanis. This is a collection of sophisticated and exclusive adult-orientated villas that lacks the beach facilities offered by the Balé. All the villas feature semi-open bathing facilities complete with outdoor shower recess and a personal pool edged by a sun deck and lounges. A handy feature is a modern kitchenette and a private butler who will make your breakfast in your villa at no extra charge. No two villas are architecturally alike and you can choose between Balinese, Javanese, Oriental, Palembang, primitive, and modern styles.

BTDC Area Nusa Dua. ✆ **0361/770777**. Fax 0361/770770. www.kayumanis.com. 20 villas. Year-round US$488–US$988. AE, MC, V. No children 15 years old and under. **Amenities:** Restaurant, Piasan (p. 180); Jacuzzi; outdoor pool; room service; spa; tennis court. *In room:* A/C, TV/DVD, hair dryer, kitchen, minibar, MP3 docking station, Wi-Fi.

St. Regis Bali ★★★ It would have to take something fairly grand to find a niche in the glut of luxury resorts in Nusa Dua but the "six-star" St. Regis fits the bill. From the private concierge who whisks you through airport immigration and baggage claim to the personal butler who is assigned to each room or villa, the emphasis at the St. Regis is on service. A number of the villas have private access to a swimmable lagoon, while other villas sit directly beachfront. Rooms and villas have Balinese and colonial-style furniture and come with private balconies and gardens. The resort also pays special attention to food, with Kayuputi, Boneka, serving delicious made-to-order, table-service buffet breakfasts with delicacies including sashimi, oysters, and foie gras, and the Gourmand Deli with not-to-be-missed ice cream.

Kawasan Pariwisata Nusa Dua Lot S6, Nusa Dua. ✆ **0361/847-8111.** Fax 0361/847-8099. www.stregis. com. 123 units. High season US$750 and up; low season US$450 and up. AE, MC, V. **Amenities:** Restaurant, Kayuputi (p. 179); bar; babysitting; bicycles; gym; outdoor pool; room service; spa; watersports. *In room:* A/C, TV/DVD, hair dryer, minibar, MP3 docking station, Wi-Fi.

Expensive

Laguna Resort & Spa Nusa Dua ★   The hotel formerly known as the Sheraton

underwent a US$7.5-million renovation and name change in 2006, though it's still managed by Starwood. Here, they call their type of luxury "indigenous" luxury. Every day features some type of cultural performance and the whole place has the feel of Indonesia's royal roots. And yet, the atmosphere of the Sheraton still lurks, though the rooms, once flower-fussy, have turned modern. The main draws remain the beachfront and the lagoonlike pool accessed directly by ladders from some of the ground-floor rooms. Large bathrooms are done in marble. Extra special treats include complimentary high tea with tableside dessert service and the midnight massage on offer in a beachfront bale after dinner. Peel me a grape, Gilbert.

Kawasan Pariwisata Nusa Dua Lot N2, Nusa Dua. ✆ **0361/771327.** Fax 0361/771326. www.luxury collection.com/bali. 271 units. High season US$400 and up; low season US$350 and up. AE, MC, V. **Amenities:** 2 restaurants, Mayang Sari Restaurant and Ocean Terrace (p. 181 and p. 180); bar; babysitting; bicycles; gym; Jacuzzi; outdoor pool; room service; spa; tennis court; watersports. *In room:* A/C, TV/DVD, hair dryer, minibar, Wi-Fi.

Wantilan Villas at the Bali Golf and Country Club   These villas are really for

golf lovers since they overlook the Bali Golf and Country Club course. Putters will enjoy the immediate accessibility to the course with priority tee times, discounted greens fees, and other guest privileges. Golf widows will enjoy the exclusive access to the private Amanusa Beach Club—a major benefit, as this is by far Bali's best-kept secret and unless you are in residence at the Amanusa it is impossible to use the facilities. Each villa has a private swimming pool and Jacuzzi with a sun deck, and fully equipped kitchen. Each bedroom is freestanding and detached with its own private bathroom. Personal cooks are on stand-by from 7am to 11pm to prepare meals either from the provided menu or according to your fancy.

Bali Golf & Country Club, Nusa Dua. ✆ **0361/771791.** Fax 0361/771797. www.wantilangolfvillas.com. 3 villas. Year-round US$345 standard; US$895 3-bedroom; US$1,195 4-bedroom. AE, MC, V. **Amenities:** Babysitting; golf course (p. 182); Jacuzzi; outdoor pool. *In room:* A/C, TV/DVD, hair dryer, Wi-Fi.

Westin Resort Nusa Dua (Kids (Value   This resort is for those who like to combine a

few hours of telecommuting with their vacation. Business travelers will appreciate the Wi-Fi, a great club lounge, and nicely appointed rooms with a safe big enough for a laptop. The hotel is also a good choice for families, with little touches for the kids including a separate check-in area, special buffet counter at breakfast, and, most important, a kids' club with complimentary babysitting all day long. With these amenities and rates as low as US$150 for a double during the low season, the Westin is a bargain for families. It's a high-quality version of a cookie-cutter experience—that is, you know what you're going to get: great service, fantastic dining, and beds so comfortable they're branded the "Heavenly."

BTDC Area Nusa Dua. ✆ **0361/771906.** Fax 0361/771908. www.westin.com. 346 units. Year-round US$300 and up. AE, MC, V. **Amenities:** Restaurant; bar; lounge; babysitting; bicycles; kids' club; gym; outdoor pool; room service; spa; tennis court; watersports. *In room:* A/C, TV/DVD, hair dryer, minibar, Wi-Fi.

Moderate

Club Med (Kids)(Value)

Club Med was the first hotel in Nusa Dua and recently finished a major renovation. But let's face it: You don't come here for the rooms or the food, you come here for your kids. On any given day, there are more than 160 kids at this resort. All-inclusive packages include all meals, alcohol—excluding champagne and cognac—and activities. The big draw is the kids' clubs (for ages 2–17) for different age brackets with age-appropriate activities, so boredom doesn't enter your child's vocabulary. Watersports include canoeing, kayaking, snorkeling, and windsurfing; games include every manner of ball game, archery, and circus games (including the trapeze). Live bands, nightly dinner shows, and baby food on the buffet make nighttime revelry just as hassle-free. Parents can participate in all the activities, as well as enjoy the spa, gym, aqua-gym classes, yoga, a six-hole golf course, and that all important, all-inclusive bar.

BTDC Area Nusa Dua, Lot 6. ✆ **0361/771521.** Fax 0361/771831. www.clubmed.com. 410 units. Prices per person all-inclusive high season US$280–US$560; low season US$240–US$480; extra charge for kids 2–4 years old US$24–US$48, 5–11 years old US$170. AE, MC, V. **Amenities:** Restaurant; bar; babysitting; kids' club; gym; Jacuzzi; outdoor pool; room service; spa; tennis court; watersports. *In room:* A/C, TV/DVD, hair dryer, minibar, Wi-Fi.

Grand Hyatt Bali

The self-styled description of being a "Balinese water palace" is a little hard to swallow given there are close to 700 rooms in four very inauthentic low-rise Balinese-style buildings at this resort. But the grand entrance with views of the immaculate beach and the water features (lagoon pool, outdoor river pool, and water slide) help the cause. Rooms are five-star standard. Ditch the kiddies at Camp Nusa (included in rates; children 3–13) and make a bee-line for the award-winning Kriya spa with its resident nutritionist and ayurvedic treatments.

BTDC Area Nusa Dua. ✆ **0361/771234.** Fax 0361/772038. www.bali.grand.hyatt.com. 648 units. High season US$280 and up; low season US$130 and up; extra charge for kids US$35 Grand room, US$60 Club room. AE, MC, V. **Amenities:** Restaurant, Nampu (p. 180); bar; babysitting; kids' club; gym; Jacuzzi; outdoor pool; room service; spa; tennis court; watersports. *In room:* A/C, TV, hair dryer, minibar.

The Nikko Hotel (Kids)

The Nikko is unique in Bali, being 15 stories high, making it about 10 stories taller than all others. The normal restriction on buildings being higher than a coconut tree has been supplanted as the hotel is built into the side of a 40m (131-ft.) cliff. The hotel is protected by dramatic cliffs and coves on either side, giving it its own private beach setting. Rooms with teak floors all have private balconies. An amphitheater features nightly entertainment, including the famous Balinese *kecak* dance. One of the more unique offerings at the Nikko is camel rides on the beach (p. 182)—the kids will love it. There is also a great children's jungle camp where you can send your little monkeys to rope climb and burn some energy. The pool facilities are superb and include an artificial beach, water volleyball and basketball areas, hot tubs and lap areas, and a water slide.

Jl. Raya Nusa Dua Selatan, Nusa Dua. ✆ **0361/773377.** Fax 0361/773388. www.nikkobali.com. 389 units. Peak season US$320–US$830; high season US$270–US$780; low season US$240–US$750. AE, MC, V.

Amenities: Restaurant, the Shore Restaurant and Bar (p. 181); bar; babysitting; kids' club; gym; Jacuzzi;
outdoor pool; room service; spa; tennis court; watersports. *In room:* A/C, TV/DVD, hair dryer, minibar, Wi-Fi.

Nusa Dua Beach Hotel and Spa (Value)   Architecturally alone in Nusa Dua is this
Balinese-styled property featuring sculptures, paintings, and carvings, making it a more sympathetic offering than the other choices on this stretch. The mature Balinese gardens, with temples and ponds with gaggles of ducks, make up for the slightly tired interiors. It's about half the price of some of the other hotels and given they are all on the same stretch of sand, this a great value. There are also nightly performances in their mini–outdoor theater that are good old-fashioned touristy fun.

Kawasan Pariwisata Nusa Dua Lot N4, Nusa Dua. ℂ **0361/771210.** Fax 0361/772617. www.nusaduahotel. com. 381 units. Peak season US$240–US$3,250; high season US$185–US$3,225; low season US$190–US$3,200. AE, MC, V. **Amenities:** Restaurant, Raja's Bali Cuisine (p. 180); bar; lounge; babysitting; bicycles; kids' club; gym; Jacuzzi; outdoor pool; spa; tennis court; watersports. *In room:* A/C, TV/DVD, hair dryer, minibar, Wi-Fi.

WHERE TO DINE

Limitless restaurants are in the hotels. The **Bali Collection** (p. 184) has 36 decent and reasonably priced Indonesian and Western cafes that often have live music and a bit of ambience at night—certainly more than you'll find in any mall during the day. Most are open daily for both lunch and dinner, though some spots are open for breakfast for early morning shoppers. Your other bet for reasonable prices and decent Indonesian fare might be to head to **Uluwatu** (p. 172) or **Jimbaran Bay** (p. 162). Unless otherwise noted, restaurants are open daily.

Very Expensive

Kayuputi ★★ SEAFOOD   Kayuputi is Bali's chic new place to "do" lunch. Serving chilled and grilled seafood dishes with sharing in mind, the freshest line-caught fish is ideal for the sashimi as a starter; choose from a selection of Sturia and Prunier caviar and seasonal imported oysters. The classy but friendly atmosphere here hits the mark. Outdoor and indoor seating sits just above the beach bales and the beautiful people below.

In the St. Regis (p. 176), Kawasan Pariwisata Nusa Dua Lot S6. ℂ **0361/847-8111.** Fax 0361/847-8099. www.stregis.com/bali. Reservations recommended. AE, MC, V. Main courses US$50; set menu US$115. Noon–5pm and 6:30–11pm.

Expensive

Faces ★ INTERNATIONAL   Faces is a destination spot, as it is one of the most relaxing restaurants on the island with its refreshingly uncomplicated cuisine. Poached lobster with wild mushroom sauté, creamy risotto, and truffle essence is a house specialty. A complimentary pickup and drop-off service is provided to guests staying in the Nusa Dua, Tanjung Benoa, and Jimbaran Bay areas.

In the Balé (p. 176), Jl. Raya Nusa Dua Selatan 76. ℂ **0361/775111.** Fax 0361/775222. www.thebale.com. Reservations recommended. No children 14 years old and under. Main courses US$20; set menu US$45. AE, MC, V. 7am–11pm.

Italian Restaurant ★ ITALIAN   As with all things Aman, the Italian Restaurant at Amanusa is just one step ahead. An incredibly generous antipasti table with simply delicious prosciutto and slivers of exquisite salami are a must. Be spoiled with the best bruschetta on Bali. Specialties include the gnocchi with spicy sausage and Napolitano sauce and a classic rendition of tiramisu. Book a table in the courtyard overlooking the pool and enjoy the nightly live *rindik* music.

In the Amanusa (p. 176), Nusa Dua. ☎ **0361/772333.** Fax 0361/772335. www.amanresorts.com. Reservations recommended. Main courses US$40; set menu upon request. AE, MC, V. 6–11pm.

Nampu JAPANESE   With the largest sake and *sho chu* selection on the island, this restaurant means business. The collection consists of 14 sakes, served either hot or cold, and nine varieties of *sho chu*, made from sweet potatoes. Prices per bottle can be less than an average bottle of wine on Bali, so sip and swig away while sampling the sashimi and sushi. The selection includes tuna, salmon, snapper, kingfish, sea bass, and yellowtail. Other favorites are *kani maki*—deep-fried soft-shell crab rolls with fish eggs—and the *karubi* beef—grilled short ribs with garlic. Nampu also has four teppanyaki tables and a menu of grilled and sautéed dishes to match.

In the Grand Hyatt Bali (p. 178), BTDC Area. ☎ **0361/771234.** www.bali.grand.hyatt.com. Reservations recommended. Main courses US$17; set menu US$50. AE, MC, V. 6–11pm.

Ocean Terrace ★★ SEAFOOD   This outdoor venue approaches the ideal for a beach restaurant. When the sun goes down and the weather permits, it's hard to beat the ambience. Fine dining options include 5- to 10- course menus prepared after a personal consultation with the chef. There are a la carte options and fresh seafood choices from the on-site aquarium. Evenings feature live jazz.

The Laguna Resort & Spa Nusa Dua (p. 177), Kawasan Pariwisata Nusa Dua Lot N2. ☎ **0361/771327.** Fax 0361/771326. www.luxurycollection.com/bali. Reservations recommended. Main courses US$25; set menu US$180 per couple. AE, DC, MC, V. 11am–11pm.

Piasan ITALIAN   Balinese Chef Ketut incorporates organic fresh vegetables into many of his dishes at the Piasan. A typical lunch for two may consist of a Caprese salad, followed by homemade fresh angel hair pasta with lobster, tomato, and cream. You can also choose from an assortment of thin-crust Italian-style pizzas. Kayumanis Private Villas do not cater to children 15 years old and younger.

In the Kayumanis Nusa Dua (p. 176), BTDC Area. ☎ **0361/770777.** Fax 0361/770770. www.kayumanis. com. Reservations recommended. Main courses US$20; set menu US$65. AE, MC, V. 11am–10pm.

Raja's Bali Cuisine BALINESE   This beachfront restaurant sits side-by-side with the main swimming pool at Nusa Dua Hotel and Spa. Balinese cuisine is rarely served outside the warungs, so if you aren't feeling adventurous, then Raja's is a good place to start. A signature dish is the *bebek betutu*, a whole duck marinated in a secret blend of 16 Balinese spices, wrapped in palm leaves, and slow cooked. Another specialty is *palem sari ulam*, steamed seafood in coconut curry pudding.

In the Nusa Dua Beach Hotel and Spa (p. 179), Kawasan Pariwisata Nusa Dua Lot N4. ☎ **0361/771210.** www.nusaduahotel.com. Reservations recommended. Main courses US$8–US$40; set menu upon request. AE, MC, V. 11am–10pm.

Moderate

Geger Beach   This is the main warung on Geger Beach run by the local *banjar*. It is a decent spot for typical Indonesian fare with beach lounges laid out in front for rent for about Rp5,000 a day. A Russian billionaire has just bought up the surrounding land, meaning the future of this stretch of beach between the Nusa Dua Bar and Grill all the way to the St. Regis hotel is up in the air. Everyone is keeping an eye on what is going to come of it, but so far, everything is pretty much business as usual. Food is typical good warung grub. Stick with simple requests like chicken satays and *nasi goreng*.

On the beach, next door to St. Regis (p. 176). © **0361/746-3117.** Main courses Rp10,000–Rp15,000. No credit cards. 8am–8pm.

Mayang Sari Restaurant INDONESIAN   While a little off-beat for an Indonesian restaurant, it's nice to see modern Indonesian cooking on offer when very few places on the island have it. Decor includes Murano glass chandeliers, the finest Balinese lace table linens, and paintings by artist Wayan Artana, renowned for his modern Balinese style. Chef Ida Bagus Oka uses a variety of authentic Indonesian recipes using local produce and a range of Indonesian herbs and spices. Our favorite is the seared Sumbawa yellowfin tuna with black pepper crust with tempeh and snake skin fruit mille-feuille, snow mushrooms, and fennel—as unusual as it is delicious. There's also nightly live piano music.

In the Laguna Resort & Spa Nusa Dua (p. 177), Kawasan Pariwisata Nusa Dua Lot N2. © **0361/771327.** www.luxurycollection.com/bali. Reservations recommended. Main courses Rp95,000–Rp360,000. AE, MC, V. Mon–Sat 7–11pm.

Nusa Dua Bar and Grill ★★ (Kids) (Finds)   INTERNATIONAL/SEAFOOD Owned by Tim, a Californian surfer in his 50s and his Balinese bride, Putu, the Nusa Dua Bar and Grill on Geger Beach is quite simply an institution. Excellent fresh fish is bought daily at the market and grilled to order with fresh vegetables and rice or potatoes. The tuna sashimi, when available, is a memorable choice. There are good smoothies, ice cold Bintang (local beer), and a funky bar with well-worn stools and a wide range of cocktails. This beach and restaurant are an expat hang, with oiled up Europeans with kids, and surfers laid-back enough to not mind the noise. This place is difficult to find but there is a free pickup and drop-off service in the Nusa Dua and surrounding areas. Call ahead for this; even if you don't know where you are, they'll find you.

Jl. Pura Geger. © **0361/743-4779.** Reservations recommended. Main courses Rp50,000–Rp150,000. No credit cards. 8am–10pm.

Nyoman's Beer Garden (Finds) INTERNATIONAL   A curious offering but pleasantly surprising if you want to leave the sterile surrounds of Nusa Dua. International and Balinese cuisine is served by a German chef and if you order a day in advance you are assured fresh lobster, *babi guling* (roast pig) or *bebek betutu* (roast duck). The beer is cold and the company laid-back and convivial. There is nightly live music.

Jl. Pantai Mengiat X. © **0361/775764.** Reservations recommended. Main courses US$4–US$30; set menu US$20. MC, V. 11am–midnight.

The Shore Restaurant and Bar ★ SEAFOOD   Designed as a contemporary interpretation of a boat on stilts, this restaurant has three very distinct levels to choose from. The lower deck seating is on the marina overlooking the beachfront; the second level is air-conditioned with full glass panels instead of walls allowing you to enjoy the view; and the top timber deck is an intimate spot for late night cocktails under the stars. The most popular dish is the seafood platter of the catch of the day, Indian Ocean rock lobsters, prawns, squid, tuna loin, and snapper filet. Needless to say, the platter is big enough to share. The surprise favorite is the terrific lasagna. Evenings feature a tapas menu for late-night grazing.

In the Nikko Hotel (p. 178), Jl. Raya Nusa Dua Selatan. © **0361/773377.** www.nikkobali.com. Reservations recommended. Main courses US$20; set menu US$45. AE, DC, MC, V. 11am–midnight.

EXPLORING NUSA DUA

With one of the most perfect stretch of **beaches** in Bali, it's hard to leave Nusa Dua. One of my favorite activities here is to just amble along the beachfront promenade at sunset

---

(Finds) **The Nusa Dua Seaweed Farmers**

Seaweed farming has long been a source of income to the communities around what we now call Nusa Dua. At the beginning of Nusa Dua's building boom in the 1980s, Suharto's regime decided there was a better use of the land than seaweed farming, and many of the traditional farmers had to leave. Fortunately, the *memula bulung* (seaweed farmers) have returned to their rightful land and continue their tradition of farming and way of life. Farmers plant and harvest along Geger Beach. The best time to catch them is at sunrise and they usually plant 1 or 2 days before the full moon. At planting time they carry their boats into the water with huge stacks of seaweed cultivated from deeper water. Indonesia is the second biggest seaweed-producing country in the world and supplies about one-fourth of the world's demand for seaweed. What you witness being harvested in Nusa Dua may end up in your cosmetics, medicine, or food stabilizers, but is rarely used with your sushi.

---

or in the early morning before it gets too hot. Another perfect sunrise/sunset activity is watching the **seaweed farmers** (above) next to **Geger Beach,** which is also the safest place for children to swim. If you're looking for a bit of activity, contact any of the **watersports** outfitters along the beach. In the bay are glass-bottom boats for snorkeling trips and many places to hire jet skis, sailboats, and catamarans.

Pasifika Museum ★   Located within the boundary of Nusa Dua, this museum displays a collection of Asian and Pacific art with some 300 paintings, including *tapa* bark paintings from Oceania, and 250 objects, including sculptures and tapestries, on permanent display in the 11 pavilions. Be sure to check out the work by Balinese artists Ida Bagus Nyoman Rai and Nyoman Gunarsa.

Bali Collection. (℃) **0361/774935.** Admission R50,000. Daily 10am–6pm.

CAMEL RIDES   *Sudan* was the name of the camel that took me for a ride. He was a friendly chap but fairly indifferent to my poking and prodding. I was introduced to him by **Bali Game Safaris** ((℃) **0361/776755;** www.balicamelsafaris.com; US$35 adults, US$20 children 5–12), out of the Nikko Hotel Bali (p. 178). The camels will put up with you for about an hour and take you on a giggle-inducing ride down the Nusa Dua beach. Daily trips leave at 9 and 10:30am or at 3 and 4:30pm.

DOLPHIN WATCHING   Bali has several dolphin-watching spots, and the best are in Nusa Dua, Tanjung Benoa, and Lovina (p. 279). In Nusa Dua you can go any time of day, whereas you have to go at sunrise or sunset in Lovina. Several tour operators will pick you up and bring you on a glass-bottom boat for a 4-hour tour up-close and personal with these gentle and smart creatures in their own habitat. Any hotel in the area can book these tours, which typically include pickup and drop-off, lunch, 3 hours dolphin watching, and insurance. Check out **Bali Star Island** ((℃) **0361/778076;** www.balistarisland.com; US$85 adults, US$55 for children 12 and under).

GOLF   **Bali Golf & Country Club** ((℃) **0361/771791;** www.baligolfandcountryclub. com; US$150 and up 18 holes; special stay and play rates available) is between the

Ayodya and the St. Regis resorts. This very good holiday course, once rated among the top five in Asia by *Fortune* magazine, starts at the beach and heads up the hill past the doors of the Amanusa Hotel. Other facilities include an excellent grass driving range with a new golf academy, Acorna Golf Institute, with a resident PGA Professional to give lessons.

SPA Most of the hotels have their own spas but we have two favorites (open daily). Designer Bill Bensley's whimsical approach to the deliciously decadent St. Regis' **Remede Spa** ★★★ (p. 176; signature rituals US$121–US$475, massage US$80–US$245, body treatment US$33–US$135; AE, MC, V; 8am–11pm) is simply inspired. The overriding theme employs lots of moons and butterflies; the best time to come is at night when the creative lighting makes the butterflies seem as if they are going to fly away. Each treatment is customized by your own spa concierge. **Laguna Resort & Spa** (p. 177; single treatment US$60–US$145; spa villa for couple, including dinner US$410; AE, MC, V; 9am–midnight) offers "midnight massages" on their beach bales facing the crashing waves. If the rhythmic movement of your treatment doesn't lull you to sleep certainly the sea air will.

SURFING At **Sri Lanka** (**best swell:** south; **best size:** the bigger the better; **best winds:** north and northwest, rainy season between Nov–Apr), the immaculate beach carries the polished persona of a private resort beach. The gentle lagoon is fantastic and safe for swimmers and there are all manner of recreational watercraft for rent. On lower tides the reef on the outer side creates and shapes perfect and fast right hand waves for competent wave-riders.

You reach the **Nusa Dua wave** (**best swell:** south; **best size:** 4–8 ft.; **best winds:** west-northwest) by heading south out of the town and either paddling over or hopping a short

Balinese Dance Performances on the Bukit Peninsula

Below is a list of Balinese dance performances you can attend while staying on the Bukit peninsula. Most are in Nusa Dua and all (except at the temple) include a Balinese buffet. Schedules are always subject to change so call ahead or ask your hotel or villa concierge about the latest schedule.

Performance	Days	Time	Cost (Rp)
Grand Hyatt Nusa Dua			
Barong	Mon	8pm	100,000–388,000
Ramayana	Tues	8pm	100,000–388,000
Kecak	Wed & Sat	8pm	100,000–388,000
Legong	Thurs	8pm	100,000–388,000
Jegog	Fri	8pm	100,000–388,000
Balinese Dance Parade	Sun	8pm	100,000–388,000
Nusa Dua Beach Hotel			
Ramayana	Tues	8pm	325,000
Legong	Fri	8pm	325,000
Pura Luhur Uluwatu			
Kecak	Daily	6pm	55,000 (no dinner)

Ashes to Ashes, Dust to Dust: Cremation

Cremation is the most important ceremony in the Balinese life cycle, as it is said to release the soul. It is a time for celebration, not sorrow, and thus is wonderfully colorful. Cremation is also an extremely costly affair: People will begin saving for their cremation in middle age. The average family spends about Rp15 million on the ceremony, about a year's wages, while wealthy families have been known to lavish hundreds of millions of rupiahs. If there is not enough money saved, families may have to wait years, sometimes more than a decade, before they can hold a cremation. In this case, bodies are buried and then exhumed after enough money has been saved and collected from the community for the cremation. The cremation is always on an auspicious day chosen by the priest from the local or nearby village, according to the Balinese calendar and the movement of the moon.

A large bamboo tower, its size and shape dictated by the caste of the dead person, is built for the cremation. A wooden life-size bull (for men) or cow (for women) is sometimes carved. On the morning of the cremation, the family of the deceased entertains friend and relatives and then the body is placed inside the bamboo tower. The village kul-kul (wooden gong) is struck and the construction is carried in noisy procession to the cremation ground by the banjar (village community members).

Cremation is the most impressive of Balinese ceremonies and usually families don't mind if you watch, although you should bring some money or a nice gift out of respect. One of the best places to see a cremation is in the Jimbaran Bay and Nusa Dua area. The cremation grounds are located in Mumbul in Nusa Dua about 700m (2,297 ft.) after McDonald's on the right-hand side as you come from Kuta. It's best to ask a local at your hotel or villa if there is one happening on the day you want to go.

boat ride from Geger Beach. For nonsurfers, you can also take a boat and all ages can gain a front-row seat to view the watery battlefield from the safety of the channel. This is one of Bali's heaviest waves, with loads of swell. With a take-off zone as large as a football field it can be easy to get stuck inside at this heavy right-hander, giving helpless fools lots of time to contemplate their erroneous wave judgment from below the surface in a natural washing machine.

SHOPPING

The less-than-swanky mall in Nusa Dua, the **Bali Collection** (© 361/771662; www. bali-collection.com) has an hourly shuttle that makes the rounds to most of the hotels. The mall sits between the Grand Hyatt Bali to the south and the Melia Bali Sol to the north. The Bali Collection feels like an outdoor mall in a middle-class suburb in America, complete with small restaurants, palm trees, and a tranquil vibe so quiet it is almost desolate. Food outlets include Starbucks, Baskin-Robbins, and, due to the influx of Russians, some Russian fare as well.

Nusa Dua isn't known for its nightlife but all of the hotels have bars for the thirsty. The cream of the crop is the **Nat King Cole Bar** at the St. Regis, which originally made the Bloody Mary famous.

4 TANJUNG BENOA

Just north of Nusa Dua lies Tanjung Benoa fishing village. The labyrinth of streets in this town makes for a good stroll, certainly more culturally interesting than sterile Nusa Dua. Tanung Benoa is a center for watersports, such as snorkeling, windsurfing, water-skiing, parasailing, and outrigger sailing, thanks to the calm protected lagoon.

For centuries the natural means of communication between this area and the rest of Bali was by boat, as this was easier than the overland route via Jimbaran. Tanjung Benoa, which appears isolated at the tip of the peninsula, was a trading port for Badung and the eastern Bukit, with a world outlook extending right across the archipelago. Its population still bears traces of this mercantile past. Chinese have lived here for centuries and a *Tatu Cina* or shrine in the local temple bears witness to this, as does the Chinese temple located next to the mosque, which is next to the Hindu temple, which is all cattycorner to the fish market.

GETTING THERE & GETTING AROUND

Tanjung Benoa is 4km (2½ miles) north from Nusa Dua. You can actually walk the beach promenade to Tanjung Benoa from Nusa Dua Beach. Taxis from the airport cost about Rp110,000.

FAST FACTS   Available for drop-ins from 8am to 8pm, with a dentist available by appointment only, is **Bali Nusa Dua Emergency Clinic,** Jl. Pratama 81, Tanjung Benoa (© 0361/771-324). A **police** post is located at Jl. Pratama, at the intersection of the Conrad Hotel and the Nusa Dua Complex in the BTDC area of Nusa Dua.

EXPLORING TANJUNG BENOA

The **Tanjung Benoa harbor** is one of the most placid spots on the island and is perfect for watersports. You can also try the "flying fish," a parasailing-like amusement using an extra-large inflatable kite. The beach is always busy. Be sure to book your watersports ahead of time from June to August as the place can be heaving with locals during the school holidays. There are plenty of operators to choose from but if you're staying in a local hotel, go with the operators they recommend or the services they offer. There will be little difference in price and you can rest easy that the operators are of a higher standard than those coming off the beach.

For spa time, go to the **Jiwa Spa** ★★, in the Conrad (p. 186; single treatment Rp750,000–Rp1,130,000; package Rp1,500,000–Rp1,550,000; AE, MC, V; daily 8am–10pm). Take your time and enjoy the private infinity pool and the relaxation lounge as well as the complimentary sauna and steam room. The kid-friendly Conrad always keeps the wee ones in mind: There is a Jiwa Spa Kids, where one of the treatments is "back scratching fun."

WHERE TO STAY

The **Royal Santrian,** Jl. Pratama Tangung Benoa (© **0361/778181;** fax 0361/776999; www.theroyalsantrian.com; 22 units; peak season $565–$795; high season $515–$745;

low season $465–$695; AE, DC, MC, V), villas are next door to our favorite spot, the Conrad. It's an excellent location. All white, bright, and brand new, the villas have their own patch of private beach and individual pools.

Expensive

The Conrad ★★★ (Kids) The most family-friendly of Bali's resorts, the Conrad has over 300m (1,000 ft.) of pristine beach fronting a calm, child-safe lagoon—and a plethora of activities. Friendly, switched-on staffers guide older kids and parents in water-sports like kayaking, parasailing, sailing, and wakeboarding; they also run the Kura Kura Kid's Club, where younger kids participate in Balinese arts and crafts, kite-making, and sand-castle-building. The rooms are spacious and contemporary (no delicate antiques to knock over—just clean-lined furniture and comfy couches); each comes with a stuffed toy monkey and rubber bath turtle. There is even a children's hair salon. The rooms have a refreshing contemporary feel with natural linen covers, dark woods, and impressive original Indonesian tribal art pieces. The on-site restaurants include the casual Eight Degrees South, and the more refined Spice, for Middle East and Far East cuisine. At East, the lobby bar, the oyster martini is a must; you can then retire to the nearest beach bale to star gaze. The Deluxe Lagoon rooms have full ocean views, and you can dive off your terrace into the lagoon.

Jl. Pratama 168, Tanjung Benoa. ✆ **0361/778788.** Fax 0361/778780. www.conradhotels.com. 360 units. High season US$310–US$650; low season US$210–US$450. AE, MC, V. **Amenities:** 3 restaurants, Eight Degrees South, Spice, and Rin (p. 187, p. 187, and p. 187); bar; babysitting; bicycles; kids' club; gym; Jacuzzi; outdoor pool; room service; spa; tennis court; watersports; Wi-Fi. *In room:* A/C, TV/DVD, hair dryer, minibar.

Moderate

Novotel Coralia Benoa Bali ★ (Kids) This hotel is slightly more upscale than your typical Novotel. The resort straddles the main street: The ocean side is more expensive and has better beach access, while the "garden" side is quiet and secluded. Better still, for the price, are the beach cabanas, which are even bigger suites in semiprivate bungalows (two per pavilion) with outdoor stone tubs. Rooms are big, bright, and airy, decorated in a minimalist Asian style. Lots of activities, including aerobics, soccer, a kids' club, and dance and cooking lessons, will keep you on the run if you like. The free shuttle to Nusa Dua is convenient for touring, but it's hard to see that you would need it. The ocean here is much deeper and better for swimming, too.

Jl. Pratama, Tanjung Benoa. ✆ **0361/772239.** Fax 0361/772237. www.novotelbali.com. 190 units. Year-round US$115–US$162 standard; US$205–US$252 beach cabana. AE, DC, MC, V. **Amenities:** 2 restaurants; 2 bars; babysitting; kids' club; fitness center; Internet; 3 outdoor pools; room service; spa; tennis court. *In room:* A/C, satellite TV, fridge, minibar.

Rumah Bali ★ (Value) This bed-and-breakfast is one of the best values in Bali. The bungalows have outdoor kitchens and generous bathrooms (with outdoor shower); deluxe bungalows get their own plunge pool. The people who run this hotel also own **Bumbu Bali** (see below) and they'll send a chef over to cook all your meals if you wish. The peaceful pool is set in a garden, while the beach is just a 5-minute walk away. If you're on a budget, you can stay here and use the beachside pool at the restaurant **Tao** (p. 188) for something close to a five-star experience.

Jl. Pratama, Tanjung Benoa. ✆ **0361/771256.** Fax 0361/771258. www.bedandbreakfastbali.com. 10 units. Year-round US$100–US$125 bungalow, plus US$20 per night high season. AE, MC, V. **Amenities:** 2 restaurants; outdoor pool; tennis court. *In room:* A/C, satellite TV, fridge, kitchen, minibar.

The main street of Tanjung Benoa has lots of empty cafes that are best avoided.

Bumbu Bali ★★ (Finds) BALINESE   At Bumbu Bali you dine in a re-creation of a Balinese village, including a central courtyard. On Wednesdays and Fridays, expect to see local dancers, gamelan players, or the odd *barong* dancer performing between tables. Swiss owner Heinz von Holzen's enthusiasm for Balinese cuisine is so strong, he has even written a book: *Bali Unveiled: The Secrets of Balinese Cuisine*. His food is the real deal and not modified for Western tastes. How can you tell? Good Balinese cuisine is spiced not spicy. Heinz's *sambal* is mixed with over 20 spices adding just the right amount of sizzle. Heinz is so insistent on using the freshest ingredients that he has his vegetables harvested overnight in the mountains and brought down to the restaurant each day. A team of four men source just 5kg (11 lbs.) of fish per day for the restaurant. Order the rijsttafel to sample the myriad of goods on offer. For something a bit more conservative, the ultra-rich green papaya soup with seafood is a meal in itself. The restaurant also hosts a cooking school.

Jl. Pratama. © **0361/771256.** Main courses Rp50,000–Rp175,000. MC, V. Daily 11am–10pm.

Eight Degrees South ★★ BARBECUE   Sample delicious barbecue and a variety of salads, pizza, sandwiches, and Asian specialties in an open-air beachside atmosphere. Behind the restaurant is the swimming pool and in front is the wide open expanse of the private beach. Three things: the Bintang is in frozen ice mugs; a very fresh salad bar is available for lunch daily; there is an excellent choice of homemade ice creams.

In the Conrad Bali (p. 186), Jl. Pratama 168. © **0361/778788.** www.conradhotels.com. Reservations recommended. Main courses US$10–US$28; set menu US$50–US$105. AE, MC, V. Daily 11am–11pm.

Spice ★ MIDDLE EASTERN   Spice takes advantage of Bali's proximity to the Spice Islands by serving Middle, Near, and Far East cuisine. They also have a tandoori oven. The new man in charge, Chef Richard Miller, has a few tricks up his sleeve to share as well and recommends the sub-primal cuts of Wagyu beef with a marbling grade of nine—which translates to "melt in your mouth."

In the Conrad Bali (p. 186), Jl. Pratama 168. © **0361/778788.** www.conradhotels.com. Reservations recommended. Main courses US$25–US$33; set menu US$70–US$105. AE, MC, V. Daily 7–11pm.

Rin ★★ JAPANESE   The menu at Rin is based on experiencing all the known flavors: salty, bitter, savory (or *unami*), sweet, and sour. The traditional flavors and seasonal ingredients of Japanese cuisine are given an eclectic twist. Take, for example, the *Chawan-mushi*, a steamed savory custard blended with foie gras that is silky and smooth yet complex.

In the Conrad Bali (p. 186), Jl. Pratama 168. © **0361/778788.** www.conradhotels.com. Reservations recommended. Main courses US$25–US$33; set menu US$70–US$105. AE, MC, V. Daily 7–11pm.

Surya Café ★★ (Finds) SEAFOOD   It doesn't get any more local than this wonderful gem. Getting to this joint is half the fun. The Surya is hidden away in a warren of waterfront shacks near the Buddhist monastery and the Chinese temple and a block from the fish market. Walk down the alleyway that connects to the side of the house and is bracketed by a billiards hall. To the right, down the alley, you can actually peer into the home of the Chinese proprietress and her Sumbanese husband. The cafe's blue hand-painted sign has images of smiling lobsters and friendly fish. Enter the restaurant at the end of the *gang* (alley) and to the right you will see live tanks with all manner of creatures on sale for your supper. The quaint restaurant serves simple, delicious, fresh seafood made to your specifications. The restaurant sits right on the harbor with fishing boats tied to the small pier to the left.

Jl. Segara Lor 21. ℂ **0361/772016.** Main courses US$3–US$5. MC, V. Daily noon–10pm.

Tao ★ (**Finds**) THAI Chef Vaewta Chookasem serves up modern Thai food at this stand-alone restaurant across the street from the Ramada. The menu has a few offerings from other Southeast Asian countries as well, but it's best to stick with the Thai. You won't be disappointed. Although they don't like to advertise it, anyone having lunch at Tao is welcome to use the beachfront Ramada pool and facilities for the day. Sunday nights feature live music.

Jl. Pratama 96. ℂ **0361/772902.** www.taobali.com. Reservations recommended. Main courses US$4–US$30; set menu US$20. AE, MC, V. Daily 10am–11pm

Ubud

*It appears that each Balinese native
From the womb to the tomb is creative,
And although the results are quite clever,
There is too much artistic endeavor.*

—Noel Coward to Charlie Chaplin

Ubud was the cultural, artistic, and spiritual heart of Bali centuries before the tanned, toned, and bejeweled began to sashay through the hallowed haunts of south Bali. Perhaps Ubud's destiny as a point of confluence was sealed in the 8th century by Rsi Markendya, a wandering priest from Java, who (legend has it) found the perfect patch for meditation where the eastern and western branches of the Wos River meet in Campuhan. This holy site is now Guning Lebah temple. Ubud's position as a center of the arts developed under Tjokorde Rai Batur, king from 1850 to 1880, a member of the Satriya family of Sukawati, who had been significant supporters of the arts and culture over the centuries.

Ubud's modern cultural prominence is a result of a fortuitous meeting of one of the scions of the House of Ubud and Walter Spies, who came to Denpasar in 1926. At the time the arts in Bali were undergoing a process of redefinition, as the traditional forms of patronage and funding, namely the rajahs and the temples, were under Dutch colonial rule and were no longer sources of wealth. Survival meant innovation and an important meeting of the minds. Walter Spies came to Ubud on the invitation of Prince Sukawati, and, together with friend and fellow artist Rudolf Bonnet, encouraged and financed individual artists in developing new styles that put art and artist ahead of tradition. This is known as the Pita Maha (p. 18).

At about this same time Bali became *the* bohemian destination for glamorous artistic society, Dorthy Lamour, Charlie Chaplin, and Noel Coward loved it, Margaret Mead and her lover Gregory Bateson got married on a ship en route to Bali, and Barbara Hutton fell head-over-heels for Walters Spies who had a different sort of partner in mind altogether.

By the early 1960s, Ubud had attained fame as a unique artists' community. Enter Arie Smit, the most well-known and longest surviving Western artist in Ubud, whose Young Artists school of painting in Penestanan earned him an enduring place in the history of Balinese art. In the following years the entire artistic region around Ubud flourished, including the enclaves of Campuhan, Penestanan, Sanggingan, Nyuhkuning, Padang Tegal, Pengosekon, and Peliatan. Nearby are the centers of wood carving at Mas and of silverware at Celuk.

Described by many as one of the world's most magical destinations, Ubud, despite the advance of yoga centers, spas, villas, and luxury hotels, remains relatively unchanged. The town has taken a stand against the encroachment of tourism and has defended its cultural practices and artistic endeavors against the influx of outsiders. By order of decree no McDonald's, Starbucks, or KFCs are allowed within its boundaries.

1 ORIENTATION

GETTING THERE & GETTING AROUND

Many hotels in the area offer pickup service, and taxis connect from the airport (Rp180,000), about an hour away. *Bemo* drop you in the center of town, while the tourist shuttles have their own stops, usually on one of the two main drags.

With the encroachment of so many smaller villages into the center of downtown, Ubud is more like an expanding minimetropolis than a sleepy royal village. Central Ubud is small enough to see on foot and hotels will generally provide regular shuttles into town. The main street is **Jalan Raya Ubud,** which runs east-west; **Monkey Forest Road** (Jl. Monkey Forest) runs perpendicular. Jalan Raya Ubud becomes Jalan Raya Campuhan (that is, the "main street" of Campuhan) to the west, which in turn becomes Jalan Raya Sayan. **Minivans** are for hire on every corner for day trips or short jaunts across town. Make sure either they have a meter or you get a fixed price before you set off. **Taxis** are few and far between in Ubud and most have arrived from the south and are looking for a fare to take them back home. **Motorbike** rental will cost about Rp50,000 to Rp75,000 for the day. **Bicycles** are available for hire at two or three street-side locations along Monkey Forest Road for about Rp10,000.

VISITOR INFORMATION, TOURS & MAPS

The **information kiosk,** on the south side of Jalan Raya Ubud (✆ **0361/973285**), near the intersection with Monkey Forest Road, is a good place to start. They have up-to-date listings of dance performances scheduled around town. For other information on good restaurants, shopping, galleries, and museums it is better to check with your villa manager or hotel concierge. Travel agencies are scattered all over town, each offering competitive prices for day trips and shuttles to other tourist areas. We recommend: **HIS Tour & Travel,** Jl. Monkey Forest (✆ **0361/972621**), **Bintang Tours,** Jl. Raya Ubud, Campuhan (✆ **0361/975992**), and **Muda Prima Holiday Tours,** Jl. Raya Mawang (✆ **0361/981465**). A local map called *Pathfinder* is a few years old, but is the most user friendly of the lot.

(*Fast Facts*) Ubud

Banks & ATMs Ubud has several banks and most will exchange cash and travelers checks. ATMs are not as prevalent as in Seminyak and Kuta but there are plenty of them around. Not all banks have ATMs.

Currency Exchange Most hotels and stores will exchange money, but the rates are poor. Several money changers are scattered about town; the best is **Central Kuta** (✆ **0361/974381**), on Jalan Raya Ubud in front of Museum Puri Lukisan, and in between Permata Bank and Animale shop.

Hospitals & Clinics The **Ubud Clinic, Medical, Laboratory Service & Pharmacy** is at Jl. Raya Campuhan 36 (✆ **0361/974911**). **Ubud Hospital** is at Jl. Dewi Sita (✆ **0361/974415**). Other services include **MF Medical Service,** Jl. Monkey Forest

(*©* **0361/971426**), and **Toyo Clinic** (medical and ambulance service), Jl. Pengosekan (*©* **0361/978078**).

Internet Access Ubud has several Internet cafes, including Pizza Bagus (p. 205). The cheapest and the fastest speed connection are **Netvice Internet,** Jl. Hanoman 35A, Padang Tegal; on Jalan Raya Ubud, **Bali 3000 Internet Cafe** (*©* **0361/978538**) and **Highway Internet Cafe** (*©* **0361/972107**); **Fairway Café & Internet,** Jl. Dewi Sita (*©* **0361/978810**); and **Triscom.net,** Jl. Kajeng 4 (*©* **0361/971898**).

Pharmacies Three local pharmacies are: **Ubud Farma,** Jl. Raya Ubud (*©* **0361/974214**); **Mua Farma,** Jl. Monkey Forest (*©* **0361/974674**); and **Ubud Pharmacy,** Jl. Raya Campuhan 36 (*©* **0361/974911**).

Police Located along Jalan Raya Ubud (*©* **0361/975316**).

Post Office The main post office is at Jl. Jembawan 1. It's open Monday to Thursday 8am to 5pm; Friday 8am to 11am; and Saturday 8am to 1pm.

2 WHERE TO STAY

Ubud is both a rare and precious experience for those seeking something beyond sun, sand, and surf. You might chose to live, as the Balinese do, in the hills surrounded by terraced rice fields, absorbing the artistic spiritually. Or you might chose to stay near town, surrounded on all sides by galleries, shops, temples, and markets. Staying at the more rural properties might mean a long walk or ride in to town, but the scenery usually makes up for it.

VERY EXPENSIVE

Amandari ★★★ (Moments) Built within Kedewatan village, the Amandari manages to balance sensitivity and opulence with its unique integration of resort and community. In the 7th century, Hindu priest Rsi Markendea came to this village from Java and founded the sacred temple (p. 208) 129 steps below the Amandari. Several times a year village ceremonies require the passage of tall, ritual palanquins and sky-high offerings gracing the heads of the village ladies. The resort itself, laid out like a fanciful Balinese village, is elegant without sacrificing local charm. The plush rooms are in huge thatch roof stone cottages. Village suites have a first-floor lounge and a cozy upstairs loft bedroom like a rustic tree house. The resort's emerald-green infinity pool mimics the color of the surroundings and blends seamlessly with the green beyond.

Kedewatan-Ubud. (*©* **0361/975333.** Fax 0361/975335. www.amanresorts.com. 30 units. Year-round US$675 and up standard; US$3,600 villa. AE, DC, MC, V. **Amenities:** Restaurant; bar; babysitting; bicycles; concierge; golf course; health club; Jacuzzi; outdoor pool; room service; spa; tennis courts. *In room:* A/C, fridge, hair dryer, minibar, Wi-Fi.

Chedi Club at Tanah Gajah ★★ (Finds) The former estate of an Indonesian architect and art collector, this property combines the family's personal art and antique collection with 5 hectares (12 acres) of grounds reminiscent of a grand English estate—albeit entirely Indonesian in design. Shimmering ponds dotted with migrant Java pond herons and Dutch colonial black swans are surrounded by terraced hills of rice paddies tended by generations of Balinese farmers. This is a terrific place for children as there is plenty

Ubud & Surrounding Villages

KEDEWATAN

SAKTI

LUNGSIAKAN

Jl. Lungsiakan

Jl. Empu Tantular

Rsi Markandya 2

Jl. Bunitan

Jl. Tegal Kuning

Sungai Ayung

Jalan Kedewatan 1

SANGGINGAN

Jalan Sanggingan

Sungai Cerik

Rsi Markandya 3

Sungai Wos

Jalan Suweta

SAMBAHAN

CAMPUHAN

Jl. Campuhan

Jl. Kedewatan 2

PENESTAWAN

Jl. Campuhan 1

SAYAN

Jalan Silang Karang

Jl. Campuhan 3

UBUD
KAJA

Jl. Kajeng

Jl. Suweta

Jl. Sriwedari

Jl. Sandat

Jl. Raya Ubud

Jl. Bisma

Jalan Monkey Forest

Jalan Sayan

Post
Office

UBUD
KELOD

Sungai Wos

Jl. Hanoman

Jl. Sugriwa

Jl. Skukma

PADANG TEGAL

Peliatan

Nyuh Kuning

NYUHKUNING

Jl. Made Lebah

PENGOSEKAN

BALI

Gilimanuk

Singaraja

Negara

Ubud

Denpasar

INDIAN
OCEAN

Nusa
Penida

ACCOMMODATIONS ■
Agung Raka Bungalows **73**
Alam Indah **65**
Alam Sari **8**
Alila Ubud **4**
Amandari **12**
Ananda Cottages **20**
Arma Resort **72**
Bali Spirit Hotel and Spa **67**
Bambu Indah **25**
Casa Luna Honeymoon
  Guesthouse **47**
Chedi Club at Tanah Gajah **79**
COMO Shambhala **3**
Four Seasons Resort at Sayan **24**
Hotel Tjampuhan **28**
Klub Kokos **10**
Komeneka Bisma **62**
Komeneka Resort **59**

Komeneka Tanggayuda **6**
Kupu Kupu Barong
  Villas & Tree Spa **5**
Made Punia's Homestay **9**
Maya Ubud Resort & Spa **84**
Taman Bebek Villas **23**
The River House **66**
The Viceroy **85**
Ubud Hanging Gardens **2**
Ubud Sari Health Resort **37**
Uma Ubud **13**
Villa Nalini **1**
Villa Puri Sayan **26**
Villa Puri Tupai **68**
Waka Di Ume **35**
Warwick Ibah Luxury Villas
  and Spa **33**

DINING ◆
Ary's Warung **46**
Bali Buddha **52**
Batan's Waru **55**
Bebek Bengil (Dirty Duck) **76**
Black Beach **53**
Cafe Lotus **40**
Cafe Moka **54**
Casa Luna **45**
CasCades Restaurant **85**
Chedi Club Restaurant **79**
Cinta Grill **61**
Coffee and Silver Cafe **63**
Gaya Restaurant **21**
Glow Restaurant **3**
Ibu Oka **44**
Kafe **58**
Kemiri **13**
Lamak **57**
Minami **16**
Mozaic **19**
Murni's Warung **32**
Nacho Mama **18**
Nasi Ayam Kedewatan **11**
Naughty Nuri's
  Warung and Grill **17**

Pizza Bagus **74**
River Café **84**
Sari Organic
  (Bodag Maliah) **34**
Siam Sally **77**
Terazo **41**
The Three Monkeys **60**
Tutmak Warung Kopi **56**
Warung Enak **75**
Warung Lada **51**
Warung Mendez **27**
West End Café **15**

ATTRACTIONS ●
Agung Rai Gallery **78**
Antonio Blanco Museum **31**
ARMA Museum of Art **71**
Botanic Garden Ubud **36**
Elephant Safari Park Lodge **7**
Gaya Fusion of Senses **21**
Genta Gallery **69**
Goa Gajah
  (Elephant Caves) **80**
Gusti Lempad's Gallery **49**
Han Snel Gallery **38**
Komaneka Fine
  Art Gallery **59**
Museum Puri Lukisan **39**
Neka Art Museum **14**
Pura Gunung Lebah **29**
Pura Kebo Edan **81**
Pura Penataran Sasih **83**
Pura Pusering Jagat **82**
Pura Saraswati **43**
Puri Saren Agung
  (Royal Palace) **48**
Rio Helmi Photo Gallery **42**
Rudana Museum **70**
Sacred Monkey
  Forest Sanctuary **64**
Seniwati Gallery **50**
Sika Contemporary
  Art Gallery **22**
Symon Studios **30**

Jalan. Raya. Andong

■ Police Station

KUTUH

Jl. Raya Pejeng Kawan

Jl. Cokorda Gede Rai

PELIATAN

DUKUH

PEJENG

Sungai Petanu

Jalan. Raya. Pejeng

Jl. Pura

TEGES

To Mas, Batuan
& Sukawati

Jalan Raya Goa Gajah

UBUD

10

WHERE TO STAY

of room to roam free in a safe environment. Extras include a private butler, evening cocktail hour, private courtyard with plunge pool, and a complimentary bar in your room with crystal decanters of gin, vodka, and whisky. Watch the farmers' daily rituals through the soaring windows of the restaurant.

Jl. Goa Gajah, Tengkulak Kaja, Ubud. © **0361/975685.** Fax 0361/975686. www.ghmhotels.com. 20 units. High season US$410 suite, US$690 pool villa, US$970 estate; low season US$360 suite, US$620 pool villa, US$920 estate. Rates include breakfast, afternoon tea, and evening drinks. AE, DC, MC, V. **Amenities:** Restaurant, Chedi Club Restaurant (p. 202); bar; babysitting; bicycles; gym; outdoor pool; room service; spa; tennis court; Wi-Fi. *In room:* A/C, TV/DVD, movie library, stereo or CD, hair dryer, minibar.

COMO Shambhala ★★★ (Moments)

If you want a retreat that rejuvenates as it relaxes you look no further than the COMO Shambhala, which calls itself "The Estate" and rightly so. Upon check-in you will be assigned PAs (personal assistants) that look after your complete program. With an ayurvedic doctor, a psychologist, a Pilates instructor, and master yogis from around the globe as well as a knock-out spa restaurant, you're bound to leave feeling better than when you arrived. The property is on the steep, bucolic Ayung River gorge. Private two- and three-bedroom villas share a common living room and pool. New one- and two-bedroom villas have their own private pools. They all have elegant furnishings, oversize and beautifully appointed bathrooms, and balconies that overlook lush jungle.

Desa Melinggih Kelod, Payangan-Gianyar. © **0361/978888.** Fax 0361/978889. www.cse.como.bz. 30 units. Year-round US$300 standard, US$450–US$1,350 suite, US$2,300 and up villa. AE, DC, MC, V. **Amenities:** 2 restaurants, Glow Restaurant (p. 202); bar; free airport transfer; babysitting; bicycles; concierge; 9 outdoor pools; aqua therapy pool; room service; spa; tennis courts; Wi-Fi. *In room:* A/C, TV/DVD, movie library, stereo or CD, fridge, hair dryer, minibar.

Four Seasons Resort at Sayan ★★

The Four Seasons, on the Ayung River, is incredibly posh, though you needn't feel intimidated. The entrance is a bit extraterrestrial: You cross a long bridge that leads to a lily pond that rests atop the lobby in an immense natural crater of rice terraces. The best rooms are right along the river. Expect Four Season's niceties like luxurious bathrooms, huge tubs, and plenty of plush towels. The design features natural fabrics and gleaming woods highlighted by precious local art and artifacts. The two-level pool follows the serpentine shape of the river below. Even if you aren't lucky enough to be in residence here go for a long lunch and enjoy the spectacular setting.

Sayan, Ubud. © **0361/977577.** Fax 0361/977588. www.fourseasons.com. 60 units. Peak season US$600–US$1,050 1-bedroom; US$2,600 2-bedroom; high season US$460–US$950 1-bedroom, US$2,400 2-bedroom; low season US$460–US$850 1-bedroom, US$2,100 2-bedroom; extra person US$100. AE, DC, MC, V. **Amenities:** 2 restaurants; bar; bicycles; health club; outdoor pool; room service; spa; Wi-Fi. *In room:* A/C, TV, stereo or CD, fridge, minibar.

Ubud Hanging Gardens ★

A bit off the radar, the Ubud Hanging Gardens is at the end of a winding road 30 minutes from Ubud by car. The property is set on a gorge so steep, it is served by a tram. Two infinity pools look out onto the jungle and the guest rooms have floor-to-ceiling windows to take full advantage of the views and they all come with their own heated infinity pools.

Desa Buahan, Ubud. © **0361/982700.** Fax 0361/982800. www.ubudhanginggardens.com. 38 villas. Year-round US$337–US$537. AE, DC, MC, V. **Amenities:** Restaurant; bar; airport transfer; Internet; 2 outdoor pools; spa. *In villa:* A/C, TV, fridge, hair dryer, minibar.

The Viceroy ★

The Viceroy has a unique and peaceful position on the slopes of the Pentanu valley near the village of Nagi, though not far from town, and has one of Ubud's best restaurants, CasCades. However one of its greatest assets is that it is family run by seasoned professionals. Plus, not long ago, a Dutch art dealer who lives in Ubud part time bequeathed pictures of his grandfather who used to be the Dutch Viceroy of this area to the Viceroy hotel. Black and white photographs showing "The Viceroy" in residence in Jakarta now grace the lobby walls.

Jl. Lanyahan, Br. Nagih, Petulu-Ubud. ℂ **0361/971777.** Fax 0361/970777. www.viceroybali.com. 11 bedrooms. High season US$950 and up; low season US$850 and up. AE, DC, MC, V. **Amenities:** Restaurant, CasCades Restaurant (p. 201); bar; lounge; babysitting; bicycles; concierge; gym; Jacuzzi; outdoor pool; room service; spa; Wi-Fi. *In room:* A/C, fan, TV/DVD, hair dryer, minibar.

EXPENSIVE

Alila Ubud   The Alila has a beautiful campus with some very mature and elegant gardens as a part of its lovely landscape. Its *pièce de résistance* however is the infinity-edge swimming pool voted one of the "50 Most Spectacular Pools in the World" by *Travel + Leisure:* It's like a cube of water in otherworldly (or at least unlikely) suspension over the spectacular gorge. The rooms could do with an upgrade (there are no bathtubs) but many overlook the stunning northern stretch of the Ayung gorge where the popular rafting trips go by. The self-contained resort is 30 minutes north of central Ubud and offers regular shuttle service. The riverbank picnics, complete with safari tents and champagne, are a real treat.

Desa Melinggih Kelod, Payangan-Gianyar. ℂ **0361/975963.** Fax 0361/975968. www.alilahotels.com. 64 units. Peak season US$245–US$510; high season US$225–US$470; low season US$185–US$390. AE, MC, V. **Amenities:** Restaurant; bar; airport transfer; babysitting; bicycles; concierge; Internet; Jacuzzi; outdoor pool; room service; sauna; spa. *In room:* A/C, TV, fridge, hair dryer, minibar.

Bambu Indah ★★ (Finds)   Savvy travelers with an environmental bent will think they have died and gone to heaven. Bambu Indah's ("Beautiful Bamboo") is the creation of the multitalented team of the Green School (p. 215). The four antique teak *joglo* have the most fantastic view of the Sayan ridge and the Ayung. Just past the swimming pool that could be mistaken for a natural pond and past the working rice fields is the temple Pura Dalem Gede Bongkasa. (The temple is not easily accessible as it requires a trek through small back roads. If you make it there, bring your own sarong and sash.) There is no cafe or restaurant on-site but home-cooked organic meals are delivered to your porch at any time of day.

Br. Baung, Sayan-Ubud. ℂ **0361/977922.** Fax 0361/974404. www.bambuindah.com. 7 villas. Peak season US$180–US$280; high season US$175–US$275; low season US$160–US$260. Rates include breakfast. MC, V. **Amenities:** Lounge; babysitting; bicycles; outdoor pool; room service; Wi-Fi. *In villa:* A/C, hair dryer, minibar.

Komaneka Resort   Komaneka manages three properties in the Ubud area. The main resort is on Monkey Forest Road and is clean, modern, and chic. Guest buildings are well away from street noise and have views of gardens and rice paddies. Accommodation is done in a cool, contemporary style with shiny marble tiles, spartan wooden furnishings, and thatch roofs. Deluxe units have unique bathrooms: Some feature outdoor showers and tubs, while others have sunken marble tubs.

The sister properties are **Komaneka Bisma** (Jl. Bisma; ℂ **0361/971933;** fax 0361/971955; 43 units; peak season US$495 suite, US$695 1-bedroom villa, US$945 2-bedroom villa; low season US$450 suite, US$650 1-bedroom villa, US$900 2-bedroom; extra bed US$45; rates include breakfast, afternoon tea, and evening drinks) by the Campuhan River valley and **Komaneka Tanggavuda** (ℂ **0361/978123;** fax 0361/973084;

20 units; peak season US$345 suite, US$395–US$445 villa; low season US$300 suite, US$350–US$400 villa; extra bed US$45; rates include breakfast, afternoon tea, and evening drinks) in Kedewatan village overlooking the river Oos, 15 minutes by car from Ubud.

Jl. Monkey Forest, Ubud. ✆ **0361/976090.** Fax 0361/977140. www.komaneka.com. 20 units. Peak season US$295 standard, US$345 suite, US$395 villa; low season US$250 deluxe, US$300 suite, US$350 villa; extra bed US$45. AE, DC, MC, V. **Amenities:** Restaurant; outdoor pool; room service; spa. *In room:* A/C, TV/DVD, CD player, fridge, minibar.

Maya Ubud Resort & Spa This fine resort is just east of central Ubud. The design makes elegant use of local materials, blended in an immaculate, contemporary style and rooms reflect a refined simplicity, with cool white and yellow tones set against the dark wood of Art Deco furnishings. Floors are river stone and ceilings are thatch. An elevator transports you down the steep valley to the riverside, where the fine spa rooms literally hang over the rushing water. The Maya is self-sufficient, but shuttle service to town keeps you connected.

Jl. Gunung Sari, Peliatan-Ubud. ✆ **0361/977888.** Fax 0361/977555. www.mayaubud.com. 108 units. Year-round US$240–US$250 standard; US$340–US$1,200 villa. AE, DC, MC, V. **Amenities:** 2 restaurants, River Café (p. 203); bar; airport transfer; bicycles; Internet; Jacuzzi; 2 outdoor pools; spa; tennis courts. *In room:* A/C, TV, fridge, hair dryer, minibar.

Taman Bebek Villas ★★ (Finds) Canadian musicologist Colin McPhee built a Balinese house on the edge of the ridge above the magnificent Ayung River valley in 1944. His house and his life in Bali were celebrated in a marvelous read, *A House in Bali* (1946). The house was a series of thatched huts within a bamboo forest. By 1980, when infamous landscape architect Made Wijaya acquired this land, only the foundations of the houses remained. Made set about re-creating and improving upon the original structures. Today Taman Bebek Villas is still a retreat where painters, writers, dancers, and scholars come for inspiration. Four new Bali Aga Suites surround the pool on the ridge. Our favorite is the Criussant Villa, a mix between Queenslander and the Malaysian styles, with wraparound verandas, spacious garden bathrooms, and colonial Dutch interiors with artworks from Made's personal collection.

Sayan, Ubud. ✆ **0361/975385.** Fax 0361/976532. www.tamanbebek.com. 5 units. Year-round US$273–US$363 bungalow; US$968 presidential suite. Rates include breakfast. AE, MC, V. **Amenities:** Cafe; bar; outdoor pool; room service; spa therapy. *In villa:* Fan, kitchenette, minibar.

Uma Ubud ★★ A sister resort to the luxurious COMO Shambhala (p. 194), this set of boutique villas are aimed at a hip, young, jet-setting audience who prefer to be close to central Ubud. White gauzy curtains cover the four-poster beds; stand-alone bathtubs are done in black-terrazzo; and some rooms have views of the surrounding rice paddies. Kemiri, the resort's main restaurant, serves lively Asian dishes.

Jl. Raya Sanggingan, Lungsiakan, Kedewatan, Ubud. ✆ **0361/972448.** Fax 0361/975686. www.como.bz. 29 units. High season US$300 standard, US$415 suite; low season US$260 standard, US$375 suite. AE, DC, MC, V. **Amenities:** Restaurant, Kemiri (p. 203); bar; babysitting; bicycles; concierge; gym; outdoor pool; room service; spa; Wi-Fi. *In room:* A/C, TV/DVD, movie library, hair dryer, minibar.

Waka Di Ume ★ This small boutique-style hotel, nestled among the rice fields of north Ubud, is a relaxing haven for those looking to escape the bustle of town. Distressed woods, *alang alang* roofs, natural colored drapes surrounding the beds, and slate and lime-washed stone filling the pathways, all contribute to an elegant, boho chic. Tuesdays and Thursdays feature special walks through the nearby rice paddies. You would hardly know you were 10 minutes from the center of town.

Jl. Suweta, Br. Sambahan, Ubud. © **0361/973178.** www.wakadiumeubud.com. 17 units. High season US$208–US$556; low season US$184–US$532. AE, DC, MC, V. **Amenities:** Restaurant; cafe; bar; lounge; babysitting; gym; Jacuzzi; outdoor pool; room service; spa; Wi-Fi (for a fee). *In room:* A/C, minibar.

Warwick Ibah Luxury Villas and Spa ★ (Finds) Reminiscent of a European estate but with Balinese design, Ibah is nestled in a dense, 2-hectare (5-acre) garden on the banks of the Campuhan. The property has been hand-crafted with the skill of Tjorkarda Raka Kerthyasa, a mask carver and a member of the Ubud royal family. Each unique villa is filled with antiques and curios from the royal family's private collection. The grottolike pool has lounge areas carved into the stone and walkways and walls covered in verdant vines. The restaurant lacks charm but you can order meals around the pool and complimentary afternoon tea with Balinese cakes is served in an outdoor bale.

Warwick Ibah, Jl. Raya Campuhan, Ubud. © **0361/974466.** Fax 0361/975686. www.warwickibah.com. 15 units. High season US$235–US$290 suite, US$445 villa; low season US$184–US$225 suite, US$340 villa. AE, MC, V. **Amenities:** Restaurant; bar; babysitting; bicycles; concierge; outdoor pool; room service; spa; Wi-Fi (for a fee). *In room:* A/C, TV/DVD, movie library, stereo or CD, hair dryer, minibar.

MODERATE

Agung Raka Bungalows Just south of central Ubud, these thatched bungalows are arranged around a series of rice paddies and surrounded by a thriving village arts community. Bungalows are basic wood-and-bamboo constructions with rudimentary outdoor bathrooms. Superior bungalows are single occupancy A-frames of teak. Bathrooms are large, modern courtyard facilities that include both a tile tub and a stone-floor shower. The suites are excellent: a dizzying spectacle of stone and marble, big enough for four and great for two.

Pengosekan Village, Ubud. © **0361/975757.** Fax 0361/975546. www.agungraka.com. 19 units. Year-round US$60 standard; US$70–US$150 bungalow. MC, V. **Amenities:** Restaurant; bar; outdoor pool. *In room:* A/C, TV, minibar.

Alam Sari ★ (Finds)(Kids) This hotel offers an excellent combination of comfort, social responsibility, setting, and low price—and is a delightful find for families, ecowarriors, and those who want to immerse themselves in Balinese culture. Everything the Alam Sari does is with a thought towards the local economy, ecology, and culture. The hotel almost exclusively employs villagers from neighboring Keliki. Environmentally friendly touches are everywhere, from solar water heaters to the use of recycled paper. Rooms are lovely, with views of the gorge and looming volcano. Traditional music is featured at night.

Keliki, Tromol Pos 03, Tegallalang, Ubud. © **0361/981420.** Fax 0361/981421. www.alamsari.com. 12 units. Year-round US$60 standard; US$70 suite; US$110–US$250 family unit. AE, MC, V. **Amenities:** Restaurant; bar; bicycles; Internet. *In room:* A/C, fridge, minibar.

Arma Resort Culture vultures can feel good about putting their feet up at the Arma Resort as the income generated from the property fuels the owner Agung Rai's other good works, such as the ARMA Museum (p. 210), the dance and drama theater, a public library, and a school. There are terrific dance and music performances here that you should try to see. The resort has a nice pool and a decent restaurant. Some sort of cultural exchange or another is likely to be going on during your stay.

Jl. Raya Pengosekan, Ubud. © **0361/975742.** Fax 0361/975332. www.armaresort.com. 23 units. High season US$115–US$245; low season US$90–US$220. Rates include breakfast. AE, MC, V. **Amenities:** 3 restaurants; cafe; lounge; babysitting; outdoor pool; room service; Wi-Fi. *In room:* A/C, hair dryer, minibar.

Bali Spirit Hotel and Spa   Not too far from central Ubud, in the village of Nyuh Kuning, this is a reasonably priced alternative to the really high-end luxury hotels. You get a great setting and comfortable rooms at a good price, without going overboard on the bells, whistles, and fees. Large, well-appointed rooms come with small kitchen nooks and decks, with local fabrics and materials employed throughout. The pool is a cozy perch with lounges overlooking the gorge, and traditional Balinese bathing pools are in the holy river below. Regular shuttles run to town.

Nyuh Kuning Village, Ubud. ✆ **0361/974013.** Fax 0361/974012. www.balispirithotel.com. 25 units. Year-round US$95–US$135 standard; US$145 villa. Rates include breakfast. AE, MC, V. **Amenities:** Restaurant; bar; bicycles; Internet; outdoor pool; room service; spa. *In room:* A/C, TV, fridge, minibar.

Casa Luna Honeymoon Guesthouse   This guesthouse has grown popular mostly through word of mouth and attracts an eclectic, artsy crowd. The guesthouse is run by writer and restaurateur Janet de Neefe who also owns **Casa Luna Restaurant** (p. 201), and the Honeymoon Bakery, and runs her own cooking classes. This place is not posh by any stretch of the imagination, and if you are looking for all the modern conveniences, look elsewhere.

Jl. Bisma, Ubud. ✆ **0361/977409.** Fax 0361/973282. www.casalunabali.com. 30 units. Year-round Rp402,500–Rp690,000. AE, MC, V. **Amenities:** 2 restaurants; bar; airport transfer; Internet; outdoor pool. *In room:* A/C, fan, minibar.

Hotel Tjampuhan ★★ (Finds)   This hotel is a tropical sanctuary with terraces that lead to a beautiful gorge, the Tjampuhan River, and the Gunung Lebah Temple. The hotel was built in 1928 for guests of the prince of Ubud and was chosen by Western artists Walter Spies and Rudolf Bonnet as headquarters for the Pita Maha. Air-conditioned rooms are larger and have better views than fan rooms. Splurge on a Raja Room (or even Spies's own villa) with verandas overlooking the gorge. There are two pondlike pools, another with cold spring water, and a sunken carved stone grotto in the shape of a mythical beast—one of the more unusual places for a massage.

Jl. Raya Campuhan, Ubud. ✆ **0361/975368.** Fax 0316/975137. http://tjampuhan.com. 67 units. Year-round US$67–US$87 standard with fan; US$90–US$110 standard with A/C; US$164 Walter Spies villa. Rates include breakfast. AE, MC, V. **Amenities:** 2 restaurants; 4 bars; babysitting; 2 outdoor pools and spring bath; spa. *In room:* A/C (in some), fan, fridge, minibar.

INEXPENSIVE

Budget choices line Monkey Forest Road and the Jalan Hanoman; better still, turn down any little alley or side street that cuts across them.

Alam Indah   The Alam Indah overlooks rice fields and is just behind Monkey Forest Road. Rooms get their names from the garden inhabitants: lily, lotus, and gardenia, to name a few. Staff are terrific with suggestions on what to do or for local tours. The breakfast is superb, with black rice pudding a must. If you're game, ask the owner Ibu Wayan and her daughter Metri for cooking classes. Be sure to book a few days in advance for the class.

Nyuhkuning, Ubud. ✆ **0361/974629.** www.alam-indah.com. 10 units. Year-round US$58–US$110; extra bed US$10. Rates include breakfast. AE, MC, V. **Amenities:** Restaurant; outdoor pool; room service. *In room:* Fan, TV.

Ananda Cottages ★   Just north of Ubud proper, Ananda Cottages is atmospheric enough for the Balinese experience you're hoping for, yet situated far enough from the town center to discourage the tourist hordes. The rice fields and thatched cottages of this bungalow campus are almost more "Balinese" than real villages you might visit (where you'll now find TVs instead of shrines, and power machines instead of hand tools). Ananda is also a spiritual place for yoga and meditation programs run every first and third week of the month; music and dance lessons are available from time to time. The cottages are brick huts with bamboo pavilion roofs. Downstairs rooms are the better choice, with outdoor tubs and patio living rooms. Upstairs rooms have modern bathrooms and small verandas. The small pool is set on an interesting raised rice terrace. The three new deluxe bungalows are very cozy and well worth the outlay.

Campuhan, Ubud. ✆ **0361/975376.** Fax 0361/975375. www.anandaubud.com. 70 units. Year-round US$70–US$80 standard without A/C; US$95–US$110 standard with A/C; US$125 bungalow; US$250 suite. AE, MC, V. **Amenities:** Restaurant; bar; babysitting; outdoor pool; room service; spa. *In room:* A/C (in some), fridge, minibar.

Klub Kokos (Kids) This is a great choice for those traveling with children. Even though its only 2.5km (1½ miles) from town, it is really off of the beaten track because of the round-about car route you need to take to reach the resort. Hence, there is no roadside traffic. As there are only seven bungalows, guests are personally looked after by their hosts Krishna Sudharsana, a renowned Balinese artist, and his Australian wife, Cathy. The restaurant has good kids' choices; there is a games room and a library for young and old. Cathy and Krishna can arrange courses on kite- or hat-making, dancing, or how to make the intricate temple offerings.

Bangkiang Sidem, Ubud. ✆ **0361/978270.** Fax 0361/978270. www.klubkokos.com. 7 units. Year-round US$70 standard; US$95–US$1152-bedroom; US$120 family unit. Rates include breakfast. MC, V. **Amenities:** Restaurant; Internet; saltwater pool; room service. *In room:* Fan.

Made Punia's Homestay This homestay is for those who are serious about getting into the spirit of things both metaphysical and artistic. Made Puni and his wife rent a comfortable house with fantastic views onto the forests and fields. About 500m (1,640 ft.) walk from the property is the village of Bangkian Sidem—but it is below the house in Made's studio where the real interest lies. Made's intricate paintings are for sale and on view and there are weekly gamelan jam sessions that you are welcome to join. Plenty of restaurants are nearby. Made will also lead you on nearby walks.

Banjar bangkiang Sidam, Ubud. ✆ **0812/397-7305.** 4 units. High season Rp350,000–Rp500,000; low season Rp250,000–Rp400,000. Rates include breakfast. No credit cards. **Amenities:** Room service. *In room:* Fan.

Ubud Sari Health Resort This was the first health retreat in Ubud. It is a good value with small cottages with real rustic charm, though it could do with a face-lift. Rooms are above a river, so let the rushing water sing you to sleep. Breakfast is served on your balcony and the staff is attentive without fawning. A garden path leads to the spa with a cold plunge pool, herbal steam bath, and sauna. Colonic fasting sessions are popular among the expat crowd that frequents this place.

Jl. Kajeng 35, Ubud. ✆ **0361/974393.** Fax 0361/976305. www.ubudsari.com. 10 units. Year-round US$35–US$75. MC, V. **Amenities:** Restaurant; babysitting; Jacuzzi; outdoor pool; room service; steam room and sauna; spa. *In room:* A/C.

VILLAS

Kupu Kupu Barong Villas & Tree Spa Kupu Kupu Barong (Gentle Butterfly) is named after the many butterflies fluttering around the resort. While taking in the Ayung River view you might just see a common sailor or a blue glassy tiger. The 34 private villas are designed in traditional but elegant Balinese architecture. The villas are ornate with slightly incongruous interiors but the oversize rooms, super-soft beds, and polished teak floors make up for the lack of style with their easy grace.

Kedewatan, Ubud. ✆ **0361/975478.** Fax 0361/975079. www.kupubarong.com. 34 villas. High season US$370 and up; low season US$320 and up. AE, DC, MC, V. **Amenities:** Restaurant; 2 bars; babysitting; bicycles; concierge; outdoor pool; room service; spa; Wi-Fi. *In villa:* A/C, TV/DVD, movie library, stereo or CD, hair dryer; minibar, MP3 docking station.

The River House ★★ ⓕ**Finds**   Nature lovers and romantics should look no further than the thatched-roof River House on the Wos. Designed by bamboo environmentalist Linda Garland, this villa is as shabby chic as it comes. Plumbing is precarious but the sounds of running river and cicadas, birdsong, and other wildlife have you forgiving the eccentricities of the house. The cozy conversation area has floor pillows and a more formal sitting area with oriental rugs on hardwood floors and antique furnishings. Staff here have withstood the test of time, events, parties, and frivolity a plenty. This was one of the main locations for the film *Eat, Pray, Love.*

Nyuhkuning, Ubud. ✆ **0361/974071.** Fax 0361/974071. www.lindagarland.com. 3 bedrooms. High season US$650; low season US$520. Meals market price. AE, MC, V. **Amenities:** Bar; babysitting; outdoor pool; room service; spa; Wi-Fi. *In room:* A/C, fan, hair dryer.

Villa Nalini   In a rural setting near a small village, this villa has an outstanding range of amenities. For starters: a movie theater, tennis court, billiards room, and industrial-strength kitchen. Despite all its high-tech extravagances there are some charming touches as well, such as a paved courtyard with a fountain containing the ruins of the original mud farm house. The owners, Ubud's royal family and patrons of the arts, have a new gamelan orchestra for the spa and their regal recitals enhance the valley ambience.

Ayung River, Ubud. ✆ **0361/731074.** Fax 0361/736391. www.elitehavensbali.com. 5 bedrooms. Peak season US$1,400; low season US$1,050. Rates include breakfast; other meals market price. AE, MC, V. **Amenities:** Bar; free airport transfer; babysitting; Jacuzzi; outdoor pool; room service; spa; tennis court; Wi-Fi. *In room:* A/C, fan, TV, hair dryer, MP3 docking station.

Villa Puri Sayan ★   There are many places to stay in Ubud but only this private villa has this view of rice terraces and the Ayung river gorge. The three-bedroom villa sits on 2,300 sq. m (24,757 sq. ft.) of exquisite tropical gardens. Sliding glass doors open onto the expansive veranda and infinity pool. Puri Sayan is tastefully decorated with overstuffed sofas, Indonesian antiques, and ornately carved Chinese opium beds.

Sayan-Ubud. ✆ **0361/974365.** Fax 0361/974365. www.villa-puri-sayan.com. 3 bedrooms. Peak season US$590; high season US$550; low season US$450. Meals market price. AE, MC, V. **Amenities:** Bar; free airport transfer; babysitting; outdoor pool; room service; spa therapy; Wi-Fi. *In room:* A/C, fan, hair dryer.

Villa Puri Tupai ★ ⓚ**Kids**   On the outskirts of Ubud in the village of Lod Tunduh, this villa has no view, but who cares? This villa is perfect for those who want to enjoy the peace and quiet and still be cosseted by a caring staff. Two Javanese *joglo* serve as the villa structure. Just beyond lies a mini topiary maze on an incredible sprawling lawn, a 25m (82-ft.) swimming pool, and an immaculate grass tennis court. A smaller *joglo* doubles as a spa or as a perfect playhouse for the kids. The walled garden makes this an ideal spot for children to safely play in the grounds.

Jl. Raya Anak Gede Rai, Br. Baung, Sayan-Ubud. ✆ **0361/981655.** Fax 0361/981655. www.villapuritupai. com. 4 bedrooms. High season US$600; low season US$400. Meals market price plus 20%. Rates include breakfast. AE, MC, V. **Amenities:** Bar; free airport transfer; babysitting; outdoor pool; room service; spa therapy; tennis court; Wi-Fi. *In room:* A/C, hair dryer.

3 WHERE TO DINE

Dining in Ubud has become as international as dining in any other metropolitan city with many international restaurants in the busy town center offering a cosmopolitan selection of Indian, Thai, American, French, Japanese, Italian, and anything south or north of the equator. Small warungs or carts *(gerobak)* sell *babi guling* (suckling pig) and other Balinese delicacies. Unless otherwise noted, restaurants are open daily.

VERY EXPENSIVE

Mozaic ★★★ INTERNATIONAL   Chef Chris Salans's constant upgrades and refinements to food and decor has turned Mozaic into one of Asia's top fine-dining destinations. Salans employs traditional French ingredients and methods but pays respect to his surroundings with Indonesian flavors such as spicy *sambal* sauce, turmeric, and cardamom. Guests choose from several six-course, constantly changing tasting menus. Highlights from a recent meal include curry butter roasted yabbies (Australian crayfish), with a delectable truffle sauce, and a crispy seared foie gras served with mango puree. The restaurant offers excellent value for money—a meal like this in the West would cost double. You can also sign up for cooking classes here.

Jl. Raya Sanggingan. ☎ **0361/975768.** www.mozaic-bali.com. Reservations recommended. Tasting menu Rp550,000–Rp1,500,000. AE, DC, MC, V. Tues–Sun 6–10:30pm.

EXPENSIVE

Ary's Warung ★ MODERN INDONESIAN   Ary's started out as a lowly warung, but as Ubud went upscale in the '90s, so did Ary's. Today, the gourmet European and Indonesian specialties here have fans from around the world. Stop in for at least one of the honey-ginger-lime drinks (with or without the booze), and kick back on a couch street side for a bit of people-watching. Though this is the place to see and be seen, Ary's is quite pleasant at night, when tranquil trance music plays and candles light every corner. Second-floor dining gives you a good view of the busy street below or the bats swooping to catch bugs at dusk. The food is good—overpriced, but good. Try the gazpacho, perfect on a hot day, or the grilled goat-cheese salad. The grilled tuna and lamb cutlets are done to perfection, and the ponzu-grilled snapper is delicious. The tasting menu (Rp220,000) includes two glasses of house wine.

Jl. Raya Ubud. ☎ **0361/975053.** Reservations recommended. Main courses Rp95,000–Rp170,000. AE, MC, V. 10am–11pm.

Casa Luna BALINESE/MEDITERRANEAN   Casa Luna serves Mediterranean and Balinese cuisine in a relaxed tropical atmosphere and is one of the key meeting places for the Ubud Writers Festival (p. 33), which was founded by the owner, Janet de Neefe. Janet and her Balinese husband also own the new Luna Bar and a cooking school (p. 213). The front of the restaurant serves breads and baked goods and an extensive menu includes kids' choices. There is weekly live jazz but times are sporadic so check ahead.

Jl. Raya Ubud. ☎ **0361/977409.** www.casalunabali.com. Reservations recommended. Main courses Rp35,000–Rp70,000; set menu Rp115,000–Rp137,000. AE, MC, V. 8am–11pm.

CasCades Restaurant ★★ ASIAN/FRENCH   CasCades serves fine French food with an Asian twist. The produce here is all fresh and local but the fine, high-quality

UBUD

10

WHERE TO DINE

meats are imported. Try the New Zealand Lamb Nori, a dish of lamb loin wrapped in feather light pastry. There are also delectable plates of pan-seared bass, river prawn, and scallops and all manner of decadent desserts. In 2008 the restaurant was honored with the Award of Excellence from *Wine Spectator U.S.A.* for their wine list of more than 160 different quality wines from around the world, which is no easy task in Bali. Adjacent to the restaurant is the Viceroy Bar, featuring a stunning lacquered long bar looking out over the dramatic river gorge.

In the Viceroy Bali (p. 194), Jl. Lanyahan. (©) **0361/972111.** www.viceroybali.com. Reservations recommended. Meat Rp150,000–Rp295,000; seafood Rp175,000–Rp490,000; set menu Rp750,000–Rp1,500,000. AE, DC, MC, V. 7am–10pm.

Chedi Club Restaurant INDONESIAN   Seemingly floating among the rice paddies, the restaurant at the Chedi Club offers a harmonious balance of Balinese and Indonesian cuisine. The glass windows make a picture perfect frame for the working rice farm in view. Much of the produce is sourced on-site from their own herb and vegetable garden. Take in a dance in the dramatic open-air amphitheater before your dinner (check for times, normally Tues and Sat in the dry season).

In the Chedi Club (p. 191), Tanah Gajah, Jl. Goa Gajah. (©) **0361/975685.** www.ghmhotels.com. Reservations recommended. Main courses Rp110,000–Rp340,000; set menu Rp250,000–Rp580,000. AE, MC, V. 7am–11pm.

Coffee and Silver Cafe EUROPEAN   Tucked away on a side road, this tiny gem literally lights up at night, with a dragon possessing red, shining eyes on top of the roof. The small but good seafood menu changes daily. Indonesian and Balinese food are also available. The emphasis here is on fresh ingredients and solid European food. The Dutch owner Carlsten is usually around answering esoteric queries that come his way about life and occasionally about what things you should see in Ubud. An attached shop sells antiques and curios. Decorative art from the Dutch colonial era sits among interesting pen and ink drawings and a mix of treasures.

Jl. Sukma 45. (©) **0361/978228.** Main courses Rp42,000–Rp119,000. AE, MC, V. Daily 8:30am–11pm.

Gaya Restaurant ASIAN/MEDITERRANEAN   This open-sided restaurant with cool breezes and stylish decor sits above the Gaya gallery (p. 211). The ceramics are made at their own studio, which produces for the likes of Armani. Gaya serves Naples-influenced cuisine and all of their breads, grissini, and desserts are baked fresh on the premises daily. The seafood linguine and the carbonara are both winners.

Jl. Raya Sayan. (©) **0361/979252.** www.gayafusion.com. Main courses Rp60,000–Rp150,000; set menu Rp165,000–Rp215,000. AE, MC, V. 7am–11pm.

Glow Restaurant ★★ HEALTH FOOD   Glow at the COMO Shambhala Estate is overseen by thoroughly innovative Chef Chris Miller who will prove to you that healthy eating doesn't mean boring and bland. Miller's spa cuisine is flavored with Balinese and Southeast Asian spices and is composed of organic and locally sourced ingredients with plenty of raw fruits and veggies, though meat and fish are also on offer. Sunday brunch is worth the trek even if you aren't a guest. The first thing that struck us was the sheer variety of dishes like gingerbread hot cakes with lemon sauce, and yellowfin tuna *tataki* with radish, black fungus, ponzu, and fried garlic. Our favorite was the roast tomato, leek, and oregano frittata with Gruyère, though a close second was the wild baby green, ocean trout gravlax, poached egg, and saffron. The *pièce de résistance* is their raw food lasagna, which has a mighty following. Pretty little local girls practice traditional dance

to the sounds of gamelan orchestra nearby under the strict tutelage of Ibu Wayan, a
known task master.

In COMO Shambhala Estate (p. 194). *©* **0361/978888.** Reservations recommended. Main courses Rp220,000–Rp320,000; dinner Rp240,000–Rp440,000. AE, DC, MC, V. 11:30am–9:30pm.

Lamak ★★ INDONESIAN   This restaurant is dramatically designed by renowned architect and landscape artist Made Wijaya and features striking steel sculpture against striking burgundy-colored walls. Before tucking into the cuisine, make a beeline for the bar with its funky cowhide bar stools and do-rag uniformed bartenders mixing up one of their signature cocktails. Lamak's kitchen offers Balinese, Indonesian, Asian, and international food but don't mistake this for fusion. The chef's dishes retain their flavorful origins through innovative interpretation. The "Small Plate" Crab Meat with young coconut, lime, and fresh mint is artfully arranged between crispy wonton sheets and is as light as it is delicious.

Jl. Monkey Forest. *©* **0361/974668.** www.lamakbali.com. Reservations recommended. Lunch Rp40,000–Rp105,000; dinner Rp45,000–Rp275,000; vegetarian Rp32,000–Rp95,000; set menu Rp150,000–Rp300,000. AE, MC, V. 11am–midnight.

Minami JAPANESE   This little restaurant is two doors down from Naughty Nuri's (p. 207), but don't expect the same crowd. Minami attracts a strong Japanese contingent and those with a more delicate palate. Start with a perfectly presented bento box with grilled fish, miso-flavored grilled beef, Japanese pickles, and shrimp tempura. In the bright and primarily white restaurant and outdoor courtyard area you can dine on high-end Japanese cuisine and then relish that second or third sake at the immaculate carved buffalo horn bar with black leather stools.

Jl. Raya Sanggingan. *©* **0361/970013.** Reservations recommended. Main courses Rp85,000–Rp210,000; set menu Rp180,000 minimum order 2 persons. MC, V. 10am–11pm.

River Café ★★ INTERNATIONAL   The main reason for dining here is the gorgeous surroundings. It's a long walk to the restaurant down some very steep steps—be prepared. Fresh baked rosemary and oregano flatbread with balsamic and olive oil was a great start to our delicious light lunch, followed by carrot soup with ginger.

In Maya Ubud Resort & Spa (p. 196), Jl. Gunung Sari Peliatan. *©* **0361/977888.** www.mayaubud.com. Reservations recommended. Pasta Rp175,000–Rp260,000; pizza Rp150,000. AE, MC, V. 10am–9pm.

MODERATE

Black Beach ★ ITALIAN   This friendly three-level restaurant is creating a bit of a buzz in quiet Ubud with its novelty factor of, you guessed it, black sand. The second-floor bar is covered in black sand from the owner's husband's beach village Sukawati. As Antonella explains, "The only thing Ubud was missing was a beach bar so we wanted to create one." The third-floor terraced restaurant has rooftop views. On the menu are 16 homemade pasta sauces as well as other Italian classics like lasagna, pizza, and fresh salads.

Jl. Hanoman 5A. *©* **0361/971353.** Pizza Rp32,000–Rp74,000; pasta Rp23,000–Rp55,000. MC, V. 7am–11pm.

Kemiri ★★ SOUTHEAST ASIAN   Kemiri is overseen by Chris Miller whose style of cooking combines Pan-Asian influences with a commitment to local ingredients. Miller's studies in nutrition and his research and interest in healthy eating are central to the estate's identity. We went with the chef's recommendation of Szechuan salt and pepper squid with green mango, long beans, peanuts, and *nuoc cham* (a Vietnamese dressing of garlic, chili, rice wine vinegar, and lime) and were hardly disappointed.

In Uma Ubud (p. 196), Jl. Raya Sanggingan. *©* **0361/972448.** Reservations recommended. Lunch Rp95,000–Rp135,000; dinner Rp130,000–Rp220,000; set menu US$60. AE, DC, MC. 6:30am–10:30pm.

Cafes, Coffee & Tea

Bali Buddha, Jl. Jembawan 1 (✆ **0361/976432**; www.balibuddha.com; main courses Rp60,000–Rp150,000; MC, V; 7am–10pm), in front of the post office to the east of town, is a happening little expat spot with a small grocery that sells fresh bread, organic vegetables, healthy snacks, supplements, and natural skin care products. The menu has organic and house-made salad-soup-sandwich standards along with Indonesian dishes, pasta, and burgers. Vegan, vegetarian, and raw dishes are also available. Upstairs is a popular juice bar—a good place to meet long-staying folks or get info off the bulletin board. It's New Age central here, more or less.

Cafe Moka, Jl. Raya Ubud (✆ **0361/972881**; main courses Rp35,000–Rp70,000; no credit cards; 8am–10pm), is a great place to pump up with some java and baked goods. Good breakfasts, croissants, and baguettes and delicate, delicious French pastries like éclairs and tarts should get your sugar rush going.

Tutmak Warung Kopi ★, on Jalan Dewi Sita, near Batan's Waru (✆ **0361/975754**; main courses Rp30,000–Rp70,000, latte Rp17,000; MC, V; 8am–11:30pm), serves the best coffee in town with great desserts, ice creams, sorbets, and a whole range of healthy treats, from salads to light lunches. There's also a good menu for kids. It is across from the soccer field so it's easy to find and extremely kid friendly.

The **West End Café** ★, Jl. Raya Sanggingan (✆ **0361/978363**; main courses Rp21,000–Rp54,000; AE, MC, V; Mon–Sat 11am–6pm), in the hip Neka Museum neighborhood, is the place for "afternoon tea" complete with scones, homemade strawberry preserves, clotted cream, tea sandwiches, and tarts. It would look right at home on the main street of an English coastal town.

TeraZo MEDITERRANEAN   The spacious interior of this hip bistro is simple yet welcoming. The extensive menu has gazpacho as a welcome starter in the tropical heat and light and delicious spring rolls. The eight-layer pie is a delicious pastry crust filled with smoked blue marlin, spinach, ricotta, and mushrooms. There are also a host of grilled items, fine pasta, and gourmet Asian-influenced dishes, such as the *nasi kuning,* yellow coconut rice with raisins, cashews, and strips of egg, or the *kue tiaun,* stir-fried rice noodles, chicken, and local greens. A tempting breakfast menu surprises with ricotta blintzes topped with honey and fresh yogurt.

Jl. Suweta. ✆ **0361/978941.** www.baligoodfood.com. Reservations recommended. Main courses Rp60,000–Rp134,000. AE, MC, V. 10am–midnight.

INEXPENSIVE

Batan's Waru EUROPEAN/INDONESIAN   Tucked away on a pleasant side street, Batan's Waru is particularly atmospheric at night, when the entrance is lit with candles. The ambitious menu has traditional dishes beyond the usual suspects, and plenty of vegetarian options. For an appetizer, try *urap pakis,* wild fern tips with roasted coconut and spices, or *lemper ayam,* chicken dumplings simmered in a banana leaf. The spicy hummus comes with grilled-pepper flatbread and tomato-mint relish. The restaurant also does smoked duck and a *babi guleng* feast, with a day's advance order, and there is a full menu of pasta, sandwiches, and light fare as well. Finish off with a perfect cup of Illy-brand espresso.

Jl. Dewi Sita. (℃) **0361/977528.** www.baligoodfood.com. Main courses Rp15,500–Rp43,000. AE, MC, V. 8am–midnight.

Bebek Bengil (Dirty Duck) ★ EUROPEAN/INDONESIAN   The Dirty Duck is the best place to try Ubud's famous dish. First stewed in local spices, then deep-fried, the duck here is delicious and not quite as oily as in other restaurants. Another way to go is the stuffed chicken with shiitake, sprouts, and spinach. The menu also features salads, sandwiches, and veggie options. Book a table toward the back, which looks out onto the paddy fields.

Padang Tegel. (℃) **0361/975489.** www.agungraka.com/bebekbengil. Main courses Rp12,500–Rp35,000. AE, DC, MC, V. 10am–10pm.

Cafe Lotus INTERNATIONAL/MODERN INDONESIAN   The food here isn't half bad, but the real reason to come to Cafe Lotus is for the chance to dine in the shadow of the Pura Saraswati temple (p. 209). The menu features good Western options, pastas and such, with some modified into fiery dishes using hot chilis, olives, and hearts of palm. Try the Balinese Satay Lilit, a mixed-fish kabob with a hint of coconut, served on skewers on a plate the size of a boat. The fresh health drinks are a delight. No beef is served due to the restaurant's proximity to the temple.

Jl. Raya Ubud. (℃) **0361/975660.** www.lotus-restaurants.com/cafe-lotus-ubud. Reservations recommended. Main courses Rp25,000–Rp54,000. AE, MC, V. 8:30am–10:30pm.

Cinta Grill INTERNATIONAL   Cinta specializes in barbecue ribs, Indonesian grilled chicken, and satay. Other specialties are Asian curries such as Javanese white chicken, South Indian fish, or North Indian chickpea with freshly ground fresh herbs, roots, and spices. There are very good Caesar salads and a first-rate carbonara and house-made tortellini with a simple classic tomato and basil. Sweet teeth will love the Dutch apple tart and chocolate fudge cake. Mojitos are the favored drink, especially during the two-for-one special from 4 to 7pm with five tropical flavors to try.

Jl. Monkey Forest. (℃) **0361/975395.** www.baligoodfood.com/cintagrill.asp. Reservations recommended. Pasta Rp48,000–Rp78,000; curries and soups Rp38,000–Rp82,000; grill Rp54,000–Rp130,000. AE, DC, MC, V. 10am–midnight.

Kafe VEGETARIAN   This is an extremely popular cafe with fantastic vegetarian mains, California-style burritos, coffee, and desserts. Upstairs houses several of the more well known NGOs in Ubud so along with vegans it is filled with a very international crowd. There is also a yoga and massage center and a gift shop with crafts from nonprofit organizations. The big notice board has all manner of local news, deals, and events.

Jl. Hanuman 44. (℃) **0361/970992.** www.balispirit.com. Main courses Rp20,000–Rp50,000. No credit cards. 8am–11pm.

Pizza Bagus ITALIAN   This is the local pizza joint of choice. There is good fresh pasta, pizza, and gelato and some of the best espresso in Ubud. They also offer Wi-Fi.

Jl. Raya Pengosekan. (℃) **0361/978520.** www.pizzabagus.com. Main courses Rp16,500–Rp39,500. MC, V. 9am–10:30pm.

Sari Organic (Bodag Maliah) ★ (Finds) ORGANIC   It is somehow reassuring to know that places like Sari Organic exist and that there are people behind them that

UBUD

10

WHERE TO DINE

believe in "making the world a better place"—their exact words. The project supports local farmers, uses organic produce, and spreads virtue as the only way to get here is on foot taking a pleasant 15-minute trek from Jalan Raya Ubud near the aqueduct down a small pathway through the farms and rice fields. When you arrive you will be pleasantly surprised by this quirky restaurant with 360-degree views of the paddy fields and wildlife. Call to reserve a table as this place is packed and popular.

Subak Sok Wayah. ✆ **0361/972087.** Reservations recommended. Main courses Rp35,000–Rp65,000. No credit cards. 8am–8pm.

Siam Sally ★★ THAI   The intrepid duo that brought us TeraZo and Cinta Grill has done it again. Good Thai food is all about getting the balance right with a bit of spice and a bit of sweet and sour. Siam Sally does it right, and all in a spectacular setting with enthusiastic service. Live jazz plays several times a week, but call ahead for the ever-changing schedule.

Jl. Raya Pengosekan. ✆ **0361/980777.** www.baligoodfood.com. Reservations recommended. Curries Rp46,000–Rp92,000; main courses Rp58,000–Rp118,000. AE, DC, MC, V. 10am–midnight.

The Three Monkeys MEDITERRANEAN   See no evil, hear no evil, eat no evil—or was that speak? The grub on offer at this bohemian cafe is eclectic and delectable. Choose from seafood, pastas, and Asian-Mediterranean dishes. There is no corkage fee for wine and at night there is a romantic feel about the place with the glow of bamboo torches lighting the evening's people-watching parade.

Jl. Hanoman, Ubud. ✆ **0361/975554.** Main courses Rp38,000–Rp59,000. MC, V. 7am–11pm.

WARUNGS

Ibu Oka ★★   Tourists and locals flock like ducks to water for the famous grilled suckling pig at Ibu Oka. The fall-off-the-bone *babi guling* is served with garlic string beans and steamed rice. The restaurant is laid out in a traditional family household compound, and diners sit at low tables, shoeless and comfortable. The ambience of clucking chickens and fighting cocks is sure to raise an eyebrow or two but this is a village warung at heart—despite the throngs of tourists who find it.

Jl. Suweta. No phone. *Babi guling* Rp25,000. No credit cards. 11am–2pm.

Murni's Warung ★   Murni's Warung was one of the first restaurants in Ubud and the simple warung has turned into a miniconglomerate. Ever-present Murni is now known as much for the antiquities and curios that she sells as far afield as the San Francisco Tribal Art Fair as she is for this Ubud establishment. Expat Ubudians have made Murni's their local watering hole since the early '80s. The fare here is simple Balinese cuisine and sandwiches. The restaurant is perched just beside the Tjampuhan suspension bridge overlooking the Tjampuhan River.

Jl. Raya Campuhan. ✆ **0361/975233.** www.murnis.com. Reservations recommended. Indonesian Rp22,000–Rp34,000; duck Rp77,000; seafood Rp43,000–Rp72,000. MC, V. 9am–10pm.

Nasi Ayam Kedewatan   This place has been around since the mid-'60s. The specialty of the house is "torn fried chicken" *(ayam goring suir)*. Owner Ibu Mangku's *sambal* is so spicy you might refry that chicken in your mouth if you aren't careful. Have plenty of steaming white rice and cold Bintang to soothe the senses.

Jl. Raya Kedewatan. ✆ **0361/974795.** Main courses start at Rp10,000. No credit cards. 9am–6pm.

Naughty Nuri's Warung and Grill ★★★ (Moments) INDONESIAN/BARBE-
CUE   Naughty Nuri's has hosted a number of memorable or unmemorable evenings
depending upon the number of martinis served. Run by Indonesian Isnuri and her
affable New Yorker husband Brian, this watering hole and restaurant is famous for its
Indonesian fare and barbecued pork spareribs. The real deal here, however, are the martinis, which celebrity chef Anthony Bourdain claims are the best outside of New York
City. Thursday is sashimi night and is packed with local Ubudians. **Nacho Mama** ★★
(✆ **0361/780-4697;** main courses Rp17,000–Rp42,000; no credit cards; 11am–10pm)
is part of Naughty Nuri's and serves burritos, tacos, and nachos and some excellent margaritas with lots of Bali limes. If Nuri's is crowded, order the ribs at Nacho Mama's down
the road.

Jl. Raya Sanggingan. ✆ **0361/977547.** Indonesian Rp20,000–Rp30,000; ribs Rp60,000; burgers
Rp48,000–Rp50,000. No credit cards. 8am–10pm.

Warung Enak INDONESIAN   The Indonesian menu here reads like a tribute to the
over 200 ethnic groups that populate these fabled islands. Here you can discover the rich
and intricate use of over 60 hand-crushed herbs and spices and lesser known nuts and
legumes that achieve strong, tangy, and always interesting flavors. Their famous rijstaffel
comes with 17 dishes and rice so that you can really taste across the archipelago. Don't
miss out on the snail satay. They are also famous for their arak cocktails, which will have
you dancing with the monkeys in no time at all.

Jl. Raya Pengosekan. ✆ **0361/972911.** www.warungenakbali.com. Main courses Rp50,000–Rp82,000;
rijstaffel Rp125,000–Rp150,000. AE, MC, V. 11am–11pm.

Warung Lada INDONESIAN   Served in traditional warung style where you point
and pick your dishes, the food here is typical warung grub like chicken, eggplant, tofu
and tempeh, vegetables, *nasi goreng, mie goreng* (fried noodles), or *soto ayam,* an Indonesian yellow soup served with boiled chicken and vegetables. You can leave here with a full
stomach for Rp50,000 for two people.

Jl. Raya Hanoman. ✆ **0361/972822.** Rice Rp3,000–Rp5,000; fish and meat Rp6,000. No credit cards.
9am–10pm.

Warung Mendez INDONESIAN   The specialty here is goat, which is much health-
ier for you than other meats due to its low fat content but difficult to cook. The owner
Chef Mendez hails from Yogyakarta and uses his old family recipes, which require sim-
mering for hours before marinating in Javanese spice paste. The goat soup, *sup iga kambing,* is made with nutmeg, ginger, cloves, cinnamon, vegetables, and a squeeze of lime.
To find this place, go up Penestanan hill and turn up the mountain road opposite the old
Beggars Bush in Tjampuhan.

Jl. Penestanan. ✆ **0361/973076.** Main courses Rp17,000–Rp47,000. No credit cards. 11am–10pm.

4 EXPLORING UBUD

TEMPLES
As you explore Ubud and make friends with the locals and expats, you will hear different
stories about the legends and histories of local temples from guides, scholars, and profes-
sors alike. There really isn't one correct answer here.

UBUD
10
EXPLORING UBUD

Goa Gajah (Elephant Caves)   One of Bali's most visited tourist sites is a grotto of elaborate stone carvings from the 9th century. The main attraction is the impressive entranceway, made of what appears to be menacing creatures and demons. Legend has it that the main protagonist was an elephant and since the carving at the entrance is elephant-like, we call this the Elephant Caves. The mouth leads into a small underground T-shaped cave measuring about 9m × 9m (30 ft. × 30 ft.) with several small ledges possibly used by priests to meditate on or even sleep. Aside from the small cave the only other thing to see here is the decorative bathing pool. On the far wall of the pool are six semi-clad female figures holding urns pouring water. Women bathe on one side and men on the other.

Bedulu Village, Blahbatu. Admission, including sarong rental, Rp6,000. Daily 7am–5:30pm.

Pura Gunung Kawi   This temple was made by King Marakata Near as an altar for King Udayana; an inscription dates the temple to A.D. 945. In the Balinese Hindu faith death consists of three phases. The first is the cremation of the body, the second is setting free the holy spirit from the spiritual body, and the third is seating the holy body in a sacred abode. Temples *(candi)* were built as the spiritual abodes of deceased kings. Here the Dewa Pitara of King Udayana is seated at the Candi Gunung Kawi temple; other altars were built for his descendants. Today the god Vishnu and goddess Sri are worshiped here as farmers and their *subak* (rice irrigation organizations) come to pray for prosperity.

Tampaksiring. Admission Rp6,000; video camera Rp5,000; camera Rp3,000. Daily 7am–5pm.

Pura Gunung Lebah   Located at Campuhan, in the gorge just 1.5km (1 mile) west of Ubud, this temple is an easy walk from the Ubud market and makes a very pleasant early morning stroll. Legend has it that in the 8th century the high priest Rsi Markandya, a holy sage who came from Java to build Besakih Temple, was spiritually attracted to the beautiful area, the confluence of two rivers. He stayed, meditated, and built a temple. Ubud was born.

Campuhan. Admission Rp10,000; video camera Rp5,000; camera Rp3,000. Daily 7am–5pm.

Pura Kebo Edan   Pura Kebo Edan, or "crazy buffalo temple," is in the east Ubud suburbs near Goa Gajah. It is said that it was built in the 12th century and while it isn't a fantastic structure it is famous for the nearly 4m (12-ft.) statue known as the Giant of Pejeng. Temple history facts are difficult to pin down but it is thought to be about 700 years old. The Giant of Pejeng is famous for his huge penis, and four of them at that. The first theory is that the animal appears in Brahmanism while others say it may represent Bima, a hero of the Mahabharata, dancing on a dead body in a myth related to the Hindu Shiva god. I like this version as in this story Bima falls in love with a woman and his desire has risen. However the penis of Bima is too big for her and she finds another lover. Bima finds them making love one day and he has them killed. It's hard to decipher the moral of the story here.

Bedulu Village. Admission Rp10,000 adults. Daily 7am–5pm.

Pura Penataran Sasih   This temple is about 4km (2½ miles) east of the center of Ubud and is best known for the hourglass-shaped drum more than 2m (6½ ft.) long, the largest single piece cast drum in the world. It is difficult to see as it is in the inner courtyard high up in a pavilion. The drum's geometric patterns are said to resemble patterns from both Irian Jaya and Vietnam. Estimates of its age vary from 1,000 to 2,000 years old; the legend of its origin says that the drum came to earth as a fallen moon, landed in a tree, and shone so brightly that it stopped a band of naughty thieves from going about their mission. Because the moon was bright both day and night, one of the thieves tried to urinate on it to stop its shining. The thief died and the moon dropped to the ground. What is actual fact is that this amazing ancient relic represents the bronze age of Southeast Asia.

Pejeng Village. Admission Rp10,000. Daily 7am–5pm.

Pura Pusering Jagat   Literally translated as the "Temple of the Navel of the World," this temple is 100m (328 ft.) south from the main road of Pura Penataran Sasih. The point of interest here is the meter-high elaborately carved holy water vessel whose exterior is sculpted with a detailed relief thought to depict the Hindu myth of "the churning of the sea of milk." There are several versions of this legend, but they all relate the story of the gods and the demons desperately trying to get their hands on the elixir of immortal life. It is nice to know that some things haven't changed since the 14th century. As the story goes, under Vishnu's guidance they set about churning this cosmic sea of milk with the aid of a holy mountain as their pestle and the serpentine *naga* as the pulleys. Carved from a single block of sandstone you can still just make out some of the figures including the undulating *naga* ropes and a number of dancing deities supporting them. In a nearby pavilion is another significant icon, the meter-high phallic lingam and its female receptacle, the yoni—an important shrine for the Balinese for infertile couples and newlyweds.

Pejeng. Admission Rp10,000. Daily 7am–5pm.

Pura Saraswati   The royal family commissioned this temple and water garden, dedicated to the Hindu goddess of art and learning, at the end of the 19th century. The main shrine is covered in fine carvings and the bale houses and giant *barong* masks are interesting. The restaurant **Cafe Lotus** (p. 205) is situated at the front so that diners can look out over the lovely grounds.

Jl. Raya Ubud. Free admission. Daily 7am–5pm.

Puri Saren Agung (Royal Palace)   From the late 19th century to the mid-1940s, this was the seat for the local ruler. It's a series of elegant and well-preserved pavilions, many decorated incongruously with colonial-era European furniture. Visitors are welcome to stroll around, though no signs explain what you are looking at. Evening dance performances are held in the courtyard, by far the best and most dramatic setting for these in Ubud. Many members of the royal family still live here and if you are lucky enough one might just show you around. There are six very basic rooms to stay in for around US$50 a night but no facilities on the grounds.

Jl. Raya Ubud. ☎ **0361/975057.** Free admission. Daily 7am–5pm.

Tirta Empul ★★★   The word *tirta* (derived from the Sanskrit) means "water" and *empul* is a Balinese word that means "spring." Balinese regard these springs as sacred and people come from miles around to bath in these waters. The temple has rice fields to the north, the Pakerisan river to the east, a palace built in Sukarno's day used as a Presidential retreat to the west, and craft stalls to the south. The temple dates from 960 B.C. in the period of the Warmadewa Dynasty. Twelve water spouts pour holy water from 12 sacred springs into a long pool; two Olympic-size pools are used for communal bathing. The main temple courtyard contains shrines and pavilions, one for Brahma, Shiva, and Krishna, one for Mt. Batur, and one for Indra (Dewi Indra).

Jl. Raya Penelokan, Tampaksiring. Admission Rp6,000. Daily 8am–6pm.

Antonio Blanco Museum ★★   This museum is an homage to Bali's famous Cata-
lan expat. Born in the Philippines, Blanco arrived here penniless, but eventually
befriended the king, married, had children, and lived the life of Riley all his days. He was
a favorite at court and the confidant of many powerful people on Bali and in Indonesia.
This grand gallery houses a collection of his homespun, baroque pornography that is as
much a romp through Blanco's sexual dalliances as anything. Some paintings feature
Blanco's raunchy prose poetry. The consummate egomaniacal artist, Blanco envisioned
this monument to himself and participated fully in its creation before shuffling off this
mortal coil in 1999. The museum grounds are a trip, with Blanco's dachshunds, monkeys, and exotic birds still ruling the roost.

Campuhan-Ubud. ℂ **0361/975502.** www.blancomuseum.com. Admission Rp50,000. Daily 9am–5pm.

ARMA Museum of Art ★★   A few kilometers south of Ubud, the Agung Rai Museum
of Art (the ARMA), is but one branch of the charming Agung Rai's empire, which includes
the museum, a commercial art gallery, a Thai restaurant, a cafe, and a resort
(p. 197) all within a stone's throw of each other. Agung Rai, one of Bali's foremost art entre-
preneurs, began his professional life peddling souvenirs in Kuta, which exposed him to local
artists. He began collecting and gained a reputation by backing local artists; with his fine eye
he began promoting their work abroad. ARMA opened with proceeds from Agung Rai's
commercial art activities and now has about 250 paintings on permanent display. The collection includes traditional Kamasan-style paintings on tree bark, works by Batuan school artists
of the '30s and '40s, and works by Walter Spies and Raden Saleh, considered the father of
Indonesian paintings. Check out Bangswaan Jawa's oil on canvas dated 1837 of an Indonesian
regent couple—the first Indonesian Western style oil painting.

Jl. Pengosekan. ℂ **0361/975742.** www.armamuseum.com. Admission Rp20,000. Daily 9am–6pm.

Neka Art Museum ★★   This museum of 400 works was founded by former school-
teacher Suteja Neka, a patron of the arts. The first gallery displays works by new and
more established Indonesian artists and operates as a commercial art gallery. Other pavilions are thematically organized. Pay special attention to the Lempad Pavilion with works
on paper by one of Bali's most revered artists, I Gusti Nyoman Lempad, and the Arie
Smit Pavilion, showcasing 50 works by the Dutch-born artist who was a personal friend
of Neka and lived on-site for many years. Don't miss the view of the Campuhan Gorge
to get a glimpse of what inspires local artists.

Jl. Raya Campuhan, Desa Kedewatan. ℂ **0361/975074.** www.museumneka.com. Admission Rp25,000.
Mon–Sat 10am–6pm; Sun noon–5pm.

Museum Puri Lukisan ★ (Finds)   The Museum Puri Lukisan is one of Bali's most
historically fascinating fine art museums. A major renovation has turned this formerly
dilapidated display into something nearly on par with the Neka Art Museum. Founded
in 1956, the collection was a joint initiative of the prince of Ubud, Tjokorda Gde Agung
Sukawati, and his close friend, Rudolf Bonnet, to showcase the ideas and artistic achieve-
ments of the Pita Maha.

Jl. Raya Ubud. ℂ **0361/975136.** www.mpl-ubud.com. Admission Rp15,000. Daily 8am–4pm.

Rudana Museum   This is the latest addition to Bali's already prolific stable of museums. Nyoman Rudana and his wife seek to promote the richness of Indonesian art to a
wider audience as well as provide a cultural education institution for the public. The

museum building was designed according to the Balinese philosophy of Tri Angga (foot,
body, and head) and Tri Mandala (inner court, middle court, and outer court). Contemporary paintings here include works by Indonesian artists Made Wianta, Nyoman Gunarsa, and Sri Hadi Suarsono.

Jl. Cok Rai Pudak 44, Peliatan. © **0361/975779.** www.museumrudana.com. Admission Rp20,000. Mon–Sat 10am–6pm; Sun noon–5pm.

ART GALLERIES
Don't pass up the free galleries around town, especially on Jalan Raya Sanggingan going north toward the more high-end resorts.

Agung Rai Gallery ★★ Agung Rai chooses his painting based on *taksu,* which is a theory of "honesty between the artist and the viewer. An artist will follow his heart or instinct. A painting that has a certain special magic does not need to be elaborated upon, the painting alone speaks." Anticipate finding some real treasures here.

Jl. Peliatan. © **0361/974562.** www.agungraigallery.com. Daily 8am–6pm.

Gaya Fusion of Senses ★★ Gaya has a strong reputation for developing contemporary art on the island. A constant stream of exhibitions show modern art by locals and foreigners in high regard, such as German Peter Dittmar, Swiss Stephan Spicher, New Yorker Pablo Gentile, and Indonesian artists Alfi, Murni, Made Wianta, and Wayan Karja. Performance art, films, and other community activities are held here. The terrace bar and restaurant (p. 202) serves the goal of "a space that integrates life and art." Every Sunday from 11am to 1pm is a free art program for children of all ages taught by top Indonesian artists who donate their time.

Jl. Raya Sayan. © **0361/979252.** www.gayafusion.com. Daily 10am–10pm.

Genta Gallery This gallery, related to the Museum Rudana, has a well-documented collection that originates from mostly Indonesian artists. Each different pavilion displays a vast range of work from landscapes of daily Balinese life or traditional objects such as *barong* to very contemporary pieces. Visit the workshop to witness the artists actually putting their ideas onto canvas.

Jl. Raya Lodtunduh 1. © **0361/974254.** www.museumrudana.com/gentagallery. Daily 9am–5pm.

Gusti Lempad's Gallery ★ Opposite the market is the former home of I Gusti Lempad, which has been in the family for well over a century. The paintings for sale are by his family but his are not for sale here (the best place to see them is at Museum Puri Lukisan and Neka Art Museum). I Gusti Nyoman Lempad, like his father and children, was a talented painter who died at the remarkable age of 116 in 1978. He originally painted in the Wayang style, but moved to a more expressive, freer style, painting and drawing in black Chinese ink on paper.

Jl. Raya Ubud. © **0361/975618.** Daily 10am–7pm.

Han Snel Gallery ★ (Finds) The small gallery of Dutch artist Han Snel is on Jalan Kajeng, a pleasant side road off Jalan Raya Ubud. Snel painted in a number of styles, but the most notable was geometric figures of Balinese landscapes and people with a slightly cubist bent. Several stunning portraits of Balinese women speak to how he met his wife: she began modeling for him at 13 and married him at 16. Examples of his paintings can be found in the other galleries in Ubud.

In Han Snel Bungalow, Jl. Kajeng. © **0361/975699.** www.hansnelbungalow.com. Daily 8am–9pm.

(Finds) A Rare Treat

The **Bali Purnati Center for the Arts,** Jl. Gunung Abang, Banjar Penataran, Negara Batuan (✆ **0361/294590;** fax 0361/294591; www.balipurnati.com), has interesting cultural exchanges and events that include performing and visual arts, music, and film. The only way to find out what is on is to call up and see if you get lucky. Opportunities to view live performances don't happen often but if they do you might catch a Wadaiko drum troupe from Japan, a stage performance of I La Galigo by renowned theater direct Robert Wilson, or the Kronos Quartet. Accommodations (eight units; year-round US$80; AE, MC, V) here are normally reserved for exchange programs and theater groups, but if you are interested in staying here just call ahead and see if there's space available.

Komaneka Fine Art Gallery   This is one of the few galleries in Bali that has ample space to show off large-scale contemporary works. The prerequisite for any foreign artist displayed here is *kontemporer,* a strong connection to the island. One of the top-selling artists here is the masterfully superior I Made Djirna who has achieved international recognition. Keen on painting women as archetypes and mothers, Djirna's women are altogether different from that of non-Balinese artists like Le Mayeur who depicted women as exotic and sexy.

Jl. Monkey Forest. ✆ **0361/976090.** http://gallery.komaneka.com. Daily 8am–8pm.

Rio Helmi Photo Gallery ★   Rio Helmi's Gallery in Ubud sells his work that celebrates the region's people and places, contemporary lifestyles, and Mahayana Buddhism. A man on a mission, Rio is quietly accomplishing the goal of photographing most of the indigenous peoples of Indonesia. His photography has been published in the *New York Times* and *Vanity Fair,* and he has also published several books including: *Bali Style, River Gems,* and *Made in Indonesia.*

Jl. Suweta. ✆ **0361/978773.** www.riohelmi.com. Daily 9am–9pm.

Seniwati Gallery ★★ (Finds)   In traditional Balinese society, activities are divided by gender and historically painting and sculpture were male territory. Of course, there have always been women painters but it was difficult for them to be shown and get their deserved recognition. In 1991 British-born Mary Northmore Aziz converted a house into a gallery for female artists. A number of the Balinese artists that she shows have been heavily influenced by one of the recognized "traditional" styles. Ni Made Suciarmi and her niece, Supini, two of Bali's top classical painters, still work on cloth polished with rice flour and grind their own pigments. Ni Wayan Warti works in the tradition of Batuan, creating paintings full of the eerie supernatural quality the Balinese call *tenget,* while Gusti Agung Galuh's paintings show a strong influence from Walter Spies.

Jl. Sriwedari 2B. ✆ **0361/975485.** www.seniwatigallery.com. Tues–Sun 9am–5pm.

Sika Contemporary Art Gallery   The owner here abhors commercial art, calling it "too sweet like candy." Instead he and his colleagues are keen on multimedia that identify with the spirit of Balinese art and culture in a nontraditional way.

Jl. Raya Campuhan. ✆ **0361/975727.** www.sikagallery.info. Daily 7:30am–6pm.

Symon Studios   Symon Studios used to be called the Art Zoo and the first thing you will notice is the sign outside that says "DANGER ART!" This weird and wonderful gallery has been a Campuhan landmark for over a quarter of century. The artist Symon hails from America's Midwest, which is a bit of an oxymoron since the primary subject matter of his paintings are of beguiling young Balinese men in various stages of undress. You get the picture. His color palate is bright and bold as Symon was influenced by both Arie Smit and Andy Warhol, not necessarily in that order.

Jl. Raya Campuhan. ℭ **0361/974721.** www.symonstudios.com. Daily 8am–8pm.

COOKING CLASSES

Classes typically include a morning at the local market and an afternoon in the kitchen. **Casa Luna Cooking School,** Jl. Raya Ubud (ℭ **0361/971257;** www.casalunabali.com; Rp300,000–Rp400,000), is run by expat Australian Janet de Neefe and her Balinese husband Ketut Suardana. Classes are held at Janet's Casa Luna Honeymoon Guesthouse (p. 198). **Ubud Hanging Gardens,** Desa Buahan (ℭ **0361/982700;** www.ubudhanging gardens.com; US$45 minimum two persons, includes lunch; p. 194), also offers classes with a market and village visit.

   Chris Salans, the renowned chef who has made Mozaic (p. 201) one of the finest restaurants in Southeast Asia, shares his prowess with the lucky few who book ahead for his remarkable cooking classes (ℭ **0361/975768;** www.mozaic-bali.com; half-day class US$90, full day US$130, professional class full day US$130; minimum four participants). Each student gets their own recipe book and apron. Even if you don't quite get it right at home you can at least look the part.

SPAS

All of the high-end resorts have good spa services and there are some mom-and-pop-type operations that will really surprise your purse strings as well as your body. Today it isn't just flower baths and foot scrubs, you will also find alternative and independent wellness centers and detox spas. Spas are open daily.

   The Mother Earth of spas, **COMO Shambhala's wellness retreat** (p. 194; single treatment US$80–US$150; AE, DC, MC, V; 10am–7pm) has tailor-made programs prescribed after consultation with a team of professionals, including ayurvedic doctors, nutritionists, and psychologists. Colonic hydrotherapy and herbal cleansers are popular here. Your specialists will prescribe daily yoga or martial arts, which help balance your *doshas*—Sanskrit for "fault" or "imbalance." Not that you would have any of those, but just in case, this is your place. Take advantage of the chlorine-free pool, with massage jets. The raw food menu is thankfully as tasty as it is nutritious.

   The spa at **Kayumanis,** Sayan (ℭ **0361/9727777;** single treatment US$35–US$300; package US$230–US$435; AE, DC, MC, V; 8am–6pm) is all about some serious pampering. A signature is "Sensory Surrender": a 6-hour treatment that begins with a brief yoga session and refreshing walk followed by a warm tea tree oil body scrub then a tea tree oil–infused bath before being wrapped in a concoction of frangipani and coconut. This is followed by a warm volcanic stone massage and then a simultaneous foot massage and facial.

   The **Kirana Spa** ★, in the Royal Pita Maha (Kedewatan; ℭ **0361/976333;** www. kiranaspa.com; 1-hr. treatments US$100, 2 hr. US$180, 3 hr. US$320, half-day US$400, 1-day US$490; AE, DC, MC, V; 9am–9pm) is a joint production between Japan's leading cosmetics company Shishedo (the first such spa outside Japan) and Ubud's royal family. The menu has just five polished and perfect treatments. You can have a spa treatment only or combine the spa time with relaxing in the gardens and swimming pool.

The **Mango Tree Spa** at Kupu Kupu Barong (p. 199; single treatment US$60–US$90, specials US$70–US$125; AE, DC, MC, V; 9am–9pm), sits in a mango tree and uses L'Occitane products. You literally have to climb a tree to reach the spa villas but fortunately stairs are provided for the tender footed.

The award-winning spa in the **Maya Ubud Resort** ★★★ (p. 196; single treatment US$60–US$75, package US$121–US$175; AE, DC, MC, V; 8am–8pm) is suspended down a gravity-defying cliff. Blending effortlessly with the colors of nature, the spa pavilions all are made with local materials and include outdoor bathtubs that sit with the waters of the Petanu River.

Spa Alila ★, in Alila Ubud (p. 195; single treatment US$45–US$65, package US$78–US$170; AE, DC, MC, V; 9am–9pm), has excellent therapists who warm up with a daily yoga session for themselves to get in the right frame of mind for working on you. The local treatments made from green tea, bamboo, and virgin coconut oil proved so popular that they have started to sell them to guests. The Alila Recovery signature massage includes techniques from Thai, Swedish, and Balinese massage.

At **Spa Hati,** Jl. Raya Andong 14 (✆ **0361/977578;** www.spahati.com; single treatment Rp70,000–Rp185,000, package Rp530,000; MC, V; 9am–9pm), you can feel good as well as do good since all of the proceeds go to support the expansion and upkeep of the Bali Hati School for children in Mas. Of the nine treatments on offer, guests can choose from a 60-minute Blissful Journey massage or Rapture, a 90-minute treatment that includes a rejuvenating body scrub and two well-trained masseuses who will massage away any remnants of jet lag.

The spa at **Four Seasons Sayan** ★★★ (p. 194; massage US$55–US$190, body treatment US$55–US$270, package US$145–US$450; AE, DC, MC, V; 9am–9pm), universally accepted as one of the best spas in Bali, has a permanent expatriate spa director, which shows how serious they are about pampering. The Suci Dara Ayurvedic experience is delivered with Indian aromatic herbal oils that will have you seeing out of your third eye. Take advantage of the new *watsu* pool and have a "rebirthing experience," which gets to your inner child with skillfully guided water stretches and movements.

UBUD OUTDOORS

One of the most enjoyable ways of seeing Ubud is **on foot,** making your way through the *gang* that zig zag through town and crossing over into the fields of rice paddies that will take you through quant villages to see farming life first hand.

BIKING Plenty of places in Ubud rent bikes and it is a lovely way to see the town and it's surrounding villages. You should expect to pay about Rp55,000 for the day. Many operators offer leisurely guided biking excursions in Ubud and down through the villages below Kintamani. **Bali Adventure Tours** (✆ **0361/721480;** www.baliadventuretours. com) ends their trip at the Elephant Safari Park (p. 216) where you can have a peak at the gentle giants without having to pay extra for entry. **Banyan Tree Cycling Tour** (✆ **08/1238798516;** www.banyantree.wikispaces.com; US$45 adults, US$35 children under 10, US$35 nonrider accompanying a rider; costs include meals, drink, and transport) begins about an hour's drive from central Ubud where you have breakfast at a restaurant with panoramic views of the mountains and rice fields. The trip is about 25km (16 miles) almost all downhill. At the end, you get a lovely home-cooked meal at the tour leader's home.

Learning to Love the Earth

The Ubud **Green School** ★★★, Jl. Raya Sibang Kaja (15 min. south of Ubud; ✆ **0361/780-5446;** www.greenschool.org; call to make a tour appointment; entrance by donation), is a spectacle better seen to be believed and could easily be the wave of the future. Visionary John Hardy and his wife, Cynthia, founded this school with the proceeds from their John Hardy jewelry brand. The school has classes from kindergarten to eighth grade with plans to expand through high school and eventually worldwide. Made almost exclusively out of bamboo, the buildings are an architectural marvel. The world's largest bamboo bridge joins the east and west sides of the campus, emblematic of the founders' goals: to connect learning with creativity; environmental responsibility with scientific knowledge; respect for self with respect for the many cultures represented in and around the school. Take a tour and be inspired.

The school also runs a day and overnight camp called **Green Camp** ★★★. Activities such as coconut tree climbing, kite making, bug hunting, and chocolate making are designed to challenge children while educating them about nature. Off-site adventures include volcano climbing, white-water rafting, mountain biking, and scuba diving. Ages range from 5 to 16 years and are residential or day programs. Check out **www.greencamp.com** for more information.

Bali Trail Blazers ★ (✆ **0361/842-7181;** www.bali-trailblazers.com; day rides US$110 per person or US$80 per person with two-person minimum, 2 days US$260, 1 week US$750, bike hire 1 week US$100, bike hire 2 weeks US$150; tours include gear, water bottle, transportation, lunch, snacks and soft drinks; longer trips include hotel, breakfast, and lunch) offers single-track off-road biking. The group has mountain trails that cross a network of farmer's tracks and motorbike paths.

RAFTING White-water rafting on the Sayan Ridge, a Level III rapid, is one of the most fun and invigorating experiences in Bali and it simply doesn't matter that it is a very touristy thing to do. It can all be a bit surreal looking up at the dense jungle above from the sacred river below. As you meander down the river at a slower pace you can take in the traditional villages and temples and see ancient stone carvings on the cliffs. Don't get too distracted because within minutes you can be dropping down a white water rapid and holding on for dear life. Contact **Sobek** ★★★, Jl. Raya Tebongkang 33 (✆ **0361/287059;** www.balisobek.com; US$79 adults, US$52 children 14 and younger; includes transportation, insurance, and lunch).

WALKING Meet in front of the Puri Lukisan Museum at 8:30am for the **Bali Nature Herbal Walk** ★ (✆ **08/123816024;** www.baliherbalwalk.com; US$18, including herbal tea, refreshing herbal drinks, Balinese cake or tropical fruits). The walk lasts until noon and exposes you to a wide range of native plants and herbs. You'll learn to identify herbs by sight, smell, and taste. On the walk you will be introduced to the plants that are used for first aid, emergencies, and more serious illnesses.

When in Rome . . .

Even if you aren't a yogi, while you are in Ubud surrounded by them why not give yoga a try? The **Yoga Barn** ★★★, Jl. Pengosekan (📞 **0361/970992;** www.theyogabarn.com; reservations recommended; single class Rp100,000, three classes Rp85,000 a class, five classes Rp80,000 a class; daily 7am–7:30pm), in the midst of the verdant *sawah* (paddy fields) off a little *gang* in Ubud's Padan Tegal, offers classes and workshops every day for every level. Internationally renowned yoga teachers, gurus, dancers, musicians, and specialists with all kinds of esoteric body knowledge and healing abilities flock to this center. You are bound to find something of interest that you possibly never even knew existed like Ecstatic Dance and Vedic Astrology. The website **www.balispirit.com** has all the information on the center's upcoming activities.

The **Bali Nature Walk** ★, Jl. Dewi Sita (📞 **08/170735914;** Rp250,000), picks you up from your hotel at about 8am. The walk starts about 30 minutes from Ubud at one of Bali's oldest temples and takes you through lush jungle and into agricultural farmland. On clear days you can see the charming temple Pura Sibi Alit.

It would be sinful to miss out on Victor Mason's famous **bird walk** ★★★ (Tjampuhan; 📞 **0361/975009;** www.balibirdwalk.com; US$33; Tues, Fri–Sun). British-bred Victor Mason leads the pack when it comes to cavorting with the birds and bees of Ubud. His famous walks start at Beggar's Bush (just over the Tjamphuhan bridge, opposite the Antonio Blanco museum) at 9am and end at Murni's restaurant (p. 206) and include lunch. Count on seeing lots of birdlife including egrets, white-breasted water hens, and the resident Java kingfisher.

Botanic Garden Ubud ★★ (Moments) These gardens, spread over 4.9 hectares (12 acres), provide an excellent look at the variety of lush island plant life. Highlights include the orchid greenhouse, a Muslim garden with a symmetrical tiled path, and the fruit tree area. A labyrinth, purportedly the first in Bali, is a surefire hit with the kids.

Kutuh Kaja. 📞 **0361/780-3904.** www.botanicgardenbali.com. Admission Rp50,000. Daily 8am–6pm.

Elephant Safari Park Lodge ★★ (Kids) The Elephant Safari Park, run by Bali Adventure Tours, is less of a safari and more of an elephant ride. These native Sumatra elephants are well cared for and live in large, lush enclosures. The owners have worked carefully with locals from Taro village, previously one of Bali's most remote and untouched villages, to make sure they leave little more than elephant tracks. A safari starts with Pachyderm 101, as knowledgeable guides discuss the animals' care and feeding, local ecology, threats to the native population, and preservation efforts. Then, along with a *mahout* (guide), you go on a galumphing trip through the jungle. A fun elephant show is staged twice daily at 12:30 and 3:30pm. The park has recently begun offering a night safari that begins at 6:45pm every night and includes an elephant talent show and a four-course dinner for US$99 and US$69 for children.

Jl. Bypass Ngurah Rai, Pesanggaran. 📞 **0361/721480.** Fax 0361/721481. www.baliadventuretours.com. Reservations recommended. Admission US$47 adults, US$73 with elephant ride; US$35 children and US$49 with elephant ride; family rates and Internet rates available. Admission includes transport, buffet lunch, and show. Daily 8am–6pm.

southern end of Monkey Forest Road. The towering tree clusters here are home to a troop of bad-tempered but photogenic primates that swing from branches, cannonball into pools, and do everything short of putting on suits and paying taxes, all to the general delight of photo-snapping visitors. Signs warn you not to feed the monkeys, but locals stand under those very signs selling you bananas and nuts for precisely that purpose. Do so if you must, but do not tease the critters, which are grumpy enough as it is—just hand them the food. Make sure you have no other food on you—they will smell it. They're also known to snatch at dangling or glittering objects and to gnaw on sandals. There's a small temple in the forest, and the track also leads to Nyuhkuning, a village known for woodcarving.

Jl. Monkey Forest. (C) **0361/971304.** www.monkeyforestubud.com. Admission Rp15,000. No credit cards. Daily 8am–6pm.

5 AROUND UBUD

Leaving the beaches behind and heading towards Ubud you might be impressed to think you are seeing a less commercial Bali, or be tempted to think this is the "real" Bali (whatever that means). However, this is a major tourist route, a sort of shopper's and collector's circuit that can leave even the most voracious shopper satisfied. Just after leaving the bypass and shortly before the Batubulan bus terminal, the center of all public transport, and heading east, you cross into the old kingdom (now the regency) of **Gianyar.** The royal house of Gianyar allied itself with the Dutch against its traditional foes in the rival palaces thus avoiding the fate of the other kingdoms whose royal lines were almost completely decimated in ritual *puputan.* This allowed them to continue their artistic endeavors and today the majority of the population is somehow involved in handicrafts and arts. Each village en route to Ubud has its own specialized handicraft or art form with roots in royal patronage.

BATUBULAN Batubulan is only about 10km (6 miles) northeast of Denpasar. This is stone carving and *barong* dance central—as if children in this village were born with a chisel in their hands and a rhythm in their walk. Performances take place every morning between 9 and 9:30am and last for about an hour. The performances are for tourists but it is a good way to kick off your shopping. This is where you will find the Ganesha of your dreams and a Buddha for your boudoir. International shipping is not a problem—if you can't resist the very large-scale pieces.

CELUK ★ (Moments) About 5km (3 miles) from Denpasar, the shops and homes of this town are filled to the gills with silver and gold. Long a center for artisans in elaborate gold jewelry for royal households, Celuk now produces jewelry for the international market. Apprentices begin young and by the time they are in their early teens are producing fine ornaments from the precious metals. Almost every family in Celuk now makes or sells gold and silver work. Prices are competitive and quality is similar. Huge tour buses park outside some of the bigger stores but don't be put off. Go to some of the smaller shops along the back lanes and you will be duly rewarded. You will be told prices are fixed but they are not. Bargain. If you are interested in buying a few gold and silver pieces check the gram rate on the Internet beforehand so you have an idea of a fair price—all gold and silver is weighed and sold by the gram.

ⓘ **Tips Getting the Real Deal**

When in **Batubulan,** make sure you are buying a carved stone piece not a cheaper mass produced artwork that is molded rather than carved from lava-stone "concrete." Unless you have a trained eye, you may not be able to tell. Always ask and look for lines that are the tell-tale signs of mold work.

Some unscrupulous carvers in **Mas** sell cheaper woods as sandalwood *(cenana),* which is an extremely expensive material mainly from East Timor. The tricks include rubbing oil on the carvings or packing them in sandalwood chips. It is hard to tell the real deal so either go to a trusted source or assume the worst and alter your price accordingly.

SUKAWATI About 5km (3 miles) south from Ubud is the **Sukawati Art Market** open dawn till dusk. Here you will find production of ceremonial umbrellas, *lamak* (the hanging decorated with Chinese coins and little mirrors seen on shrines at festival time), gold-painted *perada* cloth wrapped around shrines, and other ceremonial pieces. Tourists come by the bucket load to stock up on cheap trinkets, fabrics, baskets, and temple decorations. Be prepared to haggle. The colorful open-air food market here has literally everything under the sun. You can still see the ancient art of puppet making at the market, which is the least touristy thing about the place.

BATUAN This unique village just south of Ubud has a rich cultural legacy in both painting and the arts. The style of painting, now referred to as Batuan, originated here in the 1930s and has continued to this day. The method involves first completing a detailed black and white pen and ink drawing and then filling it in with subdued colors. These days, you can catch an occasional mobile phone or motorbike popping up in the scene. Batuan is also noted for the ancient *Gambuh* dance, which is still occasionally preformed on full moons and other special occasions. The dance form is on the edge of extinction yet is considered the ancestor of all Balinese dances. If you hear of one happening, catch it if you can.

MAS ★ Mas is just 6km (3¾ miles) south of Ubud. Woodcarving is one of Bali's most ancient arts and for centuries craftsmen have been chipping away in Mas. The woodcarvers of this old Brahamana village create both artistic sculptures as well as more traditional characters like deities, masks, or naturalist animals. Wander the back streets to see the families at work.

6 SHOPPING: ISLAND OF THE GOODS

As the artistic and cultural center of Bali, Ubud is a great base from which to source antiques and artifacts, jewelry and silver, textiles, baskets and bamboo, art, and stone and wood carvings. While most things in Ubud are within walking distance, it is worth hiring a car if you are going to hit the outer villages described above. Larger shops take credit cards but the smaller ones often are cash only. Credit card transactions normally incur a 3% commission. Most shops open daily by 9am and close by 9pm, though you'll find places that stay open as late as 10pm.

Jalan Raya Ubud, beginning at about Antonia Blanco's Museum and ending at around the Bamboo Gallery, has several great antiques and artifacts stores, art galleries, as well as the highly recommended Neka Art Museum (p. 210). **Monkey Forest Road** is lined with outlets selling beads, silver jewelry, cotton and casual apparel, paintings, fabrics, handicrafts, faux designer goods, and some tribal arts and antiques.

The **Ubud Market** ★, southeast corner of Monkey Forest Road and Jalan Raya Ubud, is open daylight hours. Booths sell handicrafts, fans, batik bags, fabrics, baskets, and jewelry. Everything is affordable but be sure and bargain. The big market is held every 3 days or so when women come in from nearby and mountain villages to sell and buy livestock, hardware, fruits, vegetables, and many other goods.

BOOKS

Ganesha Bookshop ★★ (Finds) This beloved Ubud institution with Ganesha, the god of knowledge and art, as its moniker, opened in the '80s. The owners divide their time between Sydney and Ubud and have made this intellectual haven their labor of love. The shop sells secondhand and antiquarian books and a wide variety of out-of-print books on the Indonesian archipelago. Also for sale are CDs, musical instruments, magazines and gift cards, maps, and other gift items. Jl. Raya Ubud. 𝒞 **0361/970320.** www.ganesha booksbali.com.

Periplus Bookstore Periplus publishes a huge range of books and their bookshop almost acts as a publishing center. The myriad of English titles covers literature, art, interior decoration, spirituality, cooking, and Bali and Indonesia. Tourists will find maps and the latest imported magazine to devour. Browsing isn't really encouraged as many books are wrapped in cellophane. The good selection of interactive children's books should ease the holidays. Jl. Raya Ubud. 𝒞 **0361/971803.**

GROCERIES

Bintang Supermarket There were sighs of disbelief when Ubud got its own Bintang supermarket. Such commercialism is kept at bay in this arty colony. Some however are thankful that they can now get a wide assortment of canned goods and drinks, fruits and vegetables, pastas, sauces, and dry goods. There is also a section for toiletries and other necessities. Jl. Raya Sanggingan 45. 𝒞 **0361/972972.**

Delta Dewata This excellent local supermarket stocks fresh fruits, vegetables, meats, and fish as well as household electrical items and stationery needs; it also has a decent kid's toy court with amazing bargains. Jl. Raya Andong 14. 𝒞 **0361/973049.**

FURNITURE & HOUSEWARES

Murni's Warung ★ (p. 206) is filled to the brim with Indonesian artifacts, antiques, sculptures, masks, memorabilia, and the odd remnant of the Dutch colonial area.

Design Unit Find fashionable modern Asian homewares, lamps, furniture, and the like, all very "Elle Decor," with some nifty bric-a-brac like wooden bowls and boxes. Local designers who export sell many of their goods here. The store is next door to a handy shipping company. Jl. Andong, Ubud. 𝒞 **0361/980471.**

Horizon Glassworks Ron and his wife, Ann Seivertson, run this glass studio near central Ubud and allow visitors to watch the fascinating glass blowing. Sculptures, vases, paperweights, and bowls are blown by Ron and then enhanced by his wife with swirls, dots, speckles, shards, and threads of color. Prices range from US$100 up to the thousands. Jl. Raya Ubud. 𝒞 **0361/978306.** www.horizonglassworks.com.

Island Living   On the way to Tegallalang, this vast warehouse specializes in made-to-order furniture. If you're short on time, plenty of ready-made items are for sale, such as Java chests, leather bar stools, and dinning tables; there are also planters chairs, old wheels, and furniture crafted from roots and driftwood. If you're going to have a piece made for you, bring a photo of what you're looking for and let your imagination run wild. Shipping is easy and service is good. Jl. Andong. © **0361/974064.**

Papadun   A mini Aladdin's den on all things Indonesian, Papadun has some authentic pieces mixed in with all of the touristy garb. They are a good source for the *wayang* puppets, painted masks, and an assortment of other artifacts. Jl. Raya Sanggingan (in front of Indus Restaurant). © **08/1338794377.**

Shalimar   Shalimar boutique has both antiques and some great homeware accessories like beaded table runners and matching napkins. In the antiques department you can expect to find ethnic art pieces, such as masks and *wayang* figurines. Jl. Raya Ubud 88. © **0361/977115.** www.shalimarbali.com.

The Shop ★★   The Shop is an elegant and understated approach to antiques, objects, and design. The stunning wares hail from Indonesia, Burma, Thailand, and Laos and each piece is given a letter of provenance listing details of origin, age, and cultural use. Owner Debbie's favorite piece is a reclining Burmese Buddha in alabaster. You can custom-order homewares and have them shipped anywhere in the world. The shop also sells jewelry designed by the owner and renowned American jeweler Carolyn Tyler. Jl. Raya Sayan 52. © **0361/973508.**

Toko East   Toko East has slick contemporary homewares sourced from some of the premier designers on the island. Browse the tempting treasures like Majapahit-inspired bronze works, handmade glass and ceramics, bronze garden lamps, and decorative items with sterling silver finishes, lacquered sea shell accessories, and "hyacinth" water lily weavings. Jl. Raya Ubud. © **0361/978306.** www.decko.com.

JEWELRY

Jean-Francois Fichot ★★★ (Finds)   A master craftsmen, artisan, and jeweler, Jean-Francois Fichot was one of the first artists to base his studio in Bali in the '60s. Jean-Francois does many things but his greatest gift is working with and embellishing found objects. Imagine a 15th-century Roman coin or a crystal Buddha from Tibet or an antique piece of coral from Cuba. Michael Caine and Elle McPherson like it well enough as do mere mortals. Exquisite beyond belief; go to his showroom even if you aren't looking to buy, and treat it like a museum tour. Jl. Suweta 6. © **0361/972078.** www.jf-f.com.

> (Moments)   **Take a Jewelry Tour**
>
> Visit the **John Hardy workshop** ★★★ in Mumbul near Ubud (Banjar Baturning, Mambul, Abiansemal, Badung; © **0361/469888;** www.johnhardy.com; by appointment only) and watch the production of the John Hardy jewelry brand. An organic lunch is followed by a trip to their showroom where jewelry is 50% off retail prices back home. The quality of craftsmanship here is mesmerizing.

(Finds) **The Threads of Life**

The handmade, unique textiles at **Threads of Life,** Jl. Kajeng 24 (✆ **0361/ 972187;** www.threadsoflife.com) are dyed and woven by local women thanks to the support of a nonprofit organization intent on revitalizing and sustaining this traditional Balinese art form. All proceeds support the organization's research, work, and communities.

Seraphim   Search the eclectic mix here for interesting small antique objects as well as exclusive designs of gold and silver jewelry with precious and semi-precious gemstones. Jl. Monkey Forest. ✆ **0361/971139.**

Treasures ★   The specialty here is big, distinctive pieces in 22K and 24K gold. Pieces are the result of a collaboration between local goldsmiths and international designers. All the jewelry is individually handmade by Balinese master artisans, making each piece virtually one of a kind. Pieces feature pearl, shell, and semi-precious stones. Credit cards are thankfully accepted. Jl. Raya Ubud. ✆ **0361/976697.** www.dekco.com.

TEXTILES & CLOTHING

Ani's Gallery   This shop sells batik in a myriad of colors and nontraditional motifs like flowers, butterflies, toucans, parrots, and exotic island themes like jungles with palm trees. Browse the hand-painted sarongs, kimonos, and caftans and nice selection of men's batik shirts. Tablecloths, napkins, sheets, and bedcovers are also for sale. Jl. Raya Campuhan. ✆ **0361/975431.**

Bin House   Ever since 1975 when Josephine E. Komara (nicknamed Bin) started collecting antique textiles and batik from Indonesia, she envisaged incorporating handwoven, traditional cloth into contemporary fashion. Today Bin House has five well-known lines and more than 30 outlets worldwide. The fabrics are hand-crafted from the weave, to the dye, to the finish, and can take up to a year to complete. Jl. Monkey Forest. ✆ **0361/977983.** www.binhouse.com.

Macan Tidur ★★★ **(Finds)**   This shop is an exceptional place where you are guaranteed to find a treasure that you simply can't live without. Susi is a textiles expert specializing in 18th-century textiles and has a collection that covers every part of Indonesia—you can count on reliable quality and authenticity. Bruno is both a painter and a tribal art and ancient jewelry expert. Between the two the gallery is filled to the brim with an extraordinary collection that includes sculpture, ceramics (like centuries-old Chinese porcelain salvaged from shipwrecks around Indonesia), weapons, Kris handles, baskets, and even some of Bruno's contemporary oil paintings. A nice touch is a small reference library where guests are encouraged to read about purchases they are considering or simply learn more about Indonesian art. Call ahead for an appointment with either Susi or Bruno, both generous with their knowledge. Jl. Monkey Forest. ✆ **0361/975072.** www. macantidur.com.

Wardani Shop   The best place in town for locally made *ikat* (dyed cotton), *sogket,* and *endek,* some more pricey than others. They will say "fixed price" but don't believe it. Try and get to about one-third of what is quoted. Jl. Monkey Forest. ✆ **0361/975538.**

UBUD

10

SHOPPING: ISLAND OF THE GOODS

(Finds) Dance & Cultural Performances

Every night in Ubud and the surrounding villages features several dance, music, and shadow-puppet performances. A *barong* performance at the **Royal Palace** is the best and most stimulating choice; even the kids will like it. Many of the hotels do small evening shows, inquire with your concierge.

Listings below followed by *** mean that free transport is provided from the **Ubud Tourist Information** (((C) **0361/973285**) kiosk, on Jalan Raya Ubud near the intersection of Monkey Forest Road. Get tickets and information at Ubud Tourist Information, ticket sellers on the street, or the place of the performances. The price is the same wherever you buy it.

Performance	Days	Time	Cost (Rp)
Agung Rai Museum of Art*			
Kecak Dance	Full/New Moons	7pm	100,000 (150,000 including Balinese dinner)
Mepantigan Arts	Thurs	6:30pm	100,000 75,000
Barong & Kris Dance	Fri (except Full/New Moons)	6pm	(135,000 including Balinese dinner)
Wayang Wong	Sat	7pm	75,000 (135,000 including Balinese dinner)
Legong Classic	Sun	7:30pm	75,000 (135,000 including Balinese dinner)
Bale Banjar			
Women Gamelan & Dance Group	Mon & Fri	7:30pm	65,000
Narita Dewi Gamelan & Dance	Tues	7:30pm	75,000
Chandra Wira Buana	Wed	7:30pm	75,000
Balerung Mandera*			
Legong & Barong Dance	Tues & Fri	7:30pm	100,000
Legong Dance	Fri	7:30pm	100,000
Dancers & Musician of Peliatan	Sun	7:30pm	100,000
Bentuyung Village*			
Jegog (Bamboo Gamelan)	Sun & Fri	7pm	80,000
Kertha Accomodation			
Wayang Kulit	Tues & Sat	8pm	75,000
Lotus Pond Open Stage			
Women Gamelan with Children Dancers	Tues	7:30pm	80,000
Janger Dance	Sun	7:30pm	80,000

UBUD

10

SHOPPING: ISLAND OF THE GOODS

Monkey Forest

Wayang Kulit	Tues & Sat	8pm	65,000

Oka Kartini's

Wayang Kulit	Wed, Fri, Sun	8pm	75,000

Padang Tegal

Kecak Fire & Trance Dance	Wed, Sat, Sun	7pm	75,000

Pondok Bamboo

Wayang Kulit	Mon & Thurs	8pm	75,000

Pondok Pekak

Frog Dance	Sat	7:30pm	75,000
Gamelan & Dance	Sun	7:30pm	75,000

Pura Dalem, Taman Kaja

Kecak Ramayana & Fire Dance	Mon & Fri	7:30pm	75,000
Legong Dance	Tues & Sat	7:30pm	65,000
Kecak Fire & Trance Dance	Wed & Sat	7:30pm	75,000
Jegog (Bamboo Gamelan)	Wed	7pm	80,000
Barong & Keris Dance	Thurs	7:30pm	75,000

Pura Desa Kutuh

Spirit of Bali	Tues	7:30pm	75,000
Legong Dance	Thurs	7:30pm	75,000

Pura Padang Kertha

Kecak & Fire Dance	Fri	7pm	75,000

Pura Taman Sari

Kecak Fire & Trance Dance	Thurs	7:30pm	75,000

Puri Agung, Peliatan*

Kecak (Monkey Chant Dance)	Thurs	7:30pm	80,000
Legong Dance	Sat	7:30pm	80,000

Ubud Palace

Legong Dance	Mon & Sat	7:30pm	80,000
Ramayana Ballet	Tues	7:30pm	80,000
Legong & Barong Dance	Wed	7:30pm	80,000
Legong Trance & Paradise Dance	Thurs	7:30pm	80,000
Barong & Rangda Dance	Fri	7pm	80,000
Legong of Mahabarata	Sun	7:30pm	80,000

Ubud Water Palace

Barong & Keris Dance with Children Dancers	Thurs	7:30pm	80,000
Legong Dance	Sat	7:30pm	80,000

Wantilan

Barong & Kris Dance	Mon	7pm	80,000

Yamasari Stage*

Legong Dance	Wed	7:30pm	75,000

7 UBUD AFTER DARK

Ubud's nightlife scene is growing, but it's still rather sedate. **Jazz Café,** Jl. Sukma 2, east of Monkey Forest Road (✆ **0361/976594**), has good live jazz. Monkey Forest Road has lots of little laid-back places that are more than happy to stay open late. Upscale **Lamak** (✆ **0361/974668;** www.lamakbali.com) stays up, but its scene is mostly calm. For a night of drinking and fun, hit **Naughty Nuri's** (p. 207), where most dinners turn into a romp. Next door is **Ozigo** (✆ **0812367973**) where if you have had enough of Nuri's martinis you will most likely love the live music and nightly DJ entertainment. **Café Exiles,** Jl. Pengosekan (✆ **0361/974812**) is where the disenfranchised come to fraternize, particularly on Saturday night; it's just to the southeast of central Ubud.

Central Mountains

Ubud is typically as far north as most visitors to Bali ever reach though it is still, geographically and culturally, in the south. The older communities in the mountains still adhere to strict social customs, some retain their own dialects, and many remain wary of visitors and interlopers. They may pay lip service to tourists and embrace the compensations they bring, but they are not necessarily adapting to their visitors' customs.

The central mountains remain important to all Balinese, as the mountains are the homes of their gods. Therefore, this region is a spiritual center and place of pilgrimage, where temples and their celebrations abound. Water from here is the source of much of the irrigation for rice in the south, which enhances the mountains' revered place in the hearts of the Balinese. You will see many temples devoted simply to the water goddess Dewi Danu.

You will need a car, a driver who can also translate, a map, some walking shoes, and a plan. And don't forget your sarong.

---

1 EXPLORING THE CENTRAL MOUNTAINS

Should you be coming from the north, take the mountain roads via Kubutambuhan for Kintamani or via Singaraja for Bedugul.

Most hotels and villas can arrange a driver for you if you haven't already. If you take a driver and wish to stay overnight, your hotel or villa will usually provide, at no extra charge, accommodation for your driver. You should, however, contribute to his food cost. A half- or full-day rate with a **Blue Bird** taxi may or may not cover petrol. Agree beforehand. Try not to give any money in advance. While taxis are an alternative method of travel to get into the mountains, they are not ideal for long distances in part due to their low axels.

If you have time on your hands, you can catch a **bus** from Kuta but they do not stop in all the villages and towns. To get to Bedugul and Candikuning you catch a **Perama Tours bus** (© 0361/751551 in Kuta; www.peramatour.com) from Kuta at 10am for Rp60,000 (3 hr.). For Kintamani, the Perama bus leaves at 10am for Rp150,000 (3 hr.). For those who like to travel with a chicken on their lap, a **public bus** leaves Denpasar to Singaraja, stopping in Penelokan and Kintamani for Rp20,000. Alternatively, you can catch a *bemo* from Batubulan terminal in Denpasar to Kintamani for Rp20,000.

FROM THE SOUTH

TO KINTAMANI & LAKE BATUR Various roads lead from Ubud to Kintamani, the two most obvious being either the Sayan Ridge Road or alternatively the slightly more culturally rich road just to the east that takes in the Tirtha Empul Temple and Pura Gunung Kawi complex. Both take about 2 hours. The weather noticeably turns at the top, with the village of Penelokan often surrounded in mist.

The **Sayan Ridge Road,** heading north, passes the upmarket COMO Shambala and Alila hotels, worth a stop for a lunch break.

CENTRAL MOUNTAINS

11

DANAU BATUR

 Tips **Bring Cash**

The Central Mountains have few banks and ATMs. Many places now take credit cards, but come with sufficient cash in Rupiahs. U.S. dollars can suffice, although you may not get the best exchange rates.

Before you arrive at the volcano crater's rim is a sign to **Bayung Gede,** a wonderful example of a traditional Balinese hill village. With its neat narrow lanes, ancient shrines, and well-kept steep roofed houses, it has retained its old charm and original low-lying construction.

Your **other main option** is via the road past Tirta Empul (p. 209); you also pass Pura Gunung Kawi (p. 208). Slightly menacingly, just above the beautiful temple complex of Tirtha Empul sits the **Istana,** the old Bali palace of Sukharno and now owned and occupied by his daughter, Megawati Sukarnoputri, herself a previous president of the Republic.

TO BEDUGUL   For a wonderfully scenic route bereft of the litter and villa developments that plague much of Bali, head to Papuan from the south: Take the main road via Tabanan and turn north at Antosari. Continue north from Papuan and turn east at Mayong and travel up through the hills via **Munduk.**

GETTING AROUND

It's easy to get to the central mountains, but trying to go from one village to another cross country is more difficult—as a quick glance at a map of the area will demonstrate. For example, once you are in the Batur area, to reach Bedugul, you need to drive to the north coast, along to Singaraja, and then back up the mountain road via Lake Buyan. Trying to get from one village to another can be near impossible without the assistance of a friendly hotel owner—there are no metered taxis in this region.

2 DANAU BATUR

The double caldera of Danau (Lake) Batur is 14km (8½ miles) across, 6km (4 miles) wide, and no one is quite sure how deep, although it is estimated at slightly more then 1,500m (4,921 ft.). It was once a mountain with a peak that rose some 3,000m (9,843 ft.) above sea level; now it only sits at 1,717m (5,633 ft.) and is a very active volcano. You can clearly see the plumes of smoke still rising from one of the lower spouts. The most recent eruption was in 1999 but it showed its true rage in 1917, destroying the old village of Batur and taking with it some 65,000 souls.

Farming continues on the nutrient-rich sides of the volcano and the lake feeds the neighboring rice-growing regions of Bangli, Buleleng, Gianyar, Klungkung, and Badung. Not surprisingly, the "temple at the head of the lake," Pura Ulan Danu Batur, is held in great reverence: Its priest, known as Jero Gede, is considered the island's most powerful.

Do not let the tourist circus of Penelokan discourage you from venturing further: You will find plenty more reasons to linger in the crater itself. The view is the main reason to come here; be sure to also take in the joyous winding road along the lake shore to Toya Bungkah, Pura Ulan Danu Batur, or even the hot springs (Air Panas). This area is great

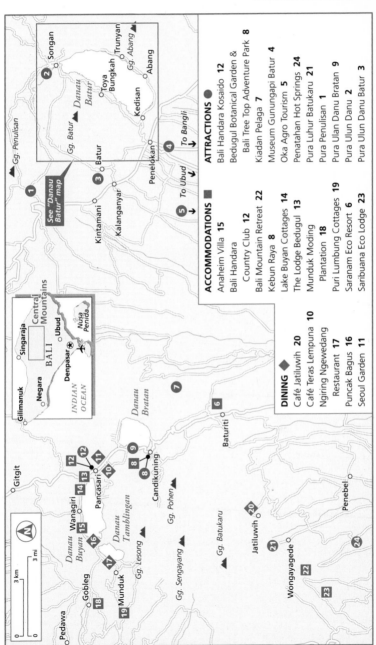

ATTRACTIONS ●

Bali Handara Kosaido **12**
Bedugul Botanical Garden &
  Bali Tree Top Adventure Park **8**
Kiadan Pelaga **7**
Museum Gunungapi Batur **4**
Oka Agro Tourism **5**
Penatahan Hot Springs **24**
Pura Luhur Batukaru **21**
Pura Penulisan **1**
Pura Ulan Danu Bratan **9**
Pura Ulun Danu **2**
Pura Ulun Danu Batur **3**

ACCOMMODATIONS ■

Anaheim Villa **15**
Bali Handara
  Country Club **12**
Bali Mountain Retreat **22**
Kebun Raya **8**
Lake Buyan Cottages **14**
The Lodge Bedugul **13**
Munduk Moding
  Plantation **18**
Puri Lumbung Cottages **19**
Saranam Eco Resort **6**
Saribuana Eco Lodge **23**

DINING ◆

Café Jatiluwih **20**
Cafe Teras Lempuna **10**
Ngiring Ngewedang
  Restaurant **17**
Puncak Bagus **16**
Seoul Garden **11**

A View of Danau Batur & Penelokan

A fantastic spectacle greets you as you come over the ridge at Penelokan and gaze down in wonder at the twin caldera of Lake Batur, yet the town itself leaves you puzzled. "What happened?" is really what you ask yourself. The further you descend into the crater, the more you find poor accommodation and service and unpleasant encounters with hawkers, and you ask yourself again, "What happened?" Surely this is one of the greatest, most spectacular natural vistas anywhere, with a beautiful lake and magnificent walking trails, and yet the whole experience is enough to turn anyone off the tourism trade. The accommodations are filthy, the food is generally expensive buffet-style catering to bus tours, and many of the trekking expeditions are essentially extortion. This is a side of Bali that you might almost wish to give a complete miss, which is a great shame as nature has created a wonder that you should be able to enjoy unimpeded. The best way to tackle this area is with an established Bali-wide trekking agency who will take you in, stay with you for the whole day, and then take you back out.

As for **Penelokan** (Rp5,000 to enter the village), it has a magnificent view to Mount Batur and, across the lake, a collection of restaurants and market stalls, and usually far too many people hustling you. The town has various hotels, with the most obvious and currently the best choice being the **Batur Lakeview Hotel** (✆ **0366/51394;** www.lakeviewhotel.info/index.htm) with eight rooms at US$40 for a superior and US$60 for a deluxe. The hotel is made of carved stone and rooms are basic, but have amazing views over the lake below.

trekking territory. If you're going to climb Mount Batur, be sure to book your trekking guide before you arrive.

However, the overall feeling around Lake Batur will be at odds with your experience of the rest of Bali and may even be, on occasion, disappointing. So much was I bothered and even stunned by the experience of the Lake Batur basin, that I had to go back a few times to ensure that I had not misinterpreted the whole place.

AROUND THE CRATER

Museum Gunungapi Batur ★   One place you should stop is the often overlooked Volcano Museum, at the entrance gates of Penelokan. Eager guides will lead you round explaining every aspect. Scale models of the volcanoes replay the various eruptions of different years; wall maps light up showing you the various active volcanoes in Indonesia (all 129 of them out of a global total of just over 500); interactive computers chart the last 26,000 years and the changing phases and shapes of Mount Batur. Head upstairs to the viewing deck where various sets of binoculars are either trained on the still smoldering crater of Batur or the rather dark and menacing village of Trunyan on the far side of the volcano. Don't forget to tip the guide, he is worth every penny.

Penelokan. ✆ **0361/67678.** www.baturmuseum.com. Admission Rp10,000. Daily 8am–5pm.

ATTRACTIONS ●
Air Panas **12**
C Bali **4**
PPPGB **5**
Toya Devasya **6**
Volcano Breeze **9**

ACCOMMODATIONS ■
Lakeside Cottages **3**
Puri Bening **10**
Under the Volcano 1 **7**
Under the Volcano 2 **11**
Under the Volcano 3 **8**

DINING ◆
Grand Pucak Sari **1**
Restaurant Gunawan **2**
Volcano Breeze **9**

CENTRAL MOUNTAINS

11

DANAU BATUR

Kintamani

The area around here is often referred to as simply Kintamani, though Kintamani itself is the rather uninspiring administrative capital; the **local market** (every 3 days) starts at 5am and is over by 10am. The main road passes through the middle of the town.

Pura Penulisan ★   Just beyond Kintamani on the road north, is Pura Penulisan, a series of five temples, which rise like a pyramid. It is considered a magical place and is often used for meditation by locals on auspicious nights.

8km (5 miles) north of Kintamani. Admission Rp1,000. Daily 7am–6pm.

Pura Ulun Danu Batur   Just outside Kintamani, on the rim of the crater, is Pura Ulan Danu Batur, Bali's most important temple after Pura Besakih, dedicated to the goddess of the lake, Ida Bhatari Dewi Danu. Today's temple is actually a reconstruction of parts of the old temple rescued from the side of the crater after the 1917 eruption. It has a *meru* with 11 tiers reflecting its importance—the god of Mount Agung has only nine—and while it is a reconstruction of separate temples, its original form dates to at least the 11th century. Oddly, you cannot actually see the lake from inside the temple. Though this is an important temple, with an important history and place in the Balinese

> ## (Finds) Oka Agro Tourism (Agro Wisata)
>
> A great place to stop on the road past Tirtha Empul (arriving via the south from Ubud), just as you reach Seribatu, is **Oka Agro Tourism** ★★, Br. Temen, Susut-Bangli (② **08/1338388422;** coffee from Rp30,000; no credit cards; daily 8am–7pm). The grandson of the owner has set up a very beautiful coffee and spice plantation that you can wander and learn about growing, harvesting, and roasting coffee. The coffee and cocoa is free to taste but they will charge you Rp30,000 per cup should you wish to try their Luwak coffee. Luwak is made of coffee beans that have been digested and excreted (whole, you will be relieved to know) by a civet and are cleaned, dried, and roasted and then served as normal coffee. The taste is slightly richer, syrupy, and with hints of caramel. It's actually very good and quite a delicacy. If you are offered some as a guest, treat it as an honor. Other spices and fruit grown on the plantation are cinnamon, vanilla, tamarind, avocado, and mangosteen. A small shop sells their harvested and processed goods.

consciousness, there are other more attractively situated temples to visit ahead of this. You will be charged Rp10,000 by the ladies outside with the sarongs if you forget to bring your own.

Kintamani. Admission including sarong Rp10,000. Daily 7am–5pm.

IN THE CRATER

The two main villages in the crater are **Toya Bungkah** and **Kedisan,** the former having more choice in terms of accommodation and restaurants, driven no doubt by the hot springs in the town. If you need to stay in the crater, then Toya Bungkah would be the more obvious choice.

Pura Ulun Danu   Not be confused with Pura Ulun Danu Batur on the rim of the caldera, this temple is at the head of Lake Batur in the crater itself. A 20-minute drive beyond Toya Bungkah, though not particularly large, this temple is highly revered for its water as the giver of life. The complex is actually a series of three temples; the one to visit is the farthest one set majestically into the side of the mountain, beyond Songan, the final village on the shore of the lake. Often before work is done in a given rice field in Bali, a priest and local farmers will travel to Lake Batur and take water from the source, which they will then carry to their lands to sprinkle on their fields. They will then pour any remaining water in to the irrigation system so that others may benefit. Given the success of rice growing in Bali, it seems to do the trick. Due to the sanctity that the Balinese place on the water, there is absolutely no swimming around here and you need to wear appropriate temple garb to enter.

Admission Rp6,000. Daily 7am–5pm.

Toya Bungkah

Certainly if you have made it in to the crater itself, you will pass through this town, either to reach the start of a trek at the head of the lake, or for the springs. This is the center of many of the trekking agencies and has budget accommodations. Despite the amount of accommodation and a number of seemingly inhabited houses, there are precious few people or even the normal signs of village life here—the whole village has the feel of a

bank holiday when everyone heads off for the day. The hot springs, **Air Panas** **231**
(Rp150,000 including lunch, drink, and towel), can be enjoyed at one of the hotels such
as the Puri Bening (p. 233) or at the specialist hot spring and spa resort, **Toya Devasya**
(© 0361/438333; www.toyadevasya.com; admission, including welcome juice and light
lunch Rp150,000; no credit cards; daily 9am–7pm), with a 20m (66-ft.) swimming pool
and several hot spring bathing areas. You do not need to stay here to use the facilities.
Various places to stop and have lunch in the town have views across the lake to the far
side with the mountains as a backdrop.

Kedisan

The other village at the base of the crater is Kedisan, which has various options for budget accommodation and also has some lovely vegetable gardens and other plants growing
down to the edge of the lake. The scenery is charming but there is not a lot going on;
whatever action there may be in the crater, it is likely more happening at Toya Bungkah.
Private boats to Trunyan leave from here. C Bali runs a small volunteer and clean-up
program here. See p. 232.

Trunyan (Overrated)

For many, the decision whether to make a trip to Trunyan is divisive. Allow me to settle
the dispute: There is no reason whatsoever why you should take a trip across a lake at an
inflated price to further the unpleasant and downright offensive way the people here
extort tourists. If you make the crossing, you'll encounter a Bali Aga village where the
main hook is that they lay their dead wrapped in a cotton shroud under an old tree that
gives off a scent that negates the stench of rotting corpses.

The trip includes a 20-minute rickety boat ride from Kedisan for upwards of
Rp1,000,000 round-trip. You will be escorted to a cemetery and then, like in the *Thriller*
music video, people will descend on you insinuating that if you do not give a suitable
offering you may well not be able to leave. Upon returning to your boat, more people
will come out of the woodwork who will tug at your arm or surround you in the hope
you will continue to toss all your money their way as you make a bolt for the boat. This
is a well-practiced stunt to rip off tourists rather than portray any form of traditional or
arcane way of life. Avoid it at all costs.

TREKKING

The whole crater area, with its staggering views, clear waters, and temperate climate is
ideal for trekking and various local tour guides will take you on escorted walks. However,
here again, you may run in to problems. This whole place is about the only area in Bali
where you need to constantly keep your wits about you. Certainly if you wish to climb
Mount Batur you will come across the motley bunch known as **PPPGB** (previously
HPPGB) or the **Association of Mount Batur Trekking Guides** (© 0361/52362). This
is the local mountain guide agency and they insist that they have the only government-
approved license that allows you to climb Mount Batur. If you wish to climb Mount
Batur, you must use one of their 62 approved guides and pay their rates—even if you
arrive with your own professional guide, you must also use one of the PPPGB (though
this will be built into your quoted price). The rates are commensurate with a monopoly
and they do not take kindly to being challenged. Unless you enjoy a degree of intimida-
tion in your negotiations, I would advise you not to. They do, however, make great
assurances that they are trained and professional.

Kayaking, Canoeing & Volunteer Work

Along with trekking around and above the lake, you can also go kayaking or canoeing on the lake. You get a much different perspective seeing the crater from the middle of the wide lake. Most trekking agencies will also offer canoeing.

One to particularly recommend is **C Bali** ★★ (✆ 0353/420541; www.c-bali. com). A 1-day tour (Rp410,000) includes both cycling and canoeing, as well as pickup from hotels elsewhere on the island and lunch. C Bali has a donation program with Kedisan village: The company accepts small donations of clothing (especially cold-weather clothing) and school supplies to pass on to the villagers and their school. Casual visitors can also participate in C Bali's Kedisan clean-up program. If you're interested in long-term volunteering (3 months), C Bali also has a Kedisan residency program.

Also be careful if your tour is to end up anywhere near Trunyan (see above), as you may find yourself being forced to pay a surcharge to get out of there. Be very clear with your guide before you start that there will be absolutely no further charges other than those that you have already paid and that there are no hidden boat trips required.

A group of up to four people will pay collectively about Rp300,000 for a short trip to the Mount Batur summit for sunrise, a 3-hour walk leaving between 4am and 5am. You should all be given head lamps and flashlights as you will be starting in darkness. A Mount Batur exploration walk of about 6 to 7 hours will set up to four of you back Rp600,000 or so and a 6-hour summit walk to Mount Abang leaving from the temple at Ulan Danu will cost the same, although this one will likely end near Trunyan and you may be surprised with a boat surcharge.

Regardless, it is all stunningly beautiful. Book a reputable agency, probably from outside the crater, come for the day, do your trek, and leave.

TREKKING AGENCIES & TOURS   Used by many locals who live in Bali, **Gede** (✆ 08/124652455) is a charming man who will take you on a guided day and explain not only the history of the area but also the flora and fauna. He will identify the local herbs and spices found on the walk and explain their local uses. When pressed, he will even play his flute, which is delightful. He charges US$100 for up to four people for half day trips. He offers a trip up Mount Batur that ends at—warning!—Trunyan (see above). You will need to pay a boatman for the return journey. Negotiate beforehand.

If you simply want a local guide who knows the mountains as well as anyone but is not part of a larger entity (and therefore without insurance), the very nice people at **Volcano Breeze** (p. 234; ✆ 0366/51824) cafe will arrange a guide for you. They are honest and have proved reliable in the past. They suggest prices of about Rp300,000 for a group of up to four for a short trip to the summit for sunrise. Note that this is the total price and not per person. They also quote about Rp600,000 for a 6- to 7-hour Mount Batur exploration trek.

Based out of Jakarta but with local representatives, **Pacto** (✆ 0221/719-6550; www. pactoltd.com; US$85 per person) runs all-day treks to Mount Batur. They also have trips throughout Bali or even other parts of Indonesia.

Clipper (✆ 08/123802675; www.clipperdiscovery.com; sunrise trek including transportation, guide, entrance fee, breakfast, PPPGB, and Clipper guide US$95) will collect you from wherever you are in Bali, take you on a tour with an experienced English-speaking guide, and then return you to your hotel. They are not cheap but costs include the full day and transportation. They do informative rainforest treks around Mount Batur as well as overnight trips to get to Mount Agung at sunrise.

Owners of the Elephant Park and long established in Bali, **Bali Adventure Tours** (✆ 0361/721480; www.baliadventuretours.com) does white-water rafting, mountain treks, and even escorted bicycle tours around Mount Batur. A 3-hour trek includes lunch and entrance to the elephant park (p. 216) for US$55; a cycling tour with the same perks is US$60.

Bali Sobek ★★★, Jl. Raya Tebongkang 33, Ubud (✆ 0361/287059; www.bali sobek.com; tour including return transfers, professional guide, and lunch US$60) does two treks: one in the jungle at Bedugul around Lake Tamblingan, which ends with a trip back across the lake in a traditional dugout canoe; the other is round Mount Batukaru through rice paddies to hot springs where you can take a dip.

The **Toya Devasya Agency** (✆ 0361/438333; www.toyadevasya.com) is specifically set up for groups. Their packages will usually include lunch at their restaurant and a dip in their hot springs (see above). They will take you canoeing, on ridge walks, downhill trekking, and they will even do an escorted and "policed" trip to Trunyan—which just means they have paid off the village in advance. An escorted trip to Trunyan for two people costs US$102 per person. A Mount Batur sunrise walk is US$94 per person for two people, including lunch and a dip in the hot springs.

WHERE TO STAY

Lakeside Cottages   At the eastern end of Toya Bungkah, this perfectly pleasant but very simple series of rooms caters mainly to trekkers. It's fine, cleanish, and, as the name suggests, the cottages are on the lake. If you are on a budget and in the area and need a bed, you can do a lot worse. Each room has hot water and terraces to take in the view of the lake. They will also arrange trekking or kayaking trips.

Toya Bungkah, Kintamani. ✆ 0366/51249. 11 units. High season US$25; low season US$23. MC. **Amenities:** Restaurant; Internet; small outdoor pool.

Puri Bening   With 29 "deluxe" double rooms and two cottages, this is the largest operation in Kintamani. The whole complex looks to have been carved from a single cement block. It has a very large, hot spring fed pool with cold plunge pool—which is about the only thing recommending it. The poor soul that we met who was staying here was hard-pressed to find any comment about the food, other than, "well, we all have to eat something."

Toya Bungkah, Kintamani. ✆ 0366/51234. www.indo.com/hotels/puribeninghayato. 31 units. Year-round Rp450,000. MC, V. **Amenities:** Restaurant; hot spring pool; plunge pool; room service. *In room:* TV.

Under the Volcano 1, 2 & 3   This is a series of separate bungalow-style accommodations along the same road, all under the same ownership but with different managers. There are a total of 22 rooms of similar decoration set up for trekkers and offer budget accommodation and cold-water showers. Volcano 2 has hot water. Again basically clean, but uninspiring.

Toya Bungkah, Kintamani. ✆ 0366/51166 for Volcano 1 & 3; ✆ 0366/52508 for Volcano 2. 22 units. Year-round Rp100,000. No credit cards. **Amenities:** Restaurant; room service.

KINTAMANI   If there is one shining light in the whole of the crater, as far as tourism infrastructure is concerned, it is **Volcano Breeze** (ℂ **0366/51824;** main courses from Rp15,000; no credit cards; daily 8am–5pm). The fish fresh from the lake is delicious and memorable. On a good day, the friendly staff will play live music; they may also try and sell you some local art which will likely have been made by the person selling it. The cafe is on the road down to the side of the lake, next door to Toya Devasya in the middle of Toya Bungkah. Next door is **Under the Volcano** (ℂ **0366/51166;** main courses Rp20,000–Rp30,000; no credit cards; daily 7am–9pm) with similar lake-caught fish and other Indonesian offerings.

AROUND PENELOKAN   On the rim of the crater on the road from Penelokan to Kintamani are a series of vast hangarlike restaurants with car parks akin to those at large sporting venues. They cater mainly to bus tourists. They all offer similar one-stop buffet-style all-you-can-eat fare, and while some do it okay, the majority rely on paying tour guides to attract their audiences. Amazingly, most of the large ones, which can host up to 600 people at a time, receive almost a third of that every day. While the majority of these mass market restaurants are off-putting, they do have great views.

At the Kintamani end of the crater's rim, **Grand Puncak Sari,** Jl. Raya Penelokan (ℂ **0366/51073;** buffet from Rp35,000; no credit cards; daily 8am–5pm), is a perfectly pleasant restaurant that does some of the best large-scale food. They freshly cook the satays in front of you and the buffet dishes are kept warm and are refreshed regularly. If you really want an experience, ask to join the Balinese lunch (Rp80,000). They make fresh *lawar* every day, both with and without fresh blood, *sambal tuang* spiced eggplant, and many other dishes, which change daily. The Balinese offering is as good as you will eat on the island, if indeed you can actually find genuine food like this outside of a ceremony.

Close to Penelokan, **Restaurant Gunawan,** Penelokan (ℂ **0366/51050;** buffet from Rp85,000; MC, V; daily 8:30am–4:30pm), is one of the better of the larger offerings, seating up to 450 people. They do a pleasant enough Indonesian and Chinese-looking buffet popular with the Korean and Japanese market.

3 BEDUGUL & DANAU BRATAN, BUYAN & TAMBLINGAN

The area around **Bedugul** village is often just referred to as simply Bedugul, though it is unclear why this would be the reference point—the daily flower, fruit, and vegetable market is Candikuning.

Though this area has a great variety of attractions, tourism here remains aimed at the local rather than the international market and the choice of accommodation and restaurants reflects this. Even the five-star golf course has a 1970s Travelodge feel. Everything appears just a little bit unloved: It's almost like the whole place was built and then forgotten about. For a truly odd experience, a group of villas on the hillside about half a mile towards Lake Bratan from the golf course look like a normal holiday resort, but upon closer inspection you see there is absolutely no one there. It's like the plague hit and everyone left town, taking the signs with them.

Bring your warm clothes. A *bemo* in between stops of Denpasar (Ubung terminal) and Singaraja's Sukasada terminal to this area costs Rp8,000.

A TOUR AROUND THE LAKES

Arriving from the south (Ubud or Seminyak), you come through the main road of Candikuning with the open-all-day market on your left. Passing this, heading down the hill, on the left is a great bread shop, **Roti Bedugul,** although their fresh bread is late to rise, being ready around 11am each morning. On the right hand side as you drop down is **Danau Bratan** with the watersports center (overpriced—you need to pay just to enter the road to the facilities) on the far side, framed majestically by the mountains behind. The town itself has little else to offer other than more shops than you care to count selling exactly the same crisps, biscuits, drinks, and basic toiletries.

Carry on out of Candikuning, away from Bedugul, along the lake shores and you will come to one of the most picturesque and most photographed of all temples, **Pura Ulan Danu Bratan** ★ (western bank of Lake Bratan; Rp10,000; daily 7am–6pm), with its formal gardens and clipped lawns set against the backdrop of the lake. Technically it is actually on the lake, built as it is on a series of small islands. It was built in reverence to the goddess of the lake and the water she provides. This is a great place to feel the natural calm of the water—just don't swim in it. These are holy waters.

This road then leads onward, past the golf course, to lakes **Buyan** and **Tamblingan.** These were actually just one lake until the early part of the 19th century when a landslide created two. The high road above the lake on the road to Munduk is possibly the best place to take in the view. There are a couple of viewing places to stop along the way.

If you're arriving via the scenic Munduk route described on p. 226, you'll see all these sites in reverse order.

EXPLORING AROUND & NEAR THE LAKES

Bali Tree Top Adventure Park ★★★ (Kids) One of Bali's most popular family attractions, the Bali Tree Top Adventure Park is a perfectly safe introduction to zip-lining and rope courses, plus you get up close and personal with the local flora. You are attached at all times by at least one rope to your mountaineer's safety harness, but normally two, which is a calming assurance when you cross between two high wire points on a swinging obstacle, with 50m (164 ft.) of fresh air between you and the ground. With the four different levels, it is fun and safe for kids from 5 years through to adults. Gloves are for sale and worth the investment.

In the Bedugul Botanical Gardens, Candikuning. (𝒞 **0361/852-0680.** www.balitreetop.com. Admission US$20 adult; US$13 children 11 and under. Daily 8:30am–6pm.

Bedugul Botanical Garden (Kebun Raya) ★★ (Finds) This wonderland is set in 160 hectares (395 acres) of landscaped and beautifully tended gardens. Opened in 1959 and currently home to almost 2,000 species of different plants, some 320 variety of orchids alone, it represents plants from the mountain areas of eastern Indonesia, areas such as Tenggara, Sulawesi, Maluku, and even Papua. The institution offers a number of scientific services and facilities in support of plant research and conservation, including a herbarium, an orchid house, seed bank, library, glass houses, nursery, and plant database. Bring a picnic.

Candikuning. (𝒞 **0368/21273.** www.kebunrayabali.com. Admission Rp7,000 per person; Rp6,000 per car. Daily 8am–6pm; some glass houses close earlier.

GOLF The **Bali Handara Kosaido** ★★ ((𝒞 **0362/22646;** www.balihandarakosaido. com; in-house guest US$70, walk-in guest US$130, golf cart US$25; AE, DC, MC, V) is possibly Bali's best-known golf course, and, built in 1974, certainly its oldest. At

> **(Finds) Kiadan Pelaga Village**
>
> The **Jaringan Ekowisata Desa (JED;** ℰ **0361/737447;** www.jed.or.id; two to four people US$75 per person, overnight US$130 per person; no credit cards), or Village Ecotourism Network, is devoted to developing sustainable ecotourism and travel in Indonesia. Through their program at Kiadan Pelaga village, you learn about the coffee-making process from managing the plantation all the way through to roasting and you meet the farmers themselves. They also grow dry rice here and if you come at the right time of year, you can take part in the harvest. You can also stay the night in the village. The basic accommodation is genuine rather than a sanitized reenactment of village life.

1,128m (3,700 ft.) above sea level, it is also possibly the only golf course in the world built in a volcano crater. It is about a 2-hour scenic drive from the Seminyak/Sanur area. Bali Handara has magnificent mountain scenery with beautiful gardens, surrounded by lush rainforest, and views over the surrounding lake. It is fair to say that both the course and the attached accommodation could do with some revitalization. However, the course remains challenging and the cooler air alone is a worthy attraction. There is a pro shop and optional golf carts.

TREKKING   You can either take an official tour with a trekking agency from the south (see chapter 5), find a local guide through your villa or hotel, or simply take a wander yourself. Plenty of trails offer walks through jungle terrain, up a mountain, or through woodland to the lakes.

You can easily find your own way along the shores of Danau Buyan. Take the turn by the police station in **Pancasari** and follow it along to the end and you will come across the start of the trail that wanders along the shores. You'll pass various spots to have a lakeside picnic. **Bali Sobek** ★★★ (℅ **0361/768050;** www.balisobek.com) offers a trek through mountain rainforest near Lake Tamblingan. Once you have crossed the lake in old-fashioned dugout canoes, the trek takes you through breathtaking tropical virgin jungle terrain.

For nature lovers, one of the best trekking routes is the challenging 7-hour trek from Lake Tamblingan to Jatiluwih. The trek takes you through dense forests, to the caldera Lubang Nagaloka ("Dragon Hideout"), along an ancient trade path used by traders for centuries, all the way to the southern slopes of Mt. Batukaru, and finally ending at Jatiluwih (p. 240), where you can enjoy the undulating paddy field views.

WHERE TO STAY

Bali Handara Country Club   With 77 rooms and a world-class golf course, this is a stay-and-play in a stunning setting, actually set in the volcano. You need not stay to play but incentive packages almost make it worthwhile. Unfortunately, while the golf course is world class, the same cannot be said of the accommodation. The rooms are in hues of cream and brown, the furniture heavy Indonesian and not very elegant; the place could do with a renovation. Stay here if it is convenient and you are a golf nut who wants to wake up overlooking the course.

Jl Taya Bedugul, Pancasari. ℅ **0362/22646.** www.balihandarakosaido.com. 77 units. Year-round US$135 course view; US$150 garden view. AE, DC, MC, V. **Amenities:** Restaurant; cafe; bar; gym; tennis court. *In room:* Satellite TV, minibar.

Kebun Raya You can now stay the night in the middle of the Botanic Gardens (see above). This very large, pavilion-style house has 14 rooms, all with balconies; rooms are smart if somewhat soulless. However, you wake up in possibly the most beautiful and, certainly the largest, tended garden in Bali with the chance to explore before everyone else.

In the Bedugul Botanical Garden (p. 235), Bedugul. © 0368/22050. 20 units. Year-round Rp360,000 deluxe; Rp550,000 suite. No credit cards. *In room:* TV.

Lake Buyan Cottages ★ (Finds)(Kids) This is an ideal place to get away for a few days with the kids. The absolutely charming if basic and slightly dated, two-bedroom cottages come with their own kitchen and fireplace with fresh firewood. The view slightly misses the lake for some reason, but it is on a large, well-tended garden with a children's play area. Take plenty of warm clothes and a roast chicken for the oven; put on the fire, and enjoy the fresh mountain air. It's too cold to have a swimming pool. Though there is no restaurant, you have your own kitchen, and they will provide an American breakfast at Rp25,000.

Jl. Raya Bedugul, Bedugul. © 0362/21351. 9 units. Year-round Rp900,000. MC, V. *In room:* TV, kitchen.

The Lodge Bedugul This brand-new villa is great fun if there is a group of you. Outside is a full-length, wraparound balcony with sweeping views out to Lake Buyan. This place comes with all the toys that you might possibly want for a party weekend away: pool table, hot tub, dart board, karaoke, and a projector film screen and surround sound. All the bedrooms are en suite. The lodge is near lakeside nature trails.

Bedugul. © 0361/745-1315. Fax 0361/288923. www.thelodgebedugul.com. 5 bedrooms. Year-round US$75 standard; US$325 villa. Rates include breakfast. MC, V (in Sanur office only); no credit cards at lodge. **Amenities:** Lounge; Jacuzzi; room service; spa. *In room:* A/C, TV, minibar.

WHERE TO DINE

There are very few places to choose from when it comes to eating in this area but we did find these two gems, both on Jalan Raya Denpasar in Bedugul. **Café Teras Lempuna** (© 0362/29312; main courses from Rp35,000; no credit cards; daily 7am–10pm) serves a mixture of simple pasta, sandwiches, and oddly, a wide selection of Japanese food. The chicken curry and the ginger pork were extremely tasty, as were most of the Japanese dishes on offer. The simple tomato and mushroom salad with miso dressing was so good I came back for it the following day. The **Seoul Garden** (© 0362/29920; main courses Rp60,000–Rp100,000; no credit cards; daily 7am–9pm) makes some of the best *kimchi* on Bali. Choose from a simple menu of pork dishes like their house specialty grilled fat with pork (Rp65,000) and my favorite, tofu with fried *kimchi*.

4 MUNDUK

Munduk is on a ridge, with one side reaching south over rice terraces and the other falling just as steeply away with views to the north coast and the seas beyond. This was the home of many weekend places for the Dutch, who came up from their administrative capital of Singaraja, and in town you can still see the evidence of colonial-era villas. The area is known for coffee as much as for walking. The main road runs right through the village.

In comparison to much of the central mountains, the people here seem softer and more congenial, similar in characteristic to lowlanders. This might have something to do with the history of Dutch influence, as this village has long been accustomed to the comings and goings of foreigners.

EXPLORING MUNDUK

A wonderful trek will take you to the traditional hillside Bali Aga villages of **Pedawa** and **Sidatapa,** where they still make sugar in the traditional way and you can admire their bamboo structures or stroll through clove and coffee plantations. For the more adventurous, is the 1,860m (6,102-ft.) peak of **Mount Lesong,** reached in 8 hours. Depending on your route, you may take in the caldera **Lubang Nagaloka,** which translates as "Dragon's Hideout." If you are not into overly stretching your legs, go in search of the infamous Luwak coffee, made from beans that have been digested and secreted by the civet. A few plantations in the area produce their own. You will need to ask around as there are no guarantees of the rodent's appearance and it all depends on the quality of the ripe beans. All hotels and villas in the area can organize the necessary guide to take you around.

If you are staying here or around, take a **plantation tour** to get an understanding not just of how the locals grow their individual crops, but also of the interdependence of each farmer on his neighbors, particularly those higher up the irrigation chain. Much of this interdependence is being protected by responsible development and leaders of the local community, for example the owner of Puri Lumbung. Most people that you ask will be happy to share their knowledge with you if they speak English.

A charming **waterfall** is at the top of Munduk; it takes about 20 minutes to walk down to and possibly 25 to get back up. It is impressive year-round, but even more so in the wet season. Clear signs on the road point the way, about two bends north of Puri Lumbung.

WHERE TO STAY

Anaheim Villa   Formerly known as the Kalaspa and on the high road above the twin lakes of Buyan and Tamblingan, the Anaheim Villa is transforming into a spa and yoga retreat. Recent investments suggest they are looking for upmarket guests. The dining villa has a very special view down to the coast. A nicely done infinity pool with wooden sun deck is below and the villas drop down the gentle hill. The well appointed villas of traditional carved stone, are self-contained, and have little terraces and views down the valley from the double beds. Plans are in the works to open the top floor of the dining villa as a restaurant which will have even more incredible views.

Buleleng, (C) **0361/727770.** www.anaheimvillas.com. 6 villas. Year-round US$125–US$225. Rates include breakfast. MC, V. **Amenities:** Restaurant; library; outdoor pool; spa; TV room.

Munduk Moding Plantation ★★ (Kids)(Moments   On the road from Bedugul to Munduk, take the turn toward Golbek and stay at this gem. This recently opened venture is a collaboration between a young local farmer who was previously trained at the Shangri-la and an international economist. The accommodations are on 5 hectares (12 acres) of coffee plantation and bring much needed vitality and service to this area. The long view down to the north coast over the pool and terrace at sunset are spectacular, with the mountains of Java in the background. The villas have an open feel and are beautifully set in natural stone with polished hardwood floors with free-standing stone baths and separate outside showers. The kitchen serves their own organic produce and offers traditional Balinese food.

It will take about 40 energetic minutes to take a complete plantation tour. The kids will enjoy strawberry picking. A guided tour with the knowledgeable manager who, before hotel school, farmed his family's land, explores surrounding plantations, the flora and fauna, and the interdependence of the farmers, their crops, and water. With a couple of horses, a tennis court, and kids' area, this is a wonderful getaway.

The owners are committed to protecting the area's natural beauty and environmental and cultural heritage and are thus developing the area with a sensitivity toward unison with the local population. With luck and hard work, they will avoid the excesses that have occurred elsewhere on the island. They also work closely with their like-minded neighbors at Puri Lumbung.

Munduk. ℂ **0362/700-5321.** www.mundukmodingplantation.com. 5 units. Year-round US$135 standard; US$160 grand suite; US$175 villas. AE, MC, V. **Amenities:** Restaurant; spa; tennis court. *In room:* TV/ DVD, stereo or CD, iPod, hair dryer, minibar.

Puri Lumbung Cottages ★★★   The best option in Munduk is this charming bungalow-style hotel. Currently you choose from 17 bungalows, although more are being added. Some are *lumbung*-style on two floors, while others are more traditional villas with each room in a different style or size. All are set in a magical garden of fruits and spices. The restaurant serves OK food, such as chicken in a basket or wok-fried pork at about Rp36,000 each, but don't get too ambitious.

Certainly the main reason for staying here is to learn and explore, but by staying here you are also helping support the local community. The owner, Nyoman Bagiarta, was an hotelier who had worked previously for an international hotel chain. He repurchased his grandfather's land and set up this hotel not just as a way to help local people through employment and supporting their traditional crafts but also to serve as a template for other hotels owned and run by Balinese. He is very respected locally, and is also the founder of the Tamblang Sacred Springs Conservation Project, devoted to educating farmers about sustainable agriculture and the preservation of indigenous trees, just slightly north of the entrance to the town and Puri Lumbung.

Puri Lumbung has daily traditional cooking as well as dance and music classes, guided tours of the nearby coffee plantations, and educational walks that focus on temples, agriculture, or history. Alternatively, you can simply sit on your balcony and take in the long view to the north coast—don't miss sunset.

Munduk. ℂ **0362/92810.** www.purilumbung.com. 17 units. Year-round US$18–US$65 standard; US$71– US$157 cottage; US$258 villa. MC, V. **Amenities:** Restaurant; spa. *In room:* Minibar (in villa only).

Saranam Eco Resort   Set on 2 hectares (5 acres) of nature's finest land on the Bedugul road, surrounded by verdant rice paddies, this offering is convenient for exploring the lower mountain region. Ten free-standing bungalows all have private terraces. While the central building is large, the rattan and bamboo furnishings, *alang alang* roofs, and garden blend unobtrusively into the hillside and surrounding terrain. The views from the restaurant and most of the rooms are possibly worth a trip in themselves. The rooms are functional, with a hot water shower and bath. The main restaurant is a popular stop for bus loads of tourists. They serve a huge welcoming buffet throughout the day.

Jalan Raya Baturiti, Kecamatan Baturiti. ℂ **0368/21038.** www.saranamresortbali.com. 35 units. Year-round US$65–US$95 standard; US$135 bungalow. Rates include breakfast. MC, V. **Amenities:** Restaurant. *In room:* TV, minibar.

Slightly more centrally positioned above the lakes Buyan and Tamblingan and just along from Puncak Bagus, **Anaheim Villa** (✆ 0361/727-770; www.anaheimvillas.com; main courses start at Rp30,000–Rp45,000; MC, V; daily 7am–9pm) serves a more formal and varied menu from other area choices. They do a very good chicken curry. The inviting **Ngiring Ngewedang Restaurant,** Munduk (✆ 08/123807010; www.ngiringngewedang. com; main courses Rp35,000–Rp60,000; MC, V; daily 7am–9pm), is perched on the bend set above the road with clear views over its own coffee plantation to the Bali lowlands. They have their own small coffee museum, will take you on a tour of their plantation, and conclude with a demonstration of the traditional methods of drying, roasting, and grinding coffee beans. The restaurant sells a variety of coffee and light meals but disappointingly they actually send their coffee to Singaraja to be processed. On the road at the Munduk end of the lake above Tamblingan, warung **Puncak Bagus,** Jl. Raya Denpasar, Banyuan (✆ 08283727637; main courses start at Rp15,000–Rp25,000; no credit cards; daily 8am–9pm), has a spectacular view of the two lakes. They serve a pleasant *nasi campur* at Rp25,000.

Firefly Suppers ★★★   Part of Big Tree Organic Farms' offerings is a once weekly dinner dubbed the Firefly Suppers, hosted by the farm's munificent and charming owners, Ben and Blair Ripple. They prepare an extravagant menu of their seasonally fresh organic produce. They also work with micro-producers from all over the region, and when pressed will talk about their part in helping educate consumers and producers alike in sustainability. The dinner is served on their farm under a banana leaf thatched roof lit by hundreds of torches. Among some of their locally harvested sustainable products is sea salt from the beaches of east Bali. The fragile crystals are collected from the brine and then dried in the wind and sun and what is left forms the miniature hollow pyramids of sea salt, which has graced the tables of both Donna Karan and French Laundry in California.

Bedugul area. ✆ 0361/954010. www.bigtreebali.com. Reservations required; location may change depending on number of reservations. 6-course meal US$50 per person. MC, V. May–Oct only.

---

5 GUNUNG BATUKARU

Bali's second highest mountain is, much of the time, mainly overlooked. Batukaru is either accessible from Tabanan (p. 288) in the southwest or through a mountain road, the turn off just below Bedugul. The Bedugul road where you turn off at **Pacung** and pass through **Jatiluwih** is one of the most enchanting low roads in Bali. The Jatiluwih area has been designated a UNESCO natural world heritage site. You pass centuries-old rice paddies with a long unspoiled view, perhaps the most spectacular of them all in Bali, to the mountains of Agung and Batur on one side, while skirting the slopes of Batukaru on the other. The ancient terraces stand as they have for hundreds of years.

The water from the natural **Penatahan Hot Springs** (Yeh Panas; about 9km/5½ miles north of Tabanan; Jl. Batukaru, Desa Penatahan; ✆ 0361/725489; admission Rp20,000; daily 8am–6pm) near the bank of the river Yeh Ho contains sulfur, potassium, and sodium, which are effective for curing skin and some other diseases. Penatahan village has a waterfall and the hot springs comes up in the middle of a temple under the big banyan tree. According to the local lore, King Jaya Wikrama suffered from a serious skin disease. Upon the minister's suggestion, the king was taken to a traditional meditation healer who received god's blessing that a hot spring should pour from the ground. The healer asked

Waka Land Cruises ★★

Waka Experience (✆ **0361/484085;** www.wakaexperience.com; adults US$82, children ages 5–10 US$42) runs tours of Jatiluwih and its surrounds in a Land Rover. The route traverses rice fields and rainforest and stops off at a traditional farmhouse, a hot spring, and an ancient quarry where the stone is still cut by traditional methods to build temples and shrines all over the island. An Indonesian and Balinese lunch is served in their restaurant in the mountains with your choice of red and white wine and even a cognac.

the king to take a bath until completely recovered. To express his gratefulness, the king then built the temple on that location.

PURA LUHUR BATUKARU This ancient temple is set against the magnificent backdrop of Batukaru mountain, at the very end of the road to the mountain. The enchanting site is often shrouded in mist. A beautiful water pavilion is reached by a floating platoon connected by hand-pulled ropes. As this is such a remote temple, swathed in outstanding and peaceful beauty, only the most determined fellow travelers will have shared your journey.

WHERE TO STAY

Bali Mountain Retreat ★ (Finds) Set on the eastern side of the slopes of Mount Batukaru, and accessed through a long (2-hr.) but rewarding drive from the lowlands, this simple offering has a great view, some nice rooms, and one of the most beautiful yoga or dance studios. The straightforward accommodation is a blend of traditional Balinese and contemporary Asian styles, ranging from well-appointed rooms in a handcrafted teak house to comfortable bungalows. Food is served buffet-style, which is more appropriate for mass market and, given the size of this operation, seems unnecessary. However it is a good place to base yourself. They will organize and advise on treks. On a good night, they will get the guitar out.

Batukaru. ✆ **08/283602645.** www.balimountainretreat.com. 5 units. High season Rp170,000–Rp910,000; low season Rp150,000–Rp828,000. MC, V. **Amenities:** Restaurant; bar/cafe; room service; spa; Wi-Fi.

Cempaka Belimbing Villas Midway between Sanda and Tabanan, with views on to the surrounding rice field and forests beyond, this large offering has 16 traditional rooms in individual villas, six with pools. Rooms are large and decently furnished if slightly sparse but the surrounding countryside and terraced fields are the draw. All rooms are individually sized: Some have bathrooms as big as the bedrooms, others have views on various sides, but all have terraces looking down the gently sloping resort, over the pool, and on to the surrounding tropical countryside.

Br. Suradadi, Belimbing, Pupuan-Tabanan. ✆ **0361/745-1178.** Fax 0361/745-1179. www.cempaka belimbing.com. 16 units. High season US$80–US$120; low season US$70–US$110; extra bed US$15. Rates include breakfast. MC, V. **Amenities:** Restaurant; bar; lounge; bicycle; Jacuzzi; outdoor pool; room service; spa. *In room:* A/C, fan, TV, minibar.

Sanda Butik Villas ★ (Finds) Just outside Sanda village, on the winding road from Papuan to Tabanan, this hotel makes a great stop-off point for journeys from the north or a relaxing get-away if you are in the warmer south. The rooms are villa-style with polished cement floors and sun rooms with full height glass walls. You almost feel as though you are sitting in the fields. They do an historic Indian curry with chutneys and *popadom* served in the charming colonial pavilion that also doubles as the living room and meeting point for their free cocktail hour—where Ted an old East-African hand serves his terribly colonial pink gin cocktails. Settle down in their library and enjoy some great books on Bali. Air-conditioning and hot water are included, but interestingly only showers and not baths.

Desa-Sanda, Pupuan-Tabanan. ℭ **08/283720055.** www.sandavillas.com. 7 units. Year-round from US$99. Rates include breakfast. MC, V. **Amenities:** Restaurant; outdoor pool; room service. *In room:* A/C, fan, TV, minifridge.

Sarinbuana Eco Lodge ★   On the slopes of Mount Batukaru, this lodge has stunning mountain views. The bungalows are furnished in a traditional style, with many pieces of furniture made from locally grown bamboo. The three-bedroom family bungalow has lots of carved timber and hand picked furniture. A huge amount of thought and a great deal of love has gone into the development of this beautiful spot.

Sarinbuana specializes in educational workshops with courses on Balinese customs, such as cooking and calligraphy. There are farming workshops on locally grown crops, including coffee and vanilla and in the right season rice planting or harvesting, although the latter is truly back-breaking. The lodge also offers special half-day seminars on sustainability or social and community projects, so you can take your knowledge back home with you. They truly practice what they preach here and what they preach we should all be listening to.

Batukaru, Tabanan. ℭ **0361/743-5198.** www.baliecolodge.com. 4 units. Year-round Rp1,000,000–Rp1,600,000. Rates include breakfast. MC, V. **Amenities:** Restaurant; lounge.

WHERE TO DINE

On the main road from Sanda south to Tabanan and at the same turn-off as Cempaka Belimbing, the remote roadside cafe **Belimbing Café (Starfruit Café),** Jl. Raya Belimbing (no phone; main courses Rp25,000; no credit cards; daily 8am–9pm), is owned by the same good folk that own the popular Café Batu Jimbar in Sanur. The view is spectacular. The extensive menu has many pasta and Indonesian dishes and does them very well. It makes an excellent lunch stop on the way north or south. Look out for their puddings.

If you could bottle a view, then **Café Jatiluwih,** Jatiluwih (ℭ **0361/815245;** sandwiches and main courses starting at Rp10,000; no credit cards; daily 9am–5pm), would be serving the most exquisite dish in town. They have *soto ayam* at Rp12,000 and a selection of sandwiches. The whole affair is aimed at the tourist market. It's worth stopping, having some local coffee, and just taking in the view.

East Bali

Dominated by the holy mountain Gunung Agung, east Bali is one of the island's most beautiful and traditional regions. It remains largely unspoiled, with not one factory marring the landscape. Here vistas of terraced rice fields and bamboo forests take the place of bars, cafes, and trendy shops. Several tourist areas are wound together by the coastal road: inland **Sidemen,** with its beautiful scenery and lush stepped vistas; **Tulamben, Padangbai,** and **Amed,** all known for their great diving and snorkeling; and **Candidasa,** a long established, if slightly tired resort.

The locals here are descendants of the Majapahits who first settled and established a court here after their flight from Java. The Regents of Klungkung were the last of the Balinese to hold out against the Dutch in 1908 and a towering monument in Semarapura commemorates the final battle. As you travel through the east, you might notice a rich variety of older customs that have managed to resist modern Javanese influence ever since their initial arrival after the 15th century.

1 EXPLORING EAST BALI

GETTING THERE

The best way to explore the east is by **car** or **motorcycle,** both easily hired or rented throughout Bali. If you don't want to hire a car, you can easily pick up a **taxi.** Negotiate a price before you leave as this is generally cheaper than letting the meter run.

Bemo run between Batubulan station and the main towns of Candidasa, Amlapura, and Klungkung. You can also catch a *bemo* from these towns to the smaller villages in the area. Prices range from Rp3,500 up to Rp15,000 and depend on what you negotiate. You are likely to pay more than the locals.

You can also get to Padangbai and Candidasa by **Perama Tours bus** (✆ **0361/751551;** www.peramatour.com) throughout the day from Kuta, Sanur, Lovina, and Ubud. Check the timetable on their website. You can arrange a drop-off at a hotel for an extra price. Prices range from Rp25,000 to Rp125,000 one-way.

GETTING AROUND

The east tends to have no authorized metered taxis. Some *bemo* operators are usually happy to drive you where you need to go. Be sure to have the phone number of your destination in case the driver isn't familiar with your destination.

You have two options for getting to the east: You can follow the **coastal road** from Sanur towards Kusamba, and then north towards Amlapura, passing Manggis en route. At Amlapura, the road forks north through Tirta Gangga and round towards Culik. At Culik you can either turn left and continue to Tulamben and the north coast, or turn right for Amed. This delightful road round the coast will end up back at Amlapura. The roads are good, if narrow, and you get a chance to see how the villagers go about their daily lives. One stop of note in Seraya is the very small open-air hand-weaving showroom

ACCOMMODATIONS ■
Alam Asmara Dive Resort **23**
Alam Batu Beach
 Bungalow Resort **52**
The Alila Resort Manggis **17**
Amankila **15**
Batu Belah **47**
Bayu Cottages Hotel
 and Restaurant **38**
Bloo Lagoon Resort **13**
Blue Moon Villa **36**
Dancing Dragon Cottage **42**
Dewa Bharata **21**
Dharma Homestay **12**
The Golden Rock **43**
Good Karma **46**
Life in Amed **37**
Mimpi Resort **48**
Nirarta Centre for Living Awareness **6**
Patal Kikian **7**
Pondok Wisata Lihat Sawah **5**
Puri Bagus **25**
Puri Sawah Villas **34**
Rama Candidasa **19**

Santai Hotel **44**
Scuba Seraya Resort **50**
Seraya Shores **29**
Siddhartha Resort **51**
Tauch Terminal Resort
 and Spa **49**
Villa Asada **18**
Villa Djamrud **33**
Villa Sasoon **24**
Villa Talia Vashti **16**
Villa Tirta Ayu **33**
Watergarden **20**
Wawa Wewe II **40**

DINING ◆
Anda Amed Resort **45**
Garpu Restaurant **19**
Komang John Café **36**
Le Warung Restaurant **13**
Life in Amed **37**
Omang Omang Café **11**
Sails **39**
Santai **44**
Vincent's **22**
Warung Kadek **41**

ATTRACTIONS ●
Budakeling **31**
Bukit Demulih **1**
Charlie's Factory **27**
Klungkung Market **4**
Nyoman Gunarsa
 Museum **3**
Pantai Kecil/
 Bias Tugal **10**
Pelangi Workshop **8**
Pura Besakih
 (Mother Temple) **26**
Pura Goa Lawah **9**
Pura Lempuyang **35**
Pura Silayukti **14**
Puri Agung
 Karangasem **30**
Sadus Tiles **8**
Taman Gili &
 Semararaja Museum **4**
Taman Tirta Gangga **32**
Taman Ujung
 Water Palace **28**
Tihingan **2**

EAST BALI

12

EXPLORING EAST BALI

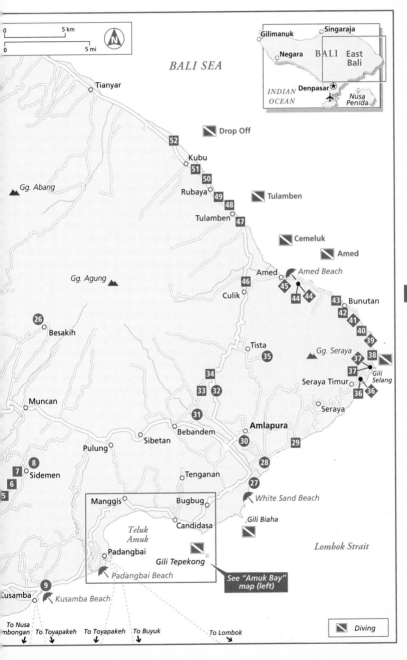

EAST BALI

12

EXPLORING EAST BALI

0   5 km
0   5 mi

BALI SEA

Tianyar

Gilimanuk   Singaraja
Negara   BALI   East Bali
INDIAN OCEAN   Denpasar   Nusa Penida

Drop Off
52
Kubu
51
50
Rubaya   49 48
Tulamben   47

Gg. Abang

Cemeluk
Amed

Gg. Agung

Amed   Amed Beach
46   45
Culik   44 44   43 Bunutan
42
41
40
39
Tista   Gg. Seraya   38
35   37 Gili Selang
Seraya Timur   37
26   34   36 36
Besakih   33 32   Seraya
31
Muncan   30
Sibetan   Bebandem   29
Pulung   28
7 8   Tenganan   27
6 Sidemen   White Sand Beach
5
Manggis   Bugbug   Gili Biaha
Teluk Amuk   Candidasa
Padangbai   Gili Tepekong   Lombok Strait
9   Padangbai Beach
Kusamba   Kusamba Beach   See "Amuk Bay" map (left)

To Nusa Lembongan To Toyapakeh To Toyapakeh To Buyuk   To Lombok

Diving

of **Threads of Life** ★★★, a nonprofit working to revitalize local weaving. Take a private tour to learn about their weaving and dying processes.

The **second option,** mostly used by visitors coming from Ubud, is, upon leaving Ubud, to head towards Gianyar, then north to Bangli and east to Rendang. Not far from Rendang is the turn to Pura Besakih (p. 252) or keep trucking on towards Amlapura traveling through Sibetan, the home of the snake fruit (p. 250).

Another scenic route worth mentioning is the road from Semarapura (Klungkung) via Sidemen and Iseh. The endless paddy field views are breathtaking.

TOURIST INFORMATION

A **tourist office** (Taman Kerta Gosa; ☎ **0366/21448,** but don't count on anyone answering; Mon–Fri 8am–2pm) is in Semarapura in the Semararaja Museum of Taman Kerta Gosa (p. 247). However, like all tourist offices in Bali, they are not set up to give you independent advice, more to sell you their commission-based tours. The tourist office in **Amlapura,** Jl. Diponegoro (☎ **0363/21196,** again, don't count on anyone answering; Mon–Fri, erratic hours), covers the whole area of Karangasem and does have a host of useful information and even has a very useful website, **www.karangasemtourism. com**, with dates for major ceremonies. The staff is helpful and able to give good information on what to see and do in the area. They can also supply you with details on area ceremonies and festivals. A similar little publication called *Agung* is available in area hotels and restaurants.

EAST BALI

12

FAST FACTS: EAST BALI

ⓕ *Fast Facts*   **East Bali**

ATMs   East Bali has few options for getting cash. While money changers are available in Candidasa, Padangbai, and Amed, ATMs are a rarity. Two ATMs are in Klungkung on the main street near the market; Padangbai has an ATM beside Hotel Madya, in front of the ferry terminal; Bangli has one ATM in the BRI bank on Jalan Kutai; your last chance is in Amlapura, outside the Hardy's supermarket. A couple of hotels may offer an ATM service with a surcharge. Always carry small change as most locals cannot change large denominations (a Rp100,000 note is the equivalent of over a week's wages).

Credit Cards   Not many places in the east take credit cards so ensure you have enough cash before heading here. Most dive resorts are able to process credit cards but may change you 2.5% to 3% surcharge.

Food   Most towns sell snacks and basics like pasta but you will not find much Western food on sale in the area.

Toiletries   Shampoo and some sun cream is available in small shops. There are no tampons for sale north of Seminyak or east of Ubud.

Wine & Alcohol   Beer is readily available in most warungs and shops in the area. However, wines and spirits can be in short supply. If you are traveling east, bring your own.

2 KLUNGKUNG (SEMARAPURA)

Klungkung is the original name of the capital of the Gelgel Regency, which changed its name in 1992 to Semarapura in tribute to the Semarapura "Palace of the God of Love." Klungkung was considered to be the highest and most important of all the regencies from the 17th century until the regency finally ceded to the Dutch in 1908. The royal family was directly descended from the emperors of the Majaphit. In 1710, Dewa Agung Jambe I, the regent of Klungkung, built Taman Gili, the royal palace. By the end of the 18th century Kerta Gosa, the so-called Halls of Justice, often referred to somewhat ambitiously as Bali's Sistine Chapel, was erected in the middle of an artificial lake. Though the Dutch made use of the Court, in 1908 they destroyed most of the rest of the palace after their bloody victory against Dewa Agung Jambe II. The fight on April 18, 1908, proceeded until the death of the last of the combatants, which included women and children. The king and many of his followers chose *puputan* (mass suicide) rather than face defeat and disgrace. The end of the battle marked the fall of the last of the Balinese kingdoms. A monument opposite Taman Gili commemorates this last stand.

EXPLORING KLUNGKUNG & THE NEARBY VILLAGES

Villagers from the nearby hills head to the city's market every 3 days, and make it a huge social event. The sprawling **Klungkung Market** has hundreds of traditional stalls selling hand-woven fabrics from nearby villages, religious paraphernalia, including the long handled Balinese ceremonial umbrellas, and lots of glittering mirrored items for the home or family shrines. A couple of stalls sell artifacts and some antiques. Be sure to haggle.

For more shopping, the main street has three antiques shops that occasionally have old textiles worth a peek. Other curiosities are mixed together with real antiques and always worth a rummage. As ever, beware of sophisticated copies.

Taman Gili & Semararaja Museum   The impressive Taman Gili, "Island Garden," in the center of Klungkung contains three important elements: Kerta Gosa, Bale Kambang, and the Semararaja Museum. Though the whole complex is sadly deteriorated due to neglect, it is still very much worth a look.

Although it has undergone many restorations since its creation, one of the best examples of Wayang painting in Bali is on the ceiling of the **Kerta Gosa.** The panels of gods and demons are arranged in nine layers. The first and lowest level depicts the five tales of Tantri, the Indonesian version of a Thousand and One Nights. The next two levels illustrate episodes of the story of Bhima Swarga who ventures into the underworld to redeem his parents' souls. During his time in hell, he battles with demons and witnesses the gruesome torture of the sinful. The fourth row depicts Garuda's search for the elixir of life; the fifth is the Balinese astrological calendar; the next three panels show the climax of the story with Bhima's visit to heaven and the rewards from the high god. The epic tale ends, gloriously, in enlightenment and justice. Kerta Gosa was considered the supreme court of Bali, where the rajah would meet with his advisors to discuss the law and human affairs. Those on trial could look up at the reliefs on the ceiling and see the moral story of Bhima Swarga and the dreadful punishments and depictions of hell and could then look further and see the panels of heaven and find consolation.

The **Bale Kambang** ★★ is surrounded by ponds and features another richly painted ceiling of the traditional Kamasan style. This building was originally the royal guards'

Dining & Breaking Records in Karangsem Regency

A *megibung* ("people eating communally") is a unique traditional meal of the Karangsem regency associated with weddings, cremations, or temple ceremonies—or anything that involves a meeting of the community.

Participants are divided into groups called *sela,* groups of eight people of the same gender, sitting cross-legged around a large woven rattan plate known as a *nare,* heaped with piles of rice. At the edge are piles of vegetables, maybe steamed *kangkung,* and *urap,* a vegetable salad of long green beans and grated coconut. Servings of pork satay, sometimes grilled pork, and a curry are dispensed by helpers and everyone tucks in—all eating with their right hand. The table cannot start to eat until eight people are seated.

If a *pedanda* (high priest) is in attendance, he eats alone, off his own plate known as a *dulang.* His or her meal consists of rice, vegetables, and duck rather than pork—unless he or she is a vegetarian. Duck symbolizes wisdom.

In 1996, 19,768 people participated in the *Guinness World Records'* largest communal eating event, consisting of the 2,452 *selas* and 152 *wanci* (special table for the high priest). Participants came from all over the Karagasem regency to help break the previous record.

headquarters and used for royal tooth-filing ceremonies. The extensively restored ceilings have decorative paintings of Balinese astrology, the story of Pan and Men Brayut and their 18 mischievous children, and the adventures of the Sutasona, the Balinese role model for nonaggressive strength and a legendary Buddhist hero who was able to turn arrows and spears, hurled at him from the gods, into flowers.

The **Semararaja Museum** has various archaeological objects, traditional artifacts, ceramics, painting, and furniture on show.

Jl. Untung Suropati 3. ✆ **0366/21448.** Admission Rp12,000. Daily 8am–6pm.

Nyoman Gunarsa Museum   This museum was built to honor the famous and powerful king Dalam Waturenggong who protected Bali from Muslim influences. It is home to a large collection of classical and contemporary Balinese artwork and work of the founder, Dr. Nyoman Gunarsa. A selection of masks, puppets, ceramics, and stone carvings dates from the 17th to 19th century. The entrance is behind the Trimurti statue and is surrounded by policemen statues.

Jl. Petigaan Banda 1. ✆ **0366/22256.** Admission Rp25,000. Mon–Sat 9am–5pm.

Tihingan ★   Located 3km (2 miles) west from Klungkung, this village is a center for gamelan makers and other traditional musical instruments. The process requires strong workers and specialist pitchers to ensure the right tone is achieved. The quality gongs from Tihingan have a global renown. A few showrooms on the main street have tradesmen at work, typically out first thing in the morning when it is cool. Though some of the showrooms will sell you gamelans, expect to pay a few million rupiah.

Kusamba   A small side road off the main Klungkung road will take you to the fishing and salt-making village of Kusamba, where the beach is lined with colorful fishing boats, salt-making huts, and rows of shallow troughs. The work of raking and sprinkling the sand with water before the filtration process starts before dawn. Seawater is carried from the ocean and poured into specially dug ponds. Once the water has evaporated, the salty residue is placed in shallow troughs, made from split palm trees, and more seawater is added. Further evaporation and purification yields fully formed, pyramid-shaped salt crystals. Some chefs consider Balinese salt to be some of the finest in the world. Buy some to help support the hard-working farmers and their families.

Pura Goa Lawah   About 2km (1¼ miles) east of Kusamba, and popularly known as the Bat Cave, this is one of the nine *kahyangan jagat* (directional temples) on Bali, which protect the island from evil spirits. Pura Goa Lawah is revered as a sacred site for Brahma, the Hindu god of creation. The dark interior is filled with a seething mass of bats that makes the walls of the cave appear to be alive. Seawater here is thought to be blessed and is brought to the mother temple of Besakih. Legend has it that a tunnel extends from the cave up to Besakih some 30km (19 miles) away, though it has yet to be discovered. The temple is one of *sad kahyangan* (six great temples of Bali) and the cave is a favored site of *nyekah* (deification of the deceased family member soul) pilgrimage. The best time to visit is during *odalan,* the temple birthday (June 1), when pilgrims flock to be blessed. Rp4,000. Parking Rp1,000. Daily 8am–5pm.

WHERE TO STAY & DINE

Klungkung doesn't have enough draw to merit staying overnight. Base yourself nearby in Ubud or Manggis instead. If you do however find yourself in the city roaming for something to eat, the best place to aim for is the **market** (see above), just behind a row of shops to the east of Taman Gosa. A selection of stalls cook up basic Indonesian fare. In the evening, the **Pasar Senggol** (night market in the same location; 5pm–midnight) has Indonesian cuisine and some Chinese-influenced offerings. It's loud and chaotic and really quite fun.

3 THE SIDEMEN VALLEY ★★

One of Bali's most scenic areas, where exceptionally beautiful verdant rice terraces tumble down hills to deep valleys, the Sidemen makes a great side trip from Ubud or a stop off on the way to Amed (p. 265). Sidemen is also known for its traditional weaving. *Songket,* a ceremonial cloth for weddings richly decorated with gold or silver thread, is one of the best known and several weaving shops along the main road sometimes offer weaving demonstrations. Look for the signs outside the shops or ask your driver who will be sure to know.

The road from Semarapura to Duda through Sidemen and Iseh, with breathtaking paddy field views among some of the most stunning in Bali, is a great way to approach Pura Besakih (p. 252). Both Walter Spies and Theo Maier resided in the countryside near Iseh to seek peace and inspiration—and to escape overcrowded Ubud.

EXPLORING SIDEMEN VALLEY

CYCLING ★★ ⓜ**Moments**   The Sidemen valley offers some of the best cycling in Bali as the roads are not as busy as others. Most hotels in the area offer free use of their mountain bikes; otherwise trips can be organized through specialist tour agents (p. 64) which include hire of bike and helmets, refreshments, lunch, and insurance.

Finds   **What to Eat in Sibetan**

Sibetan is the home of *salak* or snake fruit, an applelike fruit covered with what looks like snakeskin. If you happen to be driving by Sibetan in the dead of night or very early in the morning, stop by Sibetan market, which sells some of the best *babi guling* (roast suckling pig) around. It is all finished by 6am.

A good cycling trip begins in the heart of snake fruit country, **Selat,** and takes you through Iseh, a small mountain village down to **Sidemen.** You will cycle through valleys of uninterrupted rice terrace views, see plantations bearing a variety of crops, pass fighting cocks in baskets, and experience the daily life of the Balinese. The trip is mostly downhill and should take about 2 hours.

TREKKING   Most tour operators from the south can arrange a half- or full-day trek through the Sidemen valley. If you are staying in the area, your hotel will help you with hiring a local guide; expect to pay about Rp25,000 to Rp35,000 an hour.

Some well-trodden footpaths meander through the rice fields. With plenty of intoxicating views, crags and rivers to cross, and a smattering of temples, this is a rambler's paradise. With or without a guide, you are never too far from a road so don't worry about getting lost. Besides, you might stumble on a small village where most Balinese will welcome you with open arms and point you in the right direction.

WHITE WATER RAFTING   An exhilarating outing on the Telega Waja river begins in Muncan and takes you through 14km (9 miles) of terraced rice fields, lush tropical jungle, cascading waterfalls, and steep canyons of clean, natural spring water. Classified as a class IV river (class III being the easiest), this adventure is suitable for kids as young as 6. Book through **Sobek ★★★** (✆ **0361287059** Ubud, 0361768050 Kuta; www.balisobek.com; adult US$79, children ages 7–15 US$52; includes transfers, refreshments, lunch, and insurance).

PELANGI WORKSHOP ★★ **Finds**   Stop at the Pelangi Workshop in Sidemen village where you can see up to 40 people working on *endek* foot looms. The workshop produces some of the finest *ikat* and *songket* in Bali and is exported all over the world, including to other Balinese shop owners. Opposite the workshop is a small shop producing some traditional Lontar painting.

Jl. Soka 67. No phone. Daily 8am–5pm.

WHERE TO STAY & DINE

Nirarta Centre for Living Awareness ★   This tiny resort of six Balinese villas has magnificent views of the surrounding rice fields and mountains. Stunning scenery and organic food make this retreat a favorite for groups and health seekers. Founded by psychologist Peter Wrycza and his wife Ida Ayu who comes from a family of Balinese healers, the center follows a mix of spiritual disciplines and philosophies. Activities include meditation, meeting with high priests, trekking, and yoga.

Banjar Tabola, Sidemen. ✆ **0366/530-0636.** www.awareness-bali.com. 11 units. Year-round US$28–US$63. MC, V. **Amenities:** Restaurant.

Patal Kikian ★   Located at the top of a steep hill, not far from the center of Sidemen, is this enchanting homestay offering basic accommodation. Each bungalow has a terrace

EAST BALI

12

THE SIDEMEN VALLEY

> **Finds** **Traditional Tiles in Sidemen Village**
>
> You can buy traditional cement tiles from **Sadus Tiles** (✆ 08/5237064151;
> www.sadustiles.com). A Dutch woman and her Balinese husband create beauti-
> ful, handcrafted cement tiles, redolent of Dutch colonial Java. They make both
> traditional patterns as well as more modern designs using recently introduced
> Dutch compounds. Just watching the process is fascinating and they will wel-
> come you to the factory whether you buy or not.

perfect for enjoying the rice field views below. There is even a small pool, for those brave
enough for the cold. Ida Ayu Mas Andayani, who runs this family business, is always on
hand to share stories and show you her photo album with the likes of David Bowie and
Mick Jagger. She can also arrange trips to the local weavers or a trek. Supper under the
stars is served on your own terrace.

Sidemen. ✆ **0366/23005.** Year-round US$55–US$70. No credit cards. **Amenities:** Outdoor pool; room
service.

Pondok Wisata Lihat Sawah   This very charming family-run guesthouse is surrounded by paddy fields with breathtaking views. They also offer workshops on *songket*
weaving and can arrange hikes through the local countryside. The rooms have traditional
matting for the walls, four-poster beds, and an assortment of antique-style furniture.
They also have three private villas. The restaurant serves up a basic selection of Thai,
European, and Indonesian food.

Br. Tebola, Sidemen. ✆ **0366/5300516.** www.lihatsawah.com. 12 units. High season US$35–US$55; low
season US$30–US$50. No credit cards. **Amenities:** Restaurant; bicycles; concierge; room service. *In room:*
Fan, minibar.

4 BANGLI & GUNUNG AGUNG

Visiting Bangli, in the center of a panoramic rice-growing area, makes a great alternative
route through the east. The mountain town has a famous temple that was founded as
early as the 12th century, if not before, and the beautiful Pura Kehen is one of Bali's best.
Market days (every 3 days) are always colorful, when inhabitants from the hills come to
town to sell their wares, trade, and catch up on local gossip.

FAST FACTS   The hospital is located on Jalan Kusumayudha, just down the road from
the post office. The **police** are on Jalan Nusntara, on the road to Penelokan. The **Sasana
Budaya Arts Centre** on Jalan Sriwijaya (✆ **0366/91537**) has a tourist center (Mon–Fri
8am–3pm). The **post office** is at Jalan Kusumayudha 18.

EXPLORING BANGLI
Bukit Demulih, literally the "hill of no return," is about 3km (2 miles), about an hour's
walk, west of Bangli. At the top of the hill is a small picturesque temple and stunning
views over central Bali. En route, you will find a small holy waterfall, located in a bamboo
setting. Take a guide from your hotel.

The town, the old capital of the regency, is dominated by the *puri,* or palaces. The
Bangli court established their independence from Klungkung in the 19th century and

played an influential role in Balinese politics through to the post-independence era. Eight royal households are spread around the main crossroads. The most prominent is the **Puri Denpasar,** the palace of the last rajah of Bangli, who died 30 years ago. His descendants have restored much of the palace, and there is now a small hotel in the pavilions run by the rajah's grandson. The **royal ancestral temple** lies just to the north of the crossroads, on the western side. Huge ceremonies are held here, attended by all descendants of the royal house, including many who live in other parts of Indonesia.

Pura Dalem Penunggekan   The Temple of the Dead is a pleasant stroll away from the town center. The exterior walls depict the graphic fate of souls in heaven and hell as witnessed by Bhima while trying to retrieve the souls of his parents from hell. One panel details the lurid fate of adulterers while another portrays sinners as monkeys.

Jl Merdeka. No phone. Admission Rp5,000. Daily 7am–5pm.

Pura Kehen   The Temple of the Hearth or the Temple of Fire, the state temple of the old kingdom, is one of Bali's most beautiful temples and stands at the northeastern boundary of town, seemingly in the middle of the forest. Three copper stelae testify to its antiquity and importance. The earliest one, written in Sanskrit, seems to date to the 9th century and mentions the deity Hyang Api, the god of fire. The second is in old Balinese, and the third is in old Javanese, the latter mentioning Hyang Kehen (the same deity from the 9th century inscriptions) and indicating eight villages around Bangli that worship the deity.

The temple was constructed on eight terraces, after the manner of ancient animistic sanctuaries that are built into the southern slope of a hill, much like Pura Besakih. A flight of 38 stairs adorned with *wayang* statues leads to the main entrance, where a frightening *kala makara* demon guardian is carved on the gateway. The outer courtyard has a huge old banyan tree with a *kul kul* drum inside, as well as a flat stone for offerings. The walls are inlaid with Chinese porcelain—a common feature of ancient temples and palaces. The temple has 43 altars, including one 11-roofed *meru* to Hyang Api. Several are dedicated to the ancestors of *sudra* commoner clans such as the Ratu Pasek and Pande—which means that worshipers from all over Bali come to pray here, especially on its Odalan (Mar 3). The huge Padmasana throne in the northeastern-most corner has beautiful carvings at the back.

Jl. Sriwijaya. No phone. Admission Rp6,000. Daily 6am–6pm.

The Sasana Budaya Art Center   The Bangli area has various types of ritual *baris* or dances typical of the mountain regions, such as the *baris jojor* (eight men in a line with spears), *baris presi* or *tamiang* (eight men in a circle with leather shields), and *baris dadap* (men in pairs with bat-shaped curled shields made from holy *dadap* wood). They are performed especially at Odalans. This arts center is one of the largest in Bali and occasionally hosts dance performances—though it is not always open. Get information on show times from the tourist information office in the same building.

Jl Sriwijaya. Inquire at on-site tourist information center (Mon–Fri 8am–3pm.) for performance times.

ON THE SLOPE OF GUNUNG AGUNG

Pura Besakih (Mother Temple) ★★ (**Moments**) Bali's largest and holiest temple, Pura Besakih, is alternatively known as the "Mother Temple" and translates literally as the Temple of Spiritual Happiness. It is named after the dragon god believed to inhabit the mountain and is said to be the only temple where a Hindu of any caste can worship.

Tips   Touring Besakih

Many visitors to Besakih are appalled by the treatment they receive from guides and touts outside the entrance. Our advice is to arrange a visit to the temple with an organized tour agent. Organized tours are the best way to visit the temple as on-site guides can be intrusive and off-putting. This way, you should avoid being harassed by touts offering their services. If you do go on your own, you will be approached by guides looking to offer their services. You do not need to use a guide to view the temple. If you wish to hire an on-site guide, make sure you agree to a price beforehand. Rp20,000 to Rp30,000 should be enough.

The temple consists of between 28 and 35 separate structures depending how you count them, and although the precise origins of Pura Besakih remain unclear, the stone bases of Pura Penetaran Agung date back at least 2,000 years. This site has been used as a Hindu place of worship since at least the late 13th century, when the first Javanese conquerors settled on Bali.

Pura Besakih is about 1,000m (3,280 ft.) above sea level. Steps ascend through split gates to the main courtyard where the Trinity shrines are wrapped in cloth and decorated with flower offerings. There are a number of temples but many of their inner courtyards are closed to visitors. Eighteen separate sanctuaries belonging to different regencies and caste groups surround the main temples dedicated to Shiva, Brahma, and Vishnu. To the Balinese, visiting the temple sanctuaries is a special pilgrimage.

The mountaintop setting gives Pura Besakih an almost mystical quality, even more so if you get there for sunrise. Try to reach the temple before 9am, as after this time many tourist buses start to arrive and it can get very busy. Further, given its popularity, it also attracts the more voracious of the local touts who can make the experience a distinctly unspiritual one.

Admission Rp10,000. Daily 7am–6pm. Visitors must wear sarong and sash to enter, both of which can be purchased or rented at the entrance.

GUNUNG AGUNG

Gunung Agung, Bali's highest and, for this reason, holiest mountain, reaches just over 3,100m (10,170 ft.) and is usually at least partly obscured by cloud and mist. To the Balinese, Bali is the entire world, and Gunung Agung is the world's most sacred point. They believe that Mount Agung is a replica of Mount Meru, the central axis of the universe. And so, half way up they built Pura Besakih, the Mother Temple (see above). At some stage in their life, all Balinese must make a pilgrimage up the mountain, the closest point to heaven and where the gods live when they visit mother earth. However Mount Agung, while not a technically difficult climb, is one of Bali's biggest trekking challenges and should not be taken lightly and certainly not without a guide. Start well before dawn, armed with a strong flashlight, water, food, warm and waterproof clothing, and sensible shoes or boots. The best time for a climb is during the dry season of April through October. However as a holy mountain, climbing is not permitted when major religious events are held at the temple at Besakih, which is most of April. Check exact dates, as they operate on the Balinese calendar.

EAST BALI

12

BANGLI & GUNUNG AGUNG

The shortest and most popular route up Mount Agung is from Selat or Muncan, which involves the least walking, due to serviceable roads from either town which lead to the Pura Pasar Agung (Agung Market Temple). From this temple, the climb takes between 2 and 4 hours depending on your level of fitness. Leave by 3am at the latest if you want to get there for sunrise. The other route starts from Besakih and the climb is longer and more challenging, and only really suitable for the physically fit. From Besakih you have the option of either attacking the climb in one hit of between 5 and 6 hours or doing it with an overnight camp. Most prefer to start around 10 or 11pm arriving at the summit in time to enjoy the sunrise—rain, mist, and other climbers permitting.

At the summit on a clear morning you enjoy a 360-degree view over the Lombok Strait to Mount Rinjani and verdant Bali. Be prepared for adverse weather conditions as storms develop quickly. There are no shops along the route.

Guides are available in Besakih. We recommend: **Gung Bawa Trekking** (© 08/123878168), a reliable guide who has been trekking this mountain for years; **M&G Trekking** (© 036/341464 or 08/133153991) in Candidasa, can offer alternative routes; or **Ketut Uriada** (© 0812/3646426), based in Muncan, who is very knowledgeable about the area.

WHERE TO STAY & DINE

Bangli has a couple of places to stay with very basic accommodation. **Artha Sastra Inn,** Jl. Merdeka 5 (no phone; year-round Rp35,000–Rp50,000; cold water showers), is situated opposite the *bemo* terminal and close to the market in an old palace (the building was once the royal place of Bangli), though the grandeur is somewhat faded. The nine rooms vary enormously, so look at a few.

The **Bangli Inn,** Jl. Rambutan (© 0366/91419; year-round Rp120,000; cold water only; no shower), is the more conventional, with clean rooms built around a small court-yard.

For food during the day, the bus terminal has several stalls while the road beside the terminal transforms into a small night market *(pasar malam)* come sundown with the full range of satays, soups, and rice and noodle dishes. **Depot Murni,** Jl. Merdeka 18, just south of the town center, is a typical local warung with the usual rice and noodle offerings at inexpensive prices.

5 PADANGBAI

Fifteen minutes south of Candidasa is the little fishing village of Padangbai, with a beach aglow with the colors of wooden *prahu* boats. Simple fish restaurants and dive shops line the main road, while behind the village are dozens of small homestays and simple eateries. Just to the north is the perfect little Bloo Lagoon Beach.

GETTING THERE & GETTING AROUND

Padangbai is the main port for the ferries to Lombok (p. 303), Nusa Penida (p. 150), and the Gili Islands (p. 339). If you do decide to **rent a car** in the area, expect to pay between Rp200,000 and Rp300,000 a day. Motorbike rental will cost around Rp100,000 a day. **Perama Tours** (© 0363/41419; www.peramatour.com) offers a wide variety of **bus routes** to and from Padangbai and all round Bali. They have offices near the jetty (daily 7am–7pm). You can catch a *bemo* serving Candidasa, Amlapura, and Semarapura from

> **(Tips) Not So Valuable Visitor Information**
>
> Although they appear to be authentic, the tourist information offices in Padangbai are little more than commercial enterprises looking to offer you their tours or services.

the car park at the port entrance. If you are looking to travel south to Kuta, most **taxis** offer a fixed price of around Rp300,000.

FAST FACTS **Titi Shop** on the main Denpasar road near the ferry terminal sells toiletries and basic food requirements. A **post office** is located opposite the ferry terminal, on the right hand side near to Depot Dona.

EXPLORING PADANGBAI

Commanding a high headland at the northern end of Padangbai, **Pura Silayukti** (free admission; daily 24 hr.) is one of Bali's oldest temples. It was founded by the great Javanese Hindu sage Empu Kuturan who arrived here in the 11th century. He subsequently built a retreat on the hillside overlooking the bay, which was later to become Pura Silayukti. As one of the oldest temples, there is very little of architectural interest left to look at. The caves beneath are more interesting.

FISHING Local fishermen will take you out fishing. Expect to pay between Rp100,000 and Rp200,000 for half a day. Fishermen only fish late at night till first thing in the morning or late afternoon until sunset. Bloo Lagoon (see below) can arrange trips with their own fishing boat and are happy to cook up any catch.

SCUBA DIVING **Amuk Bay**—with Padangbai to the south and Candidasa to the north—has some of Bali's best diving. This is also Bali's premier location for sharks—but fear not, as they are mainly reef sharks with some tiger sharks and there have been no attacks reported in recent memory.

The **Bloo Lagoon,** just north of Padangbai, is the only site best suited for beginners, with its gentle white sand slope. Plus, it's a treasure-trove of marine life that includes reef sharks, rhinopias, cuttlefish, leaf scorpion fish, frogfish, lionfish, nudis, and a huge area of stag horn coral. Excellent night diving will expose you to cat sharks, Spanish dancers, crustaceans, basket stars, and hunting cephalopods.

Mimpang is an area with three rock pinnacles that break the surface and which, at the southern, deeper end (known as Shark Point), offers a spectacular wall with profuse corals, fish, and the opportunity to see pelagics.

The breathtaking **Tepekong,** a 300m-long (984-ft.) rock, is for experienced divers only due to the steep walls, cold water, and strong currents. In Tepekong's famous canyon, with its swirling waters and dramatic, craggy walls, are huge schools of sweetlips, maybe Mola-Mola (ocean sunfish), white-tip reef sharks, and turtles.

Gili Biaha ★★★, a little to the north, offers some of Bali's most stunning diving. A vast number and a great diversity of fish, sharks, and frequent pelagic visitors live against a backdrop of chiseled black walls with beautiful, healthy corals and often superb visibility. Diving here is best at slack, high tide.

The currents at Mimpang, Tepekong, and Biaha require care and respect: Not only can a gentle current become a torrential river within a matter of minutes, but both up and down currents are quite common at these sites.

EAST BALI

12

PADANGBAI

Having recently been awarded the GoEco operator status, **Geko Dive ★★**, Jl. Sila-yukti (✆ **0363/41516;** www.gekodive.com), is now one of only eight dive operators in Bali to merit this award. Established in 1997, and catering to both beginners and professionals, they offer a full range of PADI certification courses, dive assistance, and dive-and-accommodation packages. Expect to pay between US$60 and US$100 for two dives with lunch, dive computer, and local transfers.

Waterworx, Jl. Silayukti (✆ **0363/41220** office, 08/11375889 mobile; www.waterworx bali.com) offers diving and snorkeling in the area and around Nusa Penida. The SSI registered dive school has a great team that offers courses in English, French, and German. They offer courses for both PADI and SSI and offer free local pickup. Two dives, including equipment and drinks, cost between US$60 and US$105.

If you're in Seminyak and you want to dive in Padangbai, contact **AquaMarine Diving ★★★**, Jl. Raya Petitenget 2A (✆ **0361/738020;** fax 0361/738021; www.aquamarine diving.com; US$75–US$105).

SNORKELING   Padangbai has some of the best snorkeling in the east including some great places for kids to enjoy themselves without the strong currents that besiege most of Bali. Local warungs along the beaches hire out snorkel gear. One of the safest spots to snorkel is in front of the **main beach.** However, this beach can get quite crowded so you may wish to head for **Pantai Kecil,** otherwise known as Bias Tugal, to the west of the village. There are a few warungs here where you can have a simple meal and get a traditional massage. At least one new development is currently under construction up on the hill but don't let it put you off. **Bloo Lagoon ★** is also another, near-perfect small bay with some great snorkeling.

WHERE TO STAY

Most homestays are on Jalan Silayukti or in the village. Prices range from Rp40,000 (yes, only US$4) up to about Rp100,000 a night. One in particular is the **Dharma Homestay,** Jl. Silayukti (✆ **0363/41394;** Rp60,000–Rp120,000), close to the beach. The best rooms are on the top floor with stunning views over the village.

Bloo Lagoon Resort ★   Undoubtedly, this is the best place to stay in the area. Sitting on top of a hill with panoramic views, the resort consists of self-contained villas surrounding a central pool and dining area overlooking the perfect, yet small, Bloo Lagoon Beach. The resort has an ecofriendly approach and strives to integrate new energy-saving technologies; they compost, grow their own food, and recycle water. Their amphitheater occasionally hosts Balinese and Western performances. Spa Biroo overlooks the sea at the top of the hill and offers a selection of treatments from manicures and pedicures and aromatherapy massages using high-quality essential oils, to the Shama-Shama massage, a four-hand massage.

Jl. Silayukti, Padangbai. ✆ **0363/41211.** www.bloolagoon.com. 17 units. High season US$140 1-bedroom, US$170 2-bedroom, US$190 3-bedroom; low season US$120 1-bedroom, US$150 2-bedroom, US$170 3-bedroom. Discount available when booking online. AE, MC, V. **Amenities:** Restaurant (see below); babysitting; concierge; kids' club; outdoor pool; room service; spa; watersports. *In room:* A/C, fan.

WHERE TO DINE

The small **Le Warung Restaurant ★**, in the Bloo Lagoon (main courses Rp25,000–Rp50,000; AE, MC, V; daily 7:30am–10pm), uses organic produce from the garden. The chef serves simple, tasty salads, soups, and pastas with homemade sauces. Indonesian food and well-made curries are also available. Fresh juices, cappuccinos, and teas are

available all day. Nine years ago, **Omang Omang Café** ★, Jl. Silayukti ((C) **08/123638052;**
www.omangcafe.com; main courses Rp45,000–Rp70,000; no credit cards; daily 8am till
last person leaves), was the first restaurant to open in Padangbai and it is still the best
place. They cook up a selection of wholesome, organic Western and Asian fusion dishes
at very reasonable prices. The barbecue is by far the most popular choice, with memorable spareribs marinated in a secret sauce. The best choice on the Asian menu is the
chicken with cashews, though the puddings and homemade ice creams steal the show
(Rp10,000 a scoop). On Monday nights, enjoy the live jazz/blues band from 7 till 10pm.

6   MANGGIS

Some of the best quality hotels on the east coast are around Manggis. The proximity to
Candidasa makes Manggis a good alternative to staying in that resort; hiking, cycling,
and the lovely Sidemen valley are only a short drive away.

EXPLORING MANGGIS

LEARN TO COOK   Learn Balinese basics at the Alila Resort with Chef Penny Williams.
This **cooking class** ★★ (www.alilahotels.com/manggis; US$85 for half-day, US$95
seafood school, other specialty packages available; peak season incurs additional surcharge; daily) offers visitors a hands-on introduction to Balinese and Indonesian cooking.
By the end each student makes, among other things, their own perfect wok-cooked *nasi
goreng*. Delicious? Well, that's the plan, anyway.

Hire a *jukung* (local fishing boat) from the Alila hotel and hook your own fish. Once
back on land you will learn to cook a variety of tasty seafood dishes, which include a local
fish and prawn curry or fish wrapped in banana leaves.

GET A MASSAGE   At the **Alila spa** (www.alilahotels.com/manggis; single treatment
US$30–US$80, packages US$25–US$125; AE, MC, V; daily 9am–9pm), the Balinese
traditional beauty recipes use local ingredients, such as indigenous plants, fruits, herbs,
and spices. The virgin coconut oil is sourced from the local villages. A signature treatment, the "Decleor Relax with frankincense resin," is superb for jet lag and costs a reasonable US$80 for 2 hours.

VISIT TENGANAN VILLAGE   About 3km (2 miles) inland from the main road just
south of Candidasa, is a traditional village inhabited by the Bali Aga people, Bali's original inhabitants who have lived here since well before the arrival of the Javanese. Their
culture is thought to date back to just before the Majapahit Empire (1294–1478). They
do not fraternize outside of their walled community and work and live in a communal
society. Do not be fooled by their basic living conditions, the community owns large
amounts of paddy fields that are leased to other farmers from nearby villages. With rice
prices at an ultimate high, Tenganan villagers are among the wealthiest on Bali.

Tenganan is also well known for its double *ikat* weaving better known as *kamben
gringsing*—one of only three or four places in the world who still retain this skill. The
others include various spots in Japan and Gujarat in India. Excellent samples can fetch
up to several thousand dollars; most heirloom pieces are not for sale at any price. Just
outside the walled village are a number of small shops selling a fabulous array of hand-
and machine-woven textiles and baskets. Visitors are welcome to enter the village on
payment of a small donation. The best time to visit is mid-year when very traditional
pre-Hindu festivities keep the village busy for weeks on end.

(Moments) Festivals in & Around Tenganan

Plenty of wonderful festivals take place within Tenganan and the surrounding villages. In fact, this region celebrates over 200 ceremonies annually. Go to **www.karangasemtourism.com** for details; dates vary year to year. The following two events happen during **Usaba Samah,** a month-long festival held during the fifth month of the Balinese calendar (May or June).

Maling-Malingan   Every country and society have their own way of dealing with thieves. Some cultures imprison thieves for their crimes; others use harsh punishment such as amputation. In Tenganan, they have *maling-malingan*.

Preparations start early in the morning with the village elders hanging pieces of meat and bones from the ceiling of the Bale Agung (great pavilion). At 9am, two young boys steal the meat and are chased by the community through the village. The thieves are dragged back to the Bale Agung to face their punishment: They are dressed in banana leaves, necklaces, and bracelets of meat and bones, and their faces and bodies are painted white and red. Once they are made up, the thieves are paraded around the village to their embarrassment. The moral of the story is that anyone who steals will not be welcome in the village.

Mekare Kare   The symbolic *Mekare Kare* is a warrior dance between two men, armed with two pieces of thorny pandanous leaves and a *tamiang,* a shield of plaited rattan. There is no jury just a select group of men who supervise the fight, called *tukang belas.* Both warriors agree not to hit the face of their opponent, and, although there is no punishment for breaking the agreements, most men endeavor not to, for fear of losing their reputation and social prestige. The duel has no time limit and the *tukang belas* will only stop the fight when they see any sign of anger on the competitors' faces. This is not a real game as there are no winners or losers. Instead, the emphasis is on the dancing techniques.

The whole event ends with a performance of the *abwang* dance by the bachelors and maidens of village of Subak Daha. At the end of the *Mekare Kare* is a *megibung,* a communal eating ritual, where the dancers/fighters eat together in the *wantilan* or public hall. The meal is intended to wash away any bad feeling produced by the fight.

WHERE TO STAY & DINE

The Alila Resort Manggis ★★   The Alila Resort is one of the best places to stay in the area. On a former coconut plantation by the sea, the resort's acres of sweeping green lawns are anchored by a huge swimming pool. Blocks of well-designed rooms stand back at the side. This hotel has so many activities and interesting excursions to offer, that you barely need to leave unless it is with one of their well-informed guides. The beach itself is mainly pebble but don't let that put you off. The food is knock-out and afternoon tea on the lawn is a great pleasure. The restaurant **Sea Salt** ★ (reservations recommended; main courses US$70, set menus start US$25; daily 7am–10:30pm) is set in a traditional Balinese pavilion. The Australian chef uses organic food, mostly from their own garden, and local ingredients to create fresh, modern interpretations of Balinese cuisine. Take for example the Balinese risotto, or the seared salmon with local sea salt and fragrant pounded *tabieun*—an indigenous sweet, slightly numbing long pepper. A highlight is the exotic ice creams, such as cardamom, Bali coffee, and ginger flower. They occasionally host live Balinese performances.

Buitan, Manggis. ✆ **0363/41011.** Fax 0363/41015. www.alilahotels.com. 55 units. Peak season US$205–US$455; high season US$190–US$420; low season US$155–US$350. AE, MC, V. **Amenities:** Restaurant; babysitting; concierge; outdoor pool; room service; spa; watersports. *In room:* A/C, TV, hair dryer, minibar.

Amankila ★★   There is a world of over-indulged travelers known as "Aman Junkies" who base their travels around Aman locations. If you happen to be one of them, then you already know about this place; otherwise, if you have the opportunity to stay here, read on.

Amankila is nestled on a huge hillside with luxurious private villas linked by raised walkways, all enjoying spectacular views of the Indian Ocean and Nusa Penida. The spacious rooms are designer-luxurious with wooden four-poster beds, extravagant fixtures and fittings, cushioned window seats, and private terraces. Bathrooms are ballroom size, some with sunken tubs. Some villas come with their own private pool; the awe-inspiring huge main pool cascades down three levels. Not surprisingly Amankila has one of the only good, white sand beaches in the vicinity. Their beach club has a nearly 45m (148-ft.) pool, daybeds, and a beautiful restaurant. The **Beach Club** (reservations recommended; main courses US$15–US$23, set menu US$110–US$150; daily 11am–10:30pm) has an extensive lunch menu of salads, sandwiches, wood-burning-oven pizza, fish and chips, and one of the best burgers on the island. Stay the afternoon for the fine assortment of traditional high tea.

Jl. Raya Manggis, Manggis. ✆ **0363/41333.** www.amankila.com 33 units. Year-round US$750 and up standard; US$1,150 and up suite. AE, DC, MC, V. **Amenities:** 3 restaurants; bar; babysitting; bicycles; concierge; gym; outdoor pool; room service; spa; watersports. *In room:* A/C, hair dryer, minibar, MP3 docking station, Wi-Fi.

Puri Bagus ★★   Puri Bagus is a short ride from the town center and a good compromise between Candidasa's ultraluxe options and the budget stops. Pretty and romantic, this hotel is the best in its class. Set on land jutting into the ocean, with steps leading right down to the beach, the good-size bungalows are airy and light, thanks to many large windows. Cool outdoor bathrooms have hand-held showers. The pool has a deep section for scuba practice, or turning somersaults, and a shallow area for kids. Dance programs and movies are offered at night, plus there's a full range of free daily activities and good dining seaside.

Manggis. ✆ **0363/41304.** Fax 0363/41290. www.manggis.puribagus.net. 26 units. High season US$75–US$80; low season US$55–US$60. AE, DC, MC, V. **Amenities:** 2 restaurants; 2 bars; bicycles; concierge; outdoor pool; room service; nearby tennis court; watersports. *In room:* A/C, fridge, minibar.

Villa Asada ★★   Part of a group of seven villas designed by Popo Danes, the famous locally trained Balinese architect, this four-bedroom villa, 10 minutes from Candidasa, overlooks Amuk Bay. Muted cream furnishings complement the large floor-to-ceiling glass windows and doors. With open-air sitting areas, the villa enjoys the cool breeze from the ocean.

Manggis, Candidasa. ✆ **0361/731074.** Fax 0361/736391. www.villaasada.com. Peak season US$650; high season US$600; low season US$550. AE, MC, V. Rates include breakfast; other meals market price. **Amenities:** Bar; outdoor pool; spa therapy; Wi-Fi. *In room:* A/C, hair dryer.

7 CANDIDASA

Candidasa was once the main tourist resort in the area and the last large resort before Amed. Now it serves mainly for scuba diving and snorkeling. The town itself is laid out along the seashore, although the golden sand beach that people once flocked to has been destroyed. The local unscrupulous developers blew up the reef to provide building materials for hotels for the tourists who came to visit the golden sand beaches. That's a fairly clear definition of irony. The beach is now a combination of sand, pebbles, or concrete buttresses *(groynes)*, which have been installed in an attempt to reclaim some of the golden sand. The beach is impassible at high tide.

The main road passes through the town and accommodation and restaurants are laid out along either side, although the best of both are not necessarily on the seaward side. You can tell that Candidasa was very popular at one point and while the area is trying to reclaim some of its former glory, it will take many years for the beach to recover—if indeed it does. When all's said and done, Candidasa does make a good base to explore this scenic and interesting region, given its central location.

GETTING THERE & GETTING AROUND

Hotels outside the town like the **Alila** and **Amankila** (see above) offer regular shuttles into town. Most hotels offer airport pickup for a fee and most restaurants and dive shops will offer free pickup and drop-off. Motorbike rental and *bemo* are also available. **Safari** (© 0363/41707), on the main road, is a reliable and friendly tourist agency with a selection of cars, jeeps, and motorbikes.

FAST FACTS The Candidasa **clinic,** on Jl. Raya Candidasa, can provide for basic medical needs. If your hotel has no Internet, a few shops on the main street do. **Happy's** (© 0363/41019) may have slow service, but charges are low—about Rp3,000 per hour. The **police station** is on the main road at the junction to the Rama Candidasa Hotel. The **Asri Shop,** on the main street, offers postal services.

EXPLORING CANDIDASA

Although Candidasa itself does not offer any decent snorkeling or diving, the sights of Padangbai and the islands of Gili Tepekong, Gili Mimpang, and Gili Biaha are a short 10-minute boat ride away. Otherwise, the diving at Amed and Tulamben are a short drive away. For **trekking,** there are plenty of paddy field walks around Candidasa, on the slopes of Mount Agung. If you are staying in the area, ask your hotel or villa to organize a trek with a local guide.

BEACHES The imaginatively named **White Sand Beach** ★★ is one of Bali's most beautiful beaches. But please, don't tell anyone about this place. It's a secret. The entrance to the beach road is well hidden between Candidasa and Amlapura. A kilometer or so after the hamlet of Bug Bug in the village of Peraci, a very small sign denotes **Pantai Pasir Putih.** Then a kilometer or two down a rickety track (although the road is improving), through some lush countryside of small villages and beautiful temples, brings you to a stand where you buy a ticket for Rp5,000. Nearly a kilometer of white sand is unmarred by hotels, though umbrellas and loungers are waiting for you. The waters are clear blue and the coconut palms provide shade. At the southern end, a line of fishing outriggers *(jukung)* prove that this is still a working beach but left to the devices of the tourists for the best part of the day. The fancy hotels on the east coast make special outings here for their guests complete with rather unnecessary picnic lunches and icy cold drinks. About a dozen simple thatched warungs offer visitors cold drinks, beer, and either freshly caught fish or river prawns, barbecued on coconut husk fires served with rice and vegetables or maybe a salad.

CHARLIE'S FACTORY ★★   Long-term American resident, surfer Charlie Wayan Jaya (✆ 08/1337012121; www.islandmystk.com), has created his own little organic empire within a coconut grove. Known in Japanese guide books as "Soapaman Charlie," with the nearby local secret surf break now "Soapaman Point," Charlie is becoming something of a tourist attraction in his own right. His bamboo factory creates fragrant organic soaps, virgin coconut oils, cocoa butter, and creams. His palm sugar syrup gives ice cream and pancakes a whole new meaning. Follow the road from Candidasa to Amlapura. About 7km (4 miles) later turn off at the sign to Jasri. Follow the bumpy road to Jasri beach, where you will see the factory, a large bamboo pyramid.

MASSAGE & SPA   The secluded dive destination **Alam Asmara** (see below; body massage Rp250,000–Rp350,000, scrub treatment Rp450,000–Rp800,000, ocean detox Rp350,000–Rp600,000; AE, DC, MC, V; daily 9am–9pm) is for people who want to seriously get away from the crowds and prefer a quiet place to indulge in diving. After your time in the water, head for the spa for a traditional massage using techniques from both Bali and Java.

At the **Jaya Spa** at the Puri Bagus Candidasa (single treatment Rp275,000–Rp350,000, package Rp550,000; AE, MC, V; daily 9am–9pm), the Royal Balinese treatment attempts to balance body, mind, and soul and leaves you totally relaxed.

SPEAR FISHING   If you love catching big fish like mackerel and tuna, then try your hand at spear fishing. Mr. Toron, a Balinese fisherman (contact him through **Bali Dives,** Denpasar; ✆ 0361/412981 or 08/123813994; www.balidives.com; US$250 per person including boat from Sanur, US$175 per person including car to Candidasa, but not boat), is a qualified spear fisher. He knows the water around Candidasa so well that he will guarantee that you find some fish—the question is whether or not you can spear them. Lunch will be a barbecue of your own freshly caught fish on one of the nearby beaches (remind them about the barbecue before you go as they have a tendency of forgetting small details). All transfers, lunch, drinks, boat, and guide costs are included.

WHERE TO STAY
Expensive
The three-bedroom **Villa Talia Vashti** ★, Jl. Raya Candidasa (✆ 08/11147350; www. taliavashti.com; peak season US$400, low season US$250; rates include breakfast; MC, V), on its own white sand beach with spectacular ocean views, is about as upmarket as it gets in this part of town.

Villa Sasoon, Jl. Puri Bagus (✆ 0363/41511; fax 0363/41911; www.villasasoon.com; four villas; peak season US$400, low season US$300; rates include breakfast, other meals market price; AE, MC, V), is hidden in a quiet part of Candidasa. Each villa has three pavilions surrounding its own private pool. Private kitchens allow guests to cook for themselves or for the on-call chef to come in and create special meals.

Moderate
Alam Asmara Dive Resort   This bungalow-style dive resort has an on-site dive shop. The darkish rooms are nicely furnished with outdoor bathrooms. The small pool and

restaurant patio look out to the sea. This is one of the best options on the sleepy Candidasa strip. Guests receive a complimentary 50-minute massage upon arrival.

Jl. Raya Candidasa, Candidasa. ✆ **0363/41929.** Fax 0363/42101. www.alamasmara.com. 12 units. Year-round US$95. AE, DC, MC, V. **Amenities:** Restaurant; bar; airport transfers; concierge; outdoor pool; room service; spa. *In room:* A/C, TV, hair dryer, minibar.

Rama Candidasa   This large, beachfront resort set in a tropical garden is a bit large for this area, but its amenities and activities make it a good choice. The large pool has plenty of sea-facing loungers and bales. Each of the pleasantly decorated rooms comes with an ocean view or veranda and Balinese antique-styled furniture and white linen. Of the activities on offer here, choose from Balinese dance lessons, cooking classes, trekking, or yoga. If that seems too hectic, check yourself into the hotel's spa and enjoy one of the amazing acupressure massages.

Jl. Raya Sengkidu, Karangasem. ✆ **0363/41974.** Fax 0363/41975. www.ramacandidasahotel.com. 72 units. Peak season US$170–US$335; high season US$160–US$325; low season US$135–US$300; extra bed US$30. AE, DC, MC, V. **Amenities:** Restaurant (see below); bar; outdoor pool; spa; watersports; Wi-Fi. *In room:* A/C, TV/DVD, minibar.

Watergarden ★★   The simple thatched bungalows of the Watergarden may not be spectacular, but they're plenty comfortable. Each has a wide veranda overlooking the lily ponds that give the hotel its name. The best and most private rooms are at the back and have their own charming water features. In-house dining at the Watergarden Café is some of the best in town. The place has a laid-back feel that draws lots of return guests and attracts many expat locals.

Jl. Raya Candidasa, Candidasa. ✆ **0363/41540.** Fax 0363/41164. www.watergardenhotel.com. 14 units. Year-round US$125–US$165 standard; US$320 villa. AE, MC, V. **Amenities:** Restaurant; bar; airport transfer; small outdoor pool. *In room:* A/C (in some), TV, minibar, Wi-Fi.

Inexpensive

Dewa Bharata   On the north end of the main road in Candidasa, this is your typical good, basic beachside accommodation.

Jl. Raya Candidasa, Candidasa. ✆ **0363/41090.** Fax 0363/41091. www.dewabharatahotels.com. 20 units. Peak season US$26–US$36; high season US$23–US$33; low season US$20–US$30; extra bed US$5. Rates include breakfast. No credit cards. **Amenities:** Restaurant; outdoor pool. *In room:* A/C, fan, TV.

WHERE TO DINE

Vincent's (✆ **0363/41368;** www.vincentsbali.com; main courses US$6–US$11; MC, V; daily 10:30am–midnight), on the main road almost opposite the lotus lagoon, on the inland side, serves Indonesian and Western food alongside an extensive wine list and good cocktails. The large street-facing lounge area has an inviting ambience. The rear garden is great on hot summer nights.

The menu at **Garpu Restaurant,** in the Rama Candidasa Resort & Spa (reservations recommended; main courses US$15–US$30, set menu US$15–US$30; AE, DC, MC, V; daily 7am–11pm), has mainly Mediterranean and Balinese delights. Spaghetti marinara is served with an abundance of shellfish in a rich tomato sauce. You'll be tempted at dessert by their pudding, or you may simply be tempted by their cocktail list. There is a live Balinese performance every Saturday night.

8 AMLAPURA

The sprawling town of Amlapura does not have a lot to interest the tourist, although it does have a bustling marketplace. The main attractions are the three palaces, faded remnants of what was once Bali's richest and most powerful kingdom.

GETTING THERE

The best way to get here is by car and driver but there are plenty of **bemo** and **public buses** from Batubulan bus station in Denpasar to Singaraja stopping at Padangbai, Candidasa, and Gianyar en route. The bus station for Singaraja and Tirta Gangga is on the corner of Jalan Sudirman and Jalan Untung Surapati. These will cost between Rp10,000 and Rp15,000 one way. Allow about 3 hours to get here from Denpasar.

FAST FACTS   The city **hospital** is on Jalan Ngurah Rai. **Hardy's,** on Jl. Diponegoro, although a large supermarket, does not have the same assortment of Western foods as in other Hardy's in the south. There is no alcohol or beer on sale. An **apotek** is on Jalan Ngurah Rai 47. The **post office** is on Jalan Gatot Subroto.

EXPLORING AMLAPURA

The neighboring villages of **Asak, Bungaya, Subagan,** and **Timbrah,** on the road to Amlapura coming from the south, are traditional villages resembling the archaic Bali Aga village of Tenganan (p. 257). Although not as good as Tenganan, they are worth a visit especially during festival time. Watch out in June or July for the exquisite *rejang* dance performed by unmarried girls, and the *abung,* preformed by unmarried men.

West of Amlapura is **Budakeling,** known for its Buddhist Brahmin priests, whose lineage dates back to the 15th century. It is also known for the inscribers of Sanskrit *lontar* manuscripts and traditional silver and gold artisans. This is a great place to look at the work of the silversmiths who are a lot less pushy than those in Celuk (near Ubud).

The stunning scenery around Budakeling is worthy of an early morning trek. From the Lempuyang hills, you can enjoy the sights of the misty village hamlets, lush green hills, and the cool bamboo forests as the sun rises. Climb the Puncak Sari hill and get a bird's-eye view of Budakeling from the top. Bring a guide from your hotel.

Pura Lempuyang   This is one of Bali's *sad kahyangan,* six temples of the heavens. Located on the slopes of the often misty Gunung Lempuyang it sits at the top of 1,700 steps that wind their way through lavish jungle. As you ascend, the temperature drops. Views are generally awe inspiring; early morning is the best time to visit. The faithful visit Lempuyang to ask for blessings, solve domestic problems, cure sickness, or even to gain power. The major festival in Lempuyang is held every 6 months on the Thursday after Galungan (every 210 days). During the rainy season the mountain is at its most majestic, but the stone steps can be slippery.

The signposted road to Lempuyang heads off from the main road a few kilometers past Tirta Gangga. No phone. Admission by donation. Daily 24 hr.

Puri Agung Karangasem   These charming palaces display a mix of European and Balinese architecture, and a wealth of mythological creatures and figures. You can easily observe the colonial influence with its all faded grandeur. Parts of the eclectic architecture are decorated with carved *wayang* figures and others with Dutch finery. You'll see portraits of royal personages, including the last Rajah Anak Agung Gede Putu whose mesmerizing eyes make it easy to believe he was the proud husband of nine wives and father to countless children. The rajahs certainly knew how to live well. Some members of the royal family still live here.

Jl. Teuku Umar. No phone. Admission Rp10,000. Daily 8am–6pm.

Taman Tirta Gangga   Tirta Gangga, "holy water of the Ganges," was built in 1948 by the same rajah as the Taman Ujung with more opulence and certainly more success. It is believed that after a tour of the Palace of Versailles, near Paris, I Gusti Bagus Jelantik was so inspired by the architecture and fountains that he decided to build a second water palace. He wanted this water palace to be greater and more ornate than Taman Ujung. Sadly both water palaces were damaged by the 1963 eruption of Gunung Agung. But you can still enjoy the swimming pools and ornamental ponds where the last rajah bathed. The cool spring waters make it a pleasant place to linger for a few hours—though never on a Sunday, when it fills with local Balinese coming to relax or to flirt with their intendeds.

The area surrounding Tirta Gangga has acres of emerald *sawah* (rice) glittering on perfectly formed terraces making for some great trekking. If you are staying locally, ask your hotel or villa to hook you up with a local guide. Otherwise, ask the ticket office at Tirta Gangga if they can find you a guide. Expect to pay about Rp100,000 for a 4-hour trek for two people.

Tirta Gangga. No phone. Admission adult Rp5,000. Daily 6am–6pm.

Taman Ujung Water Palace   Known as Taman Soekasada Ujung by the Balinese, this was once a private retreat of I Gusti Bagus Jelantik, Karengasem's last rajah. The Taman Ujung Water Palace was built in 1919 and almost destroyed when Gunung Agung erupted in 1963. The palace was further damaged by the earthquake of 1979. Much of it was renovated in 2004 with little sympathy, but you can still see the remnants of the main pool and admire the views from higher up the hill.

Taman Ujung is sometimes the venue for upscale dinners when flickering candlelight and lavish table settings lend it a softer and more romantic atmosphere, evocative of earlier times. There are also classic Balinese dance performances and occasionally ceremonies.

Jl. Diponegoro. ✆ **0363/21383.** Admission adults Rp10,000. Daily 8am–6pm.

WHERE TO STAY

Although the palaces are worth a look there is nothing in the way of suitable accommodation in the center of Amalpura. The nearest accommodations can be found near Tirta Gangga, a few kilometers from Amlapura.

The one-bedroom **Villa Tirta Ayu** (Beautiful Spring) and two-bedroom **Villa Djamrud** (Emerald; Tirta Gangga Water Palace Villas, Desa Tirta Gangga, Amlapura; ✆ **0363/ 21383;** fax 0363/21383; www.tirtagangga-villas.com; Tirta Ayu year-round US$350–US$400; Djamrud year-round US$120–US$250; rates include breakfast; payment online) overlook the beautiful Water Palace.

Stay the night on top of a hill in the **Puri Sawah Villas,** Tirta Gangga, Karangasem (✆ **0363/21847;** four units; high season Rp200,000–Rp250,000, low season Rp150,000–Rp200,000; rates include breakfast; no credit cards), a fairly basic but pleasant place with beautiful views of the surrounding paddy fields.

Seraya Shores ★   About 6km (3¾ miles) from Amlapura, just past the Ujung Water Palace, is the cozy resort of Seraya Shores. In an old coconut plantation, the resort looks over a delightful stretch of black sand shore. The restaurant is the best value spot in the

area—another luxury. The "no menu" policy allows Chef Sasa to offer only the freshest **265**
ingredients—local market produce, organic vegetables, fresh caught fish, and sometimes,
lobster and fresh river prawns in an Indo-Euro fusion. The well-trained staff are proud
of their English skills taught by the boss, Amanda. She also organizes dive trips and
picnics to Pantai Pasir Putih (p. 260) and a fabulous drive to Amed and back through
Tirta Gangga.

Dusun Merajan, Seraya Barat. ✆ **08/1338416572.** www.serayashores.com. 7 units. High season US$80–
US$165; low season US$65–US$150; extra bed US$10. No credit cards. **Amenities:** Restaurant; bar; babysitting; outdoor pool. *In room:* Fan.

9 AMED

Amed is the generic name given to a string of villages that line the coast on Bali's northeast corner. The main north-south road roller-coasters through the fishing hamlets of
Amed, Jemeluk, Bunutan, Bangli, and Lipah and on to Banyuning and Aas, before reaching Seraya and back to Amlapura. Along the way, it passes magnificent landscapes of lofty
mountains and curving bays of crystal tourmaline waters. The pebble beaches are lined
with *jukung,* brightly painted fishing outriggers. Each morning around 7am, a spectacular sight awaits early risers, as the fishing *jukung* return, sometimes laden with catches of
baby mackerel.

Amed remained a backwater for many years, the home of hill farmers, salt makers, and
fishermen. The lack of development has become its greatest asset, as it has retained the
charm and ambience of old Bali known to only a lucky few. Now the secret is out and
small luxury hotels and villas are appearing with increasing regularity.

Amed enjoys a Mediterranean climate with two very distinct seasons. Several months
of the year are green and misty, while the other months have no rain at all and the dry
vegetation turns to gold.

GETTING THERE

If coming from the south it is easy enough to hire a car and driver for either a drop-off
or to escort you for several days. From the airport to Amed costs around Rp350,000. It
is easy to hire a motorbike or car and driver in Amed and while there are no car agencies,
drivers with cars available for day trips are easy to find.

EXPLORING AMED

You can enjoy numerous scenic and very hilly walks around Amed, which is especially
beautiful during the rainy season (Nov–Apr) when the temperature is cooler and the hills
are green and misty—a sight difficult to imagine during the hot dry months. A local
guide from your hotel is all you need to take you into the hills.

BIKING TO PASIR PUTIH   You can bike from Amed to Pantai Pasir Putih (p. 260). A
car takes guests from their hotel to one of several starting points off the main road; it is
a mainly downhill ride to the beach that follows back roads through luscious rural areas,
rarely visited by Westerners. The trip takes about 2 hours before arriving at the beach.
Cars transport guests back to their hotel. For information and bookings call **Ketut Surya**
(✆ **08/5238231850**) or **Komang Bajing** (✆ **08/124667752**).

SAILING TO THE LOMBOK GILIS IN A JUKUNG   Follow in the revered footsteps of
Victorian-era naturalist Alfred Russel Wallace and sail to Lombok (chapter 15) and the

Gili Islands (chapter 16) in a *jukung* (a local fishing boat) for a memorable, if somewhat uncomfortable, 3-hour ride (Rp350,000–Rp400,000) across the very deep Lombok Strait. By the time you read this, there should be a new traditional sailboat, complete with food and mojitos, to take guests across. You can ask Kim at Anda Amed about the new boat (🕿 **08/174737861**).

SCUBA DIVING & SNORKELING   Amed is one of Bali's top dive areas and the small bays provide many good snorkeling locations with shallow waters and few currents. Snorkeling gear is available through the dive operators. One of the best dive operators is **Euro Dive,** Lipah (🕿 **0363/23605;** fax 0363/23605), with PADI certified guides specializing in the dive sites in and around Amed as well as Tulamben, just 20 minutes away. If you're in south Bali and you want to take a diving excursion to this part of the island, contact **AquaMarine Diving,** Jl. Raya Petitenget 2A, Seminyak (🕿 **0361/738020;** fax 0361/738021; www.aquamarinediving.com; US$85).

While the marine fish life here is superb, some coral bleaching occurred in 1998 thanks to the El Niño, and although the reef is recovering, we cannot yet tell when it will reach its former glory. Conditions here, from shore or boat, are easy, with good visibility.

Amed Reef, with many different kinds of sponges and gorgonians, is home to everything from lobsters, shrimp, and goby sets to blue-spotted rays and schools of barracuda. White-tip reef sharks, Napoleon wrasse, big trevally, and large schools of bannerfish, snapper, and fusilier can be found at **Amed Wall.** The deep slope after the wall is rich in invertebrates with crinoids and commensals. **Lipah Bay,** a small black sand bay, is home to a 20m (66-ft.) steel freighter wreck encrusted with sponges, gorgonians, and coral bushes and inhabited by clouds of anthias, and parrotfish and angelfish. The deeper slope is dotted with sea fans. **Gili Selang** on Bali's eastern point can, like all exposed sites, have ripping currents and is therefore a site for experienced divers only. You may encounter white-tip reef sharks, Napoleon wrasse, turtles, and dolphins, along with low-lying, healthy corals with many moray eels, schools of fish, nudis, and pygmy seahorses. **Amed Ghost Bay** is good for muck-diving: Mimic octopus and Wonderpus, frogfishes, Ornate and Robust ghostpipefish, stonefish—we're never sure quite what we'll find there.

WHERE TO STAY

Despite its size, the **Bayu Cottages Hotel and Restaurant,** Jl. Raya Pantai Amed, Lipah (🕿 **0363/23495;** www.bayucottages.com; six units; high season US$42, low season US$34; MC, V), boutique hotel has plenty of facilities. Looking over the beach in Lipah, it has a pleasant saltwater pool and an open-air sea-view restaurant. Rooms have hot water, air-conditioning, and satellite TV.

The **Santai Hotel,** Bunutan, Amed (🕿 **0363/23487;** fax 0363/23585; www.santai bali.com; 10 units; high season US$70–US$115, low season US$50–US$90; additional person US$10, kids 11 and under US$6; rates include breakfast; MC, V), is a small older resort of 10 rooms squeezed in by the beach with a big tropical garden, a good restaurant (see below), and a large swimming pool.

Blue Moon Villa ★   British owned, and run by the ever-efficient Komang John, this small resort commands views across the bays. The rooms have big beds and filmy mosquito nets. Hot and cold water is readily available. The airy open dining room is surrounded with gardens, though some prefer to use the bales with low tables and cushions. The menu has daily specials, offering plenty of fresh fish and an eclectic mix of Indonesian and Western dishes.

Selang Beach, Amed. ℂ **0363/21428.** www.bluemoonvilla.com. 9 units. Year-round US$60–US$95 standard; US$95–US$145 suite; US$72–US$380 villa; kids under 12 US$10. MC, V. **Amenities:** Restaurant; bar; babysitting; bicycles; 2 outdoor pools; room service; spa therapy; watersports. *In room:* A/C, minibar.

Dancing Dragon Cottage ★ (Finds)

Billed as a feng shui resort, the cottages here are bright, clean, and pleasant with balconies looking out to sea. The pool and open dining room are also oriented to the sea. Elements of feng shui have been incorporated into the harmonious design by internationally recognized specialist and author Karen Kingston. She also occasionally runs international feng shui and space clearing seminars incorporating Balinese and Chinese practices here.

Amed. ℂ **0363/23521.** www.dancingdragoncottages.com. 10 units. High season US$108; low season US$96. AE, MC, V. **Amenities:** Restaurant; bar; outdoor pool; room service; Wi-Fi. *In room:* A/C, hair dryer, minibar.

The Golden Rock

Situated on a rocky knoll overlooking the sea in Aas, this lovely place is a specialized detox and cleansing retreat. Guests can check in for 4, 7, or 10 days and spend time cleansing and healing their mind, body, and spirit. The Rock offers yoga and *qigong* as well as a range of interesting sophisticated equipment designed to help guests regain their equilibrium.

Aas. No phone. www.theretreatbali.com. 4 units. Year-round 4-day €560 single, €490 shared; 7-day €905 single, €790 shared; 10-day €1,250 single, €1,050 shared. **Amenities:** Restaurant; outdoor pool; sauna and infrared sauna. *In room:* A/C, TV.

Life in Amed

This villa resort on the beach towards the southern end of the Amed strip of villages at Lean has good, if basic, facilities. Some offer both upstairs and downstairs bedrooms, making them ideal for families. Their cozy open dining area has some of the best food in Amed. The two beach bungalows require advance booking.

Lean. ℂ **0363/23152.** www.lifebali.com. 8 units. High season US$75–US$145; low season US$55–US$120. AE, MC, V. **Amenities:** Restaurant; babysitting; Internet; outdoor pool; room service; spa; watersports. *In room:* A/C, TV/DVD, hair dryer, minibar, movie library.

Inexpensive

Wawa Wewe II

Cheap and cheerful, this resort is popular with French and American tourists as well as local expats. It is often fully booked, especially during July and August. Some of the rooms look out to the sea and many have an upper mezzanine floor. Open-air bathrooms have hot and cold water. The Buddha-shaped pool is the focus of activity. The friendly staff is eager to help and can find you a motorbike to hire or may even offer to accompany you to a local village ceremony or take you sightseeing.

Lipah. ℂ **0363/23522.** 10 units. High season US$35; low season US$25. Rates include breakfast. No credit cards. **Amenities:** Restaurant; outdoor pool. *In room:* A/C, fan.

Good Karma

As a stylish, tropical paradise of bamboo huts, this rustic place is very popular with many guests who return year after year. Each of the 15 rooms look straight on to the beach, and being fan-cooled and having only cold-water showers doesn't seem to deter the guests' enthusiasm. The rooms furthest from the main building are the most private and popular. The small restaurant offers local and European dishes and some Japanese. Their seafood fried rice is worth a visit.

Jl. Culik, Amed. No phone. 18 units. Year-round US$15–US$30. No credit cards. Rates include breakfast. **Amenities:** Restaurant. *In room:* Fan.

The **Anda Amed Resort** (reservations recommended; sandwiches and wraps US$4–US$5, main courses US$4–US$8; MC, V; daily 7am–10pm) dining room looks out to sea and has a Mediterranean-inspired menu together with lots of local favorites. Their white gazpacho and salads are particularly good.

The restaurant at Blue Moon Villa, **Komang John Café** ★ (see above; reservations recommended; main courses US$5–US$10, set menu US$6–US$8; MC, V; daily 7:30am–10:30pm) attracts plenty of outside guests and has a fresh and eclectic menu. Their seared fresh tuna salad is exceptional as is their chocolate pudding cake. They have a good bar with cocktails, spirits, and wines. Most nights you'll catch Komang John and friends in the midst of a good old fashioned guitar jam session.

The tiny dining area of the **Life in Amed** (see above; main courses start at US$4; AE, MC, V; daily 7am–11pm) offers some of the best food in the area. Their arugula salad with toasted pine nuts, feta cheese, and beetroot is especially good. Live Balinese traditional music and dances can be arranged upon request.

Arguably Amed's best restaurant, **Sails**, Jl. Raya Lean, Lean (© **0363/22006;** reservations recommended during high season; main courses US$4–US$10; no credit cards; daily 11am–11pm), has fresh fish, New Zealand lamb chops, steak, very good mashed potatoes, and well-prepared local dishes.

The **Santai,** Bunutan (© **0363/23487;** www.santaibali.com; reservations recommended; main courses US$6–US$15; MC, V; daily 7am–11pm), is a long-established small resort in Jemeluk and one of the few places that has a foreign chef—from Norway no less. The menu features local grilled fish and Indonesian dishes. They also offer good espresso coffee and an impressive bar selection and wine list.

In the middle of Lipah, **Warung Kadek** (© **08/5237997885;** main courses Rp10,000–Rp60,000; no credit cards; daily 8am–9pm) offers consistently good local food and some Chinese dishes. Their sweet and sour pork is worth a visit. Juices, drinks, and cold beer are readily available.

10 TULAMBEN

This small village on the northeast coast has become a center for divers. Its raison d'être is the wreck of the Liberty, a U.S. Army supply ship that was attacked by a Japanese submarine during WWII. The dive is an easy walk-in off the beach about 25m (82 ft.) from the shore. Its deepest point is about 30m (98 ft.) and the shallowest about 5m (16 ft.). It is suitable for all levels of certification and experience. Some people stay in town, or drive from Amed or Kuta. Infrequent public minibuses to Singaraja and Amlapura are available but because the area is now focused more on tourism, these services tend to be unreliable. Hire a car and driver either on the street or through your hotel.

 Tips **Avoid the Underwater Crowds**

Because many PADI companies are now organizing day trips to Tulamben from the south, the dive sites are overcrowded after 11am. To avoid the crowds, plan to stay overnight and dive early in the morning or late in the afternoon.

EAST BALI

12

TULAMBEN

(Finds) Another Shipwreck

Both divers and snorkelers will find the **Japanese shipwreck** off Banyuning worth a visit. It is possible to wobble in from the rocky beach or hire a local fishing boat and enter the water that way. Under the trees on the beach, a small warung serves cold drinks, beer, juice, and decent local food. You can hire snorkeling gear from your hotel or from the outfitters on the beach in front of the shipwreck.

FAST FACTS   As yet, Tulamben has no ATMs, banks, money changers, Internet cafes, emergency services, or basically anything at all. The hotels and homestays usually provide shuttle services or arrange transport and sometimes Internet access.

SCUBA DIVING

Most resorts in Tulamben and on the northeast coast run their own boats and PADI operations. The best dives are early morning or night dives during the full moon.

Being on Bali's northeast coast, Tulamben Bay receives very plankton-rich waters from the Indonesian Throughflow (the major ocean current that moves from the Pacific to the Indian Ocean). This, coupled with the different physical environments found in the area, means the bay contains a stunningly diverse underwater ecosystem.

The 120m (394-ft.) U.S. Army Transport **Liberty shipwreck** ★★ lies 20m (66 ft.) offshore and offers an extraordinary density of marine life, including a huge school of big-eyed trevally, bumphead parrotfish, leaf scorpionfish, and pygmy seahorses. If you go night-diving, look out for the flashlightfish, Spanish dancers, and cephalopods.

Both the **Coral Garden** (which runs eastward from the Liberty shipwreck) and the upper area of the **Wall/Drop-off** (at the eastern end of the bay) provide wonderfully shallow dives where you're limited by air supply rather than bottom time, and yield an incredible variety of marine life from Thecacera nudis to boxer crabs to frogfish and ribbon eels in all stages of development. Deeper on the Wall/Drop-off are reef sharks, sponges, and gorgonian fans (one of 3m/10 ft. diameter), and occasional sightings of whale sharks and Mola-Mola.

Slightly north of Tulamben is **Kubu,** where conditions always seem to be calm. Here you'll also sight plentiful gorgonians, bommies with beautiful soft corals, and scores of nudis. Five minutes eastward by outrigger, **Batu Kelebit** is where you are most likely to see pelagics including—on rare occasions—dolphins. Further east, **Batu Niti** has the area's most pristine corals.

Due to the beach entry, Tulamben is also great for **snorkeling** and for the 1-day introduction to diving offered by some dive companies (although you need booties and open-heeled fins, not full-foot fins for walking on the rocky beach).

Contact **Scuba Seraya Dive,** 5 minutes south of Tulamben Bay in the Scuba Seraya Resort (p. 270; ✆ **0361/283922;** fax 0361/281347; www.scubaseraya.com; two shore dives US$75, three shore dives US$90 per person). If you're coming from the south, contact **AquaMarine Diving** ★★★, Jl. Raya Petitenget 2A, Seminyak (✆ **0361/738020;** fax 0361/738021; www.aquamarinediving.com; US$75 in Tulamben, US$85 outside Tulamben per person).

EAST BALI

12

TULAMBEN

Many more divers and tourists are coming to the northeast coast, so some warungs and would-be restaurants are springing up along the main road, but the quality and selection on offer is not convincing. Guests dine in their hotels.

Alam Batu Beach Bungalow Resort   Favored mainly by German guests, the Alam Batu has a dining area built onto a rocky promontory, pleasant gardens, and a pool. The four air-conditioned and six fan bungalows are rather dingy but have airy open bathrooms. The garden spa offers a small selection of treatments. Evening meals are communal buffets with Balinese and European dishes for Rp150,000.

Jl. Batu Pemasuh, Batu Ringgit, Kubu. ✆ **0363/23324.** www.alambatu.de. 12 units. High season US$112–US$123; boat show season (Jan–Mar) US$100–US$112. MC, V. **Amenities:** Restaurant; lounge; Internet; outdoor pool; spa; watersports. *In room:* A/C (in some), fan, minibar.

Batu Belah ★ (Finds)   At the eastern end of the village, Batu Belah is a tiny but pristine homestay with a lovely pool and restaurant, built into the rocks above the sea.

Sekar Karang, Tulamben. ✆ **08/179755214.** www.eastbaliresort.com. 4 units. Year-round US$63. Rates include breakfast. No credit cards. **Amenities:** Restaurant; outdoor pool. *In room:* A/C, fan, TV, fridge.

Mimpi Resort   This was the first resort in the area and caters mostly to German divers. The beachfront restaurant and pool area are surrounded by bougainvillea. The Ocean View rooms are the best choice but rates are rather expensive for the accommodation offered.

Tulamben. ✆ **0362/94497.** www.mimpi.com. 54 units. High season US$125–US$325; low season US$100–US$300. AE, DC, MC, V. **Amenities:** Restaurant; bar; babysitting; bicycles; concierge; Internet; outdoor pool; room service; spa; watersports. *In room:* A/C, TV (in some), hair dryer, minibar.

Scuba Seraya Resort ★   This lovely small resort with a peaceful stretch of beachfront is preferred by many world-famous underwater photographers. The eight air-conditioned cottages and four private villas (each with kitchenette, outside tub, and cushioned outside sitting area) overlooking the ocean, are built in spacious, well-tended gardens. The restaurant serves a good choice of simple, tasty international and local food all day. On-site is one of the area's best scuba-diving shops.

Tulamben. ✆ **0361/283922.** www.scubaseraya.com. 12 units. High season US$100 standard, US$190 villa; low season US$85 standard, US$175 villa. MC, V. **Amenities:** Restaurant; outdoor pool; room service; spa; watersports. *In room:* A/C, hair dryer, kitchenette.

Siddhartha Resort   A little further to the west, this brand-new resort will definitely be the best resort on the northeast coast. With 30 tastefully decorated rooms in three different price ranges and two oceanfront "dream villas," there is something to suit every budget. The resort has a 1,500 sq. m (16,145 sq. ft.) spa and a state-of-the-art PADI diving school. The restaurant serves international and Balinese dishes.

Kubu, Karangansem. No phone. www.siddhartha-bali.com. 32 units. Year-round €55–€120. Rates include breakfast. DC, V. **Amenities:** Gym; outdoor pool; room service; spa. *In room:* A/C, fan, TV/DVD (in some), minibar, pool (in villas).

Tauch Terminal Resort and Spa   This is a budget beachfront resort with bungalows and air-conditioned rooms, pool, bar, restaurant, shop, and spa. Permanently booked solid, this is not a resort for anyone who likes privacy but a must for those who prefer safety in numbers and spend most of their holiday underwater.

Banjar Kubu Village. ✆ **0361/774504.** www.tulamben.com. 24 units. Year-round US$76–US$166. AE, MC, V. **Amenities:** Restaurant; bar; babysitting; concierge; outdoor pool; room service; spa; Wi-Fi. *In room:* A/C, hair dryer, minibar.

North Bali

The North is, for most visitors to Bali, the world on the other side of the mountains. It's the wild and open side of Bali that has been the least touched by recent tourism. The majority of tourism here is contained, mercifully, to the flat lands west of Lovina. The irony is that the regency of Buleleng is central to Bali's colonial history and hosted the old capital, the port of Singaraja, the major trading post for the Dutch, Chinese, and Arabs, and the disembarkation point for generations of visitors.

1 GETTING THERE & GETTING AROUND

There is virtually no taxi service in the north. *Bemo* use Singaraja as a hub, but aren't useful for getting to small, secluded villages. Visitors rely on hired cars and drivers from the south.

You have several options for approaching north Bali. From the **south,** the obvious route is to take the main road from Denpasar, pass Lake Bratan, towards Singaraja. The road passes through hillside terraces of vegetables and fruits climbing to about 1,200m (3,937 ft.). The **east** route approaches via Tulamben or past Mount Batur. The last route, by the **west** tends to be congested with lorries ferrying workers on their way around Bali or back to Java. However if you turn off the main western road at Antosari, this will take you through the foothills of Mount Batukaru, through stunning picturesque paddy fields up through Pupuan, best known for its coffee and clove plantations.

2 TEMBOK, SEMBIRENTENG & TEJAKULA

Coming from the east and leaving Amed behind, between Kubu and Tembok the scenery changes dramatically. The dark lava stone and cactus landscape gives way to lush fruit plantations and steep hills with waterfalls. On your drive, visit the unusual pillared horse baths in the center of **Tejakula,** a village famous throughout Bali for silver crafts, unique dance performances, and *wayang wong* mask dances.

EXPLORING NEAR TEMBOK, SEMBIRENTENG & TEJAKULA

Set on the hillside overlooking the ocean, **Puri Bagus Ponjok Batu,** Jl. Raya Singaraga, Tejakula (© **0362/21430;** www.bagus-agro.com; set menu Rp65,000 or Rp75,000; cooking classes US$40; treks US$40), is a farm of 5 hectares (12 acres) that organizes simple, tasty Indonesian set lunches served in a gazebo. Cooking classes can be arranged with 2 days notice and they also undertake treks from Sembiran up to their farm, through palm plantations and over lava rock slopes. Stopping en route you can see how coconut oil is made and *arak* produced.

NORTH BALI

13

TEMBOK, SEMBIRENTENG & TEJAKULA

BALI SEA

Banyuwedang
Pejarakan
Pemuteran
Banyupoh
Pondok Sari Beach
Musi
Sanggalangit
Gerokgak
Gg. Sanglang
Gg. Musi
Celukan Bawang
Penulon
Pangkungparuk
Gg. Patas
Seririt
Banjar
Busungbui

Gilimanuk
Singaraja
North Bali
Negara   BALI
Ubud
Denpasar
INDIAN OCEAN
Nusa Penida

ATTRACTIONS ●

Atlas North Bali Pearls **5**
Banjar Air Panas **8**
Biorock Project **1**
Buddhist Wihara temple **9**
Dutch bridge **21**
Gedong Kirtya & Puri Kawan **18**
Jagaraga **29**
Klenteng Ling Gwan Kiong
  Chinese Temple **17**
Old Harbour **21**

Pura Agung Pulaki **5**
Pura Beji **23**
Pura Dalem **24**
Pura Kerta Kawat **6**
Pura Maduwe Karang **25**
Pura Melanting **6**
Pura Pabean **5**
Pura Pondok Batu **32**
Pura Puncak Manik **6**
Pura Tirta **5**
Puri Bagus Ponjok Batu **31**

Puri Kanginan Palace **20**
Reef Seen Aquatics &
  Turtle Hatchery **3**
Sawan **28**
Sudaji **27**
Suwug **26**

ACCOMMODATIONS ■

Adi Assri Resort **4**
Alam Anda **34**
Amertha Bali Villas **4**

This part of Bali is home to some of the oldest Bali Aga villages, settlements that were not influenced by the customs brought to Bali from the Javanese courts. Some of these settlements were originally ancient trading posts with India, China, and beyond as long ago as the 1st century A.D.

LES   This small village in the hills has one of the highest waterfalls in Bali, a 30m (98-ft.) cascade with a cool bathing pool called **Yeh Mampeh.** Just follow the sign to Les on the road after Tejakula and dip your toes in the cool pool.

SEMBIRAN & JULAH   From Pacung, take the steep, winding road up to **Sembiran,** an ancient Bali Aga village with lovely sea views. Ancient traditions—religious, social,

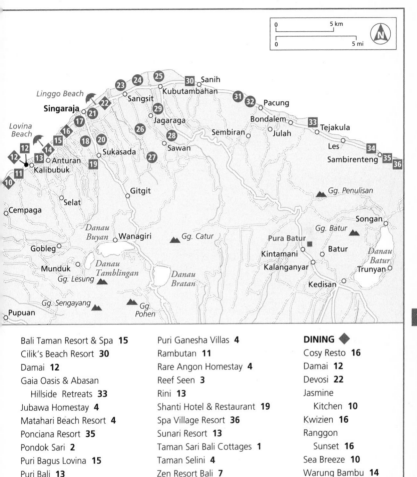

	0	5 km
	0	5 mi

		DINING ◆
Bali Taman Resort & Spa **15**	Puri Ganesha Villas **4**	Cosy Resto **16**
Cilik's Beach Resort **30**	Rambutan **11**	Damai **12**
Damai **12**	Rare Angon Homestay **4**	Devosi **22**
Gaia Oasis & Abasan	Reef Seen **3**	Jasmine
Hillside Retreats **33**	Rini **13**	Kitchen **10**
Jubawa Homestay **4**	Shanti Hotel & Restaurant **19**	Kwizien **16**
Matahari Beach Resort **4**	Spa Village Resort **36**	Ranggon
Ponciana Resort **35**	Sunari Resort **13**	Sunset **16**
Pondok Sari **2**	Taman Sari Bali Cottages **1**	Sea Breeze **10**
Puri Bagus Lovina **15**	Taman Selini **4**	Warung Bambu **14**
Puri Bali **13**	Zen Resort Bali **7**	

and architectural—are kept alive here and most of the village temples are built with round megalithic stones. Enjoy a coffee with the locals or go to one of the small village warungs. They speak their own dialect of Balinese here, and the entry and exit signs wishing you "Welcome" and "Goodbye" are in Balinese rather than the usual Indonesian. The nearby village of **Julah** is one of Bali's oldest. Look out for the giant *kemit* tree, where corpses were laid out in ancient times. There is also a large Pura Dalem (Temple of the Dead) of black local stone at the foot of the village.

PURA PONDOK BATU   This imposing temple has recently been renovated in true north Bali style. Rebuilt entirely out of the dark, austere lava stone readily available in

(**Finds**) **Bebali Weaving in Pacung**

Supported by donations and with a great deal of dedication, **Nyoman Sarmika** of Surya Indigo, keeps the ancient tradition of *bebali* weaving on back strap looms alive. Using purely natural dyes, these simple but extremely beautiful cloths said to have magical properties have been used for rites of passage in Bali for generations. Visit his small shop ((**C**) **08/123626535**) on the main road in Pacung (Tejakula, Buleleng, 20km/12 miles east of Singaraja) and chat with him about the area, too.

the north on a promontory overlooking the Bali Sea, this is one of the important temples founded by Danghyang Nirartha, the priest who came from Java in the 16th century. It is said that he performed miracles on this site.

WHERE TO STAY & DINE

Very Expensive

Spa Village Resort This heavenly destination beachside spa resort, a member of Small Luxury Hotels of the World, oozes peacefulness and calm. Their individually tailored "discovery paths" are dedicated to healing, rejuvenation, wellness, and spirituality, all with Balinese origins or using traditional techniques. Weekly programs incorporate specific dietary regimens and even training in traditional Balinese massage. All dietary needs are catered to and an extensive healthy and locally sourced menu is available to supplement your good work.

Jl. Singaraja-Amlapura 100, Desa Tembok, Tejakula-Buleleng. (**C**) **03/2783-1000** in Malaysia. Fax 0321/487397. www.spavillage.com. 31 units. Year-round US$400–US$680. Rates include meals, coffee, and tea. AE, DC, MC, V. **Amenities:** Restaurant; bar; lounge; bicycles; concierge; gym; outdoor pool; room service; spa; watersports; Wi-Fi. *In room:* A/C, TV/DVD (villa only), hair dryer, minibar, MP3 docking station.

Expensive

Alam Anda ★ (**Value**) This long-established Mediterranean-style dive resort has over 400m (1,312 ft.) of beachfront and is simple luxury at its finest. Guests choose between comfortable bungalows with air-conditioning, open bathrooms, and sea or garden views or one of the two new beachfront villas with private pools. The restaurant is patrolled by two pet ducks that come running when the popcorn is served. A lovely garden spa offers inexpensive ayurvedic treatments, which in town would be triple the price. This resort has no delusions of grandeur, is good value for your money, and on the whole quite charming. British hostess Kim is a fount of local knowledge. The hotel is often full so book ahead.

Sembirenteng, Buleleng. (**C**) **08/124656485**. www.alamanda.net. 28 units. Year-round US$125 standard; US$165–US$235 villa. MC, V. **Amenities:** Restaurant; bar; outdoor pool; room service; spa; watersports; Wi-Fi. *In room:* A/C, hair dryer, minibar.

Moderate

Ponciana Resort This is a small resort run by a Balinese woman who spent 25 years in Australia. Simply decorated bedrooms are in several traditional Balinese buildings in a garden setting or beach front. The restaurant offers a choice of inexpensive Indonesian

and Western food; choose their specialty catch of the day. The resort offers guests com- **275**
plimentary use of their kayaks and can arrange fishing trips. For those wishing to take
things even easier, a beachside bale is available for massages and other simple spa treatments.

Jl. Raya Singaraja, Amlapura. ✆ **08/12385951.** www.poncianaresortbali.com. 9 villas. Year-round
US$50–US$180. Rates include breakfast. No credit cards. **Amenities:** Restaurant; outdoor pool; room
service; Wi-Fi (for a fee). *In room:* A/C.

Inexpensive
Gaia Oasis & Abasan Hillside Retreats   This yoga retreat combines two separate
resorts, one on the beach and one in the hills. Both are ecofriendly and run as nonprofit
organizations. Seminars and healing programs are presented here by an assortment of
experts. Restaurants at both resorts offer a buffet of seafood and vegetarian dishes. Smok-
ing and alcohol are frowned upon.

Dusun Tegal Sumaga, Tejakula. ✆ **08/12385-3350.** Fax 0362/28428. www.gaia-oasis.com. 23 units. Year-
round US$31–US$75; extra bed US$28. MC, V. **Amenities:** Restaurant; babysitting; room service.

3 AIR SANIH & SURROUNDING VILLAGES

Carry on along the winding and very uneven main road through Air Sanih, a small village famous for a natural cold water spring with public bathing pools. Entry is around
Rp3,000; the springs are open 7am to 7pm.

EXPLORING NEAR AIR SANIH
This lush area just to the east of Singaraja produces the best rice in Bali. Given the
importance of rice in Balinese culture, some of the most highly decorated temples are
dedicated to the irrigation and rice goddess, Dewi Sri. Bring a picnic. Sarongs and sashes
can be borrowed at the gates for a small donation for temple upkeep.

PURA MADUWE KARANG   In Kubutambahan, this is one of the largest temples in
north Bali and is dedicated to protect the unfortunate crops that grow on land without
irrigation. The reliefs show scenes from the Ramayana epic and daily Balinese life,
together with the most photographed temple carving in Bali—a foreigner on a bicycle
wearing shorts from the Dutch era, largely attributed as portraying the first foreign artist,
W. O. J. Nieuwenkamp, who travelled around the area on his bicycle in 1904. The back
wheel is in the form of a lotus flower.

PURA BEJI   A few kilometers before Singaraja, look for the sign on the right for Pura
Beji temple in **Sangsit,** again dedicated to Dewi Sri. Dating back to the 15th century,
this unusual sandstone temple has intricate and unusual carvings reminiscent of South
America. The temple sponsors have left carved portraits on the back of the main portal.
Rest under venerable frangipani trees before taking a short walk through the rice fields
to the Pura Dalem, temple of the dead.

PURA DALEM   This temple is dedicated to Siwa and the souls of the dead with erotic
carvings reflecting a Balinese heaven and hell. The carvings of this famous temple just
outside the village also show how their peaceful village life was abruptly changed forever
by the Dutch colonialists bringing guns and terror and, later, cars and planes—heaven
being the representation of the island before the colonists arrived.

AIR SANIH & SURROUNDING VILLAGES

Back on the main road from the temple, look for the turn south towards **Jagaraga,** the site of the last tragic battle fought by 16,000 Balinese soldiers led by Gusti Jelantik against 3,000 well-armed Dutch troops in 1849. Nowadays, though, there is nothing to see.

Continue along the road into the mountains to visit the foundries of the few remaining traditional gamelan and gong makers in the village of **Sawan.** Ask the locals how to get to the nearby traditional villages of **Sudaji,** to see the marketplace with huge ancient trees, and **Suwug,** to sit at the warung in the main square built into the roots of a huge banyan tree.

WHERE TO STAY & DINE

Cilik's Beach Resort This very private property has several individually designed bungalows and one *lumbung* set in extensive and beautiful beachfront gardens. The authentic Indonesian buildings are made of timber from Kilimantan, marble from Java, red bricks from southern Bali, and bamboo from the mountains. Each bungalow is filled with a collection of antique furniture giving them a charming, homey feel. A selection of fresh, local food is cooked to order.

Air Sanih, Singaraja. ☎ **0362/26561.** Fax 0362/26561. www.ciliksbeachgarden.com. 4 units. Year-round US$125–US$210 Villa East; US$112–US$154 Villa West; US$84–US$125 Oktagonal; US$70–US$98 *lumbung*. No credit cards. **Amenities:** Restaurant; babysitting; Internet; room service; watersports and boat rental. *In room:* Stereo/CD, hair dryer.

4 SINGARAJA

Singaraja, the capital of Bali's largest regency, Buleleng, is the second most important town on the island and has a rich cultural and social history. With more than 100,000 inhabitants at the last count, this now quiet town was the important center of regional government under the Dutch for hundreds of years. Cut off by the mountains, the north developed independently from the south. It took the Dutch years of fighting before they eventually vanquished the south and finished the main Singaraja-Denpasar road. All that remains of the colonial splendor are some tree-lined boulevards and sadly, very few of the beautiful villas.

The original kingdom of Buleleng, which reached as far as Blambangan in East Java in the 17th century, was founded by the royal family of Singaraja. The direct descendants and their families still live in the palaces today, although not quite in the same style.

GETTING THERE

If you are coming, by car, from the **east,** take the coast road. From the **southeast,** drive through Kintamani and past the Batur volcano. The main road from the **west** passes through two tourist extremes, the quiet and peaceful fishing village of Pemuteran (p. 284) and the rather run-down, budget travel Lovina (p. 278). From the **south,** the winding road from the market town of Bedugul goes past the famous but overly touristy Git Git Waterfall before dropping down to the coast.

Three bus stations here have *bemo* and bus services to the rest of the island and a service to Java. The station on the eastern side of Singaraja, **Penarukan Terminal,** Jl. Surapati, serves east Bali (Amlapura, Kintamani, Gianyar) and ends in Batubulan Terminal, Denpasar, 3 hours later. **Banyuasri Terminal,** Jl. Jend Sudiman, on the western side of Singaraja, serves the western destinations of Lovina, Permuteran, and Gilimanuk (2

hr.). This service continues over to Java ending in Yogyakarta, 21 hours later. **Sukasada**
Terminal, Jl. Mayor Metra, in the south, serves Gigit, Bedugal, and ends in Ubung
Terminal, Denpasar (3 hr.). Prices range from Rp10,000 to Yeh Sanih up to Rp30,000
to Denpasar.

Taxis are not available here. Cars and drivers can be hired on the street or through the
hotels in Lovina.

FAST FACTS   Banks are open daily from 8am to 3pm. All the main Indonesian banks
have a branch in Singaraja. **Bank Mandiri,** Jl. A. Yani 60 (✆ **0362/25333**), on the main
street is easy to find. The hospitals are **Kerta Husada,** Jl. A. Yani (✆ **0362/26277**) and
the **Singaraja Public hospital Rumah Sakit Umum** on Jl. Ngurah Rai (✆ **0362/22573**).
Pharmacies, open daily from 8am until 7 or 10pm, are on Jalan A. Yani and in the Kerta
Husada. The **police station** is on Jalan Pramuka (✆ **0362/241510**). The **post office** is
on Jalan Gajah Mada 150 (✆ **0362/21788**). The **tourism office** is on Jalan Veteran 23
(✆ **0362/28170;** Mon–Fri 8am–5:30pm, Sat 8am–noon). They provide a pamphlet on
the Buleleng Regency and a Singaraja map.

EXPLORING SINGARAJA

Coming in from the east and passing the **Dutch bridge** and the **Old Harbour,** it is difficult to imagine just how important this port was in the centuries under Dutch colonialism. Just along from the large freedom fighter monument between the bridge and the
harbor, the recently renovated **Klenteng Ling Gwan Kiong Chinese Temple** ★ is well
worth a visit. All the white-painted rows of shops in this old part of town were built in
the early 1900s and have delicately carved Art Deco friezes.

PURI KAWAN & PURI KANGINAN PALACE ★   Follow the tree-lined Jalan Ngurah
Rai—with a few remaining colonial villas on each side—south towards the statue of the
winged lion symbol of Buleleng. Turn left to find Jalan Veteran 20 and the famous
Gedong Kirtya ★ (free admission; Mon–Thurs 7:30am–3:30pm, Fri 7am–12:30pm,
weekends and public holidays closed). This very special library has more than 3,000
ancient texts written in Javanese *kawi* and old Balinese script, inscribed on *lontar* palm
leaves. Founded by the Dutch, in what must have been a state of guilty conscience, the
library opened in 1928. The other collection of *prasasti* inscriptions on bronze are the
oldest examples of writing on the island. The library is part of the old Puri Kawan and
Puri Agung palace complex. Just across the road, peer through the imposing gates of the
Puri Kanginan Palace. Sometimes you can get lucky and you are invited in to have a
look and see what life must have been like for royalty in centuries gone by.

SHOPPING

Both **Pasar Banyuasri** (just off Jl. A. Yani near the imposing statue of a farmer with his
bullocks) and **Pasar Anyar** (off Jl. Diponogoro) sell everything from fresh fish to sarongs.
The **gold shops** on Jalan Sawo, off Jalan Diponogoro, sell good value jewelry appealing
to Westerners. **Hardy's** supermarket, at the north end of Jalan Ngurah Rai, is good for a
small selection of everything from imported Western food to cosmetics.

Berdikari ★, Jl. Dewi Sartika 42 (✆ **0362/22217;** daily 7am–7pm), is one of the
best shops for hand-woven *ikat* in Indonesia and home to the only silk weavers on the
island. Visitors can see the fascinating dyeing and weaving process from start to finish.
Presidents and politicians come here to buy *ikat* for formal wear and their photographs
line the walls. The expensive fabrics can also be woven to order. Prices are fixed and credit
cards are not accepted.

The handful of hotels in town caters purely to Indonesian business travelers. Although in the past it was impossible to get a decent meal in Singaraja, some little restaurants are opening up at last. **Devosi,** on Jalan A. Yani, is an airy warung overlooking rice fields on the main road to the west. Also on the beach to the west, a group of little restaurants have sprung up on Jalan Pantai Penimbangan Barat, such as **Cosy Resto** and **Ranggon Sunset,** with fresh grilled seafood and simple rice and noodle dishes at reasonable prices.

Shanti Hotel & Restaurant (Finds) Ten minutes south of Singaraja, high up in the green hills of Sambangan, this hotel and restaurant offers easy, interesting treks through beautiful scenery to nearby villages and waterfalls. In their traditional Balinese kitchen, visitors can see how coffee and coconut oil are processed by hand. The shady restaurant has an extensive menu that uses fresh local produce and creates gourmet experiences for pennies. Stay overnight in one of the two pristine rice-barn villas to really get the most out of this very special experience.

Sambangan, Singaraja. ✆ **0362/700-1331.** Fax 0362/23120. www.shanti-northbali.com. 2 units. Year-round US$60. Rates include breakfast. MC, V. **Amenities:** Restaurant; bar; room service; spa therapy. *In villa:* Fan, TV/DVD.

---

5 LOVINA

In the 1960s, five small villages were fused into one under the collective name of Lovina or "Love Indonesia," by the Rajah of Singaraja. Because he thought that the area had great potential for tourism, he published many articles in the foreign press that led to Lovina becoming a new and popular destination for the hippie crowd.

To the west of Singaraja, this long stretch of flat, black sandy beach is good for swimming, snorkeling, and dolphin- and local-fishermen-watching, and is now a favorite haunt for backpackers and northern European retirees on low budgets. Some of the locals are doing what they can to smarten Lovina up a bit, but it is perhaps a little past its sell-by date and further, has become notorious as a red-light district in recent years. But, if cheap, cheerful, and low-key is your thing, this may be the place.

A sad part of the area's history is that it has historically quarried for coral and over-fished. The coral used to be burned to make building lime for mortar—a crying shame. Happily, as an unexpected and recent addition because of tourism, the coral is now protected and the local fishermen have much better respect for how to fish the sea without destroying their own source of livelihood.

GETTING THERE & GETTING AROUND

Public *bemo* come here from Singaraja, the south, and Gilimanuk in the west, stopping all along the main road. Hop on and hold on.

Pak Komang (✆ **08/1338365761**) and his group of transportation friends are reliable, speak reasonable English, and are happy to organize a car and driver for tours or to take you anywhere on the island. **Perama Tours** (✆ **0362/41161**) has two offices in Lovina (one in the Perama Hotel) and charge reasonable rates for getting around the island. **Motorbikes** can be rented all over town at your own risk for around Rp50,000 per day. Remember, drive with caution. Like Singaraja, no **taxis** are available, only private transport with cars and drivers.

(**Warning!**) **Chasing the Dolphins of Lovina**

Everyone in Lovina will try to sell you an early morning dolphin trip. Because of the number of people involved, these trips should now be rechristened dolphin "chasing" rather than dolphin "watching," with up to 30 very loud boats involved in the hunt. Consequently, actual sightings are becoming increasingly rare and most of the dolphins have wisely moved to other locations. Expect to pay around Rp50,000 per person for a 2-hour trip.

Another annoyance involving dolphins can be found at the somewhat commercial **Melka Hotel.** Here you pay US$50 for a 20-minute swim with large dolphins kept in rather small pools. Some guests (especially young women) are scared when the dolphins become overly friendly. There have been recent tales of physical and even sexual abuse by the male dolphins on unsuspecting tourists. As this is entirely out of character for the normally sweet and docile dolphin clan, one might assume that this is retribution for their retched conditions.

FAST FACTS Lovina has two **ATMs** on the corner of the main road and Jalan Pantai Bina Ria but no banks. A number of Internet cafes are dotted around the village. The most reliable is **Spice Link,** Jl. Pantai Binaria (© 0362/41509; daily 8am–5pm). Coming from Singaraja, just after the traffic lights on the left hand side, is a small **pharmacy** and a general practitioner's surgery with a doctor on 24-hour call. The new **Tourist Police** office is just outside the Sunari Resort. The **post office** is on the main road, about 5 minutes from the village center. Open Monday to Thursday 8am to 3pm, Friday until noon, and Saturday until 1pm. A **tourist information** office (© 0362/25141) is on the main road in the center of the village and is open Monday to Thursday and Saturday 7am to 5:30pm, and Friday until 1pm.

EXPLORING LOVINA

The main draw of Lovina is the clear, calm water and its black sand beaches. Sadly, the coral reef here is not in pristine condition due to bleaching and the dynamite fishing of a past era. However, snorkelers still have plenty to see and beginning divers can use this location for introductory dives. Night diving is also very popular here.

Spice Dive, Kaliasem and Jl. Binaria (© 0362/41509; www.balispicedive.com), a PADI certified dive school, is a good place to learn to scuba dive. Although Lovina is not suitable for accomplished divers, trips can be organized to Menjangan Island or Tulamben (about 2 hr. away). Spice Dive also offers water-skiing, windsurfing, paragliding, and canoeing. Paragliding costs US$15 per session and water-skiing and wake boarding is US$20 for 20 minutes.

Sailing, fishing, and spear fishing can be done at **Kubu Lalang** hotel, Jl. Singaraja Tukadmungga (© 0362/42207). Fix your prices before you head out. Expect to pay about Rp70,000 per hour for fishing and about Rp100,000 per hour for other activities. You can also hire the fishermen to take you snorkeling (about Rp30,000 per hour). Most fishermen are part of a local village association, which allows them to use their fishing boat to ferry tourists around. Therefore prices are generally fixed.

The other big draw of Lovina is dolphin-watching (see above).

SPAS   Local black sand is added to your massage oil at the **Damai** (p. 282; ✆ **0362/ 41008;** www.damai.com; massages Rp450,000–Rp750,000, water healing Rp2,500,000 for two people; AE, DC, MC, V; daily 8am–8pm), making for a terrific scrub. Private spa pavilions can be booked for ayurvedic massages at about Rp800,000 for an hour and the ultimate six-hand massage is around Rp115,000 for an hour. A less expensive spa is **Agung's,** Jl. Damai (✆ **0362/42018;** full body massage Rp75,000–Rp95,000, facial Rp75,000–Rp125,000; no credit cards; daily 11am–7pm), but in comparison to the Damai, is a little gloomy.

SHOPPING

The artist **Made Ariana** (✆ **08/1338459153**) has made quite a name for himself, so make an appointment to visit his studio if you are interested in Balinese expressionism. **Biyu Nasak Gallery** (✆ **0362/4168**), on the main road in the center of the village, has a primitive "ancient" art collection. **Bakery Lovina** (✆ **0362/42225;** daily 7:30am– 9:30pm), on the main road, sells expensive but freshly baked bread and cakes, together with wine, alcohol, and a range of imported deli products.

WEST OF LOVINA

BANJAR & AIR PANAS   The **Buddhist Wihara temple,** in the hills behind Banjar village, is home to Bali's only Buddhist monk and is a colorful mix of Balinese and more traditional Buddhist architecture. Admission is free but a donation is expected.

The holy hot springs or **Air Panas** in Banjar village are very popular with the locals. The three hot spring bathing pools, set in well-maintained gardens, have clean changing rooms and are open to the public daily from 8am until 6pm. If you would like to take a dip in the slightly sulfurous waters, get here in the early morning and bring your own towel. A small restaurant overlooking the pools serves local dishes at reasonable prices and has some very simple rooms with beautiful garden views.

SERIRIT   All roads from Singaraja to Java and the west or to Denpasar and the south pass through **Seririt.** This small town has two banks with ATMs, a chemist, and a very understocked Hardy's Supermarket. The only local color, so to speak, is a group of Balinese ladies selling flowers for temple offerings.

Just after Seririt on the road to Gilimanuk, is the **Zen Resort Bali,** Jl. Pantai Uma Anyar (✆ **0362/93578;** fax 0362/93579; www.zenresortbali.com; 14 units; year-round US$105–US$133; MC, V), a peaceful place with simple but colorful rooms and a large swimming pool. Rates include ayurvedic, meditation, or pranayama retreats as well as special workshops available on request.

CELUKAN BAWANG   This is the most important port in north Bali although not particularly attractive. The docks are really only worth a peek if fishermen from other parts of Indonesia with their beautifully painted wooden boats happen to be visiting. The morning is the best time to find them.

GEROKGAK   Just before entering this village, look for a sign on the left to the *objek wisata alam bendungan* or reservoir. This is a peaceful place to walk or take a picnic and chances are you will be completely alone.

PENYABANGAN   Follow the sign for **Atlas North Bali Pearls** (✆ **08/123877012;** daily 10am–5pm) down a dirt road towards the beach. Ring beforehand to book one of their very interesting introductory tours. After seeing how incredibly complicated the cultivation process is, you will never look at a pearl the same way again. The little

cafe-cum-showroom serves very good coffee and offers the chance to buy a lovely local
pearl or two at relatively competitive prices.

Banyupoh

This little village is famous for two things: grapes and temples. There is no real growing season here, so do not be surprised to see a vineyard full of grapes ready for harvest next to a plot that just has new shoots.

PURA AGUNG PULAKI This has been an important place for ancestor and spirit worship since prehistoric times. The first story based on historical fact dates from the 16th century when the priest Dang Hyang Nirartha (1460–1550) came from Java with his family, bringing with him a purer form of Hinduism. He found a holy spring at Pulaki. The temple has since become one of Bali's nine most important directional temples and is also home to hordes of holy monkeys. The new temple, carved out of the mountainside, was completed in 1984 and has heavy, black lava stone buildings and ornate carvings. Visit the temple at full moon to see the colorful throngs of worshipers who come from all over Bali to pray for fortune and prosperity. A good Balinese Hindu has to pray at Pura Agung Pulaki at least once every year. Foreigners are allowed into the temple if they wear a sarong and a sash and pay a small donation.

PURA KERTA KAWAT Entering Banyupoh village, watch for a sign on the left to Pura Kerta Kawat, down a small road lined with vineyards. Balinese believe that praying here further increases prosperity.

PURA MELANTING Just along the main road is the sign for Pura Melanting, an awe-inspiring temple hidden in the forest and reached by a flight of wide stone steps. It is always frequented by a steady stream of worshipers who believe that praying here increases prosperity and good fortune. In 1997 the simple temple buildings were destroyed by a forest fire. Sadly, it has since been rebuilt in the overly ornate Neo-Balinese temple style reminiscent of Chinese temples, with no expense spared and no surface devoid of carving. Still, this is a wonderful place for meditation.

PURA PABEAN On the beach across the road from Pulaki, two huge megaliths from earlier times disappeared into the sand in the 13th century and were only rediscovered and re-erected in 1997 in their original position. Ida Bagus Tugur, an architect with no formal training, began to build a new temple on the hill behind the megaliths in 1987, using spiritual inspiration and instructions from old *lontar* palm leaf books. During excavations for the foundations, skeletons and gold jewelry were found, proving that the site could have been linked to the necropolis in Gilimanuk and other prehistoric sites in the area.

PURA PUNCAK MANIK This is a small temple built around a sacred spring high up in the hills behind Pura Melanting. You have to climb hundreds of steps and those hardy enough to reach the top are rewarded by magnificent views.

PURA TIRTA This small, recently renovated temple is famed for the spring that provides the holy water for many temple ceremonies.

WHERE TO STAY

Find a huge selection of small backpacker hotels along the main and side roads leading down to the beach throughout the Lovina villages. These cheap accommodations have different seasonal rates. If you are on a budget, it pays to shop around and compare prices. Two of the cheapest places in the center of town, close to the beach are **Rini** and

Puri Bali, on Jalan Marwar, and offer a choice of fan or air-conditioned rooms with cold or hot water, swimming pool, and a small restaurant. When they say hot water, check to see that there is hot water. Hot to them may mean tepid to you.

Expensive

Damai ★★ (Moments)   High up in the hills with lovely views of the Bali Sea from the restaurant and pool, Damai is the only place to stay out of town. Set in beautiful gardens, the older rooms are very pleasant but have no privacy. Bathrooms are small but each room has a Jacuzzi in the walled garden outside. The brand-new, Singaporean-style villas have infinity plunge pools with lovely views. The interiors are rather cool with black walls and European furniture—though somewhat incongruous with the surroundings. The spa offers an extensive range of treatments and one of only a few six-hand massages on the island—you thought four was excessive. Don't miss the large Japanese-style breakfast.

Jl. Damai, Kayu Putih, Singaraja. ℂ **0362/41008.** www.damai.com. 14 villas. High season US$185–US$875; low season US$160–US$850; extra bed US$75. Rates include breakfast. AE, DC, MC, V. **Amenities:** Restaurant, Damai (see below); babysitting; outdoor pool; room service; spa; Wi-Fi. *In room:* A/C, TV/DVD, hair dryer, minibar.

Puri Bagus Lovina   The first hotel west after Singaraja is this well-run family hotel. Villas are set far apart from each other in lovely gardens leading to the beach. The restaurant next to the double-level pool has an extensive menu. Popular romantic dinners cost US$75 and include a bottle of local wine.

Jl. Raya Seririt Gilimanuk, Desa Pemuteran, Buleleng. ℂ **0362/21430.** Fax 0362/22627. www.bagus-discovery.com. 40 villas. High season US$200–US$390; low season US$185–US$375. AE, DC, MC, V. **Amenities:** Restaurant; bar; babysitting; kids' club; outdoor pool; room service; spa; watersports; Wi-Fi (for a fee). *In villa:* A/C, hair dryer, minibar.

Moderate

Bali Taman Resort & Spa   Built in 1989, this low-end resort and spa was one of the first hotels in the area and although the rooms are clean, the decor has kept its late 1980s feel. Credit cards are accepted, which in these parts is a plus.

Jl. Raya Lovina, Lovina. ℂ **0362/41126.** www.balitamanlovina.com. 30 units. Year-round US$50–US$150. MC, V. **Amenities:** Restaurant; bar; lounge; Internet (for a fee); outdoor pool; room service; spa; tennis court. *In room:* A/C, TV, stereo or CD, hair dryer, minibar.

Rambutan (Kids)   This is a long-standing, popular family-run child-friendly resort. The children's playground even has a tree house. Two freeform pools make up for not being directly on the beach and you can rest easy while the children run around safely in the garden. The rooms are very simple, with rattan furniture, carved wooden doors, and tile floors. Restaurant prices are in U.S. dollars and include all the usual international and Indonesian favorites. The owners are avid supporters of the Singaraja Orphanage and are happy to take guests there who might like to help.

Jl. Rambutan, Lovina. ℂ **0362/41388.** Fax 0362/41621. www.rambutan.org. 28 units. High season US$20–US$187; low season US$20–US$170. MC, V. **Amenities:** Restaurant; Internet (for a fee); 2 outdoor pools; room service. *In room:* A/C, fan, TV, DVD (in villa), kitchenette (in villa), minibar.

Sunari Resort   With over 80 rooms and villas, this is the largest hotel in Lovina. Set on the beach, it has a 24-hour restaurant serving local, Chinese, and European fare. The rooms can be a bit doom and gloom, but the gardens and pool are very pleasant.

Lovina Beach. ℂ **0362/41775.** Fax 0362/41659. www.sunari.com. 83 units. Peak season US$95–US$500; high season US$90–US$495; low season US$85–US$480; extra bed US$30. MC, V. **Amenities:** Restaurant; gym; outdoor pool; room service; Wi-Fi (for a fee). *In room:* A/C, TV, minibar.

Expensive

Damai ★★ (Finds) BALINESE   Meals here are expensive but definitely worth every rupiah. The six-course tasting menu changes every evening and offers traditional Balinese dishes with Scandinavian touches; the interesting a la carte menu offers such delicacies as tuna *tataki* mahimahi on cauliflower puree with almonds. Although the food here tends to be a little overplated, it is cooked to perfection. An eight-course Champagne Brunch on Sundays (11am–2pm) is a good value at Rp245,000 (children 11 and under Rp155,000). Every night includes a Balinese performance and live music.

In the Damai (see above), Jl. Damai. ℂ **0362/41008.** www.damai.com. Main courses Rp195,000–Rp229,000; set menu Rp360,000. AE, MC, V. Daily 7am–midnight.

Moderate

Jasmine Kitchen THAI/CAFE   This little restaurant serves the usual Thai favorites and wonderfully wicked cakes baked daily. Fresh prawns in chili sauce are an excellent choice. The wine list is small with local "Wine of the Gods" on offer.

Gang Binaria, Kalibuk-Lovina. ℂ **0362/41565.** Main courses Rp26,000–Rp45,000. No credit cards. Daily 11:30am–10:30pm.

Kwizien INTERNATIONAL   This popular restaurant was taken over by a Dutch couple in 2007 and was subsequently fitted with air-conditioning and revamped. The menu features imported steaks (Rp90,000–Rp125,000 for a t-bone) and local food with rather strange dishes such as meatballs in blueberry sauce.

Jl. Raya Singaraja, Seririt-Kaliasem. ℂ **0362/42031.** www.balikwizien.com. Meat Rp50,000–Rp125,000; fish Rp80,000–Rp90,000; pasta Rp40,000–Rp55,000. MC, V. Daily 5pm–midnight.

Sea Breeze INDONESIAN/INTERNATIONAL   At the end of Jalan Pantai Binaria next to the Lovina dolphin statue, is this favorite hang-out for locals and a perfect spot for sunset drinks. Good breakfasts are served. A live band plays a few nights a week.

Jl. Pantai Binaria. ℂ **0362/41138.** Main courses Rp30,000–Rp250,000. No credit cards. Daily 8am–11pm.

Inexpensive

Warung Bambu BALINESE   On the side road to Puri Bagus, this bamboo cafe serves the best Balinese food in the area. Apart from their rijstaffel for Rp115,000 and their surprise menu for Rp175,000 per person, none of their tasty dishes are over Rp50,000. Cooking classes for a minimum of two persons have to be booked 1 day in advance and cost Rp300,000 per person. Only local wines are served. Balinese dance performances take place on Wednesday and Sunday nights.

Jl. Puri Bagus Pemaron. ℂ **0362/27080.** www.warung-bambu.mahanara.com. Main courses Rp19,000–Rp25,000. Special meals, *betutu dolong,* and Balinese Night Rp180,000, 2-person minimum. MC, V. Daily 11am–11pm.

LOVINA AFTER DARK

Most of the nightlife in Lovina takes place in the little bars and restaurants which have evening happy hour. The lone club on the main road to the east of the village is impossible to miss: It's a huge concrete eyesore, the pyramid-shaped **Volcano Club.** The disco is open from 9pm until late Wednesday to Saturday. Regular Balinese dance performances and other cultural events are organized by the **Lovina Culture Foundation** (ℂ **0362/41293**). Ring them for information on performances in town.

6 PEMUTERAN

When a small group of pioneer investors bought land in Pemuteran in the mid-1980s, they vowed to adhere to the ideals of gentle tourism and to create a hideaway for discerning visitors. Due to its being some 3 to 4 hours drive from the south, this peaceful fishing village has been more carefully developed than similar places in Bali.

Once guests have made the trip once, they tend to return. There is no nightlife, no ATMs, no hawkers on the beach, no jet skis—just a large bay, good for swimming, and a handful of small resorts each with their own restaurant and some with PADI dive centers. Everyone's goal here is to offer visitors a peaceful respite and some of the best snorkeling and diving in this part of Indonesia.

GETTING THERE & GETTING AROUND

Public *bemo* buses are available along the main road from dawn to dusk or "express" buses between Singaraja and Gilimanuk are also available. **Puri Ganesha** (see below) offers transfers by Harley-Davidson bike with a "jockey" and a car for the luggage.

If you're traveling from the south or airport before 3pm, the quickest scenic drive over the central mountains takes around 3½ hours. After 3pm, when the rush hour begins, be prepared to spend longer in the car. Transfers from Ubud take between 2½ and 3 hours; from Amed and Candidasa, around 4 hours.

Taxis as such are not available, but there is **Village Drivers Association** (🕿 08/1337903234), although their rates are higher than finding someone direct.

FAST FACTS The small **Pemuteran Clinic** (🕿 08/1915678011) has a doctor on call 24 hours who will also come to your hotel. If there is something really serious, call experienced, English-speaking **Dr. Handra** (🕿 08/123605733) who will come from Singaraja. He accepts credit cards—and charges European prices. Because this is such a rural area, **telephones** and **Internet connections,** even those using satellites, tend to be erratic. There are no Internet cafes but most of the hotels do have an Internet service for their guests, albeit not necessarily on all day.

PEMUTERAN OUTDOORS

The excellent dive school **Reef Seen Aquatics,** in the Reef Seen resort (see below; 🕿 0362/93001; www.reefseenbali.com), predominately caters to certified divers. However, they can also arrange introductory dive courses when given notice. For snorkeling, hire a local villager at one of the smaller dive concessions for Rp200,000 per day to take you to reefs in and around Pemuteran.

The fantastic **Biorock Project** ★★, in front of Taman Sari hotel, is a perfect place for kids to enjoy snorkeling. The waters in Permuteran are usually calm and visibility is clear. You can also start or end the day with a boat ride. Enjoy the sun rising or setting and you may even catch a glimpse of a whale or dolphin—but no promises. Pony rides are available along the beach. Reef Seen can organize all these activities.

The **Turtle hatchery** project based at Reef Seen educates the local community about not killing turtles or stealing their eggs. The hatchery helps raise awareness of the need for conservation while enabling the birth and growth of different species of turtles: Olive Ridley, Green, and Hawksbill. When the turtles are mature and healthy enough, they are released back into the sea. Sponsor and release your own turtle when you visit—the money all goes to a good cause.

Pemuteran's Biorock Project

By the late 1990s, a combination of coral bleaching and dynamite fishing had decimated the reefs at Pemuteran. This gave a very bleak outlook for the local residents, who relied on fishing both for their own consumption and as a draw for marine tourists, divers, and snorkelers.

However, in June 2000, the Taman Sari Resort donated US$12,000 to start the **Karang Lestari Proyek** (Coral Protection Project). This project uses low-voltage electricity to promote and accelerate coral growth on metal frames. Taman Sari Resort supplies the electricity and further funding is supplied by private donations.

The technology comes from the **Global Coral Reef Alliance** (GCRA; www.globalcoral.org) in the United States. The basic principle is that when electrodes are immersed in seawater, limestone is created, making a very strong base on which corals readily grow, sometimes five times faster than normal. This process generates a high pH level in the water, in which corals flourish, therefore more energy can be used to reproduce and build. These corals are also more resistant to environmental stress and it is believed that they will also withstand future seasonal temperature rises (the cause of coral bleaching).

The Karang Lestari Proyek, at 2.4 hectares (6 acres), is the world's largest coral-reclamation project. At present, over 40 metal frames of various shapes and sizes at depths of 5 to 10m (16–33 ft.) have a variety of hard corals growing on each, in various stages of development. Despite the fact that this is a young project, the area makes an interesting and educational day's diving.

The project is fully supported by the people of Pemuteran village. In order to restore the fish population, everyone has agreed to observe the site as a no-fishing area. They have also agreed to stop dynamite and cyanide fishing.

WHERE TO STAY & DINE
Expensive
Matahari Beach Resort ★   This peaceful, rather ornate resort with an Olympic-size pool is set in beautiful gardens. Each of the spacious, traditionally furnished rooms has a marble bathroom and garden shower but the private terraces can be a little gloomy. The resort is a Relais & Châteaux member, so expect rather formal dining in the restaurant with prices to match. Balinese music and dance performances are held regularly. The huge spa has an interesting range of treatments and a special pavilion for tea ceremonies. Outside guests are welcome at the spa if space is available, but book well in advance.

Jl. Raya Seririt Gilimanuk, Desa Pemuteran, Buleleng. ② **0362/92312.** Fax 0362/92313. www.matahari-beach-resort.com. 32 units. Year-round US$234–US$514. Rates include breakfast. AE, DC, MC, V. **Amenities:** 2 restaurants; bar; bicycles; concierge; gym; outdoor pool; room service; spa; tennis court; watersports; Wi-Fi (for a fee). *In room:* A/C, movie library, hair dryer, minibar.

Puri Ganesha Villas ★★★ (Finds)   At the far opposite end of Pemuteran Bay is one of our favorite places to visit and was voted World's Best Beach Hideaway by *Travel + Leisure.* Egyptologist, designer, and food connoisseur Diana von Cranach runs this

(Finds) Babi Guling

A few kilometers to the west is the small village of Goris, with a tidy and interesting daily market. The highlight here is the famous *babi guling* suckling pig. Queues of locals wait for the pig to be delivered every morning around 7:30am to Bali Re, a warung at the front of the market. It is so good, that even Hermès bag–toting tourists from Pemuteran have been spotted licking their fingers here. A portion costs around Rp15,000. Get there early, because once they run out for the day, that's it.

beautiful spot as though she is entertaining house guests not paying clients. The long list of celebrity repeat guests is too secretive to mention. The beautiful free-standing one- to three-bedroom villas each has its own private, 12m (39-ft.) pool. The style is Barbados-beach-house-meets-classic-Bali, with antiques and wooden floors. Many people make the journey from the south just to stay here. To top it all, Diana runs an amazing kitchen specializing in raw and living food, and alongside the daily changing menu, they also offer a raw food healing program and cooking classes.

Desa Pemuteran, Gerokgak. ℂ **0362/94766.** Fax 0362/93433. www.puriganesha.com. 4 villas. Year-round US$500–US$675. AE, MC, V. **Amenities:** Restaurant; babysitting; Internet; room service; spa. *In villa:* A/C, kitchenette, minibar, outdoor pool.

Moderate

Amertha Bali Villas   On the main road is this collection of modern, southern Bali–style one-, two-, and three-bedroom villas with private pools and a little beachfront restaurant. The villas are managed by Taman Sari Bali Cottages, just along the road. Stay in a villa near the beach because those closer to the road can be noisy.

Dusun Pemuteran, Gerokgak-Buleleng. ℂ **0362/94831.** Fax 0362/93264. www.balitamansari.com. 18 units. High season US$90–US$415; low season US$75–US$400. MC, V. **Amenities:** Restaurant; 2 outdoor pools; room service; spa; tennis court; Wi-Fi (for a fee). *In room:* A/C, TV/DVD, hair dryer, kitchenette, minibar.

Pondok Sari   Next to Taman Selini, this hotel has 30 standard rooms, four deluxe bungalows, and a villa set in tropical gardens. The beachfront restaurant serves adequate international and local fare.

Jl. Raya Seririt Gilimanuk, Pemuteran. ℂ **0362/94738.** Fax 0362/94738. www.pondoksari.com. 35 units. High season US$73–US$250; low season US$62–US$238. MC, V. **Amenities:** Restaurant; bar; lounge; outdoor pool; room service; spa. *In room:* A/C, hair dryer.

Taman Sari Bali Cottages ★   At the west end of the village, this hotel is a favorite with expats and tour groups as much for the charming cottages and easy rates as for the garden, ambience, and laid-back nature. Book early during school holidays. Rooms and villas are scattered throughout a large garden facing the sea. A small swimming pool with bar is next to the restaurant. Spa treatments are on offer.

Dusun Pemuteran, Gerokgak-Buleleng. ℂ **0362/93264.** www.balitamansari.com. 12 units. Year-round US$50–US$82 cottage; US$100–US$190 suite; US$250–US$350 villa. MC, V. **Amenities:** Restaurant; bar; babysitting; outdoor pool; room service; spa; watersports; Wi-Fi (for a fee). *In room:* A/C, TV/DVD, hair dryer, kitchenette (villa only), minibar.

Taman Selini   On the main road in the center of the village, the Taman Selini has 11 Balinese-style, tastefully decorated bungalows with terraces facing the garden and a large swimming pool. The bar has an outside lounging area by the beach opposite the popular restaurant that serves very good Greek mezze as well as Indonesian and international favorites.

Jl. Raya Seririt Gilimanuk, Pemuteran. (C) **0362/94746.** www.tamanselini.com. 12 units. Year-round US$120–US$250; extra bed US$10. MC, V. **Amenities:** Restaurant; outdoor pool; room service; Wi-Fi (for a fee). *In room:* A/C, hair dryer.

Inexpensive

Many inexpensive lodgings are on Jalan Raya Gilimanuk. Two homestays are: the **Jubawa Homestay** ((C) **0362/94745;** www.jubawa.com; 18 units; year-round Rp200,000–Rp250,000; no credit cards), just after Matahari Beach Resort, has 12 clean rooms, most of them with air-conditioning and hot water, but the main road can be noisy. The little restaurant serves frugal Balinese and Thai food. The **Rare Angon Home-stay** ((C) **0362/94747;** year-round Rp250,000–Rp350,000; MC, V), near the entrance to Taman Sari, has three clean air-conditioned rooms and a small restaurant that some-times serves fresh grilled fish.

You cannot miss the large sign for **Adi Assri Resort** ((C) **0362/94838;** fax 0362/94838; www.adiassri.com; 32 units; high season US$53–US$77; low season US$48–US$72; extra bed US$15; rates include breakfast; MC, V) on the main road after Jubawa on the beach side. This new resort has bright and airy rooms although they are possibly a bit stark, and the layout and full glass front offers little privacy. The pool area and restaurant are near the beach and spa treatments are available.

Reef Seen ((C) **0362/93001;** www.reefseenbali.com; year-round Rp500,000; MC, V) is down a dirt track just after Amertha Bali Villas. The five pleasant rooms have garden bathrooms, air-conditioning, and hot water. Chris Brown has been in Pemuteran for many years and he had the original PADI dive school in the area. He also initiated the original reef and turtle saving projects (p. 284). Village children learn and practice Bali-nese dancing here and their performances are magical.

West Bali

West Bali is best defined as the area west of Tabanan on the southern coast of Bali and the **Taman National Park.** Traveling west requires planning for at least 1 overnight with a car and driver. If you are visiting Bali for 5 days or more, a journey west is a great escape from "downtown" Bali as this area sees very few international visitors.

This 71km (44 mile) strip of volcanic sand coast is home to the Malay-speaking Bugis and Balinese Christians. Most of the population of west Bali are rice farmers, fishermen, or plantation workers and are increasingly Muslim due to the area's proximity to Java. The coastal towns of west Bali were settled by Bugis Javanese seafarers during the 17th century, who established a trading center in Negara.

1 GETTING THERE & GETTING AROUND

The west is serviced by one main road that stretches from Tabanan to the port village of Gilimanuk, the transit point for ferries to Java. Though the only misrouting possible would take you north to Singaraja or Lovina, it is not advisable to self-drive; take a car and driver. If you're planning an extended stay here, most hotels offer car or motorbike rentals or complimentary use of a car; many will also have bicycles available for guests. Driving from Denpasar to Gilimanuk takes 4 hours. Seaside and mountain villages are never more than 10km (6 miles) off the main road.

(Fast Facts   West Bali

Banks Most banks here will exchange cash and travelers checks. Major banks are in Negara and Tabanan.

Clinics & Hospitals In Tabanan, head to **Dharma Kerti Clinic,** Jl. Manik 14 (© **0361/811424**), **Tabanan Public Hospital,** Jl. Merpati 11 (© **0361/811754**), or **Gelgel Hospital,** Jl. Mawar (© **0361/811444**). In Negara, are **Negara Public Hospital,** Jl. Gelar (© **0365/41006**), and **Kerta Yasa Clinic,** Jl. Ngurah Rai 143 (© **0365/41248**).

Police Police are stationed at Jalan Pahlawan in Tabanan (© **0361/811210**), Jalan Raya Melaya, in Melaya (© **0365/41302**) and Jalan Tanah Lot (© **0361/812399**) and Jalan Pekarangan Baturiti in Tabanan (© **0361/93347**).

---

2 TABANAN

Tabanan encompasses a broad range of landscapes from the lofty peaks in the north, including Mt. Batukaru and part of Mt. Bratan with its dramatic volcanic lake, to the

ATTRACTIONS ●

Belimbingsari Catholic church **1**
Bunut Bolong **10**
Kurma Asih **6**
Margarana Monument **24**
Nirwana Bali Golf Club **17**
Palasari Protestant church **3**
Pasar Hewan (Kediri) **21**

Pura Gede Perancak **5**
Pura Luhur at Rambut Siwi **7**
Pura Taman Ayun **22**
Pura Tanah Lot **15**
Royal Palace at Kerambitan **14**
Sangeh Monkey Forest **23**
Subak Rice Museum
(The Mandala Mathika Subak) **20**

ACCOMMODATIONS ■

Dewi Sinta Restaurant & Villa **16**
Gajah Mina Beach Resort **11**
Kembang Desa Luxury Beach Villas **12**
Le Meridien Nirwana Golf Spa & Resort **17**
Medewi Beach Cottages **9**
Pondok Pisces **11**
Puri Dajuma Cottages **8**
Puri Taman Sari Hotel **25**
Shankaris **11**
Taman Wana Villas & Spa **2**
Villa Devatas **19**
Villa Zolima **11**
Waka Gangga **13**

DINING ◆

Café Nathalia **4**
Rumah Makan Puas **4**
Warung Nasi Andi Jaya **18**

INDIAN OCEAN

Bali Strait

TAMAN NASIONAL BALI BARAT
(WEST BALI NATIONAL PARK)

← To Ketapang Banyuwedang
(Java)

WEST BALI

TABANAN

14

verdant rice plains in the south. Beautiful black sand beaches between Pasut and Klating-dukuh are being developed for tourism but apart from the busy seaside temple of Tanah Lot this is a not an overly visited area. The main highway from Java passes through the gently sloping southern part of Tabanan along the coast, making it a commercial center. Tabanan is known for its dancers and gamelan musicians and was home to the famous pre-World War II dancer I Mario who perfected the kebyar dance. Tabanan is also home to one of Bali's last royal families who maintain and live in a palace (see "Royal Palace at Kerambitan," below). Mount Batukaru (p. 240) is also accessible via Tabanan.

Going west to Tabanan is simply a matter of following the signs from Denpasar and Seminyak—only one east-west road runs along Bali's southern coast.

EXPLORING IN & AROUND TABANAN

Kediri is south of Tabanan and has one of the busiest cattle markets in Bali, **Pasar Hewan.** It's not much to see unless you are in the market for livestock, but it is a small detour on the way further south to the pottery town of **Pejaten,** famous for its lovely pottery and terra-cotta tiles with figures of gods, goddesses, and *wayang* heroes. Also on sale are glazed Chinese ceramics. The prices are unbelievably cheap.

The **Margarana Monument,** 2km (1¼ miles) west of Marga (to the north of Tabanan), commemorates the November 20, 1946, battle against Dutch forces who sought to regain Bali as a colony after the departure of the Japanese. From here, one of the great figures in Balinese history, Gusti Ngurah Rai, led a band of independence fighters. Inside is a shrine in honor of Ngurah Rai and the words of his final letter ending in "Freedom or death."

On Bali's western coastline at Tanah Lot, 20 minutes drive north from Seminyak, the Greg Norman–designed championship course **Nirwana Bali Golf Club** ★★★ (in Le Meridien Resort, see below; Mon–Fri US$165, Sat & Sun US$175) opened in July 1997. It is acknowledged as one of the world's best; both *Asian Golf Monthly* and *Golf Digest* have voted the course the number one course in Indonesia. International competitions are staged here and there is a wealth of professional expertise on hand should you need lessons or guidance. The caddies here remain some of the best on the island. Golf carts with a caddy are compulsory and a drink service is provided. Lessons are available with the resident PGA professionals.

Pura Taman Ayun   East of Tabanan is a huge elegant state temple surrounded by a moat. Built in 1634 and renovated in 1937, it was the main temple of the Mengwi kingdom until 1891. It has a flowing fountain and lovingly tended grounds and is sometimes used as a background for Balinese royal feasts. Notice the *meru* dedicated to the god of fertility or "shrine of Ulun Suwi" on the east side of the main complex. The grounds house a total of 50 shrines and pavilions.

Jl. I Gusti Ngurah Rai. ✆ **0361/235600.** Admission Rp4,100. Daily 8am–6pm.

Pura Tanah Lot ★   Along the east-west road, this temple is one of the most popular and important sea temples on Bali. Proceed with caution if you chose to go. Sunset is the preferred time to visit and is thus teaming with tourists. You have to wade through a row of commercial shops and cafes before you arrive at the temple itself and aggressive touts try to sell you all manner of things. Non-Balinese are not let inside the actual temple. It is best to visit during the day before lunch. You can catch the spectacular sunsets all over the southern coast.

> **Fun Facts   To Go or Not to Go?**
>
> An old superstition says that it is bad luck if you visit Pura Tanah Lot with your fiancé before marriage and it will cause you to break up before your nuptials.

The temple is in Beraban village on a rock that is only accessible at low tide. All of the sea temples were constructed to be in sight of each other and form a chain along the coast. So from Pura Tanah Lot, look to the cliff top of Uluwatu in the distance to the south, and to the other side to the west towards Perancak near Negara.

Pura Tanah Lot is associated with the Majapahit priest Nirartha, who refashioned Balinese Hinduism in the 16th century. It remains an important prayer site and is where followers of the faith pray for the success of their crops and generally anything else associated with agriculture. Farmers in rural areas make pilgrimages to the temple to seek blessings that will safeguard their livelihood, while urban-dwelling Hindu's often visit Tanah Lot in family groups to meditate and seek spiritual guidance. Hidden among the rocks and crevices surrounding Tanah Lot are a number of black sea snakes. Although these snakes are tame, be cautious and refrain from unnecessarily aggravating them or wandering off unaccompanied. These snakes are believed to be the guardians of the temple and protect the entire area from unseen evil forces—don't let them think you are one of them.

Beraban. Admission Rp3,300. ATM on-site. Daily 7am–4:30pm.

Royal Palace at Kerambitan ★★ (**Finds**)   To the west of Tabanan is the 17th-century Puri Anyar Kerambitan. Its royal family represents Bali in its current progressive form, with roots in Balinese history dating from the 13th century. The family enjoyed great prosperity until the law of Land Reform in 1961 restricted ownership of land to 5 hectares (12 acres) per family. The family estate of then around 300 hectares (741 acres) was taken and redistributed. Under these new circumstances, it became a challenge to maintain the palace, its grounds, and many temples. The present (seventh-generation royal family) King Anak Agung Ngurah Oka Silagunadha (Bapak Oka as he prefers to be known) had a vision to "share this gift of the ancestors" with the world and he opened the palace to visits in 1967. Feasts have been presented here for the likes of from Mick Jagger, David Bowie, and Supertramp, to Prime Minister Fukuda of Japan, ministers, and ambassadors from all over the world. A drama ritual named *Tektekan,* created by Bapak Oka for royal performances, is sometimes staged under the control of priests: Daggers penetrate the flesh of men in trance portraying the fight between good and evil called *Rwa Binedha.* If you book ahead, enticing Balinese feasts can be arranged for you, too. You can also stay in one of the palace in simple rooms filled with antiques. Call well ahead of your intended stay or tour.

Desa Baturiti, Tabanan. (✆)/fax **0361/812774.** www.balipurikerambitan.web.id. Reservations required. Dinner on request at market price. AE, DC, MC, V. Open only for pre-ordered dinner and events.

Sangeh Monkey Forest   Spend a morning north of Tabanan (or a 30-minute ride from Denpasar) on 7 hectares (17 acres) of land surrounding the 17th century **Pura Bukit Sari** temple, set within groves of nutmeg trees. The majority of the monkeys here are macaques, ranging from babies to larger 10kg (22 lb.) adults. Keep a firm grip on

WEST BALI

14

TABANAN

your jewelry, glasses, and toupee as the mischievous residents are adept at snatching any object that isn't tied down and will laugh in your face while they are at it.

Jl. Imam Bonjol. © **0361/235600**. Admission Rp20,000. 24 hr.

Subak Rice Museum (The Mandala Mathika Subak)   This museum dedicated to rice cultivation in Bali features dioramas of typical rice field irrigation systems from A.D. 600 that feed the beautiful rice terraces adorning Bali's volcanic slopes. Well-versed guides explain how rice terraces are constructed, planted, and harvested using the rudimentary wooden tools on display. You will never look at a bowl of rice in quite the same way again.

Jl. Raya Kediri. © **0361/810315**. Admission Rp5,000. Daily 7am–4:30pm.

Taman Kupu Kupu (Bali Butterfly Park)   Billed as the largest butterfly park in Asia, this preserve is best seen in the early morning when the butterflies arise and take flight. The park promotes the study, breeding, and preservation of over 300 species of butterflies found in Indonesia and is home to the rare birdwing butterfly. If your children are budding entomologists this is a great opportunity to further their interests. It is 7km (4 miles) north of Tabanan on the way to Penebel.

Jl. Batukaru, Sandan Wanasari. © **0361/814282**. Admission Rp30,000. Daily 8am–5pm.

WHERE TO STAY

Expensive

Le Meridien Nirwana Golf Spa & Resort ★   This is the place to go if you are looking for a fairway to heaven. The luxurious rooms in this five-star resort sit in lush landscaped gardens and rice terraces surrounding the massive swimming pools. Rooms offer spectacular ocean views and villas have plunge pools and butler service. Sunset dinners with views of the Tanah Lot are a highlight—and possibly one of the best ways to see the temple. The golf course (see above) has spectacular ocean views, rice fields as bunkers, and four sets of tees. There is a clubhouse, shops, a driving range, spa, and massage and drink service. The Nautilus Pizzeria and Pub is great for snooker, darts, karaoke, or cheering on your team at a sporting event with a cold draft in hand.

Jl. Raya Tanah Lot, Tabanan. © **0361/815900**. Fax 0361/815901. www.starwoodhotels.com. 278 units. Year-round US$118–US$468. AE, DC, MC, V. **Amenities:** 4 restaurants; 2 bars; babysitting; bicycles; kids' club; concierge; golf course; gym; Internet (for a fee); Jacuzzi; outdoor pool; room service; spa; tennis court. *In room:* A/C, TV/DVD, movie library, stereo or CD, hair dryer, minibar.

Villa Devatas ★   This majestic villa is a low-key luxury. The stunning five-bedroom estate is set in immaculate tropical gardens with a river and rainforest at the property edge. Facilities include a pool with Jacuzzi, an air-conditioned game and media room, a spa, and an air-conditioned gym. Bathrooms are spacious with indoor and outdoor showers, fluffy towels, and Bulgari amenities.

Jl. Raya Tabanan, Cepaka. © **61416/497046**. www.balivilladevatas.com. 5 bedrooms. Peak season US$1,250 and up; high season US$600–US$1,500; low season US$550–US$1,250; extra guest US$50. Rates include breakfast. AE, MC, V. **Amenities:** Bar; babysitting; gym; Jacuzzi; 2 outdoor pools; room service; spa; Wi-Fi. *In room:* A/C, fan, TV/DVD, movie library, minibar.

Moderate

Kembang Desa Luxury Beach Villas   About 30 minutes north of Tanah Lot, these four luxury villas are spread over 3 hectares (7 acres) of land with the feeling of a grand estate with rice fields on one side and beach views on the other. The light, whitewashed wooden villas are tastefully decorated. The pool has special fiber-optic lighting that re-creates a "stars in the sky" effect. Four more beachfront villas are being built; ask if they're ready when you book.

Jl. Pantai Klecung, Tabanan. ☎ **0361/742-3964.** www.balikembangdesavillas.com. 4 villas. High season US$400; low season US$200. No credit cards. **Amenities:** Restaurant; bicycles; outdoor pool; room service; spa. *In room:* A/C, TV/DVD, movie library, stereo or CD, hair dryer, minibar, MP3 docking station.

Waka Gangga ★ Kids Finds Despite the simplicity of this resort—no TVs—you'll be spoiled by a soul-pampering spa, cozy canopy beds, and amazing views. The formula here is about reviving the spiritual self with the natural energy of the Indian Ocean and mountains. Activities include horse rides on the beach and to Pura Tanah Lot; catamaran sailing; bicycling around local villages; and Land Cruiser tours. The pool and restaurant are on Yeh Gangga beach. The individual lanais are charming and atmospheric with king-size beds, sunken bathtubs, and a garden shower. All of the lanais have views but go for one of the northernmost ones as they edge the lovely rice paddies which you can soak in from your deck. Children will have plenty of room to run around, cots are free, and babysitting is available.

Yeh Gangga, Tabanan. ☎ **0361/484085.** www.wakagangga.com. 10 units. Year-round US$230–US$470. AE, DC, MC, V. **Amenities:** Restaurant; bar; outdoor pool; room service; spa; Wi-Fi (for a fee). *In room:* A/C, fan, fridge, hair dryer, minibar.

Inexpensive
Dewi Sinta Restaurant & Villa Near the ticket office to Tanah Lot is this mid-range hotel with 27 comfortable and modern rooms dotted along a descending terrace. The open hall is a popular stage for cultural dances like the *kecak* or *legong* preformed for large tourist groups. You might be lucky enough to catch one during your stay.

Pura Tanah Lot, Tabanan. ☎ **0361/812933.** www.indo.com/hotels/dewisinta. 27 units. High season US$26–US$48; low season US$18–US$40. MC, V. **Amenities:** Restaurant; bicycles; outdoor pool; room service. *In room:* A/C, TV, minibar.

Puri Taman Sari Hotel Near the Margarana monument, in coconut groves and rice fields, this traditional Balinese compound is owned by a member of the royal family of Mengwi. They offer classes in cooking, dance, and gamelan. Bikes are also available and there are some nice walks in the area.

Umabian, Desa Peken, Kecamatan Marga. ☎ **0361/742-1165.** www.balitamansari.com. 16 units. High season US$48–US$63; low season US$40–US$55. AE, MC, V. **Amenities:** Restaurant; bicycles; outdoor pool; room service. *In room:* A/C, TV.

WHERE TO DINE
Aside from the restaurants in the hotels, on the main road in the heart of Tabanan town is **Warung Nasi Andi Jaya** where there is a painted sign of a pig on the outside but no signage with the name. Just ask anyone where it is. They serve delicious freshly roasted pork all day long at around Rp15,000 to Rp25,000 per dish. Several other warungs are along the main road; a night market is on the south side of town.

3 TABANAN TO NEGARA

Following the coast to Negara to the far west are nice views but little tourist development except for the surf colonies at **Balian** and **Medewi.** One can also go northward from Antosari passing waterfalls at **Pujungan,** south of Pupuan, a walk of a couple of kilometers to two falls, one 50m (164 ft.) in height. This road takes you through rice paddies and spice trees and descends into coffee plantations to Pupuan. The other alternative is to drive north via **Pulukan** to Pupuan. This steep and scenic road also goes through spice-growing areas and then at about 10km (6 miles) before Manggissari, this winding road will lead you through a **Bunut Bolong,** a huge ficus tree with a tunnel in it.

Because points west of Tanah Lot are infrequently visited by tourists, accommodations and dining are sparse and not up to the standards of the more developed areas of Bali. You will, however, encounter dozens of inexpensive home stays and basic bungalows for backpackers and surfers. We have selected accommodations with five or more rooms or cottages that offer ocean or mountain vistas. Bring snacks and picnic supplies.

BALIAN

Past Tabanan, 1½ hours west of Denpasar, on the coast is this beach known for sharks. Don't turn left at the first surfboard sign coming into town—it leads to the beach and nowhere else. Carry on and take a left up the hill after crossing the bridge. This will bring you to the hillside offering views to assess the waves and numerous homestays and warungs. The classic **Balian wave (best season:** dry Apr–Oct; **best swell:** south-south-west; **best size:** 3–5 ft.; **best winds:** east-northeast) is a left to the north of the river mouth but the right off the other side can get good too. Just watch out coming in on this side on lower tides as the shore break can be surprisingly heavy. Crowds can be pretty thin up this way.

Where to Stay & Dine

Gajah Mina Beach Resort ★ Located near Lalang Linggah village, this cozy little resort overlooking a white sand beach is an affordable getaway for both singles and families. The stone cottages have local antiques and comfortable furniture hand-selected by the owner. The restaurant caters to the primarily European clientele and offers a mix of simple Thai and Indonesian fare and a limited but well selected wine list. The best feature is the tourist-free beach; the famous surf break at Balian is a 10-minute walk from the resort. Natural caves and ancient stone carvings offer romantic walks on cliff tops, headlands, coconut groves, and deserted beaches nearby. The resort also serves as a yoga retreat and prepares *jamu* (healing Indonesian concoctions from local plants) and vegetarian meals.

Suraberata, Lalang Linggah, Selemadeg, Tabanan. ✆ **08/123811630.** Fax 0361/731174. www.gajah minaresort.com. 11 units. High season US$105–US$220; low season US$95–US$200. MC, V. **Amenities:** Restaurant; babysitting; bicycles; outdoor pool; room service; spa; watersports. *In room:* A/C, TV, minibar.

Pondok Pisces ★ The owners of this resort, arguably the friendliest in the Balian beach area, live on the property and personally cater to the needs of their guests. The eclectic mix of bungalows with beach and river views are each decorated with individual flavor. There's no air-conditioning, but ocean breezes and fans are all that's needed for your comfort. The restaurant serves respectable European and local fare. The staff are particularly friendly and reflect the hospitality of the resort's owners.

Balian Beach, Banjar Pengasahan, Lalang Linggah. ✆ **0361/780-1735.** www.pondokpiscesbali.com. 5 units. High season Rp265,000–Rp660,000; low season Rp250,000–Rp620,000. AE, MC, V. **Amenities:** Restaurant; cafe; babysitting; room service. *In room:* Fan, TV/DVD, movie library, fridge.

Shankaris Located on Suraberata beach, about 90 minutes from the airport, Shan-karis, formerly the Sacred River Retreat, caters to wellness sybarites interested in yoga,

Joged Bumbung: The Local Gamelan Music & Dance

The northwest Bali is known for gamelan **Joged Bumbung** ★★, played on about 15 bamboo instruments that produce mellow, haunting, soothing tones and vibrations that can be felt by the body as much as by the ears. Some of the bamboo instruments are so large that musicians actually sit on them and play them with large mallets. The best ensemble to watch is the Jegog Mebarung where two or more orchestras try to out-perform one another.

health food, and spiritual studies. The resort has well-appointed, single- and two-story villas, a vegetarian restaurant, yoga retreat, and pool overlooking the beach. Perfect for the New Age crowd, it hosts equinox solstice celebrations, drumming circles, crystal healing, and moon rituals. The Ganesha waterfall cave is a special treat for those interested in communing with the happiest of all Hindu deities.

Jl. Denpasar, Gilimanuk, Subrata, Selamadeg Barat. ℂ **0361/814992.** Fax 0361/814992. www.shankaris baliretreat.com. 13 units. Year-round US$48–US$72. MC, V. **Amenities:** Restaurant; cafe; lounge; outdoor pool; room service; Wi-Fi (for a fee). *In room:* A/C, TV.

Villa Zolima ★★ **Kids**   It's a 5-minute drive to Balian surfer beach and 10 minutes to Soka beach with its fishermen, fresh lobster, and fish from these luxurious yet understated villas. The modern tropical structures have infinity pools looking over rice fields and the ocean. Children will be in heaven in large expansive playing fields, on the trampoline, and in the adorable Swiss Family Robinson–style tree house complete with child-size furniture. The helpful villa manager greets you on arrival and a chef cooks for you and handles the grocery shopping. Most fruit and veggies come from the on-site organic garden. And, it's only an hour's drive from Seminyak.

Lalang Linggah. ℂ **0361/759668.** www.villazolima.com. 4 bedrooms. Peak season US$1,000; high season US$800; low season US$600. Rates include car with driver, airport transfers, welcome drink, breakfast, afternoon tea, and first lunch or dinner. Other meals market price. No credit cards, but bank transfers possible. MC, V. **Amenities:** Airport transfers, babysitting; outdoor pool; room service; spa therapy; Wi-Fi. *In room:* A/C, fan.

MEDEWI

After a 2½-hour drive from Kuta, a long way from the main Bali surf hub, look for the sign to **Pantai Medewi** (**best season:** dry Apr–Oct; **best swell:** south; **best size:** 4–6 ft.; **best winds:** light winds only), with its old school Bali surfing environment. Its "fatter" left waves and rippable walls are preferred by long-boarders. Barrels are rare. Bring reef-boots as the rocks are sharp, the entrance to the break is difficult, and there is an abundance of sea urchins. This is for serious surfers and not great for swimming. Go early before the winds pick up or venture out with a calm forecast in hand. Medewi is rarely crowded as few choose to make the drive. If you like surfing uncrowded waves with friendly locals and visitors, then Medewi might just be your place on the Island of the Gods.

Pura Luhur at Rambut Siwi   This is another 16th-century temple related to the history of Nirartha. Pura Luhur at Rambut (hair) Siwi means "worship of the hair." Legend has it that Nirartha gifted a lock of his hair that is stored in one of the three enclosures. The stunning cliff overlooks a long, wide stretch of beach and is between the villages of Air Satang and Yeh Embang, at the end of a 300m-long (100-ft.) side road. Look for the sign at the turn-off near the warungs.

Rp2,000 sarong rental, Rp10,000 recommended donation. Daily 7am–5pm.

Where to Stay & Dine

Medewi Beach Cottages   These cottages are ideal for surfers looking for high and long rolling waves and are lovely for those looking for serenity in rugged mountainous surrounds. These spacious cottages come with all the bells and whistles, a large and attractive pool area, and a bar and restaurant.

Pantai Medewi. ⓒ **0361/852521.** www.medewibeachcottages.com. 20 units. High season US$56–US$71; low season US$45–US$60. AE, MC, V. **Amenities:** Restaurant; bar; airport transfers; outdoor pool; room service. *In room:* A/C, TV, fridge.

Puri Dajuma Cottages ★   Travelers headed to Gilimanuk will enjoy an overnight here, the halfway point. You will be perfectly situated to explore both coastal Bali and the rarely visited mountain villages of Asah Duren and Manggissari, where cloves and *kopi* (coffee) are the staple crops. The spacious, comfortable cottages (all with ocean views) are a 2km (1¼ miles) walk from Medewi beach. The resort is family friendly, with a wading pool for the youngest of the bunch. The restaurant serves simple European and local dishes and a wide selection of vegetables and fruit organically grown in their own gardens.

Pekutatan, Negara. ⓒ **0365/43955.** www.dajuma.com. 18 units. Year-round US$147–US$162. MC, V. **Amenities:** Restaurant; bar; bicycles; Jacuzzi; outdoor pool and wading pool; room service; spa. *In room:* A/C, TV, hair dryer, minibar.

4 NEGARA & AROUND

Negara is a quiet district capital that comes to life during the famous **bull races (Makpung)** in early August. A few banks, ATMs, a post office, hospital, police station, petrol station, and Hardy's supermarket make this a good place to stop for supplies.

Until recently, buffalo were simply a means of transportation but now they pull decorated mini-carriages in races in and around Perancak. The buffalo race developed in the 1930s. The jockeys dress in traditional clothing with vests, scarves, and kris (swords). Carts are decorated in full regalia and the bulls pull them around the 2km (1¼-mile) course. Teams are divided by the river, Ljo Gading, that divides the two townships; team names are Timur (East) and Barat (West). In the Magembeng, affiliated cow race, cows can run 100m (328 ft.) in 9 seconds. However, the winners are not necessarily the fastest, as style and elegance count too.

Watch bull race practice every Sunday morning on the black sand beach Delod Berawan, which used to be home to hunted crocodiles. (Curiously enough, it is said that this sand cures rheumatism.) Mendoyo, to the north, hosts some of the best races on Bali. Get race dates from the **Bali Tourism Board** in Denpasar: ⓒ **0361/223602.** Like all things in Bali, take the start times with a grain of sand.

While in Negara, visit with the **local palm sugar farmer** in his small farm in Palasari to observe how this buttery brown sweet is harvested and processed. He also grows and processes cacao fruit that is dried, ground, and shipped to chocolate manufacturers. Book this tour through the Taman Wana (see below). Simply tip the staff from Taman Wana who will help you find the farm. Give a donation to the farmer—he will be pleasantly surprised.

PERANCAK Nirartha arrived here in 1546 where a limestone temple, **Pura Gede Perancak,** was built in commemoration. Bull races take place at **Taman Wisata Perancak** park (📞 **0365/42173**) with occasional runs for prearranged tour groups.

In Perancak village, you can visit the community-run turtle conservation program, **Kurma Asih** or Turtle Lovers Group (Rp25,000). They aim to save the overhunted turtles. Join the effort and "adopt a nest." See if you can set a baby turtle free and share the joy as he takes his first stroke in the water. Nearby are beautiful Madurese-style fishing boats in Perancak Bay.

LOLOAN TIMUR Small traditional *jukung* and sampans sail quietly up the river towards this unique Bali village south of Negara, home to a Muslim Bugis community that preserves 300-year-old traditions. Most are descendants of sailors from Sulawesi who used to be pirates and settled here at the end of the 17th century. A large mosque is in the center and Bugis-style stilt houses are in the area.

BELIMBINGSARI & PALASARI ★★ Christians were exiled to the far west by the Dutch in 1939 after attempting to convert the local Hindus and causing religious unrest in east Bali. Visit the **Catholic** (in Belimbingsari) and **Protestant churches** (in Palasari) that are monuments to Balinese, Hindu, and European design and ornamentation. The local pastors will happily show you the churches and various building projects in progress. Their Christian practice has distinct Balinese Hindu influence.

CEKIK & GILIMANUK

Near to Gilimanuk on the far west coast is Cekik, known as the entrance to Bali's only national park, **Taman Nasional Bali Barat (West Bali National Park).** People who want to start an early trek in the park have limited choices in places to stay. Try the **Hotel Lestari** (📞 **0365/61504**) for between Rp150,000 and Rp350,000 or **Hotel Sari** (📞 **0365/61264**) for Rp150,000. On the way to Gilimanuk, visit the **Jayaprana Grave.** It may be a hot hike up but the views are stunning. The grave is revered by the Balinese, who remember the sad outcome of a typical 17th-century love story here (king covets beautiful woman who loves the king's adopted son; king has son killed; beautiful woman commits suicide).

Though it is certain that Bali was populated very early in prehistoric times, few traces of these people exist. What we do have is on display at the **Museum Situs Purbakala Gilimanuk** (📞 **0365/61328;** admission Rp5,000 donation; Mon–Fri 8am–4pm), 500m (1,640 ft.) south of the ferry port. In the 1960s, archaeological excavations nearby revealed the oldest evidence of human life on Bali with figures ranging, depending on your sources, from about 3,000 to 4,000 years old. Bronze jewelry, axes, pottery, and funerary offerings are on display. Considering their value and historic importance, this could be the best 50 cents you've ever spent.

Gilimanuk is the main port for the 24-hour ferry service to Banyuwangi in East Java. No Balinese would pass through Gilimanuk without enjoying the explosive *ayam betutu* chicken dish served at the famous **Mem Tempe** warung at the top of the steps behind the little bus terminal.

WHERE TO STAY

Taman Wana Villas & Spa ★★ Finds Tucked away in the hills of Palasari, 30km (19 miles) from Bali's west coast, this luxury resort caters to visitors primarily from Europe seeking a total escape. The resort sits atop a hillside overlooking the Palasari

WEST BALI

14

NEGARA & AROUND

reservoir, rice terraces, and, in the distance, the Java Sea. The comfortable rooms are well appointed. The restaurant has a limited menu but serves vegetables and fruits from the resort's organic gardens. Hiking and biking through the nearby Palasari and Belimbing-sari villages in the early morning is an inspired start to your day. The staff will be are happy to show you around. Or take the golf carts on a guided tour.

Jl. Taman Wana, Palasari, Negara. (⟨*C*⟩ **0365/470-2208.** Fax 0365/470-2209. www.bali-tamanwana-villas. com. 27 units. Peak season US$285–US$360 standard, US$1,035 suite; high season US$270–US$345 standard, US$1,020 suite; low season US$250–US$325 standard, US$1,000 suite; extra bed US$35. DC, MC, V. **Amenities:** Restaurant; bar; babysitting; bicycles; Jacuzzi; outdoor pool; room service; spa. *In room:* A/C, TV/DVD, movie library, hair dryer, minibar.

WHERE TO DINE

As you move along the south coast to the west the local fare becomes spicier. If you like your goat satay dipped in five-alarm chili you will love eating along the southern coast. In Negara, the tidy little **Café Nathalia,** Jl. Ngurah Rai 107 (⟨*C*⟩ **0365/41161;** main courses Rp45,000–Rp90,000; MC, V; daily 11am–10pm), in the Wira Prada Hotel, is best known for its spicy Chinese food but also has some of the best *nasi goreng* and fried Indonesian noodle dishes on the southern coast. Follow your meal with a cup of high-octane local coffee. **Rumah Makan Puas,** Jl. Ngurah Rai 60 (⟨*C*⟩ **0365/41618;** main courses Rp40,000–Rp80,000; no credit cards; daily 11am–10pm), just 100m (328 ft.) from the Wira Prada hotel, is best known for its twice-cooked spicy chicken—surprisingly tender given that it is grilled and then fried.

5 TAMAN NASIONAL BALI BARAT ★

The Taman Nasional Bali Barat (West Bali Barat National Park) is teeming with wildlife unseen in east Bali. This is your chance to see a Varanus salvator devouring violet crabs or a long-tailed macaque making off with your hat and sunglasses. The only indigenous animal you won't see is the Balinese tiger—hunted to extinction in the 1930s. Its smaller cousin, the clouded leopard, still roams these forests.

West Bali National Park consists of 770 sq. km (300 sq. miles) of forest, 1,000m (3,280 ft.) of pristine beach, and outlying islands with some of the best diving and snorkeling in Indonesia. The park is surrounded by privately owned plantations and forests, which provide a buffer zone for the park's 200-plus animal species to wander and forage freely. Within the park's boundaries is savanna, monsoon forest, arid volcanic slopes, coral islands, and mangrove swamps. The volcanic peak Gunung Patas dominates the park at an elevation of 1,412m (4,632 ft.).

The park is well known as the last refuge of one of the rarest birds on earth, the Bali starling. Unfortunately, the only way to see this endangered bird is in captivity where they are being bred and released. If you are a birder, take the 2-hour walk along the beautiful **Tegal Bunder trail** to see a variety of local species such as kingfishers, sunbirds, hornbills, orioles, and the ever-present yellow vented bul-bul. Birding is best done in the early morning between 6 and 8am. Bring binoculars. You will see a variety of monkeys, including the ubiquitous long-tailed macaque and the beautiful ebony langur. Several deer species, such as barking deer and large red stags, inhabit the park and the surrounding area. Visit the **Bali Starling Pre-Release Centre** (Rp50,000; daily 8am–3pm). Here the Bali myna or jalak putih birds are being raised and saved from extinction, though

ACCOMMODATIONS ■
Hotel Lestari **12**
Hotel Sari **11**
Menjangan Resort **3**
Mimpi Resort **2**
Novus Gawana Resort & Spa **1**
Waka Shorea **6**
DINING ◆
Mem Tempe **10**

ATTRACTIONS ●
Bali Starling
  Pre-Release Center **5**
Jayaprana Grave **4**
Museum Situs
  Purbakala Gilimanuk **9**
Secret Bay
  (Gilimanuk Bay) **8**
Taman Nasional Bali Barat **7**

there are many in captivity around the world. Ask for directions at the park office in Labuan Lalang.

Menjangan Island ★★ has what are possibly Bali's best dive sites. The waters are calm and clear except in January and February when the sea is rough and windblown. The coral reef walls off Menjangan teem with angelfish, anthias, butterfly fish, and gobies. Swimming with green turtles is a highlight—your guide will know where to find them. Qualified dive shops attached to the resorts in Pemuteran (p. 284) can outfit and transport you to your chosen dive destination. Snorkeling is particularly rewarding in and around Menjangan as the waters are clear and the currents gentle.

An extremely untidy harbor is the starting point for boats to Menjangan. If you are not going through a local dive operator or hotel, expect to pay around Rp330,000 for the boat plus an extra Rp150,000 per person to cover park and guide fees for the island, insurance, and snorkel gear. Pleasant and knowledgeable English-speaking guides will be happy to take you on a day snorkeling trip to the island or to see other less frequented parts of the park. If you are not interested in water activities other than to cool off, just pack a picnic, towels, lots of sun cream, hats, and take the boat to Menjangan anyway.

> **(Moments)** **The Best Time for Wildlife Viewing**
>
> For viewing wildlife in the park, have your guide take you to a water hole where a variety of local wildlife gather in the early evenings to take their fill before retiring.

Explore the island, swim, and visit **Pura Gili Kancana,** one of Bali's oldest and most revered temples.

SCUBA DIVING & SNORKELING   A number of qualified dive centers are along the beach at Pemuteran (p. 284), the best being Kuta-based **Archipelago Dive Sarana** (© **0361/761414;** fax 0361/756944; www.archipelagodive.com) and Nusa Dua–based **Yos Diving** (© **0361/773774;** fax 0361/775439; www.yosdive.com). Two island dives cost US$95, including lunch.

Menjangan Island, part of West Bali National Park, was Bali's first internationally known diving location. Famous for wall-diving with easy conditions, Menjangan is 30 minutes from mainland Bali and offers warm waters, white sand, and visibility that can reach 50m (164 ft.) plus. Between 1997 and 1998, Menjangan's reef flats not only suffered from a population explosion of the coral-eating crown of thorns starfish but also from coral bleaching as a result of El Niño; the walls, however, were unaffected. These walls start at 10m (33 ft.) and descend to 26 to 60m (85–197 ft.) and are full of nooks and crannies, overhangs, and crevasses and are covered with Bali's highest concentration of gorgonian fans as well as soft corals and sponges. The fish life is prolific and you may see turtles. Although you can occasionally see whale sharks, there are only rare sightings of pelagics around Menjangan as the island is protected from the cold ocean currents. Various dive sites circle the island: the main three are **Garden Eel Point, Pos Two,** and **Anker Wreck,** which lies at 35 to 50m (115–164 ft.), though the calm conditions and good visibility could make it easy to forget this is a deep dive.

Secret Bay (aka Gilimanuk Bay) was Bali's first and so best-known **muck dive.** At 2km (1¼ miles) wide, 3 to 12m (10–39 ft.) deep, this is the only bay off the narrow Bali Strait (currents reach 7 knots) and acts as a large catch tank for many larval and juvenile fish and rare marine species. The water is cold and the fish fat and healthy. Unusual nudis, Banggai cardinalfish, gobies, Ambon scorpionfish, filefish, puffers, dragonets, seahorse and pipefish, juvenile Batavia batfish, and many other organisms can be seen here. Elsewhere juveniles hide to avoid predators, but here in Gilimanuk there are very few large fish, leaving the juveniles with no need to hide. The bottom is fine sand with patches of algae and sea grass, some branches, and coconuts (housing for many octopi). Night-diving yields Bobbit worms, cephalopods, wandering crustaceans, and frequent surprises.

FISHING   One of the locals can take you out for a combined fishing and snorkeling trip to the offshore reefs. Bring sun block and a picnic with plenty of beverages packed in ice. These narrow dugouts provide an invigorating downwind sail if the winds are above 5 knots. Cost is typically Rp200,000 to Rp250,000 per day. Arrange boats at the Labuan Lalang park office.

HORSEBACK RIDING   Contact Menjangan Jungle Resort (see below) for riding in and around the park. The cost for 1½ hours of riding is US$30, including a guide.

TREKKING   It is not possible to enter and explore the park alone. Choose from 2-, 4-, or 7-hour treks through the park. The bird walk normally takes 2 hours. The 4-hour trek is a leisurely passage through the foothills and the 7-hour trek is a rigorous hike to the slopes of Mount Klatakan. During the dry season it is possible to obtain an overnight camping permit. Bring mosquito repellant and netting for your overnight. All tours must be guided by locals who charge the following:

     2-hour trek: Rp150,000 for one to two persons; Rp250,000 for three to five people.

     4-hour trek: Rp200,000 for one or two persons; Rp300,000 for three to five people.

     7-hour trek: Rp400,000 for one or two persons; Rp500,000 for three to five people.

     Overnight camping guiding fees range from Rp800,000 to Rp175,000 for four people.

Guides can be booked at the park center in Cekik near Gilimanuk but there is more chance of finding someone who speaks English at the Labuan Lalang harbor office. Discuss and arrange a trek personally with one of the guides the day before. Because of the heat, try to start early in the morning.

WHERE TO STAY & DINE

Although it is possible to dive or snorkel Menjangan Island on a day trip from south Bali, because it's 3½ hours by road plus a short boat ride, it's much better to stay overnight.

Menjangan Resort ★★ (Finds) (Moments)   This nature lover's paradise and well-kept secret inside the National Park is a favorite among the local expat community due to its remote location on "the other side of Bali." The resort sits among 362 hectares (895 acres) of forest and has a beach that looks onto the Menjangan Island. Stay in the forested area at Monsoon Lodge or on a protected cove in one of the beachfront gazebos over the water and surrounded by lush mangroves. The resort has a stable of 30 horses from Australia, a yacht for day cruises, and indigenous wildlife including deer, wild boar, and amazing bird life. Take a day and nighttime safari in an open-air jeep. Dine on Indonesian or Western fare at the amazing five-story Bali Tower Bankirai Restaurant constructed from 28m-long (92-ft.) logs from Kalimantan.

In West Bali National Park. Jl. Raya Gilimanuk-Singaraja, KM. 17, Desa Pejarakan-Buleleng. (✆ **0362/94700.** Fax 0362/94708. www.menjanganresort.com. 23 units. High season US$60–US$250 standard, US$530 villa; low season US$90–US$280 standard, US$560 villa. MC, V. **Amenities:** Restaurant; cafe; bar; bicycles; Jacuzzi; outdoor pool; room service; spa; watersports; Wi-Fi. *In room:* A/C, fan, TV/DVD, hair dryer, minibar.

Mimpi Resort ★   This resort makes a great base for diving, muck diving, and snorkeling excursions in the west due to its on-site PADI dive center. The large swimming pool is lovely and there are also hot spring pools and an open restaurant by the white sand beach. The standard rooms are simple but the large, more expensive villas have private gardens and plunge pools. Some of the villas have an outside bathtub that can be filled with sulfurous water directly from the nearby hot springs.

Banyuwedang. (✆ **0362/94497.** Fax 0362/94498. www.mimpi.com. 54 units. High season US$125–US$225 standard, US$375 villa; low season US$100–US$200 standard, US$350 villa. AE, MC, V. **Amenities:** Restaurant; bar; babysitting; bicycles; concierge; Internet (for a fee); outdoor pool; room service; spa; watersports. *In room:* A/C, TV, hair dryer, minibar.

Novus Gawana Resort & Spa   Just next door to Mimpi, the rooms here are *lumbung* or traditional rice barns and the bedrooms, built into the roof, are reached by a wooden staircase. The swimming pool and restaurant overlook the mangrove bay and the national park beyond. This resort also has its own PADI dive facilities.

Banyuwedang. ⓒ **0362/94598.** Fax 0362/94598. www.novusgawana.com. 14 villas. Peak season US$300–US$400; high season US$180–US$240; low season US$150–US$200. AE, MC, V. **Amenities:** Restaurant; bar; outdoor pool; room service; spa; Wi-Fi (for a fee). *In room:* A/C, fan, stereo or CD, hair dryer, minibar.

Waka Shorea ★   In the Bali Barat National Park just across from Menjangan Island and a short 20-minute boat ride away from Labuan Lalang harbor, this outpost of the Waka chain is set on a private peninsula. Most of the rustic rooms are very pleasant and nothing if not relaxing.

Jl. Raya Seririt Km 15, Gilimanuk. ⓒ **0362/94499.** Fax 0362/94666. www.wakaexperience.com. 16 units. Year-round US$185–US$285. AE, MC, V. **Amenities:** Restaurant; bar; babysitting; Internet (for a fee); outdoor pool; room service. *In room:* A/C, fan.

Lombok

You can see Bali in Lombok, but you can't see Lombok in Bali!
—Traditional local saying

Often referred to as "Bali, 20 years ago," Lombok is finally coming into its own as a traveler's destination. Bali and Lombok are often called "sister islands," with Lombok taking the role of the shy and beautiful younger sister, overshadowed by her glamorous older sister. While many of the features that make Bali so appealing to visitors also exist on Lombok, the island is a unique and fascinating destination in its own right.

Lombok has a rich and diverse culture, which blends the traditions of the indigenous Sasak people with Balinese Hindu and Arabic influences, to name a few. Many of Lombok's traits and customs are similar to those of Java and Bali, yet its people retain traditions and beliefs unique to the island, particularly in language, cultural performances, celebrations, and the arts. Village life is based on the mainstays of farming and traditional handicraft production. The Sasak people are friendly and relatively unaffected by

tourism, with a warm tradition of hospitality to visitors.

At around 5,300 sq. km (2,046 sq. miles), Lombok is only slightly smaller than Bali. The pace on Lombok is unhurried and the atmosphere laid-back. The beaches are uncrowded and tourism enclaves are not marred by high-density development. Although the island has good infrastructure, tourism development only started in the '90s and it has had a slow, steady growth rather than a gold-rush expansion since then.

With the construction of Lombok's first international airport (p. 331) already underway, Lombok is ready to take its place as an international tourism destination. Plans are also underway for a major resort by United Arab Emirates–investment company Emaar Properties, near Kuta in south Lombok. Though the world economic downturn has tempered the pace of development, don't expect the Lombok you see today to be the same you'll see a decade from now.

1 LOMBOK IN DEPTH

A BRIEF HISTORY OF LOMBOK

The indigenous Sasak people of Lombok are descendents of a Malay race who have inhabited Lombok for at least 2,000 years. As part of the Indonesian archipelago, Java has influenced Lombok to varying degrees, conquering and incorporating the island into the Majapahit Empire in the 14th century. Today's Sasak aristocracy still claims Javanese ancestry.

The Balinese colonized Lombok in the 18th century, ruling the island for 150 years until 1894. Balinese influence has always centered in the west, where Balinese still constitute at least 10% of the population. The last king of Lombok reigned over western Lombok during the mid-1800s and oversaw the construction of an impressive number of temples. He also restricted the land rights of the Sasak aristocracy, introduced an

Frommer's Favorite Lombok Experiences

Climbing Gunung Rinjani   Demanding, frustrating, yet hugely rewarding, the climb up Mount Rinjani is a highlight of any visit to Lombok. If a climb up a 3,726m-high (12,224-ft.) volcano is too daunting, treks through the lush forests of the Rinjani National Park have their own rewards. See p. 328.

Heading to the Gili Islands   Needing no introduction, the famous islands of Gili Air, Gili Meno, and Gili Trawangan—collectively known as the Gilis—are the only destination for many travelers to Lombok. Three archetypal coral islands, surrounded by white sands, palm trees, and clear turquoise waters also have no cars, and hence no traffic or pollution. See chapter 16.

Sunning & Surfing in the Southwest & South Coasts   Few places in Indonesia have such a stunningly beautiful vista as the south coast of Lombok. This is where the island meets the Indian Ocean, whose endless rhythms have carved a series of magnificent beaches, bays, peninsulas, cliffs, and inlets into the shoreline. The climate lends itself to days wandering uncrowded beaches, sunbathing on the white sands, and swimming in calm bays. For the adventurous, the south coast is also the surfing mecca of this part of Indonesia. See p. 322 and 332.

Relaxing in Senggigi   Although Senggigi makes the perfect base for exploring the rest of Lombok, it's easy to just choose one of the beautiful resorts and spend your days here instead. The beaches are gorgeous, the resorts luxurious. See p. 316.

Catching a Local Festival   Lombok's population is a mixture of Sasak Muslims, Balinese Hindus, Chinese Buddhists, and more, and festivals and special events are held most any time of the year. Don't miss the **Bau Nyale Festival**

inflexible taxation system, and demanded forced labor of Sasak peasantry. The Sasak revolted several times in the 19th century, with Islam the unifying factor among the armies scattered and isolated across the island.

Sasak leaders approached the Dutch for help in overthrowing the Balinese in the early 1890s. The Dutch, mistakenly believing Lombok was rich in tin, obliged and the Sasak War broke out in 1894. The Balinese were soundly defeated and a number of temples and palaces were destroyed.

Over the centuries, Lombok has been populated by migrants from Java and other Indonesian islands, particularly Bugis shipbuilders and seafarers from Sulawesi. As part of the historical Spice Islands, Arab traders, Chinese, and Dutch all made their homes in Lombok and thus the island has become a melting pot of religions, cultures, beliefs, and ceremonies. The majority of the population today practices a moderate form of Islam, which is still changing and evolving with the impact of modernization and education. Most Sasak Muslims observe Islamic religious practices, such as prayer five times a day and fasting during the month of Ramadan. There are two main groups among the Sasak: **Waktu Lima,** meaning "five times" (the number of times worshipers pray per day), or Sunni Muslims, and **Wetu Telu,** "three times," nominal Muslims who combine Islamic observances with a

(p. 335) in February or March. In July, the **Senggigi Festival** is a wonderful whirl of color, culture, and sound. In October, **Perang Topat** (p. 315) at Lingsar Temple is a fascinating ritual and hilarious local fun. Catch a Gendang Beleq performance—unique to Lombok (p. 306); watch elegant Sasak *tari* dancing, with colorful and dramatic costumes; or ask a local to take you to see a traditional *nyongkolan* wedding procession in the villages, with the beautifully dressed bride and groom parading down the street accompanied by dancing crowds and the weirdly hypnotic, wailing *kecimol* (p. 306) music.

Buying Local Handicrafts   Quite a few of the crafts on sale in Bali are actually made in the villages of Lombok and are available here at a fraction of the price. Lombok **pottery** is exported throughout the world. Distinctive designs in terra cotta and earthenware are hand-thrown in the small villages, such as Masbagik, Penujak, and Banyumulek, by successive generations of potters. **Wood carving** is a Lombok specialty, particularly furniture and ornamental objects carved into intricate designs with mother-of-pearl inlay, called *cukli*. The markets and villages around **Sayang Sayang** in west Lombok, just to the east of Selaparang Airport, have a wide selection of these hand-carved items. Purchase magnificent sea trunks with beaten brass hinges and hasps, ornately carved wooden screens and room dividers, or highly polished decorative bowls and ornaments—all for bargain prices. See p. 321.

Escaping to the Cool Highlands   If the tropical heat is wearing you down, escape to the magical cool mountain retreat of the Sembalun valley. High on the northeast shoulder of Mount Rinjani, Sembalun is steeped in history and mass tourism is still a long way in the future. See p. 338.

mosaic of Hinduism, animism, and ancestor worship. Other religions, particularly Hinduism and Buddhism, peacefully coexist alongside the Muslim population.

ART, ARCHITECTURE & MUSIC

Lombok is famous for its highly collectible and distinctive hand-thrown **pottery.** Huge pots, cooking and dining implements, and ornamental pottery is crafted in the villages of Banyumeluk, Penujak, and Masbagik. Other interesting crafts include hand-carved wooden furniture, ornaments, sculpture, and finely woven cloth called *ikat. Osap,* a more rustic form of *songket* textile, is spun with cotton and is still common in many villages and available throughout the Sasak areas of the island. Old pieces can command thousands of dollars although most are yours for the price of lunch.

Examples of **Dutch colonial architecture** are still evident around the old port in Ampenan and in the administrative buildings that line the main road through Mataram. You can still see quite a few examples of old **Sasak architecture,** the traditional houses of the time before the advent of the Dutch, in the north around Bayan; in the south particularly in the villages of Rambitan and Sade; and in the small villages on the northeast coast. Traditionally, houses were very small and not very high, with a sweeping thatched roof of

> **Tips** **The Rudat**
>
> Try to catch a *rudat* performance while you are on Lombok. *Rudat* combines the-ater and military skill, with performers dressed in uniforms, wielding guns, and re-enacting their Dutch colonial military training, often with humorous, tongue-in-cheek overtones. There are no regular scheduled performances unless you arrive during the Senggigi Festival in July. Otherwise, inquire at your hotel or tour office for current cultural festivals and performances.

alang alang grass. The floors are made from dried cow dung, compressed and polished over the years. New layers of cow dung are added when the flooring wears down and the smell disappears fairly quickly. Two-story *lumbung* huts on pillars usually have woven bamboo walls and thatched *alang alang* roofs. *Lumbung* huts have a distinctive shape to the roof, which curves down from the apex and then flattens out at the eaves, like a bonnet.

Gendang Beleq ("big drums") is the distinctive music of Lombok and forms an important part of island culture. Join in almost any major event or cultural performance in Lombok and you will see a band of colorfully dressed dancers carrying huge drums across their bodies, filling the air with an irresistible beat. These drums are actually a variant of the *kendang* drum that traditionally accompanies gamelan orchestras through-out Indonesia. The barrel-shaped drum produces a deep bass tone and a characteristic high-pitched slap. The *gendang beleq* used in Lombok are distinctive because of their huge size—usually around 1.5m (5 ft.) in length and 50cm (20 in.) in diameter. Drum-mers train for years to master the drumming and maneuvering of the size and weight of the drums in skilful and graceful performance.

Kecimol music, also found on Lombok, is similar and often accompanies marriage processions through the streets of the villages. A vibrant combination of performers includes drums, gamelan, keyboard, and flutes dancing along with someone on a mega-phone mounted on a small carriage. This raucous fusion moves to an almost military marching beat. The keys are played in an Arabic style, with wailing flutes lending Eastern tones to the mix. The whole ensemble is accompanied by a vocalist singing love songs. It is an unmistakable sound, played at high volume, announcing the parade to all the vil-lages and homes it passes along the way.

EATING & DRINKING IN LOMBOK

Lombok means "chili" in Sasak, so it's no surprise that traditional Sasak food is often fiery hot. Lombok is a melting pot of cultures and this is reflected in the styles of food avail-able, ranging from Dutch-influenced breads and *martabak* to authentic Chinese cuisine, spicy Padang food from Sumatra, and traditional Indonesian fare.

Sate pusut is a delicious local satay, with meats, spices, and coconut pressed onto flat skewers and grilled. **Satay tanjung** is a tasty specialty from the Tanjung in north Lom-bok, but also found in the cities, featuring fresh fish and spices wrapped on skewers and grilled. **Lemper** are small parcels of sticky rice filled with shredded chicken or beef and spices, wrapped in coconut leaves. **Lontong** are small conical shaped cakes of rice that have been wrapped in leaves and steamed.

Lombok is famed for its specialty chicken dish **ayam taliwang** (small, free-range vil-lage chicken), which actually originates from the neighboring island of Sumbawa. A whole *ayam kampung* is grilled over coconut husks and served with *sambal. Pelecing ayam* is grilled chicken broken into pieces, added to the spicy and piquant sauce, and slowly simmered, turning the marinade into a delicious red coating.

Being a Muslim island, pork is not readily available except in the tourist areas and at Chinese restaurants and lamb is rare. Goat *(kambing)* however, is very popular. A whole young goat cooked on a spit is the meat of choice for celebrations, parties, and festive occasions, especially the Islamic festivals of Idul Adha and Eid-ul-Fitri. Beef is also freely available on Lombok and a staple in Lombok diets (unlike their Hindu cousins in Bali). **Beef *rendang*** is simmered for hours in coconut milk and spices.

Large tuna, snapper, Spanish mackerel, barracuda, and a huge variety of shellfish are found in the seas off Lombok. *Ikan* (fish) are generally served whole and baked, fried, or more often, grilled on outdoor barbecues over a fire of charcoal and coconut husks. Local *cumi cumi* (squid) and *udang* (prawns) are cooked in fiery *sambal,* braised in oyster sauce, or deep fried.

Particularly popular in Lombok are *pelecing kangkung* and *pecel,* sold from *kaki lima* and warungs everywhere. *Pelecing kangkung* is locally grown *kangkung* (a type of leafy water spinach) boiled and served with fresh bean sprouts and topped with a fiery red chili and tomato sauce. *Pecel* is a variant that combines *kangkung,* cabbage, and other vegetables, fresh bean sprouts, and sometimes tomato with spicy peanut sauce and prawn crackers. *Lalapan* is a plate of fresh cabbage, snake beans, and cucumber served with spicy *sambal.* *Beberuk* (or *Beberuq*) is a typical Sasak side dish of finely diced snake beans and small, round eggplant, with tomato, chili, shallots, lime, and spices. *Ares* is a unique dish made from the inner stem of the banana tree and mixed with coconut milk and spices. *Olah-olah* is made from the heart of banana tree flower mixed with coconut cream, mild spices, and finely chopped snake beans. *Rujak* is unripe fruit such as mango or papaya, mixed with ripe apple, guava, or pineapple, coated in a hot and sweet and sour sauce of sweet soy, palm sugar, and chilies.

> ### A Sasak Saying
> We used to store rice in our *lumbung* huts . . . now they're used to store tourists!

Despite being a Muslim island, alcohol is readily available in all the tourism areas.

2 GETTING THERE & GETTING AROUND

GETTING THERE BY AIR

Selaparang Airport (sometimes called **Mataram Airport**) is located slightly north and between the cities of Ampenan and Mataram. The airport handles domestic flights, as well as international flights from Kuala Lumpur, Malaysia, and Singapore.

Airline offices on Lombok are in Mataram: **Batavia Air,** Jl. Pejanggik; **Garuda Indonesia,** Jl. Panca Usaha 11 (© **0370/638259**); **Indonesia Air Transport (IAT),** Jl. Adi Sucipto; **Lion Air,** Jl. Sriwijaya 81 (© **0370/629111**); and **Silk Air,** Jl. Panca Usaha 11 (© **0370/628254**). In Cakranegara, **Merpati Nusantara Airlines,** Jl. Pejanggik 69 (© **0370/636745**).

FROM BALI   Lombok is only 25 minutes by air from Bali. Payment online is difficult; buy tickets direct from the airline counters at the domestic airports or through local travel agents in both Bali and Lombok. Many seats cannot be held for longer than a few

ATTRACTIONS ●
Batu Layar **18**
Chinese Cemetery **19** ·
Dive Zone & Sundancer **29**
Gerupuk **43**
Gili Genting **30**
Gunung Pengsong Temple **27**
Jeruk Manis Waterfall **47**
Jojang Spring **48**
Mawi Beach **35**
Mawun Beach **34**
Obel Obel Beach **49**
Pantai Sira & Kosaido
  Golf Course **59**
Pura Batu Bolong **17**
Pura Lingsar **24**

Pura Mayura **21**
Pura Medana **58**
Pura Meru **22**
Pura Narmada **25**
Pura Segara **20**
Pura Suranadi & Hutan
  Wisata Suranadi **26**
Selong Blanak **33**
Sendang Gile Waterfall **52**
Sweta **23**
Tanjung A'an Beach **42**

ACCOMMODATIONS ■
The Anandita **57**
The Beach Club **15**
Bola Bola Paradis **32**
Bulan Baru Hotel **1**
Gili Lampu Bungalows **45**

See "Gili Islands"
Chapter 16

BALI SEA

Gondang

57

58 53

56   Tanjung

55   54

59   56   55 54

Bangsal

X-Right

Malimbu

Senggigi

Lombok Strait

1

See "Senggigi"
map (left)

Senggigi

Gg. Punikan

2

4   3

5

6

18

19

7

Ampenan   20

8   9

Mataram ★ Sweta   22 Lingsar   24   26

11   10

Cakranegara   21   23   25   Suranadi

13   12

Narmada

14

27

15

16

*Lombok
Strait*

← To Bali

Bonjeruk

17

Gili
Nanggu
Gili
28   Tangkong Lembar

Sukarara   **Praya**

Bangko-Bangko   30

31   Gili
Gede

29

Tuan

Desert
Point

Gg. Mareje ▲

32

*Gg. Tukad
Ponggod* ▲   Pelangan

Sekotong

Mangkung

Sengkol

Rambitan

Sade

Selong
Blanak

Pengantap

33

36 37 38

INDIAN OCEAN

34 35 Kuta

*Belongas
Bay*

*Selong
Blanak*

*Tanjung
Tampa*

39

40 41

Surfing

Gili Nanggu Cottages **28**
Hati Suci Homestay **46**
Heaven on the Planet **44**
Holiday Resort **4**
Hotel Tugu Lombok **56**
Ken's Hotel **37**

Lembah Rinjani **50**
Matahari Inn **36**
Medana Resort **54**
Novotel Lombok Resort **41**
The Oberoi **55**
Puri Bunga Beach Cottages **9**

Puri Mas Boutique
  Resort & Spa **6**
Puri Mas Kerandangan
  Resort **7**
Qunci Villas **5**
Santosa Villas & Resort **3**
Secret Island Resort **31**
Senggigi Beach Hotel **13**
Sheraton Senggigi
  Beach Resort **8**
Sira Beach House **53**
Tastura Hotel **38**
Villa Sepoi Sepoi **53**
Windy Beach Resort **2**

DINING ◆
Ashtari **40**
Asmara Restaurant **10**
Café Alberto **14**
De Quake Restaurant **11**
Ketapang Café **39**
Kokok Pletok **56**
Lumbung Restaurant &
  Sunbird Café **55**
Medana Resort **54**
Pondok Senaru &
  Restaurant **51**
Square Restaurant **12**
Warung Menega **16**

LOMBOK

15

GETTING THERE & GETTING AROUND

hours so make sure you have time to spare. An alternative to booking direct is to get your hotel or tour operator to book transfers for you; the costs involved are not much more than the flight tickets.

Bali to Lombok airfares are approximately Rp385,000 to Rp450,000, depending on the season. A **Domestic Departure Tax** of Rp30,000 from Denpasar and Rp20,000 from Mataram is applicable to all travelers and is paid when you check in to your flight.

Garuda Airlines (© 08/041807807, at the Bali airport © 0370/646846; www. garuda-indonesia.com) flies a comfortable 737 jet every evening to facilitate international arrivals and departures.

Merpati Airlines (on Lombok © **0370/621111,** at the Lombok airport © 0370/ 33637, on Bali © 0361/235358; www.merpati.co.id) flies direct daily.

Indonesia Air (on Lombok © **0370/668-0210** or 0370/639589, on Bali © 0361/ 759768 or 0361/740-6929; www.iat.co.id) has two flights daily.

Trans Nusa Air (on Lombok © **0370/616-2428** or 0370/616433, on Bali © 0361/ 760218; www.transnusa.co.id) and **Trigana Air** (on Lombok © **0370/646839,** on Bali © 0361/760218; www.trigana-air.com) operates three flights daily.

FROM ELSEWHERE IN INDONESIA   Daily direct flights from Jakarta to Lombok are usually timed to connect with European flights. Lombok is easily accessible from Jakarta, Bali, Jogyakarta, and Surabaya and is an important connection for travel to the eastern islands, in particular Sumbawa, Komodo, and Flores.

Garuda Indonesia (see above) has direct flights between Lombok and Jakarta twice daily. **Lion Air** (© **0370/663444;** www.lionair.co.id) has daily flights between Lombok, Jakarta, and Surabaya. **Merpati Airlines** (see above) has flights between Lombok, Bali, Jakarta, Surabaya, Bandung, Sumbawa, Flores, Kupang, and many other Indonesian destinations. **Trans Nusa Air** (© **0370/616428** or 0370/616433; www.transnusa.co.id) flies between Lombok and Sumbawa four times a week. **Batavia Air** (© **0370/648998**; www.batavia-air.co.id) has daily flights between Lombok, Surabaya, and Jakarta.

FROM OUTSIDE INDONESIA   **Selaparang Airport** in Lombok currently handles international arrivals and has efficient and fast visa processing. **Silk Air** (a subsidiary of Singapore Airlines; © **0370/62825,** 0370/628254, 0370/628256; www.silkair.com) flies direct between Lombok and Singapore, three times a week. **Merpati Airlines** (see above) has daily flights between Lombok and Kuala Lumpur, Malaysia, with a short stopover in Surabaya.

GETTING THERE BY SEA

Padangbai Harbour provides the sea link between Bali and Lombok. **Lembar Harbour,** on Lombok, is approximately 1 hour south of Senggigi. Public ferries depart every hour

LOMBOK

15

GETTING THERE & GETTING AROUND

from 12:35am to 4:55am, then at 7:55, 8:15, 9:50am. The crossing takes approximately 4 to 5 hours and costs Rp31,000. Get to your boat a half-hour before departure. Night ferries run at 9:20, 10:25, and 11:30pm.

Perama Tours (Main office: Jl. Legian 39, Kuta, Bali; ✆ **0361/751551** or 0361/751875; www.peramatour.com) offers a complete transfer package, which includes pickup from destinations throughout Bali and Lombok, bus transfer to the local harbor, ferry ticket, and transfer from the harbor to your destination, on either island. Depending on weather and number of bookings, they may use their private boat transfer direct to the Gilis (chapter 16) and then on to Senggigi, otherwise it's the public ferry. Travel time is approximately 8 hours. The return leg from the Gilis leaves at 7am and from Senggigi at 9am. Times and prices are as follows from: Lovina, 9am, Rp450,000; Kuta, 10am, Rp350,000; Sanur, 10:15am, Rp350,000; Ubud, 11am, Rp350,000; Candidasa, 12:30pm, Rp325,000; Padangbai, 1:30pm, Rp300,000.

THE FAST BOATS   **Blue Water Express** (BWS; ✆ **0361/723479** or 08/1338418988 after hours; www.bwsbali.com) provides transfers between Bali and Gili Trawangan, stopping at Teluk Kode on Lombok. BWS operates two boats, with 25- and 15-passenger capacities, departing from Benoa Harbour, Bali, daily at 8am, arriving in Lombok at 10am; and from Gili Trawangan at 11am. BWS leaves Lombok at 11:30am, arriving in Bali at 1:30pm. Fares include air-conditioned hotel transfers in Bali. Tickets cost Rp690,000 one-way; Rp1,300,000 round-trip. Price is the same regardless of where you disembark.

Gili Cat (✆ **0361/271680;** www.gilicat.com), an Australian-built small fast ferry, departs Padangbai on Bali at 9am daily and travels to Lombok and Gili Trawangan (p. 349), before returning to Bali, departing Gili Trawangan at 11:15am. Their service also includes free transfers between Padangbai, Ubud, Kuta, and Sanur on Bali. Journey time is around 1 hour; tickets are Rp660,000 one-way; Rp1,200,000 round-trip.

Specialized Lombok Tours

Sunda Trails (✆ **0370/647390;** www.sundatrails.com) offers off-the-beaten-track tours to remote villages. Run by the enthusiastic Anita, with many years of experience traveling throughout Lombok and the nearby islands, Sunda works closely with local communities and is ideal for those with an interest in different cultures. Tours can be tailor-made for individuals or groups. Ready-made tours range from trips around Lombok and the islands to the east, tours to Mount Rinjani, trekking and trips to Komodo Island to see the Komodo dragons, and trips based on specific cultural festivals or events.

To see Lombok up close and personal, book a tour through **Lombok Biking Tours** (✆ **0370/692164**). These safe and professional bike tours are designed for all levels of fitness, from easy rides near Senggigi to challenging trips through hills and over winding roads. Friendly and experienced local guides accompany your trip on well-maintained bicycles and mountain bikes. Tours include the service of a local guide, bottled water and snacks, plus private transport to wherever your trip begins and ends. Their shop is located on the main street in Senggigi (next to Bumbu Café).

Airport taxis (dark blue) service incoming flights; a taxi counter is in the arrivals hall at the airport, with fares to various destinations around Lombok displayed (airport to center of city will cost between Rp25,000 and Rp30,000 and takes around 15 min.). Light blue **Blue Bird Taxis** (© 0370/627000) service most destinations in Lombok and are easily flagged down on the roadside. All taxis in Lombok automatically use their meters and fares are low, so there is no need to haggle prices (unlike in Bali).

Bemo (small public minibuses) also ply the routes from city to city, and from Ampenan to Senggigi on the west coast. Smaller private *bemo* (with open backs and bench seating) are available for charter, but you need good negotiating skills. It's far easier (and often more economical) to use taxis or hire a car.

Rent a car from: **Lombok Car Rentals** (© 0370/660-9477; www.lombokcarrentals. com; daily US$15–US$25); **Lombok Car Hire** (© 08/18362905; daily US$20–US$35); and **Lombok Hotel and Travel** (© 0370/665-0238; www.lombokhotel andtravel.com; daily Rp225,000–Rp550,000).

Daily motorbike rentals are available from: **Lombok Komodo** (© 0370/654846; www.lombokkomodo.com; Rp35,000–Rp75,000); **Lombok Tour and Travel** (© 0370/ 693-584; www.lombok-tourandtravel.com; Rp60,000); and **Lombok Cars** (© 0370/ 657-9425; www.lombokcars.com; US$5–US$10).

(*Fast Facts*) Lombok

Banks & ATMs In Mataram, banks are at Jalan Pejanggik 2 and Jalan Langko; in Cakranegara, you'll find banks along Jalan Pejanggik. Two banks are located on Jalan Raya Senggigi in Senggigi. ATMs are in Mataram, Senggigi, and Praya. Bring cash.

Currency Exchange Most hotels and stores will exchange money, but the rates are poor. Banks also exchange cash and traveler's checks. Try the exchange offices at Jalan Raya Senggigi km 13 (© 0370/692247) and Jalan Raya Senggigi km 10 (© 0370/693693) instead.

Hospitals & Clinics In Mataram, **Mataram General Hospital,** Jl. Pejanggik 6 (© 0370/622254); **Santo Antonius Hospital,** Jl. Koperasi 16 (© 0370/636767); **Army Hospital,** Jl. HOS Cokroaminoto 7 (© 0370/640149); Siti Hajar Islamic Hospital, Jl. Catur Warga (© 0370/623498); and **Klinik Risa Husada,** Jl. Pejanggik 115 (© 0370/625559). In Senggigi, try the **Senggigi Medical Clinic,** in Senggigi Beach Hotel (p. 318; © 0370/693856).

Internet Access In Mataram, try: **Elian Internet,** Mataram Mall; **Wartel,** Jl. Pejanggik; **Telkom,** Jl. Pendidikan 23 (© 0370/633333; 24 hr.). In Sengigga, try **Planet Internet** (© 0370/693920), **Superstar Internet,** or **Millennium Internet** (© 0370/693860; 24 hr.), all on Jl. Raya Senggigi.

Pharmacies In Mataram, **Kimia Farma,** Jl. IGK Jelantik Gosa (© 0370/624845); **Airlangga Farmasi,** Jl. Airlangga 25A (© 0370/634221); **Masyarakat Farmasi,** Jl. AA Gde Ngurah (© 0370/633547); **Kemala Hikmah Pharmacy,** Jl. Langko 64 (© 0370/646322).

Police The island's **main police office** is at Jalan Langko 77, Mataram (© 0370/ 632733). A police station is on Jalan Raya Senggigi (© 0370/693267) in Senggigi.

Post Office Lombok's main post office is at Jalan Sriwijaya 37, Mataram (☎ **0370/ 632645;** Mon–Thurs 8am–5pm, Fri till 11am, Sat till 1pm). Other offices are at Jalan Langko, Mataram (☎ **0370/631642;** Mon–Thurs 8am–4:30pm, Fri till 11am, Sat till 1pm); Jalan Raya Senggigi (Mon–Sat 8am–6pm); and in Segara Anak Cottages, south Lombok (☎ **0370/654846**).

Tourist Offices & Visitor Information In Mataram: the **West Lombok Tourist Office** is located at Jalan Suprato 20 (☎ **0370/621658;** Mon–Thurs 7:30am–2pm, Fri till 11am, Sat 8am–1pm) and the **West Nusa Tenggara Tourist Office** is at Jalan Singosari 2 (☎ **0370/634800;** Mon–Thurs 8am–2pm, Fri till 11am, Sat till 12:30pm). In Senggigi call ☎ **0370/632-733.** The tourist information center on Mount Rinjani is open daily 6am to 6pm.

3 WEST LOMBOK

West Lombok is the most developed area of the island for tourism. Just as in Bali, tourists in Lombok generally do not stay in the cities and instead head straight for the beaches. **Senggigi** (p. 316) is the main beach resort approximately 20 minutes drive from the airport. The west interior is lush with agricultural lands and mountains sheltering small picturesque towns and villages. On the coast, the wide Lombok Strait separates Lombok from Bali and forms a series of picturesque bays and beaches. This region, being closest to Bali, has a long history of Hindu settlement and traces of the old empires are still visible in the large Hindu population, temples, and traditional ceremonies.

GETTING THERE & GETTING AROUND

Dark blue airport **taxis** are available at the arrivals terminal at the airport. From the airport to the city center will cost around Rp25,000 to Rp30,000 and takes around 15 minutes. Blue Bird taxis ply the route between Senggigi and the cities, and around Senggigi, and can be hired for most destinations around the island. Yellow public *bemo* connect the cities of Ampenan, Mataram, and Cakra. Fares are around Rp5,000. To explore the cities **hire a car and driver,** rather than using taxi.

THE CITIES

The three main cities of Lombok—Ampenan, Mataram, and Cakranegara—were clearly defined in the past, but as populations have grown the three have melded together to create what is, for Lombok, an urban sprawl.

Ampenan was originally Lombok's main seaport. With its numerous cheap hotels, old buildings, plentiful *cidomo* (horse carts), gold and pearl shops, and its Arab quarter, Ampenan is a colorful town to explore in its own right. The remains of the port are at the end of the road to the west, at the intersection of the five roads of central Ampenan. This area becomes a market at night, filled with warungs and *kaki lima* (food carts) for cheap, tasty food and local flavor. Cultural shows, such as *gandrung* dance or the shadow puppet play *wayang sasak,* take place here on special holidays. Some Dutch colonial architecture is still visible toward the beach. Ampenan has a reasonably large Arab and Chinese population and you'll see an interesting Buddhist temple on the road to the old port. **Kebun Roek,** near the traffic lights in Ampenan on the road from the airport, is the site of the local market. Every day traders set up stalls selling fresh produce from around the island, local snacks, live chickens, and fresh fish in the afternoon when the fishing boats come in.

Mataram starts about 3km (2 miles) to the east of Ampenan, and is the administrative center for Lombok and Sumbawa. Numerous government offices, banks, mosques, and churches line the main street. The public hospital (Rumah Sakit Umum), the main post office, and Mataram University are all here. The cultural center **Taman Budaya** (© 0370/622428), on Jalan Majapahit, regularly presents traditional music and dance. You can often visit during rehearsal.

> **When on Lombok . . .**
>
> Be respectful of the Muslim culture, which tends to be more conservative than the Hindu culture.

Cakranegara (often abbreviated to Cakra) to the east of Mataram, is Lombok's main shopping area. The main road is lined with electronics and textile shops, bookstores, sporting goods stores, and other small businesses. The only shopping mall in Lombok is just past the monument on the main road from Mataram to Cakra. The upstairs food court has cheap local meals.

The main road continues further east to **Sweta** (almost a city in its own right) and the **Bertais Bus Terminal,** serving destinations in east Lombok and where it is possible to arrange transport to neighboring Sumbawa and to the islands of Flores and Komodo. The main road is wide and in good condition, and is the main route across Lombok to the east coast.

Exploring the Cities & Nearby Temples

While in Mataram, visit the **Provincial Museum and Cultural Centre** (Nusa Tenggara Barat Museum; Jl. Panji Tilar; © 0370/632159; admission Rp2,000; Tues–Sun 8am–noon), which houses artifacts from Lombok and Sumbawa, including exhibits on the geology, history, and culture of the islands, as well as some priceless weapons and costumes. The museum is interesting enough, if you can manage to get there when it's open.

Local temples are open daily, 10am to 5pm; admission (and occasional eel feeding) is by donation. **Pura Meru,** on Jalan Selaparang in Cakranegara, was built in 1720 by Balinese Prince Anak Agung Made Karang and is the largest temple on Lombok. The interior enclosure has 33 shrines as well as the three multitiered *meru* (mountain altar) representing the Hindu trinity. This important temple for the Balinese hosts an annual Pujawali festival, held over 5 days during the full moon in September or October, the biggest Hindu event on Lombok.

Pura Mayura, just across the street from Pura Meru, was built in 1744 as the court temple of the last Balinese kings in Lombok. A *bale kambang* (floating pavilion) in a large artificial lake is used as a meeting place. Today the palace gardens are a playground for children. The temple sits behind the sedate water gardens.

The temple of **Gunung Pengsong,** on Jalan Gajah Mada south of Mataram, sits on a hilltop with vistas of rice fields, the sea, and Gunung Rinjani. Populated by monkeys, this is the hill the Balinese aimed for in the mythic account of their initial arrival in western Lombok. In March or April, a buffalo is sacrificed here to ensure a rich harvest. The Bersih Desa, or "village purification" festival, held every year at harvest time, finds the area spruced up to honor the rice goddess, Dewi Sri.

Pura Lingsar, Desa Lingsar, Narmada, is sacred not only to Lombok's Hindu community, but also for local Muslim and Wektu Telu followers. Built around 1714, Pura Lingsar was originally dedicated to the prevailing animist beliefs of the time, and some of the original animist statues remain today. This is the only temple on Lombok where all the religions—Hindu, Buddhist, Christian, and Muslim—come together to pray for prosperity, fertility, rain, health, and general success. **Perang Topat** is an annual festival held here and features a ritualized war with rice cakes, which also serve as an offering to the Gods. Lingsar has spring-fed pools within the temple grounds and is home to large freshwater eels. Visitors are welcome to accompany a temple priest to feed them hard-boiled eggs, purchased at nearby stands.

Pura Narmada, around 10km (16 miles) east of Cakranegara in Narmada, was created circa 1805 as a replica of Gunung Rinjani and Segara Anak, the lake within Rinjani's crater. The gardens at Narmada are beautifully maintained and surround the pools and lake. Check for performances of traditional dances on special occasions. Some of the other pools at Narmada are available for swimming (modest attire, please) and are popular with local people.

Pura Suranadi, a complex of three temples a few kilometers north of Narmada in Suranadi, is the oldest and holiest of the Balinese temples in Lombok, founded by the 16th-century Javanese priest, Danghyang Nirartha. Underground streams bubble up into restored baths, used for ritual bathing. Suranadi is regarded as the place to obtain the proper holy water for Hindu cremations. Huge sacred eels live in the pools and streams here, and can sometimes be lured out with an offering of boiled eggs (purchased at a nearby stall). To see a sacred eel is considered very lucky; conversely, it is taboo to eat the eels or to contaminate their water.

Beyond Suranadi, on the main road before the temple, is **Hutan Wisata Suranadi** (Rp4,000; daily 8am–5:30pm), literally the Suranadi Tourist Forest. Stroll through the botanical garden with labeled specimens and observe birds, monkeys, and butterflies.

Shopping

Mataram Mall, Jl. Pejangik, Cakranegara (daily 9am–9pm), is Lombok's only real mall. **Hero Supermarket,** on the ground floor, is useful for some Western goods, food, and toiletries. The **Chemist** next door has imported toiletries, nutritional supplements, and medicines. McDonald's and KFC have outlets on the ground floor.

Many of Lombok's **weaving** and **basketry** industries are located near Cakranegara. Turn left at the central traffic lights and look for the market on the right near the bridge. The baskets in particular are sold in Bali at many times the Lombok price. Further east, near the Bertais bus terminal, the next large town east of Cakra, sometimes referred to as Sweta, has a huge daily market, with all kinds of goods on sale from foodstuffs, to clothing, to exotic birds, handicrafts, and more.

Where to Dine

Try **Delicio Restaurant** in the Mataram Mall (daily 9am–9pm), for Chinese and international meals, coffee, and delicious Western cakes. **Oceanic Café,** on the second floor, is great for salads and dim sum. **Elements,** on the second floor in the new wing, serves fresh juices and coffee. Across the road from the Mall is **Pizza Hut.**

Seafood Nikmat, Jl. Panca Usaha 1, Cakranegara (© **0360/634-330;** main courses Rp10,000–Rp13,500; no credit cards; daily 11am–11pm), is equally popular with locals and visitors. Ignore the less than glamorous surroundings and enjoy some of the best seafood in Lombok. Chef William trained in Australia and uses a combination of traditional cooking and Asian-fusion styles. Live lobsters swimming in the tank, fresh crabs and prawns on ice, and a selection of the best fish from the daily markets keep customers coming to Nikmat. Highly recommended is the live crab in piquant Padang sauce—a huge, delicious meal for two.

A Boat Trip

All the way up the western coast of Lombok you will find beaches full of *jukung*. Hitch a ride over to the Gilis (chapter 16) for some snorkeling and lunch. The trip should take up to an hour each way but ask before as it depends on the wind and currents. These boats do have motors so don't worry too much if you find yourself in the middle of the ocean without any wind. Book a day in advance if possible. Expect to pay about Rp250,000 for a half-day for four people.

At night, **Jalan Pejanggik** (the main street of Mataram) comes alive with many covered stalls set up along the road. Seating is basic, at plastic chairs and tables. *Ayam taliwang,* Lombok's chicken specialty, is served at many of the stalls here, together with barbecued fish and seafood, satays, and a wide range of the local fast food. Prices fall in the Rp10,000 to Rp25,000 range.

THE WEST COAST

The main road along the west coast starts at Ampenan and winds its way parallel to the beaches. Orientation and travel is easy. Heading north from Ampenan is **Pura Segara,** a Balinese sea-temple. The **Chinese cemetery,** on the main road just out of Ampenan, has interesting graves painted in bright colors with Chinese decorations.

Batu Layar, on the hill a couple of kilometers before Senggigi, has an important ancestral grave *(makam)* where Muslims picnic and pray for health and success. Lombok has many *makam,* typically the graves of important religious leaders that have become shrines. The graveyard and the nearby beach are very popular during Muslim holidays, particularly Eid-ul-Fitri (Lebaran) and at Lebaran Topat.

Nearby **Pura Batu Bolong** (literally meaning "rock with a hole"), is an interesting Hindu temple on a cliff facing Bali across the Lombok Strait. Built on a large rocky outcrop with a hole at the base, it is said that virgins were once sacrificed to the sea from the seatlike rock at the outermost point. Colorful Hindu ceremonies are held here every month at the dark and full moons, and at Hindu festival times. Admission and compulsory temple sash by donation. This is a great place to watch the sunset, with fantastic vistas across to Gunung Agung on Bali.

The **beaches** of the west coast are large sweeping bays of clean turquoise water, white sands, and coconut groves.

4 SENGGIGI

Nowhere near as large or as busy as its Bali counterparts, Senggigi is the main tourism center on Lombok and, apart from the Gili Islands, the most developed tourism area. Senggigi is a great base for exploring the rest of Lombok, with day trips within a few hours drive from town.

GETTING THERE

Senggigi is about 10km (16 miles) north of Ampenan and about 20 minutes drive from Lombok's airport. Hire a dark blue airport **taxi** from the arrivals terminal at the airport (around Rp60,000). From Lembar Harbor, either charter a *bemo* or catch a Blue Bird

taxi. It's possible to join with other travelers in sharing the cost of chartering a *bemo.*
From other destinations, taxis are the easiest form of transport.

ORIENTATION

Senggigi Beach is the large bay that forms the center of Senggigi, with the main road running parallel to the beach, and large resorts occupying the space between. The main road in Senggigi is lined with small shops, tour agencies, restaurants, bars, and nightclubs. The town has a couple of supermarkets, one BNI bank, numerous ATMs and money changers, and a post office.

Tourism development runs north along the coastal road for about 10km (16 miles). About 2km (3 miles) north is **Kerandangan Valley,** with a popular beach and some nice hotels. Past that is **Mangsit,** an accommodation alternative to Senggigi, with boutique-style hotels positioned along breathtaking bays. Furthest north is **Lendang Luar,** with two hotels—Bulan Baru and Ebano R & R—perched on the long stretch of pristine beach here.

Mainly deserted white sand beaches, flanked by coconut groves, and untouched by hotel development, continue all the way north along the main coastal road. **Malimbu** and **Nipah** are two picturesque bays good for snorkeling, swimming, and getting away from it all, less than a half-hour from Senggigi.

Teluk Nara and **Teluk Kodek** are on a large bay that forms a natural harbor, about 25km (15 miles) north of Senggigi. All the main dive operators have boats here, which transfer guests to the Gili Islands, as an alternative to nearby Bangsal Harbour. **Bangsal Harbour** (p. 325) is reached by turning left at the crossroads in Pemenang; it is easy to catch the public ferries (actually large outrigger boats) out to the Gilis, or to charter boats for island hopping from here.

WHERE TO STAY

Expensive

Sheraton Senggigi Beach Resort ★   In central Senggigi with a private stretch of beachfront, the Sheraton also has a large swimming pool with swim-up bar and fantastic water slide for the kids. Within the grounds are two private villas, set behind walls right on the beachfront. Each villa has its own courtyard garden and private pool. Ultra-luxurious furnishings and every conceivable comfort set these in a class of their own, with a price tag to match.

Senggigi Beach. ✆ **0370/693333.** www.sheraton.com/senggigi. 154 units. Peak season Rp975,000–Rp3,000,000 standard, Rp8,750,000 villa; high season Rp925,000–Rp2,950,000 standard, Rp8,700,000 villa; low season Rp725,000–Rp2,750,000 standard, Rp8,500,000 villa; extra bed Rp350,000. AE, MC, V. **Amenities:** 2 restaurants; fitness center; spa; watersports. *In room:* A/C, TV, hair dryer, minibar.

Moderate

Holiday Resort (Kids)(Value)   Formerly part of the Holiday Inn chain, but always of a superior standard, the Holiday Resort sits on its own stretch of beach in Mangsit. Comfortable rooms and chalets look out over the ocean or the lush gardens. The freeform pool overlooks the beach and has a Jacuzzi. Across the road from the main resort are the self-contained apartments. With two bedrooms, a living and dining room, and fully equipped kitchenette, these are ideal for long-term guests and families.

Senggigi Beach. ✆ **0370/693444.** www.holidayresort-lombok.com. 188 units. Peak season US$82–US$117; high season US$77–US$112; low season US$67–US$102; extra bed US$20. MC, V. **Amenities:** 2 restaurants; lounge/bar; kids' club; fitness center; spa. *In room:* A/C, hair dryer, minibar.

Puri Mas Boutique Resort & Spa   Puri Mas has two boutique properties: on the beachfront at Mangsit and set in pretty gardens in the Kerandangan Valley. Both have charming rooms and private villas, furnished with antiques and collectibles, set in lovely beachfront gardens. In Mangsit, the one-bedroom luxury villas are set within walled gardens with fantastic pools separating the bedrooms from the main living areas; the open-air garden bathrooms are delightful.

The **Puri Mas Kerandangan Resort,** Jl. Wisata Alam, Desa Kerandangan (3 units; high season US$100; low season US$95; AE, MC, V) has private Balinese-style villas set alongside a pool in beautiful gardens with lotus ponds and romantic bales. All rooms come with their own verandas and the furnishings are rather ornate with lots of carved wood typical of the Lombok style. Other amenities include available bikes, a spa, and Wi-Fi.

Jl. Raya Mangsit Beach, Senggigi. ✆ 0370/693831 (for both resorts). www.purimas-lombok.com. 24 units. High season US$103 standard, US$175 suite, US$365 villa; low season US$85 standard, US$145 suite, US$300 villa. AE, MC, V. **Amenities:** Restaurant; bar; babysitting; bicycles; concierge; outdoor pool; room service; spa. *In room:* A/C, hair dryer, minibar, Wi-Fi.

Qunci Villas ★★ (Finds)   The extremely popular Qunci Villas incorporates two fabulous boutique properties on the beachfront in Mangsit, within 100m (328 ft.) of each other. The stylish rooms and private villas with personal plunge pools feature minimalist architecture and elegant furnishings. The newer Qunci Pool Villas have a stunning infinity pool on the beachfront, with a wooden deck and sumptuous lounging platforms with big padded cushions. The Zen harmony of the buildings and the decorations uses natural tones and clean classic lines, and combines wood, stone, and flowing landscaping, so that nothing grates on the nerves. A smooth teak tree trunk is casually parked on the lawn as a garden seat; a slab of slate masquerades as a table top; a huge hollowed-out boulder creates a unique bathtub.

Jl. Raya Mangsit, Senggigi. ✆ 0370/693800. www.quncivillas.com. High season US$95 Garden View, US$115 Ocean View, US$195 villa; low season US$75 Garden View, US$95 Ocean View, US$145 villa. MC, V. **Amenities:** 2 restaurants; 2 bars; spa. *In room:* A/C, hair dryer; minibar.

Santosa Villas & Resort ★ (Kids)   This resort stretches between Senggigi Beach and the center of town. A recent renovation transformed the old hotel into a stunning resort with fountains, lotus and koi ponds, and a range of accommodation from comfortable standard rooms to spacious suites. The magnificent lagoon-style pool with arched bridges and swim-up bar commands fantastic views over the bay. Four private villas hide behind high sandstone walls, with wooden decks, garden seating, and private pools. The spacious bedrooms open onto a large and luxurious marble bathroom, with sunken bathtub and separate rain showers.

Jl. Raya Senggigi Km. 8, Senggigi. ✆ 0370/693090. www.santosavillas.com. 192 units. Year-round US$100–US$250 standard, US$400 villa, US$500 family suite; extra bed US$30. AE, MC, V. **Amenities:** 2 restaurants; lounge; outdoor pool; spa; 2 tennis courts. *In room:* A/C, TV, hair dryer, minibar.

Senggigi Beach Hotel & Pool Villa Club (Kids)   This resort occupies the entire peninsula that juts out to Senggigi Bay and faces two separate beachfronts. The hotel has a full range of activities and facilities and is good value for families. Choose from a range of different styles of rooms, from standard to bungalows, though the ocean view bungalows are the nicest. Within the grounds of the hotel, but separated from the main resort, is the **Pool Villa Club**—16 luxury villas with separate reception, entrance, and restaurant that surround a canal-style swimming pool. Local sandstone, marble, coconut wood, and ethnic decorations create a delightful ambience, while all fittings and facilities are modern. The four-person Jacuzzi on a sandstone deck beside the pool has angled doors for privacy, or can be opened up to enjoy the views.

Jl. Pantaai Senggigi, Mataram. ✆ 0370/693210. www.senggigibeachhotel.com. 150 units. High season US$75–US$170 standard, US$550 villa; low season US$55–US$150 standard, US$500 villa; extra bed

US$25. AE, DC, MC, V. **Amenities:** 3 restaurants; kids' club; outdoor pool; spa; 2 tennis courts. *In room:* A/C,
TV, hair dryer, minibar.

Inexpensive

The Beach Club (Finds)   This delightful little place is on the beach just before Senggigi and next to Café Alberto (p. 320). The beachfront bar and restaurant is popular with Lombok expats and tourists. The club has lounging bales and tables on the beach, a backpacker's cottage, and three beautiful timber bungalows with thatched roofs nestled in a beachfront garden. In the center of the pretty tropical garden is a gorgeous swimming pool, with an elevated deck and comfortable sun loungers to take in the ocean views.

Jl. Raya Batu Bolong, Senggigi. ✆ **0370/693637** or 08/1805243380. www.thebeachclublombok.com. 4 units. High season Rp380,000; low season Rp350,000. No credit cards. **Amenities:** Cafe; restaurant; bar; outdoor pool; Wi-Fi. *In room:* A/C, TV/DVD, movie library, minibar.

Bulan Baru Hotel (the New Moon) (Value)   Located a kilometer north of Windy Beach, the Bulan Baru is nestled in a pretty valley opposite a long peaceful stretch of beach. The rooms are spacious and comfortable and feature open-air garden bathrooms. The central pool has swim-up bar service. Bulan Baru is 7km (4 miles) north of Senggigi—close enough to enjoy all the facilities of the tourist resort, but far enough away to have a sense of village living.

Jl. Raya Senggigi, Setangi. ✆ **0370/693785.** 12 units. Year-round Rp250,000; extra bed Rp50,000. No credit cards. **Amenities:** Restaurant; bar; Internet; outdoor pool. *In room:* A/C, minibar.

Puri Bunga Beach Cottages   On a terraced hillside overlooking Senggigi Beach, opposite the Pasar Seni (Art Market), this was one of the first hotels in Senggigi. Choose from budget to midrange cottages. Interiors are simply decorated and rather basic, but all have private terraces with fantastic views of the stunning sunsets.

Jl. Raya Mangsit Beach, Senggigi. ✆ **0370/693013.** www.puribungalombok.com. 50 units. High season US$35–US$60; low season US$30–US$50. MC, V. **Amenities:** Restaurant; bar; babysitting; bicycles; concierge; outdoor pool; room service; watersports; Wi-Fi (for a fee). *In room:* A/C, TV, hair dryer, minibar.

Windy Beach Resort   For travelers less concerned with plush surroundings and more concerned with unwinding in a beautiful natural environment, Windy Beach is the perfect choice along this stretch. This rustic and charming property on its own beachfront in north Mangsit offers basic but comfortable rooms; the deluxe bungalows are more spacious. Walk along the peaceful white sand beach, relax and read in beachside bales, or lay by the beachfront pool to watch the stunning sunsets.

Jl. Raya Mangsit Beach, Senggigi. ✆ **0370/693191.** www.windybeach.com. 16 units. Peak season US$44–US$55; high season US$39–US$50; low season US$34–US$45; extra bed adult US$10, children 11 and below US$5. No credit cards. **Amenities:** Restaurant; outdoor pool. *In room:* A/C, hair dryer, minibar.

WHERE TO DINE

Look out for **theme dinners** and traditional dinner shows at the hotels. Shows usually feature traditional music, theater, and dance presentations by local performers and are accompanied by a reasonably priced buffet dinner. The Sheraton, Santosa, Holiday Resort, and Qunci Villas often host cultural dinner dances.

Moderate

Square Restaurant ★★ (Finds) INTERNATIONAL   Square is indisputably the fine dining choice in town. Executive Chef Wayan Budiana has been involved in the Bali restaurant scene for many years, most notably at the hugely successful Mozaic, before moving to

Lombok. The restaurant has a temperature-controlled wine cellar and one of the best-stocked bars in Lombok. Imported wines, Cuban cigars, beautifully presented meals, efficient and friendly service, and top-quality produce are all hallmarks of dining here. Foie gras has almost become the restaurant's signature dish, pan-seared and served with apple chutney and tamarind. Or try the beef tenderloin, with mashed potato and broccoli au gratin.

Jl. Raya Senggigi. ✆ **0370/664-4888.** Fax 0370/623975. www.squarelombok.com. Lunch Rp45,000–Rp70,000; dinner Rp60,000–Rp150,000; set menu Rp250,000. AE, MC, V. Daily 11am–11pm.

Warung Menega (**Finds**) BARBECUE/SEAFOOD   Slightly out of town, to the south near the Bintang Hotel, this is a similar seafood barbecue experience to those in Jimbaran on Bali. Warung Menega serves fresh local seafood barbecues every day for lunch and dinner. Tables are set up on the sand, with the waves only meters away. Wonderfully fresh snapper, barramundi, grouper, and other fish are barbecued and served whole, with rice, water spinach, and a selection of dipping sauces. Guests select fish, lobster, prawns, squid, and local clams displayed on ice near the barbecue; price is determined by weight. The local clams, topped with a piquant barbecue sauce and then lightly grilled, are seriously delicious and only Rp60,000 per kilo.

Jl. Raya Senggigi 6. ✆ **0370/663-4422.** www.menega.com. Seafood per kg; crab Rp90,000; fish Rp60,000–Rp70,000; lobster Rp300,000–Rp500,000. AE, MC, V. Daily 10am–11pm.

Inexpensive

Asmara Restaurant (**Kids**) (**Value**) GERMAN/INDONESIAN/SASAK   This has deservedly been one of Senggigi's most popular restaurants for many years. On the main street, just up from the Art Market, the restaurant offers street-side or elegant indoor dining. There is also a separate bar, billiards room, library, and PlayStation for the kids. Children are well catered to with a special menu, with sensible prices and serving sizes. The restaurant has a very good selection of local Sasak and Indonesian dishes, together with German specialties and international food. Organically grown herbs, homemade breads and yogurt, and fresh local produce set this restaurant apart from the rest. Try the locally produced pineapple wine—a dry, white wine with a subtle pineapple finish and a kick. It's the Lombok version of grappa. Special dishes of seasonal fare are available every week, and a great value three-course lunch is available every day for just Rp45,000. Every Friday night is "Stammtisch," a German tradition of "open table" (buffet), where anyone is welcome to join the table of expatriates and residents enjoying the good food and live music.

Jl. Raya Senggigi. ✆ **0370/693619.** www.asmara-group.com. Set lunch Rp45,000; Indonesian Rp30,000–Rp55,000; Western Rp60,000–Rp165,000. MC, V. Daily 7am–11pm.

Café Alberto (**Kids**) ITALIAN/SEAFOOD   On the beach, just at the south entrance to Senggigi, is one of the best Italian restaurants in Lombok. Café Alberto also has an open lounge area, a pool, and a poolside bar overlooking the ocean. Guests are invited to spend their day by the beach, swimming in the pool, lounging on the comfortable banquettes, taking advantage of the free Wi-Fi, all while enjoying the great food. Fresh seafood barbecues, authentic pastas, bruschetta, and wood-fired pizzas are Café Alberto's best dishes. Don't forget to try their homemade limoncello.

Jl. Raya Senggigi. ✆ **0370/693039** or 0370/693313. www.cafealberto.com. Indonesian Rp45,000–Rp65,000; pasta Rp48,000–Rp120,000; seafood Rp65,000–Rp185,000. MC, V. Daily 9am–midnight.

De Quake Restaurant ★ (**Finds**) SEAFOOD   This delightful find sits on the beachfront in the Pasar Seni (Art Market). Enjoy the best strawberry margaritas in town while lazing on the cushions, watching the magnificent Senggigi sunset, and dining on superbly fresh seafood. Try the scallop and cucumber salad for Rp36,000, or indulge in a seafood basket for two with lobster, king prawns, squid, fish, crab, and clams served with steamed rice, and water spinach for Rp550,000.

Art Market. ℭ **0370/693694.** www.dequake.com. Main courses Rp35,000–Rp52,000. MC, V. Daily 10am–11pm.

SENGGIGI OUTDOORS

Senggigi Reef, off the point near the Senggigi Beach Hotel, has good coral for snorkeling and, in the right conditions, some decent surf breaks. Snorkel gear can be hired from the beachside stalls. **Canoes** can be hired from the beach on the weekends and during peak tourism times. Local **outrigger boats** *(prahu)* are lined up on the beach between the Santosa Resort and the Art Market and can be chartered for trips along the coast or out to the Gili Islands. The cost is between Rp300,000 and Rp450,000, depending on the number of passengers and number of islands on your itinerary. North of Senggigi, most beaches are deserted and you can easily find your own exclusive beach for the day.

The **Senggigi wave** (**best season:** dry, Apr–Oct; **best swell:** west/southwest; **best size:** 3–5 ft.; **best winds:** southeast) is in front of the Senggigi Beach Hotel. This great right and left beach break can produce long rides when the swell is up. This wave is best on mid- to high tides and is only a short paddle from the beach. The crowds here are generally light and the peaceful serenity of surfing these white sand beaches with very few surfers can be just the ticket for those wary of the growing Bali crowds.

SHOPPING

The **Pasar Seni** (Art Market; Jl. Raya Senggigi; daily 9am–9pm) is just south of the Sheraton between the main road and Senggigi Bay, and can also be reached by the beach. The market sells handicrafts and souvenirs from around Lombok, as well as T-shirts, sarongs, and clothing. You will also find some more upmarket shops, such as Exotic Style, the Little Shop, and Treasure Chest, which all sell a great selection of gifts, homewares, jewelry, and resort wear.

Most shops are along Jalan Raya Senggigi and are open daily 9am to 9pm. **Ciokolata Boutique,** next door to Senggigi Jaya Supermarket, sells a great range of designer resort and street wear. The boutique also has a small but lovely collection of expensive and exquisite Autore pearls, grown in Lombok. **Bayan,** next to Restoran Taman, has a huge selection of Lombok handicrafts ranging from hand-carved wooden furniture, oil paintings, light shades and lamps, ceramics, and homewares at ridiculously low prices.

In the far right corner of Senggigi Plaza, is **House of Pearls,** with beautiful fresh- and saltwater pearls and jewelry.

(Tips) **Street Pearls**

Although the sellers that stroll along the streets and beachfront can be pesky, they are usually polite and will leave if you just say "No" politely and firmly. The DVDs and watches they sell will be copies, but the **pearls** are authentic and make good gifts to take home, although they may not be the best quality. A classic medium length string of white pearls should cost around Rp100,000 to Rp150,000.

SENGGIGI AFTER DARK

The hugely popular **Happy Café** ★ (✆ **0370/693984;** daily noon till late), on the corner of the main street and Senggigi Plaza, has live music nightly. Popular with expatriates, locals, and tourists, Happy Café has a laid-back friendly atmosphere and a good selection of drinks, snacks, and main meals. Most people come for the music and the fun after 9pm.

Marina Café, Jl. Raya Senggigi (✆ **0370/693136;** www.marinasenggigi.com; daily 6pm till late), is the busiest and most popular nightspot in town. Dining is available in the courtyard downstairs, and snacks are served from the bars on both levels. Marina regularly showcases top bands and DJs from around Indonesia. The regular house band plays covers of top-40 hits.

The **Sahara Club,** in Senggigi Plaza (✆ **0370/664-7077** or 0370/619-4143; daily 6pm till late; cover Fri and Sat Rp20,000), is regularly packed with locals, particularly the young and trendy set from Mataram. This Egyptian-themed club has live bands, floor shows, and top Indonesian DJs.

5 THE SOUTHWEST COAST & ISLANDS

South of Lembar Harbour, the main port on West Lombok, the southwest coast is one of the most spectacular areas on the island and remains relatively undeveloped. Thirteen largely uninhabited islands lie just off the coast. Some have simple accommodations for travelers—the Gilis of the future, no doubt.

EXPLORING THE SOUTHWEST COAST & ISLANDS

The drive itself to this stretch of coast is a worthwhile trip, as the road meanders through villages where life is untouched by tourism. Along the roadside you will see people building and repairing boats, laying out handmade bricks to dry in the sun, working in the fields, and sometimes guiding primitive wooden plows harnessed to huge water buffalo as they prepare the fields for planting. Take your time exploring and don't be afraid to wander down some of the small dirt roads toward the beaches—often deserted paradise. The local people are delightfully friendly and your hand will get tired waving to the children, who call "hello" whenever they see you.

Heading south past Lembar Harbour, toward **Sekotong** on the left side of the road, is a sealed road leading up the hill. The steep climb results in a magnificent panorama across the fields, and stretches out across the clear waters, the white coastline, and the many small dot islands. A bit further along the main road is **Taun,** a peaceful village on a wide, placid bay. Three lovely islands—Gili Nanggu, Gili Tangkong, and Gili Sudat—are easily accessible by local outrigger boats from here. A small sign in the nearby village will direct you to the local boat hire area, where you can arrange boat trips at reasonable rates.

A little further on, before the local marine culture complex (Balai Budaya Laut), is a small dirt road leading off toward **Gili Genting,** a small hill in the ocean just off the point. At high tide it is separated from the mainland by a shallow stretch of water and at low tide it is possible to walk out to explore the island. The rock formations are ancient lava flows carved into tunnels and caves by the sea and providing sheltered nooks and crannies of shade—a perfect setting for a picnic lunch.

Further south and across the road on the beachfront is **Dive Zone** (✆ **0370/660-3205;** www.divezone-lombok.com; excursion to Sekotong or Kuta US$35–US$80, to Belongas US$45–US$115), the only dive facility in this part of Lombok. Dive Zone's local experts have pioneered development of previously unknown dive sites in this area. They also offer island-hopping tours to explore the many islands around Sekotong and further south. A long jetty stretches over the sea at the Dive Zone site (one of the **Sundancer** facilities, a high-end resort under construction), with coral and fish clearly visible in the clear water below.

At the next intersection is a signpost for Labuhan Poh and Pelangan, the site of **Bola Bola Paradis** (see below).

The largest of the islands here is **Gili Gede,** appropriately meaning "Big Island." The island is easily accessed by boat from the village of Tembowong. Local boat owners will charge between Rp100,000 and Rp150,000, depending on the number of passengers. Gili Gede is one of the few islands in the area that has accommodation, **Secret Island Resort** (see below), and a newly opened resort on the other side of the island.

The surfing mecca of **Bangko Bangko** is on the far southwest tip of Lombok. Although the road deteriorates after Labuhan Poh, it is still passable for most vehicles in the dry season. The drive to the point is dotted with tiny villages, making it a worthwhile trip even for nonsurfers.

WHERE TO STAY & DINE

Bola Bola Paradis (Finds) This peaceful hotel in Pelangan is one of the few places to stay in the southwest. Funky designed rooms and comfortable lounging platforms on the terraces are set on lawns leading to the beach. Comfortable rooms are also in the main building, and have private terraces facing the beach. The restaurant can arrange fresh fish and seafood dinners. The hotel organizes snorkeling and boat trips.

Pelangan. ✆ **0817/5787355.** www.bolabolaparadis.com. 11 units. Year-round Rp275,000 standard, Rp300,000–Rp390,000 superior; Rp400,000 luxury. No credit cards. **Amenities:** Restaurant; bar; lounge; room service. *In room:* A/C, minibar.

Gili Nanggu Cottages (Finds) This is the only accommodation and restaurant on Gili Nanggu. *Lumbung* (rice barn–style) bungalows are right on the beach. Basic but comfortable, the bungalows have a bathroom and hammocks downstairs and bedrooms upstairs. Further back are cottages with air-conditioning and hot water. The carpeted floors are incongruous, but the cottages are comfortable if you intend on staying for a few days. The restaurant has fresh seafood, although prices are higher than usual. Cold beer and drinks, and a good snack menu, is available for day-trippers.

Gili Nanggu. ✆ **0370/623783.** www.gilinanggu.com. 17 units. Year-round Rp240,000–Rp350,000 standard. No credit cards. **Amenities:** Restaurant.

Secret Island Resort (Kids) (Value) These accommodations on Gili Gede are nothing fancy, but are adequate and a perfect base for exploring the surrounding islands. Choose

Lombok's (& the World's?) Greatest Wave

Desert Point (**best season:** dry Apr–Oct; **best swell:** west/southwest; **best size:** 4–8 ft.; **best winds:** southeast), voted by Australian surf magazine *Tracks* as the world's greatest wave, is located near a tiny fishing village called Bangko Bangko on the mountainous southwest tip of Lombok. As getting there is a real mission overland due to poor road conditions, many surfers prefer to surf this from the regular charter boats departing Bali's Benoa Harbour on week-long "surfaris" instead. The more intrepid and hardy adventurer can stay at the small, basic homestays that have recently sprung up in the area and wait for the notoriously fickle wave to come alive. When it does turn on, it's not unknown for helicopters to drop a load of pro surfers on the spot for the day's action. Crowds can get big, especially if the place is firing. Tricky currents separate those who should be out there from those who shouldn't, but on its prime days there are enough perfect waves to please the masses. Look out for the crowds of local kids riding pieces of wood on the tiny days.

from a range of eclectic rooms, with cottages facing the beach and a hillside villa overlooking the ocean. The resort has its own speedboat with experienced captain for fishing charters and offers snorkeling and island-hopping tours. They also offer transfers from Bali and Senggigi (and other locations by arrangement), making getting to the island easy. With no roads and very little development, a few days here offers travelers the chance to relax and recharge on a true deserted island.

SW. 12 Gilis; Sekotong, Gili Gede. ✆ 08/1803762001. www.secretislandresort.com. 12 units. High season US$25 standard, US$75 villa; low season US$20 standard, US$60 villa. No credit cards. **Amenities:** Restaurant; bar; babysitting; bicycles; watersports. *In room:* Fan, Internet (for a fee).

6 NORTH LOMBOK

Dominated by the purple peaks of the Rinjani mountain range and the majesty of Lombok's famous volcano, Gunung Rinjani, the north of the island offers stunning landscapes and long curves of deserted beaches. Jungles and rainforest with towering plantations of mahogany and teak provide ample opportunity for trekking and ecotourism. North Lombok is generally undeveloped and allows travelers to get a sense of the history and traditional roots of the island. Don't expect tourist markets or restaurants and bars catering to Westerners.

GETTING THERE & GETTING AROUND
North Lombok is reached by two main roads, both in good condition and offering different scenic routes. The **coastal road** that runs from Ampenan all the way up the west coast to the north of the island provides stunning views of the many beautiful bays and beaches of the west coast, as well as vistas over the Gili Islands and Bali.

The **Pusuk Pass,** a winding mountain road that starts in Gunungsari and runs through the mountains inland, terminates at Pemenang in the north. The pass provides wonderful views of valleys and gorges, with rivers running through the tropical forests and small villages among the trees. Families of gray monkeys live in the jungle and come down to the road to beg for food from passing motorists.

A *bemo* runs from Gunungsari through the Pusuk Pass up to the north coast (about 30 min.; Rp5,000). *Bemo* also run regularly between Ampenan and Senggigi, and less frequently from Senggigi to Bangsal and Pemenang. The best way to see the north is by hired car or motorbike, or with a car and driver.

Bangsal is at the crossroads where the main coastal road meets the Pusuk Pass Road, with Jalan Raya (main street) continuing north all the way around the island to the east coast. The road to the west only runs about 1km (less than 1 mile) to Bangsal Harbor, the main point of departure to the Gili Islands (chapter 16).

EXPLORING NORTH LOMBOK

Use a local guide, who can lead you through the jungle to waterfalls or point out places of interest, when exploring the trails of north Lombok. Negotiate a fee beforehand.

Bangsal is a pretty village with a large Balinese Hindu population, surrounded by rice fields, temples, and close to the ocean and the mountains. The village has a few small homestays, particularly on the road to the harbor, and makes a good base for exploring the north. The harbor, however, is renowned for the annoying touts and sellers who try to force travelers to charter boats and buy goods before going to the Gili Islands.

Further north, a small signposted road branches off from the main road to **Pantai Sira,** a beautiful white sand beach with good snorkeling on the offshore coral reef. This is also the site for the world-class **Kosaido Golf Course** (© **0370/640137;** US$65–US$85 greens fee and caddy).

On the tip of the next peninsula north is a small temple, **Pura Medana,** an ancient Hindu site with wonderful sunset views and a peaceful atmosphere.

Tanjung, 5km (3 miles) north of Bangsal, is a large village with numerous warungs and shops, and one of the few public telephone offices in the north. Tanjung has an interesting daily cattle market for cows, goats, and horses.

Gondang, further up the coast, is a small town near a good beach. Tiu Pupus Waterfall is a 20-minute walk beyond the end of a poorly marked, rocky road. The falls flow into a deep pool with nice swimming. The trek through the traditional Sasak village of **Kerurak** makes the effort worthwhile. Another half-hour trek from Tiu Pupus leads to **Kerta Gangga Waterfalls,** with three beautiful waterfalls set in the jungle.

The dusty, traditional village of **Segenter,** on the road to Anyar, provides a glimpse into the harsh reality of life on the island's dry side. The 300 villagers in this northern interior village eke out a basic living raising corn and beans, yet they welcome visitors with a smile and proudly share their simple life with tours through the village.

Bayan, further north, is renowned as the root of early Islam on Lombok and maintains old dance and poetic traditions, such as *kemidi rudat,* a theater performance based on the *Thousand and One Nights.* One of the oldest and most important Wetu Telu (p. 304) mosques is in Bayan, and important sacred sites from Lombok's ancient past are located nearby.

The road from Bayan leads to **Senaru,** the gateway to the **Rinjani National Park.** The pretty village in lovely scenery has fantastic views of the volcanic mountains. The **Sendang Gile waterfalls** at Senaru are among Lombok's most spectacular, even after descending the 200-plus vertical steps to stand below them. The water cascades in a steep vertical drop down the hillside into a rocky stream below.

(Moments) **A Waterfall & Jungle Trek**

Guides can be hired from the Pondok Senaru & Restaurant (p. 330) near the car park at Senaru for the less-than-an-hour trek through the jungle to the lovely **Tiu Kelep** waterfall. First, pay the modest admission fee at the gate (around Rp20,000) to Sendang Gile Waterfall, good for swimming. Negotiate an additional fee of around Rp50,000 for a guide to take you through the forest to Tiu Kelep. Climb the rocks to the hidden cave behind the falls and follow local legend that says for every pass behind the waterfall, you take 1 year off your age.

WHERE TO STAY

Hotel Tugu Lombok ★★★ (Finds) This is a destination, rather than simply a place to stay, and is unlike any other hotel on Lombok. This luxurious resort is perched on a pristine beach neighboring the Kosaido Golf Course. Tugu Lombok features hundreds of original artworks and antiques collected as a loving testament to the long forgotten, original cultures of Lombok and Java. The Bhagavat Gita suites are highly recommended for those seeking luxury in a style reminiscent of the Indonesian royalty of yesteryear. Antique furnishings, soaring ceilings, and luxurious appointments are housed in private 400-sq.-m (4,305-sq.-ft.) villas with personal plunge pools. Air-conditioning, glowing candles, and perfumed air greets the tired traveler. The modern bathrooms open into a private garden with a rain-shower. A gigantic boulder, hollowed in the center, forms a bathtub to be filled with warm water and scented flowers.

Sire Beach-Sigar Penjalin village-Tanjung. ℂ **0370/620111.** www.tuguhotels.com. 19 units. High season US$228 standard, US$293 suite, US$553 villa; low season US$175 standard, US$225 suite, US$425 villa. AE, MC, V. **Amenities:** Restaurant; bar; babysitting; bicycles; gym; outdoor pool; room service; spa; watersports. *In room:* A/C, TV/DVD, movie library, stereo or CD, hair dryer, Internet (for a fee), minibar, MP3 docking station.

Medana Resort (Value) On the road to the Oberoi, overlooking palm groves and the ocean, this small resort is not as expensive or opulent as others in the area. Medana has spacious and comfortable bungalows set on terraced banks leading to a magnificent swimming pool. Each bungalow has canopied beds, teak furnishings, and garden bathrooms with sunken bathtubs, and private terraces overlooking the palms and the glorious sunsets across the Gilis, Bali, and beyond. The resort also has its own glass-bottom boat and traditional sailing outrigger for exploring the brilliant reefs and the Gili Islands.

Jl. Medana, Tanjung. ℂ **0370/628000.** www.medanaresort.com. 6 units. Year-round US$110; extra person US$25. MC, V. **Amenities:** Restaurant; bar; outdoor pool; room service; watersports. *In room:* A/C, TV, hair dryer, minibar.

The Oberoi ★★ Like most Oberoi resorts around the world, the Lombok version is a haven for those seeking the ultimate in luxury and service. Located on the tip of the Medana peninsula, not far from the Kosaido Golf Course, the Oberoi has one of the most sublime beaches in the area, with views of the Gili Islands. The heart of the resort is the huge three-tiered infinity pool that seems to float out over the ocean. Most of the villas have private walled courtyards and swimming pools. The rooms are luxuriously appointed with huge beds, spacious living areas, and all the comforts one would expect of a world-class resort. The bathrooms are perfect, with separate vanities for him and her and ample use of marble. The garden bathtub is big enough for two, and is lined with scented oils and softly glowing candles. The other 30 luxury pavilions share the resort facilities, with cozy lounging and relaxing areas dotted around the pool and beachfront. The spa is renowned for its lavish body treatments, and an H2O Dive Centre is on the beachfront.

Medana Beach, Tanjung, Mataram. ✆ **0370/638444.** www.oberoihotels.com. 50 units. High season US$387–US$402 standard, US$1,067 and up suite, US$517–US$979 villa; low season US$320–US$365 standard, US$970 and up suite, US$470–US$890 villa. AE, DC, MC, V. **Amenities:** 2 restaurants; bar; babysitting; bicycles; concierge; gym; outdoor pool; room service; spa; tennis; watersports. *In room:* A/C, TV/DVD, movie library, stereo or CD, hair dryer, Internet (for a fee), minibar, MP3 docking station.

Villas

In addition to the hotels and resorts, several luxury private villas are on Pantai Sire, adjacent to the Kosaido Golf Course. All are suitable for families with kids.

The **Anandita** (Bali booking office ✆ **0361/730668;** www.theanandita.com; peak season US$1,395, high season US$1,175, low season US$890; AE, MC, V) is on the beachfront, down the road to the left of Hotel Tugu Lombok. The villa has four separate bedrooms and a lagoon pool with Jacuzzi. The villa would be perfect for up to four couples, or two families who want their own space and privacy.

The **Villa Sepoi Sepoi** (Singapore booking office: ✆ **65/9185-4900** in Singapore; www.sepoi-sepoi.com; peak season US$1,250, high season US$1,000, low season US$800; AE, MC, V) is a huge family villa on the beachfront, next to Sira Beach House. Rooms are built from stone and thatch with sandstone or wood floors and contemporary furnishings. Each room is furnished to reflect a theme: for example, the Chinese Room is decorated with modern red and black touches.

The **Sira Beach House** (www.sirabeachhouse.com; peak season US$1,200, high season US$1,080, low season US$960; AE, MC, V), recently renamed from Villa Nia, is a six-room villa on approximately 3 hectares (7 acres) of lawns leading to Sire Beach. The extensive property has a tennis court, a large swimming pool, and a poolside bale and barbecue. Either rent the whole villa with family or friends (12 to 14 guests), or the Master Villa (two rooms) can be rented separately. The villa has a car for private transport, as well as bicycles for guests. The friendly team can arrange special barbecues, tours, boat trips, and anything else guests require.

WHERE TO DINE

Apart from warungs and local eating houses, dining in north Lombok is limited to the upmarket resorts in the area; however, none are far from each other and it's easy to stay at one resort and dine at any of the others nearby.

Fine dining at the Oberoi (p. 326) is on top-quality local and imported produce at both the **Lumbung Restaurant** ★★ and the **Sunbird Café** ★ (AE, DC, MC, V; daily 6:30am–11pm). Continental and Asian-fusion cuisine is available at both, with the emphasis on fresh seafood. Start with seared sea scallops on soba noodles with shiitake, roasted sesame, and soy (say that five times fast) for Rp160,000 or for a main course, Indian curry chicken with basmati rice, Indian pickles, and chutney at Rp195,000, or Australian lamb with sun-dried tomato and gnocchi for Rp385,000. Expatriate guests from Bali and the Gilis often hop over by speedboat to the beachfront Sunbird Café to dine on Asian tapas (Rp75,000–Rp130,000) and sip imported wines.

The **Kokok Pletok** ★★ (a la carte US$5–US$10, set menu US$18; AE, DC, MC, V; daily 7am–11pm) in Hotel Tugu (p. 326) is a magnificent venue surrounded by statues of the rice Goddess Dewi. Breakfast includes bacon and eggs, eggs Benedict, muesli, fresh fruits, homemade yogurt, and traditional Indonesian breakfasts such as *bubur ayam* and *nasi goreng*. The resort also offers a range of theme dinners (main courses Rp110,000–Rp215,000; set menu US$35–US$40), where guests are served authentic Indonesian dishes by waiters dressed in period costumes.

Medana Resort (p. 326) is a good alternative for those staying at the Oberoi, Tugu, and other resorts at Pantai Sire with lower prices than the others. The restaurant (main courses Rp45,000–Rp60,000; MC, V; daily 8am–10pm) offers a range of Indonesian specialties, fresh seafood, and Western dishes. Try the special rijsttafel, a huge feast with dessert for two people at Rp325,000.

CLIMBING RINJANI: LOMBOK'S SACRED VOLCANO

Located on the north of the island, **Gunung Rinjani** ★★★ soars 3,726m (12,224 ft.) above sea level and is the second-highest volcano in Indonesia. Visitors from around the world come to Lombok to climb Gunung Rinjani to its crater lake or demanding summit, particularly from July to September, during the European holidays and Lombok's "high season". Gunung Rinjani is considered a "Home of the Gods" and the mountain is a pilgrimage site for prayer; pilgrims bathe in the pools and hot springs, which are said to have healing powers.

The 4km-wide (2½-miles) caldera near the top of the volcano is almost filled by a beautiful crescent-shaped lake, Danau Segara Anak (Child of the Sea Lake). The lake is around 230m (755 ft.) deep and contains plentiful fish, and is home to birds and other wildlife. A smaller volcanic cone, Gunung Baru Jari, was formed a mere couple of hundred years ago and juts from the crater's interior at the edge of the lake. Caves, waterfalls, and hot springs are around the volcano, most importantly **Aik Kalak** on the northeast of the crater, where the volcanically heated waters are said to cure illnesses, particularly skin diseases.

The northern gateway to the Rinjani National Park is at Senaru (see above). The **Rinjani National Park** (admission Rp150,000) is the nature reserve of 41,330 hectares (102,129 acres) surrounding the volcano. Senaru is the usual starting point for climbing Gunung Rinjani, with a number of trekking centers that can organize trips up the mountain. Other options, for a slightly shorter route to the summit, are Sembalun Lawang and Sembalun Bumbung (p. 338) to the northeast. Both are rustic mountain villages, with basic homestays and tour centers that can organize your trek.

The **Rinjani Trek Management Board** (RTMB; © 0370/641124 or 08/11390047; www.lombokrinjanitrek.org), originally set up and sponsored by the New Zealand government, forms a partnership between the Rinjani National Park, the tourism industry, and the local community. Cooperatives are at Rinjani Trek Centre (RTC) in Senaru and the Rinjani Information Centre (RIC) in Sembalun Lawang (p. 338). Under the guidance of the RTMB, each center is run by a stakeholders' committee who look after roster systems for guides and porters, village tours, trail maintenance, and handicraft sales. Revenue from trekking and entry fees is used for conservation, training, and management of the Rinjani Trek, thus ensuring sustainability of this natural resource for the future. In 2004 the Rinjani Trek won the World Legacy Award for Destination Stewardship. Rinjani is currently being considered for Geopark status and World Natural Heritage status by UNESCO.

Guides and porters at the trek centers have many years experience on the mountain and in Rinjani National Park, together with a vested interest in safe and ecofriendly trekking, and are therefore the recommended choice for climbing Mount Rinjani. When climbing, it is prudent to use an authorized guide, deal with a reputable trekking business, and carry as few valuables as possible with you.

Two-day, 1-night treks (US$200) are the shortest, and take visitors to the crater rim. The most popular is the 3-day, 2-night (US$310) trek which allows trekkers to climb down to the shores of the lake and enjoy a soak in the hot springs. It takes 3 to 4 days to reach the summit of the volcano (US$310), a demanding climb with magnificent views from the highest point on Lombok. Costs include entrance fee, meals, porter, return transport, alcoholic beverage, first aid, tent, bag, and mattress.

Trekking on the volcano is not for everyone. A certain level of fitness is needed and climbing to the summit is particularly strenuous. Altitudes of over 2,700m (8,858 ft.) are reached in all these treks and, even on the equator, nighttime temperatures can be very cold, with strong winds and occasional rain.

The best time to climb Gunung Rinjani is in the dry season from around April to October, or before the rainy season starts. The sunny days and cooler temperatures make this time of the year the most comfortable for climbing, and enable the clearest views of the stunning scenery both on and around the mountain.

Where to Stay & Dine

Lembah Rinjani ★, Sembalun Lawang (© **08/1803652511** or 08/5239543279; http://lembahrinjani.googlepages.com; year-round Rp175,000; no credit cards) is a charming and rustic mountain retreat on the feet of the Rinjani volcano. Rooms are basic, but very clean and comfortable, with private terraces and astounding views of the mountain, which seems to rise up immediately in front of you. The air here is clear and cold, rising up in mists when you breathe. At their restaurant, try the local curries, tasty soups, and stir-fries—all great for warming up. A house specialty is the *serbat* (a traditional Javanese drink), made with fresh cinnamon, nutmeg, ginger, and other ground spices. The staff is very knowledgeable about the area and many of them serve as guides

Tips for Trekking Mount Rinjani

- Always use a reputable trekking business and check that they have facilities to cope with emergencies.
- Never wander away on your own, even if you're an experienced climber. A number of deaths and injuries have occurred on the mountain. Loose shale and unstable surfaces are hazards.
- Use good quality, comfortable shoes and take a walking stick to help with the inclines.
- Make sure you have a warm jacket and enough clothes as it is cold on the mountain.
- Check that your trekking company is supplying sleeping bags and blankets.
- Don't try to save money by trekking on your own or using unauthorized guides.
- Licensed guides will have identification, and are experienced to handle your trek and the conditions on the mountain.
- Don't take passports or carry valuables that aren't essential to your trek.
- Please respect this natural wonder. Don't litter or leave anything on the mountain, except your footprints.

and porters for climbing the mountain. Ask for one of them to show you around or guide you on a short mountain trek. The view from the small mountain just out of town is incredible and you can see a Hindu temple half-way up.

The **Pondok Senaru & Restaurant,** Rinjani National Park, Senaru (© **0370/622868;** main courses Rp10,000–Rp25,000; No credit cards; daily 8am–9pm), presents a good value on a small hillside next to the public parking area in Senaru, at the entrance to the Rinjani National Park. Stop here for a cool drink when visiting the waterfalls (p. 325) and enjoy the fine views from the garden bales over the rice terraces and jungle-covered foothills. The restaurant serves sandwiches and Indonesian meals for lunch and dinner. Basic accommodation is also available (Rp200,000–Rp350,000; no credit cards).

7 CENTRAL LOMBOK

Lombok is divided into four governmental regions: west, central, east, and the recently created north Lombok regency. The south of the island, except for those areas bordering the west and east coasts, is therefore classified as "central Lombok." The central area, mainly on the southern slopes of the Gunung Rinjani mountain range, is cooler and more lush than the south thanks to abundant rainfall in the wet season and protection by forests and jungle throughout the rest of the year.

GETTING THERE & GETTING AROUND

The main road that runs through the cities continues east across the entire island, providing easy access to the central and eastern regions. Public buses and *bemo* run from Bertais bus terminal near Sweta, but for exploring the area properly and the small villages off the main road, private transport is essential. Alternatively, the interesting villages of the area can be explored on day trips from Senggigi or Kuta.

EXPLORING & SHOPPING CENTRAL LOMBOK

A drive through this area will take you through numerous villages specializing in traditional crafts.

About a half an hour drive southeast of Cakranegara, the town of **Praya** is the hub of the south and seat of the Central Lombok governmental administration. This is the home of the Saturday market central to many of the area's handicraft villages.

Five kilometers (3 miles) to the west of Praya is the weaving village of **Sukarara,** where *ikat* and traditional cloth is made and sold. Weavers work outside many of the shops, using antiquated back strap looms. Some of the larger pieces can take several months to weave and collectors from around the world visit this village to purchase the blankets, sarongs, and cloth.

The Thursday market is further south at **Sengkol; Beleka,** about 10km (16 miles) east of Praya, is the site of a Wednesday market. Both local markets sell food and vegetables, live chickens and fish, as well as some locally produced household goods.

Families of **Loyok,** a small dusty village on the road to Tetebatu, make traditional woven products, using rattan, grasses, and bamboo. The good-quality baskets, boxes, mats, and other weaving are often sent to Bali, where they fetch much higher prices. Prices here are cheap but, as anywhere in Indonesia, bargain anyway. Visit the shops and the family compounds out back, where several generations of the same family sit around, chatting and weaving.

On the main road east across the island, around 50km (31 miles) from the cities, a signposted road leads north to **Tetebatu,** on the southern slopes of Gunung Rinjani. This

Lombok's New International Airport

Central Lombok is the location of the new **Lombok International Airport** currently under construction and due to open in late 2010.

The airport will be located on approximately 539 hectares (1,331 acres) of open land in Tanak Awu, around 40 minutes drive south of the cities, and just off the main road to Kuta. There are plans to build a toll road linking the airport and the city, with a travelling time of around 20 minutes, and to construct a bypass road allowing fast access to the beautiful south coast.

The new airport will replace the existing Selaparang Airport in Mataram, which currently handles only short-bodied aircraft and is limited mainly to domestic flights. Phase I of the runway at the new Lombok International Airport will be suitable for landing Airbus 310s and Boeing 747s, and is within flight range of Australia, Japan, Timor, Taiwan, and Korea. Plans to lengthen the runway stretch all the way to 2028.

In the past, controversy raged over the acquisition of the land by government decree at below-market value. Today, however, most local people approve of the new airport, recognizing it as opening Lombok up to international travelers and bringing new opportunities to the predominantly agricultural communities near the airport. Some Balinese feel threatened by the international airport in Lombok, as most travelers previously had to travel to Bali to make the connection to Lombok.

area is wet and misty during rainy season, cool and lush during the dry. A nice waterfall called **Jeruk Manis** is about an hour's walk to the north of Tetebatu, through a monkey-filled forest. The scenery is lovely and the falls are worth seeing, but it's best to take a local guide with you, as there have been problems with theft in the past. Guides can be organized at any of the homestays listed below.

Near Lendang Nangka is **Jojang Spring,** with great vistas and a forest inhabited by black monkeys. In August, Sasak boxing takes place in the village.

Heading further east on the main road, a turnoff at Lenek leads to the small village of **Pringgasela.** This area is a major center for *ikat* and traditional fabrics produced by hand on old-fashioned looms. Visit the small houses and shops here to purchase the distinctive traditionally woven, colorful fabrics.

WHERE TO STAY & DINE

Accommodations and places to eat in the area are scarce. What few exist are usually basic homestays and backpacker accommodations, and basic warungs and roadside stalls. **Wisma Soedjono** (© **0376/21309** or 08/18544265; high season Rp300,000–Rp500,000, low season Rp250,000–Rp450,000; no credit cards), in Tetebatu, is set high on the hillside with views of the countryside, and is the most popular hotel and restaurant in the area. One of the original hotels in the area and family owned, the Dutch colonial–style hotel has a range of fan-cooled rooms and a pool. The more expensive rooms have hot water. The restaurant (Rp15,000–Rp30,000) serves Indonesian and Sasak food, with some Western-style snacks.

LOMBOK

15

CENTRAL LOMBOK

Also in Tetebatu, **Hakiki** (no phone; high season Rp250,000–Rp400,000, low season Rp200,000–Rp350,000; no credit cards) is a lovely place to get away from it all. Set in rice fields at the end of Waterfall Street, the lovely bungalows with fans have terraces overlooking rice fields and mountains. There is also a good restaurant.

Another option in Tetebatu is **Green Orry** (✆ **0376/22782;** high season Rp300,000–Rp400,000, low season Rp250,000–Rp350,000; no credit cards) with thatched-roof fan-cooled rooms and bungalows. The better rooms are nicely decorated, very clean and comfortable. The good restaurant serves Indonesian and Western food at reasonable prices and the hotel can arrange guides and tours in the area, as well as tickets with Perama Tours to Bali and other destinations.

8 KUTA & THE SOUTH COAST

In an island nation with seemingly infinite, sublime coastline, the south coast of Lombok surely rates among the best. **Kuta** is the south coast's main town and center of tourism development, and is the hub for exploring the southern beaches. Around 60km (37 miles) south of Mataram and about 1½ hour's drive from Senggigi, Kuta (sometimes spelled Kute) makes for a wonderful day trip from other points in Lombok, or as an alternative holiday destination in its own right. Kuta is a small haven of hotels, homestays, backpacker's hostels, and simple restaurants catering mainly to surfers. The small-scale development evokes Bali in the 1980s. Kuta and the surrounding beaches have gained an international reputation as some of the best surfing destinations in Southeast Asia.

GETTING THERE & GETTING AROUND

From the cities, head south along the main road to Praya, passing through small villages along the way. Public transport is infrequent; hire a car or motorbike, or car with a driver for a day trip. It takes around 1 hour to reach the south coast from Cakra or Ampenan; allow around 1½ hours from Senggigi.

Up in the Air: A New Megaresort for Lombok?

The south coast of Lombok is currently the site of a proposed US$600-million megaresort by United Arab Emirates investment company Emaar Properties.

An agreement signed between Emaar and the Indonesian government in 2008 allows Emaar and the state-owned Bali Tourism Development Corporation to develop 1,200 hectares (2,965 acres) along 7km (4 miles) of the Kuta and Tanjung A'an beaches over the next 12 years into a world-class resort and residential community of 10,000 luxury villas, eight hotels, and two 18-hole golf courses. It is rumored the project will include Ritz-Carlton and Armani resorts.

The global economic crisis of 2009 has since put the project in doubt, but Emaar says they will still go ahead. If the development takes place, the south coast—and Lombok by association—will be totally transformed. Investors and land speculators have been snapping up property on the south coast ever since the news broke.

Surfing on Lombok's Southern Peninsula: Ekas Bay

The south coast is where the gentle Lombok waters meet the Indian Ocean, forming great swells and surf breaks. It's easy to hire a board and a surf guide to learn to surf or access the more challenging surf breaks in the area.

Ekas Bay (Teluk Ekas; **best season:** dry Apr–Oct; **best swell:** west/south-west; **best size:** 3–5 ft.; **best winds:** southeast) on Gili Melayu, Lombok's island-like southern peninsula, is home to a variety of breaks. "Outside Ekas" is a powerful left-hander to satisfy the most power-hungry chargers. "Inside Ekas" has a much mellower wave breaking both left and right. Those not wanting an extreme challenge can surf the left-hander, with its great conditions for beginners. Ekas is never crowded and is often only surfed by guests at **Heaven On the Planet** (📞 **08/123705393** or 08/123751103; www.heavenontheplanet. co.nz; minimum 2-night stay; rates per night all-inclusive for twin share: high season AU$120 for more than 5 nights, AU$150 less than 5 nights; low season AU$100 for more than 5 nights, AU$130 less than 5 nights; no credit cards) as the surf charter boats rarely pass these waters.

EXPLORING THE SOUTH COAST

As you drive to the south, the landscape becomes much drier away from the mountains and wide fields of crops become the norm. On reaching the south coast the landscape opens up to reveal a long coastline with some of the most sublime beaches and views in Indonesia.

On the east side of the road, just before Kuta, is **Rambitan,** a village with clusters of the low, thatch-roofed homes with cow dung floors of the traditional Sasak style, as well as thatched *lumbung,* traditional rice barns. On the west side of the road is **Sade,** a hilltop village with one of the oldest mosques in Lombok, Mesjid Kuno. Both villages are interesting examples of traditional Sasak architecture and communal living in compounds, where life continues as it has for centuries. Residents act as guides for a small fee, encourage walks through either of these villages, and are happy to share a glimpse of their lifestyles with visitors.

Around 4km (2½ miles) east of Kuta is **Tanjung A'an,** with white sand and good waves for surfers. Further east is **Gerupuk,** well known as a top surf location.

To the west of Kuta are a series of beautiful beaches and bays hidden behind headlands and rolling hills, providing peaceful and secluded spots for picnics and swimming. **Mawun Beach** is around 30 minutes drive to the west and is a picturesque bay with a nice white sand beach and calm waves, perfect for swimming. **Mawi,** just west, has good right- and left-hand barrels for surfing when the swell is large enough. Further west are picturesque **Selong Blanak** and many more scenic bays and beaches, largely deserted, although the road deteriorates rapidly and the going can be rough. Use an experienced local guide with a good vehicle.

Just to the east of the main Kuta area, the beach in front of the Novotel (p. 334) is sometimes referred to as **Mandalika,** named after legendary Princess Mandalika. See the box, "Bau Nyale Festival."

WHERE TO STAY

Ken's Hotel   This smaller, Japanese-owned hotel is on the main road into Kuta, close to the beach and all amenities in town. The comfortable and clean rooms are arranged around a swimming pool, with a small restaurant alongside. Ken's offers a better class of accommodation than the other Kuta hotels catering to the surf crowd.

Kuta. ✆ **0370/655057.** Japanese only website www.kenshotel.com. High season US$120–US$465; low season US$89–US$438. AE, MC, V. **Amenities:** Restaurant; outdoor pool. *In room:* A/C, fan, TV.

Matahari Inn   In town rather than on the beach, the Matahari is one of the original hotels in Kuta and still offers good value budget accommodation. The standard rooms, basic but reasonable, are set in pretty gardens with a swimming pool. The six villas are better quality, built in Sasak style with a thatched roof, and decorated with traditional inlaid wood furniture. The spacious garden bathrooms have bathtubs and modern fittings. A good restaurant on-site serves international "tourist food" and a good selection of local dishes.

Jl. Raya Pantai, Kuta. ✆ **0370/655000.** www.indo.com/hotels/matahari. 34 units. Year-round US$19–US$53. No credit cards. **Amenities:** Restaurant; outdoor pool. *In room:* A/C, fan.

Novotel Lombok Resort ★★ (Kids)   This is the only luxury place to stay in Kuta. The Novotel sits on the pristine white sands of Mandalika Beach, just east of Kuta. The resort is built in the traditional Sasak style and blends beautifully with its surroundings through the use of natural woods, stone, and earth tones. The Pool Villas are top of the range, with lovely gardens, private swimming pools, and lounging bales. The spacious rooms are decorated in ethnic style and have gorgeous natural bathrooms. The resort itself offers so many activities and facilities, it's almost easy to never step out to explore the coast. Every day features complimentary classes for guests in subjects such as Bahasa Indonesian, pottery making, weaving, woodcarving, and more, all taught by talented locals. A range of activities is geared to children. Other options include aqua aerobics, beach volleyball, archery, diving, and snorkeling for the active; plus, the glorious body treatments offered by Vous Spa for the less energetic. **Kafe Chilli** sits under a high thatched roof on the beachfront and offers informal dining and live entertainment every night. **Empat Ikan,** dinner only, the resort's stylishly designed fine-dining restaurant, specializes in seafood.

Pantai Putri Nyale. ✆ **0370/653333.** www.novotellombok.com. 101 units. High season US$120–US$465; low season US$89–US$438. AE, MC, V. **Amenities:** 2 restaurants; kids' club; 4 outdoor pools including children's pool; spa. *In room:* A/C, TV, hair dryer, minibar.

Tastura Hotel   On the main road opposite Kuta Beach, the Tastura has a lagoon pool, restaurant, shop, and convention hall. This midrange accommodation is in a great location for exploring the area and a magnificent beach is across the road.

Jl. Raya Pantai, Kuta. ✆ **0370/655540.** tastura@telkom.net.id. 25 units. High season Rp300,000–Rp550,000; low season Rp350,000–Rp600,000. MC, V. **Amenities:** Restaurant; outdoor pool; room service. *In room:* A/C, TV, minibar.

(Warning! **Kuta Cowboys**

Just as in Kuta in Bali, Kuta Lombok has its own crowd of **Kuta cowboys** (p. 73). Drugs, particularly marijuana, are sometimes part of the scene. Penalties for drug possession and use in Indonesia are very strict: If caught, you will do jail time at the very least. Better to give this a wide berth, even if the guys are just sitting on the beach, playing guitars, and having fun.

Moments   Bau Nyale Festival

This festival (Feb or Mar) commemorates the legend of the Putri (Princess) Mandalika, who was so beautiful and adored that, when she was of marriageable age, every prince in Lombok sought her as his bride. Legend says that when she couldn't choose between the suitors and fighting broke out between the rivals, rather than throw the kingdom into chaos, she ended her life by leaping into the sea, saying, "Kuta," or "Wait for me here," in the local Sasak language.

When she disappeared into the waves, hundreds of *nyale* (sea worms) floated to the surface. Local *dukun* (priests) announced that the worms were the Princess's hair, or that her body had been transformed into the worms. Thus, every year in February or March, when the conditions are right for spawning and the *nyale* worms return to the site, locals remember the Mandalika legend.

Tens of thousands (some say up to 100,000) of revelers attend the all-night celebrations of the Bau Nyale festival. A full program of cultural performances takes place on the beachfront, the highlight being an enchanting reenactment of the Princess Mandalika legend. Young people from the villages who are normally kept separated are permitted to flirt and strut. It's also the time to compete with improvised *pantun* poetry, a ritualized form of competing in rhyming couplets.

Early in the morning, around 3am, the first worms spawn and the crowd rushes into the water to catch them, amid much laughter and excitement. Associated with fertility, the sea worms are cooked and eaten for good luck and prosperity. As part of the fertility rituals, they are ground up and placed in irrigation channels to help ensure bountiful crops.

LOMBOK

15

KUTA & THE SOUTH COAST

WHERE TO DINE

Ashtari (Finds INTERNATIONAL   On the main road out of town to the west, about 2km (1¼ miles) from central Kuta, Ashtari is set high on a hill with sublime views over Kuta and the southern beaches. Open only for breakfast and lunch, visitors love the homemade vegetarian meals and laid-back ambience. The emphasis is on fresh, organic, and natural local ingredients. Fresh juices, herbal teas, smoothies, and other delicious and healthy beverages are also available. Try a freshly baked baguette with goat's cheese, sun-dried tomatoes, avocado, and roasted aubergines, washed down with a divine rose-hip tea. There is a good selection of magazines and board games. A suspended balcony begs you to reach for your camera.

Kuta. No phone. Main courses Rp30,000–Rp150,000. No credit cards. Daily 7am–3pm.

Ketapang Café (Value INDONESIAN/WESTERN   While this humble place is nothing fancy, the food is surprisingly good and excellent value for your money. It's right in town, on the corner of the main road to the beach. The menu ranges from local and international entrees and soups, to Indonesian and Western main courses, pastas, and pizzas, all with an emphasis on fresh seafood. For starters, try the local spring rolls, filled with chicken, shrimp, and vegetables, or the chicken salad, served in a hollowed-out pineapple. Delicious main courses include the fresh fish filet cooked in ginger and lemongrass, or the exceptionally good chicken breast with snow peas and cashews.

Kuta. No phone. Main courses Rp30,000–Rp60,000. No credit cards. Daily 8am–10pm.

9 EAST LOMBOK

The east of the island is the least visited and developed, although large towns here support a thriving local population. Most people come here to catch a ferry to neighboring Sumbawa, en route to the islands of Komodo and Flores.

Many of the villages in eastern Lombok are strongly Islamic. Travelers have reported harassment in the past, although most of the people are merely curious and eager to welcome visitors to their homes. You'll likely be curious too. Without the tourism infrastructure, you'll get a close-up look at the lifestyles and culture of the Sasak people.

GETTING THERE & GETTING AROUND

East Lombok extends from Masbagik, on the main east-west road, across the island and encompasses the eastern slopes of the Rinjani mountain range down to the peninsula on the southeast corner of Lombok.

Public buses regularly travel the route across the island to **Kayangan,** the main port on the east coast. For exploring outside of these parameters, you will need private transport. Hire a car or motorbike in Senggigi, the cities, or Kuta; alternatively, you could hire a car and driver to guide you around, but be prepared to pay the costs of accommodation and meals for the driver.

EXPLORING EAST LOMBOK

The beauty of the people in this area is that, if you are stuck, they will always offer you a meal and a place to stay, in the true tradition of Sasak hospitality. Cross the island on the main road that links east to west. **Bonjeruk,** before the pottery village of Masbagik, is a village of numerous *dalang* (puppeteers) and many of the puppets for the shadow play *wayang sasak* are made here. Before you reach the coast, turn right at the road to **Selong,** the capital city and business hub of east Lombok. The atmosphere is reminiscent of a large town in the 1950s, with wide tree-lined streets and old Dutch colonial architecture.

From Selong, return to the main road, heading toward Pringgabaya and turn left at the signpost to **Sapit,** a small village on the southern slopes of (though seemingly at the top) the Rinjani mountain range, where there is one of the few hotels in the area (the Hati Suci Homestay, see below). The steep road winds through mountain villages, interspersed with pretty fields of crops and patches of jungle. Low clouds gather on the mountains and the air is cool; the view is breathtaking, with villages and fields stretched in the distance, and the rain forest extending up the peaks behind.

It is easy to continue up over the mountain and down to the main villages of Sembalun Lawang and Sembalun Bumbung (see below) on the other side. From there, the road winds down the mountain and meets up with the main coastal road in north Lombok. An alternative and challenging route is to return to the main road and travel to the east coast, from there on the main road that circumnavigates the island north.

The main east-west road intersects the coastal road at **Labuhan Lombok.** This is the main port in East Lombok, serving the shipping route from the eastern islands. The port proper is called Kayangan. Gorgeous panoramic views can be had from the hills before the harbor. Labuhan Lombok is a bustling town with plenty of warungs and eateries to refuel. A small hotel is close to the center of town, on the road out to Kayangan, for those wishing to stay, and the public ferry between Lombok and Sumbawa operates nonstop daily.

Following the main coastal road, heading north from Labuhan Lombok, the road winds past fields of tobacco and corn, with occasional glimpses of the Alas Strait, the sea separating Lombok from Sumbawa. The coastline of Sumbawa Island looms surprisingly close.

At the small town of **Transat** there is a sign for Gili Lampu Bungalows (see below), with a rough dirt road leading down to the restaurant and beach.

Labuhan Pandan is a small town on the northeast coast with shops and small warungs. The road north from Labuhan Pandan is in good condition and provides sublime views of the ocean. Small white sand-fringed islands are visible further out in the bright blue water, while the green bulk of Sumbawa Island fills the horizon.

Further north, the road winds up into the hills and the coastline drops away as it passes through small towns baking in the hot sun; sleepy houses are surrounded by fields of dry crops and browning grass. In one, an arched entrance to the football field proudly announces its creation in 1945—and it looks like the place, and pace, probably hasn't changed much since then.

The hills grow steeper and then became mountains, as the road journeys up onto the eastern slopes of the awesome Rinjani mountain range. To the left is the towering volcano, with fold after fold of mountain range swathed in green jungle.

The two huge islands of **Gili Sulat** and **Gili Lawang** stretch for miles along the coast. Both are uninhabited, as fresh water is scarce, but they have great potential for ecotourism with their intact ecosystems, ample fishing, wetlands, mangroves, and superb snorkeling and diving. Currently, the only way to visit is to organize a trip with a local fishing boat. Inquire among the fishermen on the beaches and arrange a trip with transport back at the end of the day, for around Rp350,000.

The road gradually meanders back to hug the coast on the north face of the island, passing many small bays with deserted beaches. **Obel Obel** is a long black sand beach popular with locals for picnics and swimming. Small groups of children play in the calm waters while adults enjoy the shade of the trees that line the beachfront.

Leaving the coast, the road climbs into the mountains again and becomes tough going, with large sections broken by flooding and large potholes. In one section you'll see what was obviously a major riverbed at one time, but has since collapsed by some recent disaster and filled with rock and debris. A new roadway and recently constructed bridge ride over the top of the shambles, allowing access to the remnants of the original road further on.

In **Sambelia** district, not far from the main town of Bayan (p. 325), the road gives way completely to a landscape strewn with huge rocks and boulders, tossed into piles and swept into drifts as if some insane giant had thrown marbles across the valley floor. This is the result of the floods and landslide that struck this area in January 2006. Heavy rains almost every monsoon season do some damage to these roads and whenever a new section is built, within a few years it is potholed and parts are washed out by flooding. A makeshift side track leads around the wreckage and the road continues along to the north coast. Branching off the main coastal road at **Kali Putih,** a smaller road runs inland through the mountains

---

ⓘ Tips   The East Coast Islands

These gilis, unlike the famous Gili Islands (see chapter 16) of northwest Lombok, are uninhabited and relatively unexplored. It's impossible to count all the islands, as many small coral atolls rise just above sea level, but there are at least eight.

The staff at **Gili Lampu Bungalows** (p. 338) can organize day trips and snorkeling out to Gili Lampu, reached by small outrigger boat in about 20 minutes. Boat charters can also go to any of the other islands off this section of coast.

Cultural Riches & Ancient Traditions in East Lombok

This whole area has many small villages whose people still practice the old traditions and Sasak *adat* (traditional customs). Sembalun Bumbung has retained many older cultural traditions, such as *tandang mendat*, a men's martial dance, and a unique version of *wayang wong* theater. Sembalun Bumbung has a tomb that holds the remains of a Majapahit ancestor.

Near Sembalun Lawang is one of the few remaining ancient villages on Lombok: **Desa Belek** (or ask for directions to the "Rumah Adat"). A few thatch-roofed houses stand in a crumbling compound, with other nearby homes falling into ruin. Here the culture is firmly rooted in animist beliefs, with a circle of sacred stones in the center of the compound and the spirits of the ancestors close by. The caretaker, whose family has lived here for countless generations, will guide you around and show you ancient and sacred artifacts. Staff at Lembah Rinjani (p. 329) homestay can guide you to the village. Please leave a donation.

with wonderful scenery of dense forests and huge old trees, opening up to valley vistas and towering mountain ranges.

Sembalun Bumbung and neighbor **Sembalun Lawang** are in a high, cool valley on the slopes of Gunung Rinjani, surrounded by lush fields and valleys. Both villages are alternative points to Senaru for climbing Mount Rinjani and there are a number of tour agencies that organize treks in the region, as well as several small homestays. **Rinjani Trek Management Board** (RTMB; ☎ 0370/641124 or 08/11390047; www.lombokrinjani trek.org; p. 328) operates the Rinjani Information Centre (RIC) in Sembalun Lawang. **Lembah Rinjani** (p. 329) is a small homestay at the base of Rinjani volcano. Further on, the steep, rough road through the mountains eventually leads to Sapit (p. 336).

WHERE TO STAY & DINE

Accommodation is very scarce in this part of the island. Be prepared to rough it a little, although the following places are clean and comfortable.

The **Gili Lampu Bungalows** (there's no direct contact to the Gili Lampu Bungalows itself, contact their agent Lombok Eco Logdes, Jl. Sungai Meninting 18, Ireng, Ampenan, Lombok; ☎ 0370/692179; www.lombok-ecolodge.com; no credit cards) are on the main coastal road heading north from Labuhan, look for the small town of Transat and turn right at the sign for Gili Lampu Bungalows. The six bungalows, made from coconut and woven bamboo, are basic, clean, and comfortable. The largest has two bedrooms, a fan, and a Western toilet with cold water shower. At between Rp50,000 and Rp90,000, including breakfast, they're a bargain. The beach is only about 30m (98 ft.) away from the restaurant.

Perched in the forest, almost at the top of the mountain, the **Hati Suci Homestay,** Sapit (☎ 08/1803757355; ☎ 0370/636545 Mataram; fax 370/624695; www.hatisuci. tk or www.desa-sapit.com; year-round Rp170,000; no credit cards) has rooms and bungalows on terraced slopes with wonderful views down the mountain. The rooms are very basic and the electricity supply is erratic, but there's a small restaurant and the friendly owner organizes trips to the nearby hot springs, and guides trekkers up Mount Rinjani.

The Gili Islands

The Gili Islands: Where travelers go for a few days and wind up staying a month. Situated off the northwest coast of Lombok, these mini tropical barefoot heavens have crystal-clear aquamarine seas, perfect white sand beaches, and coral reefs with drop-offs and ledges for spying turtles, manta rays, and myriad forms of aquatic life. Once considered simply a budget destination for backpackers on a side trip from Bali, the Gilis are now a popular destination in themselves and have come of age in recent years.

The quietest is the middle island, **Gili Meno.** Life unwinds at a relaxed pace and service and accommodations are suitably in line. One step slightly up the development chain is **Gili Air,** with a greater variety of restaurants, guesthouses, and villas. This is also a real working island with a permanent local population with an income outside of tourism. **Gili Trawangan,** or simply Gili T, is at the other extreme and is best known as a party island, but is no longer a one-trick pony. In recent years the addition of luxury villas with private pools, air-conditioning, freshwater showers, and 24-hour electricity has enticed the return of travelers who came here many years ago, but now feel comfortable visiting with their spouse and children. That's not to say the original magic has gone, but rather that partying is no longer the sole reason to come here.

One of the Gilis' biggest draws is scuba diving. With year-round water temperatures of about 28°C (82°F), the islands are one of the world's best places for viewing turtles and, from December to April, manta rays. Between the three islands are at least 18 accepted dive spots. The currents are strong and drift diving is the norm. Although the big dive schools with swimming pool training facilities are based on Gili T, the other islands sit marginally closer to the dive sites. It doesn't really matter which island you choose for convenience to the sites.

Each of the Gilis is completely free of cars and motorcycles with the only transportation being *cidomo* (horse-drawn carriages) and bicycles. However, be ever vigilant of the miniature horses trotting up behind you—there is only so much room on the boardwalks that circle each island.

1 GETTING TO, BETWEEN & AROUND THE GILIS

The Gilis are easily accessible from Bali by boat or plane, both taking approximately 2 hours journey door to door. From Lombok, it is just a hop, skip, and boat ride away.

Most tourists prefer to arrange private transfer services through the hotels or villas where they are staying on the Gilis. This will include pickup, meeting and greeting service, and being escorted hand-held to your suite door. Many third-party agents either in Bali or over the Internet can arrange all your transportation and accommodation needs. For those going alone the choices are as follows:

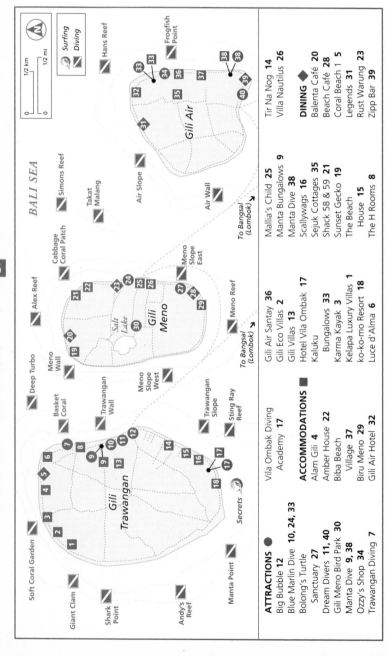

ATTRACTIONS ●
Big Bubble **12**
Blue Marlin Dive **10, 24, 33**
Bolong's Turtle
  Sanctuary **27**
Dream Divers **11, 40**
Gili Meno Bird Park **30**
Manta Dive **9, 38**
Ozzy's Shop **34**
Trawangan Diving **7**
Vila Ombak Diving
  Academy **17**

ACCOMMODATIONS ■
Alam Gili **4**
Amber House **22**
Biba Beach
  Village **37**
Biru Meno **29**
Gili Air Hotel **32**
Gili Air Santay **36**
Gili Eco Villas **2**
Gili Villas **13**
Hotel Vila Ombak **17**
Kaluku
  Bungalows **33**
Karma Kayak **3**
Kelapa Luxury Villas **1**
ko-ko-mo Resort **18**
Luce d'Alma **6**
Mallia's Child **25**
Manta Bungalows **9**
Manta Dive **38**
Scallywags **16**
Sejuk Cottages **35**
Shack 58 & 59 **21**
Sunset Gecko **19**
The Beach
  House **15**
The H Rooms **8**
Tir Na Nog **14**
Villa Nautilus **26**

DINING ◆
Balenta Café **20**
Beach Café **28**
Coral Beach 1 **5**
Legends **31**
Rust Warung **23**
Zipp Bar **39**

ⓘ Tips **Getting on the Right Boat**

Each boat heading to the Gili Islands has a strip down its bow: **white** is for Gili Air; **yellow** for Gili Meno; and **blue** for Gili Trawangan.

BY AIR

The Gilis do not have an airport and sea planes have yet to catch on. You'll have to fly first to Mataram, Lombok, and then take a boat. For information on getting to Lombok by air, see p. 307.

On arrival in Mataram, if you haven't organized private transportation, purchase a ticket from the taxi office to either **Bangsal** (public harbor) or **Teluk Nare** or **Teluk Kodek** (both private harbors). The journey takes approximately 40 minutes; cost is about Rp120,000 each way. The taxi can take you on the Monkey Forest route or the coastal route (p. 288), so you can get in a touch of sightseeing on your way. Either route takes the same amount of time and the same amount of money—although the coastal route is prettier.

BY BOAT

The trip will take you across the **Wallace Line,** a deep water boundary, running from Australia to Borneo. To the east live Asian and Australasian flora and fauna, and to the west live Asiatic. Chances are you will see dolphins and a whole array of bird life, which seem to also observe the boundary.

PUBLIC BOAT FROM BANGSAL PUBLIC HARBOUR, LOMBOK Taxis must finish their journey at the port gate which, for reasons best known to the *cidomo* drivers, is 600m (1,968 ft.) from the actual port. You can either walk these last 600m (2,000 ft.) or take the ever-present *cidomo,* although at an average of Rp30,000 per single journey it is hardly going to break the bank. Once at the harbor, buy a boat ticket from the office; do not be tempted to buy a ticket from anyone else, no matter how enticing the so-called deal may sound. Prices from the ticket office at Bangsal are fixed.

Costs (Rp) to:	Air	Meno	Trawangan
Public	8,000	9,000	10,000
Charter (up to 12)	155,000	170,000	185,000

Boats run daily 8am to 4:30pm; the journey takes approximately 40 minutes but can take longer depending on the weather.

Bangsal has a small shop selling snacks and toiletries. You can either buy here or wait until you arrive on the islands. All the islands now have their own basic stores.

FAST BOAT FROM BALI A number of direct fast boat services are now available from Bali to Gili T. No boat service is available to Gili Meno as it is too shallow; Island Getaway offers a service to Gili Air, too, if required, at no extra cost. If you are staying in Kuta, Seminyak, and Sanur, one of the most established options is Blue Water Express from **Benoa Harbour.** For those staying near Ubud, Candidasa, or the east coast, it is quicker to depart from **Pandangbai,** about 2 hours from Seminyak. Check the weather forecast before you book as the journey is far more pleasant on calm seas.

THE GILI ISLANDS

16

GETTING TO, BETWEEN & AROUND THE GILIS

The **Blue Water Express** (© 0361/723479; 08/1338418988 after hours; www.bws bali.com) departs Bali International Marina in Benoa Harbour daily at 8am and from Gili T at 11am. Journey time is 2 to 2½ hours; tickets cost Rp690,000 one-way; Rp1,300,000 round-trip.

The **Gili Cat** (© 0361/271680; www.gilicat.com) departs Padangbai (east Bali) daily at 9am; from Teluk Kode, Lombok, at 11:45am; and from Gili Trawangan at 11:15am. Journey time is around 2 hours; tickets are Rp660,000 one-way; Rp1,200,000 round-trip. Afternoon service leaves Bali at 1:30pm and Gili T at 3:30pm.

Island Getaway (© 0361/753241; www.gili-paradise.com) boats depart Benoa Harbour daily at 8am; and from Gili Trawangan at 11:30am. The trip takes 2 to 2½ hours; tickets are Rp650,000 one-way; Rp1,300,000 round-trip.

Black Pearl (© 08/17343168; www.bluewatercruises.com) leaves from Serangan Harbour at 9am and returns from Gili T at 1pm stopping at Teluk Kode. The trip takes 2½ hours; tickets are Rp680,000 one-way; Rp1,260,000 round-trip.

SHUTTLE BUS & BOAT FROM BALI If you have time or a tight budget, you may wish to experience how the locals travel. Catch the public ferry (capacity 100) from Padangbai. **Perama Tours** (main office: Legian 39, Kuta; © 0361/751551 or 0361/751875; www.peramatour.com) shuttle bus and boat service runs daily from several points on Bali by bus to Padangbai, then direct to Gili T on the slow boat. The service takes around 8 hours. Though the boat looks like it lists heavily, fear not, it has looked this way for a long time. Times and prices are from: Kuta, 10am, Rp350,000; Sanur, 10:15am, Rp350,000; Ubud, 11am, Rp350,000; Padangbai, 1:30pm, Rp300,000; Candidasa, 12:30pm, Rp325,000; Lovina, 9am, Rp450,000.

The return leg from Gili T leaves at 7am and 9am from Senggigi.

A LOCAL EXPERIENCE You can also negotiate with the local fishermen in Amed, Bali, who will sail you in their *jukung* to any of Gilis. The whole village gets involved in making these boats, carved from a single tree trunk with an outrigger on each side. The journey takes about 3 hours. It's a lovely way to see the coast, watch for sea life, and enjoy a local experience. The seats are wooden struts and the cover overhead from the sun can be inadequate where it exists. Expect to pay between Rp200,000 to Rp300,000 for the boat, which should fit up to four people. If you're on Lombok, hire a boat from the west coast (p. 310).

> (**Warning!**   **Taking the Local Boats**
>
> None of the local boats carry life jackets. With little shade, it can also get hot on the boat, so take strong sun block and a hat.

GETTING BETWEEN THE GILI ISLANDS

Tourist **boats** shuttle between the islands, running a circuit starting in Air, then on to Meno, then Trawangan then back to Meno, and finally Air twice daily. The boats leave pretty much on time, with timetables at each ferry point, and give you a chance to take in an island for the day at little cost. The fixed fares are: Air to Meno Rp17,000; Air to Gili T Rp19,500; Gili T to Meno Rp19,000. Boat times are posted in the station office. It's a good idea to check the times 1 day ahead of your planned trip.

To **charter** your own boat, you need to negotiate with one of the omnipresent boatman. The boatmen are businessmen and the price will vary depending on how wealthy they think you are. Have some sympathy, petrol is not cheap, the engines are expensive to run, and they are not guaranteed a return trip. Negotiate, but be fair.

GETTING AROUND THE GILI ISLANDS

Once on the islands the only mode of transport is nonmotorized. You can use a *cidomo* (horse-drawn cart), hire a bicycle, or just walk. What's the rush, anyway? Expect to pay between Rp20,000 and Rp30,000 for a *cidomo* for a short trip, and multiples thereof if you make stops along the way. **Bikes** can be hired throughout the islands. They are not cheap and none come with chains and locks. You will likely leave your bike outside a restaurant only to return and find it missing. Due to the size of the islands, if you walk along the road you will find it parked outside another bar. Thankfully the shop owners are understanding and no deposit is taken as no bikes leave their home island.

(Fast Facts The Gili Islands

ATMs There is only one ATM among the three islands, in front of **Hotel Vila Ombak** (p. 351), Gili T. Bring cash.

Business Hours Most restaurants on the islands are open for breakfast, lunch, and dinner, but exact times are nebulous. During high season, restaurants will open early and close late due to the influx of customers; in the low season, opening and closing times will depend on if they think customers are nearby. In low season, opening times are not guaranteed. Therefore, we have not listed opening and closing times for most restaurants.

Credit Cards You'll have the most luck trying to pay with a credit card at some of the bigger resorts, private villas, and dive schools on Gili T (with a 3% to 5% surcharge). Unless otherwise noted, accommodations and restaurants do not accept credit cards.

Doctors All of the islands have a nurse available who can treat basic first aid conditions. For more serious conditions, a doctor's surgery is available 24 hours on Gili T behind Vila Ombak.

Electricity Each of the Gilis suffer from a shortage of electricity. Sometimes the local electric company cuts the supply, so you can find yourself walking and dining under the stars. Most accommodations and restaurants on Gili Meno and Gili Air do not have backup generators, but many of the bigger resorts on Gili Trawangan do.

Etiquette The majority of Gili Islanders are Muslim, so please have respect and display as little nudity as you can. Do not sunbathe topless. Bikinis should be limited to the beach only.

Internet Access There are enough Internet cafes and shops that offer Internet access on the islands but they are all painfully slow. Expect to pay about Rp500 a minute. Some villas and premises on Gili T now offer free Wi-Fi.

Police There are no police on any of the islands, which partly accounts for the relaxed vibe. Any thefts, harassments, or complaints can be made to the island **Kepala Desa** (Head of the Village). They take crime very seriously and will go to extreme lengths to ensure the issue is cleared up, generally taking matters into their own hands. Most of the people associated with the Kepala Desa do not speak English, so always take someone from your hotel or villa with you and give them a contribution of thanks for their efforts. For insurance purposes you may need to visit the nearest police station in Mataram, Lombok.

Post Office There are no post offices on any of the islands. However, you can buy stamps from **William's Bookshop** on Gili T. Some hotels will post letters if you ask nicely.

Seasons High season is July, August, Christmas, New Years, and Nyepi (Balinese New Year, typically either Mar or Apr). Book months in advance as accommodations, though plentiful on Gili T, fill quickly and some find themselves camping on the beach (although many are there possibly because they couldn't find their way home). During low season, things are decidedly quieter. Though most accommodations prices are open to negotiation any time of the year, you'll have more success during the low season. Rainy season falls between November and April with less rain than Bali and Lombok, but it is still worth a visit during these times.

Shopping Various small kiosks sell drinks, snacks, basic food, toiletries, and suntan lotion on all three islands. Prices are considerably higher than the mainland. A few stalls and shops make and sell souvenirs items, but you're best off doing your souvenir shopping on the larger islands.

Travel Agents **Perama Tours** has offices on all the islands and can arrange transportation back to Lombok and Bali. They can also arrange a selection of tours to the nearby islands.

Water The Gilis do not have freshwater. Do not drink water from the tap. Bottled water is widely available. Make sure the bottles are sealed.

2 GILI AIR

Gili Air, "Island of Water," is the nearest island to Lombok and popular with guests on the mainland who visit for the day. This is also the most populated of the three Gilis, with just over 1,000 local inhabitants, descendants of Bugis, Mandar, and Sulawesi. The majority of accommodation here is locally owned and managed with only a few foreign-owned properties (unlike on Gili T).

FAST FACTS Ozzy's Shop (p. 347), Gili Air Hotel (p. 345), and Gecko Cafe, behind the Perama Tours office, offer **Internet.** Rent **bicycles** at Ozzy's (p. 347). The village **clinic** is behind the harbor. Ask for directions. At the time of writing, a nurse was on call from 8am to 6pm, but there is no way to know that this is always the case. The **public boat harbor Koperasi,** on the south coast bang in the middle, is open daily 8am to 5:30pm; look at the timetable on the wall for public boats.

WHERE TO STAY

The majority of lodgings are on the north and east coasts near the best snorkeling. Gili Air is still quite primitive when it comes to running water and most accommodations still only offer saltwater showers.

Biba Beach Village ★ This villa hotel and restaurant has been lovingly built by Italian owners Claudio and Sabrina making it one of the more charming places to stay on the island—if you can get a room. The interior has been carefully furnished in a traditional Indonesian style that effortlessly mixes with the modern amenities. Each bungalow has a king-size bed and a single bed. All the rooms have terraces, with chairs and tables overlooking the garden and out over the sea.

The restaurant sits directly on the beach. Dinner is served in *buruga* (open-sided thatched platforms on stilts) adorned in colorful fabrics. Claudio takes great pride in his food and the Italian menu offers a selection of freshly made pastas, *frito misto*, and gnocchi. The fresh ravioli dishes (Rp35,000) change daily. A specialty is the hand-stuffed mushroom ravioli served with a simple butter sauce. The spaghetti with fresh homemade tomato sauce is as good as it gets, and perhaps even better considering the location. The mouthwatering bruschetta is worth the visit alone.

(C) **08/1917274648.** biba69@alice.it. 3 units. US$25–US$70 standard; US$33–US$75 for 3 people. Rates include breakfast. **Amenities:** Restaurant. *In room:* A/C, fan.

Gili Air Hotel   This hotel's 29 chalets are all arranged around a garden, with direct sea views from about a dozen units. Rooms are simple, the more basic have fans and a shower room while the luxury suites offer TVs, air-conditioning, and fridge. All rooms have saltwater showers, which are only so refreshing, but freshwater is planned for the future. Nowadays the resort is looking somewhat out of date and could do with a refurbishment but has the most magnificent views from the half-dozen beachfront bales.

Thanks to the Italian owners, the food here is good and is very popular with Italian tourists. Choose from an extensive Italian menu featuring pasta, with some Indonesian favorites thrown in for good measure, or a nightly seafood and meat barbecue. During high season, the restaurant serves up crab or lobster live from the aquarium.

Prices are steep for this island, but do not be afraid to try to negotiate a better price during the low season.

(C) **0370/634435** or 0370/643580. www.hotelgiliair.com. 29 units. US$39–US$64 standard; US$53–US$78 superior; US$64–US$85 suite; US$78–US$105 luxury. Rates include breakfast. **Amenities:** Restaurant; bar; Internet; saltwater pool. *In room:* A/C (in some), TV (in some), minibar.

Gili Air Santay (Finds)   This is a great budget choice and as such gets very busy in the summer. Traditional Sulawesi bungalows are spread out in a tropical garden, about a 100m (328-ft.) stroll to the beach. All of the fan-cooled bungalows have a large balcony with hammock, and are a perfect place to laze the day away. Book well ahead if you want to stay in the high season.

The beachside restaurant Santay serves delicious, authentic Thai food as well as traditional Sasak and European foods. If you have overdone barbecue fish and had enough local fodder, this is the place to head for.

(C) **08/1803758695.** www.giliair-santay.com. 10 units. Rp100,000–Rp200,000 standard; Rp130,000–Rp400,000 bungalow; Rp300,000–Rp450,000 family unit; extra person Rp40,000. **Amenities:** Restaurant. *In room:* Fan.

Kaluku Bungalows   These seven traditional styled rice barns, all with sea views, are next door to the Blue Marlin Dive (p. 356). Dive and stay options are available. Otherwise make use of the swimming pool, one of a few on the island, and the restaurant. Accommodation is in *lumbung* bungalows with small terraces in front, double beds with luxury linens, and modern outdoor shower rooms.

(C) **0370/634387.** www.bluemarlindive.com. 7 units. Rp350,000–Rp700,000. Rates include breakfast. **Amenities:** Restaurant; bar; outdoor pool. *In room:* A/C, TV, minibar.

Manta Dive   Part of a popular chain based on Gili T, these recently built *lumbung*-style bungalows with balconies are constructed around a pool with sea views. Rooms are basic with modern amenities. Some great bars and restaurants are right in front of the dive school. They offer competitive stay and dive packages.

☎ **08/1353050462.** www.manta-dive.com 4 units. US$40–US$65. **Amenities:** Outdoor pool. *In room:* A/C, minibar.

Sejuk Cottages (**Finds**   Set back from the beach, nestled in a former coconut plantation, these Sasak-style bungalows of various shapes and sizes are uniquely designed using Lombok wood with *alang alang* roofing. The best units are the luxury bungalows with upstairs terraces. Each bungalow is named after an Indonesian plant or flower, most of which can be found in the beautifully manicured gardens. Most bungalows have two double beds making these perfect for families and small groups. The only downside is that the hotel doesn't have a restaurant of its own, but with so much on offer nearby, it's only so much of a drawback.

☎ **0370/636461** or 08/1339535387. sejukcottages@hotmail.com. 12 units. Rp150,000–Rp300,000 standard; Rp350,000–Rp675,000 superior; Rp315,000–Rp650,000 bungalow. Rates include breakfast and taxes. **Amenities:** Bar. *In room:* A/C, fan, TV (in some), fridge.

WHERE TO DINE

Most restaurants on the island offer a similar menu and with few exceptions, the quality is the same. It's a mixture of Indonesian with basic Western food, and plenty of Italian options thrown in. Try and order your food before you're hungry as the pace of service can be pretty relaxed. The **Santay** at the Gili Air Santay (see above) for Thai and **Biba ★** at Biba Beach Village (see above) for Italian are also two excellent choices. Most of the restaurants listed are nothing more than open-air beach shacks. Almost none of the restaurants have phone numbers. They do not have credit card machines.

The **Green Café** serves a selection of sandwiches, pasta, and some delicious Sasak home cooking for Rp15,000 to Rp25,000. **Munchies** (Rp10,000–Rp25,000) is popular with travelers for their reasonably priced fresh fish barbecues. They also serve local curries. Prices for fresh fish are agreed upon when you choose. **Tami's** (Rp20,000–Rp40,000) serves a variety of local cuisines mostly to day visitors from the Oberoi Hotel on Lombok. The dish to try is the delicious grilled chicken, but the rest of the menu is not much different from others on the island—and it is slightly more expensive.

The **Wiwin Café** (Rp25,000–Rp30,000) gets packed in the evening thanks to its large selection of fresh fish. The fish is weighed in front of you and you agree upon a price. Also on the menu is local and European food and some pretty good Indian curries. The bar has a large selection of local and Western booze. The attached bookshop has a good selection of secondhand books.

Zipp Bar (Rp35,000–Rp50,000) is an ideal place to pass the day. Lounge on one of the sun beds and sip cocktails until you doze. Jump in the water, and enjoy some of the best snorkeling on the island. Try a pizza from their wood-burning oven. A range of pastas, burgers, local food, and sandwiches are also available. Watch out though, you may be charged from the more expensive "tourist" menu. Same food, different prices; ask for the local menu. If you are looking for some late-night drinking, this is the place to head to. Either look out for or watch out for the crowd-pleasing full moon parties.

EXPLORING GILI AIR

Snorkeling and diving are the main focus on Gili Air. For **surfers,** one right-hand break is mostly frequented by locals rather than tourists who prefer the better known breaks at Trawangan. The break is located on the southwest coast.

The best place to enjoy **snorkeling** on Gili Air is to start on the east coast at the top of the island and drift down with the currents. If you haven't brought your own gear you can hire it from plenty of beach bars and hotels. Expect to pay about Rp20,000 for mask and fins per day. If you would prefer to explore further off shore, hire a glass-bottom boat. Owners offer a day rate rather than charging by the hour so make the most of it and spend a day cruising round all three islands stopping for a well-deserved lunch before heading back at sunset. Expect to pay about Rp50,000 per person (four-person minimum) from **Ozzy's Shop** (✆ 0370/622179; daily 8am–8pm).

For **diving,** three established groups operating on the island are **Blue Marlin Dive** (✆ 0370/634387; www.bluemarlindive.com), **Dream Divers** (✆ 0370/634547; www.dreamdivers.com), and **Manta Dive** (✆ 08/1337789047; www.manta-dive.com). All have their headquarters on Gili Trawangan. Costs are fixed across all islands so there is no haggling. You can, however, save slightly by booking online.

Cycling on Gili Air is not for those looking for a leisurely spin round the island. There are lots of areas where you will need to dismount and push. This is best done early evening or first thing in the morning when it's slightly cooler. Expect to take about an hour to an hour and a half to circumnavigate the island. A day's hire from Ozzy's Shop will cost Rp30,000.

GILI AIR AFTER DARK

As with the other Gilis, Air is famous for its full moon parties. DJs from Bali and overseas fly in to mix tunes for revelers. The best places are **Zipp Bar** (see above) and **Legends,** a reggae joint in the north with a great beachfront tree house to fall out of.

3 GILI MENO

Gili Meno, the middle of the three islands, is the smallest and quietest with few permanent inhabitants and thus retains the most original charm. Most accommodations and food options are on the eastern coast, near some of the best snorkeling. However, a few secluded snorkel spots on the north coast are worth the trek. You will also see the best sunsets here, with Mount Agung in the distance.

FAST FACTS Gili Meno has **no ATM.** Most places do not accept credit cards. A **clinic** in the center of the island is managed by a nurse and open daily. The **harbor** is on the east coast. The **Perama Tours** boat ticket office (✆ 0370/632824) is in Kontiki Meno on the southeast coast. There is a small **wartel** for Internet at the harbor.

WHERE TO STAY

Amber House Each of the bamboo bungalows at Amber House is arranged in a charming garden and has its own veranda with ocean views. What you get here is basic accommodation with limited food, but a great location thanks to its seclusion. This quiet spot is a short walk from the main drag and has a lovely beach with good snorkeling.

✆ 08/137569728. 5 units. Rp120,000–240,000. Rates include breakfast. **Amenities:** Cafe (breakfast only). In room: Fan.

Biru Meno At this quiet out-of-the-way place on the southernmost tip of the island, the only sound you will hear is the water lapping on the coral beach. The rooms are decorated with natural matting and bamboo furniture while the gardens have been creatively decorated using locally sourced implements and an abundance of flowers. Swags of coral adorn the place giving it a mystical feel in the evening. The restaurant has great pizzas from its wood-fired oven and grilled fish and curries.

📞 08/1339758968. www.birumeno.com. 8 units. Rp150,000–Rp400,000. Rates include tax and breakfast. **Amenities:** Restaurant. *In room:* Fan.

Mallia's Child   Situated right on the beach, these basic, clean bungalows are a little overpriced for what they offer, but are in a handy location if you are looking to relax in the center of the island action. It's a great place to watch the world go by, but not much else. The attached restaurant has a wood-burning pizza oven and serves all the usual Indonesian and basic Western foods. The evenings feature a good barbecue.

📞 0370/622007. .www.gilimeno-mallias.com. 8 units. US$25–US$35 standard; US$50–US$70 family room. **Amenities:** Restaurant. *In room:* Fan.

Shack 58 & 59 ★ (Finds)   This delightful villa with the ocean just meters away, is a perfect honeymooners' choice. The simply furnished bedroom has both a double bed and a single bed. A further bale and gazebos on the seafront are perfect for watching the sunrise and Mount Rinjani in the background. You will be well looked after by husband and wife team Hengkie and Nirah who serve up a wonderful barbecue under the stars. Shack 59, is set inland and is a one-room cottage with a gazebo on the waterfront.

No phone. www.shack58.com. 2 villas. 50€ Shack 58; 45€ Shack 59. Rates include breakfast and taxes. Payment available via PayPal. *In room:* A/C, fan, TV/DVD, fridge (Shack 59).

Sunset Gecko ★ (Finds)   This ecofriendly, Japanese-owned place is situated on a fantastic spot on the island's northeast coast. Its isolated position means you get a front seat to the island's most stunning sunsets. The small A-frame rooms and two-bedroom wooden house are simply furnished and adorned with *ikat* fabrics. Don't be put off by the communal washrooms, as they are clean and beautifully designed with environmentally friendly soap. The food needs improving, at the time of our visit, but the position of its comfortable oceanfront bales make up for it.

📞 08/13535667743. www.thesunsetgecko.com. 6 units. Rp150,000 standard; Rp350,000 2-bedroom. **Amenities:** Restaurant.

Villa Nautilus ★   This place is ideal for those who are not quite ready to leave behind the modern world. Each of the five stone villas has a bed almost large enough to get lost in; a plush living area with floor to ceiling windows; air-conditioning; and a balcony with sun loungers facing the sea. One villa can be turned into a family villa. This is the most luxurious accommodation you will find on the island with a price tag to match, but well worth it. The in-house **Bibi's Cafe** has a selection of Indonesian cuisine and wood-fired pizzas for Rp20,000 to Rp30,000.

📞 0370/642-1431. www.villanautilus.com. 5 villas. Year-round US$68–US$88; extra person US$20. Children 1 and under stay free in parent's room. Rates do not include tax. MC, V. **Amenities:** Restaurant. *In room:* A/C, fan.

WHERE TO DINE

As on Gili Air, most of the island restaurants do not take credit cards. When ordering, always check whether the fish is fresh or frozen. Most places offer frozen fish during the day and a fresh fish barbecue in the evening. Various restaurants serve pizzas from their own wood-burning ovens. **BiBi's Cafe,** part of Villa Nautilus (see above), is also a good choice for pizza and Indonesian food.

Located on the northeast of the island, **Balenta Café** (📞 08/1933122903; Rp20,000–50,000) is ideal for day-trippers from Gili T. The kitchen offers a daily catch served to your order or as a delicious fish satay. Stop by in advance to tell them if you are hoping to visit for lunch and dinner and would like fresh fish—that way you are guaranteed it. The restaurant also has a turtle hatchery with a breeding program.

Beach Café (Rp25,000) is a simple idyllic beach bar serving a mean curry and the usual local offerings. After supper, lie beside the fire lit on the beach in the softest sand and enjoy star gazing.

Situated bang in the middle of the main drag, visit **Rust Warung** (© 08/1805241600; Rp15,000–50,000) in the evening for one of the island's best seafood barbecues. You can often enjoy listening to someone strumming on a guitar.

EXPLORING GILI MENO

Snorkeling and **diving** ★★★ are the main attraction here. Good snorkeling is along the northwest coast, near Balenta Café. You should see lots of **sea turtles** to the north of Balenta. The other good place is off the east coast near Amber House and Shack 58. Beware of strong currents at both of these locations. Snorkeling gear is available for rent (around Rp20,000 per day, negotiate for longer) at numerous shops and restaurants around the island.

At the time of writing there is only one dive shop on Gili Meno: **Blue Marlin Dive** (© 08/1917193285; www.bluemarlindive.com). Being based in Meno means that you are slightly nearer to more of the dive sites, but apart from that there are no benefits. Prices are fixed throughout the Gilis (p. 355).

One of the nicest things to do is to take a **stroll around the island.** A few guides will show you the way, if you don't fancy getting lost on the maze of dirt tracks that crisscross the island. On the way to the charming saltwater lake in the middle of the island, you pass through small villages, coconut plantations, and fields of peanuts and maize. If you are here during the dry season (May–Oct), look out for the salt mining.

In the center of the island is **Gili Meno Bird Park** (no phone; Rp50,000; 9am–dusk), with over 300 species of birds on show, including parrots, flamingos, pelicans, eagles, and pheasants from around the world. The park has deteriorated over the years and could do with some love and attention.

Situated on the southeast coast is the small **Bolong's Turtle Sanctuary** (no phone; www.gilimenoturtles.com; by donation; 9am–dusk) with a breeding program for 500 turtles. Once their green and loggerhead turtles reach a suitable age and size they are released back into the wild.

---

4 GILI TRAWANGAN

Gili T has moved on, no longer the backpacker, mushroom-addled, hedonistic discount paradise of yesterday. "A pity," the old hands might say. Though Gili T has cast off its grungy origins—it is the only island of the three where fresh well water and air-conditioning are the norm, and new developments are opening almost weekly with levels of service previously unheard of—it's not quite on the jet-set radar, though it won't be long.

Many are drawn by the still famous party nights; others for the lack of traffic. You can cycle the island in an hour and a half; the clean white sand beaches are endless; and the social options the same. Yes, Gili T remains a party island.

This is now a serious tourist destination with coffee shops, a doctor's surgery, pool bars, pizza, sushi, boutique hotels, and luxury villas. In the last 10 years, or even just 2,

Gili T has come a long way. And while the hard-core traveler may have moved on, the essence of island life remains. It is calm, safe, and a beautiful place to hang out.

FAST FACTS   A Bank Mandiri **ATM** is in front of Hotel Vila Ombak. Queues are long and the machine sometimes runs out of money. You can get **cash advances** on Gili T, but expect to pay a hefty charge of at least 7% to 10%. A 24-hour English-speaking emergency **clinic** is well signposted just behind Vila Ombak Hotel; a nurse is available daily 8am to 6pm for basic first aid. Various places offer **Internet** access and most of the top-end villas and restaurants have Internet or even Wi-Fi. It can be very slow though. **Tara Internet** (© **08/1917903789;** Rp400 per min.) has the fastest on the island. Gili T has **no fresh water,** it is mostly well water. None of the tap water, even piped into high-end hotels, is potable. The **port** is on the east coast. Most small boats moor just north of the port on the beach. Expect to get your feet wet. **Perama Tours** is also located just north of the jetty and can assist with transportation needs and trips to outlying islands on one of their boats.

WHERE TO STAY

Most accommodation is on the east and north coasts alongside the best swimming and snorkeling. Places here are just off the main drag. Book ahead if you are traveling in July, August, and around Christmas and New Year when hotels can get booked up months in advance. When booking, one consideration to be aware of is the mosque near the jetty where the morning call to prayer starts at 5am.

A few offerings dot the west coast, but as the water is shallow and the beaches full of remnants of dead coral, there is little swimming to be done here. The roads are covered in many places, especially on the western and northern coast, in soft sand that makes it difficult for both *cidomo* and bikes. You may have to get off both at times.

Head for the north for peace and quiet. The strip of town is only a 10-minute cart ride away. Don't forget to take the driver's telephone number if you want a late return. Most *cidomo* stop running around 11pm but if you arrange ahead you will find someone to give you a lift. Failing that, it's no more than a lovely 30-minute stroll. Take a torch—or let the stars guide you.

Expensive

Gili Villas ★   One of the latest villa complexes to hit the island, these luxurious two-bedroom villas (they can be offered as one-bedrooms depending on the season and availability) have every modern convenience you will need. Fed up with the noise and chaos of the town strip, you can chill out in your own peaceful, secluded environment. Breakfast can either be served in your villa or at **Coco's** (p. 353) in the front, which is under the same ownership.

© **08/123753125.** www.gilivillasindonesia.com. 4 villas. US$175–US$225 1-bedroom; US$225–US$275 2-bedroom. Rates include breakfast, tax, and service. MC, V. **Amenities:** Babysitting; pool. *In room:* A/C, fan, satellite TV/DVD.

Kelapa Luxury Villas ★   If you want the best that Gili T has to offer, this is one to consider. This luxury set of villas stands out from the crowd with their über–design—and so does their price tag. Let the in-house chef cook up a fantasy of dishes or self-cater in your kitchen. There is talk of a tennis court and a helipad. Truly, Gili T has come a long way.

© **08/1933147723.** www.kelapavillas.com. 10 villas. US$195 1-bedroom; US$315–US$335 2-bedroom; US$355–US$390 3-bedroom; US$560–US$620 4-bedroom. High-season surcharge US$40 per night. AE, MC, V. **Amenities:** Bikes; Internet; outdoor pool; room service. *In room:* A/C, satellite TV/DVD, kitchen.

ko-ko-mo Resort ★★   The Gilis, long known for their sleepy beachside bungalows and no frills villas, are going upmarket. The ko-ko-mo villas will be the first "five star" development on Gili T, featuring one-, two-, and three-bedroom villas and a fine-dining restaurant. Husband and wife team Mathew and Di Somerton use traditional Balinese design and Javanese furniture in what they call "elegant tropical." On their dedicated patch of beach are large king-size beach beds for two, just the ticket for a lazy day with a loved one.

ⓒ **0370/642352.** www.kokomogilit.com. 9 villas. US$150 1 bedroom; US$200–US$250 2 bedrooms; US$300 3 bedrooms. AE, MC, V. **Amenities:** Restaurant, the Restaurant (p. 353); outdoor pool. *In room:* A/C, satellite TV, DVD/CD, minibar.

Moderate

The Beach House ★★   A Gili T institution, the Beach House was one of the first luxurious villa complexes on the island. Due to its success and popularity, it is usually fully booked well in advance. Choose from studio rooms and tree houses (Indonesian stilt houses), to bungalows, and the four-bedroom villa. All the units are set back from the main strip in a tropical garden with palm trees and frangipani. Each is simply decorated with modern furniture. The pool overlooks the main drag making it ideal for people-watching. If you'd prefer to hide out, several villas have private pools.

ⓒ **0370/642352.** www.beachhousegilit.com. 32 units. US$40 Tree House; US$45 studio; US$55 standard bungalow; US$85 pool bungalow; US$200 2-bed villa; US$3004-bed villa. Rates include breakfast. MC, V. **Amenities:** Restaurant; bar; outdoor pool; room service. *In room:* A/C, TV/DVD, kitchen (in villas).

Hotel Vila Ombak   This is a perennial favorite with expats over for the weekend from Bali. The resort is far larger than you would notice, with 61 rooms of varying size and quality, and it is a 5-minute walk to the center of town, but just far enough. The traditional *lumbung* huts have terraces, hammocks, and some have balconies. The quality of the food has been suspect in the past but don't let this put you off. They are currently updating and adding new bungalows and a seafront terrace.

ⓒ **0370/642336.** www.hotelombak.com. 61 units. US$110–US$140 standard; US$250 cottage. Discounts available online. AE, MC, V. **Amenities:** 2 restaurants; bar; 3-level outdoor pool with Jacuzzi; room service; spa; Wi-Fi. *In room:* A/C, satellite TV, minibar.

The H Rooms ★★   These five modern, one-bedroom interconnected villas are behind the well-known hangout Horizontal. Chill out in one of the most popular bars by day, on one of the lounges on the beach or in one of the Jacuzzis in every glam villa. The beds are fit for an emperor. With every requirement met, you will never need to leave this resort. Lie back and enjoy!

ⓒ **08/1917446052** or 0370/639248. www.thegiliislands.com. 5 villas. Rp750,000–Rp2,000,000. Rates include breakfast. MC, V. **Amenities:** Restaurant, Horizontal (p. 353); bar; room service. *In room:* A/C, fan, satellite TV/DVD, fridge, Jacuzzi.

Luce d'Alma   Though this place is billed as the only four-star hotel on the island, many other hotels offer similar levels of comfort. However, the 10 air-conditioned rooms here have modern furnishings and, unusual for Gili T, their own bath. The hotel itself has a large swimming pool, Jacuzzi, gym, and spa.

ⓒ **0370/621777.** www.lucedalmaresort.com. 10 units. US$90–US$150. MC, V. **Amenities:** Bikes; gym; Jacuzzi; outdoor pool; sauna; spa. *In room:* A/C, satellite TV/DVD, hair dryer, minibar.

Inexpensive

Alam Gili   Located on the quieter northern shore, this tranquil and traditional beachfront Indonesian-styled resort features eight spacious bungalows in a stunning tropical garden and is part of the larger family-run Alam Group. If you really want to spoil your-self, take the huge two-story "Fish Suite" with its ornate wood carvings, sea view, and air-conditioning. The beach out front has great snorkeling.

© **0361/974629.** www.alamindahbali.com. 8 units. US$55–US$75 standard; US$95 Fish Suite. Rates include breakfast. MC, V. **Amenities:** Restaurant; outdoor pool. *In room:* Fan (A/C in Fish Suite).

Gili Eco Villas   The eco name is for real here, as all the villas' electricity is harnessed from either solar panels or wind generators and they are completely off the grid. Air-conditioning, although in every room, costs extra and the owners encourage you to go without it. The profit from the air-conditioning supplement is donated to Gili Eco Trust or one of the Biorock projects in front of the resort. Even the water from the villas is recycled. And while the green credentials are impressive in themselves, the owners still manage to deliver a stunning resort of antique Javanese *joglo* houses with charming fur-nishings of reclaimed wood.

© **0361/847-6419** or 0370/636057. www.giliecovillas.com. 7 villas. US$90–US$170 1-bedroom; US$140–US$220 2-bedroom. Rates include breakfast. AE, MC, V. **Amenities:** Babysitting; massage; out-door pool; port transfers. *In villa:* A/C, DVD, kitchen.

Karma Kayak   Grace and Astrid from Holland have set up six bungalows on the quiet northern coast far from the maddening crowd. Each bungalow is simply decorated in its own individual style with *ikat* fabric. This idyllic setting is perfect for those wishing to escape the loud music and party scene. The lounging area on the beach is adorned with *beruga* (gazebos) and sun loungers. It is the perfect place on the island to chill out, enjoy a sangria, and tuck into some great tapas.

© **08/1803640538.** www.karmakayak.com. 6 units. Rp350,000–Rp600,000. Rates include breakfast and taxes. No credit cards. **Amenities:** Restaurant, Karma Kayak (p. 353). *In room:* A/C (in some).

Manta Bungalows   These *lumbung* bungalows are affiliated with the dive school **Manta Dive** (p. 346), one of the most respected dive schools on the island, and are situ-ated right behind the school. The hotel has recently completed eight new bungalows to complement the existing six, and a new swimming pool with kid-friendly area. The friendly atmosphere and great location draw many repeat guests, making this a great value for your money.

© **08/123753125.** www.manta-dive.com. 14 units. US$40–US$65. MC, V. **Amenities:** Restaurant; bar; outdoor pool. *In room:* A/C, minibar.

Scallywags ★   Located behind the WAG club, Scallywags is stylish upon first glance, so you know what to expect from the rooms. The 10 bungalows have a modern Asian style mixed with a colonial feel. Each has its own small garden with lounge furniture. The large rooms themselves have modern features such as flatscreen TVs, solar-heated water, and Internet. Each room has been soundproofed and made ecofriendly with solar panel-ing. The swimming pool area includes a large *beruga* (gazebo) at one end and a pool bar on the other. Scallywags also has its own speedboat, the *Jackie O,* which guests can use for water-skiing or other watersports. Even if you're not staying here, the restaurant is worthy of your attention.

© **0370/648792.** www.scallywagsresort.com. US$60–US$80. MC, V. **Amenities:** Restaurant, Scallywags (p. 354); bar; outdoor pool; room service; watersports. *In room:* Satellite TV, hair dryer, Internet, minibar.

Tir Na Nog   Surprisingly, this lively Irish bar has very good accommodations, set back on the other side of the road so you are no more troubled by noise and revelers than at any other places in the middle of town. The 10 villas are clean and comfortable with fresh hot water and air-conditioning. The owners of the bar also own the franchise **Ryoshi** <u>353</u> sushi restaurant next door.

📞 **0370/639463.** www.tirnanogbar.com. 10 villas. From Rp300,000. MC, V. **Amenities:** Restaurant; bar. *In room:* A/C, kitchen.

WHERE TO DINE

Don't discount the **Beach House** (p. 351; Rp20,000–Rp60,000; MC, V; daily 7am–10pm)—Gili T's original barbecue and salad bar is still going strong.

Moderate

The Restaurant ★★ AUSTRALIAN   Australian chef Mathew, the co-owner of ko-ko-mo Resort has a long history of working both in Sydney and Bali. His new venture is this upmarket restaurant, serving the finest local and imported meat and seafood. Expect to see beef carpaccio with black truffle oil and game terrine with sweet mango jam and pickled onion on the appetizers list. If that isn't enough to whet your appetite, the main courses include quail stuffed with rice and mushrooms and lobster pasta. With an impressive wine list to match, and a piano playing in the background, this will certainly be a revelation to anyone returning after a few years away.

In the ko-ko-mo Resort (p. 351). 📞 **0370/642352.** www.kokomogilit.com. Main courses Rp140,000–Rp200,000. MC, V. Daily 7am–10pm.

Inexpensive

The **Coco** cafe (no phone; Rp15,000–Rp25,000; MC, V; daily 7am–6pm), the only Illy coffee shop on the island, serves baguettes, homemade cakes, milkshakes, and fresh fruit juices. It's right on the main drag. The lovely hand-painted wall at **Gili Deli** (📞 **08/123764443;** Rp30,000–35,000; daily 8am–6pm) conjures up images of a cafe that you would expect to see in the hip area of a big city. This great little place serves up salads, wraps, and baguettes along with local coffees. The established local fish restaurant **Juku** (no phone; Rp25,000–Rp50,000; daily 7am–10pm) is popular with the expat community for its reasonably priced grilled fish. The well-known Bali-based chain **Wrap a Snapper** (📞 **0370/624217;** Rp20,000–Rp30,000; daily 7am–midnight) serves up the best fish and chips on Gili T.

Coral Beach 1 (**Finds**) PIZZA   The best pizzas on the island come busting hot, straight from a wood-burning oven at Coral Beach 1. The five bales stretched by the sea are an ideal place to lounge away the day with some of the best snorkeling on the island. If you don't manage to get one of the bales, deck chairs are on offer where you can dangle your feet directly in the water and feast away.

No phone. Main courses Rp20,000–Rp45,000. Daily 7am–10pm.

Horizontal ★ BAR/WESTERN   This bar and restaurant sits on a beach littered with sun loungers in front of one of the best snorkeling areas. The choices are endless to curb any munchies desire: Will it be pizza from the wood-burning oven or a hearty burger? Or perhaps simple nibbles such as Thai cakes, Vietnamese rice rolls, or a fresh and tasty salad? After dark, it's cocktail hour—sip on margaritas until it's time for zeds.

At the H Rooms (p. 351). 📞 **0370/639248.** www.thegiliislands.com. Rp25,000–Rp70,000. MC, V. Daily 7am–midnight.

Karma Kayak (**Finds**) TAPAS   Enjoy sunset views while tucking into the house specialties here, authentic Spanish tapas, such as *boquorones fritas,* prawns, Spanish tortilla, and all the other usual Spanish delights. The chicken satays are some of the best on the island. In the evening, a barbecue features marinated meat or fish.

In the Karma Kayak (p. 352). ✆ **08/1803640538.** Tapas Rp13,000–Rp27,000. Daily 7am–9:30pm.

Kiki Nova WARUNG   This local warung makes one of the best *nasi campur* on the island. Different every day, the dish is a selection of vegetables, fried meat, and shrimp and usually a curry. Go before 2pm, otherwise you may find it all gone.

No phone. *Nasi campur* Rp20,000. Daily 7am–5pm.

Persona INDIAN   Curries are the order of the day here. The kitchen serves up a freshly made Indian cuisine of the usual tandoori delights with nan bread. Chicken tandoori, *daal*, and *tikka masala* are all delicious. Once you have dined, lie back on one of the mattresses on the beach and enjoy a hookah.

✆ **0370/660-7233.** Main courses Rp25,000–Rp50,000. MC, V. Daily noon–10:30pm.

Scallywags ★ BARBECUE/WESTERN   From the folks that brought you the Beach House next door, this is a new favorite on the island, serving wraps, paninis, salads, and many non-Asian choices. In the evening, the place is alive with revelers feasting on barbecue fresh fish, prawns, and meat, and choosing from the salad bar and plenty of freshly made pastas. Situated right on the shore front, on the busy southern stretch, you'll get plenty of atmosphere, value, and fresh organic food. Don't forget to try their Caipirosca.

In Scallywags Resort (p. 352). ✆ **0370/648792.** www.scallywagsresort.com. Main courses Rp20,000–Rp70,000. MC, V. Daily 7am–10pm.

EXPLORING GILI TRAWANGAN

BOATING   Most villas can hire you a glass-bottom boat or will recommend a man to call. Otherwise, it's easy to arrange this through various outlets on the island. The boat people rent out their boats for a full-day or half-day to one or all of the islands. The trip usually entails stopping at a few snorkeling spots as well as one of the other islands for lunch. For a full day, don't pay more than Rp450,000 for a trip to Gili Meno and the nearby area, and Rp600,000 for all three islands.

CYCLING   Hire a bike from many of the shops along the main strip. A rental store next to Coco Cafe rents bikes from Rp25,000 a day. Don't pay any more than Rp50,000 a day although you may well hear offers higher than this. A perfect way to spend an early morning or a late afternoon is a cycle round the island. One road hugs the coast, but much of it on the south and north sides are soft sand, which make for tough going at times. Plenty of other roads crisscross the center of the island passing local houses and through small villages while keeping under the shelter of the coconut palms. A trip around the island should take an hour or two depending on your route. Take a map as there are plenty of dead-end tracks. But the island is so small, you're never too far from a friendly face to show you the way home.

DIVING ★★★   The Gili Islands may be a bit sleepy on land, but they come alive under water. With some 3,500 individual species living in the reefs and seas of Indonesia, compared with only around 1,500 species off the Great Barrier Reef, you are rarely disappointed. Some 25% of the world's reefs are in Indonesia and the Gilis offer some of the best sites with the richest diversity. Diving here offers you clear, visible, and mainly safe waters.

The area has also become globally regarded as one of the premier turtle-viewing spots (both hawksbill and Olive Ridley), with year-round water temperatures of 28°C (82°F). Other fish and marine life you are likely to see include black and white-tip reef sharks,

The Five Best Dive Spots on the Gilis

Shark Point: All levels
Location: Northside Gili Trawangan
This is probably the most popular site off Gili T and excellent for viewing larger marine life. It is a vast open area with a flat sandy bottom and a series of ridges that fall away into deeper water and progressively deeper canyons parallel to the shore. Reef sharks can be found in the canyons, and cuttlefish, stingrays, and tons of turtles in the shallows. In the past, this has been a favored hang-out for huge bump-head parrot fish.

Manta Point: All levels
Location: Southside Gili Trawangan
This gently sloping reef has a variety of hard and soft corals interspersed with bombies and large table corals that provide shelter for fish. With rarely any current, it is an excellent site to get close up with reef sharks, stingrays, cuttlefish, and octopus. At the right time of the year (Dec–Mar), as the name suggests, you may well see a passing manta ray.

Simons Reef: Advanced divers
Location: Northeast of Gili Meno
This great deep dive offers a variety of corals not seen at many of the other sites. At 30m (98 ft.) this site has a sandy bottom between large sea mounds, which rise some 20m (66 ft.) from the sea bed. Sand bar formations here are similar to sand dunes in a desert.

Hans Reef: All levels
Location: Northeast of Gili Air
Famous for its muck diving, this site provides an opportunity to view some of the smaller, stranger creatures found in these parts. Frog fish, leaf scorpion fish, sea horses, black spotted morays, spearers, pipe fish, and many types of shrimp and other macro life are here.

Deep Turbos: Advanced divers
Location: East of Gili Trawangan
This site has spectacular topography. At 30m (98 ft.), this is another site with a sandy bottom between large sea mounds. You'll find a good variety of corals, huge sea fans, and plenty of overhangs and cracks to explore. Garden eels cover the sandy bottom and barracuda, leopard sharks, and giant rays can also be seen here.

THE GILI ISLANDS

16

GILI TRAWANGAN

cuttlefish, moray eels, angel fish, ghost pipefish, pink leafed scorpion fish, blue ringed octopus, and, from December to March, manta rays.

With some 15 to 18 accepted dive sites, many suitable for beginners, and professional, internationally credited dive schools, diving options are available for all abilities. Currents however can be misleading. Attempting to swim between the islands will likely end you far out at sea.

All the PADI dive schools on the Gilis charge the same price. Prices for a single dive typically start at US$40; you'll pay US$60 for an introductory scuba course; it's US$350 for a PADI open water certificate and US$275 for an advanced open dive. You will encounter many other non-professional, non-accredited dive schools on the islands. Use on the PADI-certified ones listed below.

The schools are: **Blue Marlin Dive** (✆ 08/1339930190; www.bluemarlindive.com); **Dream Divers** (✆ 0370/634496; www.dreamdivers.com); **Big Bubble** (✆ 0370/625020; www.bigbubblediving.com); **Manta Dive** (✆ 08/123753125; www.manta-dive.com); **Vila Ombak Diving Academy** (✆ 0370/642336; www.hotelombak.com); and **Trawangan Diving** (✆ 08/1339648; www.trawangandive.com).

In recent years, increasingly destructive and more concentrated fishing practices, coupled with the increase in pollution that tourism brings, has led to reef damage. The use of heavy anchors has been addressed to some extent with the introduction of mooring buoys, and, mercifully, fishing techniques involving either dynamite or cyanide have, with the financial support of the **Gili Eco Trust** (www.giliecotrust.com), now been banned. Concern about the destruction of the reef and the need to protect the marine life and the islands' microcosm led to the creation of the Gili Eco Trust in 2001. All seven of the dive centers on the Gilis participate and anyone wishing to dive around these islands needs to pay a one-time fixed fee of Rp40,000, which goes to the trust to help pay for beach cleaning, recycling, education, and reef conservation. The Trust is expanding its programs to cover education and awareness initiatives as well as projects that help the local community develop more sustainable practices.

One of the major projects of the Trust has been **Biorock** ★★. The Biorock is an artificial structure pumped with a small electrical current which, over time, allows the development and regeneration of a coral reef system. Currently 33 reef modules are in operation and the work to date has shown remarkable results.

HORSEBACK RIDING (Moments) **Stud's Horse Riding Adventures** (✆ 08/175746079) offers beach rides and treks around the island through the coconut plantations. Most of the horses are actually ponies but there are some for the bigger boys. Take a memorable sunset ride followed by a swim in the sea.

KAYAKING (Moments) Astrid, a former kayaking medalist, will take you out on a half-day kayaking expedition via **Karma Kayak** (p. 352; Rp300,000 per person). Lunch is a picnic on the beach of Gili Meno, en route. Trips are subject to the weather and the currents on the day.

SNORKELING ★★ The best snorkeling on the island, with plenty of varieties of coral, is the **north coast** where you are virtually guaranteed to see turtles. Another popular spot is off the **east coast.** Start at the north easterly spot and be carried south by the currents. The currents can be very strong. Ask the dive schools for any advice on currents. Snorkeling kits can be rented from plenty of places on the island. Expect to pay about Rp20,000 a day.

(Moments) **Learning to Free Dive**

FreeDiveGili offers a rare opportunity to learn to free dive. An experienced Apnea Total instructor will teach you all the techniques required to enable you to dive longer and deeper. Located in Manta Dive (p. 346) on Gili T (✆ 0370/643649; www.apnea-total.com), the 2-day introductory course is US$185.

SURFING   At the southern end of the island is a fast right-handed break, better known as **Secrets.** This break is best tackled at high tide with a southwest or south swell. The wave can get big and in shallow waters and is best left to the experts.

WATERSPORTS   The **Beach House, Scallywags,** and **Kelapa Villas** (see "Where to Stay," above) can all arrange banana boats, donuts, and water-skiing. (The kids never seem to tire of the banana boat.) It's not cheap though. Expect to pay Rp700,000 for an hour and Rp400,000 for half an hour.

GILI TRAWANGAN AFTER DARK

Gili T certainly lives up to its time-honored party island reputation. For such a small island, and no matter the season, there's ample opportunity at plenty of bars and night-spots to let your hair down every night of the week. During high season, the place is rammed with revelers. If you think you're sneaky for coming here during low season, you've got another thing coming: The party seems undeterred even through the low season. Popular full moon parties feature DJs from Bali and Europe and round out the hedonistic offerings. Rotating party nights have historic followings, although with the island's popularity, more than one venue is now popular on any given night.

Monday: Blue Marlin. On the second floor of the dive school, the dance floor comes alive to the sounds of throbbing trance and tribal tunes.

Wednesday: Tir Na Nog. Or simply, "the Irish Bar," you don't need to ask for directions to this place in the evening—just follow the crowd. With dancing on the bar a nightly sport, great music, and a lively crowd, if you are enjoying your time on Gili T, you will end up here at some point. If you're not enjoying your time on Gili T, this may be just the pick-me-up.

Friday: Rudy's. An institution on Gili T, this is one of the island's original bars and it still has heaps of appeal today. Locally owned and operated, it's the place to meet people from all over the world, rubbing shoulders with expats and locals while downing their legendary magic (read: magic mushroom, legal in Indonesia) cocktails. Rudy's is a lively place any night of the week, but it's a traditional Friday-night spot.

Any night: Sama Sama. This bar has gained heaps of popularity because of the great live music and impromptu jam sessions. Some of the best reggae music can be heard here not only from the band but from the lively musical crowd.

(Warning!)   Don't Get Burned on Gili T (or Anywhere in Indonesia)

Along with Gili T's reputation as a party destination, it unfortunately also has a reputation for the availability of drugs, particularly ecstasy and cannabis. Things quieted down considerably after an undercover police crackdown in 2008. While the reputation of the island remains, the liberal drugs policy of turning a blind eye has gone for good. You may still be approached. The penalty for possession for even one seed is a minimum 4 years and for dealing, the penalty is life or death. **Avoid** contact and association with drugs and dealers **at all costs.**

Fast Facts

1 FAST FACTS: BALI & LOMBOK

BANKS Major currencies can be exchanged at most banks, money changers, and hotels. There is often a different rate for any notes smaller than US$100 and this applies to most currencies. Banking hours are Monday to Friday, 8am to 3pm. Banks in hotels usually stay open longer while money changers are generally open until early evening.

BUSINESS HOURS Most places keep daily "daylight hours," which on the equator pretty much means 6am to 6pm (or a little later).

DRUG LAWS Though you might be offered marijuana at every turn, Indonesia officially takes drug offenses very seriously. American and Australian forces have teamed up with Indonesian police to fight drugs, along with terrorism, and penalties for mere possession include long jail sentences and large fines.

ELECTRICITY Currents can be either 110 volts (50 AC) or 220 to 240 volts (50 AC).

EMBASSIES & CONSULATES **Australia:** Jl. Tantular 32, Renon, Denpasar (ⓒ **0361/241118;** Mon–Fri 8am–noon and 12:30–4pm). The Australian consulate also assists nationals of **Canada** and **New Zealand. United Kingdom:** Tirtra Nadi 20, Sanur (ⓒ **0361/270601;** Mon–Thurs 8:30am–12:30pm, Fri 11:30am–6:30pm). **United States:** Jl. Hayam Wuruk 310, Denpasar (ⓒ **0361/233605;** Mon–Fri 8am–4:30pm).

EMERGENCIES Bali has a new emergency response center that coordinates all governmental bureaus and services: dial ⓒ **112.** Otherwise, you can call the national numbers: ⓒ **110** for the police, ⓒ **118** for an ambulance, ⓒ **113** in case of fire, and ⓒ **111/115-151** for search and rescue. The Red Cross can be reached at ⓒ **26465.** (You must dial the local area code if you are using a mobile phone.) The Indonesian Red Cross is at Jalan Imam Bonjol, Km 3, Denpasar (ⓒ **0361/480282**), on Bali, and Jalan Bung Karno 29, Mataram (ⓒ **0370/623885**), on Lombok.

HOSPITALS Hospitals and clinics are listed in the Fast Facts section of each individual chapter or town. If you need a doctor or dentist, ask your hotel for a referral—many have one on call.

LIQUOR LAWS You won't find liquor in halal restaurants catering to Muslims, but there are no restrictions elsewhere. The legal drinking age is 17, but the police rarely enforce this law.

MAIL Your hotel can send mail for you, or you can go to the post office in Denpasar, at Jalan Raya Puputan Renon (ⓒ **0361/223566**). Other branches are in Kuta, Jalan Raya Kuta (ⓒ **0361/754012**), Ubud, and Sanur. For big items, packing and shipping services are in all major tourist areas, but the cost can be exorbitant. The Lombok main post office is at Jalan Sriwijaya, Mataram (ⓒ **0370/632645**).

POLICE Dial ⓒ **110** for the police.

RAMADAN During Ramadan you can still get food throughout the day on Lombok and the Gili Islands and most businesses run as usual but service is slower than normal as there is less staff. After Ramadan, the festival of Eid-ul-Fitr (a Muslim holiday celebrating the end of Ramadan) begins with a 3-day celebration. Ramadan: August 11 to September 10, 2010; August 1 to August 30, 2011. Bali sees little change during Ramadan.

TAXES Some hotels and restaurants factor government taxes (10% tax and 11% service) into their quoted prices, but most of them will put it as an additional charge.

TELEPHONES The international country code for Indonesia is **62.** Because many hotels charge a great deal even for using your calling card, you're better off using the wartel network of privately owned pay phones. There's one in every tourist center, though some work better than others. Some also have Internet access. See "Telephone Dialing at a Glance," p. 49, for details.

TIME ZONE Bali and Lombok are 8 hours ahead of Greenwich Mean Time, except during daylight saving time, which it does not observe. That's 13 hours ahead of Eastern Standard Time in the U.S.

TIPPING Tips are always welcome but not expected. Generally larger more upmarket restaurants and hotels will add between 15% and 21% to the bill to cover 10% government tax and allow something for service. As most waiters, masseurs, guides, or taxi drivers earn under Rp100,000 a day and work long hours, an appreciative tip for their hard work is always a nice thing to do. When staying at a villa, if no service has been added, allow between 5% and 10% of the total bill to be split between the staff. Make sure they are all aware, even the gardeners, as some villa managers will pocket the full amount themselves. For longer stays, a discretionary amount is acceptable. Round up taxi bills to the nearest thousand.

TOILETS Western-style toilets with seats are becoming more common than the Asian squat variety, though cheap *losmen* (homestays) and some less touristy public places still have the latter. Always carry toilet paper with you, or you might have to use your hand (the left one only, please) and the dip bucket.

VISITOR INFORMATION Before you go, browse the **Bali Tourism Board** website at www.balitourismboard.org.

The Indonesian Embassy in the in **Australia** is at 8 Darwin Ave., Yarralumla, ACT 2600 (✆ 612/62508600; www. kbri-canberra.org.au); in **New Zealand** at 70 Glen Rd., Kelburn, Wellington, New Zealand (✆ 475/8697-9899; www. indonesianembassy.org.nz); in the **U.K.** at 38 Grosvenor Sq., London W1K 2HW (✆ 020/7499-7661; www.indonesian embassy.org.uk); in the **U.S.** at 2020 Massachusetts Ave. NW, Washington D.C. 20036 (✆ 202/775-5200; www.embassy ofindonesia.org).

You can get other Bali travel information at the **Bali Government Tourism Office,** Jl. S. Parman, Renon (✆ 0361/222387; Mon–Thurs 7am–2pm, Fri 7–11am, Sat 7am–12:30pm), and at the **Department of Tourism, Post, and Telecommunications,** Jl. Raya Puputan, Niti Mandala (✆ 0361/225649; Mon–Thurs 7am–3pm, Fri till noon).

Tourist offices on Lombok can be found at: In Mataram at Jl. Suprato 20 (✆ 0370/621658; Mon–Thurs 7:30am–2pm, Fri till 11am, Sat 8am–1pm); and Jl. Singosari 2 (✆ 0370/634800; Mon–Thurs 8am–2pm, Fri till 11am, Sat till 12:30pm); and in Senggigi (✆ 0370/632733).

WATER Avoid tap water in Bali and Lombok unless properly boiled. Bottled water is available everywhere, and restaurants in tourist areas seem to use it as a matter of course, but you should always ask to be sure.

2 AIRLINE WEBSITES

AIRLINES TO & FROM BALI

Air France
www.airfrance.com

Air New Zealand
www.airnewzealand.com

Ansett Australia
www.ansett.com.au

Cathay Pacific Airways
www.cathaypacific.com

China Airlines
www.china-airlines.com

Continental Airlines
www.continental.com

Garuda Indonesia
www.garuda-indonesia.com

Japan Airlines
www.jal.co.jp

KLM
www.klm.com

Korean Air
www.koreanair.com

LTU International Airways
www.airberlin.com

Lufthansa
www.lufthansa.com

Malaysia Airline System
www.malaysiaairlines.com

Qantas Airways
www.qantas.com.au

Qatar Airways
www.qatarairways.com

Royal Brunei Airlines
www.bruneiair.com

Singapore Airlines
www.singaporeair.com

Thai Airways International
www.thaiair.com

AIRLINES TO & FROM LOMBOK

Batavia Air
www.batavia-air.co.id

Garuda Indonesia
www.garuda-indonesia.com

Lion Air
www.lionair.co.id

Merpati Airlines
www.merpati.co.id

Silk Air
www.silkair.com

Trigana Air
www.trigana-air.com

BUDGET AIRLINES

Adam Air
www.adamair.co.id

Air Asia
www.airasia.com

Jetstar (Australia)
www.jetstar.com

Hongkong Airlines
www.hongkongexpress.com

Valuair
www.jetstar.com/vf/en/index.aspx

Virgin Blue
www.virginblue.com

Basic Indonesian

The national language of Indonesia is Bahasa, but English is spoken widely where travelers to Bali congregate. On Lombok, English is less prevalent. Over 350 different dialects are spoken throughout the Indonesian archipelago but Bahasa, the national language, is spoken by over 65% of the population.

Learning simple greetings and phrases will make your visit to Bali more enjoyable for both you and the locals who take an interest in where you come from, what you do for a living, and where you are staying.

The indigenous language to Bali is "Basa Bali," spoken in the home by all Balinese natives. Basa has high, intermediate, and low versions used depending on caste and age of the person being addressed. To avoid the caste intricacies of Basa Bali most of the local people on the island speak Bahasa outside the home.

1 BASIC GRAMMAR

Bahasa is easily spoken by nonnative speakers as it is nontonal and written using the Roman alphabet. There are no plurals, genders, or tenses, making it markedly easier to pick up. The few basic rules in grammar include the following:

To indicate past tense, place the word *sudah* before the verb.
To indicate the future tense, place the word *akan* before the verb.
To form a plural, repeat the word. For example, *ayam* for chicken and *ayam-ayam* for chickens.

2 ESSENTIAL WORDS & PHRASES

English	Bahasa Indonesian
GREETINGS	
Hello.	**Halo.**
Welcome.	**Selamat dating.**
Goodbye. (See you later.)	**Sampai jumpa.**
Good morning.	**Selamat pagi.**
. . . afternoon.	**Selamat sore.**
. . . evening.	**Selamat malam.**
. . . night.	**Selamat tidur.**
Goodbye. (Person addressed is leaving.)	**Selamat jalan/Dadah.**
See you soon.	**Sampai ketemu lagi.**
USEFUL PHRASES	
Hello, how are you?	**Halo, apa kabar?**
My name is . . .	**Nama saya . . .**

English	Bahasa Indonesian
I would like . . .	Saya mau . . .
Where is . . . ?	Dimana . . . ?
the airport	bandara
the harbor	pelabuhan
the boat	kapal
a hotel	hotel
the beach	pantai
When is . . . ?	Kapan . . .
breakfast	sarapan/makan pagi
lunch	makan siang
dinner	makan malam
the performance	pertunjukan
How much is that?	Berapa harganya?
What time is it?	Jam berapa sekarang?
Do you speak English?	Apakah anda bisa berbahasa Inggris?
I do not speak Indonesian.	Saya tidak bisa berbahasa Indonesia.
Sorry, but I don't understand.	Maaf, tapi saya tidak mengerti.
Yes.	Ya.
No.	Tidak.
Not yet.	Belum.
Maybe.	Mungkin.
Please.	Tolong.
Excuse me. (To draw the attention of a person.)	Permisi.
Thank you.	Terima kasih.
I am sorry.	Maaf.
Don't mention it. ("No problem.")	Tidak apa-apa.
You are welcome.	Kembali.
Entrance	Jalan masuk
Exit	Jalan keluar
Toilet/Bathroom	Kamar mandi
Men	Pria
Women	Wanita

EMERGENCIES

I am from . . .	Saya dari Negara . . .
Help me.	Tolong.
I am lost.	Saya kesasar.
I am hurt/sick.	Saya sakit.
Call an ambulance.	Panggillah ambulans.
Call a doctor.	Panggillah Dokter.
I would like to call this number.	Saya mau telepon nomor ini.
Hospital	Rumah Sakit

English	Bahasa Indonesian	
Police	Polisi	
Fire	Kebakaran	
Pharmacy	Apotek	
Accident	Kecelakaan	
Emergency	Darurat	
Please take me to . . .	Tolong antar saya ke . . .	
I am allergic to . . .	Saya alergi . . .	
Where are the toilets?	Dimana kamar kecil?	
Leave me alone.	Jangan ganggu saya.	

NUMBERS

0	Nol	17	Tujuh belas
1	Satu	18	Delapan belas
2	Dua	19	Sembilan belas
3	Tiga	20	Dua puluh
4	Empat	30	Tiga puluh
5	Lima	40	Empat puluh
6	Enam	50	Lima puluh
7	Tujuh	60	Enam puluh
8	Delapan	70	Tujuh puluh
9	Sembilan	80	Delapan puluh
10	Sepuluh	90	Sembilan puluh
11	Sebelas	100	Seratus
12	Dua belas	1,000	Seribu
13	Tiga belas	10,000	Sepuluh ribu
14	Empat belas	100,000	Seratus ribu
15	Lima belas	1,000,000	Satu juta
16	Enam belas		

MONTHS

January	Januari	July	Juli
February	Februari	August	Agustus
March	Maret	September	September
April	April	October	Oktober
May	Mei	November	November
June	Juni	December	Desember

DAYS

Monday	Senin	Friday	Jum-at
Tuesday	Selasa	Saturday	Sabtu
Wednesday	Rabu	Sunday	Minggu
Thursday	Kamis		

ESSENTIAL WORDS & PHRASES

What time is it?	**Jam berapa sekarang?**	Next time	**Kapan-kapan**
		Hour (o'clock)	**Jam**
Today	**Hari ini**	Day	**Hari**
Tomorrow	**Besok**	Week	**Minggu**
Yesterday	**Kemarin**	Month	**Bulan**
Next week	**Minggu depan**	Year	**Tahun**

TRAVEL & SIGHTSEEING

English	Bahasa Indonesian
Please take me to . . .	**Tolong antar saya ke . . .**
How long is the trip?	**Berapa lama perjalanan?**
How do I get to . . .	**Bagaimana cara saya ke . . .**
Go right.	**Belok kanan.**
Go left.	**Belok kiri.**
Go straight.	**Jalan terus.**
At the corner.	**Di sudut.**
Next to . . .	**Di samping . . .**
Behind	**Di belakang**
In front of . . .	**Di depan . . .**
Opposite	**Di seberang**
Near to . . .	**Dekat dengan . . .**
Far from . . .	**Jauh dari . . .**
Here	**Disini**
There	**Disana**
South	**Selatan**
North	**Utara**
East	**Timur**
West	**Barat**
Stop	**Berhenti**
I am staying at . . .	**Saya tinggal di. . .**

AT THE TABLE

Restaurant	**Restoran**
What are the house specialties?	**Apa yang special disini?**
May I see a menu?	**Boleh saya lihat menu?**
I am a vegetarian.	**Saya vegetarian.**
Please don't make the food too spicy.	**Jangan dibikin terlalu pedas.**
I would like the . . .	**Saya mau . . .**
Waiter	**Mas/Mbak**
May I have the bill?	**Saya mau bayar?**
Keep the change.	**Simpan saja kembaliannya.**
Enjoy your meal/*Bon appétit.*	**Selamat makan.**

INDEX

See also Accommodations Index, below.

ABL Tours and Travel, 60
Abyss Adventures (Sanur),
68, 136
Accommodations, 5–6,
50–51. See also Accommo-
dations Index
Active vacations, 59–71
Addresses, finding, 40
Agung Rai Gallery (Ubud), 211
Agung's (Lovina), 280
Air Panas, 231, 280
Airport Left (Kuta), 87
Airport Rights (Kuta), 86–87
Air Sanih, 275–276
AJ Hackett (Kuta), 84
A-Krea (Sanur), 139
Alam Asmara (Candidasa), 261
Alam Nusa Spa (Lembongan),
144
Alila spa (Manggis), 257
Alternative health and well-
ness, 62–63
Amed, 265–268
Amed Ghost Bay, 266
Amed Reef, 266
Amlapura, 263–265
Ampenan, 313–314
Amuk Bay, 255
Andy's Gallery (Seminyak),
114
Ani's Gallery (Ubud), 221
Antonio Blanco Museum
(Ubud), 210
AquaMarine Diving, 68, 256,
266, 269
Archipelago Adventures, 64
Architecture, 20–22, 305–306
ARMA Museum of Art
(Ubud), 210
Art, Lombok, 305
Art galleries, Ubud, 211–212
Asia Transpacific Journeys, 60
Atlas North Bali Pearls
(Penyabangan), 280–281
ATMs (automated teller
machines), 40
Aussie Pub (Kuta), 91

Ayana Thallaso (Jimbaran
Bay), 155
Ayurveda, 62

Babi guling, 286
Bacio (Kuta), 91
Backroads, 60
Bagus Pub (Kuta), 91
Balangan (Uluwatu), 166, 168
Bale Kambang (Klungkung),
247–248
Bali Adventure Tours, 60, 68,
71, 214, 216, 233
Balian, 62, 294–295
Bali Antique Shop (Semin-
yak), 110
Balian wave, 294
Bali Arts Festival, 33
Bali Barrel (Kuta), 89
Bali Beach Golf Course
(Sanur), 136
Bali Belly, 43
Balibike.com, 64
Bali Bird Park (Sanur), 134
Bali Bomb Memorial (Kuta), 84
Bali Butterfly Park (Tabanan),
292
Bali Collection (Nusa Dua), 184
Bali Crystal Divers, 68, 136
Bali Deli (Seminyak), 114
Bali Discovery Tours, 59, 71
Bali Dives, 285
Bali Game Safaris (Nusa
Dua), 182
Bali Golf & Country Club
(Nusa Dua), 67, 182–183
Bali Hai, 140
Bali Handara Kosaido (Bedu-
gul), 235–236
Bali Hyatt spa (Sanur), 137
Bali International Diving Pro-
fessionals, 46
Bali Kitesurf School (Sanur),
136–137
Bali Museum (Denpasar), 116
Bali Nature Herbal Walk
(Ubud), 215
Bali Nature Walk (Ubud), 216

Balinese theater, Kuta, 90
Bali Purnati Center for the
Arts (Ubud), 212
Bali Rock (Kuta), 91
Bali Safari & Marine Park
(Sanur), 134–135
Bali Slingshot (Kuta), 84–85
Bali Spirit, 71
Bali Spirit Festival, 33
Bali Starling Pre-Release
Centre, 298–299
Bali Sunrise Tours, 68
Bali Trail Blazers (Ubud), 215
Bali Tree Top Adventure Park
(Bedugul), 235
Bamboo Blonde (Seminyak),
112
Bangko Bangko, 323
Bangli, 251–254
Bangsal, 325
Bangsal Harbour, 317
Banjar, 280
Banks, 358
Banyan Tree Cycling Tour
(Ubud), 214
Banyupoh, 281
Bat Cave (Penida), 152
Batu Abah (Penida), 153
Batuan, 218
Batubulan, 217
Batu Kelebit (near
Tulamben), 269
Batu Layar (near Senggigi),
316
Batu Niti (near Tulamben), 269
Bau Nyale Festival, 335
Bayan, 325
Bayung Gede, 226
Beaches. See also specific
beaches
    best, 4
    Candidasa, 260
    Nusa Dua, 181
    Sanur, 138
    Uluwatu, 166
The Beatles Bar (Sanur), 140
Bebali weaving, 274
Bedugul, 234–237

Bedugul Botanical Garden (Kebun Raya), 235
Beleka, 330
Belimbingsari, 297
Bemos, 39
Berdikari (Singaraja), 277
Besakih, 253
Biasa (Seminyak), 111
Biking, 63–64
    Amed, 265
    Gili Air, 347
    Gili Trawangan, 354
    Lembongan, 143
    Lombok, 311
    Sanur, 135–136
    Sidemen Valley, 249
    Ubud, 214
Bingin (Uluwatu), 166, 168
Bin House (Ubud), 221
Bintang (Seminyak), 114
Bintang Supermarket (Ubud), 219
Biorock Project (Pemuteran), 284, 285
Birds and bird-watching, 65
    Gili Meno, 349
    Penida, 152
    Sanur, 134
    Ubud, 216
    West Bali Barat National Park, 298–299
Biyu Nasak Gallery (Lovina), 280
Blackie's Warung (Lembongan), 144
Bloo Lagoon, 255, 256
Blue Marlin (Gili Trawangan), 356
Blue Oasis Beach Club (Sanur), 137
Boating and sailing, 65–66. See also Kayaking; whitewater rafting
    Gili Trawangan, 354
Body & Soul (Kuta), 88
Body Works (Seminyak), 108
Bolong's Turtle Sanctuary (Gili Meno), 349
Bonjeruk, 336
Botanic Garden Ubud, 216
Bounty, 92, 142
Bowling, Kuta, 84
Budakeling, 263
Bugs and bites, 42–43
Bukit Demulih, 251–252
Bukit Peninsula, 54, 154–188
Bulgari (Uluwatu), 167
Bull races (Makpung; Negara), 296

Bungy jumping and slingshot, Kuta, 84
Business hours, 358
Bus travel, 39
Buyan, Lake, 235
By the Sea (Seminyak), 110

Café Batu Jimbar (Sanur), 139
Cakranegara, 314
Camel rides, Nusa Dua, 182
Candidasa, 260–262
Canggu, 115–119
Canoeing, Danau Batur, 232
Carrefour (Kuta), 88
Car rentals, 38–39
Car travel, 37–38
Casa Gourmet (Seminyak), 114
Casa Luna Cooking School (Ubud), 213
Catur Eka Budi (Denpasar), 116
C Bali (Danau Batur), 232
Cekik, 297
Celuk, 217, 218
Celukan Bawang, 280
Cempaka (Kuta), 89
Ceningan, 149
Centerstage (Kuta), 92
Central Lombok, 330–332
Central Mountains, 54, 225–242
Ceremonies, 23, 30
Charlie's Factory (Candidasa), 261
Cheeky Monkeys (Sanur), 135
Chill (Seminyak), 108
Chisholm, Jack, 86
Ciokolata Boutique (Senggigi), 321
Climate, 30–31
Clipper, 68, 232
Club Double Six (Kuta), 92
Cockfights, 24
Cocoon Home (Jimbaran Bay), 158
COMO Shambhala's wellness retreat (Ubud), 213
Cooking classes, 66, 213, 257, 271
Coral Garden (Tulamben), 269
Cornershop/tuckshop (Seminyak), 111
Cozy (Kuta), 85
Crafts, 19–20, 61–62
Credit cards, 41–42
Cremation, 184

Crusoes (Kuta), 91
Crystal Bay (Penida), 152
Curl (Kuta), 89
Currency and currency exchange, 40–42
Customs regulations, 36

DaLa Spa (Kuta), 85
Damai spa (Lovina), 280
DAN (Divers' Alert Network), 69
Danau Batur, 226–234
Dance and cultural performances, 17
    Bukit Peninsula, 183
    Denpasar, 116
    Lombok, 306
    Sanur, 140
    Ubud, 222–223
Dance lessons, Sanur, 131
Dandelion (Seminyak), 110
Deejay Café (Kuta), 92
De Ja Vu (Kuta), 91
Delta Dewata (Ubud), 219
Dengue fever, 42
Denpasar, 52, 116–117
Desa Belek, 338
Desert Point (Lombok), 70, 324
Design Unit (Ubud), 219
Devosi (Singaraja), 278
Dharma Homestay (Padangbai), 256
Dietary red flags, 43
Dijon (Kuta), 88–89
Dinda Rella (Seminyak), 111
Disabilities, travelers with, 46
Discovery Mall (Kuta), 87
Disini (Seminyak), 110
Dive Zone (Senggigi), 69, 323
Dolphin watching, 182, 279
Double D Sports Bar (Kuta), 91
Dreamland (Uluwatu), 168
Drinks, 28–29
Driving infringements, 38
Driving License, International, 38
Drug laws, 358
Dry season, 30

Echo Beach (Canggu), 115
Ecotourism, 47–48
Ekas Bay, 333
Electricity, 358
Elephant Safari Park Lodge (Ubud), 216
Embassies and consulates, 358
Emergencies, 358

Ena Dive Centre & Marine Adventures (Sanur), 136
Engine Room (Kuta), 91
Entry requirements, 35–37
Espresso Bar & Pizzeria (Kuta), 91
ET Club (Seminyak), 111
Etiquette for visiting temples and ceremonies, 34
Eurodive (Amed), 68–69, 266
Exo-Fly (Uluwatu), 167

Families with children, 4–5, 46, 57–58
Fauna, 26
Festivals and special events, 31–35
Fishing, 66–67
  Candidasa, 261
  Lembongan, 145
  Menjangan, 300
  Padangbai, 255
Flora, 25–26
Food and cuisine, 26–28
  cooking classes, 66, 213, 257, 271
  Lombok, 306–307
Food stores and markets, 88
  Cakranegara, 315
  Denpasar, 116
  Jimbaran Bay, 159
  Sanur, 138–139
  Seminyak, 114
  Ubud, 219
Four Seasons Sayan (Ubud), 214
FreeDiveGili, 356

Gala Gala Underground House (Lembongan), 144
Galleria Bali (Kuta), 87
Galungan, 24, 31
Gamat Bay (Penida), 152
Gandhi Ashram, 71
G and V (Seminyak), 110
Ganesha Bookshop (Ubud), 219
Ganesha Gallery (Jimbaran Bay), 158
G.A.P. Adventures, 60
Garuda Vishnu Kencara Cultural Park (Uluwatu), 165–166
Gaya Ceramic and Design (Ubud), 61
Gaya Fusion of Senses (Ubud), 211
Gaya Spa (Kuta), 85
Gay and lesbian travelers, 45–46

Gede (Danau Batur), 232
Gedong Kirtya (Singaraja), 277
Geger Beach (Nusa Dua), 182
Geko Dive (Padangbai), 256
Gendang Beleq, 306
Genta Gallery (Ubud), 211
Geography, 25
Gerokgak, 280
Gerupuk, 333
Gili Biaha, 255
Gili Gede, 323
Gili Genting, 323
The Gili Islands, 55, 60, 339–357. See also specific islands
Gili Lawang, 337
Gilimanuk, 297
Gili Meno Bird Park, 349
Gili Selang, 266
Gili Sulat, 337
Girls Surf Retreats, 70
Glo (Seminyak), 108
Global Coral Reef Alliance, 285
Goa Gajah (Elephant Caves; Ubud), 208
Golf, 67
  Bedugul, 235–236
  Nusa Dua, 182–183
  Pantai Sira, 325
  Sanur, 136
  Tabanan, 290
Gondang, 325
Goris, 286
Green Balls (Uluwatu), 169
Green Camp (Ubud), 215
Green School (Ubud), 215
Griya Santrian Art Shop (Sanur), 139
Grocer & Grind (Seminyak), 114
Groceries. See Food stores and markets
Gudang Keramic (Sanur), 139
Gunung Agung, 252–254
Gunung Batukaru, 240–242
Gunung Pengsong, 314
Gunung Rinjani, 328
Gusti Lempad's Gallery (Ubud), 211

Han Snel Gallery (Ubud), 211
Happy Café (Senggigi), 322
Hardy, John, 8, 220
Haveli (Seminyak), 110
Henna Spa (Jimbaran Bay), 155, 158
Herbs and medicinal plants, 62
High season, 30, 31

Hiking and trekking, 67–68
  Bedugul, 236
  Candidasa, 260
  Danau Batur, 231–233
  Gili Meno, 349
  Menjangan, 301
  Sidemen Valley, 250
  Ubud, 215–216
History of Bali, 10–16
Holidays, 31
Holistic and intuitive healing, 63
Horizon Glassworks (Ubud), 219
Horseback riding, 108, 300, 356
Hospitals, 358
Hug A Bug (Sanur), 139
Hutan Wisata Suranadi, 315

Ibisa (Sanur), 138
Icon Asian Arts (Seminyak), 112
Impossibles beach (Uluwatu), 166, 168
Innuendo (Seminyak), 110–111
Insurance, 44–45
  scuba diving, 69
International Driving License, 38
Internet access, 49–50
Intrepid Travel, 60
Island Explorer Cruises, 142
Island Living (Ubud), 220
Island Promotions, 60
Itineraries, suggested, 55–58
I-to-i, 61

Jagaraga, 276
Jagatnata Temple (Denpasar), 116
Jamu Traditional Spa
  Kuta, 85
  Sanur, 137
Japanese shipwreck (off Banyuning), 269
Jari Menari (Seminyak), 109
Jayaprana Grave (Cekik), 297
Jaya Spa (Candidasa), 261
J Cuvee (Kuta), 88
Jean-Francois Fichot (Ubud), 220
JED (Jaringan Ekowisata Desa), 59, 149, 236
Jemme Jewellery (Seminyak), 113
Jenggala Ceramics (Jimbaran Bay), 158–159

Jeruk Manis, 331
Jimbaran Bay, 154–165
    accommodations, 160–162
    exploring, 155–158
    restaurants, 162–165
    shopping, 158–159
    traveling to and around,
        154–155
Jiwa Spa (Tanjung Benoa), 185
Joged Bumbung, 295
John Hardy workshop
    (Ubud), 220
Jojang Spring, 331
Joy Jewellery (Seminyak),
    111
Julah, 273
Jungle Surf (Kuta), 90
Jungutbatu (Lembongan),
    143, 147, 149–150

Kaki lima, 28
Kama Sutra (Kuta), 92
Karang Lestari Proyek (Coral
    Protection Project;
    Pemuteran), 285
Kayaking
    Danau Batur, 232
    Gili Trawangan, 357
Kayumanis (Ubud), 213
Kecimol music, 306
Kedisan, 231
Kedonganan Fish Market
    (Jimbaran Bay), 159
Kerandangan Valley, 317
Kerta Gosa (Klungkung), 247
Kerurak, 325
Kiadan Pelaga, 236
Kintamani (Danau Batur),
    229
Kirana Spa (Ubud), 213–214
Kitesurfing, 136–137
Klenteng Ling Gwan Kiong
    Chinese Temple (Singa-
    raja), 277
Klungkung (Semarapura),
    247–249
Klungkung Market, 247
Komaneka Fine Art Gallery
    (Ubud), 212
Kopi lubak, 133
Kosaido Golf Course (Pantai
    Sira), 325
Kubu (near Tulamben), 269
Kuningan, 24, 31
Kuoni, 61
Kusamba, 248–249
Kuta, 52, 72–92, 332–335
    accommodations, 73–79
    currency exchange, 73
    exploring, 84–87

getting there and around,
    72–73
hospitals, 73
nightlife, 90–92
pharmacies, 73
police, 73
post office, 73
restaurants, 79–84
safety, 73
shopping, 87–90
tourism information, 73
Kuta cowboys, 47, 73, 334
Kuta Karnival, 33
Kuta Reef, 86

Labuhan Lombok, 336
Labuhan Pandan, 337
Laguna Resort & Spa (Nusa
    Dua), 183
La Vida Loca (Kuta), 91
Legends (Kuta), 92
Legian (Seminyak), 109
Legian Pub (Kuta), 92
Le Mayeur Museum (Sanur),
    135
Lembah Rinjani, 338
Lembongan, 140–150
    accommodations, 146–148
    day trips to, 140, 142
    exploring, 143–146
    orientation, 143
    restaurants, 148–150
    traveling to, 142–143
Lendang Luar, 317
Les, 272
Liberty shipwreck
    (Tulamben), 269
Life cycle rites, 24
Lipah Bay, 266
Loloan Timur, 297
Lombok, 303–338
    banks and ATMs, 312
    central, 330–332
    getting to and around,
        307, 310–312
    history of, 303–305
    hospitals and clinics, 312
    Internet access, 312
    Kuta and the south coast,
        332–335
    north, 324–330
    police, 312
    post office, 313
    southwest coast and
        islands of, 322
    visitor information, 313
Lombok Biking Tours, 64
Lombok Golf Kosaido Coun-
    try Club, 67

Lombok International Air-
    port, 331
Lovina, 278–283
Low season, 31
Loyok, 330
Lulur Spa (Lembongan), 144

Macan Tidur (Ubud), 221
Mail, 358
Maju Jaya (Kuta), 88
Makpung (bull races; Neg-
    ara), 296
Malaria, 42–43
Malibu Point (Penida), 153
Malimbu, 317
Mambo (Kuta), 88
Manggis, 257–259
Mango Tree Spa (Ubud), 214
Mangsit, 317
Manik Organic Restaurant
    (Sanur), 139
Manik Organik Yoga Studio
    (Sanur), 138
Manta Point (Penida),
    152–153
Marcy's Surf Coaching, 70, 86
Margarana Monument (near
    Marga), 290
Marina Café (Senggigi), 322
Maru Gallery (Seminyak),
    112–113
Mas, 218
Mataram, 314
Mawi, 333
Mawun Beach, 333
Maya Ubud Resort, 214
M-Bar-Go (Kuta), 92
Medewi, 295–296
Meditation, 63
Med Medan, 32
Mekar Bhuana Conservatory
    (Sanur), 61, 134
Menjangan Island, 299
Milo's (Kuta), 88
Mimpang, 255
Mosquitoes, 42–43
Motorcycles, 39
Munduk, 237–240
Murni's Warung (Ubud), 219
Museum Gunungapi Batur
    (Danau Batur), 228
Museum Puri Lukisan (Ubud),
    210
Museum Situs Purbakala
    Gilimanuk, 297
Mushroom Bay (Lembon-
    gan), 143
    accommodations, 146–147
    restaurants, 148–150
Music, 17–18, 306

Names, 23
Natural and raw food coun-
  seling, 63
Negara, 296–298
Negara Bull Races, 33
Neka Art Museum (Ubud), 210
New Kuta Golf, 67
Ni Luh Djelantik (Seminyak),
  113
Nipah, 317
Nirarta Centre, 71
Nirwana Bali Golf Club
  (Tabanan), 67, 290
Nogo (Sanur), 138
Nusa Ceningan, 149
Nusa Dua, 174–185
    accommodations, 174,
      176–179
    exploring, 181–184
    nightlife, 185
    restaurants, 179–181
    shopping, 184
    traveling to and around, 174
Nusa Dua Festival, 33
Nusa Indah (Kuta), 90
Nusa Lembongan. *See*
  Lembongan
Nusa Penida, 150–153
Nusa Penida Bird Sanctuary,
  152
Nyepi, 32
Nyoman Gunarsa Museum
  (Klungkung), 248

Obel Obel, 337
Odalan ceremonies and
  festivals, 32
Ogoh-Ogoh day, 31–32
Oil massages, 63
Oka Agro Tourism (Danau
  Batur), 230
One World Retreats, 71
Orchard (Seminyak), 113
Outside Corner (Uluwatu), 167

Pacto (Danau Batur), 232
Padangbai, 254–257
Padang Padang (Uluwatu),
  166, 168
Paddys Bar (Kuta), 91
Paintball Bali (Uluwatu), 166
Painting, 18
Palasari, 297
Pantai Kecil (Bias Tugal), 256
Pantai Medewi, 295
Pantai Pasir Putih, 260
Pantai Sira, 325
The Pantry (Sanur), 138
Papadun (Ubud), 220

Papillon (Seminyak), 111
Paragliding, Uluwatu, 167
Pasar Delod Peken (Sanur),
  139
Pasar Hewan (Tabanan), 290
Pasar Seni (Senggigi), 321
Pasar Sindhu (Sanur), 139
Pasifika Museum (Nusa Dua),
  182
Patra Bali Resort (Kuta), 85
Paul Ropp, 88, 159
The Peak (Uluwatu), 167
Peak season, 31
Peanuts' Pub Crawl (Kuta), 90
Pecatu Indah (Bukit penin-
  sula), 170
Pedaler's Pub & Grille, 64
Pejaten, 290
Pelangi Workshop (Sidemen),
  250
Pemuteran, 284–287
Penatahan Hot Springs
  (Gunung Batukaru), 240
Penelokan, 228
Penida, 150–153
Penyabangan, 280
Perama Tours, 39, 143, 225,
  243, 254, 278, 311, 332,
  342, 344
Perancak, 297
Perang Topat, 315
Performing arts, schools, 61
Periplus Bookstore
    Kuta, 87
    Seminyak, 109
    Ubud, 219
Petitenget Temple
  (Seminyak), 108
Pita Maha, 18
Planning your trip, 30–51
    customs regulations, 36
    entry requirements, 35–37
    getting around, 37–39
    health concerns, 42–44
    money and costs, 40–42
    safety concerns, 45
    specialized travel
      resources, 45–47
    staying connected, 49–50
    traveling to Bali and
      Lombok, 37
    when to go, 30–31
Police, 358
    registration with the, 36
Pondok Pekak, 61
Popcari Sweat, 43
Poppies Gang I (Kuta), 90
Posers (Kuta), 92
Pottery classes, 61–62

PPPGB (Association of Mount
  Batur Trekking Guides),
  231–232
Prana Spa (Seminyak), 108
Praya, 330
Pringgasela, 331
Provincial Museum and
  Cultural Centre
  (Mataram), 314
Pura Agung Pulaki (Banyu-
  poh), 281
Pura Batu Bolong (near
  Senggigi), 316
Pura Beji (Sangsit), 275
Pura Besakih (Mother Temple;
  Gunung Agung), 252–253
Pura Bukit Sari (Tabanan),
  291–292
Pura Dalem (near Air Sanih),
  275
Pura Dalem Penunggekan
  (Sidemen), 252
Pura Gede Perancak, 297
Pura Gili Kancana
  (Menjangan), 300
Pura Goa Giri Putri (Penida),
  151–152
Pura Goa Lawah (near
  Kusamba), 249
Pura Gunung Kawi (Ubud),
  208
Pura Gunung Lebah (Ubud),
  208
Pura Kebo Edan (Ubud), 208
Pura Kehen (Sidemen), 252
Pura Kerta Kawat (Banyupoh),
  281
Pura Lempuyang (Amlapura),
  263
Pura Lingsar (Narmada),
  314–315
Pura Luhur at Rambut Siwi
  (Medewi), 295
Pura Luhur Batukaru
  (Gunung Batukaru), 241
Pura Luhur Uluwatu, 166
Pura Maduwe Karang
  (Kubutambahan), 275
Pura Maospahit (Denpasar),
  116
Pura Mayura (Cakranegara),
  314
Pura Melanting (Banyupoh),
  281
Pura Meru (Cakranegara), 314
Pura Narmada (Narmada), 315
Pura Pabean (Banyupoh), 281
Pura Penataran Sasih (Ubud),
  208–209

Pura Penaturan Ped (Penida), 152
Pura Penulisan (Danau Batur), 229
Pura Pondok Batu, 273–274
Pura Puncak Manik (Banyupoh), 281
Pura Pusering Jagat (Ubud), 209
Pura Saraswati (Ubud), 209
Pura Silayukti (Padangbai), 255
Pura Suranadi, 315
Pura Taman Ayun (Tabanan), 290
Pura Tanah Lot (Tabanan), 290–291
Pura Tirta (Banyupoh), 281
Pura Ulan Danu Bratan, 235
Pura Ulun Danu (Danau Batur), 229, 230
Puri Agung Karangasem (Amlapura), 263–264
Puri Bagus Ponjok Batu (Tejakula), 271
Puri Ganesha (Pemuteran), 284
Puri Kanginan Palace (Singaraja), 277
Puri Kawan (Singaraja), 277
Puri Pemecutan (Denpasar), 116
Puri Saren Agung (Royal Palace; Ubud), 209
Puru Ulun Siwi (Jimbaran Bay), 155
Pusuk Pass, 324–325

Q Bar (Kuta), 90–91
Quarzia (Seminyak), 112
Quicksilver, 153

R abies, 43
Race Track (Uluwatu), 167
Rainfall, average, 30
Rainy season, 30
Ramadan, 358–359
Rambitan, 333
Raya Antiques (Seminyak), 114
Rebab (Sanur), 137
Reef Seen Aquatics (Pemuteran), 284
Regions in brief, 52, 54–55
Registration with the police, 36
Religion (Seminyak), 112
Religion and spirituality, 22–24. See also Yoga and spiritual journeys

Religious events and festivals, 31–35
Remede Spa (Nusa Dua), 183
Rendevous (Kuta), 92
Responsible Travel, 61
Restaurants, best, 6–7
Rinjani, Mount, 328
Rinjani Country Club Golf & Resort, 67
Rinjani National Park, 325–330
Rio Helmi Photo Gallery (Ubud), 212
Rip Curl School of Surf (Arjuna), 70, 85
Ropp, Paul, 159
Royal Bali Yacht Club, 65, 137
Royal Palace (Puri Saren Agung; Ubud), 209
Royal Palace at Kerambitan (Tabanan), 291
Rudana Museum (Ubud), 210–211
Rudat, 306
Rudy's (Gili Trawangan), 357

S acred Monkey Forest Sanctuary (Ubud), 217
Sade, 333
Sadus Tiles (Sidemen), 251
Safety concerns, 45
Sahara Club (Senggigi), 322
Sailing (yachting)
    Amed, 265
    Sanur, 137
Sail Sensations, 142
Salans, Chris, 213
Salubuan Beach (Uluwatu), 167
Sama Sama (Gili Trawangan), 357
Samaya (Seminyak), 109
Sambelia, 337
Sand fleas, Uluwatu beach, 169
Sangeh Monkey Forest (Tabanan), 291–292
Sanur, 52, 54, 120–140
    accommodations, 121–130
    ATMs, 120
    banks and currency exchange, 121
    exploring, 134–135
    history of tourism in, 122
    hospitals and clinics, 121
    Internet access, 121
    nightlife, 139–140
    outdoor activities, 135–138
    pharmacies, 121

police, 121
restaurants, 130–134
shopping, 138–139
traveling to and around, 120
Sanur Deli & Annie Salon, 139
Sanur Kite Festival, 33
Sanur Village Festival, 33
Sapit, 336
Saraswati, 32
Sari Api Ceramic Studio (Ubud), 62
Sasana Budaya Art Center (Sidemen), 252
Sawan, 276
Scuba diving, 68–69
    Amed, 266
    best, 3
    Gili Air, 347
    the Gili Islands, 355–356
    Gili Meno, 349
    Gili Trawangan, 354–356
    Lembongan, 144–145
    Menjangan, 300
    Padangbai, 255–256
    Padangbai area, 255
    Pemuteran, 284
    Penida, 152–153
    Sanur, 136
    Tulamben, 269
Scuba Seraya Dive, 269
Seasons, 30–31
Seaweed farming (Nusa Dua), 182
Secret Bay (Gilimanuk Bay), 300
Segenter, 325
Sekotong, 322
Selong, 336
Selong Blanak, 333
Semararaja Museum (Klungkung), 248
Sembalun Bumbung, 338
Sembalun Lawang, 338
Sembiran, 272–273
Sembirenteng, 271–275
Seminyak, 52, 93–115
    accommodations, 96–101
    exploring, 108–109
    nightlife, 114–115
    restaurants, 101–107
    safety, 96
    shopping, 109–114
    traveling to and around, 93, 96
Seminyak Square, 109
Senaru, 325
Sendang Gile waterfalls, 325
Senggigi, 313, 316–322

Senggigi Beach, 317
Senggigi Festival, 33
Senggigi Reef, 321
Senggigi wave, 321
Seniwati Gallery (Ubud), 212
Seraphim (Ubud), 221
Seririt, 280
Shalimar (Ubud), 220
Shipping goods home, 110
The Shop (Ubud), 220
Sidemen Valley, 249–251
Sika Contemporary Art
  Gallery (Ubud), 212
Simple Konsept Store
  (Seminyak), 112
Singaraja, 276–278
Skubaskool (Seminyak), 68
Sky Garden (Kuta), 91
Snorkeling, 68–69
  Amed, 266
  best, 3
  Gili Air, 347
  Gili Meno, 349
  Gili Trawangan, 356
  Lembongan, 143, 145
  Menjangan, 300
  Padangbai, 256
  Penida, 153
  Sanur, 136
  Tulamben, 269
Sobek, 60, 68, 71, 215, 233,
  236, 250
Sound healing, 63
Spa Alila (Ubud), 214
Spa Hati (Ubud), 214
Spa on the Rocks (Jimbaran
  Bay), 155
Spas and massages, 167
  best, 7–9
  Candidasa, 261
  Jimbaran Bay, 155, 158
  Kuta, 85
  Lembongan, 144
  Lovina, 280
  Manggis, 257
  Nusa Dua, 183
  Sanur, 137
  Seminyak, 108
  Tanjung Benoa, 185
  Ubud, 213–214
Spa Venus (Seminyak), 109
Special events and festivals,
  31–35
  nonreligious, 33
Spice Dive (Lovina), 279
Spice Roads, 64
Sri Lanka (Nusa Dua), 183
Stadium Café (Kuta), 90
STA Travel, 47

Student travel, 47
Studio Perak (Ubud), 62
Studio 13 (Seminyak), 113
Subak Rice Museum
  (Tabanan), 292
Sudaji, 276
Sukarara, 330
Sukawati Art Market, 218
Suly Resort & Spa, 61
Sunda Trails, 60, 311
Sun exposure, 43
Surfer Girl (Kuta), 90
Surf Goddess Retreats, 70
Surfing, 69–70
  Bangko Bangko, 323
  Ekas Bay, 333
  Gili Trawangan, 356
  Jimbaran Bay, 158
  Kuta, 85–87
  Kuta area, 333
  Lembongan, 145–146
  Nusa Dua, 183–184
  Sanur, 138
  Uluwatu, 167–169
Surf shops, Kuta, 89–90
Surf Travel Online, 70
Suwug, 276
Sweta, 314
Swimming. See also Beaches
  Kuta, 86
  Sanur, 138
Swine flu, 42
Symon Studios (Ubud), 213

Tabanan, 288–293
Taman Budaya, 314
Taman Gili & Semararaja
  Museum (Klungkung), 247
Taman Kupu Kupu (Tabanan),
  292
Taman Nasional Bali Barat
  (West Bali Barat National
  Park), 297, 298–302
Taman Tirta Gangga
  (Amlapura), 264
Taman Ujung Water Palace
  (Amlapura), 264
Taman Werdhi Budaya Arts
  Center, 33
Tamblingan, Lake, 235
Tandjung Sari (Sanur), 140
Tanjung, 325
Tanjung A'an, 333
Tanjung Benoa, 185–188
Tarot readings, 63
Taun, 322–323
Taxes, 359
Taxis, 39
Tea Tree Spa (Kuta), 85

Tegal Bunder trail, 298
Tejakula, 271–275
Telaga (Penida), 151
Telephones and cell-
  phones, 49, 359
Teluk Kodek, 317
Teluk Nara, 317
Tembok, 271–275
Temperatures, average, 30
Temples, 22
  best, 2–3
  celebrations, 23
  Danau Batur, 229–230
  etiquette for visiting, 34
  Penida, 151–152
  Ubud, 207–209
  village and family, 23
Temples (Uluwatu), 167
Tenganan Village, 257–258
Tepekong, 255
Tetebatu, 330–331
Textiles, classes, 62–63
Textiles and weaving, 19–20
Theater, 16–17
Theta Spa (Kuta), 85
Threads of Life (Ubud), 62,
  221
Tiempo (Jimbaran Bay), 159
Tihingan, 248
Time zone, 359
Tir Na Nog (Gili Trawangan),
  357
Tirta Empul (Ubud), 209
Tiu Kelep waterfall, 326
Tjokorda Raka Swastika, 61
Toilets, 359
Toko East (Ubud), 220
Tours, 59–61
Toya Bungkah, 230–231
Toya Devasya
  Danau Batur, 233
  Toya Bungkah, 231
Toyapakeh (Penida), 152
Transat, 337
Transportation, 37–39
Travel insurance, 44–45
Treasures (Ubud), 221
Trekking. See Hiking and
  trekking
Tropicsurf, 70
Trunyan, 231
Tuban (South Kuta Beach)
  accommodations, 78–79
  restaurants, 83–84
Tubes (Kuta), 91
Tulamben, 268–270
Turtle hatchery (Pemuteran),
  284

Ubud, 54, 189–224
accommodations, 191–200
banks and currency
exchange, 190
exploring, 207–217
hospitals and clinics,
190–191
Internet access, 191
nightlife, 224
outdoor activities, 214–216
pharmacies, 191
police, 191
post office, 191
restaurants, 201–207
shopping, 218–223
traveling to and around, 190
visitor information, tours
and maps, 190
Ubud Hanging Gardens, 213
Ubud Market, 219
Ubud Writers Festival, 33
**Udayana Golf Driving Range
(Sanur), 136**
Uluwatu (shops)
Kuta, 88
Sanur, 139
Uluwatu (town), 165–174
accommodations, 169–172
restaurants, 172–174
**Uluwatu spa (Jimbaran Bay),
155**

Vi Ai Pi (Kuta), 91–92
Villa rentals, 50–51. *See also*
Accommodations Index
Visas, 35–36
Visitor information, 359
**Volcano Breeze (Danau
Batur), 232**
Volunteer work, 232

Waka Experience (Gunung
Batukaru), 241
Waka Louka Cruise, 142
Waka Maya (Sanur), 137–138
Wall/Drop-off (Tulamben), 269
Wardani Shop (Ubud), 221
**Warisan Casa (Jimbaran Bay),
159**
Water, drinking, 359
Waterbom (Kuta), 87
Waterworx (Padangbai), 256
Wayang style, 18
Weather, 30
Websites, 35
Weddings, 47
**Werdhi Budaya Arts Center
(Denpasar), 116**

**West Bali Barat National Park
(Taman Nasional Bali
Barat), 297, 298–302**
Wheelchair accessibility, 46
White Sand Beach, 260
White-water rafting, 71
Sidemen Valley, 250
Ubud, 215
Wi-Fi access, 49
**Women and single
travelers, 47**
Wood carvings and craft, 20
**World Diving Lembongan,
69, 145**

Yoga and spiritual journeys,
70–71
Yoga Barn (Ubud), 216
Yoga classes and retreats
Sanur, 138
Ubud, 216

Zen Bali, 71

ACCOMMODATIONS

**Adi Assri Resort (Pemuteran),
287**
**Adinda Hotel (Denpasar),
116–117**
**Agung Raka Bungalows
(Ubud), 197**
Ajanta Villa (Sanur), 129
Alam Anda (Buleleng), 274
**Alam Asmara Dive Resort
(Candidasa), 261–262**
**Alam Batu Beach Bungalow
Resort (Tulamben), 270**
Alam Gili (Gili Trawangan), 351
Alam Indah (Ubud), 198
Alam Kul Kul (Kuta), 77
Alam Sari (Ubud), 197
**The Alila Resort Manggis,
258–259**
Alila Ubud, 195
Alila Villas Uluwatu, 170
Alu Bali (Seminyak), 98–99
Amandari (Ubud), 191
Amankila (Manggis), 259
Amanusa (Nusa Dua), 176
Amber House (Gili Meno), 347
**Amertha Bali Villas
(Gerokgak-Buleleng), 286**
Anaheim Villa (Munduk), 238
**Ananda Cottages (Ubud),
198–199**
Anandita (Pantai Sire), 327
**Anantara Seminyak Resort &
Spa Bali, 97**

Arma Resort (Ubud), 197
Artha Sastra Inn (Bangli), 254
**Aston Legend Villas (Sanur),
128**
Atas Ombak (Seminyak), 100
**Ayana Resort & Spa (Jimba-
ran Bay), 160**
Balé (Nusa Dua), 176
**Bali Handara Country Club
(Bedugul), 236**
Bali Hyatt (Sanur), 121
**Bali Mountain Retreat
(Gunung Batukaru), 241**
Bali Niksoma (Kuta), 76
**Bali Spirit Hotel and Spa
(Ubud), 198**
**Bali Taman Resort & Spa
(Lovina), 282**
Bambu Indah (Ubud), 195
Bangli Inn, 254
Batu Belah (Tulamben), 270
**Batu Karang Resort & Day
Spa (Lembongan), 147**
Batur Lakeview Hotel, 228
**Bayu Cottages Hotel and Res-
taurant (Amed), 266**
**The Beach Club (Senggigi),
319**
**The Beach House (Gili Tra-
wangan), 351**
**Biba Beach Village (Gili Air),
344**
Biru Meno (Gili Meno), 347
**Bloo Lagoon Resort (Padang-
bai), 256**
**Blue Moon Villa (Amed),
266–267**
**Bola Bola Paradis (Pelangan),
323**
**Bulan Baru Hotel (Senggigi),
319**
**Bulgari Hotel & Resort 186
(Uluwatu), 169**
**Casa Luna Honeymoon
Guesthouse (Ubud), 198**
**Cempaka Belimbing Villas
(Pupuan-Tabanan), 241**
**Chedi Club at Tanah Gajah
(Ubud), 191, 194**
**Cilik's Beach Resort (Singa-
raja), 276**
**The Club at The Legian
(Seminyak), 97**
Club Med (Nusa Dua), 178
**Coconuts Beach Resort (Lem-
bongan), 147**
COMO Shambhala (Ubud), 194
**The Conrad (Tanjung Benoa),
186**
Damai (Singaraja), 282

Dancing Dragon Cottage (Amed), 267
Desa Seni (Canggu), 115
Dewa Bharata (Candidasa), 262
Dewi Sinta Restaurant & Villa (Tabanan), 293
Discovery Kartika Plaza Hotel (Kuta), 76
Dream Beach Bungalows (Lembongan), 148
The Dusun (Seminyak), 98
The Elysian Boutique Villa Hotel (Seminyak), 99
Emerald Villa (Sanur), 129
Flashbacks (Sanur), 123
Four Seasons Resort at Jimbaran Bay, 160
Four Seasons Resort at Sayan (Ubud), 194
Gaia Oasis & Abasan Hillside Retreats (Tejakula), 275
Gajah Mina Beach Resort (near Lalang Linggah), 294
The Gangsa (Sanur), 128
Gending Kedis Luxury Villas and Spa (Jimbaran Bay), 160
Gili Air Hotel, 345
Gili Air Santay, 345
Gili Eco Villas (Gili Trawangan), 351
Gili Lampu Bungalows (Ampenan), 338
Gili Nanggu Cottages, 323
Gili Villas (Gili Trawangan), 350
The Golden Rock (Amed), 267
Good Karma (Amed), 267
Grand Hyatt Bali (Nusa Dua), 178
Green Orry (Tetebatu), 332
Griya Santrian (Sanur), 123
Hai Tide Huts (Lembongan), 146
Hakiki (Tetebatu), 332
Hard Rock Hotel (Kuta), 76
Hati Suci (Sapit), 338
Heaven On the Planet (Ekas Bay), 333
Holiday Inn Resort (Tuban), 78
Holiday Resort (Senggigi), 317
Hotel InterContinental (Jimbaran Bay), 161
Hotel Lestari (Cekik), 297
Hotel Puri Ayu (Denpasar), 117
Hotel Santika (Tuban), 78
Hotel Sari (Cekik), 297
Hotel Tjampuhan (Ubud), 198
Hotel Tugu Lombok, 326

Hotel Vila Ombak (Gili Trawangan), 351
The H Rooms (Gili Trawangan), 351
Inna Bali (Denpasar), 117
The Istana (Uluwatu), 171
Jaringan Ekowisata Desa (Kiadan Pelaga), 236
Jimbaran Puri Bali, 161
Jubawa Homestay (Pemuteran), 287
Kaluku Bungalows (Gili Air), 345–346
Karang Kambar Estate (Uluwatu), 172
Karang Putih Villa (Uluwatu), 171
Karma Kandara Villas (Uluwatu), 172
Karma Kayak (Gili Trawangan), 352
The Kayana (Seminyak), 99
Kayumanis Jimbaran, 161
Kayumanis Nusa Dua, 176
Kebun Raya (Bedugul), 237
Kelapa Luxury Villas (Gili Trawangan), 350
Kembang Desa Luxury Beach Villas (Tabanan), 292–293
Ken's Hotel (Kuta), 333–334
Khayangan (Uluwatu), 171
Klub Kokos (Ubud), 199
ko-ko-mo Resort (Gili Trawangan), 350
Komaneka Bisma (Ubud), 195–196
Komaneka Resort (Ubud), 195–196
Komaneka Tanggavuda (Ubud), 195–196
Kubu Lalang (Lovina), 279
Kupu Kupu Barong (Tuban), 79
Kupu Kupu Barong Villas & Tree Spa (Ubud), 199–200
Laguna Resort & Spa Nusa Dua, 177
Lake Buyan Cottages (Bedugul), 237
Lakeside Cottages (Danau Batur), 233
Laksmana Villas (Seminyak), 99
La Taverna (Sanur), 123, 126
The Legian (Seminyak), 96
Lembah Rinjani (Sembalun Lawang), 329
Lembongan Island Beach Villas, 147

Lembongan Sunset Beach, 148
Le Meridien Nirwana Golf Spa & Resort (Tabanan), 292
Life in Amed (Amed), 267
The Lodge Bedugul, 237
Long House (Uluwatu), 172
Luce d'Alma (Gili Trawangan), 351–352
Made Homestay (Penida), 153
Made Punia's Homestay (Ubud), 199
Mallia's Child (Gili Meno), 347
Manta Bungalows (Gili Trawangan), 352
Manta Dive (Gili Air), 345
Mara River Safari Lodge (Sanur), 126
Matahari Beach Resort (Pemuteran), 285
Matahari Inn (Kuta), 334
Maya Ubud Resort & Spa, 196
Medana Resort (Tanjung), 326
Medewi Beach Cottages, 296
Melka Hotel (Lovina), 279
Menjangan Resort, 301
Mick's Place (Uluwatu), 170
Mimpi Resort (Menjangan), 301
Mimpi Resort (Tulamben), 270
Munduk Moding Plantation, 238–239
Mutiara Mas Bungalows (Penida), 153
Mu Uluwatu, 171
Nakula Familiar Inn (Denpasar), 117
The Nikko Hotel (Nusa Dua), 178–179
Nirarta Centre for Living Awareness (Sidemen), 250
Novotel Coralia Benoa Bali (Tanjung Benoa), 186
Novotel Lombok Resort (Kuta), 334
Novus Gawana Resort & Spa (Menjangan), 301–302
Nusa Dua Beach Hotel and Spa, 179
Nusa Lembongan Resort, 146
Oazia Spa Villas (Canggu), 115, 118
The Oberoi (Medana), 326–327
The Oberoi Bali (Seminyak), 96–97
Padma Hotel (Kuta), 77
Pantai Lima (Mengwi), 118
Parigata Villas Resort (Sanur), 128

374 Patal Kikian (Sidemen), 250–251

The Patra Bali Resort & Villas (Tuban), 79

Pavilions Private Villas (Sanur), 129–130

Playgrounds (Lembongan), 147–148

Ponciana Resort (Amlapura), 274–275

Pondok Pisces (Lalang Linggah), 294

Pondok Sari (Pemuteran), 286

Pondok Wisata Lihat Sawah (Sidemen), 251

Poppies Cottages (Kuta), 78

Puri Bagus (Manggis), 259

Puri Bagus Lovina (Buleleng), 282

Puri Bambu (Jimbaran Bay), 162

Puri Bening (Danau Batur), 233

Puri Bunga Beach Cottages (Senggigi), 319

Puri Dajuma Cottages (Medewi), 296

Puri Ganesha Villas, 285–286

Puri Lumbung Cottages (Munduk), 239

Puri Mas Boutique Resort & Spa (Senggigi), 317–318

Puri Mas Kerandangan Resort (Senggigi), 318

Puri Mesari (Sanur), 127

Puri Santrian (Sanur), 126

Puri Sawah Villas (Amlapura), 264

Puri Taman Sari Hotel (Tabanan), 293

Qunci Villas (Senggigi), 318

Rama Candidasa, 262

Ramada Bintang Bali Resort & Spa (Kuta), 77

Rambutan (Lovina), 282

Rare Angon Home-stay (Pemuteran), 287

Reef Seen (Pemuteran), 287

The River House (Ubud), 200

Royal Santrian (Tanjung Benoa), 185–186

Rumah Bali (Tanjung Benoa), 186

The Samaya (Seminyak), 97

Sanda Butik Villas (Pupuan-Tabanan), 241–242

Santai Hotel, 266

Santosa Villas & Resort (Senggigi), 318

Sanur Beach Hotel, 126–127

Sanur Paradise Plaza, 127

Saranam Eco Resort (Munduk), 239

Sarinbuana Eco Lodge (Tabanan), 242

Scallywags (Gili Trawangan), 352–353

Scuba Seraya Resort (Tulamben), 270

Secret Island Resort (Gili Gede), 323–324

Segara Village (Sanur), 127

Sejuk Cottages (Gili Air), 345

Senggigi Beach Hotel & Pool Villa Club, 318–319

Sentosa Private Villas and Spa (Seminyak), 98

Seraya Shores (Amlapura), 264–265

Shack 58 & 59 (Gili Meno), 348

Shankaris (Suraberata), 294–295

Shanti Hotel & Restaurant (Singaraja), 278

Sheraton Senggigi Beach Resort, 317

Shipwrecks Beach Villa (Lembongan), 148

Siddhartha Resort (Tulamben), 270

Silq (Seminyak), 99

Sira Beach House, 327

Spa Village Resort (Tejakula-Buleleng), 274

Sri Phala Resort & Villa (Sanur), 128

St. Regis Bali (Nusa Dua), 176–177

Sunari Resort (Lovina), 282

Sunset Gecko (Gili Meno), 348

Taman Bebek Villas (Ubud), 196

Taman Sari Bali Cottages (Pemuteran), 286

Taman Selini (Pemuteran), 287

Taman Wana (Seminyak), 98

Taman Wana Villas & Spa (Palasari), 297–298

Tandjung Sari (Sanur), 121, 123

Tastura Hotel (Kuta), 334

Tauch Terminal Resort and Spa (Tulamben), 270

Tir Na Nog (Gili Trawangan), 352

Tugu Hotel (Canggu), 118

Ubud Hanging Gardens, 194

Ubud Sari Health Resort, 199

Udayana Eco Lodge (Uluwatu), 171

Uma Ubud, 196

The Viceroy (Ubud), 194–195

Villa Aqua (Seminyak), 100

Villa Asada (Manggis), 259

Villa Bali Asri (Seminyak), 98

Villa Balquisse (Jimbaran Bay), 160–161

Villa Bulan Putih (Uluwatu), 172

Villa Coco (Kuta), 77

Villa Crusoe (Seminyak), 100

Villa de daun (Kuta), 76–77

Villa Des Indes (Seminyak), 100–101

Villa Devatas (Tabanan), 292

Villa Kubu (Seminyak), 99–100

Villa Mahapala (Sanur), 128–129

Villa Mana (Canggu), 115

Villa Nalini (Ubud), 200

Villa Nautilus (Gili Meno), 348

Villa Puri Sayan (Ubud), 200

Villa Puri Tupai (Ubud), 200

Villa Sasoon (Candidasa), 261

The Villas Bali Hotel and Spa (Seminyak), 100

Villa Sepoi Sepoi (Pantai Sire), 327

Villa Shaba (Jimbaran Bay), 162

Villa Talia Vashti (Candidasa), 261

Villa Tirta Ayu (Amlapura), 264

Villa Zolima (Lalang Linggah), 295

Under the Volcano 1, 2 & 3 (Danau Batur), 233

Waka Di Ume (Ubud), 196–197

Waka Gangga (Tabanan), 293

Waka Maya (Sanur), 123

Waka Nusa Resort (Lembongan), 146–147

Waka Shorea (Gilimanuk), 302

Wantilan Villas at the Bali Golf and Country Club (Nusa Dua), 177

Warwick Ibah Luxury Villas and Spa (Ubud), 197

Watergarden (Candidasa), 262

Wawa Wewe II (Amed), 267

Westin Resort Nusa Dua, 177–178

Windy Beach Resort (Senggigi), 319

Wisma Soedjono (Tetebatu), 331

Zen Resort Bali (Lovina), 280